D1823606

UNIX® SYSTEM V
RELEASE 4

System Administrator's
Reference Manual

UNIX Software Operation

Published by Prentice-Hall, Inc.
A Division of Simon & Schuster
Englewood Cliffs, New Jersey 07632

ACKNOWLEDGEMENT

AT&T gratefully acknowledges the X/Open Company Limited for permission to reproduce portions of its copyrighted *X/Open Portability Guide, Issue 3*.

IMPORTANT NOTE TO USERS

While every effort has been made to ensure the accuracy of all information in this document, AT&T assumes no liability to any party for any loss or damage caused by errors or omissions or by statements of any kind in this document, its updates, supplements, or special editions, whether such errors are omissions or statements resulting from negligence, accident, or any other cause. AT&T further assumes no liability arising out of the application or use of any product or system described herein; nor any liability for incidental or consequential damages arising from the use of this document. AT&T disclaims all warranties regarding the information contained herein, whether expressed, implied or statutory, *including implied warranties of merchantability or fitness for a particular purpose.* AT&T makes no representation that the interconnection of products in the manner described herein will not infringe on existing or future patent rights, nor do the descriptions contained herein imply the granting or license to make, use or sell equipment constructed in accordance with this description.

AT&T reserves the right to make changes without further notice to any products herein to improve reliability, function, or design.

TRADEMARKS

SunOS is a registered trademark of Sun Microsystems, Inc.
UNIX is a registered trademark of AT&T.

10 9 8 7 6 5 4 3 2 1

ISBN 0-13-947011-5

UNIX
PRESS
A Prentice Hall Title

P R E N T I C E   H A L L

ORDERING INFORMATION

UNIX® SYSTEM V, RELEASE 4 DOCUMENTATION

To order single copies of UNIX® SYSTEM V, Release 4 documentation, please call (201) 767-5937.

ATTENTION DOCUMENTATION MANAGERS AND TRAINING DIRECTORS:
For bulk purchases in excess of 30 copies please write to:
Corporate Sales
Prentice Hall
Englewood Cliffs, N.J. 07632.
Or call: (201) 592-2498.

ATTENTION GOVERNMENT CUSTOMERS: For GSA and other pricing information please call (201) 767-5994.

Prentice-Hall International (UK) Limited, *London*
Prentice-Hall of Australia Pty. Limited, *Sydney*
Prentice-Hall Canada Inc., *Toronto*
Prentice-Hall Hispanoamericana, S.A., *Mexico*
Prentice-Hall of India Private Limited, *New Delhi*
Prentice-Hall of Japan, Inc., *Tokyo*
Simon & Schuster Asia Pte. Ltd., *Singapore*
Editora Prentice-Hall do Brasil, Ltda., *Rio de Janeiro*

AT&T UNIX® System V Release 4

General Use and System Administration

UNIX® System V Release 4 Network User's and Administrator's Guide
UNIX® System V Release 4 Product Overview and Master Index
UNIX® System V Release 4 System Administrator's Guide
UNIX® System V Release 4 System Administrator's Reference Manual
UNIX® System V Release 4 User's Guide
UNIX® System V Release 4 User's Reference Manual

General Programmer's Series

UNIX® System V Release 4 Programmer's Guide: ANSI C
and Programming Support Tools
UNIX® System V Release 4 Programmer's Guide: Character User Interface
(FMLI and ETI)
UNIX® System V Release 4 Programmer's Guide: Networking Interfaces
UNIX® System V Release 4 Programmer's Guide: POSIX Conformance
UNIX® System V Release 4 Programmer's Guide: System Services
and Application Packaging Tools
UNIX® System V Release 4 Programmer's Reference Manual

System Programmer's Series

UNIX® System V Release 4 ANSI C Transition Guide
UNIX® System V Release 4 BSD / XENIX® Compatibility Guide
UNIX® System V Release 4 Device Driver Interface / Driver−Kernel
Interface (DDI / DKI) Reference Manual
UNIX® System V Release 4 Migration Guide
UNIX® System V Release 4 Programmer's Guide: STREAMS

Available from Prentice Hall

Introduction

This *System Administrator's Reference Manual* describes the commands, file formats, and miscellaneous facilities used by those who administer a UNIX system running on the AT&T 3B2 Computer.

Several closely-related documents contain other valuable information:

- The *System Administrator's Guide* provides procedures for and explanations of administrative tasks.

- The *User's Guide* presents an overview of the UNIX system and tutorials on how to use text editors, automate repetitive jobs, and send information to others.

- The *User's Reference Manual* describes the commands that constitute the basic software running on the AT&T 3B2 Computer.

- The *Programmer's Guide* presents an overview of the UNIX system programming environment and tutorials on various programming tools.

- The *Programmer's Reference Manual* describes the commands, system calls, subroutines, libraries, file formats, and miscellaneous facilities used by programmers.

The *System Administrator's Reference Manual* is divided into five sections:

(1M)	System Maintenance Commands and Application Programs
(4)	File Formats
(5)	Miscellaneous Facilities
(7)	Special Files
(8)	System Maintenance Procedures

Throughout this manual, numbers following a command are intended for easy cross-reference. A command with a (1M), (7), or (8) following it means that the command is in the corresponding section of this manual. A command with a (4) or (5) following it means that the command is in the corresponding section of this manual and the *Programmer's Reference Manual*. A command followed by a (1), (1C), or (1G) usually means that it is found in the *User's Reference Manual*. (Section 1 commands appropriate for use by programmers are located in the *Programmer's Reference Manual*.) A command with a (2) or (3) following it means that the command is in the corresponding section of the *Programmer's Reference Manual*.

Section 1M, "System Maintenance Commands and Application Programs," contains commands and programs that are used in administering a UNIX system.

Section 4, "File Formats," documents the structure of particular kinds of files. For example, the format of /etc/passwd is given on passwd(4) and the content of /etc/profile is explained on profile(4). In general, when a C language structure corresponds to a file format, it can be found in either the /usr/include or /usr/include/sys directories.

Section 5, "Miscellaneous Facilities," contains a variety of information. For example, a table of the octal and hexadecimal equivalents of the ASCII character set is given on ascii(5), shell environmental variables (such as HOME, PATH, LANGUAGE, etc.) are described on environ(5), and names of common AT&T terminals are listed on term(5).

Section 7, "Special Files," discusses the characteristics of system files that refer to input/output devices. The names in this section generally refer to device names for the hardware, rather than to the names of the special files themselves.

Section 8, "System Maintenance Procedures," discusses crash recovery, firmware programs, boot procedures, facility descriptions, etc.

Each section begins with a page labeled intro. Entries following the intro page are arranged alphabetically and may consist of more than one page. Some entries describe several routines, commands, etc. In such cases, the entry appears only once, alphabetized under its "primary" name. (An example of such an entry is mount(1M), which also describes the umount command.) The "secondary" commands are listed directly below their associated primary command. To learn which manual page describes a secondary command, locate its name in the middle column of the "Permuted Index" and follow across that line to the name of the manual page listed in the right column.

All entries are based on a common format, not all of whose parts always appear:

- **NAME** gives the name(s) of the entry and briefly states its purpose.

- **SYNOPSIS** summarizes the use of the program being described. A few conventions are used, particularly in Section 1M (*Commands*):

  □ Constant Width strings are literals and are to be typed just as they appear.

□ *Italic* strings usually represent substitutable argument and program names found elsewhere in the manual. (They are underlined in the typed version of the entries.)

□ Square brackets [ ] around an argument indicate that the argument is optional. When an argument is given as "name" or "file," it always refers to a *file* name.

□ Ellipses ... are used to show that the previous argument may be repeated.

■ **DESCRIPTION** provides an overview of the command.

■ **EXAMPLE(S)** gives example(s) of usage, where appropriate.

■ **FILES** gives the file names that are built into the program.

■ **SEE ALSO** offers pointers to related information.

■ **DIAGNOSTICS** discusses the diagnostic indications that may be produced. Messages that are intended to be self-explanatory are not listed.

■ **WARNINGS** points out potential pitfalls.

■ **BUGS** gives known bugs and sometimes deficiencies.

Preceding Section 1 are a "Table of Contents" (listing both primary and secondary command entries) and a "Permuted Index." Each line of the "Table of Contents" contains the name of a manual page (with secondary entries, if they exist) and an abstract of that page. Each line of the "Permuted Index" represents a permutation (or sorting) of a line from the "Table of Contents" into three columns. The lines are arranged so that a keyword or phrase begins the middle column. Use the "Permuted Index" by searching this middle column for a topic or command. When you have found the entry you want, the right column of that line lists the name of the manual page on which information corresponding to that keyword can be found. The left column contains the remainder of the permutation that began in the middle column.

Table of Contents

1. Commands

Table of Contents _____

Table of Contents

Table of Contents _____

4. File Formats

5. Miscellaneous Facilities

7. Special Files

8. System Maintenance Procedures

Permuted Index

System Administrator's Reference Manual

System Administrator's Reference Manual

System Administrator's Reference Manual

System Administrator's Reference Manual

System Administrator's Reference Manual

System Administrator's Reference Manual

System Administrator's Reference Manual

System Administrator's Reference Manual

NAME

intro – introduction to maintenance commands and application programs

DESCRIPTION

This section describes, in alphabetical order, commands that are used chiefly for system maintenance and administration purposes. The commands in this section should be used along with those listed in Section 1 of the *User's Reference Manual* and Sections 1, 2, 3, 4, and 5 of the *Programmer's Reference Manual*. References of the form *name*(1), (2), (3), (4) and (5) refer to entries in the above manuals. References of the form *name*(1M), *name*(7) or *name*(8) refer to entries in this manual.

Because of command restructuring for the Virtual File System architecture, there are several instances of multiple manual pages with the same name. For example, there are four manual pages called mount(1M). In each such case the first of the multiple pages describes the syntax and options of the generic command, that is, those options applicable to all FSTypes (file system types). The succeeding pages describe the functionality of the FSType-specific modules of the command. These pages all display the name of the FSType to which they pertain centered and in parentheses at the top of the page. Note that the administrator should not attempt to call these modules directly. The generic command provides a common interface to all of them. Thus the FSType-specific manual pages should not be viewed as describing distinct commands, but rather as detailing those aspects of a command that are specific to a particular FSType.

COMMAND SYNTAX

Unless otherwise noted, commands described in this section accept options and other arguments according to the following syntax:

name [*option*(*s*)] [*cmdarg*(*s*)]

where:

name	The name of an executable file
option	– *noargletter*(*s*) or, – *argletter*<>*optarg* where <> is optional white space
noargletter	A single letter representing an option without an argument
argletter	A single letter representing an option requiring an argument
optarg	Argument (character string) satisfying preceding *argletter*
cmdarg	Pathname (or other command argument) *not* beginning with – or, – by itself indicating the standard input

SEE ALSO

getopt(1) in the *User's Reference Manual*.
getopt(3C) in the *Programmer's Reference Manual*.

DIAGNOSTICS

Upon termination, each command returns 0 for normal termination and non-zero to indicate troubles such as erroneous parameters, bad or inaccessible data, or other inability to cope with the task at hand. It is called variously "exit code," "exit status," or "return code," and is described only where special conventions are involved.

NOTES
 Unfortunately, not all commands adhere to the standard syntax.

NAME

accept, reject – accept or reject print requests

SYNOPSIS

accept *destinations*

reject [–r *reason*] *destinations*

DESCRIPTION

accept allows the queueing of print requests for the named *destinations*. A *destination* can be either a printer or a class of printers. Run lpstat −a to find the status of *destinations*.

reject prevents queueing of print requests for the named *destinations*. A *destination* can be either a printer or a class of printers. (Run lpstat −a to find the status of *destinations*.) The following option is useful with reject.

−r *reason*   Assign a *reason* for rejection of requests. This *reason* applies to all *destinations* specified. *Reason* is reported by lpstat −a. It must be enclosed in quotes if it contains blanks. The default reason is unknown reason for existing destinations, and new destination for destinations just added to the system but not yet accepting requests.

FILES

/var/spool/lp/*

SEE ALSO

lpadmin(1M), lpsched(1M).

enable(1), lp(1), lpstat(1) in the *User's Reference Manual*.

NAME
acct: acctdisk, acctdusg, accton, acctwtmp closewtmp, utmp2wtmp — over-view of accounting and miscellaneous accounting commands

SYNOPSIS
/usr/lib/acct/acctdisk

/usr/lib/acct/acctdusg [−u *file*] [−p *file*]

/usr/lib/acct/accton [*file*]

/usr/lib/acct/acctwtmp "*reason*"

/usr/lib/acct/closewtmp

/usr/lib/acct/utmp2wtmp

DESCRIPTION
Accounting software is structured as a set of tools (consisting of both C programs and shell procedures) that can be used to build accounting systems. acctsh(1M) describes the set of shell procedures built on top of the C programs.

Connect time accounting is handled by various programs that write records into /var/adm/wtmp, as described in utmp(4). The programs described in acctcon(1M) convert this file into session and charging records, which are then summarized by acctmerg(1M).

Process accounting is performed by the UNIX system kernel. Upon termination of a process, one record per process is written to a file (normally /var/adm/pacct). The programs in acctprc(1M) summarize this data for charging purposes; acctcms(1M) is used to summarize command usage. Current process data may be examined using acctcom(1).

Process accounting and connect time accounting (or any accounting records in the tacct format described in acct(4)) can be merged and summarized into total accounting records by acctmerg (see tacct format in acct(4)). prtacct (see acctsh(1M)) is used to format any or all accounting records.

acctdisk reads lines that contain user ID, login name, and number of disk blocks and converts them to total accounting records that can be merged with other accounting records.

acctdusg reads its standard input (usually from find / −print) and computes disk resource consumption (including indirect blocks) by login. If −u is given, records consisting of those filenames for which acctdusg charges no one are placed in *file* (a potential source for finding users trying to avoid disk charges). If −p is given, *file* is the name of the password file. This option is not needed if the password file is /etc/passwd. (See diskusg(1M) for more details.)

accton alone turns process accounting off. If *file* is given, it must be the name of an existing file, to which the kernel appends process accounting records (see acct(2) and acct(4)).

acctwtmp writes a utmp(4) record to its standard output. The record contains the current time and a string of characters that describe the *reason*. A record type of ACCOUNTING is assigned (see utmp(4)). *reason* must be a string of 11 or fewer characters, numbers, $, or spaces. For example, the following are suggestions for use in reboot and shutdown procedures, respectively:

```
acctwtmp "acctg on" >> /var/adm/wtmp
acctwtmp "acctg off" >> /var/adm/wtmp
```

For each user currently logged on, `closewtmp` puts a false DEAD_PROCESS record in the `/var/adm/wtmp` file. `runacct` (see `runacct(1M)`) uses this false DEAD_PROCESS record so that the connect accounting procedures can track the time used by users logged on before `runacct` was invoked.

For each user currently logged on, `runacct` uses `utmp2wtmp` to create an entry in the file `/var/adm/wtmp`, created by `runacct`. Entries in `/var/adm/wtmp` enable subsequent invocations of `runacct` to account for connect times of users currently logged in.

FILES

`/etc/passwd`	used for login name to user ID conversions
`/usr/lib/acct`	holds all accounting commands listed in sub-class 1M of this manual
`/var/adm/pacct`	current process accounting file
`/var/adm/wtmp`	login/logoff history file

SEE ALSO

acctcms(1M), acctcon(1M), acctmerg(1M), acctprc(1M), acctsh(1M), diskusg(1M), fwtmp(1M), runacct(1M), acct(4), utmp(4)
acctcom(1) in the *User's Reference Manual*
acct(2) in the *Programmer's Reference Manual*

NAME

acctcms – command summary from per-process accounting records

SYNOPSIS

/usr/lib/acct/acctcms [-a [-p] [-o]] [-c] [-j] [-n] [-s] [-t] *files*

DESCRIPTION

acctcms reads one or more *files*, normally in the form described in acct(4). It adds all records for processes that executed identically-named commands, sorts them, and writes them to the standard output, normally using an internal summary format. The options are:

-a   Print output in ASCII rather than in the internal summary format. The output includes command name, number of times executed, total kcore-minutes, total CPU minutes, total real minutes, mean size (in K), mean CPU minutes per invocation, "hog factor", characters transferred, and blocks read and written, as in acctcom(1). Output is normally sorted by total kcore-minutes.

-c   Sort by total CPU time, rather than total kcore-minutes.

-j   Combine all commands invoked only once under "***other".

-n   Sort by number of command invocations.

-s   Any filenames encountered hereafter are already in internal summary format.

-t   Process all records as total accounting records. The default internal summary format splits each field into prime and non-prime time parts. This option combines the prime and non-prime time parts into a single field that is the total of both, and provides upward compatibility with old (i.e., UNIX System V) style acctcms internal summary format records.

The following options may be used only with the –a option.

-p   Output a prime-time-only command summary.

-o   Output a non-prime (offshift) time only command summary.

When –p and –o are used together, a combination prime and non-prime time report is produced. All the output summaries will be total usage except number of times executed, CPU minutes, and real minutes, which will be split into prime and non-prime.

A typical sequence for performing daily command accounting and for maintaining a running total is:

```
acctcms file . . . > today
cp total previoustotal
acctcms -s today previoustotal > total
acctcms -a -s today
```

SEE ALSO

acct(1M), acctcon(1M), acctmerg(1M), acctprc(1M), acctsh(1M), fwtmp(1M), runacct(1M), acct(4), utmp(4)
acctcom(1) in the *User's Reference Manual*
acct(2) in the *Programmer's Reference Manual*

NOTES
>   Unpredictable output results if −t is used on new style internal summary format files, or if it is not used with old style internal summary format files.

NAME
acctcon, acctcon1, acctcon2 – connect-time accounting

SYNOPSIS
/usr/lib/acct/acctcon [*options*]

/usr/lib/acct/acctcon1 [*options*]

/usr/lib/acct/acctcon2

DESCRIPTION
acctcon converts a sequence of login/logoff records to total accounting records (see the tacct format in acct(4)). login/logoff records are read from standard input. The file /var/adm/wtmp is usually the source of the login/logoff records, however, because it may contain corrupted records or system date changes, it should first be fixed using wtmpfix. The fixed version of file /var/adm/wtmp can then be redirected to acctcon. The tacct records are written to standard output. Here are the options for acctcon:

-l *file*   *file* is created to contain a summary of line usage showing line name, number of minutes used, percentage of total elapsed time used, number of sessions charged, number of logins, and number of logoffs. This file helps track line usage, identify bad lines, and find software and hardware oddities. Hangup, termination of login(1) and termination of the login shell each generate logoff records, so that the number of logoffs is often three to four times the number of sessions. See init(1M) and utmp(4).

-o *file*   *file* is filled with an overall record for the accounting period, giving starting time, ending time, number of reboots, and number of date changes.

acctcon is a combination of the programs acctcon1 and acctcon2. acctcon1 converts login/logoff records, taken from the fixed /var/adm/wtmp file, to ASCII output. acctcon2 reads the ASCII records produced by acctcon1 and converts them to tacct records. acctcon1 can be used with the −l and −o options, described above, as well as with the following options:

-p   Print input only, showing line name, login name, and time (in both numeric and date/time formats).

-t   acctcon1 maintains a list of lines on which users are logged in. When it reaches the end of its input, it emits a session record for each line that still appears to be active. It normally assumes that its input is a current file, so that it uses the current time as the ending time for each session still in progress. The −t flag causes it to use, instead, the last time found in its input, thus assuring reasonable and repeatable numbers for non-current files.

EXAMPLES
The acctcon command is typically used as follows:

```
acctcon -l lineuse -o reboots < tmpwtmp > ctacct
```

The acctcon1 and acctcon2 commands are typically used as follows:

```
acctcon1 -l lineuse -o reboots < tmpwtmp | sort +1n +2 > ctmp
acctcon2 < ctmp > ctacct
```

FILES

/var/adm/wtmp

SEE ALSO

acct(1M), acctcms(1M), acctmerg(1M), acctprc(1M), acctsh(1M), fwtmp(1M),
init(1M), runacct(1M), acct(4), utmp(4)
acctcom(1), login(1) in the *User's Reference Manual*
acct(2) in the *Programmer's Reference Manual*

NOTES

The line usage report is confused by date changes. Use wtmpfix (see fwtmp(1M)),
with the /var/adm/wtmp file as an argument, to correct this situation.

NAME
acctmerg – merge or add total accounting files

SYNOPSIS
/usr/lib/acct/acctmerg [–a] [–i] [–p] [–t] [–u] [–v] [*file*] . . .

DESCRIPTION
acctmerg reads its standard input and up to nine additional files, all in the tacct format (see acct(4)) or an ASCII version thereof. It merges these inputs by adding records whose keys (normally user ID and name) are identical, and expects the inputs to be sorted on those keys. Options are:

–a   Produce output in ASCII version of tacct.
–i   Input files are in ASCII version of tacct.
–p   Print input with no processing.
–t   Produce a single record that totals all input.
–u   Summarize by user ID, rather than user ID and name.
–v   Produce output in verbose ASCII format, with more precise notation for floating–point numbers.

EXAMPLES
The following sequence is useful for making "repairs" to any file kept in this format:

acctmerg –v <*file1* > *file2*

Edit *file2* as desired . . .

acctmerg –i <*file2* > *file1*

SEE ALSO
acct(1M), acctcms(1M), acctcon(1M), acctprc(1M), acctsh(1M), fwtmp(1M), runacct(1M), acct(4), utmp(4)
acctcom(1) in the *User's Reference Manual*
acct(2) in the *Programmer's Reference Manual*

NAME
acctprc, acctprc1, acctprc2 – process accounting

SYNOPSIS
/usr/lib/acct/acctprc

/usr/lib/acct/acctprc1 [*ctmp*]

/usr/lib/acct/acctprc2

DESCRIPTION
acctprc reads standard input, in the form described by acct(4), and converts it
to total accounting records (see the tacct record in acct(4)). acctprc divides
CPU time into prime time and non-prime time and determines mean memory size
(in memory segment units). acctprc then summarizes the tacct records, according to user IDs, and adds login names corresponding to the user IDs. The summarized records are then written to standard output. acctprc1 reads input in
the form described by acct(4), adds login names corresponding to user IDs, then
writes for each process an ASCII line giving user ID, login name, prime CPU time
(tics), non-prime CPU time (tics), and mean memory size (in memory segment
units). If *ctmp* is given, it is expected to contain a list of login sessions sorted by
user ID and login name. If this file is not supplied, it obtains login names from
the password file, just as acctprc does. The information in *ctmp* helps it distinguish between different login names sharing the same user ID.

From standard input, acctprc2 reads records in the form written by acctprc1,
summarizes them according to user ID and name, then writes the sorted summaries to the standard output as total accounting records.

EXAMPLES
The acctprc command is typically used as shown below:

        acctprc < /var/adm/pacct > ptacct

The acctprc1 and acctprc2 commands are typically used as shown below:

        acctprc1 ctmp </var/adm/pacct │ acctprc2 >ptacct

FILES
/etc/passwd

SEE ALSO
acct(1M), acctcms(1M), acctcon(1M), acctmerg(1M), acctsh(1M), cron(1M),
fwtmp(1M), runacct(1M), acct(4), utmp(4)
acctcom(1) in the *User's Reference Manual*
acct(2) in the *Programmer's Reference Manual*

NOTES
Although it is possible for acctprc1 to distinguish among login names that share
user IDs for commands run normally, it is difficult to do this for those commands
run from cron(1M), for example. A more precise conversion can be done using
the acctwtmp program in acct(1M). acctprc does not distinguish between users
with identical user IDs.

A memory segment of the mean memory size is a unit of measure for the number
of bytes in a logical memory segment on a particular processor.

NAME

chargefee, ckpacct, dodisk, lastlogin, monacct, nulladm, prctmp, prdaily, prtacct, runacct, shutacct, startup, turnacct – shell procedures for accounting

SYNOPSIS

/usr/lib/acct/chargefee *login-name number*

/usr/lib/acct/ckpacct [*blocks*]

/usr/lib/acct/dodisk [-o] [*files ...*]

/usr/lib/acct/lastlogin

/usr/lib/acct/monacct *number*

/usr/lib/acct/nulladm *file*

/usr/lib/acct/prctmp

/usr/lib/acct/prdaily [-1] [-c] [*mmdd*]

/usr/lib/acct/prtacct *file* ["*heading*"]

/usr/lib/acct/runacct [*mmdd*] [*mmdd state*]

/usr/lib/acct/shutacct ["*reason*"]

/usr/lib/acct/startup

/usr/lib/acct/turnacct on | off | switch

DESCRIPTION

chargefee can be invoked to charge a *number* of units to *login-name*. A record is written to /var/adm/fee, to be merged with other accounting records by runacct.

ckpacct should be initiated via cron(1M) to periodically check the size of /var/adm/pacct. If the size exceeds *blocks*, 1000 by default, turnacct will be invoked with argument *switch*. If the number of free disk blocks in the /var file system falls below 500, ckpacct will automatically turn off the collection of process accounting records via the *off* argument to turnacct. When at least 500 blocks are restored, the accounting will be activated again on the next invocation of ckpacct. This feature is sensitive to the frequency at which ckpacct is executed, usually by cron.

dodisk should be invoked by cron to perform the disk accounting functions. By default, it will use diskusg (see diskusg(1M)) to do disk accounting on the S5 file system in /etc/vfstab. If the –o flag is used, it will use acctdusg (see acct(1M)) to do a slower version of disk accounting by login directory. *files* specifies the one or more filesystem names where disk accounting will be done. If *files* are used, disk accounting will be done on these filesystems only. If the –o flag is used, *files* should be mount points of mounted filesystems. If the –o option is omitted, *files* should be the special file names of mountable filesystems.

lastlogin is invoked by runacct to update /var/adm/acct/sum/loginlog, which shows the last date on which each person logged in.

monacct should be invoked once each month or each accounting period. *number* indicates which month or period it is. If *number* is not given, it defaults to the current month (01–12). This default is useful if monacct is to executed via cron(1M) on the first day of each month. monacct creates summary files in /var/adm/acct/fiscal and restarts the summary files in /var/adm/acct/sum.

nulladm creates *file* with mode 664 and ensures that owner and group are adm. It is called by various accounting shell procedures.

prctmp can be used to print the session record file (normally /var/adm/acct/nite/ctmp created by acctcon1 (see acctcon (1M)).

prdaily is invoked by runacct to format a report of the previous day's accounting data. The report resides in /var/adm/acct/sum/rprt/mmdd where *mmdd* is the month and day of the report. The current daily accounting reports may be printed by typing prdaily. Previous days' accounting reports can be printed by using the *mmdd* option and specifying the exact report date desired. The −1 flag prints a report of exceptional usage by login id for the specified date. Previous daily reports are cleaned up and therefore inaccessible after each invocation of monacct. The −c flag prints a report of exceptional resource usage by command, and may be used on current day's accounting data only.

prtacct can be used to format and print any total accounting (tacct) file.

runacct performs the accumulation of connect, process, fee, and disk accounting on a daily basis. It also creates summaries of command usage. For more information, see runacct(1M).

shutacct is invoked during a system shutdown to turn process accounting off and append a "reason" record to /var/adm/wtmp.

startup can be invoked when the system is brought to a multi-user state to turn process accounting on.

turnacct is an interface to accton (see acct(1M)) to turn process accounting on or off. The switch argument moves the current /var/adm/pacct to the next free name in /var/adm/pacctincr (where *incr* is a number starting with 1 and incrementing by one for each additional pacct file), then turns accounting back on again. This procedure is called by ckpacct and thus can be taken care of by the cron and used to keep pacct to a reasonable size. shutacct uses turnacct to stop process accounting. startup uses turnacct to start process accounting.

FILES

/var/adm/fee	accumulator for fees
/var/adm/pacct	current file for per-process accounting
/var/adm/pacct*incr*	used if pacct gets large and during execution of daily accounting procedure
/var/adm/wtmp	login/logoff summary
/usr/lib/acct/ptelus.awk	contains the limits for exceptional usage by login ID

/usr/lib/acct/ptecms.awk	contains the limits for exceptional usage by command name
/var/adm/acct/nite	working directory
/usr/lib/acct	holds all accounting commands listed in section 1M of this manual
/var/adm/acct/sum	summary directory contains information for monacct
var/adm/acct/fiscal	fiscal reports directory

SEE ALSO

acct(1M), acctcms(1M), acctcon(1M), acctmerg(1M), acctprc(1M), cron(1M), diskusg(1M), fwtmp(1M), runacct(1M), acct(4), utmp(4)
acctcom(1) in the *User's Reference Manual*
acct(2) in the *Programmer's Reference Manual*

NAME

arp – address resolution display and control

SYNOPSIS

arp *hostname*

arp −a [*unix* [*kmem*]]

arp −d *hostname*

arp −s *hostname ether_address* [temp] [pub] [trail]

arp −f *filename*

DESCRIPTION

The arp program displays and modifies the Internet-to-Ethernet address translation tables used by the address resolution protocol [arp(7)].

With no flags, the program displays the current ARP entry for *hostname*. The host
may be specified by name or by number, using Internet dot notation.

The following options are available:

−a   Display all of the current ARP entries by reading the table from the file
        kmem (default /dev/kmem) based on the kernel file *unix* (default
        /stand/unix).

−d   Delete an entry for the host called *hostname*. This option may only be
        used by the super-user.

−s   Create an ARP entry for the host called *hostname* with the Ethernet address
        ether_address. The Ethernet address is given as six hexadecimal bytes
        separated by colons. The entry will be permanent unless the word temp is
        given in the command. If the word pub is given, the entry will be pub-
        lished, for instance, this system will respond to ARP requests for *hostname*
        even though the hostname is not its own. The word trail indicates that
        trailer encapsulations may be sent to this host.

−f   Read the file named *filename* and set multiple entries in the ARP tables.
        Entries in the file should be of the form

             hostname ether_address [temp] [pub] [trail]

        with argument meanings as given above.

SEE ALSO

ifconfig(1M), arp(7).

NAME
     automount – automatically mount NFS file systems

SYNOPSIS
     automount [–nTv] [–D *name=value*] [–M *mount-directory*]
          [–t *sub-options*] [*directory map* [–*mount-options*]] . . .

DESCRIPTION
     automount is a daemon that automatically and transparently mounts an NFS file
     system as needed. It monitors attempts to access directories that are associated
     with an automount map, along with any directories or files that reside under
     them. When a file is to be accessed, the daemon mounts the appropriate NFS file
     system. You can assign a map to a directory using an entry in a direct auto-
     mount map, or by specifying an indirect map on the command line.

     automount uses a map to locate an appropriate NFS file server, exported file sys-
     tem, and mount options. It then mounts the file system in a temporary location,
     and replaces the file system entry for the directory or subdirectory with a sym-
     bolic link to the temporary location. If the file system is not accessed within an
     appropriate interval (five minutes by default), the daemon unmounts the file sys-
     tem and removes the symbolic link. If the indicated directory has not already
     been created, the daemon creates it, and then removes it upon exiting.

     Since the name-to-location binding is dynamic, updates to an automount map are
     transparent to the user. This obviates the need to pre-mount shared file systems
     for applications that have hard coded references to files.

     If you specify the dummy directory /–, automount treats the *map* argument that
     follows as the name of a direct map. In a direct map, each entry associates the
     full pathname of a mount point with a remote file system to mount.

     If the directory argument is a pathname, the *map* argument points to a file
     called an indirect map. An indirect map contains a list of the subdirectories con-
     tained within the indicated directory. With an indirect map, it is these sub-
     directories that are mounted automatically. The *map* argument must be a full
     pathname.

     The –*mount-options* argument, when supplied, is a comma-separated list of
     mount(1M) options, preceded by a hyphen (–). If mount options are specified in
     the indicated map, however, those in the map take precedence.

     The following options are available:

     –n   Disable dynamic mounts. With this option, references through the auto-
            mount daemon only succeed when the target file system has been previ-
            ously mounted. This can be used to prevent NFS servers from cross-
            mounting each other.

     –T   Trace. Expand each NFS call and display it on the standard output.

     –v   Verbose. Log status messages to the console.

     –D *name=value*
            Assign *value* to the indicated automount (environment) variable.

−M *mount-directory*

Mount temporary file systems in the named directory, instead of /tmp_mnt.

−t *sub-options*

Specify *sub-options* as a comma-separated list that contains any combination of the following:

l *duration*

Specify a *duration*, in seconds, that a file system is to remain mounted when not in use. The default is 5 minutes.

m *interval*

Specify an *interval*, in seconds, between attempts to mount a file system. The default is 30 seconds.

w *interval*

Specify an *interval*, in seconds, between attempts to unmount file systems that have exceeded their cached times. The default is 1 minute.

ENVIRONMENT

Environment variables can be used within an automount map. For instance, if $HOME appeared within a map, automount would expand it to its current value for the HOME variable.

If a reference needs to be protected from affixed characters, enclose the variable name within braces.

USAGE

Direct/Indirect Map Entry Format

A simple map entry (mapping) takes the form:

directory [*−mount-options*] *location* ...

where directory is the full pathname of the directory to mount when used in a direct map, or the basename of a subdirectory in an indirect map. *mount-options* is a comma-separated list of mount options, and *location* specifies a remote file system from which the directory may be mounted. In the simple case, *location* takes the form:

host : *pathname*

Multiple *location* fields can be specified, in which case automount sends multiple mount requests; automount mounts the file system from the first host that replies to the mount request. This request is first made to the local net or subnet. If there is no response, any connected server may respond.

If *location* is specified in the form:

host : *path* : *subdir*

host is the name of the host from which to mount the file system, *path* is the pathname of the directory to mount, and *subdir*, when supplied, is the name of a subdirectory to which the symbolic link is made. This can be used to prevent duplicate mounts when multiple directories in the same remote file system may be accessed. With a map for /home such as:

```
able  homeboy:/home/homeboy:able
baker homeboy:/home/homeboy:baker
```

and a user attempting to access a file in /home/able, automount mounts
homeboy:/home/homeboy, but creates a symbolic link called /home/able to the
able subdirectory in the temporarily mounted file system. If a user immediately
tries to access a file in /home/baker, automount needs only to create a symbolic
link that points to the baker subdirectory; /home/homeboy is already mounted.
With the following map:

```
able  homeboy:/home/homeboy/able
baker homeboy:/home/homeboy/baker
```

automount would have to mount the file system twice.

A mapping can be continued across input lines by escaping the NEWLINE with a
backslash. Comments begin with a # and end at the subsequent NEWLINE.

Directory Pattern Matching

The & character is expanded to the value of the directory field for the entry in
which it occurs. In this case:

```
able  homeboy:/home/homeboy:&
```

the & expands to able.

The * character, when supplied as the directory field, is recognized as the
catch-all entry. Such an entry resolves to any entry not previously matched. For
instance, if the following entry appeared in the indirect map for /home:

```
*     &:/home/&
```

this would allow automatic mounts in /home of any remote file system whose
location could be specified as:

hostname:/home/*hostname*

Hierarchical Mappings

A hierarchical mapping takes the form:

directory [/ [*subdirectory*]] [−*mount-options*] *location*...
            [/ [*subdirectory*] [−*mount-options*] *location*...]...

The initial /[*subdirectory*] is optional for the first location list and mandatory for
all subsequent lists. The optional *subdirectory* is taken as a filename relative to the
directory. If *subdirectory* is omitted in the first occurrence, the / refers to the
directory itself.

Given the direct map entry:

```
/arch/src   \
/          -ro,intr  arch:/arch/src        alt:/arch/src    \
/1.0       -ro,intr  alt:/arch/src/1.0     arch:/arch/src/1.0   \
/1.0/man   -ro,intr  arch:/arch/src/1.0/man  alt:/arch/src/1.0/man
```

automount would automatically mount /arch/src, /arch/src/1.0 and
/arch/src/1.0/man, as needed, from either arch or alt, whichever host
responded first.

Direct Maps

A direct map contains mappings for any number of directories. Each directory listed in the map is automatically mounted as needed. The direct map as a whole is not associated with any single directory.

Indirect Maps

An indirect map allows you to specify mappings for the subdirectories you wish to mount under the directory indicated on the command line. It also obscures local subdirectories for which no mapping is specified. In an indirect map, each directory field consists of the basename of a subdirectory to be mounted as needed.

Included Maps

The contents of another map can be included within a map with an entry of the form

        +*mapname*

where *mapname* is a filename.

Special Maps

The −null map is the only special map currently available. The −null map, when indicated on the command line, cancels a previous map for the directory indicated.

FILES

/tmp_mnt   parent directory for dynamically mounted file systems

SEE ALSO

df(1M), mount(1M), passwd(4).

NOTES

When it receives signal number 1, automount rereads the /etc/mnttab file to update its internal record of currently-mounted file systems. If a file system mounted with automount is unmounted by a umount command, automount should be forced to reread the file.

Shell filename expansion does not apply to objects not currently mounted.

Since automount is single-threaded, any request that is delayed by a slow or non-responding NFS server will delay all subsequent automatic mount requests until it completes.

Programs that read /etc/mnttab and then touch files that reside under automatic mount points will introduce further entries to the file.

NAME
        autopush – configure lists of automatically pushed STREAMS modules

SYNOPSIS
        autopush −f *file*
        autopush −r −M *major* −m *minor*
        autopush −g −M *major* −m *minor*

DESCRIPTION
        This command allows one to configure the list of modules to be automatically
        pushed onto the stream when a device is opened. It can also be used to remove
        a previous setting or get information on a setting.

        The following options apply to autopush:

        −f   This option sets up the autopush configuration for each driver according
                to the information stored in the specified file. An autopush file consists of
                lines of at least four fields each where the fields are separated by a space
                as shown below:

                    maj_   min_   last_min_   mod1 mod2 ... modn

        The first three fields are integers that specify the major device number, minor
        device number, and last minor device number. The fields following represent the
        names of modules. If *min_* is -1, then all minor devices of a major driver
        specified by *maj_* are configured and the value for *last_min_* is ignored. If
        *last_min_* is 0, then only a single minor device is configured. To configure a
        range of minor devices for a particular major, *min_* must be less than *last_min_*.

        The last fields of a line in the autopush file represent the list of module names
        where each is separated by a space. The maximum number of modules that can
        be automatically pushed on a stream is defined to be eight. The modules are
        pushed in the order they are specified. Comment lines start with a # sign.

        −r   This option removes the previous configuration setting of the particular
                major and *minor* device number specified with the −M and −m options
                respectively. If the values of *major* and *minor* correspond to a setting of a
                range of minor devices, where *minor* matches the first minor device
                number in the range, the configuration would be removed for the entire
                range.

        −g   This option gets the current configuration setting of a particular *major* and
                minor device number specified with the −M and −m options respectively. It
                will also return the starting minor device number if the request
                corresponds to a setting of a range (as described with the −f option).

SEE ALSO
        streamio(7)
        Programmer's Guide: STREAMS

NAME

backup – initiate or control a system backup session

SYNOPSIS

backup –i [–t *table*] [–o *name*] [–m *user*] [–ne] [–s | –v] [–c *week:day* | demand]

backup [–a] [–t *table*] [–o *name*] [–m *user*] [–ne] [–c *week:day*|demand]

backup –S | –R | –C [–u *user* | –A | –j *jobid*]

DESCRIPTION

Without options, the backup command performs all backup operations specified for the current day and week of the backup rotation in the backup register. This set of backup operations is considered a single job and is assigned a backup job id which can be used to control the progress of the session. As backup operations are processed, their status is tracked [See bkstatus(1M)]. As backup operations are completed, they are recorded in the backup history log.

backup may only be executed by a user with superuser privilege.

A backup job can be controlled in three ways. It can be canceled, suspended or resumed (after being suspended).

Modes of Operator Intervention

Backup operations may require operator intervention to perform such tasks as inserting volumes into devices or confirming proper volume labels. backup provides three modes of operator interaction.

backup with no options assumes that an operator is present, but not at the terminal where the backup command was issued. This mode sends a mail message to the operator. The mail identifies the device requiring service and the volume required. The operator reads the mail message, invokes the bkoper command, responds to the prompts, and the backup operation continues.

backup –i establishes interactive mode, which assumes that an operator is present at the terminal where the backup command was issued. In this mode, bkoper is automatically invoked at the terminal where the backup command was entered. The operator responds to the prompts as they arrive.

backup –a establishes automatic mode, which assumes that no operator is available. In this mode, any backup operation that requires operator intervention fails. Backups that can be satisfied by mounted volume proceed.

Register Validations

A number of backup service databases must be consistent before the backups listed in a backup register can be performed. These consistencies can only be validated at the time backup is initiated. If any of them fail, backup will terminate. Invoking backup –ne performs the validation checks in addition to displaying the set of backup operations to be performed. The validations are:

1.   The backup method must be a default method or be an executable file in /bkup/method .

2.   The dependencies for an entry are all defined in the register. Circular dependencies (eg., entry abc depends on entry def; entry def depends on entry abc) are allowed.

3.   The device group for a destination must be defined in the device group table, /dgroup.tab [See "*Device Management*").

Options

-a   Initiates all backup operations in automatic mode; does not prompt an operator to service media.

-c *week:day* | demand
            Selects from the backup register only those backup operations for the specified week and day of the backup rotation, instead of the current day and week of the rotation. If demand is specified, selects only those backup operations scheduled to be performed on demand.

-e   This option displays an estimate of the number of volumes required to perform each backup operation.

-i   Selects interactive operation

-j *jobid* Controls only the backup job identified by *jobid*. *jobid* is a backup job id.

-m *user*   Sends mail to the named *user* when all backup operations for the backup job are complete.

-n   Displays the set of backup operations that would be performed but does not actually perform the backup operations. The display is ordered according to the dependencies and priorities specified in the backup register.

-o *name*   Initiates backup operations only on the named originating object. *name* is an item in the following form:
                 oname | *odevice*

-s   Displays a "." for each 100 (512-byte) blocks transferred to the destination device. The dots are displayed while each backup operation is progressing.

-t *table* Initiates backup operations described in the specified backup register instead of the default register, etc/bkup/bkreg.tab . *table* is a backup register.

-u *user*   Controls backup jobs started by the named *user* instead of those started by the user invoking the command. *user* is a valid login id.

-v   While each backup operation is progressing, display the name of each file or directory as soon as it has been transferred to the destination device.

-A   Controls backup jobs for all users instead of those started by the user invoking the command.

-C   Cancels backup jobs.

-R   Resumes suspended backup jobs.

-S   Suspends backup jobs.

DIAGNOSTICS

The exit codes for the backup command are the following:

0 = successful completion of the task
1 = one or more parameters to backup are invalid.
2 = an error has occurred which caused backup to fail to
     complete *all* portions of its task.

EXAMPLES

Example 1:

```
backup -i -v -c 2:1 -m admin3
```

initiates those backups scheduled for Monday of the second week in the rotation period instead of backups for the current day and week. Performs the backup in interactive mode and displays on standard output the name of each file, directory, file system partition, or data partition as soon as it is transferred to the destination device. When all backups are completed, sends mail notification to the user with login id admin3.

Example 2:

```
backup -o /usr
```

initiates only those backups from the *usr* file system that is mounted on the originating device /dev/rdsk/c1d0s2 and is labeled usr.

Example 3:

```
backup -S
```

Suspends the backup jobs requested by the invoking user.

Example 4:

```
backup -R -j back-359
```

resumes the backup operations included in backup job id back-359.

FILES

```
/etc/bkup/method/*
/etc/bkup/bkreg.tab
/etc/device.tab
/etc/dgroup.tab
```

SEE ALSO

bkhistory(1M), bkoper(1M), bkreg(1M), bkstatus(1M)

NAME
  biod – NFS daemon

SYNOPSIS
  biod [*nservers*]

DESCRIPTION
  biod starts *nservers* asynchronous block I/O daemons. This command is used on
  an NFS client to buffer read-ahead and write-behind. Four is the usual number for
  nservers.

  The biod daemons are automatically invoked in run level 3.

SEE ALSO
  mountd(1M), nfsd(1M), sharetab(4).

NAME

bkexcept – change or display an exception list for incremental backups

SYNOPSIS

bkexcept [–t *file*] [–d *patterns*]

bkexcept [–t *file*] –a | –r *patterns*

bkexcept –C [*files*]

DESCRIPTION

The bkexcept command displays a list of patterns describing files that are to be excluded when backup operations occur using incfile. The list is known as the "exception list."

bkexcept may be executed only by a user with superuser privilege.

bkexcept –a adds patterns to the list.

bkexcept –d displays patterns from the list.

bkexcept –r removes patterns from the list.

Patterns

Patterns describe individual pathnames or sets of pathnames. Patterns must conform to pathname naming conventions specified under DEFINITIONS on the intro(2) page. A pattern is taken as a filename and is interpreted in the manner of cpio. A pattern can include the shell special characters *, ?, and []. Asterisk (*) and question mark (?) will match period (.) and slash(/). Because these are shell special characters, they must be escaped on the command line.

There are three general methods of specifying entries to the exception list:

- To specify all files under a particular directory, specify the directory name (and any desired subdirectories) followed by an asterisk:

  */directory/subdirectories/**

- To specify all instances of a filename regardless of its location, specify the filename preceded by an asterisk:

  /filename

- To specify one instance of a particular file, specify the entire pathname to the file:

  /directory/subdirectories/filename

If *pattern* is a dash (–), standard input is read for a list of patterns (one per line until EOF) to be added or deleted.

Compatibility

Prior versions of the backup service created exception lists using ed syntax. bkexcept –C provides a translation facility for exception lists created by ed. The translation is not perfect; not all ed patterns have equivalents in cpio. For those patterns that have no automatic translation, an attempt at translation is made, and the translated version is flagged with the word QUESTIONABLE. The exception list translation is directed to standard output. Redirect the standard output to a translation file, review the contents of the translation file (correcting entries that were not translated properly and deleting the QUESTIONABLE flags), and then use the resulting file as input to a subsequent bkexcept −a. For example, if the translated file was named checkfile the −a option would appear as follows:

        bkexcept -a - < checkfile

Options

−t *file* The filename used in place of the default file.

−a *pattern...*

Adds *pattern* to the exception list where *pattern* is one or more patterns (comma-separated or blank-separated and enclosed in quotes) describing sets of paths.

−d *pattern...*

Displays entries in the exception list. If *pattern* begins with a slash (/), −d displays all entries whose names begin with *pattern*. If *pattern* does not begin with a slash, −d displays all entries that include *pattern* anywhere in the entry. If *pattern* is a dash (−), input is taken from standard input. *pattern* is not a pattern − it matches patterns. *pattern* a∗b matches /a∗b but does not match /adb. For files containing a carriage return, a null exception list is returned. For files of zero length (no characters), an error is returned (search of table failed).

The entries are displayed in ASCII collating sequence order (special characters, numbers, then alphabetical order).

−r *pattern...*

Removes *pattern* from the exception list. *pattern* is one or a list of patterns (comma-separated or blank-separated and enclosed in quotes) describing sets of paths. *pattern* must be an exact match of an entry in the exception list for *pattern* to be removed. Patterns that are removed are echoed to standard output, stdout.

−C [*files*]

Displays on standard output the translation of each *file* (a prior version's exception list) to the new syntax. Each *file* contains ed patterns, one per line.

If *file* is omitted, the default UNIX exception list, /etc/save.d/except, is translated. If *file* is a dash (−), input is taken from standard input, one per line.

DIAGNOSTICS

The exit codes for the bkexcept command are the following:

0 = the task completed successfully
1 = one or more parameters to bkexcept are invalid
2 = an error has occurred, causing bkexcept to fail to
    complete *all* portions of its task

EXAMPLES

Example 1:

        bkexcept -a /tmp/*,/var/tmp/*,/usr/rje/*,*/trash,

adds the four sets of files to the exception list, (all files under /tmp, all files under /var/tmp, all files under /usr/rje, and any file on the system named trash).

Example 2:

        bkexcept −d /tmp

displays the following patterns from those added to the exception list in Example 1.

        /tmp/*

        bkexcept −d tmp

displays the following patterns from those added to the exception list in Example 1.

        /tmp/*, /var/tmp/*

displays one per line, with a heading.

Example 3:

        bkexcept −r /var/tmp/*,/usr/rje/*

removes the two patterns from the exception list.

Example 4:

        bkexcept −C /save.d/old.except > trans.except

translates the file /save.d/old.except from its ed format to cpio format and sends the translations to the file trans.except. The translations of /save.d/old.except may be added to the current exception list by using bkexcept −a as follows:

        bkexcept −a − < trans.except

FILES

/etc/bkup/bkexcept.tab   the default exception list for UNIX System V Release 4.0.

/etc/save.d/except   the default exception list for UNIX pre-System V Release 4.0.

SEE ALSO

backup(1M), incfile(1M).
cpio(1), ed(1), sh(1) in the *User's Reference Manual*.
intro(2) in the *Programmer's Reference Manual*.
''The Backup Service''chapter in the *System Administrator's Guide*.

NAME
        bkhistory – report on completed backup operations

SYNOPSIS
        bkhistory [–hl] [–f *field_separator*] [–d *dates*] [–o *names*] [–t *tags*]
        bkhistory –p *period*

DESCRIPTION
        bkhistory without options reports a summary of the contents of the backup his-
        tory log, bkhist.tab. Backup operations are sorted alphabetically by tag. For
        each tag, operations are listed from most to least recent. backup(1M) updates
        this log after each successful backup operation.

        bkhistory may be executed only by a user with the superuser privilege.

        bkhistory –p assigns a rotation *period* (in weeks) for the history log; all entries
        older than the specified number of weeks are deleted from the log. The default
        rotation period is one (1) week.

  Options
        –d *dates*
                Restricts the report to backup operations performed on the specified dates.
                dates are in the date format. *day, hour, minute,* and *year,* are optional and
                will be ignored. The list of *dates* is either comma-separated or blank-
                separated and surrounded by quotes.

        –f *field_separator*
                Suppresses field wrap on the display and specifies an output field separa-
                tor to be used. The value of *c* is the character that will appear as the field
                separator on the display output. For clarity of output, do not use a
                separator character that is likely to occur in a field. For example, do not
                use the colon as a field separator character if the display will contain dates
                that use a colon to separate hours from minutes. To use the default field
                separator (tab), specify the null character ("") for *c*.

        –h   Suppresses header for the reports.

        –l   Displays a long form of the report. This produces an ls –l listing of the
                files included in the backup archive (if backup tables of contents are avail-
                able on-line).

        –o *names*
                Restricts the report to the specified originating objects (file systems or data
                partitions). *names* is a list of *onames* and/or *odevices*. [See bkreg(1M)].

                The list of names is either comma-separated or blank-separated and sur-
                rounded by quotes.

        –p *period*
                Sets the number of weeks of information that will be saved in the backup
                history table. The minimum value of *period* is 1, which is also the default
                value. the size of int. By default, *period* is 1.

−t *tags*
Restricts the report to backups with the specified *tags*. *tags* is a list of tag values as specified in the backup register. The list of *tags* is either comma-separated or blank-separated and surrounded by quotes.

DIAGNOSTICS
The exit codes for the bkhistory command are the following:

0 =   the task completed successfully
1 =   one or more parameters to bkhistory are invalid
2 =   an error has occurred, causing bkhistory to fail to complete *all* portions of its task

EXAMPLES
Example 1:

bkhistory −p 3

sets the rotation period for the history log to three weeks. Entries older than three weeks are deleted from the log.

Example 2:

bkhistory −t SpoolDai,UsrDaily,TPubsWed

displays a report of completed backup operations for the three tags listed.

Example 3:

bkhistory −l −o /usr

Displays an ls −l listing of the files that were backed up from /usr (the originating object) if there is a table of contents.

FILES

/etc/bkup/bkhist.tab	the backup history log that contains information about successfully completed backup operations
/etc/bkup/bkreg.tab	description of the backup policy established by the administrator
/var/sadm/bkup/toc	list of directories with on-line tables of contents

SEE ALSO
backup(1M), bkreg(1M).
date(1), ls(1) in the *User's Reference Manual*.

NAME

bkoper – interact with backup operations to service media insertion prompts

SYNOPSIS

bkoper [–u *users*]

DESCRIPTION

Backup operations may require an operator to insert media and to confirm proper volume labels. The bkoper command provides a mailx-like interface for these operator interactions. It begins by printing a list of headers. Each header describes a backup operation requiring interaction, the device requiring attention including the media type and label of the volume to be inserted (see EXAMPLE). The system displays prompts and the operator issues commands to resolve the backup operation. Typing a carriage return invokes the current header. If no headers have been serviced, the current header is the first header on the list. If a header has been selected and serviced, the current header is the next one following.

bkoper may be executed only by a user with superuser privilege. By default, the operator may interact only with backup operations that were started by the same user ID .

If the –u *users* option is given, the operator interacts only with backup operations started by the specified *user*(s).

Commands

! *shell-command*
        Escapes to the shell. The remainder of the line after the ! is sent to the UNIX system shell (sh) to be interpreted as a command.

=   Prints the current backup operation number.

?   Prints this summary of commands.

[p|t] [*n*]   Both the p and t options operate in the same way. Either option will interact with the backup operation described by the *n*'th header. *n* defaults to the current header number.

h   Prints the list of backup operations.

q   Quits from bkoper.

DIAGNOSTICS

The exit codes for bkoper are the following:

0 = successful completion of the task
1 = one or more parameters to bkoper are invalid.
2 = an error has occurred which caused bkoper to fail to
      complete *all* portions of its task.

EXAMPLE

A sample header is shown below. Items appearing in the header are listed in the following order: header number, job-ID, tag, originating device, destination group, destination device, destination volume labels. [See bkreg(1M) for descriptions of items.] Not every header contains values for all these fields; if a destination group is not specified in /etc/bkup/bkreg.tab, then no value for "destination group" appears in the header.

```
1 back-111 usrsun /dev/dsk/c1d0s1  disk /dev/dsk/c2d1s9 usrsave
2 back-112 fs2daily /dev/dsk/c1d0s8 ctape /dev/ctape/c4d0s2 -
```

Backup headers are numbered on the basis of arrival; the oldest header has the
lowest number. If the destination device does not have a volume label, a dash is
displayed in the header.

SEE ALSO

bkreg(1M), bkstatus(1M), getvol(1M), mailx(1).

NAME

    bkreg – change or display the contents of a backup register

SYNOPSIS

    bkreg −p *period* [−w *cweek*] [−t *table*]

    bkreg −a *tag* −o *orig* −c *weeks:days* | demand −d *ddev* −m *method* | migration
        [−b *moptions*] [−t *table*] [−D *depend*] [−P *prio*]

    bkreg −e *tag* [−o *orig*] [−c *weeks:days* | demand] [−m *method* | migration] [−d *ddev*]
        [−t *table*] [−b *moptions*] [−D *depend*] [−P *prio*]

    bkreg −r *tag* [−t *table*]

    bkreg [−A | −O | −R] [−hsv] [−t *table*] [−c *weeks*[:*days*] | demand]

    bkreg −C *fields* [−hv] [−t *table*] [−c *weeks*[:*days*] | demand] [−f *c*]

DESCRIPTION

    A backup register is a file containing descriptions of backup operations to be per-
formed on a UNIX system. The default backup register is located in
/etc/bkup/bkreg.tab. Other backup registers may be created.

    The bkreg command may be executed only by a user with superuser privilege.

    Each entry in a backup register describes backup operations to be performed on a
given disk object (called the originating object) for some set of days and weeks
during a rotation period. There may be several register entries for an object, but
only one entry may specify backup operations for an object on a specific day and
week of the rotation period. The entry describes the object, the backup method
to be used to archive the object, and the destination volumes to be used to store
the archive. Each entry has a unique *tag* that identifies it. *Tags* must conform to
file naming conventions.

Rotation Period

    Backups are performed in a rotation period specified in weeks. When the end of
a rotation period is reached, a new period begins. Rotation periods begin on
Sundays. The default rotation period is one week.

Originating Objects

    An originating object is either a raw data partition or a filesystem. An originat-
ing object is described by its originating object name, its device name, and
optional volume labels.

    Several backup operations for different originating objects may be active con-
currently by specifying priorities and dependencies. During a backup session,
higher priority backup operations are attempted before lower priority backup
operations. All backup operations of a given priority may proceed concurrently
unless dependencies are specified. If one backup is declared to be dependent on
others, it will not be started until all of its antecedents have completed successfully.

Destination Devices

    Each backup archive is written to a set of storage volumes inserted into a destina-
tion device. A destination device can have destination device group, a destination device name, media characteristics, and volume labels. Default characteristics for a medium (as specified in the device table) may be overridden (see the

"Device Management" chapter in the *System Administrator's Guide*).

Backup Methods

An originating object is backed up to a destination device archive using a method. The method determines the amount of information backed up and the representation of that information. Different methods may be used for a given originating object on different days of the rotation. Each method accepts a set of options that are specific to the method.

Several default methods are provided with the Backup service. Others methods may be added by a UNIX system site. For descriptions of the default methods, see incfile(1M), ffile(1M), fdisk(1M), fimage(1M), and fdp(1M).

A backup archive may be migrated to a different destination by specifying migration as the backup method. The device name of the originating object for a migration must have been the destination device for a previously successful backup operation. This form of backup does not re-archive the originating object. It copies an archive from one destination to another, updating the backup service's databases so that restores can still be done automatically.

Register Validations

There are items in a single backup register entry and items across register entries that must be consistent for the backup service to conduct a backup session correctly. Some of these consistencies are checked at the time the backup register is created or changed. Others can be checked only at the time the backup register is used by backup(1M). See backup(1M) for a complete list of validations.

Modes

The bkreg command has two modes: changing the contents of a backup register and displaying the contents of a backup register.

Changing Contents

bkreg −p   changes the rotation period for a backup register. The default rotation period is one week.

bkreg −a   adds an entry to a backup register. This option requires other options to be specified. These are listed below under **Options**.

bkreg −e   edits an existing entry in a backup register.

bkreg −r   removes an existing entry from a backup register.

Displaying Contents

bkreg −C   produces a customized display of the contents of a backup register.

bkreg [−A|−R|−O]
            produces a summary display of the contents of a backup register.

Options

−a   Adds a new entry to the default backup register. Options required with −a are: *tag, originating device, weeks:days, destination device*, and *method*. If other options are not specified, the following defaults are used: the default backup register is used, no method options are specified, the priority is 0, and no dependencies exist between entries.

-b *moptions*
> Each backup method supports a specific set of options that modify its behavior. *moptions* is specified as a list of options that are blank-separated and enclosed in quotes. The argument string provided here is passed to the method exactly as entered, without modification. For lists of valid options, see "The Backup Service" chapter in the *System Administrator's Guide* and the following entries in this book: fdisk(1M), fdp(1M), ffile(1M), fimage(1M), and incfile(1M).

-c *weeks:days* | demand
> Sets the week(s) and day(s) of the rotation period during which a backup entry should be performed or for which a display should be generated.
> *weeks* is a set of numbers including 1 and 52. The value of *weeks* cannot be greater than the value of **-p***period*. *weeks* is specified as a combination of lists or ranges (either comma-separated or blank-separated and enclosed in quotes). An example set of weeks is

> > `''1 3-10,13''`

> indicating the first week, each of the third through tenth weeks, and the thirteenth week of the rotation period.

> *days* is either a set of numbers between 0 (Sunday) and 6 (Saturday), or a set of abbreviations between s (Sunday) and sa (Saturday). In addition, *days* are specified as a combination of lists or ranges (either comma-separated or blank-separated and enclosed in quotes).

> demand indicates that an entry is used only when explicitly requested by

> > `backup -c demand`

-d *ddev*
> Specifies *ddev* as the destination device for the backup operation. *ddev* is of the form:

> > [*dgroup*] [: [*ddevice*] [:*dchar*] [:*dmname*]]

> where either *dgroup* or *ddevice* must be specified and *dchar* and *dmname* are optional. (Both *dgroup* and *ddev* may be specified together.) Colons delineate field boundaries and must be included as indicated above.

> *dgroup* is the device group for the destination device. [See devgroup.tab(4).] If omitted, *ddevice* must be specified.

> *ddevice* is the device name of a specific destination device. [See device.tab(4).] If omitted, *dgroup* must be specified and any available device in *dgroup* may be used.

> *dchar* describes media characteristics. If specified, they override the default characteristics for the device and group. *dchar* is of the form:

> > keyword=*value*

> where keyword is a valid device characteristic keyword (as it appears in the device table.) *dchar* entries may be separated by commas or blanks. If separated by blanks, the entire string of arguments to *ddev* must be enclosed in quotes.

dlabels is a list of volume names of the destination volumes. The list of *dlabels* must be either comma-separated or blank-separated. If blank-separated, the entire *ddev* argument must be surrounded by quotes. Each *dlabel* corresponds to a *volumename* specified on the `labelit` command. If *dlabels* is omitted, `backup` and `restore` do not validate the volume labels on this entry.

−e   Edits an existing entry. If any of the options −b, −c, −d, −m, −o, −D, or −P are present, they replace the current settings for the specified entry in the register.

−f *c*   Overrides the default output field separator. *c* is the character that will appear as the field separator on the display output. The default output field separator is colon (:).

−h   Suppresses headers when generating displays.

−m *method* | `migration`

Performs the backup using the specified *method*. Default methods are: `incfile`, `ffile`, `fdisk`, `fimage`, and `fdp`. If the method to be used is not a default method, it must appear as the executable file in the standard method directory /etc/bkup/method. `migration` indicates that the value of *orig* (following the −o option) matches the value of *ddev* during a prior backup operation. The originating object is not rearchived; it is simply copied to the location specified by *ddev* (following the −d option). The backup history (if any) and tables of contents (if any) are updated to reflect the changed destination for the original archive.

−o *orig*

Specifies *orig* as the originating object for the backup operation. *orig* is specified in the following format:

    oname : *odevice* [: *omname*]

where *oname* is the name of an originating object. For file system partitions, it is the nodename on which the file system is usually mounted, mount. For data partitions, it is any valid path name. This value is provided to the backup method and validated by `backup`. The default data partition backup methods, `fdp` and `fdisk`, do not validate this name.

odevice is the device name for the originating object. In all cases, it is a raw disk partition device name. For AT&T 3B2 computers, this name is specified in the following format: /dev/rdsk/c?d?s?.

olabel is the volume label for the originating object. For file system partitions, it corresponds to the *volumename* displayed by the `labelit` command. A data partition may have an associated volume name that appears nowhere except on the outside of the volume (where it is taped); `getvol` may be used to have an operator validate the name.

On AT&T 3B2 computers, the special data partition /dev/rdsk/c?d?s6 names an entire disk and is used when disk formatting or repartitioning is done to reference the disk's volume table of contents (VTOC). [See fmthard(1M) and prtvtoc(1M).] `backup` validates this special full disk partition with the disk volume name specified when the disk was partitioned. [See fmthard(1M).] If the disk volume name is omitted, backup does not validate the volume labels for this originating object.

-p *period*

Sets the rotation period (in weeks) for the backup register to *period*. The minimum value is 1; the maximum value is 52. By default the current week of the rotation is set to 1.

-r   Removes the specified entries from the register.

-s   Suppresses wrap-around behavior when generating displays. Normal behavior is to wrap long values within each field.

-t *table*

Uses *table* instead of the default register, bkreg.tab.

-v   Generates displays using (vertical) columns instead of (horizontal) rows. This allows more information to be displayed without encountering problems displaying long lines.

-w *cweek*

Overrides the default behavior by setting the current week of the rotation period to *cweek*. *cweek* is an integer between 1 and the value of *period*. The default is 1.

-A   Displays a report describing all fields in the register. The display produced by this option is best suited as input to a filter, since in horizontal mode it produces extremely long lines.

-C *fields*

Generates a display of the contents of a backup register, limiting the display to the specified fields. The output is a set of lines, one per register entry. Each line consists of the desired fields, separated by a field separator character. *fields* is a list of field names (either comma-separated or blank-separated and enclosed in quotes) for the fields desired. The valid field names are period, cweek, tag, oname, odevice, olabel, weeks, days, method, moptions, prio, depend, dgroup, ddevice, dchar, and dlabel.

-D *depend*

Specifies a set of backup operations that must be completed successfully before this operation may begin. *depend* is a list of *tag*(s) (either comma-separated or blank-separated and enclosed in quotes) naming the antecedent backup operations.

-f *c*   Overrides the default output field separator. *c* is the character that will appear as the field separator on the display output. The default output field separator is colon (":").

-O   Displays a summary of all originating objects with entries in the register.

-P *prio*

Sets a priority of *prio* for this backup operation. The default priority is 0; the highest priority is 100. All backup operations with the same priority may run simultaneously, unless the priority is 0. All backups with priority 0 run sequentially in an unspecified order.

-R   Displays a summary of all destination devices with entries in the register.

DIAGNOSTICS

The exit codes for bkreg are the following:

0 = the task completed successfully
1 = one or more parameters to bkreg are invalid
2 = an error has occurred, causing bkreg to fail to
    complete *all* portions of its task

Errors are reported on standard error if any of the following occurs:

1.   The tag specified in bkreg −e or bkreg −r does not exist in the backup register.

2.   The tag specified in bkreg −a already exists in the register.

EXAMPLES

Example 1:

        bkreg −p 15 −w 3

establishes a 15-week rotation period in the default backup register and sets the current week to the 3rd week of the rotation period.

Example 2:

        bkreg −a acct5 −t wklybu.tab \
        −o /usr:/dev/rdsk/c1d0s2:usr −c "2 4-6 8 10:0,2,5" \
        −m incfile −b −txE \
        −d diskette:capacity=1404:acctwkly1,acctwkly2,acctwkly3 \

adds an entry named *acct5* to the backup register named wklybu.tab. If wklybu.tab does not already exist, it will be created. The originating object to be backed up is the /usr file system on the /dev/rdsk/c1d0s2 device which is known as usr. The backup will be performed each Sunday, Tuesday, and Friday of the second, fourth through sixth, eighth, and tenth weeks of the rotation period using the incfile (incremental file) method. The method options specify that a table of contents will be created on additional media instead of in the backup history log, the exception list is to be ignored, and an estimate of the number of volumes for the archive is to be provided before performing the backup. The backup will be done to the next available diskette device using the three diskette volumes acctwkly1, acctwkly2, and acctwkly3. These volumes have a capacity of 1404 blocks each.

Example 3:

        bkreg −e services2 −t wklybu.tab \
        −o /back:/dev/rdsk/c1d0s8:back −m migration \
        −c demand −d ctape:/dev/rdsk/c4d0s3 \

changes the specifications for the backup operation named services2 on the backup table wklybu.tab so that whenever the command backup −c demand is executed, the backup that was performed to the destination device back:dev/rdsk/c1d0s2:back will be migrated from that device (now serving as the originating device) to a cartridge tape.

Example 4:

    bkreg -e pubsfri -P 10 -D develfri,marketfri,acctfri

changes the priority level for the backup operation named pubsfri to 10 and makes this backup operation dependent on the three backup operations develfri, marketfri, and acctfri. The pubsfri operation will be done only after all backup operations with priorities greater than 10 have begun and after the develfri, marketfri, and acctfri operations have been completed successfully.

Example 5:

    bkreg -c 1-8:0-6

provides the default display of the contents of the default backup register, for all weekdays for the first through eighth weeks of the rotation period. The information in the register will be displayed in the following format:

Rotation Period = 10   Current Week = 4

Originating Device: / /dev/root

Tag	Weeks	Days	Method	Options	Pri	Dgroup
rootdai	1-8	1-6	incfile			diskette
rootsp	1-8	0	ffile	-bxt	20	ctape

Originating Device: /usr /dev/dsk/c1d0s2

Tag	Weeks	Days	Method	Options	Pri	Dgroup
usrdai	1-8	1-5	incfile			diskette
usrsp	1-8	0	ffile	-bxt	15	ctape

FILES

/etc/bkup/method/*
/etc/bkup/bkreg.tab   describes the backup policy established by the administrator
/etc/dgroup.tab   lists logical groupings of devices as determined by the administrator
/etc/device.tab   describes specific devices and their attributes

SEE ALSO

backup(1M), fdisk(1M), fdp(1M), incfile(1M), ffile(1M), fimage(1M), fmthard(1M), getvol(1M), labelit(1M), mkfs(1M), mount(1M), prtvtoc(1M), restore(1M)

NAME
bkstatus – display the status of backup operations

SYNOPSIS
bkstatus [–h] [–f *field_separator*] [–j *jobids*] [–s *states* | –a] [–u *users*]

bkstatus –p *period*

DESCRIPTION
Without options, the bkstatus command displays the status of backup operations that are in progress: either active, pending, waiting or suspended. When
used with the –a option, the backup command includes failed and completed
backup operations in the display.

bkstatus –p defines the amount of status information that is saved for display.

bkstatus may only be executed by a user with superuser privilege.

Each backup operation goes through a number of states as described below. The
keyletters listed in parentheses after each state are used with the –s option and
also appear on the display.

pending (p)
> backup has been invoked and the operations in the backup register for
> the specified day are scheduled to occur.

active (a)
> The backup operation has been assigned a destination device and
> archiving is currently underway; or a suspended backup has been
> resumed.

waiting (w)
> The backup operation is waiting for operator interaction, such as
> inserting the correct volume.

suspended (s)
> The backup operation has been suspended by an invocation of backup
> –S.

failed (f)
> The backup operation failed or has been cancelled.

completed (c)
> The backup operation has completed successfully.

The –a and –s options are mutually exclusive.

Options
–a
> Include failed and completed backup operations in the display. All
> backup operations that have occurred within the rotation period are
> displayed.

–f *field_separator*
> Suppresses field wrap on the display and specifies an output field
> separator to be used. The value of *c* is the character that will appear
> as the field separator on the display output. For clarity of output, do
> not use a separator character that is likely to occur in a field. For
> example, do not use the colon as a field separator character if the

display will contain dates that use a colon to separate hours from minutes. To use the default field separator (tab), specify the null character ("") for *c*.

-h   Suppress header on the display.

-j *jobids*   Restrict the display to the specified list of backup job ids (either comma-separated or blank-separated and enclosed in quotes). [See backup(1M)].

-p *period*   Define the amount of backup status information that is saved and made available for display as *period*. *period* is the number of weeks that information is saved in /bkup/bkstatus.tab. Status information that is older than the number of weeks specified in *period* is deleted from the status table. The minimum valid entry is 1. The maximum valid entry is 52. The default is 1 week.

-s *states*   Restrict the report to backup operations with the specified *states*. *states* is a list of state key-letters (concatenated, comma-separated or blank-separated and surrounded by quotes). For example,

       apf
       a,p,f
       "a p f"

all specify that the report should only include backup operations that are active, pending or failed.

-u *users*   Restrict the display to backup operations started by the specified list of *users* (either comma-separated or blank-separated and enclosed in quotes). *users* must be in the passwd file.

DIAGNOSTICS

The exit codes for the bkstatus command are the following:

0 = successful completion of the task
1 = one or more parameters to bkstatus are invalid.
2 = an error has occurred which caused bkstatus to fail to
    complete *all* portions of its task.

EXAMPLES

Example 1:

    bkstatus -p 4

specifies that backup status information is to be saved for four weeks. Any status information older than four weeks is deleted from the system.

Example 2:

    bkstatus -a -j back-459,back-395

produces a display that shows status for the two backup jobs specified, even if they have completed or failed.

Example 3:

        bkstatus −s a,c −u "oper3 oper4"

produces a display that shows only those backup jobs issued by users oper3 and
oper4 that have a status of either active or completed.

FILES

/etc/bkup/bkstatus.tab   lists the current status of backups that have
                              occurred or are still in progress

/etc/bkup/bkreg.tab   describes the backup policy decided on by the Sys-
                              tem Administrator

SEE ALSO

backup(1M), bkhist(1M), bkreg(1M)

NAME

brc, bcheckrc – system initialization procedures

SYNOPSIS

/sbin/brc

/sbin/bcheckrc

DESCRIPTION

These shell procedures are executed via entries in /sbin/inittab by init whenever the system is booted.

First, the bcheckrc procedure checks the status of the root file system. If the root file system is found to be bad, bcheckrc repairs it.

Then, bckeckrc mounts the /stand, /proc, and /var (if it exists) file systems (/var may exist as a directory in the root file system, or as a separate file system).

The brc script performs administrative tasks related to file sharing.

After these two procedures have executed, init checks for the initdefault value in /sbin/inittab. This tells init in which run level to place the system. If, for example, initdefault is set to 2, the system will be placed in the multiuser state via the rc2 procedure.

Note that bcheckrc should always be executed before brc. Also, these shell procedures may be used for several run-level states.

SEE ALSO

fsck(1M), init(1M), rc2(1M), shutdown(1M), inittab(4), mnttab(4).

NAME
   buildsys – operating system configuration script

SYNOPSIS
   /sbin/buildsys [–s]

DESCRIPTION
   The buildsys shell script performs the activities necessary to build a new bootable operating system from single user mode. buildsys is executed by the shell
   script rc6 or during a powerup if the configuration of a new bootable operating
   system is necessary. The bootable operating system resides in /stand, and is
   generally referred to as unix.

   Building a new operating system is usually required by hardware and system
   software changes made to your system. These changes must be incorporated into
   the bootable operating system so that it has complete and correct knowledge of
   the system configuration.

   buildsys is not intended to be executed at the user level.

   buildsys performs the following activities:

   - checks and mounts the file systems listed in /etc/boot_tab (it also
     looks at /etc/vfstab to do this)

   - runs cunix to create a new unix

   - unmounts all file systems previously mounted

   - optionally reboots the system; a reboot is requested if buildsys was
     run during a powerup (i.e., the –s option was specified); if it was run
     by rc6 (no –s option), then control is returned to rc6

   If an error occurs during the configuration of a new unix, buildsys exits to a
   shell; this gives the user a chance to fix any problems that might have caused the
   configuration process to fail, or to copy a version of unix to /stand/unix that is
   known to work in order to reboot the system. Exiting this shell (using ctrl–d or
   exit), puts the machine in firmware mode. The machine can then be rebooted
   from firmware.

SEE ALSO
   cunix(1M), init(1M), rc6(1M), shutdown(1M), vfstab(4).
   System Administrator's Guide

NAME
>   captoinfo — convert a *termcap* description into a *terminfo* description

SYNOPSIS
>   captoinfo [-v ...] [-V] [-1] [-w *width*] *file* ...

DESCRIPTION
>   captoinfo looks in *file* for termcap descriptions. For each one found, an equivalent terminfo description is written to standard output, along with any comments found. A description which is expressed as relative to another description (as specified in the termcap tc = field) will be reduced to the minimum superset before being output.
>
>   If no *file* is given, then the environment variable TERMCAP is used for the filename or entry. If TERMCAP is a full pathname to a file, only the terminal whose name is specified in the environment variable TERM is extracted from that file. If the environment variable TERMCAP is not set, then the file /usr/share/lib/termcap is read.
>
>   -v   print out tracing information on standard error as the program runs. Specifying additional -v options will cause more detailed information to be printed.
>
>   -V   print out the version of the program in use on standard error and exit.
>
>   -1   cause the fields to print out one to a line. Otherwise, the fields will be printed several to a line to a maximum width of 60 characters.
>
>   -w   change the output to *width* characters.

FILES
>   /usr/share/lib/terminfo/?/*   Compiled terminal description database.

NOTES
>   captoinfo should be used to convert termcap entries to terminfo entries because the termcap database (from earlier versions of UNIX System V) may not be supplied in future releases.

SEE ALSO
>   curses(3X), infocmp(1M), terminfo(4).

NAME
checkfsys – check a file system

SYNOPSIS
checkfsys

DESCRIPTION
The checkfsys command allows you to check for and optionally repair a damaged file system. The command invokes a visual interface (the check task available through the sysadm command). The initial prompt allows you to select the device that contains the filesystem. Then you are asked to specify the type of checking. The following choices are available:

check only
> Check the file system. No repairs are attempted.

interactive fix
> Repair the file system interactively. You are informed about each instance of damage and asked if it should be repaired.

automatic fix
> Repair the file system automatically. The program applies a standard repair to each instance of damage.

The identical function is available under the sysadm menu:

> sysadm check

NOTES
While automatic and interactive checks are generally successful, they can occasionally lose a file or a file's name. Files with content but without names are put in the *file-system*/lost+found directory.

If it is important not to lose data, check the file system first to see if it appears to be damaged. If it does, use one of the repair options of the task.

DIAGNOSTICS
The checkfsys command exits with one of the following values:

0   Normal exit.

2   Invalid command syntax. A usage message is displayed.

7   The visual interface for this command is not available because it cannot invoke fmli. (The FMLI package is not installed or is corrupted.)

SEE ALSO
fsck(1M), makefsys(1M), mountfsys(1M), sysadm(1M).

NAME

chroot – change root directory for a command

SYNOPSIS

/usr/sbin/chroot *newroot command*

DESCRIPTION

chroot causes the given command to be executed relative to the new root. The meaning of any initial slashes (/) in the path names is changed for the command and any of its child processes to *newroot* . Furthermore, upon execution, the initial working directory is *newroot* .

Notice, however, that if you redirect the output of the command to a file:

chroot *newroot command* >x

will create the file x relative to the original root of the command, not the new one.

The new root path name is always relative to the current root: even if a chroot is currently in effect, the *newroot* argument is relative to the current root of the running process.

This command can be run only by the super-user.

SEE ALSO

cd(1) in the *User's Reference Manual.*
chroot(2) in the *Programmer's Reference Manual.*

NOTES

One should exercise extreme caution when referencing device files in the new root file system.

NAME

chrtbl – generate character classification and conversion tables

SYNOPSIS

chrtbl [*file*]

DESCRIPTION

The chrtbl command creates two tables containing information on character classification, upper/lower-case conversion, character-set width, and numeric formatting. One table is an array of (257*2) + 7 bytes that is encoded so a table lookup can be used to determine the character classification of a character, convert a character [see ctype(3C)], and find the byte and screen width of a character in one of the supplementary code sets. The other table contains information about the format of non-monetary numeric quantities: the first byte specifies the decimal delimiter; the second byte specifies the thousands delimiter; and the remaining bytes comprise a null terminated string indicating the grouping (each element of the string is taken as an integer that indicates the number of digits that comprise the current group in a formatted non-monetary numeric quantity).

chrtbl reads the user-defined character classification and conversion information from *file* and creates three output files in the current directory. To construct *file*, use the file supplied in /usr/lib/locale/C/chrtbl_C as a starting point. You may add entries, but do not change the original values supplied with the system. For example, for other locales you may wish to add eight-bit entries to the ASCII definitions provided in this file.

One output file, ctype.c (a C-language source file), contains a (257*2)+7-byte array generated from processing the information from *file*. You should review the content of ctype.c to verify that the array is set up as you had planned. (In addition, an application program could use ctype.c.) The first 257 bytes of the array in ctype.c are used for character classification. The characters used for initializing these bytes of the array represent character classifications that are defined in /usr/include/ctype.h; for example, _L means a character is lower case and _S|_B means the character is both a spacing character and a blank. The second 257 bytes of the array are used for character conversion. These bytes of the array are initialized so that characters for which you do not provide conversion information will be converted to themselves. When you do provide conversion information, the first value of the pair is stored where the second one would be stored normally, and vice versa; for example, if you provide <0x41 0x61>, then 0x61 is stored where 0x41 would be stored normally, and 0x61 is stored where 0x41 would be stored normally. The last 7 bytes are used for character width information for up to three supplementary code sets.

The second output file (a data file) contains the same information, but is structured for efficient use by the character classification and conversion routines (see ctype(3C)). The name of this output file is the value you assign to the keyword LC_CTYPE read in from *file*. Before this file can be used by the character classification and conversion routines, it must be installed in the /usr/lib/locale/*locale* directory with the name LC_CTYPE by someone who is super-user or a member of group bin. This file must be readable by user, group, and other; no other permissions should be set. To use the character classification and conversion tables in this file, set the LC_CTYPE environment variable appropriately (see environ(5) or setlocale(3C)).

The third output file (a data file) is created only if numeric formatting information is specified in the input file. The name of this output file is the value you assign to the keyword LC_NUMERIC read in from *file*. Before this file can be used, it must be installed in the /usr/lib/locale/*locale* directory with the name LC_NUMERIC by someone who is super-user or a member of group bin. This file must be readable by user, group, and other; no other permissions should be set. To use the numeric formatting information in this file, set the LC_NUMERIC environment variable appropriately (see environ(5) or setlocale(3C)).

The name of the locale where you install the files LC_CTYPE and LC_NUMERIC should correspond to the conventions defined in *file*. For example, if French conventions were defined, and the name for the French locale on your system is french, then you should install the files in /usr/lib/locale/french.

If no input file is given, or if the argument "−" is encountered, chrtbl reads from standard input.

The syntax of *file* allows the user to define the names of the data files created by chrtbl, the assignment of characters to character classifications, the relationship between upper and lower-case letters, byte and screen widths for up to three supplementary code sets, and three items of numeric formatting information: the decimal delimiter, the thousands delimiter and the grouping. The keywords recognized by chrtbl are:

LC_CTYPE	name of the data file created by chrtbl to contain character classification, conversion, and width information
isupper	character codes to be classified as upper-case letters
islower	character codes to be classified as lower-case letters
isdigit	character codes to be classified as numeric
isspace	character codes to be classified as spacing (delimiter) characters
ispunct	character codes to be classified as punctuation characters
iscntrl	character codes to be classified as control characters
isblank	character code for the blank (space) character
isxdigit	character codes to be classified as hexadecimal digits
ul	relationship between upper- and lower-case characters
cswidth	byte and screen width information (by default, each is one character wide)
LC_NUMERIC	name of the data file created by chrtbl to contain numeric formatting information
decimal_point	decimal delimiter
thousands_sep	thousands delimiter

grouping   string in which each element is taken as an integer that indi-
                        cates the number of digits that comprise the current group in a
                        formatted non-monetary numeric quantity.

Any lines with the number sign (#) in the first column are treated as comments
and are ignored. Blank lines are also ignored.

Characters for isupper, islower, isdigit, isspace, ispunct, iscntrl,
isblank, isxdigit, and ul can be represented as a hexadecimal or octal constant
(for example, the letter a can be represented as 0x61 in hexadecimal or 0141 in
octal). Hexadecimal and octal constants may be separated by one or more space
and/or tab characters.

The dash character (–) may be used to indicate a range of consecutive numbers.
Zero or more space characters may be used for separating the dash character
from the numbers.

The backslash character (\) is used for line continuation. Only a carriage return
is permitted after the backslash character.

The relationship between upper- and lower-case letters (ul) is expressed as
ordered pairs of octal or hexadecimal constants: *<upper-case character lower-
case character>*. These two constants may be separated by one or more space
characters. Zero or more space characters may be used for separating the angle
brackets (< >) from the numbers.

The following is the format of an input specification for cswidth:
n1:s1,n2:s2,n3:s3
where,
        n1   byte width for supplementary code set 1, required
        s1   screen width for supplementary code set 1
        n2   byte width for supplementary code set 2
        s2   screen width for supplementary code set 2
        n3   byte width for supplementary code set 3
        s3   screen width for supplementary code set 3

decimal_point and thousands_sep are specified by a single character that gives
the delimiter. grouping is specified by a quoted string in which each member
may be in octal or hex representation. For example, \3 or \x3 could be used to
set the value of a member of the string to 3.

EXAMPLE

The following is an example of an input file used to create the USA-ENGLISH code
set definition table in a file named usa and the non-monetary numeric formatting
information in a file name num–usa.

```
LC_CTYPE   usa
isupper    0x41 – 0x5a
islower    0x61 – 0x7a
isdigit    0x30 – 0x39
isspace    0x20 0x9 – 0xd
ispunct    0x21 – 0x2f    0x3a – 0x40 \
           0x5b – 0x60    0x7b – 0x7e
iscntrl    0x0 – 0x1f     0x7f
isblank    0x20
```

```
        isxdigit  0x30 - 0x39   0x61 - 0x66 \
                  0x41 - 0x46
        ul        <0x41 0x61> <0x42 0x62> <0x43 0x63> \
                  <0x44 0x64> <0x45 0x65> <0x46 0x66> \
                  <0x47 0x67> <0x48 0x68> <0x49 0x69> \
                  <0x4a 0x6a> <0x4b 0x6b> <0x4c 0x6c> \
                  <0x4d 0x6d> <0x4e 0x6e> <0x4f 0x6f> \
                  <0x50 0x70> <0x51 0x71> <0x52 0x72> \
                  <0x53 0x73> <0x54 0x74> <0x55 0x75> \
                  <0x56 0x76> <0x57 0x77> <0x58 0x78> \
                  <0x59 0x79> <0x5a 0x7a>
        cswidth            1:1,0:0,0:0
        LC_NUMERIC  num_usa
        decimal_point            .
        thousands_sep            ,
        grouping                 "\3"
```

FILES

/usr/lib/locale/*locale*/LC_CTYPE
  data files containing character classification, conversion, and character-set width information created by chrtbl

/usr/lib/locale/*locale*/LC_NUMERIC
  data files containing numeric formatting information created by chrtbl

/usr/include/ctype.h
  header file containing information used by character classification and conversion routines

/usr/lib/locale/C/chrtbl_C
  input file used to construct LC_CTYPE and LC_NUMERIC in the default locale.

SEE ALSO

environ(5).
ctype(3C), setlocale(3C) in the *Programmer's Reference Manual*.

DIAGNOSTICS

The error messages produced by chrtbl are intended to be self-explanatory. They indicate errors in the command line or syntactic errors encountered within the input file.

WARNING

Changing the files in /usr/lib/locale/C will cause the system to behave unpredictably.

NAME

ckbinarsys – determine whether remote system can accept binary messages

SYNOPSIS

ckbinarsys [–S] –s *remote_system_name* –t *content_type*

DESCRIPTION

Because rmail can transport binary data, it may be important to determine whether a particular remote system (typically the next hop) can handle binary data via the chosen transport layer agent (uux, SMTP, etc.)

ckbinarsys consults the file /etc/mail/binarsys for information on a specific remote system. ckbinarsys returns its results via an appropriate exit code. An exit code of zero implies that it is OK to send a message with the indicated content type to the system specified. An exit code other than zero indicates that the remote system cannot properly handle messages with binary content.

The absence of the binarsys file will cause ckbinarsys to exit with a non-zero exit code.

Command-line arguments are:

–s *remote_system_name*
    Name of remote system to look up in /etc/mail/binarsys

–t *content_type*   Content type of message to be sent. When invoked by rmail, this will be one of two strings: text or binary, as determined by mail independent of any Content–Type: header lines that may be present within the message header. All other arguments are treated as equivalent to binary.

–S   Normally, ckbinarsys will print a message (if the binary mail is rejected) which would be suitable for rmail to return in the negative acknowledgement mail. When –S is specified, no message will be printed.

FILES

/etc/mail/binarsys
/usr/lib/mail/surrcmd/ckbinarsys

SEE ALSO

mailsurr(4), binarsys(4)
mail(1), uux(1) in the *User's Reference Manual.*

NAME
ckbupscd – check file system backup schedule

SYNOPSIS
ckbupscd [–m]

DESCRIPTION
ckbupscd consults the file /etc/bupsched and prints the file system lists from lines with date and time specifications matching the current time. If the –m flag is present, an introductory message in the output is suppressed so that only the file system lists are printed. Entries in the bupsched file are printed under the control of cron.

The file bupsched should contain lines of four or more fields, separated by spaces or tabs. The first three fields (the schedule fields) specify a range of dates and times. The rest of the fields constitute a list of names of file systems to be printed if ckbupscd is run at some time within the range given by the schedule fields. The general format is:

time[,time] day[,day] month[,month] fsyslist

where:

time   Specifies an hour of the day (0 through 23), matching any time within that hour, or an exact time of day (0:00 through 23:59).

day   Specifies a day of the week (sun through sat) or day of the month (1 through 31).

month   Specifies the month in which the time and day fields are valid. Legal values are the month numbers (1 through 12).

fsyslist   The rest of the line is taken to be a file system list to print.

Multiple time, day, and month specifications may be separated by commas, in which case they are evaluated left to right.

An asterisk (*) always matches the current value for the field in which it appears.

A line beginning with a sharp sign (#) is interpreted as a comment and ignored.

The longest line allowed (including continuations) is 1024 characters.

EXAMPLES
The following are examples of lines which could appear in the /etc/bupsched file.

06:00–09:00 fri 1,2,3,4,5,6,7,8,9,10,11 /applic
Prints the file system name /applic if ckbupscd is run between 6:00 A.M. and 9:00 A.M. any Friday during any month except December.

00:00–06:00,16:00–23:59 1,2,3,4,5,6,7 1,8 /
Prints a reminder to backup the root (/) file system if ckbupscd is run between the times of 4:00 P.M. and 6:00 A.M. during the first week of August or January.

FILES

/etc/bupsched   specification file containing times and file system to back up

SEE ALSO

cron(1M).

echo(1), sh(1), sysadm(1) in the *User's Reference Manual*.

NOTES

ckbupscd will report file systems due for backup if invoked any time in the window. It does not know that backups may have just been done.

ckbupscd will be removed in the next release of System V.

NAME

ckdate, errdate, helpdate, valdate – prompts for and validates a date

SYNOPSIS

ckdate [–Q] [–W *width*] [–f *format*] [–d *default*] [–h *help*] [–e *error*] [–p *prompt*]
[–k *pid* [–s *signal*]]

errdate [–W] [–e *error*] [–f *format*]
helpdate [–W] [–h *help*] [–f *format*]
valdate [–f *format] input*

DESCRIPTION

ckdate prompts a user and validates the response. It defines, among other
things, a prompt message whose response should be a date, text for help and
error messages, and a default value (which will be returned if the user responds
with a carriage return). The user response must match the defined format for a
date.

All messages are limited in length to 70 characters and are formatted automatically. Any white space used in the definition (including newline) is stripped.
The –W option cancels the automatic formatting. When a tilde is placed at the
beginning or end of a message definition, the default text will be inserted at that
point, allowing both custom text and the default text to be displayed.

If the prompt, help or error message is not defined, the default message (as
defined under NOTES) will be displayed.

Three visual tool modules are linked to the ckdate command. They are errdate
(which formats and displays an error message), helpdate (which formats and
displays a help message), and valdate (which validates a response). These
modules should be used in conjunction with FML objects. In this instance, the
FML object defines the prompt. When *format* is defined in the errdate and
helpdate modules, the messages will describe the expected format.

The options and arguments for this command are:

–Q	Specifies that quit will not be allowed as a valid response.
–W *width*	Specifies that prompt, help and error messages will be formatted to a line length of *width*.
–f *format*	Specifies the format against which the input will be verified. Possible formats and their definitions are:

%b = abbreviated month name
%B = full month name
%d = day of month (01 - 31)
%D = date as %m/%d/%y (the default format)
%e = day of month (1 - 31; single digits are preceded by a blank)
%h = abbreviated month name (jan, feb, mar)
%m = month number (01 - 12)
%y = year within century (e.g. 89)
%Y = year as CCYY (e.g. 1989)

-d *default*   Defines the default value as *default*.
                The default does not have to meet the format criteria.
-h *help*   Defines the help messages as *help*.
-e *error*   Defines the error message as *error*.
-p *prompt*   Defines the prompt message as *prompt*.
-k *pid*   Specifies that process ID *pid* is to be sent a signal if the user chooses
                to abort.
-s *signal*   Specifies that the process ID *pid* defined with the -k option
                is to be sent signal `signal` when quit is chosen. If no signal is
                specified, SIGTERM is used.
input   Input to be verified against format criteria.

EXIT CODES

0 = Successful execution
1 = EOF on input
2 = Usage error
3 = User termination (quit)
4 = Garbled format argument

NOTES

The default prompt for ckdate is:

        Enter the date [?,q]:

The default error message is:

        ERROR - Please enter a date, using the following format: *<format>*.

The default help message is:

        Please enter a date, using the following format: *<format>*.

When the quit option is chosen (and allowed), q is returned along with the return
code 3. The valdate module will not produce any output. It returns zero for
success and non-zero for failure.

NAME

ckgid, errgid, helpgid, valgid – prompts for and validates a group id

SYNOPSIS

ckgid [–Q] [–W width] [–m] [–d default] [–h help] [–e error] [–p prompt]
[–k pid [–s signal]]

errgid [–W] [–e error]
helpgid [–W] [–m] [–h help]
valgid input

DESCRIPTION

ckgid prompts a user and validates the response. It defines, among other things,
a prompt message whose response should be an existing group ID, text for help
and error messages, and a default value (which will be returned if the user
responds with a carriage return).

All messages are limited in length to 70 characters and are formatted automatically. Any white space used in the definition (including newline) is stripped.
The –W option cancels the automatic formatting. When a tilde is placed at the
beginning or end of a message definition, the default text will be inserted at that
point, allowing both custom text and the default text to be displayed.

If the prompt, help or error message is not defined, the default message (as
defined under NOTES) will be displayed.

Three visual tool modules are linked to the ckgid command. They are errgid
(which formats and displays an error message), helpgid (which formats and
displays a help message), and valgid (which validates a response). These
modules should be used in conjunction with FML objects. In this instance, the
FML object defines the prompt.

The options and arguments for this command are:

–Q	Specifies that quit will not be allowed as a valid response.
–W width	Specifies that prompt, help and error messages will be formatted to a line length of width.
–m	Displays a list of all groups when help is requested or when the user makes an error.
–d default	Defines the default value as default. The default is not validated and so does not have to meet any criteria.
–h help	Defines the help messages as help.
–e error	Defines the error message as error.
–p prompt	Defines the prompt message as prompt.
–k pid	Specifies that process ID pid is to be sent a signal if the user chooses to abort.
–s signal	Specifies that the process ID pid defined with the –k option is to be sent signal signal when quit is chosen. If no signal is specified, SIGTERM is used.
input	Input to be verified against /etc/group

EXIT CODES
>   0 = Successful execution
>   1 = EOF on input
>   2 = Usage error
>   3 = User termination (quit)

NOTES
>   The default prompt for ckgid is:
>
>>   `Enter the name of an existing group [?,q]:`
>
>   The default error message is:
>
>>   `ERROR - Please enter the name of an existing group.`
>>   *(if the —m option of* ckgid *is used, a list of valid groups is displayed here)*
>
>   The default help message is:
>
>>   `Please enter an existing group name.`
>>   *(if the —m option of* ckgid *is used, a list of valid groups is displayed here)*
>
>   When the quit option is chosen (and allowed), q is returned along with the return code **3**. The `valgid` module will not produce any output. It returns zero for success and non-zero for failure.

NAME

ckint – display a prompt; verify and return an integer value

SYNOPSIS

ckint [–Q] [–W *width*] [–b *base*] [–d *default*] [–h *help*] [–e *error*] [–p *prompt*]
[–k *pid* [–s signal]]

errint [–W] [–b *base*] [–e *error*]
helpint [–W] [–b *base*] [–h *help*]
valint [–b *base*] *input*

DESCRIPTION

ckint prompts a user, then validates the response. It defines, among other
things, a prompt message whose response should be an integer, text for help and
error messages, and a default value (which will be returned if the user responds
with a carriage return).

All messages are limited in length to 70 characters and are formatted automatically. Any white space used in the definition (including newline) is stripped.
The –W option cancels the automatic formatting. When a tilde is placed at the
beginning or end of a message definition, the default text will be inserted at that
point, allowing both custom text and the default text to be displayed.

If the prompt, help or error message is not defined, the default message (as
defined under NOTES) will be displayed.

Three visual tool modules are linked to the ckint command. They are errint
(which formats and displays an error message), helpint (which formats and
displays a help message), and valint (which validates a response). These
modules should be used in conjunction with FML objects. In this instance, the
FML object defines the prompt. When *base* is defined in the errint and helpint
modules, the messages will include the expected base of the input.

The options and arguments for this command are:

–Q   Specifies that quit will not be allowed as a valid response.

–W   Specifies that prompt, help and error messages will be formatted to a line
length of *width*.

–b   Defines the base for input. Must be 2 to 36, default is 10.

–d   Defines the default value as *default*. The default is not validated and so
does not have to meet any criteria.

–h   Defines the help messages as *help*.

–e   Defines the error message as *error*.

–p   Defines the prompt message as *prompt*.

–k   Specifies that process ID *pid* is to be sent a signal if the user chooses to
abort.

–s   Specifies that the process ID *pid* defined with the –k option is to be sent
signal signal when quit is chosen. If no signal is specified, SIGTERM is
used.

       input   Input to be verified against *base* criterion.

EXIT CODES

       0 = Successful execution

       1 = EOF on input

       2 = Usage error

       3 = User termination (quit)

NOTES

       The default base 10 prompt for ckint is:

```
Enter an integer [?,q]:
```

The default base 10 error message is:

```
ERROR - Please enter an integer.
```

The default base 10 help message is:

```
Please enter an integer.
```

The messages are changed from "integer" to "base *base* integer" if the base is set to a number other than 10.

When the quit option is chosen (and allowed), q is returned along with the return code 3. The **valint** module will not produce any output. It returns zero for success and non-zero for failure.

NAME

ckitem – build a menu; prompt for and return a menu item

SYNOPSIS

ckitem [–Q] [–W *width*] [–uno] [–f *file*] [–l *label*] [[–i *invis*] [, ...]] [–m *max*]
[–d *default*] [–h *help*] [–e *error*] [–p *prompt*] [–k *pid* [–s *signal*]] [*choice* [...]]

erritem [–W] [–e *error*] [*choice* [...]]
helpint [–W] [–h *help*] [*choice* [...]]

DESCRIPTION

ckitem builds a menu and prompts the user to choose one item from a menu of
items. It then verifies the response. Options for this command define, among
other things, a prompt message whose response will be a menu item, text for
help and error messages, and a default value (which will be returned if the user
responds with a carriage return).

By default, the menu is formatted so that each item is prepended by a number
and is printed in columns across the terminal. Column length is determined by
the longest choice. Items are alphabetized.

All messages are limited in length to 70 characters and are formatted automatically. Any white space used in the definition (including newline) is stripped.
The –W option cancels the automatic formatting. When a tilde is placed at the
beginning or end of a message definition, the default text will be inserted at that
point, allowing both custom text and the default text to be displayed.

If the prompt, help or error message is not defined, the default message (as
defined under NOTES) will be displayed.

Two visual tool modules are linked to the ckitem command. They are erritem
(which formats and displays an error message) and helpitem (which formats and
displays a help message). These modules should be used in conjunction with
FML objects. In this instance, the FML object defines the prompt. When *choice* is
defined in these modules, the messages will describe the available menu choice
(or choices).

The options and arguments for this command are:

–Q   Specifies that quit will not be allowed as a valid response.

–W   Specifies that prompt, help and error messages will be formatted to a line
      length of *width*.

–u   Specifies that menu items should be displayed as an unnumbered list.

–n   Specifies that menu items should not be displayed in alphabetical order.

–o   Specifies that only one menu token will be returned.

–f   Defines a file, *file*. which contains a list of menu items to be displayed.
      [The format of this file is: token<tab>description. Lines beginning
      with a pound sign (#) are designated as comments and ignored.]

–l   Defines a label, *label*, to print above the menu.

-i   Defines invisible menu choices (those which will not be printed in the menu). (For example, "all" used as an invisible choice would mean it is a legal option but does not appear in the menu. Any number of invisible choices may be defined.) Invisible choices should be made known to a user either in the prompt or in a help message.

-m   Defines the maximum number of menu choices allowed.

-d   Defines the default value as *default*. The default is not validated and so does not have to meet any criteria.

-h   Defines the help messages as *help*.

-e   Defines the error message as *error*.

-p   Defines the prompt message as *prompt*.

-k   Specifies that the process ID *pid* is to be sent a signal if the user chooses to abort.

-s   Specifies that process ID *pid* defined with the -k option is to be sent signal *signal* when quit is chosen. If no signal is specified, SIGTERM is used.

choice Defines menu items. Items should be separated by white space or newline.

SEE ALSO
allocmenu(3X)
printmenu(3X)
setinvis(3X)
setitems(3X)

EXIT CODES
0 = Successful execution
1 = EOF on input
2 = Usage error
3 = User termination (quit)
4 = No choices from which to choose

NOTES
The user may input the number of the menu item if choices are numbered or as much of the string required for a unique identification of the item. Long menus are paged with 10 items per page.

When menu entries are defined both in a file (by using the -f option) and also on the command line, they are usually combined alphabetically. However, if the -n option is used to suppress alphabetical ordering, then the entries defined in the file are shown first, followed by the options defined on the command line.

The default prompt for ckitem is:

```
Enter selection [?,??,q]:
```

One question mark will give a help message and then redisplay the prompt. Two question marks will give a help message and then redisplay the menu label, the menu and the prompt.

The default error message is:

```
ERROR - Does not match an available menu selection.
Enter one of the following:
- the number of the menu item you wish to select
- the token associated withe the menu item,
- partial string which uniquely identifies the token for the
menu item
- ?? to reprint the menu
```

The default help message is:

```
Enter one of the following:
- the number of the menu item you wish to select
- the token associated with the menu item,
- partial string which uniquely identifies the token for the
menu item
- ?? to reprint the menu
```

When the quit option is chosen (and allowed), q is returned along with the return code 3.

NAME

ckkeywd – prompts for and validates a keyword

SYNOPSIS

ckkeywd [-Q] [-W *width*] [-d *default*] [-h *help*] [-e *error*] [-p *prompt*]
[-k *pid* [-s *signal*]] [*keyword* [...]]

DESCRIPTION

ckkeywd prompts a user and validates the response. It defines, among other things, a prompt message whose response should be one of a list of keywords, text for help and error messages, and a default value (which will be returned if the user responds with a carriage return). The answer returned from this command must match one of the defined list of keywords.

All messages are limited in length to 70 characters and are formatted automatically. Any white space used in the definition (including newline) is stripped. The -W option cancels the automatic formatting. When a tilde is placed at the beginning or end of a message definition, the default text will be inserted at that point, allowing both custom text and the default text to be displayed.

If the prompt, help or error message is not defined, the default message (as defined under NOTES) will be displayed.

-Q   Specifies that quit will not be allowed as a valid response.

-W   Specifies that prompt, help and error messages will be formatted to a line length of *width*.

-d   Defines the default value as *default*. The default is not validated and so does not have to meet any criteria.

-h   Defines the help messages as *help*.

-e   Defines the error message as *error*.

-p   Defines the prompt message as *prompt*.

-k   Specifies that process ID *pid* is to be sent a signal if the user chooses to abort.

-s   Specifies that the process ID *pid* defined with the -k option is to be sent signal `signal` when quit is chosen. If no signal is specified, SIGTERM is used.

keyword

Defines the keyword, or list of keywords, against which the answer will be verified.

EXIT CODES

0 = Successful execution
1 = EOF on input
2 = Usage error
3 = User termination (quit)
4 = No keywords from which to choose

NOTES

The default prompt for **ckkeywd** is:

```
Enter selection [keyword,[...],?,q]:
```

The default error message is:

```
ERROR - Does not match any of the valid selections.
Please enter one of the following keywords:
keyword[,...]
```

The default help message is:

```
Please enter one of the following keywords:
keyword[,...]
```

When the quit option is chosen (and allowed), **q** is returned along with the return code 3.

NAME

ckpath – display a prompt; verify and return a pathname

SYNOPSIS

ckpath [-Q] [-W width] [-a|l] [-b|c|g|y] [-n|[o|z]] [-rtwx] [-d default]
[-h help] [-e error] [-p prompt] [-k pid [-s signal]]

errpath [-W] [-a|l] [-b|c|g|y] [-n|[o|z]] [-rtwx] [-e error]
helppath [-W] [-a|l] [-b|c|g|y] [-n|[o|z]] [-rtwx] [-h help]
valpath [-a|l] [-b|c|g|y] [-n|[o|z]] [-rtwx] input

DESCRIPTION

ckpath prompts a user and validates the response. It defines, among other things, a prompt message whose response should be a pathname, text for help and error messages, and a default value (which will be returned if the user responds with a carriage return).

The pathname must obey the criteria specified by the first group of options. If no criteria is defined, the pathname must be for a normal file that does not yet exist. If neither -a (absolute) or -l (relative) is given, then either is assumed to be valid.

All messages are limited in length to 70 characters and are formatted automatically. Any white space used in the definition (including newline) is stripped. The -W option cancels the automatic formatting. When a tilde is placed at the beginning or end of a message definition, the default text will be inserted at that point, allowing both custom text and the default text to be displayed.

If the prompt, help or error message is not defined, the default message (as defined under NOTES) will be displayed.

Three visual tool modules are linked to the ckpath command. They are errpath (which formats and displays an error message), helppath (which formats and displays a help message), and valpath (which validates a response). These modules should be used in conjunction with FACE objects. In this instance, the FACE object defines the prompt.

The options and arguments for this command are:

-Q   Specifies that quit will not be allowed as a valid response.

-W   Specifies that prompt, help and error messages will be formatted to a line length of width.

-a   Pathname must be an absolute path.

-l   Pathname must be a relative path.

-b   Pathname must be a block special file.

-c   Pathname must be a character special file.

-g   Pathname must be a regular file.

-y   Pathname must be a directory.

-n   Pathname must not exist (must be new).

-o   Pathname must exist (must be old).

-z   Pathname must have a length greater than 0 bytes.

-r   Pathname must be readable.

-t   Pathname must be creatable (touchable). Pathname will be created if it does not already exist.

-w   Pathname must be writable.

-x   Pathname must be executable.

-d   Defines the default value as *default*. The default is not validated and so does not have to meet any criteria.

-h   Defines the help messages as *help*.

-e   Defines the error message as *error*.

-p   Defines the prompt message as *prompt*.

-k   Specifies that process ID *pid* is to be sent a signal if the user chooses to abort.

-s   Specifies that the process ID *pid* defined with the -k option is to be sent signal `signal` when quit is chosen. If no signal is specified, SIGTERM is used.

input   Input to be verified against validation options.

EXIT CODES
0 = Successful execution
1 = EOF on input
2 = Usage error
3 = User termination (quit)
4 = Mutually exclusive options

NOTES
The text of the default messages for ckpath depends upon the criteria options that have been used. An example default prompt for ckpath (using the -a option) is:

    Enter a pathname [?,q]:

An example default error message (using the -a option) is:

    ERROR - Invalid pathname entered. A pathname is a filename, optionally preceded by parent directories.

An example default help message is:

    A pathname is a filename, optionally preceded by parent directories. The pathname you enter:
    - must contain 1 to {NAME_MAX} characters
    - must not contain a spaces or special characters

NAME_MAX is a system variable that is defined in limits.h.

When the quit option is chosen (and allowed), q is returned along with the return code 3. The valpath module will not produce any output. It returns zero for success and non-zero for failure.

NAME

ckrange – prompts for and validates an integer

SYNOPSIS

ckrange [–Q] [–W width] [–l lower] [–u upper] [–b base] [–d default] [–h help]
[–e error] [–p prompt] [–k pid [–s signal]]

errange [–W] [–l lower] [–u upper] [–e error]
helprange [–W] [–l lower] [–u upper] [–h help]
valrange [–l lower] [–u upper] [–b base] input

DESCRIPTION

ckrange prompts a user and validates the response. It defines, among other
things, a prompt message whose response should be an integer in the range
specified, text for help and error messages, and a default value (which will be
returned if the user responds with a carriage return).

This command also defines a range for valid input. If either the lower or upper
limit is left undefined, then the range is bounded on only one end.

All messages are limited in length to 70 characters and are formatted automatically. Any white space used in the definition (including newline) is stripped.
The –W option cancels the automatic formatting. When a tilde is placed at the
beginning or end of a message definition, the default text will be inserted at that
point, allowing both custom text and the default text to be displayed.

If the prompt, help or error message is not defined, the default message (as
defined under NOTES) will be displayed.

Three visual tool modules are linked to the ckrange command. They are
errange (which formats and displays an error message), helprange (which formats and displays a help message), and valrange (which validates a response).
These modules should be used in conjunction with FACE objects. In this
instance, the FACE object defines the prompt.

The options and arguments for this command are:

–Q   Specifies that quit will not be allowed as a valid response.

–W   Specifies that prompt, help and error messages will be formatted to a line
       length of width.

–l   Defines the lower limit of the range as lower. Default is the machine's
       largest negative integer or long.

–u   Defines the upper limit of the range as upper. Default is the machine's
       largest positive integer or long.

–b   Defines the base for input. Must be 2 to 36, default is 10.

–d   Defines the default value as default. The default is not validated and so
       does not have to meet any criteria.

–h   Defines the help messages as help.

-e   Defines the error message as *error*.

-p   Defines the prompt message as *prompt*.

-k   Specifies that process ID *pid* is to be sent a signal if the user chooses to abort.

-s   Specifies that the process ID *pid* defined with the -k option is to be sent signal `signal` when quit is chosen. If no signal is specified, SIGTERM is used.

input   Input to be verified against upper and lower limits and base.

EXIT CODES

0 = Successful execution
1 = EOF on input
2 = Usage error
3 = User termination (quit)

NOTES

The default base 10 prompt for `ckrange` is:

Enter an integer between *lower_bound* and *upper_bound* [q,?]:

The default base 10 error message is:

ERROR — Please enter an integer between *lower_bound* and *upper_bound*.

The default base 10 help message is:

Please enter an integer between *lower_bound* and *upper_bound*.

The messages are changed from "integer" to "base *base* integer" if the base is set to a number other than 10.

When the quit option is chosen (and allowed), q is returned along with the return code 3. The `valrange` module will not produce any output. It returns zero for success and non-zero for failure.

NAME

    ckstr – display a prompt; verify and return a string answer

SYNOPSIS

    ckstr [–Q] [–W width] [[–r regexp] [...]] [–l length] [–d default] [–h help] [–e error]
    [–p prompt] [–k pid [–s signal]]

    errstr [–W] [–e error]
    helpstr [–W] [–h help]
    valstr input

DESCRIPTION

    ckstr prompts a user and validates the response. It defines, among other things, a prompt message whose response should be a string, text for help and error messages, and a default value (which will be returned if the user responds with a carriage return).

    The answer returned from this command must match the defined regular expression and be no longer than the length specified. If no regular expression is given, valid input must be a string with a length less than or equal to the length defined with no internal, leading or trailing white space. If no length is defined, the length is not checked. Either a regular expression or a length must be given with the command.

    All messages are limited in length to 70 characters and are formatted automatically. Any white space used in the definition (including newline) is stripped. The –W option cancels the automatic formatting. When a tilde is placed at the beginning or end of a message definition, the default text will be inserted at that point, allowing both custom text and the default text to be displayed.

    If the prompt, help or error message is not defined, the default message (as defined under NOTES) will be displayed.

    Three visual tool modules are linked to the ckstr command. They are errstr (which formats and displays an error message), helpstr (which formats and displays a help message), and valstr (which validates a response). These modules should be used in conjunction with FACE objects. In this instance, the FACE object defines the prompt.

    The options and arguments for this command are:

    –Q   Specifies that quit will not be allowed as a valid response.

    –W   Specifies that prompt, help and error messages will be formatted to a line length of width.

    –r   Specifies a regular expression, regexp, against which the input should be validated. May include white space. If multiple expressions are defined, the answer must match only one of them.

    –l   Specifies the maximum length of the input.

    –d   Defines the default value as default. The default is not validated and so does not have to meet any criteria.

-h   Defines the help messages as *help*.

-e   Defines the error message as *error*.

-p   Defines the prompt message as *prompt*.

-k   Specifies that process ID *pid* is to be sent a signal if the user chooses to abort.

-s   Specifies that the process ID *pid* defined with the -k option is to be sent signal `signal` when quit is chosen. If no signal is specified, SIGTERM is used.

input   Input to be verified against format length and/or regular expression criteria.

EXIT CODES
0 = Successful execution
1 = EOF on input
2 = Usage error
3 = User termination (quit)

NOTES
The default prompt for ckstr is:

    Enter an appropriate value [?,q]:

The default error message is dependent upon the type of validation involved. The user will be told either that the length or the pattern matching failed.

The default help message is also dependent upon the type of validation involved. If a regular expression has been defined, the message is:

    Please enter a string which matches the following pattern:
    regexp

Other messages define the length requirement and the definition of a string.

When the quit option is chosen (and allowed), q is returned along with the return code 3. The valstr module will not produce any output. It returns zero for success and non-zero for failure.

NAME
>   cktime – display a prompt; verify and return a time of day

SYNOPSIS
>   cktime [-Q] [-W width] [-f format] [-d default] [-h help] [-e error] [-p prompt]
>   [-k pid [-s signal]]
>
>   errtime [-W] [-e error] [-f format]
>   helptime [-W] [-h help] [-f format]
>   valtime [-f format] input

DESCRIPTION
>   cktime prompts a user and validates the response. It defines, among other
>   things, a prompt message whose response should be a time, text for help and
>   error messages, and a default value (which will be returned if the user responds
>   with a carriage return). The user response must match the defined format for the
>   time of day.
>
>   All messages are limited in length to 70 characters and are formatted automati-
>   cally. Any white space used in the definition (including newline) is stripped.
>   The -W option cancels the automatic formatting. When a tilde is placed at the
>   beginning or end of a message definition, the default text will be inserted at that
>   point, allowing both custom text and the default text to be displayed.
>
>   If the prompt, help or error message is not defined, the default message (as
>   defined under NOTES) will be displayed.
>
>   Three visual tool modules are linked to the cktime command. They are errtime
>   (which formats and displays an error message), helptime (which formats and
>   displays a help message), and valtime (which validates a response). These
>   modules should be used in conjunction with FML objects. In this instance, the
>   FML object defines the prompt. When format is defined in the errtime and
>   helptime modules, the messages will describe the expected format.
>
>   The options and arguments for this command are:
>
>   -Q   Specifies that quit will not be allowed as a valid response.
>
>   -W   Specifies that prompt, help and error messages will be formatted to a line
>   length of width.
>
>   -f   Specifies the format against which the input will be verified. Possible for-
>   mats and their definitions are:
>
>   %H = hour (00 - 23)
>   %I = hour (00 - 12)
>   %M = minute (00 - 59)
>   %p = ante meridian or post meridian
>   %r = time as %I:%M:%S %p
>   %R = time as %H:%M (the default format)
>   %S = seconds (00 - 59)
>   %T = time as %H:%M:%S

-d Defines the default value as *default*. The default is not validated and so does not have to meet any criteria.

-h Defines the help messages as *help*.

-e Defines the error message as *error*.

-p Defines the prompt message as *prompt*.

-k Specifies that process ID *pid* is to be sent a signal if the user chooses to abort.

-s Specifies that the process ID *pid* defined with the -k option is to be sent signal `signal` when quit is chosen. If no signal is specified, `SIGTERM` is used.

input Input to be verified against format criteria.

EXIT CODES
 0 = Successful execution
 1 = EOF on input
 2 = Usage error
 3 = User termination (quit)
 4 = Garbled format argument

NOTES
The default prompt for `cktime` is:

 Enter the time of day [?,q]:

The default error message is:

 ERROR - Please enter the time of day, using the following format:
 <format>

The default help message is:

 Please enter the time of day, using the following format:
 <format>

When the quit option is chosen (and allowed), q is returned along with the return code **3**. The `valtime` module will not produce any output. It returns zero for success and non-zero for failure.

NAME
ckuid – prompts for and validates a user ID

SYNOPSIS
ckuid [–Q] [–W *width*] [–m] [–d *default*] [–h *help*] [–e *error*] [–p *prompt*]
[–k *pid* [–s *signal*]]

erruid [–W] [–e *error*]
helpuid [–W] [–m] [–h *help*]
valuid *input*

DESCRIPTION
ckuid prompts a user and validates the response. It defines, among other things,
a prompt message whose response should be an existing user ID, text for help
and error messages, and a default value (which will be returned if the user
responds with a carriage return).

All messages are limited in length to 70 characters and are formatted automatically. Any white space used in the definition (including newline) is stripped.
The –W option cancels the automatic formatting. When a tilde is placed at the
beginning or end of a message definition, the default text will be inserted at that
point, allowing both custom text and the default text to be displayed.

If the prompt, help or error message is not defined, the default message (as
defined under NOTES) will be displayed.

Three visual tool modules are linked to the ckuid command. They are erruid
(which formats and displays an error message), helpuid (which formats and
displays a help message), and valuid (which validates a response). These
modules should be used in conjunction with FML objects. In this instance, the
FML object defines the prompt.

The options and arguments for this command are:

–Q   Specifies that quit will not be allowed as a valid response.

–W   Specifies that prompt, help and error messages will be formatted to a line
length of *width*.

–m   Displays a list of all logins when help is requested or when the user
makes an error.

–d   Defines the default value as *default*. The default is not validated and so
does not have to meet any criteria.

–h   Defines the help messages as *help*.

–e   Defines the error message as *error*.

–p   Defines the prompt message as *prompt*.

–k   Specifies that process ID *pid* is to be sent a signal if the user chooses to
abort.

–s   Specifies that the process ID *pid* defined with the –k option is to be sent
signal signal when quit is chosen. If no signal is specified, SIGTERM is
used.

      input   Input to be verified against /etc/passwd.

EXIT CODES

      0 = Successful execution
      1 = EOF on input
      2 = Usage error
      3 = User termination (quit)

NOTES

      The default prompt for ckuid is:

          `Enter the login name of an existing user [?,q]:`

      The default error message is:

          `ERROR - Please enter the login name of an existing user.`
          `Select the help option (?) for a list of valid login names.`
          (Last line appears only if the −m *option of* ckuid *is used)*

      The default help message is:

          `Please enter the login name of an existing user.`
          (If the −m *option of* ckuid *is used, a list of valid groups is also displayed.)*

      When the quit option is chosen (and allowed), q is returned along with the return code 3. The valuid module will not produce any output. It returns zero for success and non-zero for failure.

NAME

    ckyorn – prompts for and validates yes/no

SYNOPSIS

    ckyorn [–Q] [–W *width*] [–d *default*] [–h *help*] [–e *error*] [–p *prompt*]
    [–k *pid* [–s *signal*]]

    erryorn [–W] [–e *error*]
    helpyorn [–W] [–h *help*]
    valyorn *input*

DESCRIPTION

    ckyorn prompts a user and validates the response. It defines, among other things, a prompt message for a yes or no answer, text for help and error messages, and a default value (which will be returned if the user responds with a carriage return).

    All messages are limited in length to 70 characters and are formatted automatically. Any white space used in the definition (including newline) is stripped. The –W option cancels the automatic formatting. When a tilde is placed at the beginning or end of a message definition, the default text will be inserted at that point, allowing both custom text and the default text to be displayed.

    If the prompt, help or error message is not defined, the default message (as defined under NOTES) will be displayed.

    Three visual tool modules are linked to the ckyorn command. They are erryorn (which formats and displays an error message), helpyorn (which formats and displays a help message), and valyorn (which validates a response). These modules should be used in conjunction with FACE objects. In this instance, the FACE object defines the prompt. sp The options and arguments for this command are:

    –Q   Specifies that quit will not be allowed as a valid response.

    –W   Specifies that prompt, help and error messages will be formatted to a line length of *width*.

    –d   Defines the default value as *default*. The default is not validated and so does not have to meet any criteria.

    –h   Defines the help messages as *help*.

    –e   Defines the error message as *error*.

    –p   Defines the prompt message as *prompt*.

    –k   Specifies that process ID *pid* is to be sent a signal if the user chooses to abort.

    –s   Specifies that the process ID *pid* defined with the –k option is to be sent signal signal when quit is chosen. If no signal is specified, SIGTERM is used.

    input   Input to be verified as y, yes, Y, Yes, YES or n, no, N, No, NO.

EXIT CODES
>   0 = Successful execution
>   1 = EOF on input
>   2 = Usage error
>   3 = User termination (quit)

NOTES
>   The default prompt for ckyorn is:
>
>   Yes or No [y,n,?,q]:
>
>   The default error message is:
>
>   ERROR - Please enter yes or no.
>
>   The default help message is:
>
>   To respond in the affirmative, enter y, yes, Y, or YES.
>   To respond in the negative, enter n, no, N, or NO.

When the quit option is chosen (and allowed), q is returned along with the return code 3. The **valyorn** module will not produce any output. It returns zero for success and non-zero for failure.

NAME

cmpress – re-link file system to remove fragmentation

SYNOPSIS

/usr/sbin/cmpress

DESCRIPTION

cmpress re-links the input file system to improve access time by cleaning up fragmentation of files throughout the file system. The file system must be mounted in order for this procedure to find the file system and determine its characteristics.

cmpress uses a 3B2 Computer cartridge tape for intermediate storage. The file system is first copied onto the tape, the old file system is removed and the free block list is sorted into sequential order, then the file system is copied back onto the disk so that file system blocks that previously were scattered throughout the file system are in contiguous space.

Notice that the file system is destroyed during the process of compressing it. For this reason it is strongly recommended that an up-to-date backup of the file system be made before the file system is compressed. In the event of a mishap during file system compression the file system could be restored from the backup.

Since the file system is destroyed during the compression process, it is not possible to compress the root file system. The cmpress command will reject the file system name / if it is entered.

Compressing any file system except /usr can be done through the sysadm command. An example of such a file compression is given below. Compressing the /usr file system is somewhat more complex a process, since the sysadm facilities reside in the /usr file system. A scheme for compressing /usr is given in the examples.

EXAMPLES

To compress a file system named applic, the following command would be issued:

              sysadm   tapemgmt

When the tape management facilities menu is displayed, select the compress facility and answer the questions posed by the shell procedure. This compress facility invokes the /usr/sbin/cmpress procedure.

To compress the /usr file system the UNIX system has to be in single user mode with the /usr file system mounted. The following sequence of commands will take the system from multiuser to single user mode, compress the /usr file system, then return the system to multiuser mode. Notice that any work going on in the system at the time that the system is changed to single user mode will be terminated, so this process should be done at a time when there are no other users logged in, and no background tasks are being done. It should be done only from the console from the root login.

First check to see how /usr is mounted.

> mount

Make note of the /dev/dsk/c?d?s? information, as you will need it later.

Now take the system down to single user mode.

> init 1

Lots of messages will now appear, and you will need to log back in as root.

Now mount the /usr file system. Use the /dev/dsk/c?d?s? information from the mount command above.

> mount /dev/dsk/c?d?s? /usr

Now compress the file system

> /usr/sbin/cmpress /dev/rSA/ctape?

The procedure will pose a series of questions. As the compression process runs it will display a series of messages indicating its progress.

When compression is complete the following commands will unmount the /usr file system and return the system to multi user mode. Many messages will be displayed during this process.

> umount /dev/dsk/c1d0s2
> init 2

SEE ALSO

sysadm(1M)

DIAGNOSTICS

The diagnostic messages are intended to be self explanatory.

NOTES

As mentioned above, since the compression of the file system entails its destruction and restoration it is strongly recommended that a backup copy of the file system be made before its compression is attempted.

NAME

colltbl – create collation database

SYNOPSIS

colltbl [*file* | –]

DESCRIPTION

The colltbl command takes as input a specification file, *file*, that describes the collating sequence for a particular language and creates a database that can be read by strxfrm(3C) and strcoll(3C). strxfrm(3C) transforms its first argument and places the result in its second argument. The transformed string is such that it can be correctly ordered with other transformed strings by using strcmp(3C), strncmp(3C) or memcmp(3C). strcoll(3C) transforms its arguments and does a comparison.

If no input file is supplied, *stdin* is read.

The output file produced contains the database with collating sequence information in a form usable by system commands and routines. The name of this output file is the value you assign to the keyword codeset read in from *file*. Before this file can be used, it must be installed in the /usr/lib/locale/*locale* directory with the name LC_COLLATE by someone who is super-user or a member of group bin. *locale* corresponds to the language area whose collation sequence is described in *file*. This file must be readable by user, group, and other; no other permissions should be set. To use the collating sequence information in this file, set the LC_COLLATE environment variable appropriately (see environ(5) or setlocale(3C)).

The colltbl command can support languages whose collating sequence can be completely described by the following cases:

- Ordering of single characters within the codeset. For example, in Swedish, V is sorted after U, before X and with W (V and W are considered identical as far as sorting is concerned).

- Ordering of "double characters" in the collation sequence. For example, in Spanish, ch and ll are collated after c and l, respectively.

- Ordering of a single character as if it consists of two characters. For example, in German, the "sharp s", β, is sorted as ss. This is a special instance of the next case below.

- Substitution of one character string with another character string. In the example above, the string β is replaced with ss during sorting.

- Ignoring certain characters in the codeset during collation. For example, if – were ignored during collation, then the strings re-locate and relocate would be equal.

- Secondary ordering between characters. In the case where two characters are sorted together in the collation sequence, (i.e., they have the same "primary" ordering), there is sometimes a secondary ordering that is used if two strings are identical except for characters that have the same primary ordering. For example, in French, the letters e and è have the same primary ordering but e comes before è in the secondary ordering. Thus the word lever would be ordered before lèver, but lèver would be sorted before levitate. (Note that if **e** came before **è** in the primary ordering, then **lèver** would be sorted after **levitate**.)

The specification file consists of three types of statements:

1. **codeset**   *filename*

   filename is the name of the output file to be created by **colltbl**.

2. **order is**   *order_list*

   order_list is a list of symbols, separated by semicolons, that defines the collating sequence. The special symbol, **...**, specifies symbols that are lexically sequential in a short-hand form. For example,

           order is   a;b;c;d;...;x;y;z

   would specify the list of lower_case letters. Of course, this could be further compressed to just **a;...;z**.

   A symbol can be up to two bytes in length and can be represented in any one of the following ways:

   - the symbol itself (e.g., **a** for the lower-case letter **a**),

   - in octal representation (e.g., **\141** or **0141** for the letter **a**), or

   - in hexadecimal representation (e.g., **\x61** or **0x61** for the letter **a**).

   Any combination of these may be used as well.

   The backslash character, **** , is used for continuation. No characters are permitted after the backslash character.

   Symbols enclosed in parenthesis are assigned the same primary ordering but different secondary ordering. Symbols enclosed in curly brackets are assigned only the same primary ordering. For example,

           order is   a;b;c;ch;d;(e;è);f;...;z;\
                       {1;...;9};A;...;Z

   In the above example, **e** and **è** are assigned the same primary ordering and different secondary ordering, digits 1 through 9 are assigned the same primary ordering and no secondary ordering. Only primary ordering is assigned to the remaining symbols. Notice how double letters can be specified in the collating sequence (letter **ch** comes between **c** and **d**).

   If a character is not included in the **order is** statement it is excluded from the ordering and will be ignored during sorting.

3. **substitute** *string* **with** *repl*

   The **substitute** statement substitutes the string *string* with the string *repl*. This can be used, for example, to provide rules to sort the abbreviated month names numerically:

```
substitute "Jan" with "01"
substitute "Feb" with "02"
        .
        .
        .
substitute "Dec" with "12"
```

A simpler use of the **substitute** statement that was mentioned above was to substitute a single character with two characters, as with the substitution of β with **ss** in German.

The **substitute** statement is optional. The **order is** and **codeset** statements must appear in the specification file.

Any lines in the specification file with a **#** in the first column are treated as comments and are ignored. Empty lines are also ignored.

EXAMPLE

The following example shows the collation specification required to support a hypothetical telephone book sorting sequence.

The sorting sequence is defined by the following rules:

a.   Upper and lower case letters must be sorted together, but upper case letters have precedence over lower case letters.

b.   All special characters and punctuation should be ignored.

c.   Digits must be sorted as their alphabetic counterparts (e.g., 0 as **zero**, 1 as **one**).

d.   The **Ch, ch, CH** combinations must be collated between C and D.

e.   V and W, v and w must be collated together.

The input specification file to **colltbl** will contain:

```
codeset     telephone

order is     A;a;B;b;C;c;CH;Ch;ch;D;d;E;e;F;f;\
             G;g;H;h;I;i;J;j;K;k;L;l;M;m;N;n;O;o;P;p;\
             Q;q;R;r;S;s;T;t;U;u;{V;W};{v;w};X;x;Y;y;Z;z

substitute "0" with "zero"
substitute "1" with "one"
substitute "2" with "two"
substitute "3" with "three"
substitute "4" with "four"
substitute "5" with "five"
substitute "6" with "six"
substitute "7" with "seven"
substitute "8" with "eight"
substitute "9" with "nine"
```

FILES

/lib/locale/*locale*/LC_COLLATE
> LC_COLLATE database for *locale*

/usr/lib/locale/C/colltbl_C
> input file used to construct LC_COLLATE in the default locale.

SEE ALSO

memory(3C), setlocale(3C), strcoll(3C), string(3C), strxfrm(3C), environ(5) in the *Programmer's Reference Manual*.

NAME
comsat, in.comsat - biff server

SYNOPSIS
in.comsat

DESCRIPTION
comsat is the server process which listens for reports of incoming mail and notifies users who have requested to be told when mail arrives. It is invoked as needed by inetd(1M), and times out if inactive for a few minutes.

comsat listens on a datagram port associated with the biff service specification [see services(4)] for one line messages of the form

   user@mailbox-offset

If the *user* specified is logged in to the system and the associated terminal has the owner execute bit turned on (by a biff y), the *offset* is used as a seek offset into the appropriate mailbox file and the first 7 lines or 560 characters of the message are printed on the user's terminal. Lines which appear to be part of the message header other than the From, To, Date, or Subject lines are not printed when displaying the message.

FILES
/var/utmp   who's logged on and on what terminals

SEE ALSO
services(4), inetd(1M).

NOTES
The message header filtering is prone to error.

NAME
    crash – examine system images

SYNOPSIS
    /usr/sbin/crash [–d dumpfile] [–n namelist] [–w]

DESCRIPTION
    The crash command is used to examine the system memory image of a running
    or a crashed system by formatting and printing control structures, tables, and
    other information. Command line arguments to crash are *dumpfile, namelist,* and
    outputfile.

    dumpfile is the file containing the system memory image. The default *dumpfile* is
    /dev/mem. The system image can also be /dev/ifdsk06, if the first floppy of a
    system dump is taken with the sysdump firmware command; or it can be the
    pathname of a file produced by the ldsysdump command.

    The text file *namelist* contains the symbol table information needed for symbolic
    access to the system memory image to be examined. The default *namelist* is
    /stand/unix. If a system image from another machine is to be examined, the
    corresponding text file must be copied from that machine.

    When the crash command is invoked, a session is initiated. The output from a
    crash session is directed to *outputfile.* The default *outputfile* is the standard out-
    put.

    Input during a crash session is of the form:

        function [*argument...*]

    where *function* is one of the crash functions described in the "FUNCTIONS" sub-
    section of this manual page, and *arguments* are qualifying data that indicate which
    items of the system image are to be printed.

    The default for process-related items is the current process for a running system
    or the process that was running at the time of the crash for a crashed system. If
    the contents of a table are being dumped, the default is all active table entries.

    The following function options are available to crash functions wherever they
    are semantically valid.

    –e   Display every entry in a table.

    –f   Display the full structure.

    –p   Interpret all address arguments in the command line as physical
                    addresses. If they are not physical addresses, results are incon-
                    sistent.

    –s *process*   Specify a process slot other than the default.

    –w *file*   Redirect the output of a function to *file.*

    The functions mode, defproc, and redirect correspond to the function options
    –p, –s, and –w. The mode function may be used to set the address translation
    mode to physical or virtual for all subsequently entered functions; defproc sets
    the value of the process slot argument for subsequent functions; and redirect
    redirects all subsequent output.

Output from crash functions may be piped to another program in the following way:

> function [argument...] ! shell_command

For example,

> mount ! grep rw

writes all mount table entries with an rw flag to the standard output. The redirection option (-w) cannot be used with this feature.

Depending on the context of the function, numeric arguments are assumed to be in a specific radix. Counts are assumed to be decimal. Addresses are always hexadecimal. Table address arguments larger than the size of the function table are interpreted as hexadecimal addresses; those smaller are assumed to be decimal slots in the table. Default bases on all arguments may be overridden. The C conventions for designating the bases of numbers are recognized. A number that is usually interpreted as decimal is interpreted as hexadecimal if it is preceded by 0x and as octal if it is preceded by 0. Decimal override is designated by 0d, and binary by 0b.

Aliases for functions may be any uniquely identifiable initial substring of the function name. Traditional aliases of one letter, such as p for proc, remain valid.

Many functions accept different forms of entry for the same argument. Requests for table information accept a table entry number, a physical address, a virtual address, a symbol, a range, or an expression. A range of slot numbers may be specified in the form a−b where a and b are decimal numbers. An expression consists of two operands and an operator. An operand may be an address, a symbol, or a number; the operator may be +, −, *, /, &, or | . An operand that is a number should be preceded by a radix prefix if it is not a decimal number (0 for octal, 0x for hexadecimal, 0b for binary). The expression must be enclosed in parentheses. Other functions accept any of these argument forms that are meaningful.

Two abbreviated arguments to crash functions are used throughout. Both accept data entered in several forms. They may be expanded into the following:

> table_entry = table entry | address | symbol | range | expression
>
> start_addr = address | symbol | expression

FUNCTIONS

? [−w file]
> List available functions.

! command
> Escape to the shell and execute command.

as [−e] [−f] [−w file] [proc ...]
> Print information on process segments.

base [−w file] number ...
> Print number in binary, octal, decimal, and hexadecimal. A number in a radix other than decimal should be preceded by a prefix that indicates its radix as follows: 0x, hexadecimal; 0, octal; and 0b, binary.

buffer [–w *file*] [–*format*] *bufferslot*

buffer [–w *file*] [–format] [–p] *start_addr*
> Alias: b.
> Print the contents of a buffer in the designated format. The following for-
> mat designations are recognized: –b, byte: –c, character; –d, decimal; –x,
> hexadecimal; –o, octal; and, –i, inode. If no format is given, the previous
> format is used. The default format at the beginning of a crash session is
> hexadecimal.

bufhdr [–f] [–w *file*] [[–p] *table_entry* ...]
> Alias: buf.
> Print system buffer headers. The –f option produces different output
> depending on whether the buffer is local or remote (contains RFS data).

callout [–w *file*]
> Alias: c.
> Print the callout table.

class [–w *file*] [*table_entry* ...]
> Print information about process scheduler classes.

dbfree [–w *file*] [*class* ...]
> Print free streams data block headers. If a class is entered, only data block
> headers for the class specified is printed.

dblock [–e] [–w *file*] [–c *class* ...]

dblock [–e] [–w *file*] [[–p] *table_entry* ...]
> Print allocated streams data block headers. If the class option (–c) is used,
> only data block headers for the class specified is printed.

defproc [–w *file*] [–c]

defproc [–w *file*] [*slot*]
> Set the value of the process slot argument. The process slot argument
> may be set to the current slot number (–c) or the slot number may be
> specified. If no argument is entered, the value of the previously set slot
> number is printed. At the start of a crash session, the process slot is set
> to the current process.

dis [–w *file*] [–a] *start_addr* [*count*]

dis [–w *file*] [–a] –c [*count*]
> Disassemble *count* instructions starting at *start_addr*. The default count is 1.
> The absolute option (–a) specifies a non-symbolic disassembly. The –c
> option can be used in place of *start_addr* to continue disassembly at the
> address at which a previous disassembly ended.

dispq [–w *file*] [*table_entry* ...]
> Print the dispatcher (scheduler) queues.

ds [–w *file*] *virtual_address* ...
> Print the data symbol whose address is closest to, but not greater than, the
> address entered.

file [-e] [-w *file*] [[-p] *table_entry* ...]
    Alias: f.
    Print the file table.

findaddr [-w *file*] *table slot*
    Print the address of *slot* in *table*. Only tables available to the size func-
    tion are available to findaddr.

findslot [-w *file*] *virtual_address* ...
    Print the table, entry slot number, and offset for the address entered.
    Only tables available to the size function are available to findslot.

fs [-w *file*] [[-p] *table_entry* ...]
    Print the file system information table.

gdp [-e] [-f] [-w *file*] [[-p] *table_entry* ...]
    Print the gift descriptor protocol table.

help [-w *file*] *function* ...
    Print a description of the named function, including syntax and aliases.

inode [-e] [-f] [-w *file*] [[-p] *table_entry* ...]
    Alias: i.
    Print the inode table, including file system switch information.

kfp [-w *file*] [-s *process*] [-r]

kfp [-w *file*] [-s *process*] [*value*]
    Print the kernel frame pointer (kfp) for the start of a kernel stack trace.
    The kfp value can be set using the value argument or the reset option
    (-r), which sets the kfp through the nvram (non-volatile RAM). If no
    argument is entered, the current value of the kfp is printed.

kmastat [-w *file*]
    Print kernel memory allocator statistics.

lck [-e] [-w *file*] [[-p] *table_entry* ...]
    Alias: l.
    Print record locking information. If the -e option is used or table address
    arguments are given, the record lock list is printed. If no argument is
    entered, information on locks relative to inodes is printed.

linkblk [-e] [-w *file*] [[-p] *table_entry* ...]
    Print the linkblk table.

major [-w *file*] [*entry* ...]
    Print the MAJOR table.

map [-w *file*] *mapname* ...
    Print the map structure of the given mapname.

mbfree [-w *file*]
    Print free streams message block headers.

mblock [-e] [-w *file*] [[-p] *table_entry* ...]
    Print allocated streams message block headers.

mmu [-w *file*]

> Alias: **regs**.
> Print memory management unit registers. These registers are not available on a running system.

mode [-w *file*] [*mode*]

> Set address translation of arguments to virtual (v) or physical (p) mode. If no mode argument is given, the current mode is printed. At the start of a crash session, the mode is virtual.

mount [-e] [-w *file*] [[-p] *table_entry* ...]

> Alias: **m, vfs**.
> Print information about mounted file systems.

nm [-w *file*] *symbol* ...

> Print value and type for the given symbol.

nvram [-w *file*] *type*

> Print information from non-volatile RAM. *type* may be **fwnvr** for firmware nvram, **unxnvr** for UNIX nvram, **systate** for system state nvram, or **errlog** for nvram error log information.

od [-p] [-w *file*] [-*format*] [-*mode*] [-s *process*] *start_addr* [*count*]

> Alias: **rd**.
> Print *count* values starting at *start_addr* in one of the following formats: character (-c), decimal (-d), hexadecimal (-x), octal (-o), ASCII (-a), or hexadecimal/character (-h), and one of the following modes: long (-1), short (-t), or byte (-b). The default mode for character and ASCII formats is byte; the default mode for decimal, hexadecimal, and octal formats is long. The format -h prints both hexadecimal and character representations of the addresses dumped; no mode needs to be specified. When format or mode is omitted, the previous value is used. At the start of a crash session, the format is hexadecimal and the mode is long. If no count is entered, 1 is assumed.

page [-e] [-w*file*] [[-p] *table_entry* ...]

> Print information about pages.

pcb [-w *file*] [-u] [*process*]

pcb [-w *file*] [-k] [*process*]

pcb [-w *file*] [[-p] -i *start_addr*]

> Print the process control block. If no arguments are given, the active pcb for the current process is printed. The user option (-u) prints the user pcb and the kernel option (-k) prints the kernel pcb associated with the process. The interrupt option (-i) prints the interrupt pcb located at *start_addr*.

prnode [-e] [-w *file*] [[-p] *table_entry* ...]

> Print information about the private data of processes being traced.

proc [-e] [-f] [-w *file*] [[-p] *table_entry* ... #*procid* ...]

proc [-f] [-w *file*] [-r]
> Alias: p.
> Print the process table. Process table information may be specified in two ways. First, any mixture of table entries and process IDs may be entered. Each process ID must be preceded by a *. Alternatively, process table information for runnable processes may be specified with the runnable option (-r).

ptbl [-w *file*] [-s*process*] *section segment* [*count*]

ptbl [-w *file*] [-s*process*] [-p] *addr* [*count*]
> Print information on page descriptor tables.

pty [-f] [-e] [-w *file*] [-s] [-h] [-l]
> Print the pseudo ttys presently configured. The -l, -h and -h options give information about the STREAMS modules ldterm, ptem and pckt, respectively.

qrun [-w *file*]
> Print the list of scheduled streams queues.

queue [-e] [-w *file*] [[-p] *table_entry* ...]
> Print streams queues.

quit Alias: q.
> Terminate the crash session.

rcvd [-e] [-f] [-w *file*] [[-p] *table_entry* ...]
> Print the receive descriptor table.

rduser [-e] [-f] [-w *file*] [[-p] *table_entry* ...]
> Print the receive descriptor user table.

redirect [-w *file*] [-c]

redirect [-w *file*] [*newfile*]
> Used with a file name, redirects output of a crash session to *newfile*. If no argument is given, the file name to which output is being redirected is printed. Alternatively, the close option (-c) closes the previously set file and redirects output to the standard output.

resource [-e] [-w *file*] [[-p] *table_entry* ...]
> Print the advertise table.

rtdptbl [-w *file*] [*table_entry* ...]
> Print the real-time scheduler parameter table. See rt_dptbl(4).

rtproc [-w *file*]
> Print information about processes in the real-time scheduler class.

sdt [-e] [-w *file*] [-s *process*] *section*

sdt [-e] [-w *file*] [-s *process*] [-p] *start_addr* [*count*]
> The segment descriptor table for the named memory section is printed. Alternatively, the segment descriptor table starting at *start_addr* for *count* entries is printed. If no count is given, a count of 1 is assumed.

search [–p] [–w *file*] [–m *mask*] [–s *process*] *pattern start_addr length*
> Print the words in memory that match *pattern*, beginning at the *start_addr* for *length* words. The mask is ANDed (&) with each memory word and the result compared against the pattern. The mask defaults to 0xffffffff.

size [–w *file*] [–x] [*structure_name* ...]
> Print the size of the designated structure. The (–x) option prints the size in hexadecimal. If no argument is given, a list of the structure names for which sizes are available is printed.

sndd [–e] [–f] [–w *file*] [[–p] *table_entry* ...]
> Print the send descriptor table.

snode [–e] [–f] [–w *file*] [[–p] *table_entry* ...]
> Print information about open special files.

sram [–w *file*]
> Alias: **srams**
> Print the MMU segment table values.

srmount [–e] [–w *file*] [[–p] *table_entry* ...]
> Print the server mount table.

stack [–w *file*] [–u] [*process*]

stack [–w *file*] [–k] [*process*]

stack [–w *file*] [[–p] –i *start_addr*]
> Alias: **s**.
> Dump the stack. The (–u) option prints the user stack. The (–k) option prints the kernel stack. The (–i) option prints the interrupt stack starting at *start_addr*. If no arguments are entered, the kernel stack for the current process is printed. The interrupt stack and the stack for the current process are not available on a running system.

stat [–w *file*]
> Print system statistics.

stream [–e] [–f] [–w *file*] [[–p] *table_entry* ...]
> Print the streams table.

strstat [–w *file*]
> Print streams statistics.

trace [–w *file*] [–r] [*process*]

trace [–w *file*] [[–p] –i *start_addr*]
> Alias: **t**.
> Print stack trace. The kfp value is used with the –r option; the **kfp** function prints or sets the kfp (kernel frame pointer) value. The interrupt option prints a trace of the interrupt stack beginning at *start_addr*. The interrupt stack trace and the stack trace for the current process are not available on a running system.

ts [−w *file*] *virtual_address* ...
    Print text symbol closest to the designated address.

tsdptbl [−w *file*] [*table_entry* ...]
    Print the time-sharing scheduler parameter table. See ts_dptbl(4).

tsproc [−w *file*]
    Print information about processes in the time-sharing scheduler class.

tty [−e] [−f] [−l] [−w *file*] [−t *type* [[−p] *table_entry* ...]]

tty [−e] [−f] [−l] [−w *file*] [[−p] *start_addr*]
    Valid types: pp, iu.
    Print the tty table. If no arguments are given, the tty table for both tty
    types is printed. If the −t option is used, the table for the single tty type
    specified is printed. If no argument follows the type option, all entries in
    the table are printed. A single tty entry may be specified using *start_addr*.
    The −l option prints the line discipline information.

uinode [−e] [−f] [−w *file*] [[−p] *table_entry* ...]
    Alias: ui.
    Print the ufs inode table.

user [−f] [−w *file*] [*process*]
    Alias: u.
    Print the ublock for the designated process.

var [−w *file*]
    Alias: v.
    Print the tunable system parameters.

vfs [−e] [−w *file*] [[−p] *table_entry* ...]
    Alias: mount, m.
    Print information about mounted file systems.

vfssw [−w *file*] [[−p] *table_entry* ...]
    Print information about configured file system types.

vnode [−w *file*] [[−p] *vnode_addr* ...]
    Print information about vnodes.

vtop [−w *file*] [−s process] *start_addr* ...
    Print the physical address translation of the virtual address *start_addr*.

FILES

/dev/mem	system image of currently running system
/dev/ifdsk06	used to access system image on floppy diskette

SEE ALSO

ldsysdump(1M), firmware(8).

NAME
cron – clock daemon

SYNOPSIS
/usr/sbin/cron

DESCRIPTION
The cron command starts a process that executes commands at specified dates and times. Regularly scheduled commands can be specified according to instructions found in crontab files in the directory /var/spool/cron/crontabs. Users can submit their own crontab file via the crontab command. Commands which are to be executed only once may be submitted via the at command.

cron only examines crontab files and at command files during process initialization and when a file changes via the crontab or at commands. This reduces the overhead of checking for new or changed files at regularly scheduled intervals.

Since cron never exits, it should be executed only once. This is done routinely through /sbin/rc2.d/S75cron at system boot time. /usr/sbin/cron.d/FIFO is used as a lock file to prevent the execution of more than one cron.

To keep a log of all actions taken by cron, CRONLOG=YES (by default) must be specified in the /etc/default/cron file. If CRONLOG=NO is specified, no logging is done. Keeping the log is a user configurable option since cron usually creates huge log files.

FILES

/usr/sbin/cron.d	main cron directory
/etc/default/cron	used to maintain a log
/usr/sbin/cron.d/FIFO	used as a lock file
/usr/sbin/cron.d/log	accounting information
/var/spool/cron	spool area

SEE ALSO
at(1), crontab(1), sh(1) in the *User's Reference Manual*.

DIAGNOSTICS
A history of all actions taken by cron are recorded in /usr/sbin/cron.d/log.

NAME

cunix – configure a new bootable operating system

SYNOPSIS

cunix [–a "*ld_args*"] [–b *boot_dir*] [–c *config_dir*] [–d] [–f system] [–g]
[–i *loader_directive_file*] [–l *link_ed*] [–o *outfile*] [–r *raw_disk*] [–v]

DESCRIPTION

The cunix command creates a new bootable operating system file from the object files (drivers) specified in the given system file.

The configuration of a new bootable operating system is usually done when new hardware or software is added to or removed from the system; most frequently it is done during a powerup or reboot of the system. The cunix command allows this procedure to be performed at the user level, without a powerdown or system reboot. The options to cunix also allow the user to create customized input files for the configuration process, and to choose the location for the resulting bootable operating system.

Both COFF and ELF format object files can be used as input to cunix.

The options to cunix are as follows:

–a   Pass the specified *ld_args* as arguments to the link editor; the entire set of arguments must be enclosed in double quotes, with each argument surrounded by white space. By default (no –a specified), –x is passed to the link editor as an argument for COFF format object files (directs the link editor to omit local symbols from the output symbol table, saving some space in the output file); if one or more object files is in ELF format, then no loader arguments are passed by default. The link editor ld is used by default, unless another is specified with the –l option (see below).

–b   *boot_dir* specifies the directory where driver object files reside; the default is /boot.

–c   *config_dir* specifies the directory that contains working files for cunix; the default is /config.

–d   Build the operating system with debug mode on; the default is debug mode off. Debug mode populates the sys3bsym symbol table with symbols from the kernel object file and drivers specified in the system file. The –d option causes cunix to use more disk space and time. The sys3bsym table is accessible through the sys3b system call.

–f   system specifies the file that contains configuration information; the default is /stand/system.

–g   Do not remove *config_dir*/conf.o file after the bootable operating system has been created; the default is to remove conf.o. The directory *config_dir* is either /config or the directory specified by –c, above.

–i   *loader_directive_file* to be used for configuration; a *loader_directive_file* specifies memory locations for loading the operating system at boot time. A *loader_directive_file* for a COFF system is called an ifile, while a *loader_directive_file* for an ELF system is called a mapfile. Normally, it is

not necessary to specify a *loader_directive_file*. Only use the −i option
with a custom *loader_directive_file*.

−l   Use the *link_ed* link editor to bind object files; the link editor ld is used
        by default. See NOTES.

−o   *outfile* specifies the output file name for the bootable operating system;
        the default is /stand/unix_test.

−r   The *raw_disk* where the root file system resides; the default is
        /dev/rSA/disk1.

−v   Verbose mode on; cunix displays all the modules and drivers being
        linked. The default is verbose mode off.

NOTES

Do not execute a separate ld ... −o /stand/unix command for the operating
system; the output file is processed by cunix after loading.

FILES

/boot_dir/★	drivers to be configured into the operating system
*/config_dir/*conf.o	object file created by cunix
*/config_dir/*ifile★	loader directive file(s) for COFF system
*/config_dir/*mapfile★	loader directive file(s) for ELF system
/stand/system	system file
/stand/unix	bootable operating system
/usr/bin/ld	default link editor
/dev/rSA/disk1	default location of root file system

SEE ALSO

buildsys(1M), mkboot(1M), rc6(1M), system(4).
ld(1), sys3b(2) in the *Programmer's Reference Manual*.
System Administrator's Guide.

NAME

dcopy (generic) – copy file systems for optimal access time

SYNOPSIS

dcopy [–F *FSType*] [–V] [*current_options*] [–o *specific_options*] *inputfs outputfs*

DESCRIPTION

dcopy copies file system *inputfs* to *outputfs*. *inputfs* is the device file for the existing file system; *outputfs* is the device file to hold the reorganized result. For the
most effective optimization *inputfs* should be the raw device and *outputfs* should
be the block device. Both *inputfs* and *outputfs* should be unmounted file systems.

current_options are options supported by the s5-specific module of dcopy. Other
FSTypes do not necessarily support these options. *specific_options* indicate suboptions specified in a comma-separated list of suboptions and/or keyword-attribute
pairs for interpretation by the *FSType*-specific module of the command.

The options are:

–F   Specify the *FSType* on which to operate. The *FSType* should either be
         specified here or be determinable from /etc/vfstab by matching the
         inputfs (device) with an entry in the table.

–V   Echo the complete command line, but do not execute the command.
         The command line is generated by using the options and arguments
         provided by the user and adding to them information derived from
         /etc/vfstab. This option should be used to verify and validate the
         command line.

–o   Specify FSType-specific options.

NOTE

This command may not be supported for all FSTypes.

FILES

/etc/vfstab   list of default parameters for each file system

SEE ALSO

vfstab(4).
Manual pages for the FSType-specific modules of dcopy.

NAME

dcopy (s5) – copy s5 file systems for optimal access time

SYNOPSIS

dcopy [–F s5] [*generic_options*] [–s*X*] [–a*n*] [–d] [–v] [–f*fsize*[:*isize*]] *inputfs outputfs*

DESCRIPTION

generic_options are options supported by the generic dcopy command.

With no options, dcopy copies files from *inputfs* compressing directories by removing vacant entries, and spacing consecutive blocks in a file by the optimal rotational gap.

The options are:

–F s5　　Specifies the s5-FSType. Need not be supplied if the information may be obtained from /etc/vfstab by matching the *inputfs* device with an entry in the file.

–s*X*　　Supply device information for creating an optimal organization of blocks in a file. *X* must be of the form *cylinder size:gap size*.

–a*n*　　Place the files not accessed in *n* days after the free blocks of the destination file system If no *n* is specified then no movement occurs.

–d　　Leave order of directory entries as is. The default is to move subdirectories to the beginning of directories.

–v　　Reports how many files were processed and how big the source and destination freelists are.

–f *fsize*[:*isize*]

　　Specify the *outputfs* file system (*fsize*) and inode list (*isize*) sizes in logical blocks. If the suboption (or :*isize*) is not given, the values from *inputfs* are used.

dcopy catches interrupts and quits and reports on its progress. To terminate dcopy, send a quit signal followed by an interrupt or quit.

NOTES

fsck should be run on the new file system created by dcopy before it is mounted.

FILES

/etc/mnttab　　list of file systems currently mounted

SEE ALSO

generic dcopy(1M), fsck(1M), mkfs(1M).

NAME

dd – convert and copy a file

SYNOPSIS

dd [option=value] ...

DESCRIPTION

dd copies the specified input file to the specified output with possible conversions. The standard input and output are used by default. The input and output block sizes may be specified to take advantage of raw physical I/O.

option	values
if=*file*	input file name; standard input is default
of=*file*	output file name; standard output is default
ibs=*n*	input block size *n* bytes (default 512)
obs=*n*	output block size *n* bytes (default 512)
bs=*n*	set both input and output block size, superseding *ibs* and *obs*; also, if no conversion is specified, preserve the input block size instead of packing short blocks into the output buffer (this is particularly efficient since no in-core copy need be done)
cbs=*n*	conversion buffer size (logical record length)
files=*n*	copy and concatenate *n* input files before terminating (makes sense only where input is a magnetic tape or similar device)
skip=*n*	skip *n* input blocks before starting copy (appropriate for magnetic tape, where *iseek* is undefined)
iseek=*n*	seek *n* blocks from beginning of input file before copying (appropriate for disk files, where *skip* can be incredibly slow)
oseek=*n*	seek *n* blocks from beginning of output file before copying
seek=*n*	identical to *oseek*, retained for backward compatibility
count=*n*	copy only *n* input blocks
conv=ascii	convert EBCDIC to ASCII
ebcdic	convert ASCII to EBCDIC
ibm	slightly different map of ASCII to EBCDIC
block	convert new-line terminated ASCII records to fixed length
unblock	convert fixed length ASCII records to new-line terminated records
lcase	map alphabetics to lower case
ucase	map alphabetics to upper case
swab	swap every pair of bytes
noerror	do not stop processing on an error (limit of 5 consecutive errors)
sync	pad every input block to *ibs*
... , ...	several comma-separated conversions

Where sizes are specified, a number of bytes is expected. A number may end with k, b, or w to specify multiplication by 1024, 512, or 2, respectively; a pair of numbers may be separated by x to indicate multiplication.

cbs is used only if `ascii`, *unblock*, *ebcdic*, *ibm*, or *block* conversion is specified. In the first two cases, *cbs* characters are copied into the conversion buffer, any specified character mapping is done, trailing blanks are trimmed and a new-line is added before sending the line to the output. In the latter three cases, characters are read into the conversion buffer and blanks are added to make up an output record of size *cbs*. If *cbs* is unspecified or zero, the `ascii`, *ebcdic*, and *ibm* options convert the character set without changing the block structure of the input file; the *unblock* and *block* options become a simple file copy.

After completion, dd reports the number of whole and partial input and output blocks.

EXAMPLE

This command will read an EBCDIC tape blocked ten 80-byte EBCDIC card images per tape block into the ASCII file *x*:

```
dd  if=/dev/rmt/0h  of=x  ibs=800  obs=8k  cbs=80  conv=ascii,lcase
```

Note the use of raw magnetic tape. dd is especially suited to I/O on the raw physical devices because it allows reading and writing in arbitrary block sizes.

SEE ALSO

cp(1)

NOTES

Do not use dd to copy files between filesystems having different block sizes.

Using a blocked device to copy a file will result in extra nulls being added to the file to pad the final block to the block boundary.

DIAGNOSTICS

f+p records in(out)   numbers of full and partial blocks read(written)

NAME
      delsysadm – sysadm interface menu or task removal tool

SYNOPSIS
      delsysadm *task* | [-r] *menu*

DESCRIPTION
      The delsysadm command deletes a *task* or *menu* from the sysadm interface and
      modifies the interface directory structure on the target machine.

      task | *menu*   The logical name and location of the menu or task within the
                       interface menu hierarchy. Begin with the top menu main and
                       proceed to where the menu or the task resides, separating each
                       name with colons. See EXAMPLES.

      If the -r option is used, this command will recursively remove all sub-menus
      and tasks for this menu. If the -r option is not used, the menu must be empty.

      delsysadm should only be used to remove items added as "on-line" changes
      with the edsysadm command. Such an addition will have a package instance
      tag of ONLINE. If the task or menu (and its sub-menus and tasks) have any
      package instance tags other than ONLINE, you are asked whether to continue
      with the removal or to exit. Under these circumstances, you probably do not
      want to continue and you should rely on the package involved to take the
      necessary actions to delete this type of entry.

      The command exits successfully or provides the error code within an error mes-
      sage.

EXAMPLES
      To remove the nformat task, execute:

      delsysadm main:applications:ndevices:nformat.

DIAGNOSTICS
      0 Successful execution
      2 Invalid syntax
      3 Menu or task does not exist
      4 Menu not empty
      5 Unable to update interface menu structure

NOTES
      Any menu that was originally a placeholder menu (one that only appears if sub-
      menus exist under it) will be returned to placeholder status when a deletion
      leaves it empty.

      When the -r option is used, delsysadm checks for dependencies before removing
      any subentries. (A dependency exists if the menu being removed contains an
      entry placed there by an application package). If a dependency is found, the user
      is shown a list of packages that depend on the menu being deleted and asked
      whether or not to continue. If the answer is yes, the menu and all of its menus
      and tasks are removed (even those shown to have dependencies). If the answer is
      no, the menu is not deleted.

delsysadm should only be used to remove menu or task entries that have been added to the interface with edsysadm.

SEE ALSO
    edsysadm(1M), sysadm(1M).

NAME

`devattr` – lists device attributes

SYNOPSIS

`devattr` [–v] *device* [*attribute* [. . .]]

DESCRIPTION

`devattr` displays the values for a device's attributes. The display can be presented in two formats. Used without the –v option, only the attribute values are shown. Used with the –v option, the attributes are shown in an *attribute=value* format. When no attributes are given on the command line, all attributes for the specified device are displayed in alphabetical order by attribute name. If attributes are given on the command line, only those are shown and they are displayed in command line order.

The options and arguments for this command are:

–v   Specifies verbose format. Attribute values are displayed in an *attribute=value* format.

device   Defines the device whose attributes should be displayed. Can be the pathname of the device or the device alias.

attribute   Defines which attribute, or attributes, should be shown. Default is to show all attributes for a device. See the `putdev`(1M) manual page for a complete listing and description of available attributes.

ERRORS

The command will exit with one of the following values:

0 = successful completion of the task.

1 = command syntax incorrect, invalid option used, or internal error occurred.

2 = device table could not be opened for reading.

3 = requested device could not be found in the device table.

4 = requested attribute not defined for specified device.

FILES

`/etc/device.tab`

SEE ALSO

`devattr`(3X), `listdev`(3X), `putdev`(1M).

NAME
devfree – release devices from exclusive use

SYNOPSIS
devfree *key* [*device* [. . .]]

DESCRIPTION
devfree releases devices from exclusive use. Exclusive use is requested with the command devreserv.

When devfree is invoked with only the *key* argument, it releases all devices that have been reserved for that *key*. When called with *key* and *device* arguments, devfree releases the specified devices that have been reserved with that *key*.

The arguments for this command are:

key   Designates the unique key on which the device was reserved.

device Defines device that this command will release from exclusive use. Can be the pathname of the device or the device alias.

ERRORS
The command will exit with one of the following values:

0 = successful completion of the task.

1 = command syntax incorrect, invalid option used, or internal error occurred.

2 = device table or device reservation table could not be opened for reading.

3 = reservation release could not be completely fulfilled because one or more of the devices was not reserved or was not reserved on the specified key.

FILES
/etc/device.tab
/etc/devlkfile

NOTES
The commands devreserv and devfree are used to manage the availability of devices on a system. These commands do not place any constraints on the access to the device. They serve only as a centralized bookkeeping point for those who wish to use them. Processes that do not use devreserv may concurrently use a device with a process that has reserved that device.

SEE ALSO
devfree(3X), devreserv(1), devreserv(3X), reservdev(3X).

NAME

      devinfo − print device specific information

SYNOPSIS

      /usr/lbin/devinfo −i | −p *special*

DESCRIPTION

      The devinfo command is used to print device specific information about disk devices on standard out.

      The options have the following effect:

      −i   prints the following device information:

```
Device name              Software version
Drive id number          Device blocks per cylinder
Device bytes per block   Number of device partitions with
                           a block size greater than zero
```

      −p   prints the following device partition information:

```
Device name              Device major and minor numbers
Partition start block    Number of blocks allocated to
                           the partition
Partition flag           Partition tag
```

      This command is used by various other commands to obtain device specific information for the making of file systems and determining partition information.

SEE ALSO

      prtvtoc(1M).

NAME

devnm – device name

SYNOPSIS

/usr/sbin/devnm [*name*...]

DESCRIPTION

The devnm command identifies the special file associated with the mounted file system where the argument *name* resides. One or more *name*s can be specified.

This command is most commonly used by the brc command to construct a mount table entry for the root device.

EXAMPLE

The command:

/usr/sbin/devnm /usr

produces:

/dev/dsk/c1d0s2 /usr

if /usr is mounted on /dev/dsk/c1d0s2.

FILES

/dev/dsk/*
/etc/mnttab

SEE ALSO

brc(1M), mnttab(4).

NAME
devreserv – reserve devices for exclusive use

SYNOPSIS
devreserv [key [devicelist [...]]]

DESCRIPTION
devreserv reserves devices for exclusive use. When the device is no longer required, use devfree to release it.

devreserv reserves at most one device per devicelist. Each list is searched in linear order until the first available device is found. If a device cannot be reserved from each list, the entire reservation fails.

When devreserv is invoked without arguments, it lists the devices that are currently reserved and shows to which key it was reserved. When devreserv is invoked with only the key argument, it lists the devices that are currently reserved to that key.

The arguments for this command are:

key   Designates a unique key on which the device will be reserved. The key must be a positive integer.

devicelist   Defines a list of devices that devreserv will search to find an available device. (The list must be formatted as a single argument to the shell.)

EXAMPLE
To reserve a floppy disk and a cartridge tape:

```
$ key=$$
$ echo "The current Process ID is equal to: $key"
The Current Process ID is equal to: 10658
$ devreserv $key diskette1 ctape1
```

To list all devices currently reserved:

```
$ devreserv
disk1        2423
diskette1    10658
ctape1       10658
```

To list all devices currently reserved to a particular key:

```
$ devreserv $key
diskette1
ctape1
```

ERRORS
The command will exit with one of the following values:

0 = successful completion of the task.

1 = command syntax incorrect, invalid option used, or internal error occurred.

2 = device table or device reservation table could not be opened for reading.

3 = device reservation request could not be fulfilled.

FILES

    /etc/device.tab
    /etc/devlkfile

NOTES

The commands **devreserv** and **devfree** are used to manage the availability of devices on a system. Their use is on a participatory basis and they do not place any constraints on the actual access to the device. They serve as a centralized bookkeeping point for those who wish to use them. To summarize, devices which have been reserved cannot be used by processes which utilize the device reservation functions until the reservation has been canceled. However, processes that do not use device reservation may use a device that has been reserved since such a process would not have checked for its reservation status.

SEE ALSO

devfree(1), devfree(3X), devreserv(3X), reservdev(3X).

NAME
df (generic) – report number of free disk blocks and files

SYNOPSIS
df [–F *FSType*] [–begklntV] [*current_options*] [–o *specific_options*] [*directory | special | resource...*]

DESCRIPTION
df prints the allocation portions of the generic superblock for mounted or unmounted file systems, directories or mounted resources. *directory* represents a valid directory name. If *directory* is specified df reports on the device that contains the *directory*. *special* represents a special device (e.g., /dev/dsk/c1d0s8). *resource* is an RFS/NFS resource name. If arguments to df are pathnames, df produces a report on the file system containing the named file.

current_options are options supported by the s5-specific module of df. Other FSTypes do not necessarily support these options. *specific_options* indicate suboptions specified in a comma-separated list of suboptions and/or keyword-attribute pairs for interpretation by the *FSType*-specific module of the command.

The options are:

–F	Specify the *FSType* on which to operate. This is only needed if the file system is unmounted. The *FSType* should be specified here or be determinable from /etc/vfstab by matching the *mount_point*, *special*, or *resource* with an entry in the table.
–b	Print only the number of kilobytes free.
–e	Print only the number of files free.
–g	Print the entire statvfs structure. Used only for mounted file systems. Can not be used with *current_options* or with the –o option. This option will override the –b, –e, –k, –n, and –t options.
–k	Print allocation in kilobytes. This option should be invoked by itself because its output format is different from that of the other options.
–l	Report on local file systems only. Used only for mounted file systems. Can not be used with *current_options* or with the –o option.
–n	Print only the *FSType* name. Invoked with no arguments this option prints a list of mounted file system types. Used only for mounted file systems. Can not be used with *current_options* or with the –o option.
–t	Print full listings with totals. This option will override the –b, –e, and –n options.
–V	Echo the complete command line, but do not execute the command. The command line is generated by using the options and arguments provided by the user and adding to them information derived from /etc/mnttab or /etc/vfstab. This option should be used to verify and validate the command line.
–o	Specify FSType-specific options.

If no arguments or options are specified, the free space on all local and remotely mounted file systems is printed.

NOTES

The −F option is intended for use with unmounted file systems.

This command may not be supported for all FSTypes.

FILES

/dev/dsk/*	
/etc/mnttab	mount table
/etc/vfstab	list of default parameters for each file system

SEE ALSO

mount(1M), mnttab(4), vfstab(4).
statvfs(2) in the *Programmer's Reference Manual*.
Manual pages for the FSType-specific modules of df.

NAME

df (s5) – report number of free disk blocks and i-nodes for **s5** file systems

SYNOPSIS

df [**–F s5**] [*generic_options*] [**–f**] [*directory* | *special*...]

DESCRIPTION

generic_options are options supported by the generic **df** command.

The **df** command prints out the number of free blocks and free i-nodes in **s5** file systems or directories by examining the counts kept in the super-blocks. The *special* device name (e.g., **/dev/dsk/c1d0s2**) or mount point *directory* name (e.g., **/usr**) must be specified. If *directory* is specified, the report presents information for the device that contains the directory.

The options are:

–F s5   Specifies the **s5**-FSType.

–f   An actual count of the blocks in the free list is made, rather than taking the figure from the super-block.

NOTE

The **–f** option can be used with the **–t**, **–b**, and **–e** options. The **–k** option overrides the **–f** option.

FILES

/dev/dsk/*

SEE ALSO

generic **df**(1M).

NAME

df (ufs) – report free disk space on ufs file systems

SYNOPSIS

df [–F ufs] [*generic_options*] [–o i] [*directory* | *special*]

DESCRIPTION

generic_options are options supported by the generic df command.

df displays the amount of disk space occupied by ufs file systems, the amount of used and available space, and how much of the file system's total capacity has been used.

Note that the amount of space reported as used and available is less than the amount of space in the file system; this is because the system reserves a fraction of the space in the file system to allow its file system allocation routines to work well. The amount reserved is typically about 10%; this may be adjusted using tunefs(1M). When all the space on the file system except for this reserve is in use, only the super-user can allocate new files and data blocks to existing files. When the file system is overallocated in this way, df may report that the file system is more than 100% utilized.

The options are:

–F ufs

Specifies the ufs-FSType.

–o Specify ufs file system specific options. The available option is:

i Report the number of used and free inodes. May not be used with *generic_options*.

NOTES

df calculates its results differently for mounted and unmounted file systems. For unmounted systems the numbers reflect the 10% reservation mentioned above. For this reason, the available space reported by the generic command may differ from the available space reported by this module.

The –b and –e options override the –t option.

FILES

/etc/mnttab   list of file systems currently mounted

SEE ALSO

generic df(1M), du(1M), quot(1M), tunefs(1M), mnttab(4)

NAME

    dfmounts – display mounted resource information

SYNOPSIS

    dfmounts [−F *fstype*] [−h] [−o *specific_options*] [*restriction* ...]

DESCRIPTION

    dfmounts shows the local resources shared through a distributed file system *fstype* along with a list of clients that have the resource mounted. If *restriction* is not specified, dfmounts displays remote resources mounted on the local system. *Specific_options* as well as the availability and semantics of *restriction* are specific to particular distributed file system types.

    If dfmounts is entered without arguments, all remote resources currently mounted on the local system are displayed, regardless of file system type.

    The output of dfmounts consists of an optional header line (suppressed with the −h flag) followed by a list of lines containing whitespace-separated fields. For each resource, the fields are:

        resource server pathname clients

    where

resource	Specifies the resource name that must be given to the mount(1M) command.
server	Specifies the system from which the resource was mounted.
pathname	Specifies the pathname that must be given to the share(1M) command.
clients	Lists the systems, comma-separated, by which the resource was mounted. Clients are listed in the form *domain.*, *domain.system*, or *system*, depending on the file system type.

    A field may be null. Each null field is indicated by a hyphen (−) unless the remainder of the fields on the line are also null. In this case, it may be omitted.

    Fields with whitespace are enclosed in quotation marks (" ").

FILES

    /etc/dfs/fstypes

SEE ALSO

    dfshares(1M), mount(1M), share(1M), unshare(1M).

NAME

dfmounts – display mounted NFS resource information

SYNOPSIS

dfmounts [–F nfs] [–h] [*server* ...]

DESCRIPTION

dfmounts shows the local resources shared through Network File System, along with a list of clients that have mounted the resource. The –F flag may be omitted if NFS is the only file system type listed in the file **/etc/dfs/fstypes**.

The *server* option displays information about the resources mounted from each server, where *server* can be any system on the network. If no server is specified, then *server* is assumed to be the local system.

dfmounts without options displays all remote resources mounted on the local system, regardless of file system type.

The output of dfmounts consists of an optional header line (suppressed with the –h flag) followed by a list of lines containing whitespace-separated fields. For each resource, the fields are:

> *resource server pathname clients* ...

where

resource	Specifies the resource name that must be given to the mount(1M) command.
server	Specifies the system from which the resource was mounted.
pathname	Specifies the pathname that must be given to the share(1M) command.
clients	A comma-separated list of systems that have mounted the resource.

FILES

/etc/dfs/fstypes

SEE ALSO

mount(1M), share(1M), unshare(1M).

NAME

dfmounts – display mounted RFS resource information

SYNOPSIS

dfmounts [–F rfs] [–h] [resource_name ...]

DESCRIPTION

dfmounts shows the local resources shared through Remote File Sharing, along with a list of clients that have mounted the resource. The –F flag may be omitted if rfs is the first file system type listed in the file /etc/dfs/fstypes.

The output of *dfmounts* consists of an optional header line (suppressed with the –h flag) followed by a list of lines containing whitespace-separated fields. For each resource, the fields are:

resource server pathname clients ...

where

resource	Specifies the resource name that must be given to the mount(1M) command.
server	Specifies the system from which the resource was mounted.
pathname	Specifies the full pathname that must be given to the share(1M) command.
clients	A comma-separated list of systems that have mounted the resource.

A field may be null. Each null field is indicated by a hyphen (–) unless the remainder of the fields on the line are also null. In this case, it may be omitted.

FILES

/etc/dfs/fstypes

SEE ALSO

dfmounts(1M), share(1M), unshare(1M), fumount(1M), mount(1M)

NAME
dfshares – list available resources from remote or local systems

SYNOPSIS
dfshares [–F *fstype*] [–h] [–o *specific_options*] [*server* ...]

DESCRIPTION
dfshares provides information about resources available to the host through a distributed file system of type *fstype*. *Specific_options* as well as the semantics of *server* are specific to particular distributed file systems.

If dfshares is entered without arguments, all resources currently shared on the local system are displayed, regardless of file system type.

The output of dfshares consists of an optional header line (suppressed with the –h flag) followed by a list of lines containing whitespace-separated fields. For each resource, the fields are:

resource server access transport description ...

where

resource	Specifies the resource name that must be given to the mount(1M) command.
server	Specifies the name of the system that is making the resource available.
access	Specifies the access permissions granted to the client systems, either ro (for read-only) or rw (for read/write). If **dfshares** cannot determine access permissions, a hyphen (–) is displayed.
transport	Specifies the transport provider over which the *resource* is shared.
description	Describes the resource.

A field may be null. Each null field is indicated by a hyphen (–) unless the remainder of the fields on the line are also null. In this case, it may be omitted.

FILES
/etc/dfs/fstypes

SEE ALSO
dfmounts(1M), mount(1M), share(1M), unshare(1M).

NAME

dfshares – list available NFS resources from remote systems

SYNOPSIS

dfshares [–F nfs] [–h] [*server* ...]

DESCRIPTION

dfshares provides information about resources available to the host through Network File System. The –F flag may be omitted if NFS is the first file system type listed in the file /etc/dfs/fstypes.

The query may be restricted to the output of resources available from one or more servers.

The *server* option displays information about the resources shared by each server, where *server* can be any system on the network. If no server is specified, then *server* is assumed to be the local system.

dfshares without arguments displays all resources shared on the local system, regardless of file system type.

The output of dfshares consists of an optional header line (suppressed with the –h flag) followed by a list of lines containing whitespace-separated fields. For each resource, the fields are:

> *resource server access transport*

where

resource	Specifies the resource name that must be given to the mount(1M) command.
server	Specifies the system that is making the resource available.
access	Specifies the access permissions granted to the client systems; however, dfshares cannot determine this information for an NFS resource and populates the field with a hyphen (–).
transport	Specifies the transport provider over which the *resource* is shared; however, dfshares cannot determine this information for an NFS resource and populates the field with a hyphen (–).

FILES

/etc/dfs/fstypes

SEE ALSO

share(1M), unshare(1M), mount(1M).

NAME
dfshares – list available RFS resources from remote systems

SYNOPSIS
dfshares [–F rfs] [–h] [*server* ...]

DESCRIPTION
dfshares provides information about resources available to the host through Remote File Sharing. The –F flag may be omitted if RFS is the first file system type listed in the file /etc/dfs/fstypes.

The query may be restricted to the output of resources available from one or more servers. If no *server* is specified, all resources in the host's domain are displayed. A *server* may be given in the following form:

system	Specifies a system in the host's domain.
domain.	Specifies all systems in *domain*.
domain.system	Specifies *system* in *domain*.

The output of dfshares consists of an optional header line (suppressed with the –h flag) followed by a list of lines containing whitespace-separated fields. For each resource, the fields are:

> *resource server access transport description ...*

where

resource	Specifies the resource name that must be given to the mount(1M) command.
server	Specifies the system that is making the resource available.
access	Specifies the access permissions granted to the client systems, either ro (for read-only) or rw (for read and write).
transport	Specifies the transport provider over which the *resource* is shared.
description	Describes the resource.

A field may be null. Each null field is indicated by a hyphen (–) unless the remainder of the fields on the line are also null. In this case, it may be omitted.

ERRORS
If your host machine cannot contact the domain name server, or the argument specified is syntactically incorrect, an error message is sent to standard error.

FILES
/etc/dfs/fstypes

SEE ALSO
share(1M), unshare(1M), mount(1M)

NAME

disks – adds /dev/entries for hard disks in the Equipped Device Table

SYNOPSIS

/sbin/disks

DESCRIPTION

disks will search the Equipped Device Table (EDT) to see which hard disks are equipped. For each equipped hard disk, the following steps are performed:

1. The /dev/dsk and /dev/rdsk directories are checked for an entry with the name c[slot]d?s6, where [slot] is the slot the disk controller board is plugged into (0 for the disks controlled by the integral disk controller on the system board). The ? is the number of the disk attached to the controller. The system board disk controller is capable of controlling two disks: 0 and 1.

2. If either entry is not found, disks creates /dev/dsk and /dev/rdsk entries for the disk. The /dev/SA and /dev/rSA entries are created and linked to the c[slot]d?s6 entry in /dev/dsk and /dev/rdsk respectively. The /dev/SA and /dev/rSA entries are named diskx where x is the lowest unused number for disk entries. A message is printed indicating that /dev files have been created.

disks is called each time the system is booted. It must also be called after "sysadm rmdisk" to restore the /dev entries so the disk can be repartitioned.

FILES

/dev/dsk/*	entries for the hard disk for general use
/dev/rdsk/*	
/dev/SA/*	entries for the hard disk for use by System Administration
/dev/rSA/*	

SEE ALSO

sysadm(1) in the *User's Reference Manual*.

NAME
diskusg – generate disk accounting data by user ID

SYNOPSIS
/usr/lib/acct/diskusg [*options*] [*files*]

DESCRIPTION
diskusg generates intermediate disk accounting information from data in *files,* or the standard input if omitted. diskusg output lines on the standard output, one per user, in the following format: *uid   login   #blocks*

where
uid   the numerical user ID of the user.
login   the login name of the user; and
#blocks   the total number of disk blocks allocated to this user.

diskusg normally reads only the inodes of file systems for disk accounting. In this case, *files* are the special filenames of these devices.

diskusg recognizes the following options:

-s   the input data is already in diskusg output format. diskusg combines all lines for a single user into a single line.

-v   verbose. Print a list on standard error of all files that are charged to no one.

-i *fnmlist*   ignore the data on those file systems whose file system name is in *fnmlist*. *fnmlist* is a list of file system names separated by commas or enclosed within quotes. diskusg compares each name in this list with the file system name stored in the volume ID [see labelit(1M)].

-p *file*   use *file* as the name of the password file to generate login names. /etc/passwd is used by default.

-u *file*   write records to *file* of files that are charged to no one. Records consist of the special file name, the inode number, and the user ID.

The output of diskusg is normally the input to acctdisk [see acct(1M)] which generates total accounting records that can be merged with other accounting records. diskusg is normally run in dodisk [see acctsh(1M)].

EXAMPLES
The following will generate daily disk accounting information for root on /dev/dsk/c1d0s0:

diskusg /dev/dsk/c1d0s0 | acctdisk > disktacct

FILES
/etc/passwd   used for user ID to login name conversions

# SEE ALSO
acct(1M), acctsh(1M), acct(4)

NOTES
diskusg only works for S5 file systems. acctdusg (see acct (1M)) works for all file systems, but is slower than diskusg.

NAME

    dispadmin – process scheduler administration

SYNOPSIS

    dispadmin –l

    dispadmin –c *class* –g [–r *res*]

    dispadmin –c *class* –s *file*

DESCRIPTION

    The dispadmin command displays or changes process scheduler parameters while the system is running.

    The –l option lists the scheduler classes currently configured in the system.

    The –c option specifies the class whose parameters are to be displayed or changed. Valid *class* values are RT for the real-time class and TS for the time-sharing class.

    The –g option gets the parameters for the specified class and writes them to the standard output. Parameters for the real-time class are described on rt_dptbl(4). Parameters for the time-sharing class are described on ts_dptbl(4).

    When using the –g option you may also use the –r option to specify a resolution to be used for outputting the time quantum values. If no resolution is specified, time quantum values are in milliseconds. If *res* is specified it must be a positive integer between 1 and 1000000000 inclusive, and the resolution used is the reciprocal of *res* in seconds. For example, a *res* value of 10 yields time quantum values expressed in tenths of a second; a *res* value of 1000000 yields time quantum values expressed in microseconds. If the time quantum cannot be expressed as an integer in the specified resolution, it is rounded up to the next integral multiple of the specified resolution.

    The –s option sets scheduler parameters for the specified class using the values in *file*. These values overwrite the current values in memory—they become the parameters that control scheduling of processes in the specified class. The values in *file* must be in the format output by the –g option. Moreover, the values must describe a table that is the same size (has same number of priority levels) as the table being overwritten. Super-user privileges are required in order to use the –s option.

    The –g and –s options are mutually exclusive: you may not retrieve the table at the same time you are overwriting it.

    dispadmin does some limited sanity checking on the values supplied in *file* to verify that they are within their required bounds. The sanity checking, however, does not attempt to analyze the effect that the new values have on the performance of the system. Inappropriate values can have a dramatic negative effect on system performance. See the *System Administrator's Guide* for more information.

EXAMPLES

    The following command retrieves the current scheduler parameters for the real-time class from kernel memory and writes them to the standard output. Time quantum values are in microseconds.

        dispadmin –c RT –g –r 1000000

The following command overwrites the current scheduler parameters for the real-time class with the values specified in rt.config.

```
dispadmin -c RT -s rt.config
```

The following command retrieves the current scheduler parameters for the time-sharing class from kernel memory and writes them to the standard output. Time quantum values are in nanoseconds.

```
dispadmin -c TS -g -r 1000000000
```

The following command overwrites the current scheduler parameters for the time-sharing class with the values specified in ts.config.

```
dispadmin -c TS -s ts.config
```

DIAGNOSTICS

dispadmin prints an appropriate diagnostic message if it fails to overwrite the current scheduler parameters due to lack of required permissions or a problem with the specified input file.

SEE ALSO

priocntl(1), priocntl(2), rt_dptbl(4), ts_dptbl(4)

NAME

>   dispgid – displays a list of all valid group names

SYNOPSIS

>   dispgid

DESCRIPTION

>   dispgid displays a list of all group names on the system (one group per line).

EXIT CODES

>   0 = Successful execution
>   1 = Cannot read the group file

NAME

      dispuid – displays a list of all valid user names

SYNOPSIS

      dispuid

DESCRIPTION

      dispuid displays a list of all user names on the system (one line per name).

EXIT CODES

      0 = Successful execution

      1 = Cannot read the password file

NAME
    dname – print Remote File Sharing domain and network names
SYNOPSIS
    dname [– D *domain*] [– N *netspeclist*] [–dna]
DESCRIPTION
    dname prints or defines a host's Remote File Sharing domain name or the
    network(s) used by Remote File Sharing as transport provider(s). When used
    with d, n, or a options, dname can be run by any user to print the domain name,
    transport provider name(s), or both. Only a user with root permission can use
    the –D *domain* option to set the domain name for the host or –N *netspeclist* to set
    the network specification used for Remote File Sharing. *netspeclist* is a comma-
    separated list of transport providers (*tp1,tp2,...*). The value of each transport pro-
    vider is the network device name, relative to the */dev* directory. For example, the
    STARLAN NETWORK uses starlan.

    domain must consist of no more than 14 characters, consisting of any combination
    of letters (upper and lower case), digits, hyphens (–), and underscores (_).

    When dname is used to change a domain name, the host's password is removed.
    The administrator will be prompted for a new password the next time Remote
    File Sharing is started [rfstart(1M)].

    If dname is used with no options, it will default to dname –d.
NOTES
    You cannot use the –N or –D options while Remote File Sharing is running.
SEE ALSO
    rfstart(1M).

NAME
   drvinstall – install/uninstall a driver

SYNOPSIS
   /usr/sbin/drvinstall [–m *master*] [–d *object*] [–s *system*]
   [–o *directory*] [–c *minor*] –v *version* [–ufbnx]

DESCRIPTION
   The drvinstall command accepts an *object* file, master file and system file as
   inputs, and creates the corresponding specially formatted file for use in the
   configuration of a new bootable operating system. In addition, the master and
   system files may be modified. The –u option is used for uninstalling a driver.
   Pathnames specified for the options below can be either relative or absolute pathnames.

   –m *master*
         specifies the path name of the master directory to be used. One or both
         of the –m or –d options must be specified, and at least one must specify a
         file name as the last component of the path name. If this flag is omitted,
         the /etc/master.d directory is used.

   –d *object*
         specifies the path name of the input *object* directory to be used. One or
         both of the –m or –d options must be specified, and at least one must
         specify a file name as the last component of the path name. If this flag is
         omitted, the /boot directory is used.

   –s *system*
         specifies the path name of the system file to be used. If this flag is omit-
         ted, the /stand/system file is used.

   –o *directory*
         specifies the path name of the output bootable file. If this flag is omitted,
         the /boot directory is used.

   –c *minor*
         specifies the *minor* number to be inserted at the end of an INCLUDE state-
         ment for the driver. The INCLUDE statement is inserted in the *system* file.
         Minor is optional in an INCLUDE and specifies the quantity (default of 1)
         of minor devices to be controlled by the driver. If the driver is a
         hardware driver, –c is ignored.

   –v *version*
         specifies the *version* number of the drvinstall command compatible with
         the master file being used. The –v option is required on the command
         line and currently supports "1.0".

   –u   specifies that the named driver is to be uninstalled. A driver dependency
         check is made and if a dependency is found, a warning message is issued
         and the command is aborted. If no dependency is found, then drvin-
         stall will:

- Remove the bootable *object* file.
- Replace the major number with a "–" in the `master` file if the driver is a software driver.
- Delete the INCLUDE statement from the `system` file if the driver is not a hardware driver.
- Print the major number if the driver is a software driver.

–f   when used with the –u option, disables the dependency check. This results in the driver being uninstalled regardless of dependencies.

–b   inhibits generation of the *object* file. This option is ignored for uninstall.

–n   Inhibits any edit of the `system` file.

–x   Enables debugging output.

For any driver installed, `drvinstall` calls the `mkboot` command to produce a bootable *object* file. The resultant output file is placed into the directory determined by the –o argument.

If the driver to be installed is a software driver, `drvinstall` will:

- Assign a major number to that driver if there is a "–" entry in the major number field of the associated `master` file entry. The `drvinstall` command expects any unused field of the `master` file to be filled with a "–".

  The major numbers available for software drivers on AT&T 3B2 Computers are 30–71 inclusive. The remaining major numbers are reserved for hardware devices, used by integral drivers, or reserved for SCSI devices. The `drvinstall` command determines the available major numbers by scanning all existing files in /etc/master.d for major numbers; it then assigns the first unused number in the above range (note that the directory specified by *master* on the command line is not searched for major numbers). This value replaces the corresponding "–" value in the major number field of the `master` file.

- Print the major number found or assigned in the `master` file.

If the driver to be installed is not a hardware driver (it is, e.g., a software driver or a loadable type of module), `drvinstall` will insert an INCLUDE statement for the driver in the `system` file.

SEE ALSO
cunix(1M), mkboot(1M).
master(4), system(4) in the *Programmer's Reference Manual*.

DIAGNOSTICS
The major number assigned or found for a software driver is printed on stdout. A zero is returned for success and a non-zero is returned for failures.

NAME
>   du – summarize disk usage

SYNOPSIS
>   du [–sar] [*name* ...]

DESCRIPTION
>   The du command reports the number of blocks contained in all files and (recursively) directories within each directory and file specified. The block count includes the indirect blocks of the file. If no *name*s are given, the current directory is used.
>
>   The optional arguments are as follows:
>
>   –s   causes only the grand total (for each of the specified *name*s) to be given.
>
>   –a   causes an output line to be generated for each file.
>
>   If neither –s or –a is specified, an output line is generated for each directory only.
>
>   –r   will cause du to generate messages about directories that cannot be be read, files that cannot be opened, etc., rather than being silent (the default).
>
>   A file with two or more links is only counted once.

NOTES
>   If the –a option is not used, non-directories given as arguments are not listed.
>
>   If there are links between files in different directories where the directories are on separate branches of the file system hierarchy, du will count the excess files more than once.
>
>   Files with holes in them will get an incorrect block count.

SEE ALSO
>   The ''File System Administration'' chapter in the *System Administrator's Guide*.

NAME
      editsa – add/delete entry from software application file

SYNOPSIS
      /usr/sbin/editsa –i *slot HWNAME SWNAME*

      /usr/sbin/editsa –r *SWNAME*

      /usr/sbin/editsa –l

DESCRIPTION
      The editsa command is used to add, delete or list entries in the software appli-
      cation file, /dgn/.edt_swapp. It is primarily used in application installation
      scripts to modify the software application file. This file allows a software driver,
      SWNAME, to be associated with a specific board in a specific AT&T 3B2 Com-
      puter expansion slot. The file /dgn/.edt_swapp is a data base which is read by
      the firmware program filledt to update the *name* field for designated Equipped
      Device Table (EDT) entries. editsa performs various checks to ensure the
      request will result in a valid system configuration.

      The valid uses of editsa are as shown above and an error will be returned if not
      properly entered. The option and argument definitions are as follows:

      –i   Specifies that the corresponding entry should be added to the
                   software application file.

      slot   The slot entry in the EDT for which the board, *HWNAME*, is to be
                   replaced by the argument specified as *SWNAME*.

      HWNAME The name of the hardware device (e.g. PORTS, ISC, NI) for which the
                   EDT entry is being renamed.

      SWNAME The name of the driver which is being dynamically assigned to a
                   hardware device or removed as a valid entry in the software applica-
                   tion file.

      –r   All entries which match the *SWNAME* specified in the command line
                   will be removed from the software application file.

      –l   Prints a formatted display of the software application file.

FILES
      /stand/filledt
      /dgn/.edt_swapp
      /dgn/edt_data

SEE ALSO
      edittbl(1M), firmware(8).

DIAGNOSTICS
      All errors from editsa are fatal and return an error code of 1 with the exception
      of a warning message for the case when the *HWNAME* specified does not match
      the EDT entry for the slot requested on the command line. This warning returns
      an error code of 2.

NAME
     edittbl – edit edt_data file
SYNOPSIS
     /usr/sbin/edittbl –d |–s {–g |–i |–1 |–r} [–t] [*file*]

     /usr/sbin/edittbl –B *bus_type* {–g |–i |–1 |–r} [–t] [*file*]

DESCRIPTION
     The edittbl command is a user-level utility that permits changes to edt_data
     files. These files are used by firmware programs (see firmware(8)) during con-
     struction of the Equipped Device Table (EDT).

     Note that only one of the –g, –i, –1, and –r options may be specified in either of
     the forms shown above.

     edittbl prints the option list when no arguments are specified. The options and
     arguments are:

     –d   Selects the device look-up table for the system bus. This option cannot be
            used with the –B option.

     –s   Selects the sub-device look-up table for the system bus. This option can-
            not be used with the –B option.

     –g   Generates the default entries for the selected look-up table(s). This
            overwrites any entries that are currently in the selected look-up table(s).
            For the device table, these base entries are SBD and PORTS. For the sub-
            device table, they are NULL, FD5, HD10, HD30, HD72, HD72A, HD72B,
            HD72C, HD43, and HD72D.

     –i   Specifies that new entries are to be added to the selected table(s). The ID
            codes for table entries and the input are compared; only new codes are
            installed. The formats for entries are described below. An EOF or "."
            ends the data input.

     –1   Specifies that the selected table(s) are to be listed.

     –r   Specifies that entries are to be removed from either table. The ID codes of
            the table are compared to the input; entries with codes that match the
            input are removed. The format is identical to that for the –i option and is
            listed below. An EOF or "." ends the data input.

     –t   Suppresses the program headings and user prompts; warnings and errors
            are not affected. This option is primarily useful in installation and remo-
            val scripts.

     –B   Specifies that the edt_data file for *bus_type* is to be edited. Currently the
            only bus type supported is scsi. If this option is not specified, the sys-
            tem bus edt_data file will be edited.

     file   The user may specify a target path name for the utilities. The default for
            the –d and –s options is ./edt_data. For the –B option and the scsi bus
            type, *file* is where the target controller information is to be placed; the
            default for the –B scsi option is /edt/SCSI/edt_data.

INPUT FORMAT
Data for installation/removal is entered as hex format numbers or character strings, one line for each table entry. The data fields must be supplied in the sequence described below.

Devices

ID_code
Number between 0x0 and 0xffff that a device uses to identify itself. For extended devices (such as SCSI), add 0x10000 to the ID_code. ID codes are administered by AT&T.

name
Field name for a device. Device names are administered by AT&T. This string is also the file name that DGMON loads to diagnose a device.

rq_size
Number between 0x0 and 0xff for the count of entries in a device's job request queue.

cq_size
Number between 0x0 and 0xff for the count of entries in a device's job completion queue.

boot_device
Determines whether a device may be used to boot programs. A "1" means that it is bootable; a "0" means that it is not.

word_size
Shows the word size of a device I/O bus. A "1" is used for devices with a 16 bit bus word; a "0" is used for devices with an 8 bit bus word.

brd_size
Specifies the I/O connector slots that a device requires. A "1" indicates that two slots are needed, while a "0" means that one is required.

smart_board
Determines whether a device is intelligent, i.e., requires downloaded code for normal operation or supports subdevices. A "1" indicates an intelligent device; a "0" specifies a "dumb" device.

cons_cap
Shows whether a device can support the system console terminal. A "1" is used for devices that can, a "0" for those that cannot.

cons_file
Shows whether a device needs downloaded code to support the console interface when cons_cap has a value of "1". A "0" in this field means that the device can support a system console terminal with PROM-based code. A "1" in this field means downloaded code is needed. cons_file must have the value of "0" when cons_cap is "0".

Subdevices

ID_code
Number between 0x0 and 0xffff for the code that identifies a subdevice. Subdevice ID codes are administered by AT&T.

subdev_name
String (maximum of 9 characters) for a subdevice name. Subdevice names are administered by AT&T.

dev_name
String (maximum of 9 characters) for the device name with which the subdevice is associated.

EXAMPLES

Generate and list the base entries for both the device and subdevice tables, saving the results in ./edt_data.

```
edittbl -g -l -s -d
```

Install subdevice entries with new ID codes from the file subdev.in into the existing file ./edt_data.

```
edittbl -i -s < subdev.in
```

List the device table entries found in /dgn/edt_data

```
edittbl -l -d /dgn/edt_data
```

FILES

```
/dgn/edt_data
/edt/SCSI/edt_data
/etc/scsi/edittbl
```

NAME
edquota – edit user quotas

SYNOPSIS
edquota [–p *proto_user*] *username...*
edquota –t

DESCRIPTION
edquota is a quota editor. One or more users may be specified on the command line. For each user a temporary file is created with an ASCII representation of the current disk quotas for that user for each mounted ufs file system that has a quotas file, and an editor is then invoked on the file. A null entry is used if no quotas file exists for a file system. The quotas may then be modified, new quotas added, etc. Upon leaving the editor, edquota reads the temporary file and modifies the binary quota files to reflect the changes made.

The editor invoked is vi(1) unless the EDITOR environment variable specifies otherwise.

Only the super-user may edit quotas. In order for quotas to be established on a file system, the root directory of the file system must contain a file, owned by root, called quotas. See quotaon(1M) for details.

proto_user and username can be numeric, corresponding to the uid of a user. Unassigned uids may be specified; unassigned names may not. In this way, default quotas can be established for users who are later assigned a uid.

The options are:

–p   Duplicate the quotas of the *proto_user* specified for each *username* specified. This is the normal mechanism used to initialize quotas for groups of users.

–t   Edit the soft time limits for each file system. If the time limits are zero, the default time limits in /usr/include/sys/fs/ufs_quota.h are used. Time units of sec(onds), min(utes), hour(s), day(s), week(s), and month(s) are understood. Time limits are printed in the greatest possible time unit such that the value is greater than or equal to one.

FILES
quotas	quota file at the file system root
/etc/mnttab	table of mounted file systems

SEE ALSO
quota(1M), quotacheck(1M), quotaon(1M), repquota(1M), vi(1)

NAME
edsysadm – sysadm interface editing tool

SYNOPSIS
edsysadm

DESCRIPTION
edsysadm is an interactive tool that adds or changes either menu and task definitions in the sysadm interface. It can be used to make changes directly on-line on a specific machine or to create changes that will become part of a software package. The command creates the administration files necessary to achieve the requested changes in the interface and either places them in the appropriate place for on-line changes or saves them to be included in a software package.

edsysadm presents several screens, first prompting for which type of menu item you want to change, menu or task, and then for what type of action to take, add or change. When you select add, a blank menu or task definition (as described below) is provided for you to fill in. When you select change, a series of screens is presented to help identify the definition you wish to change. The final screen presented is the menu or task definition filled in with its current values, which you can then edit.

The menu definition prompts and their descriptions are:

Menu Name
: The name of the new menu (as it should appear in the lefthand column of the screen). This field has a maximum length of 16 alphanumeric characters.

Menu Description
: A description of the new menu (as it should appear in the righthand column of the screen). This field has a maximum length of 58 characters and can consist of any alphanumeric character except at sign (@), carat (ˆ), tilde (˜), back grave ('), grave ('), and double quotes (").

Menu Location
: The location of the menu in the menu hierarchy, expressed as a menu pathname. The pathname should begin with the main menu followed by all other menus that must be traversed (in the order they are traversed) to access this menu. Each menu name must be separated by colons. For example, the menu location for a menu entry being added to the Applications menu is main:applications. *Do not include the menu name in this location definition.* The complete pathname to this menu entry will be the menu location plus the menu name defined at the first prompt.

: This is a scrollable field, showing a maximum of 50 alphanumeric characters at a time.

Menu Help File Name

Pathname to the item help file for this menu entry. If it resides in the directory from which you invoked edsysadm, you do not need to give a full pathname. If you name an item help file that does not exist, you are placed in an editor (as defined by $EDITOR) to create one. The new file is created in the current directory and named Help.

The task definition prompts and their descriptions are:

Task Name

The name of the new task (as it should appear in the lefthand column of the screen). This field has a maximum length of 16 alphanumeric characters.

Task Description

A description of the new task (as it should appear in the righthand column of the screen). This field has a maximum length of 58 characters and can consist of any alphanumeric character except at sign (@), carat (^), tilde (~), back grave (`), grave ('), and double quotes (").

Task Location

The location of the task in the menu hierarchy, expressed as a pathname. The pathname should begin with the main menu followed by all other menus that must be traversed (in the order they are traversed) to access this task. Each menu name must be separated by colons. For example, the task location for a task entry being added to the applications menu is main:applications. *Do not include the task name in this location definition.* The complete pathname to this task entry will be the task location as well as the task name defined at the first prompt.

This is a scrollable field, showing a maximum of 50 alphanumeric characters at a time.

Task Help File Name

Pathname to the item help file for this task entry. If it resides in the directory from which you invoked edsysadm, you do not need to give a full pathname. If you name an item help file that does not exist, you are placed in an editor (as defined by $EDITOR) to create one. The new file is created in the current directory and named Help.

Task Action

The FACE form name or executable that will be run when this task is selected. This is a scrollable field, showing a maximum of 58 alphanumeric characters at a time. This pathname can be relative to the current directory as well as absolute.

Task Files

Any FACE objects or other executables that support the task action listed above and might be called from within that action. *Do not include the help file name or the task action in this list.* Pathnames can be relative to the current directory as well as absolute. A dot (.) implies "all files in the current directory" and includes files in subdirectories.

This is a scrollable field, showing a maximum of 50 alphanumeric characters at a time.

Once the menu or task has been defined, screens for installing the menu or task or saving them for packaging are presented. The package creation or on-line installation is verified and you are informed upon completion.

NOTES

For package creation or modification, this command automatically creates a menu information file and a **prototype** file in the current directory (the directory from which the command is executed). The menu information file is used during package installation to modify menus in the menu structure. A **prototype** file is an installation file which gives a listing of package contents. The **prototype** file created by edsysadm lists the files defined under task action and gives them the special installation class of "admin". The contents of this **prototype** file must be incorporated in the package **prototype** file.

For on-line installation, edsysadm automatically creates a menu information file and adds or modifies the interface menu structure directly.

The item help file must follow the format shown in the *Application Programmer's Guide* in the "Customizing the Administration Interace" chapter or in the *System Administrator's Guide* in the "Customizing the sysadm Interface" appendix.

SEE ALSO

delsysadm(1M), pkgmk(1), prototype(4), sysadm(1M)

NAME
errdump – print error log

SYNOPSIS
/usr/sbin/errdump

DESCRIPTION
This command displays on the system console the error log contained in the system's nonvolatile ram. The display contains the previous saved system state, the last 5 panic messages and their time of occurrence, and an indication of the log's sanity.

DIAGNOSTICS
The phrase "not superuser" is displayed if the command is invoked by other than the super-user. The super-user is anyone logged in under the root directory from the console port.

EXAMPLE
The following is an example of the printout in response to the errdump command.

```
#
#
#
#
# errdump
nvram status:    sane

csr:      0x0648   (floppy)   (unassigned)   (clock)   (uart)

psw:      rsvd CSH_F_D QIE CSH_D OE NZVC TE IPL CM PM R I ISC TM FT
             0      1   0    1   0   0  0   f  0  0 1 0  5  0  3

r3:       0x00049001
r4:       0x00000081
r5:       0x00000000
r6:       0x40091348
r7:       0x0001a13f
r8:       0x4008edd8
oap:      0x400816d8
opc:      0x400083bc
osp:      0x40081700
ofp:      0x40081700
isp:      0x40080008
pcbp:     0x40041a40

fltar:    0xc0021140
fltcr:    reqacc   xlevel   ftype
          0xa      0x0      0x0

          srama            sramb
[0]       0x02034800       0x0000011f
```

```
    [1]      0x02035100      0x00000030
    [2]      0x02035860      0x00000074
    [3]      0x02035c00      0x00000015
             Panic log

    [0]      Thu Sep 20 09:51:36 1984
             KERNEL DATA ALIGNMENT ERROR

    [1]      Thu Sep 20 09:51:37 1984
             KERNEL DATA ALIGNMENT ERROR

    [2]      Thu Sep 20 09:51:40 1984
             KERNEL DATA ALIGNMENT ERROR

    [3]      Thu Sep 20 09:52:21 1984
             KERNEL DATA ALIGNMENT ERROR

    [4]      Fri Sep 21 05:50:10 1984
             SYSTEM PARITY ERROR INTERRUPT
```

SEE ALSO

System Administrator's Guide.

NAME

fdisk – create (recover) a complete disk archive

SYNOPSIS

fdisk −B [−dovAENV] *bkjobid odname opartdev odlab descript*

fdisk −RC [−dovAENV] *odname opartdev descript rsjobid*

DESCRIPTION

The fdisk command is invoked as a child process by other shell commands. The command name, fdisk, is read either from the *bkhist.tab* or the bkreg −m command and option. The −B, −R, and −C options are passed to fdisk by the shell commands *backup* and *restore*. The other options are passed from the bkhist.tab file or the bkreg −p command and option. The arguments are sent to fdisk from various locations in the backup service.

fdisk −B is invoked as a child process by backup to record the formatting information required to recreate the entire disk as it existed at the time of the archiving operation. The formatting information consists of the disk's volume name (not to be confused with the volume name associated with each filesystem partition on the disk), the partitions sizes and locations, and volume names. The resulting backup is a data file, including the results of a prtvtoc command that provides the information required to recreate the disk. The backup is recorded in the backup history log, /etc/bkup/bkhist.tab.

fdisk −RC is invoked as a child process by rsoper to reconstruct a disk using the formatting information previously archived, and to issue the appropriate restore requests to repopulate the most recent data on the disk. The archive is assumed to have been created by fdisk −B. It contains data describing the format of the disk and the names of the filesystems and data partitions that were present on it at the time of the archiving operation.

The arguments to fdp are defined as follows:

bkjobid   the job id assigned by backup. The method uses the *bkjobid* when it creates history log entries.

odname   the name of the data partition that is to be backed up. Unused by fdisk, but supplied by backup for command-line compatibility with other archiving methods.

opartdev   the name of the raw (character) device (partition of the disk) that represents the entire disk

odlab   the volume name on the filesystem [see labelit(1M)]. Unused by fdisk, but supplied by backup for command-line compatibility with other archiving methods.

descript   is a description for a destination device in the form:

        dgroup:dname:dchar:dlabels

dgroup specifies a device group [see devgroup.tab(4)].
dname specifies a particular device name [see device.tab(4)].
dchars specifies characteristics associated with the device. If specified, dchar overrides the defaults for the specified device and group. (See device.tab(4) for a further description of device characteristics).

dlabels specifies the volume names for the media to be used for reading or writing the archive.

rsjobid   the job id assigned by `restore`.

Options

Some options are only significant during `fdisk` −B invocations; they are accepted but ignored during `fdisk` −R invocations because the command is invoked and options are specified automatically by `restore`. These options are flagged with an asterisk (*).

d*   Inhibits recording the archive in the backup history log.

o   Permits the user to override media insertion requests [see `getvol`(1M) and the description of the −o option].

v*   Validates the archive as it is written. A checksum is computed as the archive is being written; as each medium is completed, it is re-read and the checksum recomputed to verify that each block is readable and correct. If either check fails, the medium is considered unreadable. If −A has been specified, the archiving operation fails; otherwise, the operator is prompted to replace the failed medium.

A   Establishes automated mode, (i.e., does not prompt the user to insert or remove media).

E*   Reports an estimate of media usage for the archive; then performs the backup.

N*   Reports an estimate of media usage for the archive; does not perform the backup.

V*   Generates the name and type of each partition on the disk as its formatting information is read-to or written-from the destination device.

User Interactions

The connection between an archiving method and `backup` is more complex than a simple fork/exec or pipe. `backup` is responsible for all interactions with the user, either directly, or through `bkoper`. Therefore, `fdisk` neither reads from standard-input nor writes to standard-output or standard-error. A method library must be used [see `libbrmeth`(3)] to communicate reports (estimates, filenames, periods, status, etc.) to `backup`.

DIAGNOSTICS

The exit codes for `fdisk` are the following:

0 = successful completion of the task
1 = one or more parameters to `fdisk` are invalid.
2 = an error has occurred which caused `fdisk` to fail to
    complete *all* portions of its task.

FILES

`/etc/bkup/bkhist.tab` lists the labels of all volumes that have been used for backup operations

/etc/bkup/bklog	logs errors generated by the backup methods and the backup command
/etc/bkup/rslog	logs errors generated by the restore methods and the restore command

SEE ALSO

backup(1M), device.tab(4), fdp(1), ffile(1), fimage(1), fmthard(1M), getvol(1M), incfile(1), labelit(1M), libbrmeth(3), prtvtoc(1M), restore(1M), rsoper(1M)

NAME

> fdp – create, or restore from, a full file system archive

SYNOPSIS

> fdp –B [–dovAENS] [–c *count*] *bkjobid odpname odpdev odplab descript*
>
> fdp –RC [–dovAENS] [–c *count*] *odpname odpdev redpname redev rsjobid descript*

DESCRIPTION

> The fdp command is invoked as a child process by other shell commands. The command name, fdp, is read either from the *bkhist.tab* file or the bkreg –m command and option. The –B, –R, and –C options are passed to fdp by the shell commands backup, and restore. The other options are passed from the bkhist.tab file or the bkreg –p command and option. The arguments are sent to fdp from various locations in the backup service.
>
> fdp –B is invoked as a child process by the backdaemon command to perform a backup of the data partition *odpdev* (the originating data partition). All blocks in the data partition are archived. The resulting backup is created in the format described on dd(1). The backup is recorded in the backup history log, /etc/bkup/bkhist.tab.
>
> fdp –RC is invoked as a child process by the rsoper command to restore the entire data partition from an archive created by fdp –B. The data partition archive is assumed to be in the format described on dd(1). *dd(1) format.*
>
> The arguments to fdp are defined as follows:
>
> *bkjobid*   the job id assigned by *backup*. The method uses the *bkjobid* when it creates history log entries.
>
> *odpname*   the name of the data partition that is to be backed up. Unused by fdp, but supplied by backup for command-line compatibility with other archiving methods.
>
> *odpdev*   the name of the block special device on which the data partition resides.
>
> *odplab*   the volume name on the file system [see labelit(1M)]. Unused by fdp, but supplied by backup for command-line compatibility with other archiving methods.
>
> *descript*   is a description for a destination device in the form:
> > *dgroup:dname:dchar:dlabels*
> *dgroup* specifies a device group [see devgroup.tab(4)].
> *dname* specifies a particular device name [see device.tab(4)].
> *dchars* specifies characteristics associated with the device. If specified, *dchar* overrides the defaults for the specified device and group. [See device.tab(4) for a further description of device characteristics].
> *dlabels* specifies the volume names for the media to be used for reading or writing the archive.
>
> *rsjobid*   the job id assigned by restore.

redev   if non-null, the partition to be restored to instead of *ofsdev*.

redpname   unused, but provided for consistency with other methods.

Options

Some options are only significant during fdp −B invocations; they are accepted but ignored during fdp −R invocations because the command is invoked and options are specified automatically by restore. These options are flagged with an asterisk (*).

c*count   Archives or restores only the first *count* (512 byte) blocks of data in the data partition.

d*   Inhibits recording the archive in the backup history log.

o   Permits the user to override media insertion requests [see getvol(1M) and the description of the −o option].

v*   Validates the archive as it is written. A checksum is computed as the archive is being written; as each medium is completed, it is re-read and the checksum recomputed to verify that each block is readable and correct. If either check fails, the medium is considered unreadable. If −A has been specified, the archiving operation fails; otherwise, the operator is prompted to replace the failed medium.

A   Establishes automated mode, (i.e., does not prompt the user to insert or remove media).

E*   Reports an estimate of media usage for the archive; then performs the backup.

N*   Reports an estimate of media usage for the archive; does not perform the backup.

S   Displays a period (.) for every 100 (512 byte) blocks read-from or written-to the archive on the destination device.

User Interactions

The connection between an archiving method and backup is more complex than a simple fork/exec or pipe. The backup command is responsible for all interactions with the user, either directly, or through the bkoper command. Therefore, fdp neither reads from standard-input nor writes to standard-output or standard-error. A method library must be used [see libbrmeth(3)] to communicate reports (estimates, filenames, periods, status, etc.) to backup.

DIAGNOSTICS

The exit codes for fdp are the following:

0   successful completion of the task
1   one or more parameters to fdp are invalid.
2   an error has occurred which caused fdp to fail to complete all portions of its task.

FILES

`/etc/bkup/bkexcept.tab`	lists the files that are to be excluded from an incremental file system backup.
`/etc/bkup/bkhist.tab`	lists the labels of all volumes that have been used for backup operations.
`/etc/bkup/rsstatus.tab`	tracks the status of all restore requests from users.
`/etc/bkup/bklog`	logs errors generated by the backup methods and the backup command
`/etc/bkup/rslog`	logs errors generated by the restore methods and the restore command
`$TMP/filelist$$`	temporarily stores a table of contents for a backup archive.

SEE ALSO

backup(1M), device.tab(4), fdp(1), ffile(1), fimage(1), getvol(1M), incfile(1), labelit(1M), libbrmeth(3), prtvtoc(1M), rsoper(1M),

NAME
   ff (generic) – list file names and statistics for a file system

SYNOPSIS
   ff [–F *FSType*] [–V] [*current_options*] [–o *specific_options*] *special* ...

DESCRIPTION
   ff reads the files and directories of the *special* file. I-node data is saved for files
   which match the selection criteria which is either the *inode* number and/or *inode*
   age. Output consists of the path name and other file information. Output fields
   are positional. The output is produced in i-node order. The default line produced by ff is:

       path-name i-number

   current_options are options supported by the s5-specific module of ff. Other
   FSTypes do not necessarily support these options. *specific_options* indicate suboptions specified in a comma-separated list of suboptions and/or keyword-attribute
   pairs for interpretation by the *FSType*-specific module of the command.

   The options are:

   –F   Specify the *FSType* on which to operate. The *FSType* should either be
               specified here or be determinable from /etc/vfstab by matching the
               special with an entry in the table.

   –V   Echo the complete command line, but do not execute the command.
               The command line is generated by using the options and arguments
               provided by the user and adding to them information derived from
               /etc/vfstab. This option should be used to verify and validate the
               command line.

   –o   Specify FSType-specific options.

NOTE
   This command may not be supported for all FSTypes.

FILES
   /etc/vfstab   list of default parameters for each file system

SEE ALSO
   ncheck(1M), vfstab(4).
   find(1) in the *User's Reference Manual*.
   Manual pages for the FSType-specific modules of ff.

NAME

    ff (s5) – display i-list information

SYNOPSIS

    ff [**-F s5**] [*generic_options*] [**-I**] [**-l**] [**-p***prefix*] [**-s**] [**-u**] [**-a***n*] [**-m***n*] [**-c***n*] [**-n***file*]
    [**-i***i-node-list*] *special...*

DESCRIPTION

    generic_options are options supported by the generic **ff** command.

    ff reads the i-list and directories of the *special* file, assuming it is an **s5** file sys-
tem. I-node data is saved for files which match the selection criteria. Output
consists of the path name for each saved i-node, plus other file information
requested using the print *options* below. Output fields are positional. The output
is produced in i-node order; fields are separated by tabs. The default line produced by **ff** is:

        path-name i-number

    The path name is preceded by a . (dot) unless the **-p** option is specified.

    The maximum information the command will provide is:

        path-name i-number size uid

    The argument *n* in the *option* descriptions that follow is used as a decimal integer
(optionally signed), where + *n* means more than *n*, – *n* means less than *n*, and *n*
means exactly *n*. A day is defined as a 24 hour period.

    The options are:

-F s5	Specifies the **s5**-FSType.
-I	Do not print the i-node number after each path name.
-l	Generate a supplementary list of all path names for multiply-linked files.
-p*prefix*	The specified *prefix* will be added to each generated path name. The default is . (dot).
-s	Print the file size, in bytes, after each path name.
-u	Print the owner's login name after each path name.
-a*n*	Select if the i-node has been accessed in *n* days.
-m*n*	Select if the i-node has been modified in *n* days.
-c*n*	Select if the i-node has been changed in *n* days.
-n*file*	Select if the i-node has been modified more recently than the argu- ment *file*.
-i*i-node-list*	Generate names for only those i-nodes specified in *i-node-list*. *i-node-list* is a list of numbers separated by commas and without spaces.

NOTE

If the −1 option is not specified, only a single path name out of all possible ones is generated for a multiply-linked i-node. If −1 is specified, all possible names for every linked file on the file system are included in the output. However, no selection criteria apply to the names generated.

SEE ALSO

generic ff(1M), ncheck(1M).
find(1) in the *User's Reference Manual*.

NAME
ff (ufs) – list file names and statistics for a ufs file system

SYNOPSIS
ff [–F ufs] [*generic_options*] [–o a, m, s] *special* ...

DESCRIPTION
generic_options are options supported by the generic ff command.

ff reads the i-list and directories of the *special* file, assuming it is a file system. Inode data is saved for files which match the selection criteria. Output consists of the path name for each saved inode, plus other file information requested using the options below. Output fields are positional. The output is produced in inode order; fields are separated by TAB characters. The default line produced by ff is:

    path-name i-number

The options are:

–F ufs
    Specifies the ufs-FSType.

–o   Specify ufs file system specific options. The options available are:

    a   Print the '.' and '. .' directory entries.

    m   Print mode information.

    s   Print only special files and files with set-user-ID mode.

NOTE
If the –l option is not specified, only a single path name out of all possible ones is generated for a multiply-linked inode. If –l is specified, all possible names for every linked file on the file system are included in the output. However, no selection criteria apply to the names generated.

SEE ALSO
find(1), generic ff(1M), ncheck(1M).

NAME

  ffile – create, or restore from, a full file system archive

SYNOPSIS

  `ffile` –B [–dlmortvAENSV] *bkjobid ofsname ofsdev ofslab descript*

  `ffile` –RC [–dlmortvAENSV] *ofsname ofsdev refsname redev rsjobid descript*

  `ffile` –RF [–dlmortvAENSV] *ofsname ofsdev descript rsjobid:uid:date:type:name*
  [:[*rename*]:[*inode*]] ...

DESCRIPTION

  The `ffile` command is invoked as a child process by other shell commands. The
  command name, `ffile`, is read either from the `bkhist.tab` file or the `bkreg` –m
  command and option. The –B, –R, –F, and –C options are passed to `ffile` by
  the shell commands `backup`, `restore`, and `urestore`. The other options are
  passed from the `bkhist.tab` or the `bkreg` –p command and option. The arguments are sent to `ffile` from various locations in the backup service.

  `ffile` –B is invoked as a child process by `bkdaemon` to perform a full backup of
  the file system *ofsname* (the originating file system). All files in *ofsname* are
  archived. The resulting backup is created in the format described on cpio(4).
  The backup is recorded in the backup history log,
  `/usr/oam/bkrs/tables/bkhist.tab`.

  `ffile` –RC and RF are invoked as child processes by `rsoper` to extract files from
  an full file system archive created by `ffile` –B. The file system archive is
  assumed to be in the format described on cpio(4).

  If the –RC option is selected, the entire file system is restored.

  If the –RF option is specified, only selected objects from the archive are restored.
  Each 7-tuple, composed of *rsjobid:uid:date:type:name:rename:inode*, specifies an
  object to be restored from the file system archive. The 7-tuple objects come to
  `ffile` from `rsstatus.tab`.

  The arguments to `ffile` are defined as follows:

  bkjobid   the job id assigned by `backup`. The method uses the *bkjobid* when it
          creates history log and table-of-contents entries.

  ofsname   the name of the file system that is to be backed up.

  ofsdev   the name of the block special device on which the file system resides.

  ofslab   the volume name on the file system [see `labelit`(1M)].

  descript   is a description for a destination device in the form:

          dgroup:dname:dchar:dlabels

          dgroup specifies a device group [see `devgroup.tab`(4)].
          dname specifies a particular device name [see `device.tab`(4)].
          dchars specifies characteristics associated with the device. If specified,
          dchar overrides the defaults for the specified device and group. [See
          `device.tab`(4) for a further description of device characteristics.]
          dlabels specifies the volume names for the media to be used for read-
          ing or writing the archive.

refsname if non-null, the name of the file system to be restored to instead of *ofsname*. At least one of *refsname* and *redev* must be null.

redev if non-null, the partition to be restored to instead of *ofsdev*. At least one of *refsname* and *redev* must be null.

rsjobid the restore jobid assigned by **restore** or **urestore**.

uid the real uid of the user who requested the object to be restored. It must match the uid of the owner of the object at the time the archive was made, or it must be the superuser uid.

date the newest "last modification time" that is acceptable for a restorable object. The object is restored from the archive immediately older than this date. *date* is a hexadecimal representation of the date and time provided by the **time** system call [see **time**(2)].

type either **F** or **D**, indicating that the object is a file or a directory, respectively.

name the name the object had in the file system archive.

rename the name that the object should be restored to (it may differ from the name the object had in the file system archive). If omitted, the object is restored to *name*.

inode the inode number of the object as it was stored in the file system archive. *[inode]* is not used by **ffile −R**, and is provided only for command-line compatibility with other restoration methods.

Options
Some options are only significant during **ffile −B** invocations; they are accepted but ignored during **ffile −R** invocations because the command is invoked and options are specified automatically by **restore**. These options are flagged with an asterisk (*).

d* Inhibits recording of the archive in the backup history log.

l* Creates a long form of the backup history log that includes a table-of-contents for the archive. This includes the data used to generate a listing of each file in the archive (like that produced by the **ls −l** command).

m* Mounts the originating file system read-only before starting the backup and remounts it with its original permissions after completing the backup. Cannot be used with **root** or **/usr** file systems.

o Permits the user to override media insertion requests [see **getvol**(1M) and the description of the −o option].

r* Includes remotely mounted resources in the archive.

t* Creates a table of contents for the backup on additional media instead of in the backup history log.

v* Validates the archive as it is written. A checksum is computed as the archive is being written; as each medium is completed, it is re-read and the checksum recomputed to verify that each block is readable and correct. If either check fails, the medium is considered unreadable. If –A has been specified, the archiving operation fails; otherwise, the operator is prompted to replace the failed medium.

A   Establishes automated mode, (i.e., does not prompt the user to insert or remove media).

E*   Reports an estimate of media usage for the archive; then performs the backup.

N*   Reports an estimate of media usage for the archive; does not perform the backup.

S   Displays a period (.) for every 100 (512 byte) blocks read-from or written-to the archive on the destination device.

V   Displays the name of each file written-to or extracted-from the archive on the destination device.

User Interactions

The connection between an archiving method and backup is more complex than a simple fork/exec or pipe. The backup command is responsible for all interactions with the user, either directly, or through bkoper. Therefore, ffile neither reads from standard-input nor writes to standard-output or standard-error. A method library must be used [see libbrmeth(3)] to communicate reports (estimates, filenames, periods, status, etc.) to backup.

DIAGNOSTICS

The exit codes for ffile are the following:
0   successful completion of the task
1   one or more parameters to ffile are invalid.
2   an error has occurred which caused ffile to fail to complete all portions of its task.

FILES

/usr/oam/bkrs/tables/bkexcept.tab
                       lists the files that are to be excluded from an incremental file system backup.

/usr/oam/bkrs/tables/bkhist.tab
                       lists the labels of all volumes that have been used for backup operations.

/usr/oam/bkrs/tables/rsstatus.tab
                       tracks the status ofall restore requests from users.

/usr/oam/bkrs/logs/bklog   logs errors generated by the backup methods and the backup command

/usr/oam/bkrs/logs/rslog   logs errors generated by the restore methods and the restore command

$TMP/filelist$$ temporarily stores a table of contents for a backup archive.

SEE ALSO

backup(1M), bkoper(1M) cpio(1), cpio(4), device.tab(4), fdp(1), ffile(1), fimage(1), getvol(1M), incfile(1), labelit(1M), libbrmeth(3), ls(1), restore(1M), rsoper(1M), time(2), urestore(1)

NAME

fimage − create, restore an image archive of a filesystem

SYNOPSIS

fimage −B [−dlmotuvAENS] *bkjobid ofsname ofsdev ofslab descript*

fimage −RC [−dlmotuvAENS] *ofsname ofsdev refsname redev rsjobid descript*

fimage −RF [−dlmotuvAENS] *ofsname ofsdev descript rsjobid:uid:date:type:name*
[:[*rename*]:[*inode*]] ...

DESCRIPTION

The fimage command is invoked as a child process by other shell commands. The command name, fimage, is read either from the bkhist.tab file or the bkreg −m command and option. The −B, −R, −F, and −C options are passed to fimage by the shell commands backup, restore, and urestore described below. The other options are passed from the bkhist.tab file or the bkreg −p command and option. The arguments are sent to fimage from various locations in the backup service. fimage neither reads from standard-input nor writes to standard-output or standard-error.

fimage −B is invoked as a child process by bkdaemon to perform an image backup of the filesystem *ofsname* (the originating filesystem). All files in *ofsname* are archived. The resulting backup is created in the format described on volcopy(1M). The backup is recorded in the backup history log, /etc/bkup/bkhist.tab.

fimage −RC and −RF are invoked as child processes by the rsoper command to extract files from an image archive created by fimage −B. The filesystem archive is assumed to be in the format described on volcopy format.

If the −RC option is selected, the entire filesystem is restored.

If the −RF option is specified, only selected objects from the archive are restored. Each 7-tuple, composed of *rsjobid:uid:date:type:name:rename:inode*, specifies an object to be restored from the filesystem archive. The 7-tuple objects come to fimage from the rsstatus.tab file.

The arguments to fimage are defined as follows:

bkjobid   the job id assigned by backup. The method uses the *bkjobid* when it creates history log and table-of-contents entries.

ofsname   the name of the file system that is to be backed up.

ofsdev   the name of the block special device on which the file system resides.

ofslab   the volume name on the file system [see labelit(1M)].

descript   is a description for a destination device in the form:

        dgroup:dname:dchar:dlabels

dgroup specifies a device group [see devgroup.tab(4)].
dname specifies a particular device name [see device.tab(4)].
dchars specifies characteristics associated with the device. If specified, *dchar* overrides the defaults for the specified device and group. [See device.tab(4) for a further description of device characteristics.] *dlabels* specifies the volume names for the media to be used for reading or writing the archive.

refsname   if non-null, the name of the file system to be restored to instead of *ofsname*. At least one of *refsname* and *redev* must be null.

redev   if non-null, the partition to be restored to instead of *ofsdev*. At least one of *refsname* and *redev* must be null.

rsjobid   the restore jobid assigned by `restore` or `urestore`.

uid   the real uid of the user who requested the object to be restored. It must match the uid of the owner of the object at the time the archive was made, or it must be the superuser uid.

date   the newest "last modification time" that is acceptable for a restorable object. The object is restored from the archive immediately older than this date. *date* is a hexadecimal representation of the date and time provided by the `time` system call [see `time`(2)].

type   either F or D, indicating that the object is a file or a directory, respectively.

name   the name the object had in the file system archive.

rename   the name that the object should be restored to (it may differ from the name the object had in the file system archive). If omitted, the object is restored to *name*.

inode   the inode number of the object as it was stored in the file system archive. *[inode]* is not used by `ffile` −R, and is provided only for command-line compatibility with other restoration methods.

Options

Some options are only significant during `fimage` −B invocations; they are accepted but ignored during `fimage` −R invocations because the command is invoked and options are specified automatically by `restore`. These options are flagged with an asterisk (*).

d*   Inhibits recording the archive in the backup history log.

l*   Creates a long form of the backup history log that includes a table-of-contents for the archive. This includes the data used to generate a listing of each file in the archive (like that produced by the `ls` −l command).

m*   Mounts the originating filesystem read-only before starting the backup and remounts it with its original permissions after completing the backup. Cannot be used with `root` or `/usr` filesystems.

o   Permits the user to override media insertion requests [see `getvol`(1M) and the description of the −o option].

t*   Creates a table of contents for the backup on additional media instead of in the backup history log.

u*   Unmounts the originating filesystem before the backup is begun. After the backup is complete, remounts the filesystem under its original permission. This option cannot be used with a `root` or `usr` filsystem. The −u option overrides the −m option.

v*	Validates the archive as it is written. A checksum is computed as the archive is being written; as each medium is completed, it is re-read and the checksum recomputed to verify that each block is readable and correct. If either check fails, the medium is considered unreadable. If −A has been specified, the archiving operation fails; otherwise, the operator is prompted to replace the failed medium.
A	Do not prompt the user for removable media operations (automated operation).
E*	Reports an estimate of media usage for the archive; then performs the backup.
N*	Reports an estimate of media usage for the archive; does not perform the backup.
S	Displays a period (.) for every 100 (512 byte) blocks read-from or written-to the archive on the destination device.

User Interactions

The connection between an archiving method and backup is more complex than a simple fork/exec or pipe. The backup command is responsible for all interactions with the user, either directly, or through bkoper. Therefore, ffile neither reads from standard-input nor writes to standard-output or standard-error. A method library must be used [see libbrmeth(3)] to communicate reports (estimates, filenames, periods, status, etc.) to backup.

DIAGNOSTICS

The exit codes for ffile are the following:

0 successful completion of the task
1 one or more parameters to ffile are invalid.
2 an error has occurred which caused ffile to fail to complete all portions of its task.

FILES

/etc/bkup/bkhist.tab	lists the labels of all volumes that have been used for backup operations.
/etc/bkup/rsstatus.tab	tracks the status ofall restore requests from users.
/etc/bkup/bklog	logs errors generated by the backup methods and the backup command
/etc/bkup/rslog	logs errors generated by the restore methods and the restore command
$TMP/filelist$$	temporarily stores a table of contents for a backup archive.

SEE ALSO

backup(1M), bkoper(1M) device.tab(4), fdp(1), ffile(1), fimage(1), getvol(1M), incfile(1), labelit(1M), libbrmeth(3), ls(1), restore(1M), rsoper(1M), time(2), urestore(1), volcopy(1M)

NAME

finc – fast incremental backup

SYNOPSIS

/usr/sbin/finc [*selection-criteria*] *file-system raw-tape*

DESCRIPTION

finc selectively copies the input *file-system* to the output *raw-tape*. The cautious will want to mount the input *file-system* read-only to ensure an accurate backup, although acceptable results can be obtained in read-write mode. The tape must be previously labelled by labelit. The selection is controlled by the *selection-criteria*, accepting only those inodes/files for whom the conditions are true.

It is recommended that production of a finc tape be preceded by the ff command, and the output of ff be saved as an index of the tape's contents. Files on a finc tape may be recovered with the frec command.

The argument *n* in the *selection-criteria* which follow is used as a decimal integer (optionally signed), where +*n* means more than *n*, −*n* means less than *n*, and *n* means exactly *n*. A day is defined as a period of 24 hours.

−a *n*	True if the file has been accessed in *n* days.
−m *n*	True if the file has been modified in *n* days.
−c *n*	True if the i-node has been changed in *n* days.
−n *file*	True for any file which has been modified more recently than the argument *file*.

EXAMPLES

To write a tape consisting of all files from file-system /usr modified in the last 48 hours:

```
finc   −m   −2   /dev/rdsk/c1d0s2   /dev/rSA/ctape1
```

SEE ALSO

ff(1M), frec(1M), labelit(1M).
cpio(1) in the *User's Reference Manual*.

NOTE

The raw device is required when providing both the file system and the tape to finc. Failure to do so will cause an error.

NAME

fingerd, in.fingerd – remote user information server

SYNOPSIS

in.fingerd

DESCRIPTION

fingerd implements the server side of the Name/Finger protocol, specified in RFC 742. The Name/Finger protocol provides a remote interface to programs which display information on system status and individual users. The protocol imposes little structure on the format of the exchange between client and server. The client provides a single command line to the finger server which returns a printable reply.

fingerd waits for connections on TCP port 79. Once connected it reads a single command line terminated by a <RETURN-LINE-FEED> which is passed to finger(1). fingerd closes its connections as soon as the output is finished.

If the line is null (only a RETURN-LINEFEED is sent) then finger returns a default report that lists all users logged into the system at that moment.

If a user name is specified (for instance, eric<RETURN-LINE-FEED>) then the response lists more extended information for only that particular user, whether logged in or not. Allowable names in the command line include both login names and user names. If a name is ambiguous, all possible derivations are returned.

FILES

/var/utmp	who is logged in
/etc/passwd	for users' names
/var/adm/lastlog	last login times
$HOME/.plan	plans
$HOME/.project	projects

SEE ALSO

finger(1)

Harrenstien, Ken, *NAME/FINGER*, RFC 742, Network Information Center, SRI International, Menlo Park, Calif., December 1977.

NOTES

Connecting directly to the server from a TIP or an equally narrow-minded TELNET-protocol user program can result in meaningless attempts at option negotiation being sent to the server, which will foul up the command line interpretation. fingerd should be taught to filter out IAC's and perhaps even respond negatively (IAC *will not)* to all option commands received.

NAME

    fltboot – set default boot parameters

SYNOPSIS

    /usr/sbin/fltboot

DESCRIPTION

    The fltboot command provides the supporting routines for setting or modifying the default boot parameters of the AT&T 3B2 Computer, which are held in Non-Volatile RAM (NVRAM) in firmware. The boot parameters are the default boot program and the default boot device.

    The fltboot command is interactive, so no command line parameters are required. Two prompts are displayed, one for changing the default boot program, and one for changing the default boot device. Pressing RETURN without entering a value at either prompt leaves the current value unchanged.

    The default boot program name appears within brackets in the following firmware prompt:

        Enter name of program to execute [   ]:

    As delivered, the default boot program name is NULL, as evidenced by the empty brackets above (i.e., there is no default in the delivered system, a file name must be entered).

    The default boot device appears within brackets in the following firmware prompt:

        Enter Load Device Option Number [1 (HD72)]:

    The number and device in brackets indicate the default boot device (HD72 in the above example). As delivered, the default boot device is your hard disk (normally the first hard disk connected to the first integral disk controller, if you have more than one).

    Pressing RETURN at either prompt invokes the default value shown in brackets. A NULL boot program name results in the listing of the contents of the first stand partition on the chosen device (after the Load Device is entered).

SEE ALSO

    firmware(8).

    System Administrator's Guide.

NAME
fmtflop – physically format diskettes

SYNOPSIS
/usr/sbin/fmtflop [−v] *special_file*

DESCRIPTION
fmtflop physically formats the media inserted in the diskette drive. The −v
option verifies that the diskette is correctly formatted. The *special_file* is the path
name of the diskette drive (e.g., /dev/rdsk/c0d0s6).

fmtflop formats DOUBLE-SIDED media with 512 byte sectors, 9 sectors per
track, and 80 tracks. Before executing fmtflop, the diskette must be placed in
the drive and the latch closed.

SEE ALSO
if(7).

DIAGNOSTICS
An error message is returned if the format or verify fails. If this occurs, remove
the diskette and reinsert it to make sure it is properly seated, then try entering
the command a second time. If the command fails again (especially on the same
area of the disk) the diskette is probably bad and must be discarded.

The error message process lock failed is returned if the command is
attempted by someone other than the super-user.

NAME

fmthard – populate VTOC on hard disks

SYNOPSIS

/usr/sbin/fmthard [–c *core_disk_type*] [–d *data*] [–i] [–s *datafile*]
[–n *volume_name*] /dev/rdsk/[ct]?d?s?

DESCRIPTION

The fmthard command creates (or updates) the VTOC (Volume Table of Contents) on hard disks. The /dev/rdsk/[ct]?d?s? file must be the character special file of the device where the new VTOC is to be installed.

OPTIONS

The following options apply to fmthard:

–d *data*

> The *data* argument of this option is a string representing the information
> for a particular partition in the current VTOC. The string must be of the
> format *part:tag:flag:start:size* where *part* is the partition number, *tag* is the
> ID tag of the partition, *flag* is the set of permission flags, *start* is the start-
> ing sector number of the partition, and *size* is the number of sectors in the
> partition. See the description of the *datafile* below for more information on
> these fields.

–i

> Lets the command create the desired VTOC table, but prints the informa-
> tion to standard output instead of modifying the VTOC on the disk.

–n *volume_name*

> Allows the disk to be given a *volume_name* up to 8 characters long.

–c *core_disk_type*

> The three core disk configurations are: "0" (single disk configuration), "1"
> (first disk of a dual disk configuration), and "2" (second disk of a dual
> disk configuration). Core disk configuration requires disk size to be at
> least 32MB.

Disk Configuration	Partition	Used For
0	0	root
	1	swap
	2	usr
	8	var
	9	home (remaining space)
1	0	root
	1	swap
	8	home (remaining space)
2	2	usr
	8	var
	a	home2 (remaining space)

–s *datafile*

> The VTOC is populated according to a *datafile* created by the user. The
> *datafile* format is described below. This option causes all of the disk parti-
> tion timestamp fields to be set to zero.

If no options are given, a default VTOC is created with partition **a** (see the description of the −c option, above) as the only mountable partition. Every VTOC generated by fmthard will also have partition 6 (the whole disk) and partition 7 (the boot partition). Partition 6 is the only partition that can overlap others.

The *datafile* contains one specification line for each partition, starting with partition 0. Each line is delimited by a new-line character (\n). If the first character of a line is an asterisk (*), the line is treated as a comment. Each line is composed of entries that are position-dependent, separated by "white space" and having the following format:

> *partition   tag   flag   starting_sector   size_in_sectors*

where the entries have the following values.

partition   The partition number: 0-15 decimal or 0x0-0xf hexadecimal.

tag   The partition tag: a two-digit hex number. The following are reserved codes: 0x01 (V_BOOT), 0x02 (V_ROOT), 0x03 (V_SWAP), 0x04 (V_USR), 0x05 (V_BACKUP), 0x06 (V_STAND), 0x07 (V_VAR) and 0x08(V_HOME).

flag   The flag allows a partition to be flagged as unmountable or read only, the masks being: V_UNMNT 0x01, and V_RONLY 0x10. For mountable partitions use 0x00.

starting sector   The sector number (decimal) on which the partition starts.

size in sectors   The number (decimal) of sectors occupied by the partition.

Note that you can save the output of a prtvtoc command to a file, edit the file, and use it as the *datafile* argument to the −s option.

SEE ALSO
prtvtoc(1M), newboot(1M).

NOTES
Special care should be exercised when overwriting an existing VTOC, as incorrect entries could result in current data being inaccessible. As a precaution, save the old VTOC.

After using fmthard on a bootable drive, you must execute newboot on that drive. newboot should also be executed after mirroring any partition on a bootable disk (executing either sysadm rootsetup or sysadm mirror).

If newboot is not executed after fmthard, then the drive will become unbootable and may require a partial restore. Do not do a partial restore while root and /usr are mirrored.

When using the −s option, the user must allocate at least two sectors, beginning with sector 0, for the VTOC. This is normally designated as partition 7. Failure to allocate space for the VTOC may result in overwriting the VTOC, thereby destroying the disk partitioning information.

NAME

format – physically format a SCSI hard disk

SYNOPSIS

/usr/sbin/format [–v] [–n] /dev/rdsk/[ct]?d?s6

DESCRIPTION

This command physically formats a Small Computer System Interface (SCSI) hard disk.

The super-user may use the format command in single-user state to prepare SCSI hard disks for use. The following options may be used with format:

–v   verifies that the formatted SCSI hard disk is correct.

–n   formatting is suppressed.

When a SCSI disk is formatted, a Physical Description (PD) Sector is placed at SCSI logical block zero.

SEE ALSO

Formatting in the SCSI *Operation Manual.*

NOTES

This command destroys any data that might be on the disk. It not be run in the background with other processes running. It cannot format non-SCSI hard disks.

DIAGNOSTICS

The format command exits with one of three values:

0   means NORMAL (or TRUE)

1   means execution errors

2   means bad command usage

NAME

frec – recover files from a backup tape

SYNOPSIS

/usr/sbin/frec [–p *path*] [–f *reqfile*] *raw_tape i_number*:*name* . . .

DESCRIPTION

frec recovers files from the specified *raw_tape* backup tape written by volcopy or finc, given their *i_numbers*. The data for each recovery request will be written into the file given by *name* .

The –p option allows you to specify a default prefixing *path* different from your current working directory. This will be prefixed to any *names* that are not fully qualified (i.e. that do not begin with / or ./). If any directories are missing in the paths of recovery *names*, they will be created.

–p *path*   Specifies a prefixing *path* to be used to fully qualify any names that do not start with / or ./.

–f *reqfile*   Specifies a file which contains recovery requests. The format is *i_number:newname*, one per line.

EXAMPLES

To recover a file, *i_number* 1216 when backed-up, into a file named junk in your current working directory:

```
frec /dev/rSA/ctape1 1216:junk
```

To recover files with *i_numbers* 14156, 1232, and 3141 into files /usr/src/cmd/a, /usr/src/cmd/b and /usr/joe/a.c:

```
frec –p /usr/src/cmd /dev/rSA/ctape1 14156:a 1232:b \
      3141:/usr/joe/a.c
```

SEE ALSO

ff(1M), finc(1M), labelit(1M), volcopy(1M).
cpio(1) in the *User's Reference Manual*.

NOTES

While paving a path (i.e., creating the intermediate directories contained in a pathname) frec can only recover inode fields for those directories contained on the tape and requested for recovery.

NAME

fromsmtp – receive RFC822 mail from SMTP

SYNOPSIS

fromsmtp [–d] [–h *host*] [–s *sender*] to ...

DESCRIPTION

fromsmtp reads an RFC822 message from its standard input, does some conversion of the message to make it acceptable to UNIX System mail, and pipes the result to rmail. The *to* arguments are passed as arguments to rmail. fromsmtp is normally invoked by smtpd to deliver incoming mail messages.

The –d option may be used for debugging fromsmtp. It will cause the command line for rmail to be echoed to standard output, as well as the results of the message (after conversion). The message will not be given to rmail when this option is used.

The –h *host* option may be used to prepend a host or network name to the front of the sender path in the From line at the beginning of the message. This is useful if you need to identify which of several possible networks a message was received from (for possible use in replying).

The –s *sender* option is used to give a default sender name, in case fromsmtp cannot determine the name of the sender from the message it reads. If this option is not used, the default sender name unknown will be used.

FILES

/usr/bin/rmail   where converted mail is piped to

SEE ALSO

rmail(1M), smtpd(1M)
RFC822 – Standard for the Format of ARPA Internet Text Messages

NAME

fsba – file system block analyzer

SYNOPSIS

/usr/sbin/fsba [–b *target_block_size*] *file-system1* [*file-system2* ...]

DESCRIPTION

The **fsba** command determines the disk space required to store the data from an existing file system in a new file system with the specified logical block size. Each *file-system* listed on the command line refers to an existing file system and should be specified by device name (e.g., /dev/rdsk/c1d0s2).

The *target_block_size* specifies the logical block size in bytes of the new file system. Valid target block sizes are 512, 1024, and 2048. Default target block size is 1024. A block size of 2048 is supported only if the 2K file system package is installed.

The **fsba** command prints information about how many 512-byte disk sectors are allocated to store the data in the old (existing) file system and how many would be required to store the same data in a new file system with the specified logical block size. It also prints the number of allocated and free i-nodes for the existing file system.

If the number of free sectors listed for the new file system is negative, the data will not fit in the new file system unless the new file system is larger than the existing file system. The new file system must be made at least as large as the number of sectors listed by **fsba** as allocated for the new file system. The maximum size of the new file system is limited by the size of the disk partition used for the new file system.

Note that it is possible to specify a *target_block_size* that is smaller than the logical block size of the existing file system. In this case the new file system would require fewer sectors to store the data.

SEE ALSO

mkfs(1M), prtvtoc(1M).

NAME

fsck (generic) – check and repair file systems

SYNOPSIS

fsck [–F *FSType*] [–V] [–m] [*special* ...]

fsck [–F *FSType*] [–V] [*current_options*] [–o *specific_options*] [*special* ...]

DESCRIPTION

fsck audits and interactively repairs inconsistent conditions for file systems. If the file system is inconsistent the user is prompted for concurrence before each correction is attempted. It should be noted that some corrective actions will result in some loss of data. The amount and severity of data loss may be determined from the diagnostic output. The default action for each correction is to wait for the user to respond **yes** or **no**. If the user does not have write permission fsck defaults to a no action.

The file system should be unmounted when fsck is used. If this is not possible, care should be taken that the system is quiescent and that it is rebooted immediately afterwards if the file system is a critical one, for example **root**.

current_options are options supported by the **s5**-specific module of fsck. Other *FSTypes* do not necessarily support these options. *specific_options* indicate suboptions specified in a comma-separated list of suboptions and/or keyword-attribute pairs for interpretation by the *FSType*-specific module of the command.

special represents a block or character special device (e.g., /dev/rdsk/c1d0s8). It is preferable that a character special device be used. fsck will not work on a block device if it is mounted. If *special* is not supplied, fsck looks through /etc/vfstab and executes fsck for all character specials in the fsckdev field of /etc/vfstab for which there is a numeric entry in the fsckpass field.

The options are:

–F   Specify the *FSType* on which to operate. The *FSType* should either be specified here or be determinable from /etc/vfstab by matching the *special* with an entry in the table.

–V   Echo the complete command line, but do not execute the command. The command line is generated by using the options and arguments provided by the user and adding to them information derived from /etc/vfstab. This option should be used to verify and validate the command line.

–m   Check but don't repair. This option checks that the file system is suitable for mounting.

–o   Specify *FSType*-specific options.

NOTE

This command may not be supported for all *FSTypes*.

FILES

/etc/vfstab   list of default parameters for each file system

NAME

  fsck (bfs) - check and repair **bfs** file systems

SYNOPSIS

  fsck [-F bfs] [*generic_options*] [*special...*]

  fsck [-F bfs] [*generic_optionsi*] [-y | -n] [*special...*]

DESCRIPTION

  generic_options are options supported by the generic **fsck** command.

  fsck checks to see if compaction was in process but was not completed, perhaps as a result of a system crash. If it was, **fsck** completes the compaction of the file [see **fs_bfs**(4)].

  The options are:

  -y   Assume a yes response to all questions asked by **fsck**.

  -n   Assume a no response to all questions asked by **fsck**.

SEE ALSO

  checkfsys(1M), generic fsck(1M), mkfs(1M), fs_bfs(4)
  chapter 5 of the *System Administrator's Guide*.

SEE ALSO
      checkfsys(1M), mkfs(1M), vfstab(4).
      Manual pages for the *FSType*-specific modules of fsck.

NAME

fsck (s5) – check and repair s5 file systems

SYNOPSIS

fsck [–F s5] [*generic_options*] [*special...*]

fsck [–F s5] [*generic_options*] [–y] [–n] [–p] [–s*X*] [–S*X*] [–t*file*] [–l] [–q] [–D] [–f]
[*special...*]

DESCRIPTION

generic_options are options supported by the generic fsck command.

The options are:

–F s5   Specifies the s5-FSType.

–y   Assume a **yes** response to all questions asked by fsck.

–n   Assume a **no** response to all questions asked by fsck; do not open the
           file system for writing.

–p   Correct inconsistencies that can be fixed automatically, that is, incon-
           sistencies that are deemed harmless and can be fixed without
           confirmation by the administrator. Examples of such inconsistencies
           are unreferenced i-nodes, incorrect counts in the superblocks, and
           missing blocks in the free list.

–s*X*   Ignore the actual free list and (unconditionally) reconstruct a new one
           by rewriting the super-block of the file system. The file system should
           be unmounted while this is done; if this is not possible, care should be
           taken that the system is quiescent and that it is rebooted immediately
           afterwards. This precaution is necessary so that the old, bad, in-core
           copy of the superblock will not continue to be used, or written on the
           file system.

           The –s*X* suboption allows for creating an optimal free-list organiza-
           tion.

           If *X* is not given, the values used when the file system was created are
           used. The format of *X* is *cylinder size:gap size*.

–S*X*   Conditionally reconstruct the free list. This suboption is like –s*X*
           above except that the free list is rebuilt only if there were no
           discrepancies discovered in the file system. Using S will force a no
           response to all questions asked by fsck. This suboption is useful for
           forcing free list reorganization on uncontaminated file systems.

–t*file*   If fsck cannot obtain enough memory to keep its tables, it uses a
           scratch file. If the t option is specified, the *file* named is used as the
           scratch file, if needed. Without the t option, fsck will prompt the
           user for the name of the scratch file. The file chosen should not be on
           the file system being checked, and if it is not a special file or did not
           already exist, it is removed when fsck completes.

–l   identify damaged files by their logical names

-q   Quiet `fsck`. Unreferenced `fifos` will silently be removed. If `fsck` requires it, counts in the superblock will be automatically fixed and the free list salvaged.

-D   Directories are checked for bad blocks. Useful after system crashes.

-f   Fast check. Check block and sizes and check the free list. The free list will be reconstructed if it is necessary.

Inconsistencies checked are as follows:

1. Blocks claimed by more than one i-node or the free list.
2. Blocks claimed by an i-node or the free list outside the range of the file system.
3. Incorrect link counts.
4. Size checks:
    Incorrect number of blocks.
    Directory size not 16-byte aligned.
5. Bad i-node format.
6. Blocks not accounted for anywhere.
7. Directory checks:
    File pointing to unallocated i-node.
    I-node number out of range.
8. Super Block checks:
    More than 65536 i-nodes.
    More blocks for i-nodes than there are in the file system.
9. Bad free block list format.
10. Total free block and/or free i-node count incorrect.

Orphaned files and directories (allocated but unreferenced) are, with the user's concurrence, reconnected by placing them in the `lost+found` directory, if the files are nonempty. The user will be notified if the file or directory is empty or not. Empty files or directories are removed, as long as the n suboption is not specified. `fsck` will force the reconnection of nonempty directories. The name assigned is the i-node number.

NOTE

Checking the raw device is almost always faster.

I-node numbers for . and . . in each directory are not checked for validity.

SEE ALSO

checkfsys(1M), crash(1M), generic fsck(1M), mkfs(1M), ncheck(1M), fs(4).

NAME

    fsck (ufs) − file system consistency check and interactive repair

SYNOPSIS

    fsck [−**F ufs**] [*generic_options*] [*special* ...]

    fsck [−**F ufs**] [*generic_options*] [(−**y**|−**Y**) | (−**n**|−**N**)] [−**o p,b=#,w**] [*special* ....]

DESCRIPTION

    generic_options are options supported by the generic **fsck** command. *current_options* are options supported by the **s5**-specific module of the **fsck** command.

    fsck audits and interactively repairs inconsistent conditions on file systems. In this case, it asks for confirmation before attempting any corrections. Inconsistencies other than those mentioned above can often result in some loss of data. The amount and severity of data lost can be determined from the diagnostic output.

    fsck corrects innocuous inconsistencies such as: unreferenced inodes, too-large link counts in inodes, missing blocks in the free list, blocks appearing in the free list and also in files, or incorrect counts in the super block, automatically. It displays a message for each inconsistency corrected that identifies the nature of, and file system on which, the correction is to take place. After successfully correcting a file system, **fsck** prints the number of files on that file system, the number of used and free blocks, and the percentage of fragmentation.

    The default action for each correction is to wait for the operator to respond either **yes** or no. If the operator does not have write permission on the file system, **fsck** will default to a −**n** (no corrections) action.

    Inconsistencies checked are as follows:

- Blocks claimed by more than one inode or the free list.
- Blocks claimed by an inode or the free list outside the range of the file system.
- Incorrect link counts.
- Incorrect directory sizes.
- Bad inode format.
- Blocks not accounted for anywhere.
- Directory checks, file pointing to unallocated inode, inode number out of range, absence of '.' and '. .' as the first two entries in each directory.
- Super Block checks: more blocks for inodes than there are in the file system.
- Bad free block list format.
- Total free block and/or free inode count incorrect.

    Orphaned files and directories (allocated but unreferenced) are, with the operator's concurrence, reconnected by placing them in the lost+found directory. The name assigned is the inode number. If the lost+found directory does not exist, it is created. If there is insufficient space its size is increased.

A file system may be specified by giving the name of the block or character special device on which it resides, or by giving the name of its mount point.

The options are:

−F ufs
>   Specifies the ufs-FSType.

−y | −Y
>   Assume a yes response to all questions asked by fsck.

−n | −N
>   Assume a no response to all questions asked by fsck; do not open the file system for writing.

−o
>   Specify ufs file system specific suboptions. These suboptions can be any combination of the following:
>
>   p   Check the filesystem non-interactively. Exit if there is a problem requiring intervention.
>
>   b=#   Use the block specified as the super block for the file system. Block 32 is always an alternate super block.

NOTES
Checking the character special device is almost always faster.

SEE ALSO
checkfsys(1M), crash(1M), generic fsck(1M), mkfs(1M), ufs(4).

NAME

fsdb (generic) – file system debugger

SYNOPSIS

fsdb [–F *FSType*] [–V] [*current_options*] [–o *specific_options*] *special*

DESCRIPTION

fsdb is a file system debugger which allows for the manual repair of a file system after a crash. *special* is a special device used to indicate the file system to be debugged. fsdb is intended for experienced users only. *FSType* is the file system type to be debugged. Since different *FSTypes* have different structures and hence different debugging capabilities the manual pages for the *FSType*-specific fsdb should be consulted for a more detailed description of the debugging capabilities.

current_options are options supported by the s5-specific module of fsdb. Other *FSTypes* do not necessarily support these options. *specific_options* indicate suboptions specified in a comma-separated list of suboptions and/or keyword-attribute pairs for interpretation by the *FSType*-specific module of the command.

The options are:

–F   Specify the *FSType* on which to operate. The *FSType* should either be specified here or be determinable from /etc/vfstab by matching the *special* with an entry in the table.

–V   Echo the complete command line, but do not execute the command. The command line is generated by using the options and arguments provided by the user and adding to them information derived from /etc/vfstab. This option should be used to verify and validate the command line.

–o   Specify *FSType*-specific options.

NOTE

This command may not be supported for all *FSTypes*.

FILES

/etc/vfstab   list of default parameters for each file system

SEE ALSO

mkfs(1M), vfstab(4).
Manual pages for the *FSType*-specific modules of fsdb.

NAME

fsdb (s5) – s5 file system debugger

SYNOPSIS

fsdb [**-F s5**] [*generic_options*] [**-z** *i-number*] *special* [**-**]

DESCRIPTION

generic_options are options supported by the generic **fsdb** command.

fsdb can be used to patch up a damaged **s5** file system after a crash. It has conversions to translate block and i-numbers into their corresponding disk addresses. Also included are mnemonic offsets to access different parts of an i-node. These greatly simplify the process of correcting control block entries or descending the file system tree.

fsdb contains several error-checking routines to verify i-node and block addresses. These can be disabled if necessary by invoking **fsdb** with the optional – argument or by the use of the O symbol. (**fsdb** reads the i-size and f-size entries from the superblock of the file system as the basis for these checks.)

The options are:

    -F s5   Specifies the **s5**-FSType.

    -z *i-number*   Clear the i-node identified by *i-number*. Non-interactive.

Numbers are considered decimal by default. Octal numbers must be prefixed with a zero. During any assignment operation, numbers are checked for a possible truncation error due to a size mismatch between source and destination.

fsdb reads a block at a time and will therefore work with raw as well as block I/O. A buffer management routine is used to retain commonly used blocks of data in order to reduce the number of read system calls. All assignment operations result in an immediate write-through of the corresponding block.

The symbols recognized by **fsdb** are:

#	absolute address
i	convert from i-number to i-node address
b	convert to block address
d	directory slot offset
+ , –	address arithmetic
q	quit
> , <	save, restore an address
=	numerical assignment
=+	incremental assignment
=–	decremental assignment
="	character string assignment
O	error checking flip flop
p	general print facilities
f	file print facility
B	byte mode
W	word mode

| D | double word mode |
| ! | escape to shell |

The print facilities generate a formatted output in various styles. The current address is normalized to an appropriate boundary before printing begins. It advances with the printing and is left at the address of the last item printed. The output can be terminated at any time by typing the delete character. If a number follows the p symbol, that many entries are printed. A check is made to detect block boundary overflows since logically sequential blocks are generally not physically sequential. If a count of zero is used, all entries to the end of the current block are printed. The print options available are:

i	print as i-nodes
d	print as directories
o	print as octal words
e	print as decimal words
c	print as characters
b	print as octal bytes

The f symbol is used to print data blocks associated with the current i-node. If followed by a number, that block of the file is printed. (Blocks are numbered from zero.) The desired print option letter follows the block number, if present, or the f symbol. This print facility works for small as well as large files. It checks for special devices and that the block pointers used to find the data are not zero.

Dots, tabs, and spaces may be used as function delimiters but are not necessary. A line with just a new-line character will increment the current address by the size of the data type last printed. That is, the address is set to the next byte, word, double word, directory entry or i-node, allowing the user to step through a region of a file system. Information is printed in a format appropriate to the data type. Bytes, words and double words are displayed with the octal address followed by the value in octal and decimal. A .B or .D is appended to the address for byte and double word values, respectively. Directories are printed as a directory slot offset followed by the decimal i-number and the character representation of the entry name. I-nodes are printed with labeled fields describing each element.

The following mnemonics are used for i-node examination and refer to the current working i-node:

md	mode
ln	link count
uid	user ID number
gid	group ID number
sz	file size
a #	data block numbers (0 − 12)
at	access time
mt	modification time
maj	major device number
min	minor device number

EXAMPLES

386i	prints i-number 386 in an i-node format. This now becomes the current working i-node.
ln=4	changes the link count for the working i-node to 4.
ln=+1	increments the link count by 1.
fc	prints, in ASCII, block zero of the file associated with the working i-node.
2i.fd	prints the first 32 directory entries for the root i-node of this file system.
d5i.fc	changes the current i-node to that associated with the 5th directory entry (numbered from zero) found from the above command. The first logical block of the file is then printed in ASCII.
512B.p0o	prints the superblock of this file system in octal.
2i.a0b.d7=3	changes the i-number for the seventh directory slot in the root directory to 3. This example also shows how several operations can be combined on one command line.
d7.nm="*name*"	changes the name field in the directory slot to the given string. Quotes are optional when used with nm if the first character is alphabetic.
a2b.p0d	prints the third block of the current i-node as directory entries.

SEE ALSO

fsck(1M), generic fsdb(1M).

dir(4), fs(4) in the *Programmers Reference Manual*

NAME

   fsdb (ufs) – ufs file system debugger

SYNOPSIS

   fsdb [−F ufs] [*generic_options*] [−z *i-number*] *special*

DESCRIPTION

   generic_options are options supported by the generic **fsdb** command.

   The options are:

   −F ufs

   > Specifies the **ufs**-FSType.

   −z *i-number*

   > Clear the i-node identified by *i-number*. Non-interactive.

SEE ALSO

   fsck(1M), generic fsdb(1M), dir(4), ufs(4)

NAME

    fstyp (generic) – determine file system type

SYNOPSIS

    fstyp [–v] *special*

DESCRIPTION

    fstyp allows the user to determine the file system type of unmounted file systems using heuristic programs.

    An **fstyp** module for each file system type to be checked is executed; each of these modules applies some appropriate heuristic to determine whether the supplied *special* file is of the type for which it checks. If it is, the program prints on standard output the usual file-system identifier for that type and exits with a return code of 0; if none of the modules succeed, the error message **unknown_fstyp (no matches)** is returned and the exit status is 1. If more than one module succeeds the error message **unknown_fstyp (multiple matches)** is returned and the exit status is 2.

    The options are:

    –v   Produce verbose output. This is usually information about the file systems superblock and varies across different *FSTypes*.

NOTES

    The use of heuristics implies that the result of **fstyp** is not guaranteed to be accurate.

NAME
ftpd – file transfer protocol server

SYNOPSIS
in.ftpd [−dl] [−t*timeout*] *host.socket*

DESCRIPTION
ftpd is the Internet File Transfer Protocol (FTP) server process. The server is invoked by the Internet daemon inetd(1M) each time a connection to the FTP service [see services(4)] is made, with the connection available as descriptor 0 and the host and socket the connection originated from (in hex and decimal respectively) as argument.

Inactive connections are timed out after 90 seconds.

The following options are available:

−t*timeout*
> Set the inactivity timeout period to *timeout,* in seconds. The FTP server will timeout an inactive session after 15 minutes.

Requests
The FTP server currently supports the following FTP requests; case is not distinguished.

Request	Description
ABOR	abort previous command
ACCT	specify account (ignored)
ALLO	allocate storage (vacuously)
APPE	append to a file
CDUP	change to parent of current working directory
CWD	change working directory
DELE	delete a file
HELP	give help information
LIST	give list files in a directory (ls −lg)
MKD	make a directory
MODE	specify data transfer *mode*
NLST	give name list of files in directory (ls)
NOOP	do nothing
PASS	specify password
PASV	prepare for server-to-server transfer
PORT	specify data connection port
PWD	print the current working directory

QUIT	terminate session
RETR	retrieve a file
RMD	remove a directory
RNFR	specify rename-from file name
RNTO	specify rename-to file name
STOR	store a file
STOU	store a file with a unique name
STRU	specify data transfer *structure*
TYPE	specify data transfer *type*
USER	specify user name
XCUP	change to parent of current working directory
XCWD	change working directory
XMKD	make a directory
XPWD	print the current working directory
XRMD	remove a directory

The remaining FTP requests specified in RFC 959 are recognized, but not implemented.

The FTP server will abort an active file transfer only when the ABOR command is preceded by a Telnet Interrupt Process (IP) signal and a Telnet Synch signal in the command Telnet stream, as described in RFC 959.

ftpd interprets file names according to the globbing conventions used by sh(1). This allows users to utilize the metacharacters: * ? [ ] { } ~

ftpd authenticates users according to three rules.

1)   The user name must be in the password data base, /etc/passwd, and not have a null password. In this case a password must be provided by the client before any file operations may be performed.

2)   The user name must not appear in the file /etc/ftpusers.

3)   If the user name is anonymous or ftp, an anonymous FTP account must be present in the password file (user ftp). In this case the user is allowed to log in by specifying any password (by convention this is given as the client host's name).

In the last case, ftpd takes special measures to restrict the client's access privileges. The server performs a chroot(2) command to the home directory of the ftp user. In order that system security is not breached, it is recommended that the ftp subtree be constructed with care; the following rules are recommended.

home_directory
        Make the home directory owned by ftp and unwritable by anyone.

home_directory/usr/bin
> Make this directory owned by the super-user and unwritable by anyone. The program ls(1) must be present to support the list commands. This program should have mode 111.

home_directory/etc
> Make this directory owned by the super-user and unwritable by anyone. Copies of the files passwd(4), group(4), and netconfig must be present for the ls command to work properly. These files should be mode 444.

home_directory/pub
> Make this directory mode 777 and owned by ftp. Users should then place files which are to be accessible via the anonymous account in this directory.

home_directory/dev
> Make this directory owned by the super-user and unwritable by anyone. Change directories to this directory and do the following:

```
FTP="`grep ^ftp: /etc/passwd | cut -d: -f6`"
MAJORMINOR="`ls -l /dev/tcp | nawk '{ gsub(/,/, ""); print $5, $6}'`"
mknod $FTP/dev/tcp c $MAJORMINOR
chmod 666 $FTP/dev/tcp
```

SEE ALSO
ftp(1), getsockopt(3N), passwd(4), services(4).

Postel, Jon, and Joyce Reynolds, *File Transfer Protocol (FTP)*, RFC 959, Network Information Center, SRI International, Menlo Park, Calif., October 1985.

NOTES
The anonymous account is inherently dangerous and should be avoided when possible.

The server must run as the super-user to create sockets with privileged port numbers. It maintains an effective user id of the logged in user, reverting to the super-user only when binding addresses to sockets. The possible security holes have been extensively scrutinized, but are possibly incomplete.

/etc/ftpusers contains a list of users who cannot access the system; the format of the file is one username per line.

NAME

fumount – forced unmount of an advertised resource

SYNOPSIS

fumount [-w *sec*] *resource*

DESCRIPTION

fumount unadvertises *resource* and disconnects remote access to the resource. The –w *sec* causes a delay of *sec* seconds prior to the execution of the disconnect.

When the forced unmount occurs, an administrative shell script is started on each remote computer that has the resource mounted (/usr/bin/rfuadmin). If a grace period of seconds is specified, rfuadmin is started with the fuwarn option. When the actual forced unmount is ready to occur, rfuadmin is started with the fumount option. See the rfuadmin(1M) manual page for information on the action taken in response to the forced unmount.

This command is restricted to the super-user.

ERRORS

If *resource* (1) does not physically reside on the local machine, (2) is an invalid resource name, (3) is not currently advertised and is not remotely mounted, or (4) the command is not run with super-user privileges, an error message will be sent to standard error.

SEE ALSO

adv(1M), mount(1M), rfuadmin(1M), rfudaemon(1M), rmount(1M), unadv(1M).

NAME
    fusage – disk access profiler

SYNOPSIS
    fusage [[*mount_point*] | [*advertised_resource*] | [*block_special_device*] [...]]

DESCRIPTION
    When used with no options, fusage reports block I/O transfers, in kilobytes, to
    and from all locally mounted file systems and advertised Remote File Sharing
    resources on a per client basis. The count data are cumulative since the time of
    the mount. When used with an option, fusage reports on the named file system,
    advertised resource, or block special device.

    The report includes one section for each file system and advertised resource and
    has one entry for each machine that has the directory remotely mounted, ordered
    by decreasing usage. Sections are ordered by device name; advertised resources
    that are not complete file systems will immediately follow the sections for the file
    systems they are in.

SEE ALSO
    adv(1M), mount(1M), df(1M), crash(1M).

NAME
fuser – identify processes using a file or file structure

SYNOPSIS
/usr/sbin/fuser [-[c|f]ku] *files* | *resources* [[-] [[c|f]ku] files | resources] ...

DESCRIPTION
fuser outputs the process IDs of the processes that are using the *files* or remote *resources* specified as arguments. Each process ID is followed by a letter code, interpreted as follows: if the process is using the file as 1) its current directory, the code is c, 2) its root directory, the code is r, 3) an open file, the code is o, or 4) its text file, the code is t. For block special devices with mounted file systems, all processes using any file on that device are listed. For remote resource names, all processes using any file associated with that remote resource (Remote File Sharing) are reported. For all other types of files (text files, executables, directories, devices, etc.) only the processes using that file are reported.

The following options may be used with fuser:

-c   may be used with files that are mount points for file systems. With that option the report is for use of the mount point and any files within that mounted file system.

-f   when this is used, the report is only for the named file, not for files within a mounted file system.

-u   the user login name, in parentheses, also follows the process ID.

-k   the SIGKILL signal is sent to each process. Since this option spawns kills for each process, the kill messages may not show up immediately [see kill(2)].

If more than one group of files are specified, the options may be respecified for each additional group of files. A lone dash cancels the options currently in force.

The process IDs are printed as a single line on the standard output, separated by spaces and terminated with a single new line. All other output is written on standard error.

Any user with permission to read /dev/kmem and /dev/mem can use fuser. Only the super-user can terminate another user's process

FILES
/stand/unix   for system namelist
/dev/kmem   for system image
/dev/mem   also for system image

NOTE
If an RFS resource from a pre System V Release 4 server is mounted, fuser can only report on use of the whole file system, not on individual files within it.

Because fuser works with a snapshot of the system image, it may miss processes that begin using a file while fuser is running. Also, processes reported as using a file may have stopped using it while fuser was running. These factors should discourage the use of the -k option.

SEE ALSO

mount(1M).
ps(1) in the *User's Reference Manual.*
kill(2), signal(2) in the *Programmer's Reference Manual.*

NAME

    fwtmp, wtmpfix – manipulate connect accounting records

SYNOPSIS

    /usr/lib/acct/fwtmp [-ic]
    /usr/lib/acct/wtmpfix [*files*]

DESCRIPTION

    fwtmp reads from the standard input and writes to the standard output, converting binary records of the type found in /var/adm/wtmp to formatted ASCII records. The ASCII version is useful when it is necessary to edit bad records.

    The argument -ic is used to denote that input is in ASCII form, and output is to be written in binary form.

    wtmpfix examines the standard input or named files in utmp.h format, corrects the time/date stamps to make the entries consistent, and writes to the standard output. A – can be used in place of *files* to indicate the standard input. If time/date corrections are not performed, acctcon will fault when it encounters certain date-change records.

    Each time the date is set, a pair of date change records are written to /var/adm/wtmp. The first record is the old date denoted by the string "old time" placed in the line field and the flag OLD_TIME placed in the type field of the utmp structure. The second record specifies the new date and is denoted by the string new time placed in the line field and the flag NEW_TIME placed in the type field. wtmpfix uses these records to synchronize all time stamps in the file.

    In addition to correcting time/date stamps, wtmpfix will check the validity of the name field to ensure that it consists solely of alphanumeric characters or spaces. If it encounters a name that is considered invalid, it will change the login name to INVALID and write a diagnostic to the standard error. In this way, wtmpfix reduces the chance that acctcon will fail when processing connect accounting records.

FILES

    /var/adm/wtmp
    /usr/include/utmp.h

SEE ALSO

    acct(1M),   acctcms(1M),   acctcon(1M),   acctmerg(1M),   acctprc(1M),
    acctsh(1M), runacct(1M), acct(4), utmp(4)
    acctcom(1), ed(1) in the *User's Reference Manual*
    acct(2) in the *Programmer's Reference Manual*

NAME
>   gencc – create a front-end to the cc command

SYNOPSIS
>   gencc

DESCRIPTION
>   The gencc command is an interactive command designed to aid in the creation of
>   a front-end to the cc command. Since hard-coded pathnames have been elim-
>   inated from the C Compilation System (CCS), it is possible to move pieces of the
>   CCS to new locations without recompilation. The new locations of moved pieces
>   can be specified through the –Y option to the cc command. However, it is incon-
>   venient to supply the proper –Y options with every invocation of the cc com-
>   mand. Further, if a system administrator moves pieces of the CCS, such move-
>   ment should be invisible to users.
>
>   The front-end to the cc command that gencc generates is a one-line shell script
>   that calls the cc command with the proper –Y options specified. The front-end to
>   the cc command will also pass all user-supplied options to the cc command.
>
>   gencc prompts for the location of each tool and directory that can be respecified
>   by a –Y option to the cc command. If no location is specified, it assumes that
>   that piece of the CCS has not been relocated. After all the locations have been
>   prompted for, gencc will create the front end to the cc command.
>
>   gencc creates the front-end to the cc command in the current working directory
>   and gives the file the same name as the cc command. Thus, gencc can not be
>   run in the same directory containing the actual cc command. Further, if a system
>   administrator has redistributed the CCS, the actual cc command should be placed
>   in a location that is not typically in a user's path (e.g., /usr/lib). Such place-
>   ment will prevent users from accidentally invoking the cc command without
>   using the front-end.

NOTES
>   gencc does not produce any warnings if a tool or directory does not exist at the
>   specified location. Also, gencc does not actually move any files to new locations.
>   The gencc command is obsolete.

FILES
>   ./cc   front-end to cc

SEE ALSO
>   cc(1).

NAME

　　getdev – lists devices based on criteria

SYNOPSIS

　　getdev [–ae] [*criteria* [...]] [*device* [...]]

DESCRIPTION

　　getdev generates a list of devices that match certain criteria. The criteria includes a list of attributes (given in expressions) and a list of devices. If no criteria is given, all devices are included in the list.

　　Devices must satisfy at least one of the criteria in the list unless the –a option is used. Then, only those devices which match all of the criteria in a list will be included.

　　Devices which are defined on the command line and which match the criteria are included in the generated list. However, if the –e flag is used, the list becomes a set of devices to be *excluded* from the list.

Criteria Expression Types

　　There are four possible expression types which the criteria specified in the *criteria* argument may follow:

attribute=value　　Selects all devices whose attribute *attribute* is defined and is equal to *value*.

attribute!=value　　Selects all devices whose attribute *attribute* is defined and does not equal *value*.

attribute:*　　Selects all devices which have the attribute *attribute* defined.

attribute!:*　　Selects all devices which do not have the attribute *attribute* defined.

　　　　　　See the putdev(1M) manual page for a complete listing and description of available attributes.

Options and Arguments

　　The options and arguments for this command are:

–a　　Specifies that a device must match all criteria to be included in the list generated by this command. The flag has no effect if no criteria are defined.

–e　　Specifies that the list of devices which follows on the command line should be *excluded* from the list generated by this command. (Without the –e the named devices are *included* in the generated list.) The flag has no effect if no devices are defined.

criteria　　Defines criteria that a device must match to be included in the generated list. Should be given in expressions.

device　　Defines devices which should be included in the generated list. Can be the pathname of the device or the device alias.

ERRORS

The command will exit with one of the following values:

0 = Successful completion of the task.

1 = Command syntax incorrect, invalid option used, or internal error occurred.

2 = Device table could not be opened for reading.

FILES

/etc/device.tab

SEE ALSO

devattr(1), getdgrp(1), putdev(1), putdgrp(1), getdev(3X).

NAME

getdgrp – lists device groups which contain devices that match criteria

SYNOPSIS

getdgrp [–ael] [*criteria* [. . .]] [*dgroup* [. . .]]

DESCRIPTION

getdgrp generates a list of device groups that contain devices matching the given criteria. The criteria is given in the form of expressions.

criteria can be one expression or a list of expressions which a device must meet for its group to be included in the list generated by getdgrp. If no criteria is given, all device groups are included in the list.

Devices must satisfy at least one of the criteria in the list. However, the –a flag can be used to define that a "logical and" operation should be performed. Then, only those groups containing devices which match all of the criteria in a list will be included.

dgroup defines a set of device groups to be included in the list. Device groups that are defined and which contain devices matching the criteria are included. However, if the –e flag is used, this list defines a set of device groups to be excluded. When the –e option is used and criteria is also defined, the generated list will include device groups containing devices which match the criteria and are not in the command line list.

Criteria Expression Types

There are four possible expressions types:

attribute=value   Selects all device groups with a member whose attribute *attribute* is defined and is equal to *value*.

attribute!=value Selects all device groups with a member whose attribute *attribute* is defined and does not equal *value*.

attribute:＊   Selects all device groups with a member which has the attribute *attribute* defined.

attribute!:＊   Selects all device groups with a member which does not have the attribute *attribute* defined.

See the putdev(1M) manual page for a complete listing and description of available attributes.

Options and Arguments

The options and arguments for this command are:

–a   Specifies that a device must match all criteria before a device group to which it belongs can be included in the list generated by this command. The flag has no effect if no criteria are defined.

–e   Specifies that the list of device groups on the command line should be *excluded* from the list generated by this command. (Without the –e the named device groups are the only ones which can be *included* in the generated list.) The flag has no effect if no device groups are defined.

-l	Specifies that all device groups (subject to the -e option and the *dgroup* list) should be listed even if they contain no valid device members. This option has no affect if *criteria* is specified on the command line.
criteria	Defines criteria that a device must match before a device group to which it belongs can be included in the generated list.
dgroup	Defines device groups which should be included in or excluded from the generated list.

ERRORS

The command will exit with one of the following values:

0 = successful completion of the task.

1 = command syntax incorrect, invalid option used, or internal error occurred.

2 = device table or device group table could not be opened for reading.

FILES

/etc/device.tab
/etc/dgroup.tab

SEE ALSO

devattr(1), getdev(1), putdev(1), putdgrp(1), getdgrp(3X).

NAME
getmajor – print major number(s) of hardware devices

SYNOPSIS
/usr/sbin/getmajor *name* | *ID_code*

DESCRIPTION
The getmajor command prints all major numbers for the requested device found in the system Equipped Device Table (EDT). Slot and major numbers are the same for boards that are installed directly into the backplane slots of the computer. *ID_code* is a number between 0x0 and 0xffff that a device uses to identify itself.

Devices that are on extended buses (e.g., Small Computer System Interface (SCSI) target controllers) do not have board ID codes. The proper way to use getmajor with these devices is /usr/sbin/getmajor *name*.

DIAGNOSTICS
If successful, a zero is returned. If *name* or *ID_code* is not found, a blank line is printed and the return code is nonzero.

SEE ALSO
editttbl(1M), prtconf(1M).

NAME

gettable – get DoD Internet format host table from a host

SYNOPSIS

gettable *host*

DESCRIPTION

gettable is a simple program used to obtain the DoD Internet host table from a hostname server. The indicated *host* is queried for the table. The table, if retrieved, is placed in the file hosts.txt.

gettable operates by opening a TCP connection to the port indicated in the service specification for hostname. A request is then made for all names and the resultant information is placed in the output file.

gettable is best used in conjunction with the htable(1M) program which converts the DoD Internet host table format to that used by the network library lookup routines.

SEE ALSO

htable(1M)

Harrenstien, Ken, Mary Stahl, and Elizabeth Feinler, *HOSTNAME Server*, RFC 953, Network Information Center, SRI International, Menlo Park, Calif., October 1985.

NOTES

Should allow requests for only part of the database.

NAME

getty – set terminal type, modes, speed, and line discipline

SYNOPSIS

/usr/lib/saf/ttymon [–h] [–t *timeout*] *line* [*speed* [*type* [*linedisc*]]]

/usr/lib/saf/ttymon –c *file*

DESCRIPTION

getty is a symbolic link to /usr/lib/saf/ttymon. It is included for compatibility with previous releases for the few applications that still call getty directly. getty can only be executed by the superuser, that is, by a process with the user ID root. Initially getty prints the login prompt, waits for the user's login name, and then invokes the login command. getty attempts to adapt the system to the terminal speed by using the options and arguments specified on the command line.

line The name of a TTY line in /dev to which getty is to attach itself. getty uses this string as the name of a file in the /dev directory to open for reading and writing.

–h If the –h flag is not set, a hangup will be forced by setting the speed to zero before setting the speed to the default or specified speed.

–t *timeout*
specifies that getty should exit if the open on the line succeeds and no one types anything in *timeout* seconds.

speed The *speed* argument is a label to a speed and TTY definition in the file /etc/ttydefs. This definition tells getty at what speed to run initially, what the initial TTY settings are, and what speed to try next, should the user indicate, by pressing the BREAK key, that the speed is inappropriate. The default *speed* is 300 baud.

type and *linedisc*
These options are obsolete and will be ignored.

–c *file* The –c option is no longer supported. Instead use sttydefs –l to list the contents of the /etc/ttydefs file and perform a validity check on the file.

When given no optional arguments, getty specifies the following: The *speed* of the interface is set to 300 baud, either parity is allowed, new-line characters are converted to carriage return-line feed, and tab expansion is performed on the standard output. getty types the login prompt before reading the user's name a character at a time. If a null character (or framing error) is received, it is assumed to be the result of the user pressing the BREAK key. This will cause getty to attempt the next *speed* in the series. The series that getty tries is determined by what it finds in /etc/ttydefs.

FILES

/etc/ttydefs

SEE ALSO

ct(1C), sttydefs(1M), tty(7), ttymon(1M).
login(1) in the *User's Reference Manual*.
ioctl(2) in the *Programmer's Reference Manual*.

NAME
>   getvol – verifies device accessibility

SYNOPSIS
>   getvol −n [−l *label*] *device*
>   getvol [−f|−F] [−wo] [−l *label*|−x *label*] *device*

DESCRIPTION
>   getvol verifies that the specified device is accessible and that a volume of the
>   appropriate medium has been inserted. The command is interactive and displays
>   instructional prompts, describes errors, and shows required label information.

>   Options and arguments for this command are:

>   −n   Runs the command in non-interactive mode. The volume is assumed to
>   be inserted upon command invocation.

>   −l   Specifies that the label *label* must exist on the inserted volume (can be
>   overriden by the −o option).

>   −f   Formats the volume after insertion, using the format command defined
>   for this device in the device table.

>   −F   Formats the volume after insertion and places a file system on the dev-
>   ice. Also uses the format command defined for this device in the device
>   table.

>   −w   Allows administrator to write a new label on the device. User is
>   prompted to supply the label text. This option is ineffective if the −n
>   option is enabled.

>   −o   Allows the administrator to override a label check.

>   −x   Specifies that the label *label* must exist on the device. This option should
>   be used in place of the −l option when the label can only be verified by
>   visual means. Use of the option causes a message to be displayed asking
>   the administrator to visually verify that the label is indeed *label*.

>   *device* Names the device which should be verified for accessibility.

ERRORS
>   The command will exit with one of the following values:

>   0 = successful completion of the task.

>   1 = command syntax incorrect, invalid option used, or internal error occurred.

>   3 = device table could not be opened for reading.

NOTES
>   This command uses the device table to determine the characteristics of the device
>   when performing the volume label checking.

FILES
>   /etc/device.tab

SEE ALSO
>   getvol(3X).

NAME

groupadd – add (create) a new group definition on the system

SYNOPSIS

groupadd [–g gid [–o]] group

DESCRIPTION

The groupadd command creates a new group definition on the system by adding the appropriate entry to the /etc/group file.

The following options are available:

–g gid   The group id for the new group. This group id must be a non-negative decimal integer below MAXUID as defined in the <param.h> header file. The group ID defaults to the next available (unique) number above the highest number currently assigned. For example, if groups 100, 105, and 200 are assigned as groups, the next default group number will be 201. (Group IDs from 0-99 are reserved.)

–o   This option allows the gid to be duplicated (non-unique).

group   A string of printable characters that specifies the name of the new group. It may not include a colon (:) or newline (\n).

FILES

/etc/group

SEE ALSO

groupdel(1M), groupmod(1M), logins(1M), useradd(1M), userdel(1M), usermod(1M), users(1).

DIAGNOSTICS

The groupadd command exits with one of the following values:

0   Success.

2   Invalid command syntax. A usage message for the groupadd command is displayed.

3   An invalid argument was provided to an option.

4   gid is not unique (when –o option is not used).

9   group is not unique.

10   Cannot update the /etc/group file.

NAME
groupdel – delete a group definition from the system

SYNOPSIS
groupdel *group*

DESCRIPTION
The groupdel command deletes a group definition from the system. It deletes the appropriate entry from the /etc/group file.

The following options are available:

group   A string of printable characters that specifies the group to be deleted.

FILES
/etc/group

SEE ALSO
groupadd(1M),   groupmod(1M),   logins(1M),   useradd(1M),   userdel(1M), usermod(1M), users(1).

DIAGNOSTICS
The groupdel command exits with one of the following values:

0   Success.

2   Invalid command syntax. A usage message for the groupdel command is displayed.

6   group does not exist.

10   Cannot update the /etc/group file.

NAME

   groupmod – modify a group definition on the system

SYNOPSIS

   groupmod [–g *gid* [–o]] [–n *name*] group

DESCRIPTION

   The groupmod command modifies the definition of the specified group by modifying the appropriate entry in the /etc/group file.

   The following options are available:

   -g *gid*   The group id for the new group. This group id must be a non-negative
            decimal integer below MAXUID as defined in <param.h>. The group ID
            defaults to the next available (unique) number above 99. (Group IDs from
            0-99 are reserved.)

   -o   This option allows the *gid* to be duplicated (non-unique).

   -n *name*

            A string of printable characters that specifies a new name for the group.
            It may not include a colon (:) or newline (\n).

   group   The current name of the group to be modified.

FILES

   /etc/group

SEE ALSO

   groupadd(1M),   groupdel(1M),   logins(1M),   useradd(1M),   userdel(1M),
   usermod(1M), users(1).

DIAGNOSTICS

   The groupmod command exits with one of the following values:

   0   Success.

   2   Invalid command syntax. A usage message for the groupmod command is
            displayed.

   3   An invalid argument was provided to an option.

   4   *gid* is not unique (when the –o option is not used).

   6   *group* does not exist.

   9   *name* already exists as a group name.

   10   Cannot update the /etc/group file.

NAME
hdeadd – add/delete hdelog (Hard Disk Error Log) reports

SYNOPSIS
/usr/sbin/hdeadd −a [*aoptions*]

/usr/sbin/hdeadd −d [*doptions*]

/usr/sbin/hdeadd −e [[−D] *major minor*]

/usr/sbin/hdeadd −f *filename*

/usr/sbin/hdeadd −r [−D] *major minor filename*

/usr/sbin/hdeadd −s [−D] *major minor filename*

DESCRIPTION
This command is part of the bad block handling utility. It may be used only by the super-user for manually adding or deleting disk error reports recorded by **hdelogger**. These include disk errors reported while in firmware mode and disk errors that cause the system to PANIC.

hdeadd may be used to print the list of equipped disks or to determine if a specific disk device is on the list. In addition, this command has some options that are for use in testing the feature.

The following options may be used with **hdeadd**:

−a   hdeadd allows a Hard Disk Error (HDE) report to be added manually to the HDE Log of a disk.

−d   hdeadd allows a specific report or a range of reports to be deleted from the HDE Log of a disk.

−e   prints out the list of major/minor device numbers of the equipped hard disks. If the *major* and *minor* device numbers are also provided, it determines if that specification is an equipped hard disk. The result is both printed on the standard output and is used to determine the exit status. A NORMAL (or TRUE) exit means it is an equipped disk.

−f   the file specified by *filename* is assumed to contain a canned set of HDE Log manipulations. Each line of text contains one specification in the command argument form, starting with a −a or a −d option.

−s   saves a copy of the HDE Log of the specified (by *major/minor* device number) disk in the file specified by *filename*.

−r   restores the HDE Log of the specified disk from the file specified by *filename*.

The valid *aoptions* are only hard disk error specifications.

The valid *doptions* are either a hard disk error specification or an error range specification.

A hard disk error specification includes the following values:

−D *maj min*   Specifies the major device number (*maj*) and minor device number (*min*) of the disk.

-b *blockno*   Normal form: Specifies the physical disk block number in integer counter form (i.e., treating the disk as a simple stream of blocks). Physical disk block numbering starts with zero meaning sector 0 of track 0 of cylinder 0. This is the normal form that is reported by the operating system.

-B *cyl trk sec*   Alternate form: Specifies the physical disk block number in terms of its physical cylinder number (*cyl*), track number within cylinder (*trk*), and sector number within track (*sec*). This alternate form is available to cover the possibility of a non-operating system detector reporting block numbers in this hardware form.

-t *mmddhhmm[yy]*
    Optional: Specifies the time of day when the error actually occurred. If omitted when adding reports, the current time is used. If omitted when deleting reports, any reports for the given block are deleted.

An error range specification includes the following values:

-D *maj min*   Specifies the major device number (*maj*) and minor device number (*min*) of the disk.

-F *mmddhhmm[yy]*
    Optional: Specifies the "from" time for the time interval being purged. If omitted, zero (the beginning of time) is used.

-T *mmddhhmm[yy]*
    Optional: Specifies the "to" time for the time interval being purged. If omitted, the end of time is used. The range comparisons include the end values of the range in the purge.

FILES
/dev/hdelog

SEE ALSO
hdefix(1M), hdelogger(1M), hdelog(7).
Bad Block Handling in the *System Administrator's Guide*.

DIAGNOSTICS
The HDE commands exit with one of three values:

0   means NORMAL, or TRUE

1   means bad command usage or execution errors

2   means BAD BLOCKS or FALSE (but command executed successfully)

NAME

hdefix – report or change bad block mapping on a hard disk device

SYNOPSIS

/sbin/hdefix –p [–D *major minor*]

/sbin/hdefix –a [–D *major minor* [–b *blockno* ...]]

/sbin/hdefix –a [–D *major minor* [–B *cyl trk sec* ...]]

DESCRIPTION

The hdefix command is part of the bad block handling utility. This command maps bad blocks to surrogate images in an area not accessible by the user.

Before attempting to execute hdefix, the system must be brought to the single-user state using the command init s. Only super-user can use hdefix to print a list of blocks currently mapped to surrogate images on the equipped hard disk devices or to change the mapping of these blocks.

When the mapping to surrogate images is changed, block initialization is performed. If the original block can be read, its data is written to the new surrogate image to prevent data loss. If the original block is unreadable, zeros are written to the new surrogate image. This will usually result in some data loss.

If the block is associated with a file system, the file system may be damaged as a result of the mapping change. To handle this situation, the file system is marked dirty, which means the fsck command must be run before the file system can be used, and a system reboot is forced after all other bad block processing is complete. If the block is a data block of a file, that file will be corrupted, even after this recovery has finished.

The following options may be used with hdefix:

–p   prints a report that shows both the functional blocks and currently mapped bad blocks. If a specific hard disk device is specified (by giving its *major* and *minor* device numbers), only the report for that hard disk device is printed. If no particular hard disk device is specified, a report is given for each equipped disk.

–D   used to specify the *major* device number and *minor* device number of a hard disk device.

–a   used to map new bad blocks. If no arguments follow the –a option, all equipped hard disk devices are processed, using the HDE Log on each hard disk device to determine which blocks to map. If a specific hard disk device is specified, only that disk device is processed. If one or more block numbers are specified, those blocks are mapped, instead of using the block numbers listed in HDE Log. This is the only way to map an unreadable block containing the HDE Log.

–b *blockno*   specifies the physical hard disk block number. Physical hard disk block numbering starts with zero, meaning block (sector) 0 of track 0 of cylinder 0. The *blockno* value ranges from block number 0 through the maximum number of blocks on a particular hard disk drive minus 1.

-B *cyl trk sec*
                 specifies the physical disk block number in terms of its physical
                 cylinder number (*cyl*), track number within cylinder (*trk*), and sector
                 (block) number within track (*sec*). This alternate form is available
                 for reporting bad block data obtained without using the normal sys-
                 tem capabilities (e.g., off-line diagnostics provided by the manufac-
                 turer). This option is not supported on SCSI disks.

FILES
        /dev/hdelog

SEE ALSO
        fsck(1M), init(1M), hdeadd(1M), hdelogger(1M), hdelog(7).
        Bad Block Handling in the *System Administrator's Guide*.

RETURN CODES
        The hdefix command exits with one of three values:

        0   means NORMAL (or TRUE)

        1   means bad command usage or execution errors

        2   means BAD BLOCKS (or FALSE) (but command executed successfully)

NAME

hdelogger − Hard Disk Error status report command and Log Daemon

SYNOPSIS

/usr/sbin/hdelogger [−s] [−f] [−D maj min]

DESCRIPTION

This command is part of the bad block handling utility. It is executed automatically by the init in run levels 2, 3 and 4.

The hdelogger command serves two purposes. When run by the init process [process 1 − see init(1M)], this command performs the functions of the Hard Disk Error (HDE) Log Daemon. These functions include providing summaries of outstanding errors during system startup and shutdown transitions, along with adding new errors to HDE Logs and giving the revised status summaries as errors are reported by hard disk drivers. When run as the daemon, no options are used.

When run as a normal command (process 1 is not its parent), this command provides on the spot reports of outstanding errors as recorded in the HDE Logs of equipped hard disks. You must be the super-user to run the command this way. The following options control report generation:

−s   Specifies that summary reports are to be generated. The summary report provides sufficient information for normal bad block handling operations. This is the default.

−f   Specifies that full reports are to be generated. This is intended mainly for testing the bad block handling feature, but is available in case additional detail is needed for troubleshooting complicated problems.

−D *maj min* Restricts the report generation to a specific hard disk. If this option is omitted, reports will be generated for all equipped hard disks.

FILES

/dev/hdelog

SEE ALSO

hdeadd(1M), hdefix(1M), hdelog(7).
Bad Block Handling, in the *System Administrator's Guide*.

DIAGNOSTICS

The HDE commands exit with one of three values:

0   means NORMAL, or TRUE

1   means bad command usage or execution errors

2   means BAD BLOCKS or FALSE (but command executed successfully)

NAME
htable – convert DoD Internet format host table

SYNOPSIS
htable *filename*

DESCRIPTION
htable converts a host table in the format specified by RFC 952 to the format used by the network library routines. Three files are created as a result of running htable: hosts, networks, and gateways. The hosts file is used by the gethostent(3N) routines in mapping host names to addresses. The networks file is used by the getnetent(3N) routines in mapping network names to numbers. The gateways file is used by the routing daemon in identifying passive Internet gateways; see routed(1M) for an explanation.

If any of the files localhosts, localnetworks, or localgateways are present in the current directory, the file's contents is prepended to the output file without interpretation. This allows sites to maintain local aliases and entries which are not normally present in the master database.

htable is best used in conjunction with the gettable(1M) program which retrieves the DoD Internet host table from a host.

FILES
localhosts
localnetworks
localgateways

SEE ALSO
gethostent(3N), getnetent(3N), gettable(1M), routed(1M).

Harrenstien, Ken, Mary Stahl, and Elizabeth Feinler, *DoD Internet Host Table Specification*, RFC 952, Network Information Center, SRI International, Menlo Park, Calif., October 1985.

NOTES
Does not properly calculate the gateways file.

NAME

   id – print the user name and ID, and group name and ID

SYNOPSIS

   id [–a]

DESCRIPTION

   id displays the calling process's ID and name. It also displays the group ID and
   name. If the real effective IDs do not match, both are printed.

   The –a option reports all the groups to which the invoking process belongs. ID,
   and your username. If your real and effective IDs do not match, both are printed.

   The –a option reports all the groups to which the invoking user belongs.

SEE ALSO

   getuid(2) in the *Programmer's Reference Manual.*

NAME
idload – Remote File Sharing user and group mapping

SYNOPSIS
idload [–n] [–g g_rules] [–u u_rules] [directory]
idload –k

DESCRIPTION
idload is used on Remote File Sharing server machines to build translation tables for user and group ids. It takes your /etc/passwd and /etc/group files and produces translation tables for user and group ids from remote machines, according to the rules set down in the u_rules and g_rules files. If you are mapping by user and group name, you will need copies of remote /etc/passwd and /etc/group files. If no rules files are specified, remote user and group ids are mapped to MAXUID+1 (this is an id number that is one higher than the highest number you could assign on your system.)

By default, the remote password and group files are assumed to reside in /etc/dfs/rfs/auth.info/domain/nodename/[passwd | group]. The directory argument indicates that some directory structure other than /etc/dfs/rfs/auth.info contains the domain/nodename passwd and group files. (nodename is the name of the computer the files are from and domain is the domain that computer is a member of.)

You must run idload to put the mapping into place. Global mapping will take effect immediately for machines that have one of your resources currently mounted. Mapping for other specific machines will take effect when each machine mounts one of your resources.

-n   This is used to do a trial run of the id mapping. No translation table will be produced, however, a display of the mapping is output to the terminal (stdout).

-k   This is used to print the idmapping that is currently in use. (Specific mapping for remote machines will not be shown until that machine mounts one of your resources.)

-u u_rules The u_rules file contains the rules for user id translation. The default rules file is /etc/dfs/rfs/auth.info/uid.rules.

-g g_rules The g_rules file contains the rules for group id translation. The default rules file is /etc/dfs/rfs/auth.info/gid.rules.

This command is restricted to the super-user.

Rules
The rules files have two types of sections (both optional): global and host. There can be only one global section, though there can be one host section for each computer you want to map.

The global section describes the default conditions for translation for any machines that are not explicitly referenced in a host section. If the global section is missing, the default action is to map all remote user and group ids from undefined computers to MAXUID+1. The syntax of the first line of the global section is:

global

A host section is used for each machine or group of machines that you want to map differently from the global definitions. The syntax of the first line of each host section is:

host *name* ...

where *name* is replaced by the full name of a computer (*domain.nodename*).

The format of a rules file is described below. (All lines are optional, but must appear in the order shown.)

```
global
default local | transparent
exclude remote_id-remote_id | remote_id
map remote_id:local
```

```
host  domain.nodename [domain.nodename...]
default local | transparent
exclude remote_id-remote_id | remote_id | remote_name
map remote:local | remote | all
```

Each of these instruction types is described below.

The line

default *local* | transparent

defines the mode of mapping for remote users that are not specifically mapped in instructions in other lines. transparent means that each remote user and group id will have the same numeric value locally unless it appears in the exclude instruction. *local* can be replaced by a local user name or id to map all users into a particular local name or id number. If the default line is omitted, all users that are not specifically mapped are mapped into a "special guest" login id.

The line

exclude *remote_id-remote_id* | *remote_id* | *remote_name*

defines remote ids that will be excluded from the default mapping. The exclude instruction must precede any map instructions in a block. You can use a range of id numbers, a single id number, or a single name. (*remote_name* cannot be used in a global block.)

The line

map *remote:local* | *remote* | all

defines the local ids and names that remote ids and names will be mapped into. *remote* is either a remote id number or remote name; *local* is either a local id number or local name. Placing a colon between a *remote* and a *local* will give the value on the left the permissions of the value on the right. A single *remote* name or id will assign the user or group permissions of the same local name or id. all is a predefined alias for the set of all user and group ids found in the local /etc/passwd and /etc/group files. (You cannot map by remote name in global blocks.)

Note: idload will always output warning messages for map all, since password files always contain multiple administrative user names with the same id number. The first mapping attempt on the id number will succeed, each subsequent attempts will produce a warning.

Remote File Sharing doesn't need to be running to use idload.

EXIT STATUS

On successful completion, idload will produce one or more translation tables and return a successful exit status. If idload fails, the command will return an exit status of zero and not produce a translation table.

ERRORS

If (1) either rules file cannot be found or opened, (2) there are syntax errors in the rules file, (3) there are semantic errors in the rules file, (4) host password or group information could not be found, or (5) the command is not run with super-user privileges, an error message will be sent to standard error. Partial failures will cause a warning message to appear, though the process will continue.

FILES

/etc/passwd
/etc/group
/etc/rfs/auth.info/*domain*/*nodename*/[user | group]
/etc/rfs/auth.info/uid.rules
/etc/rfs/auth.info/gid.rules

SEE ALSO

mount(1M).
"Remote File Sharing" chapter of the *System Administrator's Guide* for detailed information on ID mapping.

NAME

    ifconfig – configure network interface parameters

SYNOPSIS

    ifconfig *interface* [*address_family*] [*address* [*dest_address*]] [*parameters*]
        [netmask *mask*] [broadcast *address*] [metric *n*]

    ifconfig *interface* [*protocol_family*]

DESCRIPTION

    ifconfig is used to assign an address to a network interface and/or to configure network interface parameters. ifconfig must be used at boot time to define the network address of each interface present on a machine; it may also be used at a later time to redefine an interface's address or other operating parameters. Used without options, ifconfig displays the current configuration for a network interface. If a protocol family is specified, ifconfig will report only the details specific to that protocol family. Only the super-user may modify the configuration of a network interface.

    The *interface* parameter is a string of the form name unit, for example emd1. The interface name –a is reserved, and causes the remainder of the arguments to be applied to each address of each interface in turn.

    Since an interface may receive transmissions in differing protocols, each of which may require separate naming schemes, the parameters and addresses are interpreted according to the rules of some address family, specified by the *address_family* parameter. The address families currently supported are ether and inet. If no address family is specified, inet is assumed.

    For the DARPA Internet family (inet), the address is either a host name present in the host name data base [see hosts(4)], or a DARPA Internet address expressed in the Internet standard dot notation. Typically, an Internet address specified in dot notation will consist of your system's network number and the machine's unique host number. A typical Internet address is 192.9.200.44, where 192.9.200 is the network number and 44 is the machine's host number.

    For the ether address family, the address is an Ethernet address represented as $x:x:x:x:x:x$ where x is a hexadecimal number between 0 and ff. Only the super-user may use the ether address family.

    If the *dest_address* parameter is supplied in addition to the *address* parameter, it specifies the address of the correspondent on the other end of a point to point link.

OPTIONS

    The following *parameters* may be set with ifconfig:

    up   Mark an interface up. This may be used to enable an interface after an ifconfig down. It happens automatically when setting the first address on an interface. If the interface was reset when previously marked down, the hardware will be re-initialized.

    down   Mark an interface down. When an interface is marked down, the system will not attempt to transmit messages through that interface. If possible, the interface will be reset to disable reception as well. This action does not automatically disable routes using the interface.

trailers   (inet only) Enable the use of a trailer link level encapsulation when sending. If a network interface supports trailer encapsulation, the system will, when possible, encapsulate outgoing messages in a manner which minimizes the number of memory to memory copy operations performed by the receiver. This feature is machine-dependent, and therefore not recommended. On networks that support the Address Resolution Protocol [see arp(7)]; currently, only 10 Mb/s Ethernet), this flag indicates that the system should request that other systems use trailer encapsulation when sending to this host. Similarly, trailer encapsulations will be used when sending to other hosts that have made such requests.

-trailers   Disable the use of a trailer link level encapsulation.

arp   Enable the use of the Address Resolution Protocol in mapping between network level addresses and link level addresses (default). This is currently implemented for mapping between DARPA Internet addresses and 10Mb/s Ethernet addresses.

-arp   Disable the use of the Address Resolution Protocol.

metric n Set the routing metric of the interface to n, default 0. The routing metric is used by the routing protocol [routed(1M)]. Higher metrics have the effect of making a route less favorable; metrics are counted as addition hops to the destination network or host.

netmask *mask*
     (inet only) Specify how much of the address to reserve for subdividing networks into sub-networks. The mask includes the network part of the local address and the subnet part, which is taken from the host field of the address. The mask can be specified as a single hexadecimal number with a leading 0x, with a dot-notation Internet address, or with a pseudo-network name listed in the network table networks(4). The mask contains 1's for the bit positions in the 32-bit address which are to be used for the network and subnet parts, and 0's for the host part. The mask should contain at least the standard network portion, and the subnet field should be contiguous with the network portion. If a + (plus sign) is given for the netmask value, then the network number is looked up in the /etc/netmasks file.

broadcast *address*
     (inet only) Specify the address to use to represent broadcasts to the network. The default broadcast address is the address with a host part of all 0's. A + (plus sign) given for the broadcast value causes the broadcast address to be reset to a default appropriate for the (possibly new) Internet address and netmask. Note that the arguments of ifconfig are interpreted left to right, and therefore

```
ifconfig -a netmask + broadcast +
```

and

```
ifconfig -a broadcast + netmask +
```

may result in different values being assigned for the interfaces' broadcast addresses.

EXAMPLES

If your workstation is not attached to an Ethernet, the emd1 interface should be marked down as follows:

```
ifconfig emd1 down
```

To print out the addressing information for each interface, use

```
ifconfig -a
```

To reset each interface's broadcast address after the netmasks have been correctly set, use

```
ifconfig -a broadcast +
```

FILES

/dev/nit
/etc/netmasks

SEE ALSO

netstat(1M), netmasks(4).

DIAGNOSTICS

Messages indicating the specified interface does not exist, the requested address is unknown, or the user is not privileged and tried to alter an interface's configuration.

NAME
incfile – create, restore an incremental filesystem archive

SYNOPSIS
incfile –B [–dilmortvxAENSV] *bkjobid ofsname ofsdev ofslab descript*

incfile –T *bkjobid tocfname descript*

incfile –RC [–dilmortvxAENSV] *ofsname ofsdev refsname redev rsjobid descript*

incfile –RF [–dilmortvxAENSV] *ofsname ofsdev descript rsjobid:uid:date:type:name*
[:[rename]:[inode]] ...

DESCRIPTION
incfile is invoked as a child process by other shell commands. The command
name, incfile, is read either from the bkhist.tab file or the bkreg –m command and option. The –B, –T, –R, –F, and –C options are passed to incfile
by the shell commands backup, restore, and *urestore(1)* described below. The
minus options are passed from the bkhist.tab file or the bkreg –p command
and option. The arguments are sent to incfile from various locations in the
backup service.

incfile –B is invoked as a child process by the bkdaemon command to perform
an incremental backup of the filesystem *ofsname* (the originating filesystem). All
files in *ofsname* that have been modified or have had an inode change since the
last full backup are archived. The resulting backup is created in cpio file format.
The backup is recorded in the backup history log, /etc/bkup/bkhist.tab.

bkjobid
> the job id assigned by backup. The method uses the *bkjobid* when it
> creates history log and table-of-contents entries.

ofsname
> the name of the filesystem that is to be backed up.

ofsdev the name of the UNIX block special device on which the filesystem
resides.

ofslab the volume name on the filesystem [see labelit(1M)].

descript
> is a description for a destination device in the form:
> > *dgroup:dname:dchar:dlabels*
> *dgroup* specifies a device group [see devgroup.tab(4)].
> *dname* specifies a particular device name [see device.tab(4)].
> *dchars* specifies characteristics associated with the device. If specified,
> *dchar* overrides the defaults for the specified device and group. [See
> device.tab(4) for a further description of device characteristics].
> *dlabels* specifies the volume names for the media to be used for reading or
> writing the archive.

incfile –T is invoked as a child process by the backup to archive a table-of-
contents on the volumes described by *descript*.

tocfname
> the name of the file containing the table-of-contents.

incfile −RC and incfile −RF are invoked as child processes by the rsoper command to extract files from an incremental filesystem archive created by incfile −B. The filesystem archive is assumed to be in cpio format.

If the −RC option is selected, all files recorded in the archive are restored.

refsname
> if non-null, the name of the filesystem to be restored to instead of *ofsname*.

redev   if non-null, the partition to be restored to instead of *ofsdev*.

At least one of *refsname* and *redev* must be null.

If the −RF option is specified, only selected objects from the archive are restored. Each 7-tuple, composed of *rsjobid:uid:date:type:name:rename:inode*, specifies an object to be restored from the filesystem archive. The 7-tuple objects come to incfile from the rsstatus.tab file.

rsjobid the restore jobid assigned by restore or urestore.

uid   the real uid of the user who requested the object to be restored. It must match the uid of the owner of the object at the time the archive was made, or it must be the superuser uid.

date   the newest "last modification time" that is acceptable for a restorable object. The object is restored from the archive immediately older than this date. *date* is a hexadecimal representation of the date and time provided by the time system call.

type   either F or D, indicating that the object is a file or a directory, respectively.

name   the name the object had in the filesystem archive.

rename
> the name that the object should be restored to (it may differ from the name the object had in the filesystem archive). If omitted, the object is restored to *name*.

inode   the inode number of the object as it was stored in the filesystem archive. *[inode]* is not used by incfile −R, and is provided only for command-line compatibility with other restoral methods.

Options
Some options are only significant during incfile −B invocations; they are accepted but ignored during incfile −R invocations because the command is invoked and options are specified automatically by restore. These options are flagged with an asterisk (*).

d*   Inhibits the recording of the archive in the backup history log.

i*   Excludes from the backup those files that have only had an inode change.

l*   Creates a long form of the backup history log that includes a table of contents for the archive. This includes the data used to generate a listing of each file in the archive like that produced by the ls −l command.

m*   Mounts the originating filesystem read-only before starting the backup and remounts it with its original permissions after completing the backup. Cannot be used with root or /usr filesystems.

o   Permits the user to override media insertion requests [see the getvol(1M), −o option].

r*   Includes remotely mounted resources in the archive.

t*   Creates a table of contents for the backup on additional media instead of in the backup history log.

v*   Validates the archive as it is written. A checksum is computed as the archive is being written; as each medium is completed, it is re-read and the checksum is recomputed to verify that each block is readable and correct. If either check fails, the medium is considered unreadable. If −A has been specified, the archiving operation fails; otherwise, the operator is prompted to replace the failed medium.

x*   Ignores the exception list; backs up all changed or modified files.

A   Establishes automated mode, (i.e., does not prompt the user to insert or remove media).

E*   Reports an estimate of media usage for the archive, then performs the backup.

N*   Reports an estimate of media usage for the archive, but does not perform the backup.

S   Displays a period (.) for every 100 (512 byte) blocks read-from or written-to the archive on the destination device.

V   Displays the name of each file written-to or extracted-from the archive on the destination device.

User Interactions

The connection between an archiving method and the backup command is more complex than a simple fork/exec or pipe. The backup command is responsible for all interactions with the user, either directly, or through the bkoper command. Therefore, incfile neither reads from standard-input nor writes to standard-output or standard-error. A method library must be used [see librmeth(3)] to communicate reports (estimates, filenames, periods, status, etc.) to the backup command.

DIAGNOSTICS

The exit codes for incfile are the following:

0 = successful completion of the task
1 = one or more parameters to incfile are invalid.
2 = an error has occurred which caused incfile to fail to
    complete *all* portions of its task.

FILES

/etc/bkup/bkexcept.tab	lists the files that are to be excluded from an incremental filesystem backup.
/etc/bkup/bkhist.tab	lists the labels of all volumes that have been used for backup operations.
/etc/bkup/rsstatus.tab	tracks the status of all restore requests from users.
/etc/bkup/bklog	lists errors generated by the backup methods and the **backup** command.
/etc/bkup/rslog	logs errors generated by the restore methods and the **restore** command.
$TMP/filelist$$	temporarily stores a table of contents for a backup archive.

SEE ALSO

backup(1M), bkoper(1M) cpio(1), cpio(4), device.tab(4), fdp(1), ff(1M),
ffile(1), fimage(1), getvol(1M), incfile(1), labelit(1M), libbrmeth(3), ls(1),
restore(1M), rsoper(1M), time(2)

NAME

inetd – Internet services daemon

SYNOPSIS

inetd [–d] [–s] [*configuration-file*]

DESCRIPTION

inetd, the Internet services daemon, is normally run at boot time by the Service Access Facility (SAF). When started, inetd reads its configuration information from *configuration-file*, the default being /etc/inetd.conf. See inetd.conf(4) for more information on the format of this file. It listens for connections on the Internet addresses of the services that its configuration file specifies. When a connection is found, it invokes the server daemon specified by that configuration file for the service requested. Once a server process exits, inetd continues to listen on the socket.

The –s option allows you to run inetd "stand-alone," outside the Service Access Facility (SAF).

Rather than having several daemon processes with sparsely distributed requests each running concurrently, inetd reduces the load on the system by invoking Internet servers only as they are needed.

inetd itself provides a number of simple TCP-based services. These include echo, discard, chargen (character generator), daytime (human readable time), and time (machine readable time, in the form of the number of seconds since midnight, January 1, 1900). For details of these services, consult the appropriate RFC, as listed below, from the Network Information Center.

inetd rereads its configuration file whenever it receives a hangup signal, SIGHUP. New services can be activated, and existing services deleted or modified in between whenever the file is reread.

SEE ALSO

comsat(1M), ftpd(1M), rexecd(1M), rlogind(1M), rshd(1M), telnetd(1M), tftpd(1M), inetd.conf(4).

Postel, Jon, "Echo Protocol," RFC 862, Network Information Center, SRI International, Menlo Park, Calif., May 1983.

Postel, Jon, "Discard Protocol," RFC 863, Network Information Center, SRI International, Menlo Park, Calif., May 1983.

Postel, Jon, "Character Generater Protocol," RFC 864, Network Information Center, SRI International, Menlo Park, Calif., May 1983.

Postel, Jon, "Daytime Protocol," RFC 867, Network Information Center, SRI International, Menlo Park, Calif., May 1983.

Postel, Jon, and Ken Harrenstien, "Time Protocol," RFC 868, Network Information Center, SRI International, Menlo Park, Calif., May 1983.

NAME

infocmp – compare or print out *terminfo* descriptions

SYNOPSIS

infocmp [–d] [–c] [–n] [–I] [–L] [–C] [–r] [–u] [–s d|i|l|c] [–v] [–V]
[–1] [–w *width*] [–A *directory*] [–B *directory*] [*termname* ...]

DESCRIPTION

infocmp can be used to compare a binary terminfo entry with other terminfo entries, rewrite a terminfo description to take advantage of the use= terminfo field, or print out a terminfo description from the binary file (term) in a variety of formats. In all cases, the boolean fields will be printed first, followed by the numeric fields, followed by the string fields.

Default Options

If no options are specified and zero or one *termnames* are specified, the –I option will be assumed. If more than one *termname* is specified, the –d option will be assumed.

Comparison Options [–d] [–c] [–n]

infocmp compares the terminfo description of the first terminal *termname* with each of the descriptions given by the entries for the other terminal's *termnames*. If a capability is defined for only one of the terminals, the value returned will depend on the type of the capability: F for boolean variables, –1 for integer variables, and NULL for string variables.

–d   produces a list of each capability that is different between two entries. This option is useful to show the difference between two entries, created by different people, for the same or similar terminals.

–c   produces a list of each capability that is common between two entries. Capabilities that are not set are ignored. This option can be used as a quick check to see if the –u option is worth using.

–n   produces a list of each capability that is in neither entry. If no *termnames* are given, the environment variable TERM will be used for both of the *termnames*. This can be used as a quick check to see if anything was left out of a description.

Source Listing Options [–I] [–L] [–C] [–r]

The –I, –L, and –C options will produce a source listing for each terminal named.

–I   use the terminfo names
–L   use the long C variable name listed in <term.h>
–C   use the termcap names
–r   when using –C, put out all capabilities in termcap form

If no *termnames* are given, the environment variable TERM will be used for the terminal name.

The source produced by the –C option may be used directly as a termcap entry, but not all of the parameterized strings may be changed to the termcap format. infocmp will attempt to convert most of the parameterized information, but anything not converted will be plainly marked in the output and commented out. These should be edited by hand.

All padding information for strings will be collected together and placed at the beginning of the string where termcap expects it. Mandatory padding (padding information with a trailing '/') will become optional.

All termcap variables no longer supported by terminfo, but which are derivable from other terminfo variables, will be output. Not all terminfo capabilities will be translated; only those variables which were part of termcap will normally be output. Specifying the –r option will take off this restriction, allowing all capabilities to be output in *termcap* form.

Note that because padding is collected to the beginning of the capability, not all capabilities are output. Mandatory padding is not supported. Because termcap strings are not as flexible, it is not always possible to convert a terminfo string capability into an equivalent termcap format. A subsequent conversion of the termcap file back into terminfo format will not necessarily reproduce the original terminfo source.

Some common terminfo parameter sequences, their termcap equivalents, and some terminal types which commonly have such sequences, are:

terminfo	termcap	Representative Terminals
%p1%c	%.	adm
%p1%d	%d	hp, ANSI standard, vt100
%p1%'x'%+%c	%+x	concept
%i	%i	ANSI standard, vt100
%p1%?%'x'%>%t%p1%'y'%+%;	%>xy	concept
%p2 is printed before %p1	%r	hp

Use= Option [–u]

–u   produces a terminfo source description of the first terminal *termname* which is relative to the sum of the descriptions given by the entries for the other terminals *termnames*. It does this by analyzing the differences between the first *termname* and the other *termnames* and producing a description with use= fields for the other terminals. In this manner, it is possible to retrofit generic terminfo entries into a terminal's description. Or, if two similar terminals exist, but were coded at different times or by different people so that each description is a full description, using infocmp will show what can be done to change one description to be relative to the other.

A capability will get printed with an at-sign (@) if it no longer exists in the first *termname*, but one of the other *termname* entries contains a value for it. A capability's value gets printed if the value in the first *termname* is not found in any of the other *termname* entries, or if the first of the other *termname* entries that has this capability gives a different value for the capability than that in the first *termname*.

The order of the other *termname* entries is significant. Since the terminfo compiler tic does a left-to-right scan of the capabilities, specifying two use= entries that contain differing entries for the same capabilities will produce different results depending on the order that the entries are given in. infocmp will flag any such inconsistencies between the other *termname* entries as they are found.

Alternatively, specifying a capability *after* a use= entry that contains that capability will cause the second specification to be ignored. Using infocmp to recreate a description can be a useful check to make sure that everything was specified correctly in the original source description.

Another error that does not cause incorrect compiled files, but will slow down the compilation time, is specifying extra use= fields that are superfluous. infocmp will flag any other *termname* use= fields that were not needed.

Other Options [−s d | i | l | c] [−v] [−V] [−1] [−w *width*]

−s   sorts the fields within each type according to the argument below:

d   leave fields in the order that they are stored in the *terminfo* database.

i   sort by *terminfo* name.

l   sort by the long C variable name.

c   sort by the *termcap* name.

If the −s option is not given, the fields printed out will be sorted alphabetically by the terminfo name within each type, except in the case of the −C or the −L options, which cause the sorting to be done by the termcap name or the long C variable name, respectively.

−v   prints out tracing information on standard error as the program runs.

−V   prints out the version of the program in use on standard error and exit.

−1   causes the fields to be printed out one to a line. Otherwise, the fields will be printed several to a line to a maximum width of 60 characters.

−w   changes the output to *width* characters.

Changing Databases [−A *directory*] [−B *directory*]

The location of the compiled terminfo database is taken from the environment variable TERMINFO . If the variable is not defined, or the terminal is not found in that location, the system terminfo database, usually in /usr/share/lib/terminfo, will be used. The options −A and −B may be used to override this location. The −A option will set TERMINFO for the first *termname* and the −B option will set TERMINFO for the other *termnames*. With this, it is possible to compare descriptions for a terminal with the same name located in two different databases. This is useful for comparing descriptions for the same terminal created by different people.

FILES

/usr/share/lib/terminfo/?/*   Compiled terminal description database.

SEE ALSO

curses(3X), captoinfo(1M), terminfo(4), tic(1M).

NAME

init, telinit – process control initialization

SYNOPSIS

/sbin/init [0123456SsQqabc]

/sbin/telinit [0123456SsQqabc]

DESCRIPTION

init

init is a general process spawner. Its primary role is to create processes from information stored in the file /sbin/inittab [see inittab(4)].

At any given time, the system is in one of eight possible run levels. A run level is a software configuration of the system under which only a selected group of processes exist. The processes spawned by init for each of these run levels is defined in /sbin/inittab. init can be in one of eight run levels, 0–6 and S or s (run levels S and s are identical). The run level changes when a privileged user runs /sbin/init. This user-spawned init sends appropriate signals to the original init spawned by the operating system when the system was booted, telling it which run level to change to.

The following are the arguments to init.

0   shut the machine down so it is safe to remove the power. Have the machine remove power if it can.

1   put the system in system administrator mode. All file systems are mounted. Only a small set of essential kernel processes are left running. This mode is for administrative tasks such as installing optional utility packages. All files are accessible and no users are logged in on the system.

2   put the system in multi-user mode. All multi-user environment terminal processes and daemons are spawned. This state is commonly referred to as the multi-user state.

3   start the remote file sharing processes and daemons. Mount and advertise remote resources. Run level 3 extends multi-user mode and is known as the remote-file-sharing state.

4   is available to be defined as an alternative multi-user environment configuration. It is not necessary for system operation and is usually not used.

5   Stop the UNIX system and go to the firmware monitor.

6   Stop the UNIX system and reboot to the state defined by the init-default entry in /sbin/inittab.

a,b,c   process only those /sbin/inittab entries having the a, b, or c run level set. These are pseudo-states, which may be defined to run certain commands, but which do not cause the current run level to change.

Q,q   re-examine /sbin/inittab.

S,s   enter single-user mode. When this occurs, the terminal which exe-
       cuted this command becomes the system console. This is the only
       run level that doesn't require the existence of a properly formatted
       /sbin/inittab file. If this file does not exist, then by default the
       only legal run level that init can enter is the single-user mode.
       When the system comes up to S or s, file systems for users' files
       are not mounted and only essential kernel processes are running.
       When the system comes down to S or s, all mounted file systems
       remain mounted, and all processes started by init that should
       only be running in multi-user mode are killed. In addition, any
       process that has a utmp entry will be killed. This last condition
       insures that all port monitors started by the SAC are killed and all
       services started by these port monitors, including ttymon login
       services, are killed. Other processes not started directly by init
       will remain running. For example, cron remains running.

When a UNIX system is booted, init is invoked and the following occurs. First,
init looks in /sbin/inittab for the initdefault entry [see inittab(4)]. If
there is one, init will usually use the run level specified in that entry as the initial run level to enter. If there is no initdefault entry in /sbin/inittab, init
requests that the user enter a run level from the virtual system console. If an S or
s is entered, init goes to the single-user state. In the single-user state the virtual
console terminal is assigned to the user's terminal and is opened for reading and
writing. The command /sbin/su is invoked and a message is generated on the
physical console saying where the virtual console has been relocated. Use either
init or telinit, to signal init to change the run level of the system. Note that
if the shell is terminated (via an end-of-file), init will only re-initialize to the
single-user state if the /sbin/inittab file does not exist.

If a 0 through 6 is entered, init enters the corresponding run level. Run levels
0, 5, and 6 are reserved states for shutting the system down. Run levels 2, 3, and
4 are available as multi-user operating states.

If this is the first time since power up that init has entered a run level other
than single-user state, init first scans /sbin/inittab for boot and bootwait
entries [see inittab(4)]. These entries are performed before any other processing
of /sbin/inittab takes place, providing that the run level entered matches that
of the entry. In this way any special initialization of the operating system, such
as mounting file systems, can take place before users are allowed onto the system.
init then scans /sbin/inittab and executes all other entries that are to be processed for that run level.

To spawn each process in /sbin/inittab, init reads each entry and for each
entry that should be respawned, it forks a child process. After it has spawned all
of the processes specified by /sbin/inittab, init waits for one of its descen-
dant processes to die, a powerfail signal, or a signal from another init or telinit process to change the system's run level. When one of these conditions
occurs, init re-examines /sbin/inittab. New entries can be added to
/sbin/inittab at any time; however, init still waits for one of the above three
conditions to occur before re-examining /sbin/inittab. To get around this,

init Q or init q command wakes init to re-examine /sbin/inittab immediately.

When init comes up at boot time and whenever the system changes from the single-user state to another run state, init sets the ioctl(2) states of the virtual console to those modes saved in the file /etc/ioctl.syscon. This file is written by init whenever the single-user state is entered.

When a run level change request is made init sends the warning signal (SIGTERM) to all processes that are undefined in the target run level. init waits five seconds before forcibly terminating these processes via the kill signal (SIGKILL).

When init receives a signal telling it that a process it spawned has died, it records the fact and the reason it died in /var/adm/utmp and /var/adm/wtmp if it exists [see who(1)]. A history of the processes spawned is kept in /var/adm/wtmp.

If init receives a powerfail signal (SIGPWR) it scans /sbin/inittab for special entries of the type powerfail and powerwait. These entries are invoked (if the run levels permit) before any further processing takes place. In this way init can perform various cleanup and recording functions during the powerdown of the operating system.

telinit

telinit, which is linked to /sbin/init, is used to direct the actions of init. It takes a one-character argument and signals init to take the appropriate action.

FILES

/sbin/inittab
/var/adm/utmp
/var/adm/wtmp
/etc/ioctl.syscon
/dev/console

SEE ALSO

ttymon(1M), shutdown(1M), inittab(4), utmp(4), utmpx(4), termio(7).
login(1), sh(1), stty(1), who(1) in the *User's Reference Manual*.
kill(2) in the *Programmer's Reference Manual*.

DIAGNOSTICS

If init finds that it is respawning an entry from /sbin/inittab more than ten times in two minutes, it will assume that there is an error in the command string in the entry, and generate an error message on the system console. It will then refuse to respawn this entry until either five minutes has elapsed or it receives a signal from a user-spawned init or telinit. This prevents init from eating up system resources when someone makes a typographical error in the inittab file or a program is removed that is referenced in /sbin/inittab.

When attempting to boot the system, failure of init to prompt for a new run level may be because the virtual system console is linked to a device other than the physical system console.

NOTES

init and `telinit` can be run only by a privileged user.

The **S** or **s** state must not be used indiscriminately in the `/sbin/inittab` file. A good rule to follow when modifying this file is to avoid adding this state to any line other than the `initdefault`.

If a default state is not specified in the `initdefault` entry in `/sbin/inittab`, state **6** is entered. Consequently, the system will loop, that is, it will go to firmware and reboot continuously.

If the `utmp` file cannot be created when booting the system, the system will boot to state "s" regardless of the state specified in the *initdefault* entry in `/etc/inittab`. This can happen if the `/var` filesystem is not accessible.

NAME
          install – install commands

SYNOPSIS
          /usr/sbin/install [-c *dira*] [-f *dirb*] [-i] [-n *dirc*] [-m *mode*] [-u *user*] [-g *group*]
          [-o] [-s] *file* [*dirx* ...]

DESCRIPTION
          The `install` command is most commonly used in "makefiles" [see make(1)] to
          install a *file* (updated target file) in a specific place within a file system. Each *file*
          is installed by copying it into the appropriate directory, thereby retaining the
          mode and owner of the original command. The program prints messages telling
          the user exactly what files it is replacing or creating and where they are going.

          If no options or directories (*dirx* ...) are given, `install` will search a set of
          default directories (/bin, /usr/bin, /etc, /lib, and /usr/lib, in that order) for
          a file with the same name as *file*. When the first occurrence is found, `install`
          issues a message saying that it is overwriting that file with *file*, and proceeds to
          do so. If the file is not found, the program states this and exits without further
          action.

          If one or more directories (*dirx* ...) are specified after *file*, those directories will
          be searched before the directories specified in the default list.

          The meanings of the options are:

          -c *dira*   Installs a new command (*file*) in the directory specified by
                             dira, only if it is not found. If it is found, `install` issues a
                             message saying that the file already exists, and exits
                             without overwriting it. May be used alone or with the -s
                             option.

          -f *dirb*   Forces *file* to be installed in given directory, whether or not
                             one already exists. If the file being installed does not
                             already exist, the mode and owner of the new file will be
                             set to 755 and bin, respectively. If the file already exists,
                             the mode and owner will be that of the already existing file.
                             May be used alone or with the -o or -s options.

          -i   Ignores default directory list, searching only through the
                             given directories (*dirx* ...). May be used alone or with any
                             other options except -c and -f.

          -n *dirc*   If *file* is not found in any of the searched directories, it is
                             put in the directory specified in *dirc*. The mode and owner
                             of the new file will be set to 755 and bin, respectively.
                             May be used alone or with any other options except -c and
                             -f.

          -m *mode*   The mode of the new file is set to *mode*.

          -u *user*   The owner of the new file is set to *user*.

-g *group*   The group id of the new file is set to *group*. Only available to the superuser.

-o   If *file* is found, this option saves the "found" file by copying it to OLD*file* in the directory in which it was found. This option is useful when installing a frequently used file such as /bin/sh or /lib/saf/ttymon, where the existing file cannot be removed. May be used alone or with any other options except -c.

-s   Suppresses printing of messages other than error messages. May be used alone or with any other options.

SEE ALSO
make(1).

NAME

killall – kill all active processes

SYNOPSIS

/usr/sbin/killall [*signal*]

DESCRIPTION

killall is used by /usr/sbin/shutdown to kill all active processes not directly related to the shutdown procedure.

killall terminates all processes with open files so that the mounted file systems will be unbusied and can be unmounted.

killall sends *signal* [see kill(1)] to all processes not belonging to the above group of exclusions. If no *signal* is specified, a default of **9** is used.

FILES

/usr/sbin/shutdown

SEE ALSO

fuser(1M), shutdown(1M).
kill(1), ps(1) in the *User's Reference Manual.*
signal(2) in the *Programmer's Reference Manual.*

WARNINGS

The killall command can be run only by the super-user.

NAME

labelit (generic) – provide labels for file systems

SYNOPSIS

labelit [–F *FSType*] [–V] [*current_options*] [–o *specific_options*] *special* [*operands*]

DESCRIPTION

labelit can be used to provide labels for unmounted disk file systems or file systems being copied to tape.

The *special* name should be the disk partition (e.g., /dev/rdsk/c0d0s6), or the cartridge tape (e.g., /dev/rSA/ctape1). The device may not be on a remote machine. *operands* are *FSType*-specific and the manual page of the *FSType*-specific labelit command should be consulted for a detailed description.

current_options are options supported by the s5-specific module of labelit. Other *FSTypes* do not necessarily support these options. *specific_options* indicate suboptions specified in a comma-separated list of suboptions and/or keyword-attribute pairs for interpretation by the *FSType*-specific module of the command.

The options are:

–F   specify the *FSType* on which to operate. The *FSType* should either be specified here or be determinable from /etc/vfstab by matching the *special* with an entry in the table.

–V   echo complete command line. This option is used to verify and validate the command line. Additional information obtained via a /etc/vfstab lookup is included in the output. The command is not executed.

–o   Specify *FSType*-specific options.

NOTE

This command may not be supported for all FSTypes.

FILES

/etc/vfstab   list of default parameters for each file system

SEE ALSO

makefsys(1M), vfstab(4).
Manual pages for the FSType-specific modules of labelit.

NAME

    labelit (s5) – provide labels for s5 file systems

SYNOPSIS

    labelit [–F s5] [*generic_options*] [–n] *special* [*fsname volume*]

DESCRIPTION

generic_options are options supported by the generic labelit command.

labelit can be used to provide labels for unmounted s5 disk file systems or s5 file systems being copied to tape.

With the optional arguments omitted, labelit prints current label values.

The *special* name should be the disk partition (e.g., /dev/rdsk/c0d0s6), or the cartridge tape (e.g., /dev/rSA/ctape1). The device may not be on a remote machine.

The *fsname* argument represents the mounted name (e.g., root, u1, etc.) of the file system.

Volume may be used to equate an internal name to a volume name applied externally to the disk pack, diskette or tape.

For file systems on disk, *fsname* and *volume* are recorded in the superblock.

The options are:

–F s5   Specifies the s5-FSType. Used to ensure that an s5 file system is labelled.

–n   Provides for initial tape labeling only (This destroys the previous contents of the tape).

SEE ALSO

generic labelit(1M), makefsys(1M), s5_specific mount(1M).
fs(4) in the *Programmer's Reference Manual*.

NAME

labelit (ufs) – provide labels for ufs file systems

SYNOPSIS

labelit [–F ufs] [*generic_options*] *special* [*fsname volume*]

DESCRIPTION

generic_options are options supported by the generic labelit command.

labelit can be used to provide labels for unmounted disk file systems or file systems being copied to tape.

If neither *fsname* nor *volume* is specified, labelit prints the current values.

The *special* name should be the physical disk section (for example, /dev/dsk/c0d0s6), or the cartridge tape (for example, /dev/SA/ctape1). The device may not be on a remote machine.

The *fsname* argument represents the mounted name (for example, **root, u1**, etc.) of the file system.

Volume may be used to equate an internal name to a volume name applied externally to the disk pack, diskette, or tape.

The option is:

–F ufs
    Specifies the ufs-FSType.

SEE ALSO

generic labelit(1M), makefsys(1M), ufs(4).

NAME

    `ldsysdump` – load system dump from floppy diskettes

SYNOPSIS

    `/usr/sbin/ldsysdump` *destination_file*

DESCRIPTION

    The `ldsysdump` command loads the memory image files from the floppy diskettes used to take a system dump and recombines them into a single file on the hard disk suitable for use by the `crash` command. The *destination_file* is the name of the hard disk file into which the data from the diskettes will be loaded.

    When invoked, `ldsysdump` begins an interactive procedure that prompts the user to insert the diskettes to be loaded. The user has the option of quitting the session at any time. This allows only the portion of the system image needed to be dumped.

EXAMPLES

    This example loads the three floppies produced via the `sysdump` command on a machine equipped with 2 MB of memory.

```
$ldsysdump /var/tmp/cdump

Insert first sysdump floppy.
Enter 'c' to continue, 'q' to quit: c

Loading sysdump
..................................................................
.......................................

Insert next sysdump floppy.
Enter 'c' to continue, 'q' to quit: c

Loading more sysdump
..................................................................
........................................

Insert next sysdump floppy.
Enter 'c' to continue, 'q' to quit: c

Loading more sysdump
..................................................................
.......................................

3 Sysdump files coalesced, 4096 (512 byte) blocks
$
```

FILES

    `/dev/dsk/c0d0s6` device used for floppy access

SEE ALSO

crash(1M), sysdump(8).

ulimit(2) in the *Programmer's Reference Manual.*

DIAGNOSTICS

If a floppy diskette is inserted out of sequence a message is printed. The user is allowed to insert a new one and continue the session.

NOTES

Since the 3B2 computer can be equipped with up to 4 MB of memory, the *destination_file* can become quite large. The file size limit must be set large enough to hold a file of this size.

NAME

led – flash green LED

SYNOPSIS

/etc/led [–f] [–o]

DESCRIPTION

led is used to turn on the green LED (light emitting diode) located on the exterior of the cabinet. The main purpose is to signal particular phases of the boot procedure. The options are as follows:

–f   sets the green LED to a flashing state via the **sys3b** system call.

–o   sets the green LED to a constant on state via the **sys3b** system call.

SEE ALSO

sys3b(2) in the *Programmer's Reference Manual.*

NOTES

This command can be run only by the super-user.

NAME
>   link, unlink – link and unlink files and directories

SYNOPSIS
>   /usr/sbin/link *file1 file2*
>   /usr/sbin/unlink *file*

DESCRIPTION
>   The link command is used to create a file name that points to another file.
>   Linked files and directories can be removed by the unlink command; however, it
>   is strongly recommended that the rm and rmdir commands be used instead of
>   the unlink command.
>
>   The only difference between ln and link and unlink is that the latter do exactly
>   what they are told to do, abandoning all error checking. This is because they
>   directly invoke the link and unlink system calls.

SEE ALSO
>   rm(1) in the *User's Reference Manual*.
>   link(2), unlink(2) in the *Programmer's Reference Manual*.

NOTES
>   These commands can be run only by the super-user.

NAME

listdgrp – lists members of a device group

SYNOPSIS

listdgrp *dgroup* ...

DESCRIPTION

listdgrp displays the members of the device groups specified by the *dgroup* list.

ERRORS

This command will exit with one of the following values:

0 = successful completion of the task.

1 = command syntax incorrect, invalid option used, or internal error occurred.

2 = device group table could not be opened for reading.

3 = device group *dgroup* could not be found in the device group table.

EXAMPLE

To list the devices that belong to group partitions:

```
$ listdgrp partitions
root
swap
usr
```

FILES

/etc/dgroup.tab

SEE ALSO

putdgrp(1).

NAME
listen – network listener daemon

SYNOPSIS
/usr/lib/saf/listen [–m *devstem*] *net_spec*

DESCRIPTION
The listen process "listens" to a network for service requests, accepts requests when they arrive, and invokes servers in response to those service requests. The network listener process may be used with any connection-oriented network (more precisely, with any connection-oriented transport provider) that conforms to the Transport Interface (TLI) specification.

The listener internally generates a pathname for the minor device for each connection; it is this pathname that is used in the utmp entry for a service, if one is created. By default, this pathname is the concatenation of the prefix /dev/*netspec* with the decimal representation of the minor device number. When the –m *devstem* option is specified, the listener will use *devstem* as the prefix for the pathname. In either case, the representation of the minor device number will be at least two digits (e.g., 05 or 27), but will be longer when necessary to accommodate minor device numbers larger than 99.

SERVER INVOCATION
When a connection indication is received, the listener creates a new transport endpoint and accepts the connection on that endpoint. Before giving the file descriptor for this new connection to the server, any designated STREAMS modules are pushed and the configuration script is executed, if one exists. This file descriptor is appropriate for use with either TLI (see especially t_sync(3N)) or the sockets interface library.

By default, a new instance of the server is invoked for each connection. When the server is invoked, file descriptor 0 refers to the transport endpoint, and is open for reading and writing. File descriptors 1 and 2 are copies of file descriptor 0; no other file descriptors are open. The service is invoked with the user and group IDs of the user name under which the service was registered with the listener, and with the current directory set to the HOME directory of that user.

Alternatively, a service may be registered so that the listener will pass connections to a standing server process through a FIFO or a named STREAM, instead of invoking the server anew for each connection. In this case, the connection is passed in the form of a file descriptor that refers to the new transport endpoint. Before the file descriptor is sent to the server, the listener interprets any configuration script registered for that service using doconfig(3N), although doconfig is invoked with both the NORUN and NOASSIGN flags. The server receives the file descriptor for the connection in a strrecvfd structure via an I_RECVFD ioctl(2).

For more details about the listener and its administration, see nlsadmin(1M).

FILES
/etc/saf/*pmtag*/*

SEE ALSO
> nlsadmin(1M), pmadm(1M), sac(1M), sacadm(1M),
> doconfig(3N), nlsgetcall, nlsprovider(3N),
> streamio(7).
> *Network Programmer's Guide*

NOTES
> When passing a connection to a standing server, the user and group IDs con-
> tained in the strrecvfd structure will be those for the listener (that is, they will
> both be 0); the user name under which the service was registered with the listener
> is not reflected in these IDs.
>
> When operating multiple instances of the listener on a single transport provider,
> there is a potential race condition in the binding of addresses during initialization
> of the listeners if any of their services have dynamically assigned addresses. This
> condition would appear as an inability of the listener to bind a static-address ser-
> vice to its otherwise valid address, and would result from a dynamic-address ser-
> vice having been bound to that address by a different instance of the listener.

NAME
     logins – list user and system login information

SYNOPSIS
     logins [–dmopstuxa] [–g groups] [–l logins]

DESCRIPTION
     This command displays information on user and system logins. Contents of the
     output is controlled by the command options and can include the following: user
     or system login, user id number, /etc/passwd account field value (user name or
     other information), primary group name, primary group id, multiple group
     names, multiple group ids, home directory, login shell, and four password aging
     parameters. The default information is the following: login id, user id, primary
     group name, primary group id and the account field value from /etc/passwd.
     Output is sorted by user id, displaying system logins followed by user logins.

     –d   Selects logins with duplicate uids.

     –m   Displays multiple group membership information.

     –o   Formats output into one line of colon-separated fields.

     –p   Selects logins with no passwords.

     –s   Selects all system logins.

     –t   Sorts output by login instead of by uid.

     –u   Selects all user logins.

     –x   Prints an extended set of information about each selected user. The
          extended information includes home directory, login shell and password
          aging information, each displayed on a separate line. The password infor-
          mation consists of password status (PS for passworded, NP for no pass-
          word or LK for locked). If the login is passworded, status is followed by
          the date the password was last changed, the number of days required
          between changes, and the number of days allowed before a change is
          required. The password aging information shows the time interval that
          the user will receive a password expiration warning message (when log-
          ging on) before the password expires.

     –a   Adds two password expiration fields to the display. The fields show how
          many days a password can remain unused before it automatically
          becomes inactive and the date that the password will expire.

     –g   Selects all users belonging to group, sorted by login. Multiple groups can
          be specified as a comma-separated list.

     –l   Selects the requested login. Multiple logins can be specified as a comma-
          separated list.

NOTES
     Options may be used together. If so, any login matching any criteria will be
     displayed. When the –l and –g options are combined, a user will only be listed
     once, even if they belong to more than one of the selected groups.

NAME

    lpadmin – configure the LP print service

SYNOPSIS

    lpadmin −p *printer options*

    lpadmin −x *dest*

    lpadmin −d [*dest*]

    lpadmin −S *print-wheel* −A *alert-type* [−W *minutes*] [−Q *requests*]

DESCRIPTION

    lpadmin configures the LP print service by defining printers and devices. It is used to add and change printers, to remove printers from the service, to set or change the system default destination, to define alerts for printer faults, and to mount print wheels.

Adding or Changing a Printer

    The first form of the lpadmin command (lpadmin −p *printer options*) is used to configure a new printer or to change the configuration of an existing printer. The following *options* may appear in any order.

    −A *alert-type* [−W *minutes*]

        The −A option is used to define an alert to inform the administrator when a printer fault is detected, and periodically thereafter, until the printer fault is cleared by the administrator. The *alert-types* are:

        mail   Send the alert message via mail [see mail(1)] to the administrator.

        write   Write the message to the terminal on which the administrator is logged in. If the administrator is logged in on several terminals, one is chosen arbitrarily.

        quiet   Do not send messages for the current condition. An administrator can use this option to temporarily stop receiving further messages about a known problem. Once the fault has been cleared and printing resumes, messages will again be sent when another fault occurs with the printer.

        none   Do not send messages; any existing alert definition for the printer will be removed. No alert will be sent when the printer faults until a different alert-type (except quiet) is used.

        shell-command

            Run the *shell-command* each time the alert needs to be sent. The shell command should expect the message in standard input. If there are blanks embedded in the command, enclose the command in quotes. Note that the mail and write values for this option are equivalent to the values mail *user-name* and write *user-name* respectively, where *user-name* is the current name for the administrator. This will be the login name of the person submitting this command unless he or she has used the su command to change to another user ID. If the su command has been used to change the user ID, then the *user-name* for the new ID is used.

list   Display the type of the alert for the printer fault. No change is made to the alert.

The message sent appears as follows:

The printer *printer* has stopped printing for the reason given below. Fix the problem and bring the printer back on line. Printing has stopped, but will be restarted in a few minutes; issue an enable command if you want to restart sooner. Unless someone issues a change request

lp -i *request-id* -P ...

to change the page list to print, the current request will be reprinted from the beginning.

The reason(s) it stopped (multiple reasons indicate reprinted attempts):

reason

The LP print service can detect printer faults only through an adequate fast filter and only when the standard interface program or a suitable customized interface program is used. Furthermore, the level of recovery after a fault depends on the capabilities of the filter.

If the *printer* is all, the alerting defined in this command applies to all existing printers.

If the −W option is not used to arrange fault alerting for *printer*, the default procedure is to mail one message to the administrator of *printer* per fault. This is equivalent to specifying −W once or −W 0. If *minutes* is a number greater than zero, an alert will be sent at intervals specified by *minutes*.

−c *class*
Insert *printer* into the specified *class*. *Class* will be created if it does not already exist.

−D *comment*
Save this *comment* for display whenever a user asks for a full description of *printer* [see lpstat(1)]. The LP print service does not interpret this comment.

−e *printer*₁
Copy the interface program of an existing *printer₁ to be the interface program for printer*. (Options −i *and* −m *may not be specified with this option.*)

−F *fault-recovery*
This option specifies the recovery to be used for any print request that is stopped because of a printer fault, according to the value of *fault-recovery*:

continue
Continue printing on the top of the page where printing stopped. This requires a filter to wait for the fault to clear before automatically continuing.

`beginning`
> Start printing the request again from the beginning.

`wait`   Disable printing on *printer* and wait for the administrator or a user to enable printing again.

> During the wait the administrator or the user who submitted the stopped print request can issue a change request that specifies where printing should resume. (See the −i option of the lp command.) If no change request is made before printing is enabled, printing will resume at the top of the page where stopped, if the filter allows; otherwise, the request will be printed from the beginning.

−f allow:*form-list*
−f deny:*form-list*
> Allow or deny the forms in *form-list* to be printed on *printer*. By default no forms are allowed on a new printer.

> For each printer, the LP print service keeps two lists of forms: an "allow-list" of forms that may be used with the printer, and a "deny-list" of forms that may not be used with the printer. With the −f allow option, the forms listed are added to the allow-list and removed from the deny-list. With the −f deny option, the forms listed are added to the deny-list and removed from the allow-list.

> If the allow-list is not empty, only the forms in the list may be used on the printer, regardless of the contents of the deny-list. If the allow-list is empty, but the deny-list is not, the forms in the deny-list may not be used with the printer. All forms can be excluded from a printer by specifying −f deny:all. All forms can be used on a printer (provided the printer can handle all the characteristics of each form) by specifying −f allow:all.

> The LP print service uses this information as a set of guidelines for determining where a form can be mounted. Administrators, however, are not restricted from mounting a form on any printer. If mounting a form on a particular printer is in disagreement with the information in the allow-list or deny-list, the administrator is warned but the mount is accepted. Nonetheless, if a user attempts to issue a print or change request for a form and printer combination that is in disagreement with the information, the request is accepted only if the form is currently mounted on the printer. If the form is later unmounted before the request can print, the request is canceled and the user is notified by mail.

> If the administrator tries to specify a form as acceptable for use on a printer that doesn't have the capabilities needed by the form, the command is rejected.

> Note the other use of −f, with the −M option, below.

−h   Indicate that the device associated with the printer is hardwired. If neither of the mutually exclusive options, −h and −l, is specified, this option is assumed.

−I *content-type-list*

Allow *printer* to handle print requests with the content types listed in a *content-type-list*. If the list includes names of more than one type, the names must be separated by commas or blank spaces. (If they are separated by blank spaces, the entire list must be enclosed in double quotes.)

The type simple is recognized as the default content type for files in the UNIX system. A simple type of file is a data stream containing only printable ASCII characters and the following control characters.

Control Character	Octal Value	Meaning
backspace	10_8	move back one character, except at beginning of line
tab	11_8	move to next tab stop
linefeed (newline)	12_8	move to beginning of next line
form feed	14_8	move to beginning of next page
carriage return	15_8	move to beginning of current line

To prevent the print service from considering simple a valid type for the printer, specify either an explicit value (such as the printer type) in the *content-type-list*, or an empty list. If you do want simple included along with other types, you must include simple in the *content-type-list*.

Except for simple, each *content-type* name is freely determined by the administrator. If the printer type is specified by the −T option, then the printer type is implicitly considered to be also a valid content type.

−i *interface*

Establish a new interface program for *printer*. *Interface* is the pathname of the new program. (The −e and −m options may not be specified with this option.)

−l

Indicate that the device associated with *printer* is a login terminal. The LP scheduler (lpsched) disables all login terminals automatically each time it is started. (The −h option may not be specified with this option.)

−M −f *form-name* [−a [−o filebreak]]

Mount the form *form-name* on *printer*. Print requests that need the pre-printed form *form-name* will be printed on *printer*. If more than one printer has the form mounted and the user has specified any (with the −d option of the lp command) as the printer destination, then the print request will be printed on the one printer that also meets the other needs of the request.

The page length and width, and character and line pitches needed by the form are compared with those allowed for the printer, by checking the capabilities in the terminfo database for the type of printer. If the form requires attributes that are not available with the printer, the administrator is warned but the mount is accepted. If the form lists a print wheel as mandatory, but the print wheel mounted on the printer is different, the administrator is also warned but the mount is accepted.

If the −a option is given, an alignment pattern is printed, preceded by the same initialization of the physical printer that precedes a normal print request, with one exception: no banner page is printed. Printing is assumed to start at the top of the first page of the form. After the pattern is printed, the administrator can adjust the mounted form in the printer and press return for another alignment pattern (no initialization this time), and can continue printing as many alignment patterns as desired. The administrator can quit the printing of alignment patterns by typing q.

If the −o filebreak option is given, a formfeed is inserted between each copy of the alignment pattern. By default, the alignment pattern is assumed to correctly fill a form, so no formfeed is added.

A form is "unmounted" either by mounting a new form in its place or by using the −f none option. By default, a new printer has no form mounted.

Note the other use of −f without the −M option above.

−M −S *print-wheel*
    Mount the *print-wheel* on *printer*. Print requests that need the *print-wheel* will be printed on *printer*. If more than one printer has *print-wheel* mounted and the user has specified any (with the −d option of the lp command) as the printer destination, then the print request will be printed on the one printer that also meets the other needs of the request.

    If the *print-wheel* is not listed as acceptable for the printer, the administrator is warned but the mount is accepted. If the printer does not take print wheels, the command is rejected.

    A print wheel is "unmounted" either by mounting a new print wheel in its place or by using the option −S none. By default, a new printer has no print wheel mounted.

    Note the other uses of the −S option without the −M option described below.

−m *model*
    Select *model* interface program, provided with the LP print service, for the printer. (Options −e and −i may not be specified with this option.)

−o *printing-option*
    Each −o option in the list below is the default given to an interface program if the option is not taken from a preprinted form description or is not explicitly given by the user submitting a request [see lp(1)]. The only −o options that can have defaults defined are listed below.

        length=*scaled-decimal-number*
        width=*scaled-decimal-number*
        cpi=*scaled-decimal-number*
        lpi=*scaled-decimal-number*
        stty='*stty-option-list*'

The term "scaled-decimal-number" refers to a non-negative number used to indicate a unit of size. The type of unit is shown by a "trailing" letter attached to the number. Three types of scaled decimal numbers can be used with the LP print service: numbers that show sizes in centimeters (marked with a trailing c); numbers that show sizes in inches (marked with a trailing i); and numbers that show sizes in units appropriate to use (without a trailing letter), that is, lines, characters, lines per inch, or characters per inch.

The first four default option values must agree with the capabilities of the type of physical printer, as defined in the `terminfo` database for the printer type. If they do not, the command is rejected.

The *stty-option-list* is not checked for allowed values, but is passed directly to the `stty` program by the standard interface program. Any error messages produced by `stty` when a request is processed (by the standard interface program) are mailed to the user submitting the request.

For each printing option not specified, the defaults for the following attributes are defined in the `terminfo` entry for the specified printer type.

```
length
width
cpi
lpi
```

The default for `stty` is

```
stty='9600 cs8 -cstopb -parenb ixon
      -ixany opost -olcuc onlcr -ocrnl -onocr
      -onlret -ofill nl0 cr0 tab0 bs0 vt0 ff0'
```

You can set any of the −o options to the default values (which vary for different types of printers), by typing them without assigned values, as follows:

```
length=
width=
cpi=
lpi=
stty=
```

−o nobanner

Allow a user to submit a print request specifying that no banner page be printed.

−o banner

Force a banner page to be printed with every print request, even when a user asks for no banner page. This is the default; you must specify −o nobanner if you want to allow users to be able to specify −o nobanner with the `lp` command.

−r *class*

Remove *printer* from the specified *class*. If *printer* is the last member of *class*, then *class* will be removed.

−S *list*

Allow either the print wheels or aliases for character sets named in *list* to be used on the printer.

If the printer is a type that takes print wheels, then *list* is a comma or space separated list of print wheel names. (Enclose the list with quotes if it contains blanks.) These will be the only print wheels considered mountable on the printer. (You can always force a different print wheel to be mounted, however.) Until the option is used to specify a list, no print wheels will be considered mountable on the printer, and print requests that ask for a particular print wheel with this printer will be rejected.

If the printer is a type that has selectable character sets, then *list* is a comma or blank separated list of character set name "mappings" or aliases. (Enclose the list with quotes if it contains blanks.) Each "mapping" is of the form

known-name=alias

The *known-name* is a character set number preceded by cs (such as cs3 for character set three) or a character set name from the Terminfo database entry csnm. [See terminfo(4) in the *Programmer's Reference Manual*.] If this option is not used to specify a list, only the names already known from the Terminfo database or numbers with a prefix of cs will be acceptable for the printer.

If *list* is the word none, any existing print wheel lists or character set aliases will be removed.

Note the other uses of the −S with the −M option described above.

−s *system-name*[!*printer-name*]
    Make a remote printer (one that must be accessed through another system) accessible to users on your system. *System-name* is the name of the remote system on which the remote printer is located; it must be listed in the systems table (/etc/lp/Systems). *Printer-name* is the name used on the remote system for that printer. For example, if you want to access *printer*$_1$ on *system*$_1$ and you want it called *printer*$_2$ on your system, enter −p *printer*$_2$ −s *system*$_1$!*printer*$_1$

−T *printer-type-list*
    Identify the printer as being of one or more *printer-type*s. Each *printer-type* is used to extract data from the terminfo database; this information is used to initialize the printer before printing each user's request. Some filters may also use a *printer-type* to convert content for the printer. If this option is not used, the default *printer-type* will be unknown; no information will be extracted from terminfo so each user request will be printed without first initializing the printer. Also, this option must be used if the following are to work: −o cpi, −o lpi, −o width, and −o length options of the lpadmin and lp commands, and the −S and −f options of the lpadmin command.

    If the *printer-type-list* contains more than one type, then the *content-type-list* of the −I option must either be specified as simple, as empty (−I ""), or not specified at all.

−u allow: *login-ID-list*
−u deny: *login-ID-list*

Allow or deny the users in *login-ID-list* access to the printer. By default all users are allowed on a new printer. The *login-ID-list* argument may include any or all of the following constructs:

login-ID	a user on any system
system-name ! *login-ID*	a user on system *system-name*
system-name ! all	all users on system *system-name*
all ! *login-ID*	a user on all systems
all	all users on all systems

For each printer the LP print service keeps two lists of users: an "allow-list" of people allowed to use the printer, and a "deny-list" of people denied access to the printer. With the −u allow option, the users listed are added to the allow-list and removed from the deny-list. With the −u deny option, the users listed are added to the deny-list and removed from the allow-list.

If the allow-list is not empty, only the users in the list may use the printer, regardless of the contents of the deny-list. If the allow-list is empty, but the deny-list is not, the users in the deny-list may not use the printer. All users can be denied access to the printer by specifying −u deny:all. All users may use the printer by specifying −u allow:all.

−U *dial-info*

The −U option allows your print service to access a remote printer. (It does not enable your print service to access a remote printer service.) Specifically, −U assigns the "dialing" information *dial-info* to the printer. *Dial-info* is used with the dial routine to call the printer. Any network connection supported by the Basic Networking Utilities will work. *Dial-info* can be either a phone number for a modem connection, or a system name for other kinds of connections. Or, if −U direct is given, no dialing will take place, because the name direct is reserved for a printer that is directly connected. If a system name is given, it is used to search for connection details from the file /etc/uucp/Systems or related files. The Basic Networking Utilities are required to support this option. By default, −U direct is assumed.

−v *device*

Associate a *device* with *printer*. *Device* is the path name of a file that is writable by lp. Note that the same *device* can be associated with more than one printer.

Restrictions

When creating a new printer, one of three options (−v, −U, or −s) must be supplied. In addition, only one of the following may be supplied: −e, −i, or −m; if none of these three options is supplied, the model standard is used. The −h and −l options are mutually exclusive. Printer and class names may be no longer than 14 characters and must consist entirely of the characters A-Z, a-z, 0-9 and _ (underscore). If −s is specified, the following options are invalid: −A, −e, −F, −h, −i, −l, −M, −m, −o, −U, −v, and −W.

Removing a Printer Destination

The −x *dest* option removes the destination *dest* (a printer or a class), from the LP print service. If *dest* is a printer and is the only member of a class, then the class will be deleted, too. If *dest* is all, all printers and classes are removed. No other *options* are allowed with −x.

Setting/Changing the System Default Destination

The −d [*dest*] option makes *dest*, an existing printer or class, the new system default destination. If *dest* is not supplied, then there is no system default destination. No other *options* are allowed with −d.

Setting an Alert for a Print Wheel

−S *print-wheel* −A *alert-type* [−W *minutes*] [−Q *requests*]

The −S *print-wheel* option is used with the −A *alert-type* option to define an alert to mount the print wheel when there are jobs queued for it. If this command is not used to arrange alerting for a print wheel, no alert will be sent for the print wheel. Note the other use of −A, with the −p option, above.

The *alert-types* are:

mail   Send the alert message via the mail command to the administrator.

write   Write the message, via the write command, to the terminal on which the administrator is logged in. If the administrator is logged in on several terminals, one is arbitrarily chosen.

quiet   Do not send messages for the current condition. An administrator can use this option to temporarily stop receiving further messages about a known problem. Once the *print-wheel* has been mounted and subsequently unmounted, messages will again be sent when the number of print requests reaches the threshold specified by the −Q option.

none   Do not send messages until the −A option is given again with a different *alert-type* (other than quiet).

shell-command

Run the *shell-command* each time the alert needs to be sent. The shell command should expect the message in standard input. If there are blanks embedded in the command, enclose the command in quotes. Note that the mail and write values for this option are equivalent to the values mail *user-name* and write *user-name* respectively, where *user-name* is the current name for the administrator. This will be the login name of the person submitting this command unless he or she has used the su command to change to another user ID. If the su command has been used to change the user ID, then the *user-name* for the new ID is used.

list   Display the type of the alert for the print wheel on standard output. No change is made to the alert.

The message sent appears as follows:

```
The print wheel print-wheel needs to be mounted
on the printer(s):
printer (integer₁ requests)
integer₂ print requests await this print wheel.
```

The printers listed are those that the administrator had earlier specified were candidates for this print wheel. The number $integer_1$ listed next to each printer is the number of requests eligible for the printer. The number $integer_2$ shown after the printer list is the total number of requests awaiting the print wheel. It will be less than the sum of the other numbers if some requests can be handled by more than one printer.

If the *print-wheel* is **all**, the alerting defined in this command applies to all print wheels already defined to have an alert.

If the **–W** option is not given, the default procedure is that only one message will be sent per need to mount the print wheel. Not specifying the **–W** option is equivalent to specifying **–W** once or **–W** 0. If *minutes* is a number greater than zero, an alert will be sent at intervals specified by *minutes*.

If the **–Q** option is also given, the alert will be sent when a certain number (specified by the argument *requests*) of print requests that need the print wheel are waiting. If the **–Q** option is not given, or *requests* is 1 or the word **any** (which are both the default), a message is sent as soon as anyone submits a print request for the print wheel when it is not mounted.

FILES

```
/var/spool/lp/*
/etc/lp
```

SEE ALSO

accept(1M), lpsched(1M), and lpsystem(1M).
enable(1), lp(1), lpstat(1), and stty(1) in the *User's Reference Manual*.
dial(3C), terminfo(4) in the *Programmer's Reference Manual*.

NAME

　　lpfilter – administer filters used with the LP print service

SYNOPSIS

　　lpfilter −f *filter-name* −F *path-name*
　　lpfilter −f *filter-name* −
　　lpfilter −f *filter-name* −i
　　lpfilter −f *filter-name* −x
　　lpfilter −f *filter-name* −l

DESCRIPTION

　　The lpfilter command is used to add, change, delete, and list a filter used with the LP print service. These filters are used to convert the content type of a file to a content type acceptable to a printer. One of the following options must be used with the lpfilter command: −F *path-name* (or − for standard input) to add or change a filter; −i to reset an original filter to its factory setting; −x to delete a filter; or −l to list a filter description.

　　The argument all can be used instead of a *filter-name* with any of these options. When all is specified with the −F or − option, the requested change is made to all filters. Using all with the −i option has the effect of restoring to their original settings all filters for which predefined settings were initially available. Using the all argument with the −x option results in all filters being deleted, and using it with the −l option produces a list of all filters.

Adding or Changing a Filter

　　The filter named in the −f option is added to the filter table. If the filter already exists, its description is changed to reflect the new information in the input.

　　The filter description is taken from the *path-name* if the −F option is given, or from the standard input if the − option is given. One of the two must be given to define or change a filter. If the filter named is one originally delivered with the LP print service, the −i option will restore the original filter description.

　　When an existing filter is changed with the −F or − option, items that are not specified in the new information are left as they were. When a new filter is added with this command, unspecified items are given default values. (See below.)

　　Filters are used to convert the content of a request into a data stream acceptable to a printer. For a given print request, the LP print service will know the following: the type of content in the request, the name of the printer, the type of the printer, the types of content acceptable to the printer, and the modes of printing asked for by the originator of the request. It will use this information to find a filter or a pipeline of filters that will convert the content into a type acceptable to the printer.

　　Below is a list of items that provide input to this command, and a description of each item. All lists are comma or space separated.

　　　　Input types: *content-type-list*
　　　　Output types: *content-type-list*
　　　　Printer types: *printer-type-list*
　　　　Printers: *printer-list*
　　　　Filter type: *filter-type*

          Command: *shell-command*
          Options: *template-list*

Input types   This gives the types of content that can be accepted by the filter. (The default is **any**.)

Output types

        This gives the types of content that the filter can produce from any of the input content types. (The default is **any**.)

Printer types

        This gives the type of printers for which the filter can be used. The LP print service will restrict the use of the filter to these types of printers. (The default is **any**.)

Printers   This gives the names of the printers for which the filter can be used. The LP print service will restrict the use of the filter to just the printers named. (The default is **any**.)

Filter type   This marks the filter as a **slow** filter or a **fast** filter. Slow filters are generally those that take a long time to convert their input. They are run unconnected to a printer, to keep the printers from being tied up while the filter is running. If a listed printer is on a remote system, the filter type for it must have the value **slow**. Fast filters are generally those that convert their input quickly, or those that must be connected to the printer when run. These will be given to the interface program to run connected to the physical printer.

Command   This specifies the program to run to invoke the filter. The full program pathname as well as fixed options must be included in the *shell-command*; additional options are constructed, based on the characteristics of each print request and on the **Options** field. A command must be given for each filter.

        The command must accept a data stream as standard input and produce the converted data stream on its standard output. This allows filter pipelines to be constructed to convert data not handled by a single filter.

Options   This is a comma separated list of templates used by the LP print service to construct options to the filter from the characteristics of each print request listed in the table later.

        In general, each template is of the following form:

          keyword pattern = replacement

        The *keyword* names the characteristic that the template attempts to map into a filter specific option; each valid *keyword* is listed in the table below. A *pattern* is one of the following: a literal pattern of one of the forms listed in the table, a single asterisk (*), or a regular expression. If *pattern* matches the value of the characteristic, the template fits and is used to generate a filter specific option. The *replacement* is what will be used as the option.

Regular expressions are the same as those found in the ed(1) or vi(1) commands. This includes the \(...\) and \n constructions, which can be used to extract portions of the *pattern* for copying into the *replacement*, and the &, which can be used to copy the entire *pattern* into the *replacement*.

The *replacement* can also contain a *; it too, is replaced with the entire *pattern*, just like the & of ed(1).

lp Option	Characteristic	*keyword*	Possible *patterns*
-T	Content type (input)	INPUT	*content-type*
N/A	Content type (output)	OUTPUT	*content-type*
N/A	Printer type	TERM	*printer-type*
-d	Printer name	PRINTER	*printer-name*
-f, -o cpi=	Character pitch	CPI	*integer*
-f, -o lpi=	Line pitch	LPI	*integer*
-f, -o length=	Page length	LENGTH	*integer*
-f, -o width=	Page width	WIDTH	*integer*
-P	Pages to print	PAGES	*page-list*
-S	Character set	CHARSET	*character-set-name*
	Print wheel	CHARSET	*print-wheel-name*
-f	Form name	FORM	*form-name*
-y	Modes	MODES	*mode*
-n	Number of copies	COPIES	*integer*

For example, the template

    MODES landscape = -l

shows that if a print request is submitted with the -y landscape option, the filter will be given the option -l. As another example, the template

    TERM * = -T *

shows that the filter will be given the option -T *printer-type* for whichever *printer-type* is associated with a print request using the filter.

As a last example, consider the template

    MODES prwidth\=\(.*\) = -w\1

Suppose a user gives the command

    lp -y prwidth=10

From the table above, the LP print service determines that the -y option is handled by a MODES template. The MODES template here works because the *pattern* prwidth\=\(.*\) matches the prwidth=10 given by the user. The *replacement* -w\1 causes the LP print service to generate the filter option -w10.

If necessary, the LP print service will construct a filter pipeline by concatenating several filters to handle the user's file and all the print options. (See sh(1) for a description of a pipeline.) If the print service constructs a filter pipeline, the INPUT and OUTPUT values used for each filter in the pipeline are the types of the input and output for that filter, not for the entire pipeline.

Deleting a Filter

The −x option is used to delete the filter specified in *filter-name* from the LP filter table.

Listing a Filter Description

The −l option is used to list the description of the filter named in *filter-name*. If the command is successful, the following message is sent to standard output:

```
Input types: content-type-list
Output types: content-type-list
Printer types: printer-type-list
Printers: printer-list
Filter type: filter-type
Command: shell-command
Options: template-list
```

If the command fails, an error message is sent to standard error.

SEE ALSO

lpadmin(1M).

lp(1) in the *User's Reference Manual*.

NAME
    lpforms – administer forms used with the LP print service

SYNOPSIS
    lpforms −f *form-name options*
    lpforms −f *form-name* −A *alert-type* [−Q *minutes*] [−W *requests*]

DESCRIPTION
    The lpforms command is used to administer the use of preprinted forms, such as
    company letterhead paper, with the LP print service. A form is specified by its
    form-name. Users may specify a form when submitting a print request [see lp(1)].
    The argument all can be used instead of *form-name* with either of the command
    lines shown above. The first command line allows the administrator to add,
    change, and delete forms, to list the attributes of an existing form, and to allow
    and deny users access to particular forms. The second command line is used to
    establish the method by which the administrator is alerted that the form *form-
    name* must be mounted on a printer.

    With the first lpforms command line, one of the following options must be used:

    −F *pathname*   To add or change form *form-name*, as specified by the infor-
                        mation in *pathname*

    −   To add or change form *form-name*, as specified by the infor-
                        mation from standard input

    −x   To delete form *form-name* (this option must be used
                        separately; it may not be used with any other option)

    −l   To list the attributes of form *form-name*

Adding or Changing a Form

    The −F *pathname* option is used to add a new form, *form-name*, to the LP print ser-
    vice, or to change the attributes of an existing form. The form description is
    taken from *pathname* if the −F option is given, or from the standard input if the −
    option is used. One of these two options must be used to define or change a
    form. *Pathname* is the path name of a file that contains all or any subset of the
    following information about the form.

    Page length: *scaled–decimal–number*$_1$
    Page width: *scaled–decimal–number*$_2$
    Number of pages: *integer*
    Line pitch: *scaled–decimal–number*$_3$
    Character pitch: *scaled–decimal–number*$_4$
    Character set choice: *character-set/print-wheel* [mandatory]
    Ribbon color: *ribbon-color*
    Comment:
    comment
    Alignment pattern: [*content-type*]
    content

    The term "scaled-decimal-number" refers to a non-negative number used to indi-
    cate a unit of size. The type of unit is shown by a "trailing" letter attached to the
    number. Three types of scaled decimal numbers can be used with the LP print

service: numbers that show sizes in centimeters (marked with a trailing c); numbers that show sizes in inches (marked with a trailing i); and numbers that show sizes in units appropriate to use (without a trailing letter), that is, lines, characters, lines per inch, or characters per inch.

Except for the last two lines, the above lines may appear in any order. The Comment: and *comment* items must appear in consecutive order but may appear before the other items, and the Alignment pattern: and the *content* items must appear in consecutive order at the end of the file. Also, the *comment* item may not contain a line that begins with any of the key phrases above, unless the key phrase is preceded with a > sign. Any leading > sign found in the *comment* will be removed when the comment is displayed. Case distinctions in the key phrases are ignored.

When this command is issued, the form specified by *form-name* is added to the list of forms. If the form already exists, its description is changed to reflect the new information. Once added, a form is available for use in a print request, except where access to the form has been restricted, as described under the –u option. A form may also be allowed to be used on certain printers only.

A description of each form attribute is below:

Page length and Page Width
> Before printing the content of a print request needing this form, the generic interface program provided with the LP print service will initialize the physical printer to handle pages *scaled–decimal–number*$_1$ long, and *scaled–decimal–number*$_2$ wide using the printer type as a key into the terminfo database.

The page length and page width will also be passed, if possible, to each filter used in a request needing this form.

Number of pages
> Each time the alignment pattern is printed, the LP print service will attempt to truncate the *content* to a single form by, if possible, passing to each filter the page subset of 1-*integer*.

Line pitch and Character pitch
> Before printing the content of a print request needing this form, the interface programs provided with the LP print service will initialize the physical printer to handle these pitches, using the printer type as a key into the terminfo database. Also, the pitches will be passed, if possible, to each filter used in a request needing this form. *Scaled-decimal-number*$_3$ is in lines per centimeter if a c is appended, and lines per inch otherwise; similarly, *scaled–decimal–number*$_4$ is in characters per centimeter if a c is appended, and characters per inch otherwise. The character pitch can also be given as elite (12 characters per inch), pica (10 characters per inch), or compressed (as many characters per inch as possible).

Character set choice
> When the LP print service alerts an administrator to mount this form, it will also mention that the print wheel *print-wheel* should be used on those printers that take print wheels. If printing with this form is to be done on

a printer that has selectable or loadable character sets instead of print wheels, the interface programs provided with the LP print service will automatically select or load the correct character set. If mandatory is appended, a user is not allowed to select a different character set for use with the form; otherwise, the character set or print wheel named is a suggestion and a default only.

Ribbon color
> When the LP print service alerts an administrator to mount this form, it will also mention that the color of the ribbon should be *ribbon-color*.

Comment
> The LP print service will display the *comment* unaltered when a user asks about this form [see lpstat(1)].

Alignment pattern
> When mounting this form an administrator can ask for the *content* to be printed repeatedly, as an aid in correctly positioning the preprinted form. The optional *content-type* defines the type of printer for which *content* had been generated. If *content-type* is not given, simple is assumed. Note that the *content* is stored as given, and will be readable only by the user lp.

When an existing form is changed with this command, items missing in the new information are left as they were. When a new form is added with this command, missing items will get the following defaults:

Page Length: 66
Page Width: 80
Number of Pages: 1
Line Pitch: 6
Character Pitch: 10
Character Set Choice: any
Ribbon Color: any

Deleting a Form
The −x option is used to delete the form *form-name* from the LP print service.

Listing Form Attributes
The −l option is used to list the attributes of the existing form *form-name*. The attributes listed are those described under **Adding and Changing a Form,** above. Because of the potentially sensitive nature of the alignment pattern, only the administrator can examine the form with this command. Other people may use the lpstat command to examine the non-sensitive part of the form description.

Allowing and Denying Access to a Form
The −u option, followed by the argument allow:*login-ID-list* or −u deny:*login-ID-list* lets you determine which users will be allowed to specify a particular form with a print request. This option can be used with the −F or − option, each of which is described above under **Adding or Changing a Form.**

The *login-ID-list* argument may include any or all of the following constructs:

login-ID	A user on any system
system_name!*login-ID*	A user on system *system_name*
system_name!all	All users on system *system_name*
all!*login-ID*	A user on all systems
all	All users on all systems

The LP print service keeps two lists of users for each form: an "allow-list" of people allowed to use the form, and a "deny-list" of people that may not use the form. With the −u allow option, the users listed are added to the allow-list and removed from the deny-list. With the −u deny option, the users listed are added to the deny-list and removed from the allow-list. (Both forms of the −u option can be run together with the −F or the − option.)

If the allow-list is not empty, only the users in the list are allowed access to the form, regardless of the contents of the deny-list. If the allow-list is empty but the deny-list is not, the users in the deny-list may not use the form, (but all others may use it). All users can be denied access to a form by specifying −f deny:all. All users can be allowed access to a form by specifying −f allow:all. (This is the default.)

Setting an Alert to Mount a Form

The −f *form-name* option is used with the −A *alert-type* option to define an alert to mount the form when there are queued jobs which need it. If this option is not used to arrange alerting for a form, no alert will be sent for that form.

The method by which the alert is sent depends on the value of the *alert-type* argument specified with the −A option. The *alert-types* are:

mail   Send the alert message via the mail command to the administrator.

write   Write the message, via the write command, to the terminal on which the administrator is logged in. If the administrator is logged in on several terminals, one is arbitrarily chosen.

quiet   Do not send messages for the current condition. An administrator can use this option to temporarily stop receiving further messages about a known problem. Once the form *form-name* has been mounted and subsequently unmounted, messages will again be sent when the number of print requests reaches the threshold specified by the −Q option.

none   Do not send messages until the −A option is given again with a different *alert-type* (other than quiet).

shell-command

Run the *shell-command* each time the alert needs to be sent. The shell command should expect the message in standard input. If there are blanks embedded in the command, enclose the command in quotes. Note that the mail and write values for this option are equivalent to the values mail *login-ID* and write *login-ID* respectively, where *login-ID* is the current name for the administrator. This will be the login name of the person submitting this command unless he or she has used the su command to change to another login-ID. If the su command has been used to change the user ID, then the *user-name* for the new ID is used.

list   Display the type of the alert for the form on standard output. No change is made to the alert.

The message sent appears as follows:

```
The form form-name needs to be mounted
on the printer(s):
printer (integer₁ requests).
integer₂ print requests await this form.
Use the ribbon-color ribbon.
Use the print-wheel print wheel, if appropriate.
```

The printers listed are those that the administrator had earlier specified were candidates for this form. The number *integer₁* listed next to each printer is the number of requests eligible for the printer. The number *integer₂* shown after the list of printers is the total number of requests awaiting the form. It will be less than the sum of the other numbers if some requests can be handled by more than one printer. The *ribbon-color* and *print-wheel* are those specified in the form description. The last line in the message is always sent, even if none of the printers listed use print wheels, because the administrator may choose to mount the form on a printer that does use a print wheel.

Where any color ribbon or any print wheel can be used, the statements above will read:

```
Use any ribbon.
Use any print-wheel.
```

If *form-name* is any, the alerting defined in this command applies to any form for which an alert has not yet been defined. If *form-name* is all, the alerting defined in this command applies to all forms.

If the −W option is not given, the default procedure is that only one message will be sent per need to mount the form. Not specifying the −W option is equivalent to specifying −W once or −W 0. If *minutes* is a number greater than 0, an alert will be sent at intervals specified by *minutes*.

If the −Q option is also given, the alert will be sent when a certain number (specified by the argument *requests*) of print requests that need the form are waiting. If the −Q option is not given, or the value of *requests* is 1 or any (which are both the default), a message is sent as soon as anyone submits a print request for the form when it is not mounted.

Listing the Current Alert

The −f option, followed by the −A option and the argument list is used to list the type of alert that has been defined for the specified form *form-name*. No change is made to the alert. If *form-name* is recognized by the LP print service, one of the following lines is sent to the standard output, depending on the type of alert for the form.

 − When *requests* requests are queued:
   alert with *shell-command* every *minutes* minutes

 − When *requests* requests are queued:
   write to *user-name* every *minutes* minutes

 − When *requests* requests are queued:
   mail to *user-name* every *minutes* minutes

 − No alert

The phrase **every** *minutes* **minutes** is replaced with once if *minutes* (−W *minutes*) is 0.

Terminating an Active Alert

The −A quiet option is used to stop messages for the current condition. An administrator can use this option to temporarily stop receiving further messages about a known problem. Once the form has been mounted and then unmounted, messages will again be sent when the number of print requests reaches the threshold *requests*.

Removing an Alert Definition

No messages will be sent after the −A none option is used until the −A option is given again with a different *alert-type*. This can be used to permanently stop further messages from being sent as any existing alert definition for the form will be removed.

SEE ALSO

lpadmin(1M), terminfo(4).

lp(1) in the *User's Reference Manual.*

NAME

lpsched, lpshut, lpmove − start/stop the LP print service and move requests

SYNOPSIS

/usr/lib/lp/lpsched
lpshut
lpmove *requests dest*
lpmove *dest*$_1$ *dest*$_2$

DESCRIPTION

lpsched starts the LP print service; this can be done only by root or lp.

lpshut shuts down the print service. All printers that are printing at the time lpshut is invoked will stop printing. When lpsched is started again, requests that were printing at the time a printer was shut down will be reprinted from the beginning.

lpmove moves requests that were queued by lp between LP destinations. The first form of the lpmove command shown above (under SYNOPSIS) moves the named *requests* to the LP destination *dest*. *Requests* are request-IDs as returned by lp. The second form of the lpmove command will attempt to move all requests for destination *dest*$_1$ to destination *dest*$_2$; lp will then reject any new requests for *dest*$_1$.

Note that when moving requests, lpmove never checks the acceptance status [see accept(1M)] of the new destination. Also, the request-IDs of the moved request are not changed, so that users can still find their requests. The lpmove command will not move requests that have options (content type, form required, and so on) that cannot be handled by the new destination.

If a request was originally queued for a class or the special destination any, and the first form of lpmove was used, the destination of the request will be changed to *new-destination*. A request thus affected will be printable only on *new-destination* and not on other members of the class or other acceptable printers if the original destination was any.

FILES

/var/spool/lp/*

SEE ALSO

accept(1M), lpadmin(1M).
enable(1), lp(1), lpstat(1) in the *User's Reference Manual*.

NAME

lpsystem – register remote systems with the print service

SYNOPSIS

lpsystem [–t *type*] [–T *timeout*] [–R *retry*] [–y "*comment*"] *system-name* [*system-name* ...]

lpsystem –l [*system-name* ...]

lpsystem –r *system-name* [*system-name* ...]

lpsystem –A

DESCRIPTION

The lpsystem command is used to define parameters for the LP print service, with respect to communication (via a high-speed network such as STARLAN or TCP/IP) with remote systems. Only a privileged user (that is, the owner of the login root) may execute the lpsystem command.

Specifically, the lpsystem command is used to define remote systems with which the local LP print service can exchange print requests. These remote systems are described to the local LP print service in terms of several parameters that control communication: type, retry and timeout. These parameters are defined in /etc/lp/Systems. You can edit this file with a text editor (such as vi) but editing is not recommended.

The *type* parameter defines the remote system as one of two types: s5 (System V Release 4) or bsd (SunOS). The default type is s5.

The *timeout* parameter specifies the length of time (in minutes) that the print service should allow a network connection to be idle. If the connection to the remote system is idle (that is, there is no network traffic) for N minutes, then drop the connection. (When there is more work the connection will be reestablished.) Legal values are n, 0, and N, where N is an integer greater than 0. The value n means "never time out"; 0 means "as soon as the connection is idle, drop it." The default is n.

The *retry* parameter specifies the length of time to wait before trying to reestablish a connection to the remote system, when the connection was dropped abnormally (that is, a network error). Legal values are n, 0, and N, where N is an integer greater than 0 and it means "wait N minutes before trying to reconnect. (The default is 10 minutes.) The value n means "do not retry dropped connections until there is more work"; 0 means "try to reconnect immediately."

The *comment* argument allows you to associate a free form comment with the system entry. This is visible when lpsystem –l is used.

System-name is the name of the remote system from which you want to be able to receive jobs, and to which you want to be able to send jobs.

The command lpsystem –l [*system-name*] will print out a description of the parameters associated with *system-name* (if a system has been specified), or with all the systems in its database (if *system-name* has not been specified).

The command lpsystem –r *system-name* will remove the entry associated with *system-name*. The print service will no longer accept jobs from that system or send jobs to it, even if the remote printer is still defined on the local system.

The command **lpsystem −A** will print out the TCP/IP address of the local machine in a format to be used when configuring the local port monitor to accept requests from a SunOS system.

NOTES:

With respect to /etc/lp/Systems, this information is relatively minimal with repect to controlling network communications. Network addresses and services are handled by the Netconfig and Netdir facilities (see the "Network Services" chapter in the *System Administrator's Guide* for a discussion of network addresses and services.) Port monitors handle listening for remote service requests and routing the connection to the print service (see the "Service Access" chapter in the *System Administrator's Guide* for a discusion of port monitors.)

If the Netconfig and Netdir facilities are not set up properly, out-bound remote print service probably will not work. Similarly, if the local port monitors are not set up to route remote print requests to the print service, then service for remote systems will not be provided. (See "Allowing Remote Systems to Access Local Printers" and "Configuring a Local Port Monitor" in the "Print Service" chapter of the *System Administrator's Guide* to find out how to do this.)

With respect to the semantics of the *timeout* and *retry* values, the print service uses one process for each remote system with which it communicates, and it communicates with a remote system only when there is work to be done on that system or work being sent from that system.

The system initiating the connection is the "master" process and the system accepting the connection is the "slave" process. This designation serves only to determine which process dies (the slave) when a connection is dropped. This helps prevent there from being more than one process communicating with a remote system. Furthermore, all connections are bi-directional, regardless of the master/slave designation. You cannot control a system's master/slave designation. Now, keeping all this information in mind, if a master process times out, then both the slave and master will exit. If a slave times out, then it is possible that the master may still live and retry the connection after the retry interval. Therefore, one system's resource management strategy can effect another system's strategy.

With respect to lpsystem −A: a SunOS system (described with −t bsd) can be connected to your system only via TCP/IP, and print requests from a SunOS system can come in to your machine only via a special port (515). The address given to you from lpsystem will be the address of your system and port 515. This address is used by your TCP/IP port monitor (see sacadm(1M) and nlsadmin(1M)) to "listen" on that address and port, and to route connections to the print service. (This procedure is discussed in the "Service Access" chapter of the *System Administrator's Guide*.) The important point here is that this is where you get the address refered to in that procedure.

The command lpsystem −A will not work if your system name and IP address are not listed in /etc/inet/hosts and the printer service is not listed in /etc/inet/services.

FILES

/var/spool/lp/* /etc/lp/*

SEE ALSO

netconfig(4)
Network Programmer's Guide
System Administrator's Guide

NAME
lpusers – set printing queue priorities

SYNOPSIS
lpusers −d *priority-level*
lpusers −q *priority-level* −u *login-ID-list*
lpusers −u *login-ID-list*
lpusers −q *priority-level*
lpusers −l

DESCRIPTION
The lpusers command is used to set limits to the queue priority level that can be assigned to jobs submitted by users of the LP print service.

The first form of the command (with −d) sets the system-wide priority default to *priority-level*, where *priority-level* is a value of 0 to 39, with 0 being the highest priority. If a user does not specify a priority level with a print request [see lp(1)], the default priority is used. Initially, the default priority level is 20.

The second form of the command (with −q and −u) sets the default highest *priority-level* (0-39) that the users in *login-ID-list* can request when submitting a print request. The *login-ID-list* argument may include any or all of the following constructs:

login-ID	A user on any system
system_name!*login-ID*	A user on the system *system_name*
system_name!all	All users on system *system_name*
all!*login-ID*	A user on all systems
all	All users on all systems

Users that have been given a limit cannot submit a print request with a higher priority level than the one assigned, nor can they change a request already submitted to have a higher priority. Any print requests submitted with priority levels higher than allowed will be given the highest priority allowed.

The third form of the command (with −u) removes any explicit priority level for the specified users.

The fourth form of the command (with −q) sets the default highest priority level for all users not explicitly covered by the use of the second form of this command.

The last form of the command (with −l) lists the default priority level and the priority limits assigned to users.

SEE ALSO
lp(1) in the *User's Reference Manual*.

NAME

mail_pipe – invoke recipient command for incoming mail

SYNOPSIS

mail_pipe [-x *debug_level*] -r *recipient* -R *path_to_sender* -c *content_type* -S *subject*

DESCRIPTION

When a new mail message arrives, the mail command first checks if the recipient's mailbox indicates that the message is to be forwarded elsewhere (to some other recipient or as the input to some command). If the message is to be piped into a recipient-specified command, mail invokes mail_pipe to do some validation and then execute the command in the context of the recipient.

Command-line arguments are:

-x *debug_level*	Turn on debugging for this invocation. See the description of the -x option for the mail command for details.
-r *recipient*	The recipient's login id.
-R *path_to_sender*	The return address to the message's originator.
-c *content_type*	The value of the Content-Type: header line in the message.
-S *subject*	The value of the Subject: header line in the message if present.

mail_pipe is installed as a setuid-to-root process, thus enabling itself to change it's user and group ids to that of the recipient as necessary.

When invoked, mail_pipe performs the following steps (if a step fails, the exit code is noted as [*N*]):
- Validate invocation arguments [1].
- Verify that recipient name is ≤ 14 characters long [2].
- Verify that the setgid flag for the recipient mailbox is set [3].
- Open /var/mail/*recipient* [4].
- Verify that recipient's mailbox starts with the string Forward to [5].
- Find pipe symbol indicating start of command string in recipient mailbox [6].
- Find entry for recipient in /etc/passwd [7].
- Set gid to recipient's gid [8].
- Set uid to recipient's uid [9].
- Change current directory to recipient's login directory [10].
- Allocate space to hold newly exec'ed environment for recipient command [11].
- Parse the recipient command, performing any %*keyword* expansions required. See the 'Forwarding mail' section of mail(1), for more information regarding %*keyword* substitutions [12].
- Execute recipient command [13 if exec fails, otherwise exit code from recipient command itself].

FILES

/etc/passwd	to identify sender and locate recipients
/var/mail/*recipient*	incoming mail for *recipient*; that is, the mail file
/tmp/MLDBG*	debug trace file

/usr/lib/mail/mail_pipe   mail_pipe program

SEE ALSO
     mail(1), notify(1), vacation(1)

NAME

makefsys – create a file system

SYNOPSIS

makefsys

DESCRIPTION

The makefsys command allows you to create a file system.

The command invokes a visual interface (the make task available through the sysadm command).

The initial prompt allows you to select the device on which to create the file system. After selecting the device, you are asked some further questions before the file system is created.

The identical function is available under the sysadm menu:

sysadm make

DIAGNOSTICS

The makefsys command exits with one of the following values:

0   Normal exit.

2   Invalid command syntax. A usage message is displayed.

7   The visual interface for this command is not available because it cannot invoke fmli. (The FMLI package is not installed or is corrupted.)

SEE ALSO

checkfsys(1M), labelit(1M), mkfs(1M), mountfsys(1M), sysadm(1M).

NAME

migration − move an archive from one set of volumes to another

SYNOPSIS

migration −B [−dlmotuvAENS] bkjobid ofsname ofsdev ofslab descript

DESCRIPTION

migration is invoked as a child process by bkdaemon(1M) to move an existing archive made by some other arbitrary method to a new set of volumes. The existing backup history log entry of the archive is updated to reflect the new volumes and destination information of the archive.

bkjobid is the job id assigned by backup(1M). ofsdev is the name of the UNIX raw (character) device on which the archive resides. *ofslab* is the volume label on the archive [see labelit(1M)]. *descript* is a description for a destination device in the form:

dgroup:dname:dchar:dlabels

dgroup specifies a device group. dname specifies a device name. *dchars* specifies characteristics for the specified device and group (see device.tab(4) for a further description of device characteristics). *dlabels* specifies the media names for the media to be used for the archive.

Options

d*   Do not update the backup history log entry for the archive.

l*   Create a long form of the backup history log that includes a table-of-contents for the archive. This includes the data used to generate an *ls -l*-like listing of each file in the archive.

m*   Mount the originating filesystem read-only before starting the backup and remount it with its original permissions after completing the backup.

o   Permit the user to override media insertion requests (see getvol(1M) −o).

t*   Create a table of contents for the backup on additional media instead of in the backup history log.

u*   Unmount the originating filesystem before performing the backup and remount it with its original permissions after completing the backup.

v*   Validate the archive as it is written. A checksum is computed as the archive is being written; as each medium is completed, it is re-read and the checksum recomputed to verify that each block is readable and correct. If either check fails, the medium is considered unreadable. If −A has been specified, the archiving operation fails; otherwise, the operator is prompted to replace the failed medium.

A   Do not prompt the user for removable media operations (automated operation).

E*   Report an estimate of media usage for the archive; then perform the
        backup.

N*   Report an estimate of media usage for the archive; do not perform the
        backup.

S*   Generate a period (.) for every 100 (512 byte) blocks read-from or
        written-to the archive on the destination device.

User Interactions

The connection between an archiving method and backup(1M) is more complex
than a simple fork/exec or pipe. backup(1M) is responsible for all interactions
with the user, either directly, or through bkoper(1M). Therefore, migration neither reads from standard-input nor writes to standard-output or standard-error.
A method library must be used [see libbrmeth(3)] to communicate reports (estimates, periods, status, etc.) to backup(1M).

DIAGNOSTICS

If migration successfully completes its task, it exits with a 0 status. If any of the
parameters to migration are invalid, it exits with a 1 status. If any error occurs
which causes migration to fail to complete *all* portions of its task, it exits with a
2 status.

Errors are reported if any of the following occur:

1.   −t is specified together with −A.

2.   −A is specified together with −o.

3.   −t is specified and the destination device does not support removable
     media.

4.   −A is specified and more than one removable medium is required.

5.   Unrecoverable errors occurred in trying to read or write the destination
     device.

6.   −m is specified and the originating filesystem could not be mounted read-
     only.

7.   −m is specified and the originating filesystem could not be unmounted.

8.   −o is not specified and insufficient media names are supplied in *descript*.

9.   −u is specified and the filesystem could not be unmounted.

10. −u is specified and the filesystem could not be remounted.

FILES

/usr/oam/bkrs/tables/bkhist.tab
$TMP/filelist$$

SEE ALSO

awk(1), backup(1M), device.tab(4), getvol(1M), grep(1), labelit(1M), lib-
brmeth(3), ls(1), prtvtoc(1M), restore(1M), rsoper(1M), sed(1), time(2),
urestore(1M).

NAME

mkboot – convert an object file to a bootable object file

SYNOPSIS

/usr/sbin/mkboot [–m *master*] [–d *directory*] –k *kernel_obj* [–f *kernel_master*]

/usr/sbin/mkboot [–m *master*] [–d *directory*] *obj_file*

DESCRIPTION

The mkboot command is used to create a new object file from a previous object file and its associated master file; the new object file can be used by the cunix program to configure a new bootable operating system.

Typically, a user makes changes to one or more files in the directory /etc/master.d [files in this directory are called master files, and are in the format specified in the master(4) manual page].

Then, the user executes a mkboot command (with appropriate options) from the /boot directory; the /boot directory is used to hold all device driver object files that must be configured into the bootable operating system so that the operating system correctly reflects the current configuration of the machine.

One mkboot command must be executed for each master file changed. The mkboot command updates the existing object file in /boot with the changes made to its associated master file.

After executing all necessary mkboot commands, the user then either configures a new bootable operating system from firmware mode and reboots the system, or uses the cunix command to configure a new bootable operating system at the user level.

The user must specify either the –k option with the kernel object file name (usually KERNEL), or the name of another object file to be changed (usually a file in /boot). The object file name used can be a relative or full pathname, and can have an optional .o suffix.

If the –k option is used, the master file name kernel is assumed; –f can be used to specify a master file other than kernel to build the *kernel_obj* object.

If *obj_file* is specified instead of –k, the named *obj_file* must have an associated file in /etc/master.d; the name of the associated master file is the name of the *obj_file* in lowercase letters, without any path prefix or .o suffix.

If you are making a new object file for the kernel, you must use the –k option to specify the kernel object file; if you process a kernel object file without the –k option, the resulting object file will be unusable by cunix (an error is returned by cunix that says that no object was flagged as the kernel; this flag is added to the object file only when –k is specified).

The –m and –d options are used to specify alternate locations for master files and object files output by mkboot:

–m *master*   This option specifies the directory containing the master files to be used for the object file. The default *master* directory is /etc/master.d.

−d *directory*   This option specifies the directory to be used for storing the new object file. The default output *directory* is /boot.

To create a new object file, the applicable master file is read and the configuration information is extracted. Then, the old object file is read from the current directory, and changed to reflect the new configuration information. The resulting new object file is written to the output directory specified by the −d option or to /boot. It is given the same name as specified by *obj_file* or *kernel_obj*, in uppercase letters and without any .o suffix.

Note that if the output directory is the same as the current working directory when mkboot is executed, then the output object file overwrites the previous object file residing in the directory.

EXAMPLE
        mkboot −m newmaster gentty.o

This will read the file named gentty from the directory newmaster for the gentty device configuration data, take the file gentty.o from the current directory, and create the object file /boot/GENTTY for use in configuring a new operating system.

        cd /boot; mkboot −k KERNEL

This will read the file named kernel from the directory /etc/master.d for the new kernel configuration data, take the file KERNEL from the current directory, and create the /boot/KERNEL object file.

        cd /boot; mkboot sem

This will read the file named sem from the /etc/master.d directory, take the file SEM from the current directory (/boot), and place the output file in /boot/SEM.

DIAGNOSTICS
        mkboot FILE   (FILE does not exist)

        mkboot: FILE: cannot open: No such file or directory

        mkboot −d dir SEM   (dir does not exist)

        mkboot: dir: cannot open: No such file or directory
        mkboot: SEM; not processed

SEE ALSO
        cunix(1M), master(4)

        System Administrator's Guide

NAME
mkfifo – make FIFO special file

SYNOPSIS
mkfifo path ...

DESCRIPTION
mkfifo creates the FIFO special files named by its argument list. The arguments are taken sequentially, in the order specified; and each FIFO special file is either created completely or, in the case of an error or signal, not created at all.

For each *path* argument, the mkfifo command behaves as if the function mkfifo [see mkfifo(3C)] was called with the argument *path* set to *path* and the *mode* set to the bitwise inclusive OR of S_IRUSR, S_IWUSR, S_IRGRP, S_IWGRP, S_IROTH and S_IWOTH.

If errors are encountered in creating one of the special files, mkfifo writes a diagnostic message to the standard error and continues with the remaining arguments, if any.

SEE ALSO
mkfifo(3C) in the *Programmer's Reference Manual*.

DIAGNOSTICS
mkfifo returns exit code 0 if all FIFO special files were created normally; otherwise it prints a diagnostic and returns a value greater than 0.

NAME

mkfs (generic) – construct a file system

SYNOPSIS

mkfs [–F *FSType*] [–V] [–m] [*current_options*] [–o *specific_options*] *special* [*operands*]

DESCRIPTION

mkfs constructs a file system by writing on the *special* file; *special* must be the first argument. The file system is created based on the *FSType, specific_options* and *operands* specified on the command line. mkfs waits 10 seconds before starting to construct the file system. During this time the command can be aborted by entering a delete (DEL).

operands are *FSType*-specific and the *FSType* specific manual page of mkfs should be consulted for a detailed description.

current_options are options supported by the s5-specific module of mkfs. Other *FSTypes* do not necessarily support these options. *specific_options* indicate suboptions specified in a comma-separated list of suboptions and/or keyword-attribute pairs for interpretation by the *FSType*-specific module of the command.

The options are:

–F Specify the *FSType* to be constructed. The *FSType* should either be specified here or be determinable from /etc/vfstab by matching the *special* with an entry in the table.

–V Echo the complete command line, but do not execute the command. The command line is generated by using the options and arguments provided by the user and adding to them information derived from /etc/vfstab. This option should be used to verify and validate the command line.

–m Return the command line which was used to create the file system. The file system must already exist. This option provides a means of determining the command used in constructing the file system. It cannot be used with *current_options, specific_options*, or *operands*. It must be invoked by itself.

–o Specify *FSType*-specific options.

NOTES

This command may not be supported for all *FSTypes*.

FILES

/etc/vfstab   list of default parameters for each file system

SEE ALSO

makefsys(1M), vfstab(4).
Manual pages for the *FSType*-specific modules of mkfs.

NAME

    mkfs (bfs) – construct a boot file system

SYNOPSIS

    mkfs [−F bfs] *special blocks* [*inodes*]

DESCRIPTION

    mkfs is used to create a boot file system, which is a contiguous flat file system, to hold the bootable programs and data files necessary for the boot procedure.

    The argument *special* is the device special file that refers to the partition on which the file system is to be created. The *blocks* argument is used to specify the size of the file system. The block size is automatically 512 bytes.

    The *inodes* argument specifies the number of files that the file system will hold.

NOTES

    This file system is intended to hold the bootable files and data files for the boot procedure. Use as a general purpose file system is not recommended.

SEE ALSO

    See the *System Administrator's Guide* for more information about the boot file system.

NAME

mkfs (s5) – construct an s5 file system

SYNOPSIS

mkfs [–F s5] [*generic_options*] *special*

mkfs [–F s5] [*generic_options*] [–b *block_size*] *special blocks[:i-nodes]* [*gap blocks/cyl*]

mkfs [–F s5] [*generic_options*] [–b *block_size*] *special proto* [*gap blocks/cyl*]

DESCRIPTION

generic_options are options supported by the generic mkfs command.

mkfs constructs an s5 file system by writing on the *special* file using the values found in the remaining arguments of the command line. mkfs builds a file system with a root directory and a lost+found directory.

The options are:

–F s5   Specifies an s5-FSType.

–b *blocksize*

Specifies the logical block size for the file system. The logical block size is the number of bytes read or written by the operating system in a single I/O operation. Valid values for *blocksize* are 512, 1024, and 2048. The default is 1024.

If the second argument to mkfs is a string of digits, the size of the file system is the value of *blocks* interpreted as a decimal number. This is the number of *physical* (512 byte) disk blocks the file system will occupy. If the number of i-nodes is not given, the default is approximately the number of *logical* blocks divided by 4. mkfs builds a file system with a single empty directory on it. The boot program block (block zero) is left uninitialized.

If the second argument is the name of a file that can be opened, mkfs assumes it to be a prototype file *proto*, and will take its directions from that file. The prototype file contains tokens separated by spaces or new-lines. A sample prototype specification follows (line numbers have been added to aid in the explanation):

```
1.    /dev/c1d0s0
2.    4872 110
3.    d--777 3 1
4.    usr    d--777 3 1
5.           sh     ---755 3 1 /sbin/sh
6.           ken    d--755 6 1
7.           $
8.           b0     b--644 3 1 0 0
9.           c0     c--644 3 1 0 0
10.          slnk   l--777 2 2 /var/tmp
11.          $
12.    $
```

Line 1 in the example is the name of a file to be copied onto block zero as the bootstrap program.

Line 2 specifies the number of *physical* (512 byte) blocks the file system is to occupy and the number of i-nodes in the file system.

Lines 3-10 tell mkfs about files and directories to be included in this file system.

Line 3 specifies the root directory.

Lines 4-6 and 8-10 specify other directories and files.

Line 10 specifies the symbolic link slnk set up in /usr and containing /var/tmp.

The $ on line 7 tells mkfs to end the branch of the file system it is on, and continue from the next higher directory. The $ on lines 11 and 12 end the process, since no additional specifications follow.

File specifications give the mode, the user ID, the group ID, and the initial contents of the file. Valid syntax for the contents field depends on the first character of the mode.

The mode for a file is specified by a 6-character string. The first character specifies the type of the file. The character range is −bcdl to specify regular, block special, character special, directory, and symbolic link files respectively. The second character of the mode is either u or − to specify set-user-id mode or not. The third is g or − for the set-group-id mode. The rest of the mode is a 3 digit octal number giving the owner, group, and other read, write, execute permissions (see *chmod*(1)).

Two decimal number tokens come after the mode; they specify the user and group IDs of the owner of the file.

If the file is a regular file, the next token of the specification may be a path name whence the contents and size are copied. If the file is a block or character special file, two decimal numbers follow which give the major and minor device numbers. If the file is a directory, mkfs makes the entries . and .. and then reads a list of names and (recursively) file specifications for the entries in the directory. As noted above, the scan is terminated with the token $.

The *gap blocks/cyl* argument in both forms of the command specifies the rotational gap and the number of blocks/cylinder. The following values are recommended for the devices available on the 3B2:

NAME
    mkfs (ufs) – construct a ufs file system

SYNOPSIS
    mkfs [–F ufs] [*generic_options*] *special*
    mkfs [–F ufs] [*generic_options*] [–o *specific_options*] *special size*

DESCRIPTION
    generic_options are options supported by the generic mkfs command.

    mkfs constructs a file system by writing on the special file *special* unless the '–o
    N' flag has been specified. The numeric *size* specifies the number of sectors in the
    file system. mkfs builds a file system with a root directory and a lost+found
    directory [see fsck(1M)]. The number of inodes is calculated as a function of the
    file system size.

    The options are:

    –F ufs
        Specifies the ufs-FSType.

    –o   Specify ufs file system specific options. The following options are available:

        N   Do not write the file system to the *special* file. This suboption gives
                 all the information needed to create a file system but does not
                 create it.

        nsect   The number of sectors per track on the disk. The default is 18.

        ntrack   The number of tracks per cylinder on the disk. The default is 9.

        bsize   The primary block size for files on the file system. It must be a
                 power of two, currently selected from 4096 or 8192 (the default).

        fragsize
                 The fragment size for files on the file system. The *fragsize*
                 represents the smallest amount of disk space that will be allocated
                 to a file. It must be a power of two currently selected from the
                 range 512 to 8192. The default is 1024.

        cgsize   The number of disk cylinders per cylinder group. This number
                 must be in the range 1 to 32. The default is 16.

        free   The minimum percentage of free disk space allowed. Once the file
                 system capacity reaches this threshold, only a privileged user is
                 allowed to allocate disk blocks. The default value is 10%.

        rps   The rotational speed of the disk, in revolutions per second. The
                 default is 60.

        nbpi   The number of bytes for which one inode block is allocated. This
                 parameter is currently set at one inode block for every 2048 bytes.

        opt   Space or time optimization preference; s specifies optimization for
                 space, t specifies optimization for time. The default is t.

apc   The number of alternates per cylinder (SCSI devices only). The
       default is 0.

gap   The expected time (in milliseconds) to service a transfer completion
       interrupt and initiate a new transfer on the same disk. It is used to
       decide how much rotational spacing to place between successive
       blocks in a file. The default is 4.

NOTES

The value of the nbpi operand in the output of mkfs −m is always 2048, even if
the file system was created with some other value.

SEE ALSO

fsck(1M), generic mkfs(1M), dir(4), ufs(4).

NAME

mknod – make a special file

SYNOPSIS

/sbin/mknod *name* b | c *major minor*

/sbin/mknod *name* p

DESCRIPTION

mknod makes a directory entry for a special file.

In the first case, *name* is the special file to be created. The second argument is b to indicate a block-type special file or c to indicate a character-type. The last two arguments are numbers specifying the *major* and *minor* device numbers; these may be either decimal or octal. The assignment of major device numbers is specific to each system. You must be the super-user to use this form of the command.

The second case is used to create a FIFO (named pipe).

NOTES

If mknod is used to create a device in a remote directory (Remote File Sharing), the major and minor device numbers are interpreted by the server.

SEE ALSO

mknod(2) in the *Programmer's Reference Manual*.

NAME

montbl – create monetary database

SYNOPSIS

montbl [–o *outfile*] *infile*

DESCRIPTION

The montbl command takes as input a specification file, *infile*, that describes the formatting conventions for monetary quantities for a specific locale.

–o *outfile*   Write the output on *outfile*; otherwise, write the output on a file named LC_MONETARY.

The output of montbl is suitable for use by the localeconv() function (see localeconv(3C)). Before *outfile* can be used by localeconv(), it must be installed in the /usr/lib/locale/*locale* directory with the name LC_MONETARY by someone who is super-user or a member of group bin. *locale* is the locale whose monetary formatting conventions are described in *infile*. This file must be readable by user, group, and other; no other permissions should be set. To use formatting conventions for monetary quantities described in this file, use setlocale(3C) to change the locale for category LC_MONETARY to *locale* [see setlocale(3C)].

Once installed, this file will be used by the localeconv() function to initialize the monetary specific fields of a structure of type struct lconv. For a description of each field in this structure, see localeconv(3C).

```
struct        lconv        {
        char *decimal_point;            /* "." */
        char *thousands_sep;            /* "" (zero length string) */
        char *grouping;                 /* "" */
        char *int_curr_symbol;          /* "" */
        char *currency_symbol;          /* "" */
        char *mon_decimal_point;        /* "" */
        char *mon_thousands_sep;        /* "" */
        char *mon_grouping;             /* "" */
        char *positive_sign;            /* "" */
        char *negative_sign;            /* "" */
        char int_frac_digits;           /* CHAR_MAX */
        char frac_digits;               /* CHAR_MAX */
        char p_cs_precedes;             /* CHAR_MAX */
        char p_sep_by_space;            /* CHAR_MAX */
        char n_cs_precedes;             /* CHAR_MAX */
        char n_sep_by_space;            /* CHAR_MAX */
        char p_sign_posn;               /* CHAR_MAX */
        char n_sign_posn;               /* CHAR_MAX */
};
```

The specification file specifies the value of each struct lconv member, except for the first three members, *decimal_point*, *thousands_sep*, and *grouping* which are set by the LC_NUMERIC category of setlocale(3C). Each member's value is given on a line with the following format:

> *keyword* <white space> *value*

where *keyword* is identical to the `struct lconv` field name and *value* is a quoted string for those fields that are a `char *` and an integer for those fields that are an `int`. For example,

```
int_curr_symbol          "ITL."
int_frac_digits          0
```

will set the international currency symbol and the number of fractional digits to be displayed in an internationally formatted monetary quantity to `ITL.` and 0, respectively.

Blank lines and lines starting with a # are taken to be comments and are ignored. A character in a string may be in octal or hex representation. For example, \141 or \x61 could be used to represent the letter 'a'. If there is no specification line for a given structure member, then the default 'C' locale value for that member is used (see the values in comments in the `struct lconv` definition above).

Given below is an example of what the specification file for Italy would look like:

```
# Italy

int_curr_symbol          "ITL."
currency_symbol          "L."
mon_decimal_point        ""
mon_thousands_sep        "."
mon_grouping             "\3"
positive_sign            ""
negative_sign            "-"
int_frac_digits          0
frac_digits              0
p_cs_precedes            1
p_sep_by_space           0
n_cs_precedes            1
n_sep_by_space           0
p_sign_posn              1
n_sign_posn              1
```

FILES

/usr/lib/locale/*locale*/LC_MONETARY
      LC_MONETARY database for *locale*

/usr/lib/locale/C/montbl_C
      input file used to construct LC_MONETARY in the default locale.

SEE ALSO

localeconv(3C), setlocale(3C) in the *Programmer's Reference Manual*.

NAME

mount, umount (generic) – mount or unmount file systems and remote resources

SYNOPSIS

mount [–v |–p]

mount [–F *FSType*] [–V] [*current_options*] [–o *specific_options*] {*special* | *mount_point*}

mount [–F *FSType*] [–V] [*current_options*] [–o *specific_options*] *special mount_point*

umount [–V] [–o *specific_options*] {*special* | *mount_point*}

DESCRIPTION

File systems other than root (/) are considered removable in the sense that they can be either available to users or unavailable. mount notifies the system that *special*, a block special device or a remote resource, is available to users from the *mount_point* which must already exist; it becomes the name of the root of the newly mounted *special* or resource.

mount, when entered with arguments, validates all arguments except for the device name and invokes a *FSType* specific mount module. If invoked with no arguments, mount lists all the mounted file systems from the mount table. If invoked with any of the following partial argument lists, for example, one of *special* or *mount_point* or when both arguments are specified but no *FSType* is specified mount will search /etc/vfstab to fill in the missing arguments: *FSType, special, mount_point*, and *specific_options*. It will then invoke the *FSType*-specific mount module.

Most *FSTypes* do not have a umount specific module. If one exists it is executed otherwise the generic unmounts the file systems. If the –o option is specified the umount specific module is always executed.

current_options are options supported by the s5-specific module of mount and umount. Other *FSTypes* do not necessarily support these options. *specific_options* indicate suboptions specified in a comma-separated list of suboptions and/or keyword-attribute pairs for interpretation by the *FSType*-specific module of the command.

The options are:

–v   Print the output in a new style. The new output has the *FSType* and flags displayed in addition to the old output. The *mount_point* and *special* fields are reversed.

–p   Print the list of mounted file systems in the /etc/vfstab format.

–F   used to specify the *FSType* on which to operate. The *FSType* must be specified or must be determinable from /etc/vfstab while mounting a file system.

–V   Echo the complete command line, but do not execute the command. The command line is generated by using the options and arguments provided by the user and adding to them information derived from /etc/vfstab. This option should be used to verify and validate the command line.

       −o   used to specify *FSType*-specific options.

mount can be used by any user to list mounted file systems and resources. Only a super-user can mount or unmount file systems.

NOTES

The old output format will be phased out in a future release and all output will be in the new −v format. The most significant changes are the addition of two new fields to show the *FSType* and flags and the reversal of the *mount_point* and *special* name.

mount adds an entry to the mount table /etc/mnttab; umount removes an entry from the table.

FILES

       /etc/mnttab   mount table
       /etc/vfstab   list of default parameters for each file system.

SEE ALSO

       setmnt(1M), mountfsys(1M), umountfsys(1M), mnttab(4), vfstab(4).
       Manual pages for the *FSType*-specific modules of mount.

NAME
        mount (bfs) - mount bfs file systems

SYNOPSIS
        mount [-F bfs] [*generic_options*] [-r] [-o *specific_options*] {*special* | *mount_point*}
        mount [-F bfs] [*generic_options*] [-r] [-o *specific_options*] *special* | *mount_point*

DESCRIPTION
        generic_options are options supported by the generic mount command.

        mount attaches a bfs file system to the file system hierarchy at the pathname
        location *mount_point*, which must already exist. If *mount_point* has any contents
        prior to the mount operation, these are hidden until the file system is unmounted.

        The options are:

        -F bfs   specify the bfs FSType

        -r   mount the file system read-only

        -o   specify the bfs-specific suboptions. The following suboptions are
                  available:

                  rw | ro   - read/write or read-only
                             Default is read/write.

        Only a privileged user can mount file systems.

FILES
        /etc/mnttab

SEE ALSO
        generic mount(1M), mountfsys(1M), umountfsys(1M), mount(2), mnttab(4)

NAME

    mount – mount remote NFS resources

SYNOPSIS

    mount [–F nfs] [–r] [–o *specific_options*] [*resource mountpoint*]

DESCRIPTION

The mount command attaches a named *resource* to the file system hierarchy at the pathname location *mountpoint*, which must already exist. If *mountpoint* has any contents prior to the mount operation, the contents remain hidden until the *resource* is once again unmounted.

If the resource is listed in the **vfstab** file, the command line can specify either *resource* or *mountpoint*, and mount will consult **vfstab** for more information. If the –F option is omitted, mount will take the file system type from **vfstab**.

mount maintains a table of mounted file systems in **/etc/mnttab**, described in mnttab(4).

The following options are available to the mount command:

–r   Mount the specified file system read-only.

–o *specific_options*

    Specify file system specific options in a comma-separated list of words from the list below.

rw | ro	*resource* is mounted read-write or read-only. The default is **rw**.
suid | nosuid	Setuid execution allowed or disallowed. The default is **suid**.
remount	If a file system is mounted read-only, remounts the file system read-write.
bg | fg	If the first attempt fails, retry in the background, or, in the foreground. The default is **fg**.
retry=*n*	The number of times to retry the mount operation. The default is 10000.
port=*n*	The server IP port number. The default is NFS_PORT.
grpid	Create a file with its GID set to the effective GID of the calling process. This behavior may be overridden on a per-directory basis by setting the set-GID bit of the parent directory; in this case, the GID is set to the GID of the parent directory [see open(2) and mkdir(2)]. Files created on file systems that are *not* mounted with the grpid option will obey BSD semantics; that is, the GID is unconditionally inherited from that of the parent directory.
rsize=*n*	Set the read buffer size to *n* bytes.
wsize=*n*	Set the write buffer size to *n* bytes.
timeo=*n*	Set the NFS timeout to *n* tenths of a second.
retrans=*n*	Set the number of NFS retransmissions to *n*.
soft | hard	Return an error if the server does not respond, or continue the retry request until the server responds.

intr	Allow keyboard interrupts to kill a process that is hung while waiting for a response on a hard-mounted file system.
secure	Use a more secure protocol for NFS transactions.
noac	Suppress attribute caching.
acregmin=*n*	Hold cached attributes for at least *n* seconds after file modification.
acregmax=*n*	Hold cached attributes for no more than *n* seconds after file modification.
acdirmin=*n*	Hold cached attributes for at least *n* seconds after directory update.
acdirmax=*n*	Hold cached attributes for no more than *n* seconds after directory update.
actimeo=*n*	Set *min* and *max* times for regular files and directories to *n* seconds.

NFS FILE SYSTEMS

Background vs. Foreground

File systems mounted with the bg option indicate that mount is to retry in the background if the server's mount daemon [mountd(1M)] does not respond. mount retries the request up to the count specified in the retry=*n* option. Once the file system is mounted, each NFS request made in the kernel waits timeo=*n* tenths of a second for a response. If no response arrives, the time-out is multiplied by 2 and the request is retransmitted. When the number of retransmissions has reached the number specified in the retrans=*n* option, a file system mounted with the soft option returns an error on the request; one mounted with the hard option prints a warning message and continues to retry the request.

Read-Write vs. Read-Only

File systems that are mounted rw (read-write) should use the hard option.

Secure File Systems

The secure option must be given if the server requires secure mounting for the file system.

File Attributes

The attribute cache retains file attributes on the client. Attributes for a file are assigned a time to be flushed. If the file is modified before the flush time, then the flush time is extended by the time since the last modification (under the assumption that files that changed recently are likely to change soon). There is a minimum and maximum flush time extension for regular files and for directories. Setting actimeo=*n* extends flush time by *n* seconds for both regular files and directories.

EXAMPLES

To mount a remote file system: mount −F nfs serv:/usr/src /usr/src
To hard mount a remote file system: mount −o hard serv:/usr/src /usr/src

FILES

/etc/mnttab   table of mounted file systems
/etc/dfs/fstypes   default distributed file system type
/etc/vfstab   table of automatically mounted resources

SEE ALSO

mountall(1M), mount(2), umount(2), mnttab(4).

NOTES

If the directory on which a file system is to be mounted is a symbolic link, the file system is mounted on *the directory to which the symbolic link refers,* rather than being mounted on top of the symbolic link itself.

NAME

    mount – mount remote resources

SYNOPSIS

    mount [–F rfs] [–o nocaching][,ro|rw] [,suid|nosuid] [–cr] *resource directory*

DESCRIPTION

    The mount command makes a remote *resource* available to users from the mount point *directory*. The command adds an entry to the table of mounted devices, /etc/mnttab.

    If multiple transport providers are installed and administrators attempt to mount a resource over them, the transport providers should be specified as network IDs in the /etc/netconfig file. The NETPATH environment variable can be used to specify the sequence of transport providers mount will use to attempt a connection to a server machine (NETPATH=tcp:starlan). If only one transport provider is installed and /etc/netconfig has not been set up, all resources will be mounted over this transport provider by default.

    The following options are available:

        –o *suboption*

            nocaching   Disable client caching.

            [rw|ro]   *resource* is to be mounted read/write or read-only. The default is read/write.

            [suid|nosuid] set-uid bits are to be obeyed or ignored, respectively, on execution. The default is nosuid.

        –c   Disable client caching. This is the same as –o nocaching.

        –r   *resource* is to be mounted read-only. If the *resource* is write-protected, this flag, or the –o ro flag, must be used.

FILES

    /etc/mnttab
    /etc/netconfig
    /etc/vfstab

SEE ALSO

    umount(1M),   share(1M),   fuser(1M),   unshare(1M),   dfshares(1M), dfmounts(1M), netconfig(4), mnttab(4), vfstab(1M)

NAME

    mount (s5) – mount an s5 file system

SYNOPSIS

    mount [−F s5] [*generic_options*] [−r] [−o *specific_options*] {*special* | *mount_point*}
    mount [−F s5] [*generic_options*] [−r] [−o *specific_options*] *special mount_point*

DESCRIPTION

    generic_options are options supported by the generic mount command.

    mount notifies the system that *special*, an s5 block special device, is available to users from the *mount_point* which must exist before mount is called; it becomes the name of the root of the newly mounted *special*.

    The options are:

    −F s5   Specify an s5 FSType.

    −r   Mount the file system read-only.

    −o   Specify s5-specific suboptions. The suboptions are:

           rw | ro   Read/write or read-only. Default is rw.

           suid | nosuid
                Setuid is honored or ignored on execution Default is suid.

           remount Used in conjunction with rw. A file system mounted read-only can be *remounted* read-write. Fails if the file system is not currently mounted or if the file system is mounted rw. Option is in force only when specified.

    Only a privileged user can mount file systems.

FILES

    /etc/mnttab   mount table

SEE ALSO

    generic mount(1M), mountfsys(1M), setmnt(1M).
    mount(2), setuid(2), mnttab(4) in the *Programmer's Reference Manual*.

NAME

mount (ufs) − mount **ufs** file systems

SYNOPSIS

mount [−F ufs] [*generic_options*] [−r] [−o *specific_options*] { *special* | *mount_point* }

mount [−F ufs] [*generic_options*] [−r] [−o *specific_options*] *special mount_point*

DESCRIPTION

mount attaches a **ufs** file system to the file system hierarchy at the pathname location *mount_point*, which must already exist. If *mount_point* has any contents prior to the mount operation, these remain hidden until the file system is once again unmounted.

The options are:

−F ufs

> Specifies the **ufs**-FSType.

−r   Mount the file system read-only.

−o   Specify **ufs** file system specific options. If invalid options are specified, a warning message is printed and the invalid options are ignored. The following options are available:

> f   Fake an /etc/mnttab entry, but do not actually mount any file systems. Parameters are not verified.
>
> n   Mount the file system without making an entry in /etc/mnttab.
>
> rw | ro
> > Read/write or read-only. Default is **rw**.
>
> nosuid
> > By default the file system is mounted with setuid execution allowed. Specifying **nosuid** overrides the default and causes the file system to be mounted with setuid execution disallowed.
>
> remount
> > Used in conjunction with **rw**. A file system mounted read-only can be *remounted* read-write. Fails if the file system is not currently mounted or if the file system is mounted **rw**.

NOTES

If the directory on which a file system is to be mounted is a symbolic link, the file system is mounted on the directory to which the symbolic link refers, rather than on top of the symbolic link itself.

FILES

/etc/mnttab   table of mounted file systems

SEE ALSO

generic mount(1M), mountfsys(1M), umountfsys(1M), mkdir(2), mount(2), unmount(2), open(2), mnttab(4).

NAME

mountall, umountall – mount, unmount multiple file systems

SYNOPSIS

mountall [–F *FSType*] [–l | –r] [*file_system_table*]
umountall [–F *FSType*] [–k] [–l | –r]

DESCRIPTION

These commands may be executed only by a privileged user.

mountall is used to mount file systems according to a *file_system_table*. (/etc/vfstab is the default file system table.) The special file name "–" reads from the standard input. If the dash is specified, then the standard input must be in the same format as /etc/vfstab. With no arguments mountall restricts the mount to all systems with automnt field set to **yes** in the *file_system_table*.

Before each file system is mounted, a sanity check is done using fsck [see fsck(1M)] to see if it appears mountable. If the file system does not appear mountable, it is fixed, using fsck, before the mount is attempted.

umountall causes all mounted file systems except **root**, /proc, /var, and /usr to be unmounted. If the *FSType* is specified mountall and umountall limit their actions to the *FSType* specified.

The options are:

–F   Specify the File System type to be mounted or unmounted. If *FSType* is specified the action is limited to file systems of this *FSType*.

–l   Limit the action to local file systems.

–r   Limit the action to remote file system types.

–k   Send a *SIGKILL* signal to processes that have files opened.

DIAGNOSTICS

No messages are printed if the file systems are mountable and clean.

Error and warning messages come from fsck(1M) and mount(1M).

SEE ALSO

fsck(1M), fuser(1M), mount(1M), vfstab(4), mnttab(4).
signal(2) in the *Programmer's Reference Manual*.

NAME

  mountd – NFS mount request server

SYNOPSIS

  mountd [–n]

DESCRIPTION

  mountd is an RPC server that answers file system mount requests. It reads the file
  /etc/dfs/sharetab, described in sharetab(4), to determine which file systems
  are available for mounting by which machines. It also provides information as to
  what file systems are mounted by which clients. This information can be printed
  using the dfmounts(1M) command.

  The mountd daemon is automatically invoked in run level 3.

  With the –n option, mountd does not check that the clients are root users.
  Though this option makes things slightly less secure, it does allow older versions
  (pre-3.0) of client NFS to work.

FILES

  /etc/dfs/sharetab

SEE ALSO

  dfmounts(1M), sharetab(4).

NAME
     mountfsys, umountfsys – mount, unmount a file system

SYNOPSIS
     mountfsys
     umountfsys

DESCRIPTION
     The mountfsys command mounts a file system so that users can read from it and
     write to it. The umountfsys command unmounts the file system.

     The command invokes a visual interface (the mount or unmount tasks available
     through the sysadm command).

     The initial prompt for both commands allows you to select the device on which
     to mount/unmount the file system.

     For the mountfsys command, you are asked to select how the file system is to be
     mounted; for example, read-only or read/write.

     The identical functions are available under the sysadm menu:

     sysadm mount

     sysadm unmount

DIAGNOSTICS
     Both mountfsys and umountfsys exit with one of the following values:

     0   Normal exit.

     2   Invalid command syntax. A usage message is displayed.

     7   The visual interface for this command is not available because it cannot
              invoke fmli. (The fmli package is not installed or is corrupt.)

NOTES
     For a removable medium, once the disk is mounted it must not be removed from
     the disk drive until it has been unmounted. Removing the disk while it is still
     mounted can cause severe damage to the data on the disk.

SEE ALSO
     checkfsys(1M),   labelit(1M),   makefsys(1M),   mkfs(1M),   mount(1M),
     sysadm(1M).

NAME
    mvdir – move a directory

SYNOPSIS
    /usr/sbin/mvdir *dirname name*

DESCRIPTION
    mvdir moves directories within a file system. *dirname* must be a directory. If
    name does not exist, it will be created as a directory. If *name* does exist, and is a
    directory, *dirname* will be created as *name/dirname. dirname* and *name* may not be
    on the same path; that is, one may not be subordinate to the other. For example:

                mvdir x/y x/z

    is legal, but

                mvdir x/y x/y/z

    is not.

SEE ALSO
    mkdir(1), mv(1) in the *User's Reference Manual.*

WARNINGS
    Only the super-user can use mvdir.

NAME
     named, in.named – Internet domain name server

SYNOPSIS
     in.named [–d *level*] [–p *port*] [[–b] *bootfile*]

DESCRIPTION
     named is the Internet domain name server. It is used by hosts on the Internet to
     provide access to the Internet distributed naming database. See RFC 1034 and
     RFC 1035 for more details. With no arguments named reads /etc/named.boot
     for any initial data, and listens for queries on a privileged port.

     The following options are available:

     –d *level*
               Print debugging information. *level* is a number indicating the level of
               messages printed.

     –p *port*
               Use a different *port* number.

     –b *bootfile*
               Use *bootfile* rather than /etc/named.boot.

EXAMPLE
```
;
;      boot file for name server
;
; type           domain                source file or host
;
domain           berkeley.edu
primary          berkeley.edu     named.db
secondary  cc.berkeley.edu 10.2.0.78 128.32.0.10
cache                             named.ca
```
     The domain line specifies that berkeley.edu is the domain of the given server.

     The primary line states that the file named.db contains authoritative data for
     berkeley.edu. The file named.db contains data in the master file format,
     described in RFC 1035, except that all domain names are relative to the origin; in
     this case, berkeley.edu (see below for a more detailed description).

     The secondary line specifies that all authoritative data under cc.berkeley.edu
     is to be transferred from the name server at 10.2.0.78. If the transfer fails it
     will try 128.32.0.10, and continue for up to 10 tries at that address. The secon-
     dary copy is also authoritative for the domain.

     The cache line specifies that data in named.ca is to be placed in the cache (typi-
     cally such data as the locations of root domain servers). The file named.ca is in
     the same format as named.db.

     The master file consists of entries of the form:

```
$INCLUDE < filename >
$ORIGIN < domain >
< domain > < opt_ttl > < opt_class > < type > < resource_record_data >
```

where *domain* is . for the root, @ for the current origin, or a standard domain name. If *domain* is a standard domain name that does not end with ., the current origin is appended to the domain. Domain names ending with . are unmodified.

The *opt_ttl* field is an optional integer number for the time-to-live field. It defaults to zero.

The *opt_class* field is currently one token, IN for the Internet.

The *type* field is one of the following tokens; the data expected in the *resource_record_data* field is in parentheses.

A	A host address (dotted quad).
NS	An authoritative name server (domain).
MX	A mail exchanger (domain).
CNAME	The canonical name for an alias (domain).
SOA	Marks the start of a zone of authority (5 numbers). See RFC 1035.
MB	A mailbox domain name (domain).
MG	A mail group member (domain).
MR	A mail rename domain name (domain).
NULL	A null resource record (no format or data).
WKS	A well know service description (not implemented yet).
PTR	A domain name pointer (domain).
HINFO	Host information (cpu_type OS_type).
MINFO	Mailbox or mail list information (request_domain error_domain).

FILES

/etc/named.boot	name server configuration boot file
/etc/named.pid	the process ID
/var/tmp/named.run	debug output
/var/tmp/named_dump.db	dump of the name servers database

SEE ALSO

kill(1), signal(3), resolver(3N), resolve.conf(4).

Mockapetris, Paul, *Domain Names - Concepts and Facilities*, RFC 1034, Network Information Center, SRI International, Menlo Park, Calif., November 1987.

Mockapetris, Paul, *Domain Names - Implementation and Specification*, RFC 1035, Network Information Center, SRI International, Menlo Park, Calif., November 1987.

Mockapetris, Paul, *Domain System Changes and Observations*, RFC 973, Network Information Center, SRI International, Menlo Park, Calif., January 1986.

Partridge, Craig, *Mail Routing and the Domain System*, RFC 974, Network Information Center, SRI International, Menlo Park, Calif., January 1986.

NOTES

The following signals have the specified effect when sent to the server process using the kill(1) command.

SIGHUP   Reads /etc/named.boot and reloads database.

SIGINT   Dumps the current database and cache to /var/tmp/named_dump.db.

SIGUSR1   Turns on debugging; each subsequent SIGUSR1 increments debug level.

SIGUSR2   Turns off debugging completely.

NAME

ncheck (generic) − generate a list of path names vs i-numbers

SYNOPSIS

ncheck [−F *FSType*] [−V] [*current_options*] [−o *specific_options*] [*special...*]

DESCRIPTION

ncheck with no options generates a path-name vs. i-number list of all files on *special*. If *special* is not specified on the command line the list is generated for all *specials* in /etc/vfstab for entries which have a numeric *fsckpass*. *special* is a block special device on which the file system exists.

current_options are options supported by the s5-specific module of ncheck. Other *FSTypes* do not necessarily support these options. *specific_options* indicate suboptions specified in a comma-separated list of suboptions and/or keyword-attribute pairs for interpretation by the *FSType*-specific module of the command.

The options are:

−F   Specify the *FSType* on which to operate. The *FSType* should either be specified here or be determinable from /etc/vfstab by finding an entry in the table that has a numeric *fsckpass* field and a matching *special* if specified.

−V   Echo the complete command line, but do not execute the command. The command line is generated by using the options and arguments provided by the user and adding to them information derived from /etc/vfstab. This option should be used to verify and validate the command line.

−o   used to specify *FSType* specific options if any.

NOTE

This command may not be supported for all *FSTypes*.

FILES

/etc/vfstab   list of default parameters for each file system

SEE ALSO

vfstab(4)

Manual pages for the *FSType*-specific modules of ncheck.

NAME
ncheck (s5) – generate path names versus i-numbers for **s5** file systems

SYNOPSIS
ncheck [–**F** **s5**] [*generic_options*] [–**i** *i-number...*] [–**a**] [–**s**] [*special...*]

DESCRIPTION
generic_options are options supported by the generic **ncheck** command.

ncheck generates a path-name vs. i-number list of all files on the specified *special* device(s). Names of directory files are followed by "/." .

The options are:

–**F** **s5**   Specifies the **s5**-FSType.

–**i** *i-number*
              Limits the report to those files whose i-numbers follow. The *i-numbers* must be separated by commas without spaces.

–**a**   Allows printing of the names "." and "..", which are ordinarily suppressed.

–**s**   Limits the report to special files and files with set-user-ID mode. This option may be used to detect violations of security policy.

DIAGNOSTICS
If the file system structure is not consistent, **??** denotes the parent of a parentless file and a path-name beginning with ... denotes a loop.

SEE ALSO
generic ncheck(1M).

NAME
    ncheck (ufs) – generate pathnames versus i-numbers for **ufs** file systems

SYNOPSIS
    ncheck [–F ufs] [*generic_options*] [–i *i-list*] [–a] [–s] [–o m] [*special ...*]

DESCRIPTION
    generic_options are options supported by the generic ncheck command.

    ncheck generates a pathname versus i-number list of files for the **ufs** file system. Names of directory files are followed by "/. ".

    The options are:

    –F ufs
        Specifies the **ufs**-FSType.

    –i *i-list*
        Limits the report to the files on the i-list that follows. The i-list must be separated by commas without spaces.

    –a   Allows printing of the names "." and "..", which are ordinarily suppressed.

    –s   Limits the report to special files and files with set-user-ID mode. This option may be used to detect violations of security policy.

    –o   Specify **ufs** file system specific options. The available option is:

        m   Print mode information.

DIAGNOSTICS
    When the file system structure is improper, '??' denotes the parent of a parentless file and a pathname beginning with '. . .' denotes a loop.

SEE ALSO
    generic ncheck(1M)

NAME

netstat – show network status

SYNOPSIS

netstat [–aAn] [–f *addr_family*] [system] [core]

netstat [–n] [–s] [–i | –r] [–f *addr_family*] [system] [core]

netstat [–n] [–I *interface*] *interval* [system] [core]

DESCRIPTION

netstat displays the contents of various network-related data structures in various formats, depending on the options you select.

The first form of the command displays a list of active sockets for each protocol. The second form selects one from among various other network data structures. The third form displays running statistics of packet traffic on configured network interfaces; the *interval* argument indicates the number of seconds in which to gather statistics between displays.

The default value for the **system** argument is /unix; for *core*, the default is /dev/kmem.

The following options are available:

–a   Show the state of all sockets; normally sockets used by server processes are not shown.

–A   Show the address of any protocol control blocks associated with sockets; used for debugging.

–i   Show the state of interfaces that have been auto-configured. Interfaces that are statically configured into a system, but not located at boot time, are not shown.

–n   Show network addresses as numbers. netstat normally displays addresses as symbols. This option may be used with any of the display formats.

–r   Show the routing tables. When used with the –s option, show routing statistics instead.

–s   Show per-protocol statistics. When used with the –r option, show routing statistics.

–f *addr_family*
      Limit statistics or address control block reports to those of the specified *addr_family*, which can be one of:

               inet   For the AF_INET address family, or
               unix   For the AF_UNIX family.

–I *interface*
      Highlight information about the indicated *interface* in a separate column; the default (for the third form of the command) is the interface with the most traffic since the system was last rebooted. *interface* can be any valid interface listed in the system configuration file, such as emd1 or lo0.

DISPLAYS
Active Sockets (First Form)
The display for each active socket shows the local and remote address, the send and receive queue sizes (in bytes), the protocol, and the internal state of the protocol.

The symbolic format normally used to display socket addresses is either:

> *hostname.port*

when the name of the host is specified, or:

> *network.port*

if a socket address specifies a network but no specific host. Each hostname and *network* is shown according to its entry in the /etc/hosts or the /etc/networks file, as appropriate.

If the network or hostname for an address is not known (or if the −n option is specified), the numerical network address is shown. Unspecified, or wildcard, addresses and ports appear as *. For more information regarding the Internet naming conventions, refer to inet(7).

TCP Sockets
The possible state values for TCP sockets are as follows:

CLOSED	Closed. The socket is not being used.
LISTEN	Listening for incoming connections.
SYN_SENT	Actively trying to establish connection.
SYN_RECEIVED	Initial synchronization of the connection under way.
ESTABLISHED	Connection has been established.
CLOSE_WAIT	Remote shut down; waiting for the socket to close.
FIN_WAIT_1	Socket closed; shutting down connection.
CLOSING	Closed, then remote shutdown; awaiting acknowledgement.
LAST_ACK	Remote shut down, then closed; awaiting acknowledgement.
FIN_WAIT_2	Socket closed; waiting for shutdown from remote.
TIME_WAIT	Wait after close for remote shutdown retransmission.

Network Data Structures (Second Form)
The form of the display depends upon which of the −i or −r options you select. If you specify more than one of these options, netstat selects one in the order listed here.

Routing Table Display
The routing table display lists the available routes and the status of each. Each route consists of a destination host or network, and a gateway to use in forwarding packets. The *flags* column shows the status of the route (U if up), whether the route is to a gateway (G), and whether the route was created dynamically by a redirect (D).

Direct routes are created for each interface attached to the local host; the gateway field for such entries shows the address of the outgoing interface.

The refcnt column gives the current number of active uses per route. Connection-oriented protocols normally hold on to a single route for the duration of a connection, whereas connectionless protocols obtain a route while sending to the same destination.

The use column displays the number of packets sent per route.

The *interface* entry indicates the network interface utilized for the route.

Cumulative Traffic Statistics (Third Form)

When the *interval* argument is given, netstat displays a table of cumulative statistics regarding packets transferred, errors and collisions, the network addresses for the interface, and the maximum transmission unit (mtu). The first line of data displayed, and every 24th line thereafter, contains cumulative statistics from the time the system was last rebooted. Each subsequent line shows incremental statistics for the *interval* (specified on the command line) since the previous display.

SEE ALSO

iostat(1M), trpt(1M), vmstat(1M), hosts(4), networks(4), protocols(4), services(4).

NOTES

The notion of errors is ill-defined.

The kernel's tables can change while netstat is examining them, creating incorrect or partial displays.

NAME

newboot – load boot programs onto the hard disk boot partition

SYNOPSIS

/usr/sbin/newboot [–y] /usr/lib/boot /usr/lib/mboot *boot_special*

DESCRIPTION

newboot copies the named boot programs to the specified *boot_special* hard disk partition; unless the current directory is /usr/lib, you must specify full pathnames for the boot programs.

The *boot_special* section of a hard disk is typically the first 100, 512-byte blocks on the device, and has a file name of the form /dev/rdsk/c?d?s7; it can be identified using prtvtoc and looking for the partition with the tag of 1 (BOOT) and size of 100 blocks. You must specify the raw (character) device name.

If the –y option is not specified, you are prompted for confirmation before the *boot_special* partition is overwritten.

The mboot program is the 512-byte micro-boot file loaded by the boot device firmware; its main function is to load and execute the larger boot program.

The boot program is the boot program for hard disks that loads and executes the bootable operating system (unix).

NOTES

Installing bad boot programs may make the affected disk unbootable. Be sure you have a good backup copy of the disk before newboot is run.

DIAGNOSTICS

newboot returns an error if the specified boot programs are not found. Either change directory to /usr/lib or use the full pathnames of the programs (i.e., /usr/lib/mboot, /usr/lib/boot).

SEE ALSO

cunix(1M), mkfs(1M), mkboot(1M), prtvtoc(1M).
System Administrator's Guide

NAME

newgrp – log in to a new group

SYNOPSIS

newgrp [–] [group]

DESCRIPTION

newgrp changes a user's real and effective group ID. The user remains logged in and the current directory is unchanged. The user is always given a new shell, replacing the current shell, by newgrp, regardless of whether it terminated successfully or due to an error condition (i.e., unknown group).

Exported variables retain their values after invoking newgrp; however, all unexported variables are either reset to their default value or set to null. System variables (such as PS1, PS2, PATH, MAIL, and HOME), unless exported by the system or explicitly exported by the user, are reset to default values. For example, a user has a primary prompt string (PS1) other than $ (default) and has not exported PS1. After an invocation of newgrp, successful or not, the user's PS1 will now be set to the default prompt string $. Note that the shell command export [see the sh(1) manual page] is the method to export variables so that they retain their assigned value when invoking new shells.

With no arguments, newgrp changes the user's group IDs (real and effective) back to the group specified in the user's password file entry. This is a way to exit the effect of an earlier newgrp command.

If the first argument to newgrp is a –, the environment is changed to what would be expected if the user actually logged in again as a member of the new group.

A password is demanded if the group has a password and the user is not listed in /etc/group as being a member of that group.

FILES

/etc/group   system's group file

/etc/passwd   system's password file

SEE ALSO

login(1), sh(1) in the *User's Reference Manual*.
group(4), passwd(4), environ(5) in the *System Administrator's Reference Manual*.
see intro(2) "Effective User ID and Effective Group ID" in *Programmer's Reference Manual*

NAME
      nfsd – NFS daemon
SYNOPSIS
      nfsd [–a] [–p *protocol*] [–t *device*] [*nservers*]
DESCRIPTION
      nfsd starts the daemons that handle client file system requests.

      The following options are recognized:

      –a   start nfsd's over all available connectionless transports

      –p *protocol*   start nfsd's over the specified protocol

      –t *device*   start nfsd's for the transport specified by the given device

      nservers   the number of file system request daemons to start.

      nservers should be based on the load expected on this server. Four is the usual
      number of *nservers*.

      The nfsd daemons are automatically invoked in run level 3.

FILES
      .nfsXXX   client machine pointer to an open-but-unlinked file
SEE ALSO
      biod(1M), mountd(1M), sharetab(4).

NAME

    nlsadmin – network listener service administration

SYNOPSIS

    /usr/sbin/nlsadmin -x
    /usr/sbin/nlsadmin [*options*] *net_spec*
    /usr/sbin/nlsadmin [*options*] -N *port_monitor_tag*
    /usr/sbin/nlsadmin -V
    /usr/sbin/nlsadmin -c *cmd* | -o *streamname* [-p *modules*] \
       [-A *address* | -D] [-R *prognum*:*versnum*]

DESCRIPTION

    nlsadmin is the administrative command for the network listener process(es) on a machine. Each network has at least one instance of the network listener process associated with it; each instance (and thus, each network) is configured separately. The listener process "listens" to the network for service requests, accepts requests when they arrive, and invokes servers in response to those service requests. The network listener process may be used with any network (more precisely, with any connection-oriented transport provider) that conforms to the transport provider specification.

    nlsadmin can establish a listener process for a given network, configure the specific attributes of that listener, and start and kill the listener process for that network. nlsadmin can also report on the listener processes on a machine, either individually (per network) or collectively.

    The list below shows how to use nlsadmin. In this list, *net_spec* represents a particular listener process. Specifically, *net_spec* is the relative path name of the entry under /dev for a given network (that is, a transport provider). *address* is a transport address on which to listen and is interpreted using a syntax that allows for a variety of address formats. By default, *address* is interpreted as the symbolic ASCII representation of the transport address. An *address* preceded by a \x will let you enter an address in hexadecimal notation. Note that *address* must appear as a single word to the shell and thus must be quoted if it contains any blanks.

    Changes to the list of services provided by the listener or the addresses of those services are put into effect immediately.

    nlsadmin may be used with the following combinations of options and arguments:

nlsadmin   gives a brief usage message.

nlsadmin -x   reports the status of all of the listener processes installed on this machine.

nlsadmin *net_spec*
        prints the status of the listener process for *net_spec*.

nlsadmin -q *net_spec*
        queries the status of the listener process for the specified network, and reflects the result of that query in its exit code. If a listener process is active, nlsadmin will exit with a status of 0; if no process is active, the exit code will be 1; the exit code will be greater than 1 in case of error.

nlsadmin −v *net_spec*
> prints a verbose report on the servers associated with *net_spec*, giving the service code, status, command, and comment for each. It also specifies the uid the server will run as and the list of modules to be pushed, if any, before the server is started.

nlsadmin −z *service_code net_spec*
> prints a report on the server associated with *net_spec* that has service code *service_code*, giving the same information as in the −v option.

nlsadmin −q −z *service_code net_spec*
> queries the status of the service with service code *service_code* on network *net_spec*, and exits with a status of 0 if that service is enabled, 1 if that service is disabled, and greater than 1 in case of error.

nlsadmin −l *address net_spec*
> changes or set the transport address on which the listener listens (the general listener service). This address can be used by remote processes to access the servers available through this listener (see the −a option, below).
>
> If *address* is just a dash ("−"), nlsadmin will report the address currently configured, instead of changing it.
>
> A change of address takes effect immediately.

nlsadmin −t *address net_spec*
> changes or sets the address on which the listener listens for requests for terminal service but is otherwise similar to the −l option above. A terminal service address should not be defined unless the appropriate remote login software is available; if such software is available, it must be configured as service code 1 (see the −a option, below).

nlsadmin −i *net_spec*
> initializes an instance of the listener for the network specified by *net_spec*; that is, creates and initializes the files required by the listener as well as starting that instance of the listener. Note that a particular instance of the listener should be initialized only once. The listener must be initialized before assigning addresses or services.

nlsadmin −a *service_code* [−p *modules*] [−w *name*] −c *cmd* −y *comment net_spec*
> adds a new service to the list of services available through the indicated listener. *service_code* is the code for the service, *cmd* is the command to be invoked in response to that service code, comprised of the full path name of the server and its arguments, and *comment* is a brief (free-form) description of the service for use in various reports. Note that *cmd* must appear as a single word to the shell; if arguments are required the *cmd* and its arguments must be enclosed in quotation marks. The *comment* must also

appear as a single word to the shell. When a service is added, it is initially enabled (see the −e and −d options, below).

Service codes are alphanumeric strings, and are administered by AT&T. The numeric service codes 0 through 100 are reserved for internal use by the listener. Service code 0 is assigned to the nlps server, which is the service invoked on the general listening address. In particular, code 1 is assigned to the remote login service, which is the service automatically invoked for connections to the terminal login address.

If the −p option is specified, then *modules* will be interpreted as a list of STREAMS modules for the listener to push before starting the service being added. The modules are pushed in the order they are specified. *modules* should be a comma-separated list of modules, with no white space included.

If the −w option is specified, then *name* is interpreted as the user name from /etc/passwd that the listener should look up. From the user name, the listener obtains the user ID, the group ID(s), and the home directory for use by the server. If −w is not specified, the default is to use the user name listen.

A service must explicitly be added to the listener for each network on which that service is to be available. This operation will normally be performed only when the service is installed on a machine, or when populating the list of services for a new network.

nlsadmin −r *service_code net_spec*

    removes the entry for the *service_code* from that listener's list of services. This is normally done only in conjunction with the deinstallation of a service from a machine.

nlsadmin −e *service_code net_spec*
nlsadmin −d *service_code net_spec*

    enables or disables (respectively) the service indicated by *service_code* for the specified network. The service must previously have been added to the listener for that network (see the −a option, above). Disabling a service will cause subsequent service requests for that service to be denied, but the processes from any prior service requests that are still running will continue unaffected.

nlsadmin −s *net_spec*
nlsadmin −k *net_spec*

    starts and kills (respectively) the listener process for the indicated network. These operations will normally be performed as part of the system startup and shutdown procedures. Before a listener can be started for a particular network, it must first have been initialized (see the −i option, above). When a listener is killed, processes that are still running as a result of prior service requests will continue unaffected.

Under the Service Access Facility, it is possible to have multiple instances of the listener on a single *net_spec*. In any of the above commands, the option −N *port_monitor_tag* may be used in place of the *net_spec* argument. This argument specifies the tag by which an instance of the listener is identified by the Service Access Facility. If the −N option is not specified (i.e., the *net_spec* is specified in the invocation), then it will be assumed that the last component of the *net_spec* represents the tag of the listener for which the operation is destined. In other words, it is assumed that there is at least one listener on a designated *net_spec*, and that its tag is identical to the last component of the *net_spec*. This listener may be thought of as the primary, or default, listener for a particular *net_spec*.

nlsadmin is also used in conjunction with the Service Access Facility commands. In that capacity, the following combinations of options can be used:

nlsadmin −V

> writes the current version number of the listener's administrative file to the standard output. It is used as part of the sacadm command line when sacadm add a port monitor to the system.

nlsadmin −c *cmd* | −o *streamname* [−p *modules*] [−A *address* | −D] \
[−R *prognum* : *versnum*]

> formats the port monitor-specific information to be used as an argument to pmadm(1M).

> The −c option specifies the full path name of the server and its arguments. *cmd* must appear as a single word to the shell, and its arguments must therefor be surrounded by quotes.

> The −o option specifies the full path name of a FIFO or named STREAM through which a standing server is actually receiving the connection.

> If the −p option is specified, then *modules* will be interpreted as a list of STREAMS modules for the listener to push before starting the service being added. The modules are pushed in the order in which they are specified. *modules* must be a comma-separated list, with no white space included.

> If the −A option is specified, then *address* will be interpreted as the server's private address. The listener will monitor this address on behalf of the service and will dispatch all calls arriving on this address directly to the designated service. This option may not be used in conjunction with the −D option.

> If the −D option is specified, then the service is assigned a private address dynamically, that is, the listener will have the transport provider select the address each time the listener begins listening on behalf of this service. For RPC services, this option will be often be used in conjunction with the −R option to register the dynamically assigned address with the rpcbinder. This option may not be used in conjunction with the −A option.

> When the −R option is specified, the service is an RPC service whose address, program number, and version number should be registered with the rpcbinder for this transport provider. This registration is performed each time the listener begins listening on behalf of ththe service. *prognum* and *versnum* are the program number and version number, respectively, of the RPC service.

nlsadmin may be invoked by any user to generate reports but all operations that affect a listener's status or configuration are restricted to privileged users.

The options specific to the Service Access Facility may not be mixed with any other options.

SEE ALSO

listen(1M), pmadm(1M), rpcbind(1M), sacadm(1M)
Network Programmer's Guide

NOTES

Dynamically assigned addresses are not displayed in reports as statically assigned addresses are.

NAME
nslookup – query name servers interactively

SYNOPSIS
nslookup [–l] [*address*]

DESCRIPTION
nslookup is an interactive program to query ARPA Internet domain name servers. The user can contact servers to request information about a specific host or print a list of hosts in the domain.

OPTIONS
–l   Use the local host's name server instead of the servers in /etc/resolve.conf. (If /etc/resolve.conf does not exist or does not contain server information, the –l option does not have any effect).

address   Use the name server on the host machine with the given Internet address.

USAGE
Overview
The Internet domain name-space is tree-structured, with four top-level domains at present:

COM   commercial establishments

EDU   educational institutions

GOV   government agencies

MIL   MILNET hosts

If you are looking for a specific host, you need to know something about the host's organization in order to determine the top-level domain it belongs to. For instance, if you want to find the Internet address of a machine at UCLA , do the following:

- Connect with the root server using the root command. The root server of the name space has knowledge of the top-level domains.

- Since UCLA is a university, its domain name is ucla.edu. Connect with a server for the ucla.edu domain with the command server ucla.edu. The response will print the names of hosts that act as servers for that domain. Note: the root server does not have information about ucla.edu, but knows the names and addresses of hosts that do. Once located by the root server, all future queries will be sent to the UCLA name server.

- To request information about a particular host in the domain (for instance, locus), just type the host name. To request a listing of hosts in the UCLA domain, use the ls command. The ls command requires a domain name (in this case, ucla.edu) as an argument.

If you are connected with a name server that handles more than one domain, all lookups for host names must be fully specified with its domain. For instance, the domain harvard.edu is served by seismo.css.gov, which also services the css.gov and cornell.edu domains. A lookup request for the host aiken in the harvard.edu domain must be specified as aiken.harvard.edu. However, the

> set domain = *name*

and

> set defname

commands can be used to automatically append a domain name to each request.

After a successful lookup of a host, use the `finger` command to see who is on the system, or to finger a specific person. To get other information about the host, use the

> set querytype = *value*

command to change the type of information desired and request another lookup. (`finger` requires the type to be A.)

Commands

To exit, type Ctrl-D (EOF). The command line length must be less than 80 characters. An unrecognized command will be interpreted as a host name.

host [*server*]

> Look up information for *host* using the current default server or using *server* if it is specified.

server *domain*
lserver *domain*

> Change the default server to *domain*. `lserver` uses the initial server to look up information about *domain* while `server` uses the current default server. If an authoritative answer can't be found, the names of servers that might have the answer are returned.

root

> Changes the default server to the server for the root of the domain name space. Currently, the host `sri-nic.arpa` is used; this command is a synonym for `lserver sri-nic.arpa`.) The name of the root server can be changed with the `set root` command.

finger [*name*]

> Connect with the finger server on the current host, which is defined by a previous successful lookup for a host's address information (see the `set querytype` =A command). As with the shell, output can be redirected to a named file using > and >>.

ls [-ah]

> List the information available for *domain*. The default output contains host names and their Internet addresses. The –a option lists aliases of hosts in the domain. The –h option lists CPU and operating system information for the domain. As with the shell, output can be redirected to a named file using > and >>. When output is directed to a file, hash marks are printed for every 50 records received from the server.

view *filename*

> Sort and list the output of the `ls` command with more(1).

help
?   Print a brief summary of commands.

set *keyword* [= *value*] This command is used to change state information that
affects the lookups. Valid keywords are:

    all   Prints the current values of the various options to set. Informa-
           tion about the current default server and host is also printed.

    [no] deb[ug]
           Turn debugging mode on. A lot more information is printed about
           the packet sent to the server and the resulting answer. The default
           is nodebug.

    [no] def[*name*]
           Append the default domain name to every lookup. The default is
           nodefname.

    do [main] = *filename*
           Change the default domain name to *filename*. The default domain
           name is appended to all lookup requests if defname option has
           been set. The default is the value in /etc/resolve.conf.

    q [querytype] = *value*
           Change the type of information returned from a query to one of:

           A   The host's Internet address (the default).
           CNAME The canonical name for an alias.
           HINFO The host CPU and operating system type.
           MD   The mail destination.
           MX   The mail exchanger.
           MB   The mailbox domain name.
           MG   The mail group member.
           MINFO The mailbox or mail list information.

           (Other types specified in the RFC883 document are valid, but are
           not very useful.)

    [no] recurse
           Tell the name server to query other servers if it does not have the
           information. The default is recurse.

    ret [ry] = *count*
           Set the number of times to retry a request before giving up to
           count. When a reply to a request is not received within a certain
           amount of time (changed with set timeout), the request is resent.
           The default is *count* is 2.

    ro [ot] = *host*
           Change the name of the root server to *host*. This affects the root
           command. The default root server is sri-nic.arpa.

t [timeout] = *interval*

> Change the time-out for a reply to *interval* seconds. The default *interval* is 10 seconds.

[no] v[c]

> Always use a virtual circuit when sending requests to the server. The default is novc.

FILES

/etc/resolve.conf   initial domain name and name server addresses.

SEE ALSO

named(1M), resolver(3N), resolve.conf(4), RFC 882, RFC 883.

DIAGNOSTICS

If the lookup request was not successful, an error message is printed. Possible errors are:

Time-out

> The server did not respond to a request after a certain amount of time (changed with set timeout = *value*) and a certain number of retries (changed with set retry = *value*).

No information

> Depending on the query type set with the set querytype command, no information about the host was available, though the host name is valid.

Non-existent domain

> The host or domain name does not exist.

Connection refused
Network is unreachable

> The connection to the name or finger server could not be made at the current time. This error commonly occurs with finger requests.

Server failure

> The name server found an internal inconsistency in its database and could not return a valid answer.

Refused

> The name server refused to service the request.

The following error should not occur and it indicates a bug in the program.

Format error

> The name server found that the request packet was not in the proper format.

NAME

nsquery – Remote File Sharing name server query

SYNOPSIS

nsquery [–h] [*name*]

DESCRIPTION

nsquery provides information about resources available to the host from both the local domain and from other domains. All resources are reported, regardless of whether the host is authorized to access them. When used with no options, nsquery identifies all resources in the domain that have been advertised as sharable. A report on selected resources can be obtained by specifying *name*, where *name* is:

nodename	The report will include only those resources available from *nodename*.
domain.	The report will include only those resources available from *domain*.
domain.nodename	The report will include only those resources available from *domain.nodename*.

When the name does not include the delimiter ".", it will be interpreted as a *nodename* within the local domain. If the name ends with a delimiter ".", it will be interpreted as a domain name.

The information contained in the report on each resource includes its advertised name (*domain.resource*), the read/write permissions, the server (*nodename.domain*) that advertised the resource, and a brief textual description.

When –h is used, the header is not printed.

A remote domain must be listed in your rfmaster file in order to query that domain.

EXIT STATUS

If no entries are found when nsquery is executed, the report header is printed.

SEE ALSO

adv(1M), unadv(1M), rfmaster(4).

NOTES

If your host cannot contact the domain name server, an error message will be sent to standard error.

NAME

passmgmt – password files management

SYNOPSIS

passmgmt −a *options name*
passmgmt −m *options name*
passmgmt −d *name*

DESCRIPTION

The passmgmt command updates information in the password files. This command works with both /etc/passwd and /etc/shadow.

passmgmt −a adds an entry for user *name* to the password files. This command does not create any directory for the new user and the new login remains locked (with the string *LK* in the password field) until the passwd(1) command is executed to set the password.

passmgmt −m modifies the entry for user *name* in the password files. The name field in the /etc/shadow entry and all the fields (except the password field) in the /etc/passwd entry can be modified by this command. Only fields entered on the command line will be modified.

passmgmt −d deletes the entry for user *name* from the password files. It will not remove any files that the user owns on the system; they must be removed manually.

The following options are available:

−c *comment* A short description of the login. It is limited to a maximum of 128 characters and defaults to an empty field.

−h *homedir* Home directory of *name*. It is limited to a maximum of 256 characters and defaults to /usr/*name*.

−u *uid* UID of the *name*. This number must range from 0 to the maximum non-negative value for the system. It defaults to the next available UID greater than 99. Without the −o option, it enforces the uniqueness of a UID.

−o This option allows a UID to be non-unique. It is used only with the −u option.

−g *gid* GID of the *name*. This number must range from 0 to the maximum non-negative value for the system. The default is 1.

−s *shell* Login shell for *name*. It should be the full pathname of the program that will be executed when the user logs in. The maximum size of *shell* is 256 characters. The default is for this field to be empty and to be interpreted as /usr/bin/sh.

−l logname
    This option changes the *name* to logname. It is used only with the −m option.

The total size of each login entry is limited to a maximum of 511 bytes in each of the password files.

FILES

/etc/passwd,
/etc/shadow,
/etc/opasswd,
/etc/oshadow

SEE ALSO

useradd(1M), userdel(1M), usermod(1M), passwd(4), and shadow(4) in the *System Administrator's Reference Manual.*
passwd(1) in the *User's Reference Manual.*

DIAGNOSTICS

The passmgmt command exits with one of the following values:

0   Success.

1   Permission denied.

2   Invalid command syntax. Usage message of the passmgmt command will be displayed.

3   Invalid argument provided to option.

4   UID in use.

5   Inconsistent password files (e.g., *name* is in the /etc/passwd file and not in the /etc/shadow file, or vice versa).

6   Unexpected failure. Password files unchanged.

7   Unexpected failure. Password file(s) missing.

8   Password file(s) busy. Try again later.

9   *name* does not exist (if −m or −d is specified), already exists (if −a is specified), or logname already exists (if −m −l is specified).

NOTES

You cannot use a colon or carriage return as part of an argument because it is interpreted as a field separator in the password file.

This command will be removed in a future release. Its functionality has been replaced and enhanced by useradd, userdel, and usermod. These commands are currently available.

NAME

ping – send ICMP ECHO_REQUEST packets to network hosts

SYNOPSIS

ping *host* [*timeout*]

/usr/sbin/ping [–s] [–lrRv] *host* [*packetsize*] [*count*]

DESCRIPTION

ping utilizes the ICMP protocol's ECHO_REQUEST datagram to elicit an ICMP ECHO_RESPONSE from the specified *host* or network gateway. If *host* responds, ping will print *host* is alive on the standard output and exit. Otherwise after *timeout* seconds, it will write no answer from *host*. The default value of *timeout* is 20 seconds.

When the –s flag is specified, ping sends one datagram per second, and prints one line of output for every ECHO_RESPONSE that it receives. No output is produced if there is no response. In this second form, ping computes round trip times and packet loss statistics; it displays a summary of this information upon termination or timeout. The default datagram packet size is 64 bytes, or you can specify a size with the *packetsize* command-line argument. If an optional *count* is given, ping sends only that number of requests.

When using ping for fault isolation, first ping the local host to verify that the local network interface is running.

OPTIONS

–1   Loose source route. Use this option in the IP header to send the packet to the given host and back again. Usually specified with the –R option.

–r   Bypass the normal routing tables and send directly to a host on an attached network. If the host is not on a directly-attached network, an error is returned. This option can be used to ping a local host through an interface that has been dropped by the router daemon [see routed(1M)].

–R   Record route. Sets the IP record route option, which will store the route of the packet inside the IP header. The contents of the record route will only be printed if the –v option is given, and only be set on return packets if the target host preserves the record route option across echos, or the –1 option is given.

–v   Verbose output. List any ICMP packets, other than ECHO_RESPONSE, that are received.

SEE ALSO

ifconfig(1M), netstat(1M), rpcinfo(1M), icmp(7).

NAME

pkgadd – transfer software package to the system

SYNOPSIS

pkgadd [–d *device*] [–r *response*] [–n] [–a *admin*] [*pkginst1* [*pkginst2*[...]]]

pkgadd –s *spool* [–d *device*] [*pkginst1* [*pkginst2*[...]]]

DESCRIPTION

pkgadd transfers the contents of a software package from the distribution medium or directory to install it onto the system. Used without the –d option, pkgadd looks in the default spool directory for the package (var/spool/pkg). Used with the –s option, it reads the package to a spool directory instead of installing it.

–d   Installs or copies a package from *device*. *device* can be a full path name to a directory or the identifiers for tape, floppy disk or removable disk (for example, /var/tmp, /dev/diskette, or diskette1). It can also be the device alias.

–r   Identifies a file or directory, *response*, which contains output from a previous pkgask session. This file supplies the interaction responses that would be requested by the package in interactive mode. *response* must be a full pathname.

–n   Installation occurs in non-interactive mode. The default mode is interactive.

–a   Defines an installation administration file, *admin*, to be used in place of the default administration file. The token none overrides the use of any *admin* file, and thus forces interaction with the user. Unless a full path name is given, pkgadd looks in the var/sadm/install/admin directory for the file.

pkginst   Specifies the package instance or list of instances to be installed. The token all may be used to refer to all packages available on the source medium. The format *pkginst*.* can be used to indicate all instances of a package.

–s   Reads the package into the directory *spool* instead of installing it.

When executed without options, pkgadd users /var/spool/pkg (the default spool directory).

NOTES

When transferring a package to a spool directory, the –r, –n, and –a options cannot be used.

The –r option can be used to indicate a directory name as well as a filename. The directory can contain numerous *response* files, each sharing the name of the package with which it should be associated. This would be used, for example, when adding multiple interactive packages with one invocation of pkgadd. Each package would need a *response* file. If you create response files with the same name as the package (*i.e. package1* and *package2*), then name the directory in which these files reside after the –r.

The −n option will cause the installation to halt if any interaction is needed to complete it.

NAME

pkgask — stores answers to a request script

SYNOPSIS

pkgask [–d *device*] –r *response pkginst* [*pkginst* [...]]

DESCRIPTION

pkgask allows the administrator to store answers to an interactive package (one with a request script). Invoking this command generates a *response* file that is then used as input at installation time. The use of this *response* file prevents any interaction from occurring during installation since the file already contains all of the information the package needs.

–d   Runs the request script for a package on *device*. *device* can be a directory pathname or the identifiers for tape, floppy disk or removable disk (for example, /var/tmp, /dev/diskette, and /dev/dsk/c1d0s0). The default device is the installation spool directory.

–r   Identifies a file or directory, which should be created to contain the responses to interaction with the package. The name must be a full pathname. The file, or directory of files, can later be used as input to the pkgadd command.

pkginst   Specifies the package instance or list of instances for which request scripts will be created. The token all may be used to refer to all packages available on the source medium.

NOTES

The –r option can be used to indicate a directory name as well as a filename. The directory name is used to create numerous *response* files, each sharing the name of the package with which it should be associated. This would be used, for example, when you will be adding multiple interactive packages with one invocation of pkgadd. Each package would need a *response* file. To create multiple response files with the same name as the package instance, name the directory in which the files should be created and supply multiple instance names with the pkgask command. When installing the packages, you will be able to identify this directory to the pkgadd command.

SEE ALSO

installf(1M), pkgadd(1M), pkgchk(1), pkgmk(1), pkginfo(1), pkgparam(1), pkgproto(1), pkgtrans(1), pkgrm(1M), removef(1M).

NAME

pkgchk – check accuracy of installation

SYNOPSIS

pkgchk [-l |-acfqv] [-nx] [-p *path1*[, *path2* ...] [-i *file*] [*pkginst*...]

pkgchk -d *device* [-l |v] [-p *path1*[, *path2* ...] [-i *file*] [*pkginst*...]

pkgchk -m *pkgmap* [-e *envfile*] [-l |-acfqv] [-nx] [-i *file*]
        [-p *path1*[, *path2* ...]]

DESCRIPTION

pkgchk checks the accuracy of installed files or, by use of the -l option, displays
information about package files. The command checks the integrity of directory
structures and the files. Discrepancies are reported on stderr along with a
detailed explanation of the problem.

The first synopsis defined above is used to list or check the contents and/or attributes of objects that are currently installed on the system. Package names may be
listed on the command line, or by default the entire contents of a machine will be
checked.

The second synopsis is used to list or check the contents of a package which has
been spooled on the specified device, but not installed. Note that attributes cannot be checked for spooled packages.

The third synopsis is used to list or check the contents and/or attributes of
objects which are described in the indicated *pkgmap*.

The option definitions are:

-l   Lists information on the selected files that make up a package. It is not
        compatible with the a, c, f, g, and v options.

-a   Audits the file attributes only, does not check file contents. Default is to
        check both.

-c   Audits the file contents only, does not check file attributes. Default is to
        check both.

-f   Corrects file attributes if possible. If used with the -x option, it removes
        hidden files. When pkgchk is invoked with this option it creates direc-
        tories, named pipes, links and special devices if they do not already exist.

-q   Quiet mode. Does not give messages about missing files.

-v   Verbose mode. Files are listed as processed.

-n   Does not check volatile or editable files. This should be used for most
        post-installation checking.

-x   Searches exclusive directories, looking for files which exist that are not in
        the installation software database or the indicated *pkgmap* file.

-p   Only checks the accuracy of the pathname or pathnames listed. *pathname*
        can be one or more pathnames separated by commas (or by white space,
        if the list is quoted).

-i   Reads a list of pathnames from *file* and compares this list against the installation software database or the indicated *pkgmap* file. Pathnames which are not contained in *inputfile* are not checked.

-d   Specifies the device on which a spooled package resides. *device* can be a directory pathname or the identifiers for tape, floppy disk or removable disk (for example, /var/tmp or /dev/diskette).

-m   Requests that the package be checked against the pkgmap file *pkgmap*.

-e   Requests that the pkginfo file named as *envfile* be used to resolve parameters noted in the specified pkgmap file.

pkginst
         Specifies the package instance or instances to be checked. The format *pkginst*.* can be used to check all instances of a package. The default is to display all information about all installed packages.

SEE ALSO
    pkgadd(1M), pkgask(1M), pkginfo(1), pkgrm(1M), pkgtrans(1).

NAME
    pkginfo – display software package information

SYNOPSIS
    pkginfo [–q|x|l] [–p|i] [–a *arch*] [–v *version*]
            [–c *category1*, [*category2*[, ...]]] [*pkginst*[,*pkginst*[, ...]]]

    pkginfo [–d *device* [–q|x|l] [–a *arch*] [–v *version*]
            [–c *category1*, [*category2*[, ...]]] [*pkginst*[,*pkginst*[, ...]]]

DESCRIPTION
    pkginfo displays information about software packages which are installed on the
    system (with the first synopsis) or which reside on a particular device or direc-
    tory (with the second synopsis). Only the package name and abbreviation for
    pre-SVR4 packages will be included in the display.

    The options for this command are:

    –q   Does not list any information, but can be used from a program to
              check (*i.e.*, query) whether or not a package has been installed.

    –x   Designates an extracted listing of package information. It contains the
              package abbreviation, package name, package architecture (if available)
              and package version (if available).

    –l   Designates long format, which includes all available information about
              the designated package(s).

    –p   Designates that information should be presented only for partially
              installed packages.

    –i   Designates that information should be presented only for fully
              installed packages.

    –a   Specifies the architecture of the package as *arch*.

    –v   Specifies the version of the package as *version*. "All compatible ver-
              sions" can be requested by preceding the version name with a tilde (˜).
              Multiple white space is replaced with a single space during version
              comparison.

    –c   Selects packages to be display based on the category *category*.
              (Categories are defined in the category field of the pkginfo file.) If
              more than one category is supplied, the package must only match one
              of the list of categories. The match is not case specific.

    pkginst   Designates a package by its instance. An instance can be the package
              abbreviation or a specific instance (for example, inst.1 or
              inst.beta). All instances of package can be requested by inst.*.

    –d   Defines a device, *device*, on which the software resides. *device* can be a
              directory pathname or the identifiers for tape, floppy disk, removable
              disk, *etc.* The special token "spool" may be used to indicate the
              default installation spool directory.

NOTES

Without options, `pkginfo` lists the primary category, package instance, and name of all completely installed and partially installed packages. One line per package selected is produced.

The −p and −i options are meaningless if used in conjunction with the −d option.

The options −q, −x, and −l are mutually exclusive.

`pkginfo` cannot tell if a pre-SVR4 package is only partially installed. It is assumed that all pre-SVR4 packages are fully installed.

SEE ALSO

pkgadd(1M), pkgask(1M), pkgchk(1M), pkgrm(1M), pkgtrans(1).

NAME

pkgparam – displays package parameter values

SYNOPSIS

pkgparam [–v][–d *device*] *pkginst* [*param*[...]]]
pkgparam –f *file* [–v] [*param*[...]]]

DESCRIPTION

pkgparam displays the value associated with the parameter or parameters
requested on the command line. The values are located in either the pkginfo file
for *pkginst* or from the specific file named with the –f option.

One parameter value is shown per line. Only the value of a parameter is given
unless the –v option is used. With this option, the output of the command is in
this format:

> *parameter1='value1'*
> *parameter2='value2'*
> *parameter3='value3'*

If no parameters are specified on the command line, values for all parameters
associated with the package are shown.

Options and arguments for this command are:

–v   Specifies verbose mode. Displays name of parameter and its value.

–d   Specifies the *device* on which a *pkginst* is stored. It can be a directory
pathname or the identifiers for tape, floppy disk or removable disk (for
example, /var/tmp, /dev/diskette, and /dev/dsk/c1d0s0). The
default device is the installation spool directory. If no instance name is
given, parameter information for all packages residing in *device* is shown.

–f   Requests that the command read *file* for parameter values.

pkginst   Defines a specific package instance for which parameter values should be
displayed. The format *pkginst*.* can be used to indicate all instances of a
package.

param   Defines a specific parameter whose value should be displayed.

ERRORS

If parameter information is not available for the indicated package, the command
exits with a non-zero status.

NOTES

The –f synopsis allows you to specify the file from which parameter values
should be extracted. This file should be in the same format as a pkginfo file. As
an example, such a file might be created during package development and used
while testing software during this stage.

SEE ALSO

pkgmk(1), pkgparam(3x), pkgproto(1), pgktrans(1).

NAME

pkgrm – removes a package from the system

SYNOPSIS

pkgrm [–n] [–a *admin*] [*pkginst1* [*pkginst2*[...]]]

pkgrm –s *spool* [*pkginst*]

DESCRIPTION

pkgrm will remove a previously installed or partially installed package from the system. A check is made to determine if any other packages depend on the one being removed. The action taken if a dependency exists is defined in the admin file.

The default state for the command is in interactive mode, meaning that prompt messages are given during processing to allow the administrator to confirm the actions being taken. Non-interactive mode can be requested with the –n option.

The –s option can be used to specify the directory from which spooled packages should be removed.

The options and arguments for this command are:

–n	Non-interactive mode. If there is a need for interaction, the command will exit. Use of this option requires that at least one package instance be named upon invocation of the command.
–a	Defines an installation administration file, *admin*, to be used in place of the default *admin* file.
–s	Removes the specified package(s) from the directory "spool."
pkginst	Specifies the package to be removed. The format *pkg_abbrev.** can be used to remove all instances of a package.

SEE ALSO

installf(1M), pkgadd(1M), pkgask(1M), pkgchk(1), pkginfo(1), pkgmk(1), pkgparam(1), pkgproto(1), pkgtrans(1), removef(1M).

NAME

pkgtrans – translate package format

SYNOPSIS

pkgtrans [-ions] *device1* *device2* [*pkginst1* [*pkginst2* [. . .]]]

DESCRIPTION

pkgtrans translates an installable package from one format to another. It translates:

a file system format to a datastream

a datastream to a file system format

a file system format to another file system format

The options and arguments for this command are:

-i   Copies only the pkginfo and pkgmap files.

-o   Overwrites the same instance on the destination device, package instance will be overwritten if it already exists.

-n   Creates a new instance if any instance of this package already exists.

-s   Indicates that the package should be written to *device2* as a datastream rather than as a file system. The default behavior is to write a file system format on devices that support both formats.

device1   Indicates the source device. The package or packages on this device will be translated and placed on *device2*.

device2   Indicates the destination device. Translated packages will be placed on this device.

pkginst   Specifies which package instance or instances on *device1* should be translated. The token all may be used to indicate all packages. *pkginst*.* can be used to indicate all instances of a package. If no packages are defined, a prompt shows all packages on the device and asks which to translate.

NOTES

Device specifications can be either the special node name (/dev/diskette) or the device alias (diskette1). The device spool indicates the default spool directory. Source and destination devices may not be the same.

By default, pkgtrans will not transfer any instance of a package if any instance of that package already exists on the destination device. Use of the –n option will create a new instance if an instance of this package already exists. Use of the –o option will overwrite the same instance if it already exists. Neither of these options are useful if the destination device is a datastream.

EXAMPLE

The following example translates all packages on the floppy drive /dev/diskette and places the translations on /tmp.

```
pkgtrans /dev/diskette /tmp all
```

The next example translates packages pkg1 and pkg2 on /tmp and places their translations (i.e., a datastream) on the 9track1 output device.

```
pkgtrans /tmp 9track1 pkg1 pkg2
```

The next example translates pkg1 and pkg2 on tmp and places them on the diskette in a datastream format.

```
pkgtrans -s /tmp /dev/diskette pkg1 pkg2
```

SEE ALSO

installf(1M), pkgadd(1M), pkgask(1M), pkginfo(1), pkgmk(1), pkgparam(1), pkgproto(1), pkgrm(1M), removef(1M).

NAME

pmadm – port monitor administration

SYNOPSIS

pmadm –a [–p *pmtag* | –t *type*] –s *svctag* –i id –m *pmspecific*
–v *ver* [–f xu] [–y *comment*] [–z *script*]

pmadm –r –p *pmtag* –s *svctag*

pmadm –e –p *pmtag* –s *svctag*

pmadm –d –p *pmtag* –s *svctag*

pmadm –l [–t *type* | –p *pmtag*] [–s *svctag*]

pmadm –L [–t *type* | –p *pmtag*] [–s *svctag*]

pmadm –g –p *pmtag* –s *svctag* [–z *script*]

pmadm –g –s *svctag* –t *type* –z *script*

DESCRIPTION

pmadm is the administrative command for the lower level of the Service Access
Facility hierarchy, that is, for service administration. A port may have only one
service associated with it although the same service may be available through
more than one port. In order to uniquely identify an instance of a service the
pmadm command must identify both the port monitor or port monitors through
which the service is available (–p or –t) and the service (–s). See the option
descriptions below.

pmadm performs the following functions:

- add or remove a service
- enable or disable a service
- install or replace a per-service configuration script
- print requested service information

Any user on the system may invoke pmadm to request service status (–l or –L) or
to print per-service configuration scripts (–g without the –z option). pmadm with
other options may be executed only by a privileged user.

The options have the following meanings:

–a   Add a service. pmadm adds an entry for the new service to the port
         monitor's administrative file. Because of the complexity of the options
         and arguments that follow the –a option, it may be convenient to use a
         command script or the menu system to add services. If you use the
         menu system, enter sysadm ports, then choose the port_services
         option.

–d   Disable a service. Add x to the flag field in the entry for the service
         svctag in the port monitor's administrative file. This is the entry used by
         port monitor *pmtag*. See the –f option, below, for a description of the
         flags available.

-e   Enable a service. Remove x from the flag field in the entry for the service *svctag* in the port monitor administrative file. This is the entry used by port monitor *pmtag*. See the -f option, below, for a description of the flags available.

-f xu   The -f option specifies one or both of the following two flags which are then included in the flag field of the entry for the new service in the port monitor's administrative file. If the -f option is not included, no flags are set and the default conditions prevail. By default, a new service is enabled and no utmp entry is created for it. A -f option without a following argument is illegal.

> x   Do not enable the service *svctag* available through port monitor *pmtag*.

> u   Create a utmp entry for service *svctag* available through port monitor *pmtag*.

-g   Print, install, or replace a per-service configuration script. The -g option with a -p option and a -s option prints the per-service configuration script for service *svctag* available through port monitor *pmtag*. The -g option with a -p option, a -s option, and a -z option installs the per-service configuration script contained in the file *script* as the per-service configuration script for service *svctag* available through port monitor *pmtag*. The -g option with a -s option, a -t option, and a -z option installs the file *script* as the per-service configuration script for service *svctag* available through any port monitor of type *type*. Other combinations of options with -g are invalid.

-i id   id is the identity that is to be assigned to service *svctag* when it is started. id must be an entry in /etc/passwd.

-l   The -l option requests service information. Used by itself and with the options described below it provides a filter for extracting information in several different groupings.

> -l   By itself, the -l option lists all services on the system.

> -l -p *pmtag*   Lists all services available through port monitor *pmtag*.

> -l -s *svctag*   Lists all services with tag *svctag*.

> -l -p *pmtag* -s *svctag*
>   Lists service *svctag*.

> -l -t *type*   Lists all services available through port monitors of type *type*.

> -l -t *type* -s *svctag*
>   Lists all services with tag *svctag* available through a port monitor of type *type*.

Other combinations of options with -l are invalid.

-L   The -L option is identical to the -l option except that output is printed
            in a condensed format.

-m *pmspecific*
            pmspecific is the port monitor-specific portion of the port monitor admin-
            istrative file entry for the service.

-p *pmtag*
            Specifies the tag associated with the port monitor through which a ser-
            vice (specified as -s *svctag*) is available.

-r   Remove a service. When pmadm removes a service, the entry for the ser-
            vice is removed from the port monitor's administrative file.

-s *svctag*
            Specifies the service tag associated with a given service. The service tag
            is assigned by the system administrator and is part of the entry for the
            service in the port monitor's administrative file.

-t *type*   Specifies the the port monitor type.

-v *ver*   Specifies the version number of the port monitor administrative file. The
            version number may be given as

                  -v `pmspec -V`

            where *pmspec* is the special administrative command for port monitor
            pmtag. This special command is ttyadm for ttymon and nlsadmin for
            listen. The version stamp of the port monitor is known by the com-
            mand and is returned when *pmspec* is invoked with a -V option.

-y *comment*
            Associate *comment* with the service entry in the port monitor administra-
            tive file.

-z *script*
            Used with the -g option to specify the name of the file that contains the
            per-service configuration script. Modifying a configuration script is a
            three-step procedure. First a copy of the existing script is made (-g
            alone). Then the copy is edited. Finally, the copy is put in place over
            the existing script (-g with -z).

OUTPUT

If successful, pmadm will exit with a status of 0. If it fails for any reason, it will
exit with a nonzero status.

Options that request information write the requested information to the standard
output. A request for information using the -l option prints column headers and
aligns the information under the appropriate headings. In this format, a missing
field is indicated by a hyphen. A request for information in the condensed format using the -L option prints the information in colon-separated fields; missing
fields are indicated by two successive colons. # is the comment character.

EXAMPLES

Add a service to a port monitor with tag pmtag. Give the service the tag svctag.
Port monitor-specific information is generated by specpm The service defined by
svctag will be invoked with identity root.

```
pmadm -a -p pmtag -s svctag -i root -m `specpm -a arg1 -b arg2` \
    -v `specpm -V`
```

Add a service with service tag svctag, identity guest, and port monitor-specific information generated by specpm to all port monitors of type type:

```
pmadm -a -s svctag -i guest -t type -m `specpm -a arg1 -b arg2` \
    -v `specpm -V`
```

Remove the service svctag from port monitor pmtag:

```
pmadm -r -p pmtag -s svctag
```

Enable the service svctag available through port monitor pmtag:

```
pmadm -e -p pmtag -s svctag
```

Disable the service svctag available through port monitor pmtag:

```
pmadm -d -p pmtag -s svctag
```

List status information for all services:

```
pmadm -l
```

List status information for all services available through the port monitor with tag ports:

```
pmadm -l -p ports
```

List the same information in condensed format:

```
pmadm -L -p ports
```

List status information for all services available through port monitors of type listen:

```
pmadm -l -t listen
```

Print the per-service configuration script associated with the service svctag available through port monitor pmtag:

```
pmadm -g -p pmtag -s svctag
```

FILES
```
/etc/saf/pmtag/_config
/etc/saf/pmtag/svctag
/var/saf/pmtag/*
```

SEE ALSO

doconfig(3n), sacadm(1M), sac(1M).

NAME

powerdown – stop all processes and turn off the power

SYNOPSIS

powerdown [–y | –Y]

DESCRIPTION

The powerdown command brings the system to a state where nothing is running and then turns off power.

The command invokes a visual interface (the powerdown task available through the *sysadm(1M)* command).

You are asked questions that control how much warning the other users are given. The options are:

–y   prevents the questions from being asked and just gives the warning messages. There is a 60-second pause between the warning messages.

–Y   is the same as –y except that it has no pause between messages. It is the fastest way to bring the system down.

The identical function is available under the sysadm menu:

sysadm powerdown

This command may be assigned a password with the sysadm systemsetup password(1M) command.

FILES

/usr/sbin/shutdown – invoked by powerdown

DIAGNOSTICS

The powerdown command exits with one of the following values:

0   Normal exit.

2   Invalid command syntax. A usage message is displayed.

7   The visual interface for this command is not available because it cannot invoke fmli. (The FMLI package is not installed or is corrupt.)

SEE ALSO

shutdown(1M), sysadm(1M).

NAME
    profiler: prfld, prfstat, prfdc, prfsnap, prfpr − UNIX system profiler
SYNOPSIS
    /usr/sbin/prfld [*system_namelist*]
    /usr/sbin/prfstat on
    /usr/sbin/prfstat off
    /usr/sbin/prfdc *file* [*period* [*off_hour*]]
    /usr/sbin/prfsnap *file*
    /usr/sbin/prfpr *file* [*cutoff* [*system_namelist*]]
DESCRIPTION
    prfld, prfstat, prfdc, prfsnap, and prfpr form a system of programs to facili-
    tate an activity study of the UNIX operating system.

    prfld is used to initialize the recording mechanism in the system. It generates a
    table containing the starting address of each system subroutine as extracted from
    system_namelist.

    prfstat is used to enable or disable the sampling mechanism. Profiler overhead
    is less than 1% as calculated for 500 text addresses. prfstat will also reveal the
    number of text addresses being measured.

    prfdc and prfsnap perform the data collection function of the profiler by copy-
    ing the current value of all the text address counters to a file where the data can
    be analyzed. prfdc will store the counters into *file* every *period* minutes and will
    turn off at *off_hour* (valid values for *off_hour* are 0−24). prfsnap collects data at
    the time of invocation only, appending the counter values to *file*.

    prfpr formats the data collected by prfdc or prfsnap. Each text address is con-
    verted to the nearest text symbol (as found in *system_namelist*) and is printed if
    the percent activity for that range is greater than *cutoff*.

FILES
    /dev/prf   interface to profile data and text addresses

    /stand/unix   default for system namelist file

NAME

    prtconf – print system configuration

SYNOPSIS

    /usr/sbin/prtconf

DESCRIPTION

    The prtconf command prints the system configuration information which includes the memory and peripheral configuration. This information is displayed every time the system is initialized to multiuser mode.

EXAMPLES

    To print the configuration of the 3B2 Computer, execute:

    # /usr/sbin/prtconf

    AT&T 3B2 SYSTEM CONFIGURATION:

    Memory size: 2 Megabytes
    System Peripherals:

Device Name	Subdevices	Extended Subdevices
SBD		
	Floppy Disk	
	30 Megabyte Disk	
	72 Megabyte Disk	
SCSI		
	SD00 ID1	
		67 Megabyte Disk ID0
		67 Megabyte Disk ID1
		135 Megabyte Disk ID2
		135 Megabyte Disk ID3
NI		
PORTS		
CTC		

NAME

   prtvtoc – print the VTOC of a block device

SYNOPSIS

   /usr/sbin/prtvtoc *device*

DESCRIPTION

   The prtvtoc command allows the contents of the VTOC (volume table of contents) to be viewed. The command can be used only by the super-user.

   The *device* name must be the file name of a raw device in the form of
   /dev/rdsk/c?d?s? or /dev/rdsk/c?t?d?s6?.

EXAMPLE

   The command line entry and system response shown below are for a 72-mega-
   byte hard disk:

```
# prtvtoc /dev/rdsk/c1d0s6
* /dev/rdsk/c1d0s6 partition map
*
* Dimension:
*      512 bytes/sector
*       18 sectors/track
*       11 tracks/cylinder
*      198 sectors/cylinder
*      754 cylinders
*      754 accessible cylinders
*
* Flags:
*    1: unmountable
*   10: read-only
*
*
*                      First   Sector  Last
* PartitionTag   Flags  Sector  Count   Sector  Mount Directory
      0      2    00    19040   23460   42499   /
      1      3    01      100   18940   19039
      2      4    00    29552  119344  148895   /usr
      3      6    00    24552    5000   29551   /stand
      6      0    01        0  148896  148895
      7      1    01        0     100      99

#
```

Codes for TAG are:

NAME	NUMBER
UNASSIGNED	0
BOOT	1
ROOT	2
SWAP	3
USR	4
BACKUP	5
STAND	6

FLAG indicates how the partition is to be mounted.

NAME	NUMBER
MOUNTABLE, READ AND WRITE	00
NOT MOUNTABLE	01
MOUNTABLE, READ ONLY	10

SEE ALSO
  fmthard(1M).

CAVEAT
  The mount command does not check the "not mountable" bit.

NAME

pump – Download B16 or X86 a.out file to a peripheral board

SYNOPSIS

/sbin/pump /dev/*devname* file

DESCRIPTION

The pump command will read a B16 or X86 a.out file's sections into a buffer according to the physical address of the section. The command can be used only by the super-user. pump expects a section in the a.out file called .start. Once it has found this section, pump will inform the peripheral to start executing at the address that it found in .start after it has downloaded the a.out file.

There are four phases of the pump operation:

reset   This phase will cause a hardware reset on the peripheral.

download   This phase will download the a.out file to the peripheral.

force call to function
                 This phase will inform the peripheral to start executing at the address found in the .start section.

sysgen   This phase will sysgen the peripheral. It allows normal functioning of the peripheral to occur.

Error Messages

pump error: *UNIX_error_number* – Can't get status of /dev/*devname*

There may be no /dev/*devname*.

pump Error: *error_number* – ioctl call

The ioctl call failed. The *error_number* returned can be a UNIX system error number or, in the case of the NI, an error number of 208. Error number 208 is a timeout message. The peripheral board did not respond in time to the request made of it (this is not the only error, see intro(2) for a complete list).

Can't open a.out filename for reading!

The error may be that there is no such file or the permissions are such that the file cannot be read [see chmod(1)].

Error: Object file is not in b16 or x86 common object format

The file to be downloaded to the peripheral is not a B16 or X86 a.out file.

Section size is too big for the buffer

The **a.out** file may be greater that the 32K bytes that is the limit of RAM on the peripheral.

Error: No section name called .start

pump needs .start for the starting address that the peripheral needs to execute the downloaded code.

pump: /dev/*devname* returned a CIO FAULT during phase

The peripheral encountered a hardware fault during one of the phases of the pump.

pump: /dev/*devname* returned a CIO Invalid Queue Entry during phase

The peripheral did not understand the command phase that was issued by pump.

pump: /dev/*devname* did not respond during phase

The UNIX system driver called may not have understood the command.

pump: A timeout has occurred on /dev/*devname* during phase

The peripheral did not respond to one of the commands given.

pump: There was no return code for /dev/*devname* during phase

The return code that was given may have been corrupted.

SEE ALSO
intro(2), a.out(4).

NAME

putdev – edits device table

SYNOPSIS

putdev −a *alias* [*attribute=value* [. . .]]

putdev −m *device attribute=value* [*attribute=value* [. . .]]

putdev −d *device* [*attribute* [. . .]]

DESCRIPTION

putdev can add a new device to the device table, modify an existing device description or remove a device entry from the table. The first synopsis is used to add a device. The second synopsis is used to modify existing entries by adding or changing attributes. If a specified attribute is not defined, this option adds that attribute to the device definition. If it is already defined, it modifies the attribute definition. The third synopsis is used to delete either an entire device entry or, if the attribute argument is used, to delete an attribute assignment for a device.

The options and arguments for this command are:

−a   Adds a device to the device table using the specified attributes. The device must be referenced by its *alias*.

−m   Modifies a device entry in the device table. If an entry already exists, it adds any specified attributes that are not defined. It also modifies any attributes which already have a value with the value specified with this command.

−d   Removes a device from the device table, when executed without the *attributes* argument. Used with the *attribute* argument, it deletes the given attribute specification for *device* from the table.

alias   Designates the alias of the device to be added.

device   Designates the pathname or alias of the device whose attribute is to be added, modified, or removed.

attribute   Designates a device attribute to be added or modified. Can be any of the device attributes described under NOTES except alias. This prevents an accidental modification or deletion of a device's alias from the table.

value   Designates the value to be assigned to a device's attribute.

NOTES

The following list shows all of the attributes which can be defined for a device:

alias   The unique name by which a device is known. No two devices in the database may share the same alias name. The name is limited in length to 14 characters and should contain only alphanumeric characters and also the following special characters if they are escaped with a backslash: underscore ( ), dollar sign ($), hyphen (-), and period (.).

bdevice	The pathname to the block special device node associated with the device, if any. The associated major/minor combination should be unique within the database and should match that associated with the cdevice field, if any. (It is the administrator's responsibility to ensure that these major/minor numbers are unique in the database.)
capacity	The capacity of the device or of the typical volume, if removable.
cdevice	The pathname to the character special device node associated with the device, if any. The associated major/minor combination should be unique within the database and should match that associated with the bdevice field, if any. (It is the administrator's responsibility to ensure that these major/minor numbers are unique in the database.)
cyl	Used by the command specified in the mkfscmd attribute.
desc	A description of any instance of a volume associated with this device (such as floppy diskette).
dpartlist	The list of disk partitions associated with this device. Used only if type=disk. The list should contain device aliases, each of which must have type=dpart.
dparttype	The type of disk partition represented by this device. Used only if type=dpart. It should be either fs (for filesystem) or dp (for data partition).
erasecmd	The command string that, when executed, erases the device.
fmtcmd	The command string that, when executed, formats the device.
fsname	The filesystem name on the file system administered on this partition, as supplied to the /usr/sbin/labelit command. This attribute is specified only if type=dpart and dparttype=fs.
gap	Used by the command specified in the mkfscmd attribute.
mkfscmd	The command string that, when executed, places a file system on a previously formatted device.
mountpt	The default mount point to use for the device. Used only if the device is mountable. For disk partitions where type=dpart and dparttype=fs, this attribute should specify the location where the partition is normally mounted.
nblocks	The number of blocks in the filesystem administered on this partition. Used only if type=dpart and dparttype=fs.
ninodes	The number of inodes in the filesystem administered on this partition. Used only if type=dpart and dparttype=fs.
norewind	The name of the character special device node that allows access to the serial device without rewinding when the device is closed.

pathname	Defines the pathname to an i-node describing the device (used for non-block or character device pathnames, such as directories).
type	A token that represents inherent qualities of the device. Standard types include: 9-track, ctape, disk, directory, diskette, dpart, and qtape.
volname	The volume name on the filesystem administered on this partition, as supplied to the /usr/sbin/labelit command. Used only if type=dpart and dparttype=fs.
volume	A text string used to describe any instance of a volume associated with this device. This attribute should not be defined for devices which are not removable.

ERRORS

The command will exit with one of the following values:

0 = successful completion of the task.

1 = command syntax incorrect, invalid option used, or internal error occurred.

2 = device table could not be opened for reading or new device table could not be created.

3 = if executed with the −a option, indicates that an entry in the device table with the alias *alias* already exits. If executed with the −m or −d options, indicates that no entry exists for device *device*.

4 = indicates that −d was requested and one or more of the specified attributes were not defined for the device.

FILES

/etc/device.tab

SEE ALSO

devattr(1), putdgrp(1M).

NAME

    putdgrp – edits device group table

SYNOPSIS

    putdgrp [–d] *dgroup* [*device* [. . .]]

DESCRIPTION

    putdgrp modifies the device group table. It performs two kinds of modification. It can modify the table by creating a new device group or removing a device group. It can also change group definitions by adding or removing a device from the group definition.

    When the command is invoked with only a *dgroup* specification, the command adds the specified group name to the device group table if it does not already exist. If the –d option is also used with only the *dgroup* specification, the command deletes the group from the table.

    When the command is invoked with both a *dgroup* and a *device* specification, it adds the given device name (or names) to the group definition. When invoked with both arguments and the –d option, the command deletes the device name (or names) from the group definition.

    When the command is invoked with both a *dgroup* and a *device* specification and the device group does not exist, it creates the group and adds the specified devices to that new group.

    The options and arguments for this command are:

    –d   Deletes the group or, if used with *device*, the device from a group definition.

    dgroup Specifies a device group name.

    device   Specifies the pathname or alias of the device that is to added to or deleted from the device group.

ERRORS

    The command will exit with one of the following values:

    0 = successful completion of the task.

    1 = command syntax incorrect, invalid option used, or internal error occurred.

    2 = device group table could not be opened for reading or a new device group table could not be created.

    3 = if executed with the –d option, indicates that an entry in the device group table for the device group *dgroup* does not exist and so cannot be deleted. Otherwise, indicates that the device group *dgroup* already exists and cannot be added.

    4 = if executed with the –d option, indicates that the device group *dgroup* does not have as members one or more of the specified devices. Otherwise, indicates that the device group *dgroup* already has one or more of the specified devices as members.

EXAMPLE

To add a new device group:

        putdgrp floppies

To add a device to a device group:

        putdgrp floppies diskette2

To delete a device group:

        putdgrp -d floppies

To delete a device from a device group:

        putdgrp -d floppies diskette2

FILES

/etc/dgroup.tab

SEE ALSO

listdgrp(1), putdev(1M).

NAME
pwck, grpck – password/group file checkers

SYNOPSIS
/usr/sbin/pwck [*file*]
/usr/sbin/grpck [file]

DESCRIPTION
pwck scans the password file and notes any inconsistencies. The checks include validation of the number of fields, login name, user ID, group ID, and whether the login directory and the program-to-use-as-shell exist. The default password file is /etc/passwd.

grpck verifies all entries in the group file. This verification includes a check of the number of fields, group name, group ID, whether any login names belong to more than NGROUPS_MAX groups and that all login names appear in the password file. The default group file is /etc/group.

FILES
/etc/group
/etc/passwd

SEE ALSO
group(4), passwd(4).

DIAGNOSTICS
Group entries in /etc/group with no login names are flagged.

NAME
pwconv – Installs and updates /etc/shadow with information from /etc/passwd

SYNOPSIS
pwconv

DESCRIPTION
The pwconv command creates and updates /etc/shadow with information from /etc/passwd.

If the /etc/shadow file does not exist, this command will create /etc/shadow with information from /etc/passwd. The command populates /etc/shadow with the user's login name, password, and password aging information. If password aging information does not exist in /etc/passwd for a given user, none will be added to /etc/shadow. However, the last changed information will always be updated.

If the /etc/shadow file does exist, the following tasks will be performed:

Entries that are in the /etc/passwd file and not in the /etc/shadow file will be added to the /etc/shadow file.

Entries that are in the /etc/shadow file and not in the /etc/passwd file will be removed from /etc/shadow.

Password attributes (e.g., password and aging information) that exist in an /etc/passwd entry will be moved to the corresponding entry in /etc/shadow.

The pwconv program is a privileged system command that cannot be executed by ordinary users.

FILES
/etc/passwd, /etc/shadow, /etc/opasswd, /etc/oshadow

SEE ALSO
passwd(1), passmgmt(1M)

DIAGNOSTICS
The pwconv command exits with one of the following values:

0   SUCCESS.

1   Permission denied.

2   Invalid command syntax.

3   Unexpected failure. Conversion not done.

4   Unexpected failure. Password file(s) missing.

5   Password file(s) busy. Try again later.

NAME

  quot – summarize file system ownership

SYNOPSIS

  quot [–acfhnv] [*filesystem*]

DESCRIPTION

  quot displays the number of blocks (1024 bytes) in the named *filesystem* currently owned by each user. There is a limit of 2048 blocks. Files larger than this will be counted as a 2048 block file, but the total blocks count will be correct.

  The options are:

  –a   Generate a report for all mounted file systems.

  –c   Display three columns giving a file size in blocks, the number of files of that size, and a cumulative total of blocks containing files of that size or a smaller size.

  –f   Display count of number of files as well as space owned by each user. This options is incompatible with the –c and –v options.

  –h   Estimate the number of blocks in the file — this does not account for files with holes in them.

  –n   Attach names to the list of files read from standard input. quot –n cannot be used alone, because it expects data from standard input. For example, the pipeline ncheck filesystem | sort +0n | quot –n filesystem will produce a list of all files and their owners. This option is incompatible with all other options.

  –v   In addition to the default output, display three columns containing the number of blocks not accessed in the last 30, 60, and 90 days.

NOTES

  This command may only be used by a privileged user.

FILES

  /etc/mnttab   mounted file systems
  /etc/passwd   to get user names

SEE ALSO

  du(1M)

NAME

   quota – display a user's disk quota and usage

SYNOPSIS

   quota [–v] [*username*]

DESCRIPTION

   quota displays users' disk usage and limits. Only a privileged user may use the optional *username* argument to view the limits of other users.

   quota without options displays only warnings about mounted file systems where usage is over quota. Remotely mounted file systems which do not have quotas turned on are ignored.

   username can be numeric, corresponding to the uid of a user.

   The –v option displays user's quotas on all mounted file systems where quotas exist.

FILES

   /etc/mnttab   list of currently mounted filesystems

SEE ALSO

   edquota(1M), quotaon(1M), quotactl(2).

NAME
    quotacheck – file system quota consistency checker

SYNOPSIS
    quotacheck [–v] [–p] *filesystem...*
    quotacheck [–apv]

DESCRIPTION
    quotacheck examines each file system, builds a table of current disk usage, and
    compares this table against that stored in the disk quota file for the file system. If
    any inconsistencies are detected, both the quota file and the current system copy
    of the incorrect quotas are updated (the latter only occurs if an active file system
    is checked).

    quotacheck expects each file system to be checked to have a quota file named
    quotas in the root directory. If none is present, quotacheck will ignore the file
    system.

    quotacheck accesses the character special device in calculating the actual disk
    usage for each user. Thus, the file systems checked should be quiescent while
    quotacheck is running.

    The options are:

    –v   Indicate the calculated disk quotas for each user on a particular file sys-
            tem. quotacheck normally reports only those quotas modified.

    –a   Check the file systems indicated in /etc/mnttab to be read-write with
            disk quotas. Only those file systems that have "rq" in the mntopts field of
            the /etc/vfstab file are checked.

    –p   Run parallel passes on the required file systems.

FILES
    /etc/mnttab   mounted file systems
    /etc/vfstab   list of default parameters for each file system

SEE ALSO
    quotaon(1M), quotactl(2).

NAME
quotaon, quotaoff – turn file system quotas on and off

SYNOPSIS
quotaon [-v] *filesystem...*
quotaon [-av]

quotaoff [-v] *filesystem...*
quotaoff [-av]

DESCRIPTION
quotaon announces to the system that disk quotas should be enabled on one or more file systems. The file systems specified must be mounted at the time. The file system quota files must be present in the root directory of the specified file system and be named quotas.

quotaoff announces to the system that file systems specified should have any disk quotas turned off.

The options for quotaon are:

-a   All file systems in /etc/mnttab marked read-write with quotas will have their quotas turned on. This option is normally used at boot time to enable quotas. It applies only to file systems that have "rq" in the mntopts field of the /etc/vfstab file.

-v   Display a message for each file system where quotas are turned on.

The options for quotaoff are:

-a   Force all file systems in /etc/mnttab to have their quotas disabled. This option applies only to file systems that have "rq" in the mntopts field of the /etc/vfstab file.

-v   Display a message for each file system affected.

These commands update the status field of devices located in /etc/mnttab to indicate when quotas are on or off for each file system.

FILES
/etc/mnttab   mounted file systems /etc/vfstab list of default parameters for each file system

SEE ALSO
mnttab(4), vfstab(4)

NAME

rarpd – DARPA Reverse Address Resolution Protocol server

SYNOPSIS

rarpd *interface* [*hostname*]

/usr/sbin/rarpd -a

DESCRIPTION

rarpd starts a daemon that responds to Reverse Address Resolution Protocol (RARP) requests. The daemon forks a copy of itself that runs in background. It must be run as root.

RARP is used by machines at boot time to discover their Internet Protocol (IP) address. The booting machine provides its Ethernet Address in a RARP request message. Using the ethers and hosts databases, rarpd maps this Ethernet Address into the corresponding IP address which it returns to the booting machine in an RARP reply message. The booting machine must be listed in both databases for rarpd to locate its IP address. rarpd issues no reply when it fails to locate an IP address.

In the first synopsis, the *interface* parameter names the network interface upon which rarpd is to listen for requests. The *interface* parameter takes the "name unit" form used by ifconfig(1M). The second argument, *hostname*, is used to obtain the IP address of that interface. An IP address in "decimal dot" notation may be used for *hostname*. If *hostname* is omitted, the address of the interface will be obtained from the kernel. When the first form of the command is used, rarpd must be run separately for each interface on which RARP service is to be supported. A machine that is a router may invoke rarpd multiple times, for example:

```
/usr/sbin/rarpd emd1 host
/usr/sbin/rarpd emd2 host-backbone
```

In the second synopsis, rarpd locates all of the network interfaces present on the system and starts a daemon process for each one that supports RARP.

FILES

/etc/ethers
/etc/hosts

SEE ALSO

ifconfig(1M), ethers(4), hosts(4), netconfig(4), boot(8).

Finlayson, Ross, Timothy Mann, Jeffrey Mogul, and Marvin Theimer, *A Reverse Address Resolution Protocol*, RFC 903, Network Information Center, SRI International, Menlo Park, Calif., June 1984.

NAME

    rc0 – run commands performed to stop the operating system

SYNOPSIS

    /sbin/rc0

DESCRIPTION

    This file is executed at each system state change that needs to have the system in an inactive state. It is responsible for those actions that bring the system to a quiescent state, traditionally called "shutdown".

    There are three system states that require this procedure. They are state 0 (the system halt state), state 5 (the firmware state), and state 6 (the reboot state). Whenever a change to one of these states occurs, the rc0 procedure is run. The entry in /sbin/inittab might read:

        s0:056:wait:/sbin/rc0 >/dev/console 2>&1 </dev/console

    Some of the actions performed by rc0 are carried out by files in the directory /usr/sbin/shutdown.d and files beginning with K in /sbin/rc0.d. These files are executed in ASCII order (see FILES below for more information), terminating some system service. The combination of commands in rc0 and files in /usr/sbin/shutdown.d and /sbin/rc0.d determines how the system is shut down.

    The recommended sequence for rc0 is:

    Stop System Services and Daemons.

        Various system services (such as 3BNET Local Area Network or LP Spooler) are gracefully terminated.

        When new services are added that should be terminated when the system is shut down, the appropriate files are installed in /usr/sbin/shutdown.d and /sbin/rc0.d.

    Terminate Processes

        SIGTERM signals are sent to all running processes by killall(1M). Processes stop themselves cleanly if sent SIGTERM.

    Kill Processes

        SIGKILL signals are sent to all remaining processes; no process can resist SIGKILL.

        At this point the only processes left are those associated with rc0 and processes 0 and 1, which are special to the operating system.

    Unmount All File Systems

        Only the root file system (/) remains mounted.

Depending on which system state the systems end up in (0, 5, or 6), the entries in /sbin/inittab will direct what happens next. If the /sbin/inittab has not defined any other actions to be performed as in the case of system state 0, then the operating system will have nothing to do. It should not be possible to get the system's attention. The only thing that can be done is to turn off the power or possibly get the attention of a firmware monitor. The command can be used only by the super-user.

FILES

The execution by /usr/bin/sh of any files in /usr/sbin/shutdown.d occurs in ASCII sort-sequence order. See rc2(1M) for more information.

SEE ALSO

killall(1M), rc2(1M), shutdown(1M).

NAME
rc2 – run commands performed for multi-user environment

SYNOPSIS
/sbin/rc2

DESCRIPTION
This file is executed via an entry in /sbin/inittab and is responsible for those initializations that bring the system to a ready-to-use state, traditionally state 2, called the "multi-user" state.

The actions performed by rc2 are found in files in the directory /etc/rc.d and files beginning with S in /sbin/rc2.d. These files are executed by /usr/bin/sh in ASCII sort-sequence order (see FILES for more information). When functions are added that need to be initialized when the system goes multi-user, an appropriate file should be added in /sbin/rc2.d.

The functions done by the rc2 command and associated /sbin/rc2.d files include:

Setting and exporting the TIMEZONE variable.

Setting-up and mounting the user (/usr) file system.

Cleaning up (remaking) the /tmp and /var/tmp directories.

Loading the network interface and ports cards with program data and starting the associated processes.

Starting the cron daemon by executing /usr/sbin/cron.

Cleaning up (deleting) uucp locks status, and temporary files in the /var/spool/uucp directory.

Other functions can be added, as required, to support the addition of hardware and software features.

EXAMPLES
The following are prototypical files found in /sbin/rc2.d. These files are prefixed by an S and a number indicating the execution order of the files.

MOUNTFILESYS
```
#   Set up and mount file systems

cd /
/sbin/mountall /etc/fstab
```

RMTMPFILES
```
#   clean up /tmp
rm -rf /tmp
mkdir /tmp
chmod 777 /tmp
chgrp sys /tmp
chown sys /tmp
```

```
uucp
    #      clean-up uucp locks, status, and temporary files

    rm -rf /var/spool/locks/*
```

The file /etc/TIMEZONE is included early in rc2, thus establishing the default time zone for all commands that follow.

FILES

Here are some hints about files in /etc/rc.d:

The order in which files are executed is important. Since they are executed in ASCII sort—sequence order, using the first character of the file name as a sequence indicator will help keep the proper order. Thus, files starting with the following characters would be:

    [0–9]. very early
    [A–Z]. early
    [a–n]. later
    [o–z]. last

    3.mountfs

Files in /etc/rc.d that begin with a dot (.) will not be executed. This feature can be used to hide files that are not to be executed for the time being without removing them. The command can be used only by the super-user.

Files in /sbin/rc2.d must begin with an S or a K followed by a number and the rest of the file name. Upon entering run level 2, files beginning with S are executed with the start option; files beginning with K, are executed with the stop option. Files beginning with other characters are ignored.

SEE ALSO

shutdown(1M).

NAME

     rc6 – run commands performed to stop and reboot the operating system

SYNOPSIS

     /usr/sbin/rc6

DESCRIPTION

     The shell script rc6 is run whenever a transition to run state 6 is requested either
     through init 6 or shutdown −i6.

     The sequence of events in rc6 is as follows:

     •   check to see if a new bootable operating system (/stand/unix) needs to
            be built; if so, build one by running the buildsys command

     •   unmount all file systems

     Then init executes the initdefault entry in the /sbin/inittab file to bring
     the system to the operating state defined by that entry.

     Note that if an error occurs while buildsys is building a new bootable operating
     system, a shell is spawned that will exit only to firmware state; [see
     buildsys(1M)].

SEE ALSO

     buildsys(1M), cunix(1M), init(1M), rc0(1M), rc2(1M), shutdown(1M), init-
     tab(4).
     System Administrator's Guide

NAME

     rdate – set system date from a remote host

SYNOPSIS

     rdate *hostname*

DESCRIPTION

     rdate sets the local date and time from the *hostname* given as an argument. You must be super-user on the local system. Typically **rdate** can be inserted as part of a startup script.

NAME
>   relogin – rename login entry to show current layer

SYNOPSIS
>   /usr/lib/layersys/relogin [−s] [*line*]

DESCRIPTION
>   The relogin command changes the terminal *line* field of a user's utmp entry to
>   the name of the windowing terminal layer attached to standard input. write
>   messages sent to this user are directed to this layer. In addition, the who com-
>   mand will show the user associated with this layer. relogin may only be
>   invoked under layers.
>
>   relogin is invoked automatically by layers to set the utmp entry to the terminal
>   line of the first layer created upon startup, and to reset the utmp entry to the real
>   line on termination. It may be invoked by a user to designate a different layer to
>   receive write messages.
>
>   −s   Suppress error messages.
>
>   *line*   Specifies which utmp entry to change. The utmp file is searched for an
>   entry with the specified *line* field. That field is changed to the line asso-
>   ciated with the standard input. (To learn what lines are associated with
>   a given user, say jdoe, type ps −f −u jdoe and note the values shown
>   in the TTY field [see ps(1)]).

FILES
>   /var/adm/utmp   database of users versus terminals

SEE ALSO
>   layers(1), mesg(1), ps(1), who(1), write(1), in the *User's Reference Manual*.
>   utmp(4).

DIAGNOSTICS
>   Returns 0 upon successful completion, 1 otherwise.

NOTES
>   relogin will fail, if *line* does not belong to the user issuing the relogin com-
>   mand or standard input is not associated with a terminal.

NAME

repquota – summarize quotas for a file system

SYNOPSIS

repquota [–v] *filesystem*...

repquota [–av]

DESCRIPTION

repquota prints a summary of the disk usage and quotas for the specified file systems. For each user the current number of files and amount of space (in kilobytes) is printed, along with any quotas created with edquota.

The options are:

–a   Report on all file systems that have "rq" in the mntopts field of the /etc/vfstab file.

–v   Report all quotas, even if there is no usage.

Only privileged users may view quotas which are not their own.

SEE ALSO

edquota(1M), quota(1M), quotacheck(1M), quotaon(1M)

NAME
    restore – initiate restores of filesystems, data partitions, or disks

SYNOPSIS
    restore [–o *target*] [–d *date*] [–mn] [–s | v] –P *partdev*

    restore [–o *target*] [–d *date*] [–mn] [–s | v] –S *odevice*

    restore [–o *target*] [–d *date*] [–mn] [–s | v] –A *partdev*

DESCRIPTION
    restore posts requests for the restore of a data partition, a filesystem partition, or a disk from system-maintained archives. If the appropriate archive containing the required partition is online, the partition is restored immediately. If not, a request to restore the specified archive of the partition is posted to a restore status table. The restore status table is /etc/bkup/rsstatus.tab. The restore request is assigned a restore jobid that can be used to monitor the progress of the restore or to cancel it. A restore request that has been posted must later be resolved by an operator (see rsoper(1M)).

    restore may be executed only by a user with superuser privilege.

    If restore –A *partdev* is issued, the fdisk(1M) (full disk recovery) method is used to repartition and repopulate disk *partdev*. *partdev* is the name of the device that refers to the entire disk. For the AT&T 3B2, it is /dev/rdsk/c1d?s6.

Options
    –d *date*   Restores the partition as of *date*. This may or may not be the latest archive. See getdate(1M) for valid date formats.

    –m   If the restore cannot be carried out immediately, this option notifies the invoking user (via mail(1M)) when the request has been completed.

    –n   Displays a list of all archived versions of the object contained in the backup history log, but does not attempt to restore the object.

    –o *target* Instead of restoring directly to the specified object (*partdev* or *fsdev*), this option restores the archive to *target*. *target* is of the form:
                         [*oname*][:*odev*]
                 where *oname* is the name of the filesystem to be restored to (for –S archives) and *odev* is the name of the partition to be restored to (for –P and –A archives).

    –s   While a restore operation is occurring, displays a "." for each 100 (512-byte) blocks transferred from the destination device.

    –v   Displays the name of each object as it is restored. Only those archiving methods that restore named directories and files (incfile, ffile) support this option.

    –A *partdev* Initiates restore of the entire disk *partdev*.

    –P *partdev* Initiates restore of the data partition *partdev*.

          −S *odevice* Initiates restore of the filesystem partition *odevice*.

DIAGNOSTICS

The exit codes for **restore** are the following:

0 = the task completed successfully
1 = one or more parameters to **restore** are invalid
2 = an error has occurred, causing **restore** to fail to
        complete *all* portions of its task

EXAMPLES

Example 1:

          restore −m −S /usr

posts a request to restore the most current archived version of /usr. If the restore cannot be carried out immediately, notify the invoking user when the request has been completed.

Example 2:

          restore −o /dev/rdsk/c1d0s8 −P /dev/rdsk/c1d1s2

posts a request that the archived data partition /dev/rdsk/c1d1s2 be restored to the target device partition /dev/rdsk/c1d0s8.

Example 3:

          restore −d "december 1, 1987" −A /dev/rdsk/c1d0s6

posts a request for the restore of the entire disk */dev/rdsk/c1d0s6*. The restore should be made as of December 1, 1987.

Example 4:

          restore −n −P /dev/rdsk/c1d0s1

requests the system to display the backup date and an 1s −1 listing from the backup history log of all archived versions of the data partition /dev/rdsk/c1d0s1. The data partition is not restored.

FILES

/etc/bkup/bkhist.tab	lists the labels of all volumes that have been used for backup operations
/etc/bkup/rsstatus.tab	lists the status of all restore requests from users
/etc/bkup/rsnotify.tab	lists the email address of the operator to be notified whenever restore requests require operator intervention

SEE ALSO

fdisk(1M), mail(1M), rsnotify(1M), rsoper(1M), rsstatus(1M), urestore(1M), ursstatus(1M).
getdate(3C) in the *Programmer's Reference Manual*.

NAME
rexecd – remote execution server

SYNOPSIS
in.rexecd *host.port*

DESCRIPTION
rexecd is the server for the rexec(3N) routine. The server provides remote execution facilities with authentication based on user names and encrypted passwords. It is invoked automatically as needed by inetd(1M), and then executes the following protocol:

1) The server reads characters from the socket up to a null (\0) byte. The resultant string is interpreted as an ASCII number, base 10.

2) If the number received in step 1 is non-zero, it is interpreted as the port number of a secondary stream to be used for the stderr. A second connection is then created to the specified port on the client's machine.

3) A null terminated user name of at most 16 characters is retrieved on the initial socket.

4) A null terminated, encrypted, password of at most 16 characters is retrieved on the initial socket.

5) A null terminated command to be passed to a shell is retrieved on the initial socket. The length of the command is limited by the upper bound on the size of the system's argument list.

6) rexecd then validates the user as is done at login time and, if the authentication was successful, changes to the user's home directory, and establishes the user and group protections of the user. If any of these steps fail the connection is aborted with a diagnostic message returned.

7) A null byte is returned on the connection associated with the stderr and the command line is passed to the normal login shell of the user. The shell inherits the network connections established by rexecd.

SEE ALSO
inetd(1M)

DIAGNOSTICS
All diagnostic messages are returned on the connection associated with the stderr, after which any network connections are closed. An error is indicated by a leading byte with a value of 1 (0 is returned in step 7 above upon successful completion of all the steps prior to the command execution).

username too long
>   The name is longer than 16 characters.

password too long
>   The password is longer than 16 characters.

command too long
>   The command line passed exceeds the size of the argument list (as configured into the system).

Login incorrect.
>   No password file entry for the user name existed.

Password incorrect.
>   The wrong password was supplied.

No remote directory.
>   The chdir command to the home directory failed.

Try again.
>   A fork by the server failed.

/usr/bin/sh: ...
>   The user's login shell could not be started.

NOTES

Indicating Login incorrect as opposed to Password incorrect is a security breach which allows people to probe a system for users with null passwords.

A facility to allow all data exchanges to be encrypted should be present.

NAME

rfadmin – Remote File Sharing domain administration

SYNOPSIS

rfadmin

rfadmin –a *hostname*

rfadmin –r *hostname*

rfadmin –p [–t *transport1,transport2,...*]

rfadmin –q

rfadmin –o *option*

DESCRIPTION

rfadmin is used to add and remove hosts, and their associated authentication information, from a *domain*/passwd file on a Remote File Sharing primary domain name server. It is also used to transfer domain name server responsibilities from one machine to another. Used with no options, rfadmin returns the *hostname* of the current domain name server for the local domain on each of the transport providers that span the domain.

rfadmin can only be used to modify domain files on the primary domain name server (–a and –r options). If domain name server responsibilities are temporarily passed to a secondary domain name server, that computer can use the –p option to pass domain name server responsibility back to the primary. The command can be directed to a specific set of transport providers by using the –t option with a comma-separated list of transport providers. Any host can use rfadmin with no options to print information about the domain. The user must have root permissions to use this command, except in the case when the –q option is used.

–a *hostname*	Add a host to a domain that is served by this domain name server. *hostname* must be of the form *domain.nodename*. It creates an entry for *hostname* in the *domain*/passwd file and prompts for an initial authentication password; the password prompting process conforms with that of passwd(1).
–r *hostname*	Remove a host, *hostname*, from its domain by removing it from the *domain*/passwd file.
–p	Used to pass the domain name server responsibilities back to a primary or to a secondary name server.
–t *transport1, transport2 ...*	Select transport provider(s). The –t option is used only with the –p option.
–q	Tells if RFS is running.
–o *option*	Sets RFS system option. *option* is one of the following: loopback – Enable loop back facility. This allows a resource advertised by a computer to be mounted by the same computer. loopback is off by default.

noloopback - Turn off the loop back facility. noloopback is the default.

loopmode - Check if the loop back facility is on or off.

ERRORS

When used with the −a option, if *hostname* is not unique in the domain, an error message will be sent to standard error.

When used with the −r option, if (1) *hostname* does not exist in the domain, (2) *hostname* is defined as a domain name server, or (3) there are resources advertised by *hostname*, an error message will be sent to standard error.

When used with the −p option to change the domain name server, if there are no backup name servers defined for *domain*, an error message will be sent to standard error.

FILES

/etc/rfs/auth.info/*domain*/passwd

For each *domain*, this file is created on the primary, copied to all secondaries, and copied to all hosts that want to do password verification of hosts in the *domain*.

SEE ALSO

passwd(1), dname(1M), rfstart(1M), rfstop(1M), umount(1M).

NAME

    rfpasswd – change Remote File Sharing host password

SYNOPSIS

    rfpasswd

DESCRIPTION

    rfpasswd updates the Remote File Sharing authentication password for a host; processing of the new password follows the same criteria as passwd(1). The updated password is registered at the domain name server (/etc/dfs/rfs/auth.info/*domain*/passwd) and replaces the password stored at the local host (/etc/dfs/rfs/loc.passwd file).

    This command is restricted to the super-user.

    NOTE: If you change your host password, make sure that hosts that validate your password are notified of this change. To receive the new password, hosts must obtain a copy of the *domain*/passwd file from the domain's primary name server. If this is not done, attempts to mount remote resources may fail!

ERRORS

    If (1) the old password entered from this command does not match the existing password for this machine, (2) the two new passwords entered from this command do not match, (3) the new password does not satisfy the security criteria in passwd(1), (4) the domain name server does not know about this machine, or (5) the command is not run with super-user privileges, an error message will be sent to standard error. Also, Remote File Sharing must be running on your host and your domain's primary name server. A new password cannot be logged if a secondary is acting as the domain name server.

FILES

    /etc/dfs/rfs/auth.info/*domain*/passwd
    /etc/dfs/rfs/loc.passwd

SEE ALSO

    rfstart(1M), rfadmin(1M).
    passwd(1) in the *User's Reference Manual*.

NAME

rfstart – start Remote File Sharing

SYNOPSIS

rfstart [–v] [–p *primary_addr*]

DESCRIPTION

rfstart starts Remote File Sharing and defines an authentication level for incoming requests. (This command can only be used after the domain name server is set up and your computer's domain name and network specification have been defined using dname(1M).)

–v   Specifies that verification of all clients is required in response to initial incoming mount requests; any host not in the file /etc/rfs/auth.info/*domain*/passwd for the domain they belong to, will not be allowed to mount resources from your host. If –v is not specified, hosts named in *domain*/passwd will be verified. Other hosts will be allowed to connect without verification.

–p *primary_addr*
    Indicates the primary domain name server for your domain. *primary_addr* can specify any of the following: the network address of the primary name server for a domain (*addr*); a list of address tuples when RFS is used over multiple transport providers (*transport1:addr1,transport2:addr2, ...*). An example of each type of specification follows:

        –p *addr*
        –p *transport1:addr1,transport2:addr2, ...*

    If the –p option is not specified, the address of the domain name server is taken from the associated rfmaster files. The –p *addr* specification is valid only when one transport provider is being used. See the rfmaster(1M) manual page for a description of the valid address syntax.

If the host password has not been set, rfstart will prompt for a password. The password prompting process must match the password entered for your machine at the primary domain name server (see rfadmin(1M)). If you remove the loc.passwd file or change domains, you will also have to reenter the password.

Also, when rfstart is run on a domain name server, entries in the rfmaster(4) file are syntactically validated.

This command is restricted to the super-user.

ERRORS

If syntax errors are found when validating an rfmaster(4) file, a warning describing each error will be sent to standard error.

An error message will be sent to standard error if any of the following conditions are true:

    1. remote file sharing is already running
    2. there is no communications network
    3. a domain name server cannot be found

        4. a domain name server does not recognize the machine
        5. the command is run without super-user privileges

Remote file sharing will not start if a host password in /etc/rfs/<transport>/loc.passwd is corrupted. If you suspect this has happened, remove the file and run rfstart again to reenter your password.

NOTE: rfstart will NOT fail if your host password does not match the password on the domain name server. You will simply receive a warning message. However, if you try to mount a resource from the primary, or any other host that validates your password, the mount will fail if your password does not match the one that the host has listed for your machine.

FILES

    /etc/rfs/<transport>/rfmaster
    /etc/rfs/<transport>/loc.passwd

SEE ALSO

    share(1M), dname(1M), mount(1M), rfadmin(1M), rfstop(1M), unshare(1M).
    rfmaster(4) in the *Programmer's Reference Manual*.

NAME

rfstop – stop the Remote File Sharing environment

SYNOPSIS

rfstop

DESCRIPTION

rfstop disconnects a host from the Remote File Sharing environment until another rfstart(1M) is executed.

When executed on the domain name server, the domain name server responsibility is moved to a secondary name server as designated in the rfmaster(4) file. If there is no designated secondary name server rfstop will issue a warning message, Remote File Sharing will be stopped, and name service will no longer be available to the domain.

This command is restricted to the super-user.

ERRORS

If (1) there are resources currently advertised by this host, (2) resources from this machine are still remotely mounted by other hosts, (3) there are still remotely mounted resources in the local file system tree, (4) rfstart(1M) had not previously been executed, or (5) the command is not run with super-user privileges, an error message will be sent to standard error and Remote File Sharing will not be stopped.

SEE ALSO

adv(1M), mount(1M), rfadmin(1M), rfstart(1M), unadv(1M), rfmaster(4).

NAME
rfuadmin – Remote File Sharing notification shell script

SYNOPSIS
/etc/rfs/rfuadmin *message remote_resource* [*seconds*]

DESCRIPTION
The rfuadmin administrative shell script responds to unexpected Remote File Sharing events, such as broken network connections and forced unmounts, picked up by the rfudaemon process. This command is not intended to be run directly from the shell.

The response to messages received by rfudaemon can be tailored to suit the particular system by editing the rfuadmin script. The following paragraphs describe the arguments passed to rfuadmin and the responses.

disconnect *remote_resource*
> A link to a remote resource has been cut. rfudaemon executes rfuadmin, passing it the message disconnect and the name of the disconnected resource. rfuadmin sends this message to all terminals using wall(1):

> *Remote_resource* has been disconnected from the system.

> Then it executes fuser(1M) to kill all processes using the resource, unmounts the resource [umount(1M)] to clean up the kernel, and starts rmount to try to remount the resource.

fumount *remote_resource*
> A remote server machine has forced an unmount of a resource a local machine has mounted. The processing is similar to processing for a disconnect.

fuwarn *remote_resource seconds*
> This message notifies rfuadmin that a resource is about to be unmounted. rfudaemon sends this script the fuwarn message, the resource name, and the number of seconds in which the forced unmount will occur. rfuadmin sends this message to all terminals:

> *Remote_resource* is being removed from the system in # seconds.

SEE ALSO
fumount(1M), rmount(1M), rfudaemon(1M), rfstart(1M).
wall(1) in the *User's Reference Manual.*

BUGS
The console must be on when Remote File Sharing is running. If it's not, rfuadmin will hang when it tries to write to the console (wall) and recovery from disconected resources will not complete.

NAME

rfudaemon – Remote File Sharing daemon process

SYNOPSIS

/etc/rfs/rfudaemon

DESCRIPTION

The rfudaemon command is started automatically by rfstart(1M) and runs as a daemon process as long as Remote File Sharing is active. Its function is to listen for unexpected events, such as broken network connections and forced unmounts, and execute appropriate administrative procedures.

When such an event occurs, rfudaemon executes the administrative shell script rfuadmin, with arguments that identify the event. This command is not intended to be run from the shell. Here are the events:

DISCONNECT

A link to a remote resource has been cut. rfudaemon executes rfuadmin, with two arguments: disconnect and the name of the disconnected resource.

FUMOUNT

A remote server machine has forced an unmount of a resource a local machine has mounted. rfudaemon executes rfuadmin, with two arguments: fumount and the name of the disconnected resource.

GETUMSG

A remote user-level program has sent a message to the local rfudaemon. Currently the only message sent is *fuwarn*, which notifies rfuadmin that a resource is about to be unmounted. It sends rfuadmin the *fuwarn*, the resource name, and the number of seconds in which the forced unmount will occur.

LASTUMSG

The local machine wants to stop the rfudaemon [rfstop(1M)]. This causes rfudaemon to exit.

SEE ALSO

rfstart(1M), rfuadmin(1M).

NAME
rlogind – remote login server

SYNOPSIS
in.rlogind *host.port*

DESCRIPTION
rlogind is the server for the rlogin(1) program. The server provides a remote login facility with authentication based on privileged port numbers.

rlogind is invoked by inetd(1M) when a remote login connection is established, and executes the following protocol:

1)   The server checks the client's source port. If the port is not in the range 0-1023, the server aborts the connection. The client's address and port number are passed as arguments to rlogind by inetd in the form *host.port* with host in hexadecimal and port in decimal.

2)   The server checks the client's source address. If an entry for the client exists is both /etc/hosts and /etc/hosts.equiv, a user logging in from the client is not prompted for a password. If the address is associated with a host for which no corresponding entry exists in /etc/hosts, the user is prompted for a password, regardless of whether or not an entry for the client is present in /etc/hosts.equiv [see hosts(4) and hosts.equiv(4)].

Once the source port and address have been checked, rlogind allocates a pseudo-terminal and manipulates file descriptors so that the slave half of the pseudo-terminal becomes the stdin, stdout, and stderr for a login process. The login process is an instance of the login(1) program, invoked with the −r option. The login process then proceeds with the authentication process as described in rshd(1M), but if automatic authentication fails, it reprompts the user to login as one finds on a standard terminal line.

The parent of the login process manipulates the master side of the pseudo-terminal, operating as an intermediary between the login process and the client instance of the rlogin program. In normal operation, a packet protocol is invoked to provide Ctrl–S / Ctrl–Q type facilities and propagate interrupt signals to the remote programs. The login process propagates the client terminal's baud rate and terminal type, as found in the environment variable, TERM; see environ(4).

SEE ALSO
inetd(1M), hosts(4), hosts.equiv(4).

DIAGNOSTICS
All diagnostic messages are returned on the connection associated with the stderr, after which any network connections are closed. An error is indicated by a leading byte with a value of 1.

Hostname for your address unknown.
        No entry in the host name database existed for the client's machine.

```
Try again.
```
A *fork* by the server failed.

```
/usr/bin/sh: ...
```
The user's login shell could not be started.

NOTES

The authentication procedure used here assumes the integrity of each client machine and the connecting medium. This is insecure, but is useful in an "open" environment.

A facility to allow all data exchanges to be encrypted should be present.

NAME

   rmntstat – display mounted resource information

SYNOPSIS

   rmntstat [–h] [*resource*]

DESCRIPTION

   When used with no options, rmntstat displays a list of all local Remote File
   Sharing resources that are remotely mounted, the local path name, and the
   corresponding clients. rmntstat returns the remote mount data regardless of
   whether a resource is currently advertised; this ensures that resources that have
   been unadvertised but are still remotely mounted are included in the report.
   When a *resource* is specified, rmntstat displays the remote mount information
   only for that resource. The –h option causes header information to be omitted
   from the display.

EXIT STATUS

   If no local resources are remotely mounted, rmntstat will return a successful exit
   status.

ERRORS

   If *resource* (1) does not physically reside on the local machine or (2) is an invalid
   resource name, an error message will be sent to standard error.

SEE ALSO

   mount(1M), fumount(1M), unadv(1M).

NAME
     rmnttry – attempt to mount queued remote resources
SYNOPSIS
     /etc/rfs/rmnttry [resource ...]
DESCRIPTION
     rmnttry sequences through the pending mount requests stored in
     /etc/rfs/rmnttab, trying to mount each resource. If a mount succeeds, the
     resource entry is removed from the /etc/rfs/rmnttab file.

     If one or more resource names are supplied, mounts are attempted only for those
     resources, rather than for all pending mounts. Mounts are not attempted for
     resources not present in the /etc/rfs/rmnttab file (see rmount(1M)). If a mount
     invoked from rmnttry takes over 3 minutes to complete, rmnttry aborts the
     mount and issues a warning message.

     rmnttry is typically invoked from a cron entry in
     /var/spool/cron/crontabs/root to attempt mounting queued resources at
     periodic intervals. The default strategy is to attempt mounts at 15 minute inter-
     vals. The cron entry for this is:
          10,25,40,55 * * * * /etc/rfs/rmnttry >/dev/null
FILES
     /etc/rfs/rmnttab pending mount requests
SEE ALSO
     mount(1M), rmount(1M), rumount(1M), mnttab(4).
     crontab(1) in the User's Reference Manual.
DIAGNOSTICS
     An exit code of 0 is returned if all requested mounts succeeded, 1 is returned if
     one or more mounts failed, and 2 is returned for bad usage.

NAME

rmount – queue remote resource mounts

SYNOPSIS

/usr/sbin/rmount [–d[r] *resource directory*]

DESCRIPTION

rmount queues a remote resource for mounting. The command enters the resource request into /etc/rfs/rmnttab, which is formatted identically to mnttab(4). rmnttry(1M) is used to poll entries in this file.

When used without arguments, rmount prints a list of resources with pending mounts along with their destined directories, modes, and date of request. The resources are listed chronologically, with the oldest resource request appearing first.

The following options are available:

–d   indicates that the *resource* is a remote resource to be mounted on directory.

–r   indicates that the *resource* is to be mounted read-only. If the *resource* is write-protected, this flag must be used.

FILES

/etc/rfs/rmnttab pending mount requests

SEE ALSO

mount(1M), rmnttry(1M), rumount(1M), rmountall(1M), mnttab(4).

DIAGNOSTICS

An exit code of 0 is returned upon successful completion of rmount. Otherwise, a non-zero value is returned.

NAME
rmountall, rumountall – mount, unmount Remote File Sharing resources

SYNOPSIS
/usr/sbin/rmountall [–] " *file-system-table* " [...]
/usr/sbin/rumountall [–k]

DESCRIPTION
rmountall is a Remote File Sharing command used to mount remote resources according to a *file-system-table*. (/etc/vfstab is the recommended *file-system-table*.) rmountall also invokes the rmnttry command, which attempts to mount queued resources. The special file name "–" reads from the standard input.

rumountall causes all mounted remote resources to be unmounted and deletes all resources that were queued from rmount. The –k option sends a SIGKILL signal, via fuser, to processes that have files open.

These commands may be executed only by the super-user.

The format of the *file-system-table* is as follows:

column 1   block special file name of file system

column 2   mount-point directory

column 3   –r if to be mounted read-only; –d if remote resource

column 4   file system type (not used with Remote File Sharing)

column 5+   ignored

Columns are separated by white space. Lines beginning with a pound sign (#) are comments. Empty lines are ignored.

SEE ALSO
fuser(1M), mount(1M), rfstart(1M), rmnttry(1M), rmount(1M),
sysadm(1) in the *User's Reference Manual*.
signal(2) in the *Programmer's Reference Manual*.

DIAGNOSTICS
No messages are printed if the remote resources are mounted successfully.

Error and warning messages come from mount(1M).

NAME

route – manually manipulate the routing tables

SYNOPSIS

route [–fn] { add | delete } { *destination* | default } [host | net] [*gateway* [*metric*]]

DESCRIPTION

route manually manipulates the network routing tables normally maintained by the system routing daemon, routed(1M), or through default routes and redirect messages from routers. route allows the super-user to operate directly on the routing table for the specific host or network indicated by *destination*. default is available for gateways to use after all other routes have been attempted. The *gateway* argument, if present, indicates the network gateway to which packets should be addressed. The *metric* argument indicates the number of hops to the *destination*. The *metric* is required for *add* commands; it must be zero if the destination is on a directly-attached network, and nonzero if the route utilizes one or more gateways.

The add command instructs route to add a route to *destination*. delete deletes a route.

Routes to a particular host must be distinguished from those to a network. The optional keywords net and host force the destination to be interpreted as a network or a host, respectively. Otherwise, if the destination has a local address part of INADDR_ANY, then the route is assumed to be to a network; otherwise, it is presumed to be a route to a host. If the route is to a destination connected by a gateway, the *metric* parameter should be greater than 0. If adding a route with metric 0, the gateway given is the address of this host on the common network, indicating the interface to be used directly for transmission. All symbolic names specified for a *destination* (except default) or *gateway* are looked up in the hosts database using gethostbyname(3N). If this lookup fails, then the name is looked up in the networks database using getnetbyname(3N).

OPTIONS

–f   Flush the routing tables of all gateway entries. If this is used in conjunction with one of the commands described above, route flushes the gateways before preforming the command.

–n   Prevents attempts to print host and network names symbolically when reporting actions. This is useful, for example, when all name servers are down on your local net, so you need a route before you can contact the name server.

FILES

/etc/hosts
/etc/networks

SEE ALSO

ioctl(2), gethostbyname(3N), getnetbyname(3N), routing(4N), routed(1M).

DIAGNOSTICS
> add [host | net] *destination : gateway*
>> The specified route is being added to the tables. The values printed are from the routing table entry supplied in the ioctl(2) call.
>
> delete [host | net] *destination : gateway*
>> The specified route is being deleted.
>
> *destination* done
>> When the −f flag is specified, each routing table entry deleted is indicated with a message of this form.
>
> Network is unreachable
>> An attempt to add a route failed because the gateway listed was not on a directly-connected network. Give the next-hop gateway instead.
>
> not in table
>> A delete operation was attempted for an entry that is not in the table.
>
> routing table overflow
>> An add operation was attempted, but the system was unable to allocate memory to create the new entry.

NAME

routed – network routing daemon

SYNOPSIS

in.routed [−qstv] [*logfile*]

DESCRIPTION

routed is invoked at boot time to manage the network routing tables. The routing daemon uses a variant of the Xerox NS Routing Information Protocol in maintaining up to date kernel routing table entries.

In normal operation routed listens on udp(4P) socket 520 (decimal) for routing information packets. If the host is an internetwork router, it periodically supplies copies of its routing tables to any directly connected hosts and networks.

When routed is started, it uses the SIOCGIFCONF ioctl(2) to find those directly connected interfaces configured into the system and marked up (the software loopback interface is ignored). If multiple interfaces are present, it is assumed the host will forward packets between networks. routed then transmits a *request* packet on each interface (using a broadcast packet if the interface supports it) and enters a loop, listening for *request* and *response* packets from other hosts.

When a *request* packet is received, routed formulates a reply based on the information maintained in its internal tables. The *response* packet generated contains a list of known routes, each marked with a hop count metric (a count of 16, or greater, is considered infinite). The metric associated with each route returned provides a metric relative to the sender.

request packets received by routed are used to update the routing tables if one of the following conditions is satisfied:

(1)   No routing table entry exists for the destination network or host, and the metric indicates the destination is reachable (that is, the hop count is not infinite).

(2)   The source host of the packet is the same as the router in the existing routing table entry. That is, updated information is being received from the very internetwork router through which packets for the destination are being routed.

(3)   The existing entry in the routing table has not been updated for some time (defined to be 90 seconds) and the route is at least as cost effective as the current route.

(4)   The new route describes a shorter route to the destination than the one currently stored in the routing tables; the metric of the new route is compared against the one stored in the table to decide this.

When an update is applied, routed records the change in its internal tables and generates a *response* packet to all directly connected hosts and networks. routed waits a short period of time (no more than 30 seconds) before modifying the kernel's routing tables to allow possible unstable situations to settle.

In addition to processing incoming packets, routed also periodically checks the routing table entries. If an entry has not been updated for 3 minutes, the entry's metric is set to infinity and marked for deletion. Deletions are delayed an additional 60 seconds to insure the invalidation is propagated throughout the internet.

Hosts acting as internetwork routers gratuitously supply their routing tables every 30 seconds to all directly connected hosts and networks.

Supplying the −s option forces routed to supply routing information whether it is acting as an internetwork router or not. The −q option is the opposite of the −s option. If the −t option is specified, all packets sent or received are printed on the standard output. In addition, routed will not divorce itself from the controlling terminal so that interrupts from the keyboard will kill the process. Any other argument supplied is interpreted as the name of file in which routed's actions should be logged. This log contains information about any changes to the routing tables and a history of recent messages sent and received which are related to the changed route. The −v option allows a logfile to be created showing the changes made to the routing tables with a timestamp.

In addition to the facilities described above, routed supports the notion of distant *passive* and *active* gateways. When routed is started up, it reads the file gateways to find gateways which may not be identified using the SIOGIFCONF ioctl. Gateways specified in this manner should be marked passive if they are not expected to exchange routing information, while gateways marked active should be willing to exchange routing information (that is, they should have a routed process running on the machine). Passive gateways are maintained in the routing tables forever and information regarding their existence is included in any routing information transmitted. Active gateways are treated equally to network interfaces. Routing information is distributed to the gateway and if no routing information is received for a period of the time, the associated route is deleted.

The gateways is comprised of a series of lines, each in the following format:

> < net | host > *filename1* gateway *filename2* metric *value* < passive |
> active >

The net or host keyword indicates if the route is to a network or specific host.

filename1 is the name of the destination network or host. This may be a symbolic name located in networks or hosts, or an Internet address specified in dot notation; see inet(3N).

filename2 is the name or address of the gateway to which messages should be forwarded.

value is a metric indicating the hop count to the destination host or network.

The keyword passive or active indicates if the gateway should be treated as passive or active (as described above).

FILES

/etc/gateways   for distant gateways
/etc/networks
/etc/hosts

SEE ALSO

ioctl(2), inet(7), udp(7).

NOTES

The kernel's routing tables may not correspond to those of routed for short periods of time while processes utilizing existing routes exit; the only remedy for this is to place the routing process in the kernel.

routed should listen to intelligent interfaces, such as an IMP, and to error protocols, such as ICMP, to gather more information.

NAME
rshd – remote shell server

SYNOPSIS
in.rshd *host.port*

DESCRIPTION
rshd is the server for the rsh(1) program. The server provides remote execution facilities with authentication based on privileged port numbers.

rshd is invoked by inetd(1M) each time a shell service is requested, and executes the following protocol:

1) The server checks the client's source port. If the port is not in the range 0-1023, the server aborts the connection. The clients host address (in hex) and port number (in decimal) are the argument passed to rshd.

2) The server reads characters from the socket up to a null (\0) byte. The resultant string is interpreted as an ASCII number, base 10.

3) If the number received in step 1 is non-zero, it is interpreted as the port number of a secondary stream to be used for the stderr. A second connection is then created to the specified port on the client's machine. The source port of this second connection is also in the range 0-1023.

4) The server checks the client's source address. If the address is associated with a host for which no corresponding entry exists in the host name data base [see hosts(4)], the server aborts the connection.

5) A null terminated user name of at most 16 characters is retrieved on the initial socket. This user name is interpreted as a user identity to use on the server's machine.

6) A null terminated user name of at most 16 characters is retrieved on the initial socket. This user name is interpreted as the user identity on the client's machine.

7) A null terminated command to be passed to a shell is retrieved on the initial socket. The length of the command is limited by the upper bound on the size of the system's argument list.

8) rshd then validates the user according to the following steps. The remote user name is looked up in the password file and a chdir is performed to the user's home directory. If the lookup or fails, the connection is terminated. If the chdir fails, it does a chdir to / (root). If the user is not the super-user, (user ID 0), the file /etc/hosts.equiv is consulted for a list of hosts considered equivalent. If the client's host name is present in this file, the authentication is considered successful. If the lookup fails, or the user is the super-user, then the file .rhosts in the home directory of the remote user is checked for the machine name and identity of the user on the client's machine. If this lookup fails, the connection is terminated.

9) A null byte is returned on the connection associated with the stderr and the command line is passed to the normal login shell of the user. The shell inherits the network connections established by rshd.

FILES

/etc/hosts.equiv

SEE ALSO

rsh(1)

DIAGNOSTICS

The following diagnostic messages are returned on the connection associated with the stderr, after which any network connections are closed. An error is indicated by a leading byte with a value of 1 (0 is returned in step 9 above upon successful completion of all the steps prior to the command execution).

locuser too long
> The name of the user on the client's machine is longer than 16 characters.

remuser too long
> The name of the user on the remote machine is longer than 16 characters.

command too long
> The command line passed exceeds the size of the argument list (as configured into the system).

Hostname for your address unknown.
> No entry in the host name database existed for the client's machine.

Login incorrect.
> No password file entry for the user name existed.

Permission denied.
> The authentication procedure described above failed.

Can't make pipe.
> The pipe needed for the stderr was not created.

Try again.
> A *fork* by the server failed.

NOTES

The authentication procedure used here assumes the integrity of each client machine and the connecting medium. This is insecure, but is useful in an open environment.

A facility to allow all data exchanges to be encrypted should be present.

NAME

rsnotify – display or modify the information identifying the individual in charge of restore requests

SYNOPSIS

rsnotify [–u *user*]

DESCRIPTION

rsnotify without options displays the name of the person who is to receive mail(1M) notifications whenever restore requests require operator intervention. The display includes the date the individual was assigned.

rsnotify may only be executed by a user with superuser privileges.

Options

–u *user*

assigns *user* to be the one to receive restore notifications. *user* is the user's login ID. If *user* is null, rsnotify mails the notices to root. *user* must be in the passwd file.

DIAGNOSTICS

The exit codes for rsnotify are the following:

0 = the task completed successfully
1 = one or more parameters to rsnotify are invalid
2 = an error has occurred, causing rsnotify to fail to
    complete all portions of its task

EXAMPLES

Example 1:

        rsnotify –u oper3

assigns the individual with login ID oper3 as the one to be notified when a restore request needing operator intervention is initiated.

FILES

/etc/bkup/rsnotify.tab   provides the electronic mail address of the operator to be notified whenever restore requests require operator intervention

/etc/bkup/rsstatus.tab   tracks the status of all restore requests from users

SEE ALSO

getvol(1M), restore(1M), rsstatus(1M), urestore(1M).

NAME

    rsoper – service pending restore requests and service media insertion prompts

SYNOPSIS

    rsoper –d *ddev* [–j *jobids*] [–u *user*] [–m *method*] [–n] [–s|v] [–t]
        [–o *oname*[:*odevice*]]

    rsoper –r *jobid*

    rsoper –c *jobid*

DESCRIPTION

    rsoper –d identifies media containing backup archives of file systems and data partitions, and allows an operator to complete pending restore(1M) and urestore(1M) requests. rsoper takes information about the archive entered on the command line and matches it against pending restore or urestore requests in the restore status table. rsoper then invokes the proper archiving method to read the archive and extract requested files, directories, and data partitions. As subsequent archive volumes are needed, the operator is requested to insert or mount the appropriate archive volumes. See getvol(1M).

    Depending on the information available in bkhist.tab and the volume labeling technique (internal or external), all options and arguments listed below may not be required. If required fields are omitted, rsoper issues an error message indicating the information that is needed. The command can then be reissued with the appropriate fields specified.

    rsoper may be executed only by a user with superuser privileges.

    rsoper –r removes a pending restore job from the restore status table (see rsstatus(1M) and ursstatus(1M)) and notifies the requesting user that the job has been marked complete.

    rsoper –c removes a pending restore job from the restore status table (see rsstatus(1M) and ursstatus(1M)) and notifies the requesting user that the job has been canceled.

Options

    –c *jobid*   Cancels a pending restore request and notifies the originating user that the request has been canceled.

    –d *ddev*   Describes the device that will be used to read the archive containing the required file system or data partition. *ddev* is of the form:

        ddevice[:[*dchar*][:[*dmnames*]]]

        ddevice is the device name for the device; see device.tab(4). *dchar* describes characteristics associated with the device. *dchar* is of the form:

        [density=*density*] [blk_fac=*blockingfactor*] [mntpt=*dir*]

        If mntpt=*dir* is specified, *ddevice* is assumed to be a file system partition and *dir* is the place in the UNIX directory structure where *ddevice* will be mounted. This is valid only for fimage(1M) archives. *dmnames* is a list of volume labels, separated by either commas or blanks. If the list is blank separated, the entire *ddev* argument must be surrounded by quotes.

-j *jobids*   Limits the scope of the request to the jobs specified. *jobids* is a list of restore job IDs (either comma separated or blank separated and surrounded by quotes).

-m *method*   Assumes the archive on the first volume in the destination device was created by the *method* archiving operation. Valid *methods* are: incfile, ffile, fimage, fdp, fdisk, and any customized methods in the /etc/bkup/method directory. This option is required if the backup history log is not available, if the log does not include information about the specified archive or if rsoper cannot determine the format of the archive.

-n   Displays attributes of the specified destination device but does not attempt to service pending restore requests.

-o *oname*[:*odevice*]

               Specifies the originating file system partition or data partition to be restored. *oname* is the name of the the originating file system. It may be null. *odevice* is the device name of the originating file system or data partition. This option is required if the backup history log is not available or does not include information about the specified archive.

-r *jobid*   Removes the restore request for the specified job.

-s   While a restore operation is occurring, this option displays a period (.) for each 100 (512-byte) blocks transferred from the destination device.

-t   Assumes that the volume inserted in the destination device contains a table of contents for an archive. This option is required if the backup history log is not available, if the log does not include information about the specified archive, or if rsoper cannot determine the format of the volume.

-u *user*   Restricts restores to those requested by the user specified.

-v   Displays the name of each object as it is restored. Only those archiving methods that restore named directories and files (incfile and ffile) support this option.

DIAGNOSTICS

The exit codes for rsoper are the following:

0 = the task completed successfully
1 = one or more parameters to rsoper are invalid
2 = an error has occurred, causing rsoper to fail to
    complete all portions of its task

If a method reports that no part of a restore request was completed, rsoper reports this fact to the user.

EXAMPLES

Example 1:

        rsoper −d /dev/tape/c4d0s2

asks the restore service to read the archive volume that has been inserted into the device /dev/tape/c4d0s2. The service will attempt to resolve any restore requests that can be satisfied by the archive volume.

Example 2:

The following example assumes that the backup history table contains a record of backups performed and that the restore status table contains a record of the restore requests. The command line

        rsoper −d /dev/ctape:density=1600:USRLBL1 −v −u clerk1

instructs the restore service to perform only pending restore requests from the rsstatus.tab table issued by clerk1. The restore procedures are to be done from the cartridge tape labeled USRLBL1, with a density of 1600 bps. The restore service will display on the operator terminal the names of the files and directories as they are successfully restored.

Example 3:

The following example assumes that the backup history table no longer contains a log of the requested backup operations. With that assumption:

rsoper −d /dev/diskette2:blk_fac=2400:arc.dec79 −m incfile −o /usr2

instructs the restore service to perform a restore of the /usr2 file system using the incremental restore method. The /usr2 file system is to be restored from archived diskettes with a blocking factor of 2400. The diskettes containing the archive are labeled "arc.dec79.a," "arc.dec79.b," and "arc.dec79.c."

Example 4:

        rsoper −c rest−737b

cancels the restore request with the job ID rest−737b.

FILES

/etc/bkup/bkhist.tab	−	lists the labels of all volumes that have been used for backup operations
/etc/bkup/rsstatus.tab	−	lists the status of all restore requests from users
/etc/bkup/rsnotify.tab	−	lists the electronic mail address of the operator to be notified whenever restore requests require operator intervention
/etc/bkup/method	−	a directory that contains the programs used for various backup methods

SEE ALSO

fdisk(1M), fdp(1M), ffile(1M), fimage(1M), getvol(1M), incfile(1M), restore(1M), rsnotify(1M), rsstatus(1M), urestore(1M), ursstatus(1M).
mail(1) in the *User's Reference Manual*.
getdate(3C), device.tab(4) in the *Programmer's Reference Manual*.

NAME

rsstatus – report the status of posted restore requests

SYNOPSIS

rsstatus [-h] [-d *ddev*] [-f *field_separator*] [-j *jobids*] [-u *users*]

DESCRIPTION

With no options, rsstatus reports the status of all pending restore requests that are posted in the restore status table.

rsstatus may be executed only by a user with superuser privileges.

Volume labels marked with an asterisk in the output of this command are table of contents volumes.

Options

-d *ddev*   Restricts the report to pending restore jobs that could be satisfied by the specified device type or volumes. *ddev* describes the device or volumes used to select requests to be restored. *ddev* is of the form:

[*dtype*][:*dlabels*]

dtype is a device type (such as diskette, cartridge tape, or 9-track tape). If specified, restrict the report to posted requests that could be satisfied by volumes of the type specified.

dlabels is a list of volume names corresponding to the *volumename* displayed by the labelit command. *dlabels* may be either comma-separated or blank-separated and surrounded by quotes. If specified, restrict the report to posted requests that could be satisfied by an archive residing on the specified volumes.

-f *field_separator*

Suppresses field wrap and specifies an output field separator to be used. *field_separator* is the character that will appear as the field separator in the output displayed. To make sure the output is clear, avoid using a character (for a separator) that is likely to appear in a field. For example, do not use a colon as a field separator if the display will contain dates in which a colon is used to separate hours from minutes.

-h   Suppresses the header for the report.

-j *jobids*   Restricts the report to the jobs specified. *jobids* is a list of restore job IDs (either comma-separated or blank-separated and surrounded by quotes).

-u *users*   Restricts the report to requests submitted by the specified *users* (either comma-separated or blank-separated and surrounded by quotes). *users* must be listed in the passwd file.

DIAGNOSTICS

The exit codes for rsstatus are the following:

0 = successful completion of the task
1 = one or more parameters to rsstatus are invalid.
2 = an error has occurred which caused rsstatus to fail to complete all portions of its task.

EXAMPLES

Example 1:

    `rsstatus −d diskette`

reports the status of those posted restore requests that can be satisfied by inserting diskettes into a diskette drive.

Example 2:

    `rsstatus −j rest−354a,rest−429b`

reports the status of only the two posted restore requests for which job IDs are specified.

FILES

`/etc/bkup/rsstatus.tab` — tracks the status of all restore requests from users

SEE ALSO

restore(1M), urestore(1M), ursstatus(1M).
dgroup.tab(4), device.tab(4) in the *Programmer's Reference Manual.*

NAME

rumount – cancel queued remote resource request

SYNOPSIS

/etc/rfs/rumount *resource* ...

DESCRIPTION

rumount cancels a request for one or more resources that are queued for mount. The entries for the resources are deleted from /etc/rfs/rmnttab.

FILES

/etc/rfs/rmnttab — pending mount requests

SEE ALSO

mount(1M), rmnttry(1M), rmount(1M), rumountall(1M), mnttab(4).

DIAGNOSTICS

An exit code of 0 is returned if rumount completes successfully. A 1 is returned if the resource requested for dequeuing is not in /etc/rfs/rmnttab. A 2 is returned for bad usage or an error in reading or writing /etc/rfs/rmnttab.

NAME
> rwhod, in.rwhod – system status server

SYNOPSIS
> in.rwhod

DESCRIPTION
> rwhod is the server which maintains the database used by the rwho(1) and rup-time(1) programs. Its operation is predicated on the ability to broadcast messages on a network.

> rwhod operates as both a producer and consumer of status information. As a producer of information it periodically queries the state of the system and constructs status messages which are broadcast on a network. As a consumer of information, it listens for other rwhod servers' status messages, validating them, then recording them in a collection of files located in the directory /var/spool/rwho.

> The rwho server transmits and receives messages at the port indicated in the rwho service specification, see services(4). The messages sent and received, are of the form:

```
struct      outmp {
      char  out_line[8];      /* tty name */
      char  out_name[8];      /* user id */
      long  out_time;  /* time on */
};

struct      whod {
      char  wd_vers;
      char  wd_type;
      char  wd_fill[2];
      int   wd_sendtime;
      int   wd_recvtime;
      char  wd_hostname[32];
      int   wd_loadav[3];
      int   wd_boottime;
            struct      whoent {
            struct         outmp we_utmp;
            int   we_idle;
      } wd_we[1024 / sizeof (struct whoent)];
};
```

> All fields are converted to network byte order prior to transmission. The load averages are as calculated by the w(1) program, and represent load averages over the 5, 10, and 15 minute intervals prior to a server's transmission. The host name included is that returned by the gethostname(2) system call. The array at the end of the message contains information about the users logged in to the sending machine. This information includes the contents of the utmp(4) entry for each non-idle terminal line and a value indicating the time since a character was last received on the terminal line.

Messages received by the rwho server are discarded unless they originated at a rwho server's port. In addition, if the host's name, as specified in the message, contains any unprintable ASCII characters, the message is discarded. Valid messages received by rwhod are placed in files named whod. *hostname* in the directory /var/spool/rwho. These files contain only the most recent message, in the format described above.

Status messages are generated approximately once every 60 seconds. rwhod performs an nlist(3) on /stand/unix every 10 minutes to guard against the possibility that this file is not the system image currently operating.

FILES

/var/spool/rwho

SEE ALSO

rwho(1), ruptime(1), w(1), gethostname(3), nlist(3), utmp(4).

NOTES

This service takes up progressively more network bandwidth as the number of hosts on the local net increases. For large networks, the cost becomes prohibitive.

rwhod should relay status information between networks. People often interpret the server dying as a machine going down.

NAME

    sac – service access controller

SYNOPSIS

    sac –t *sanity_interval*

DESCRIPTION

    The Service Access Controller (SAC) is the overseer of the server machine. It is started when the server machine enters multiuser mode. The SAC performs several important functions as explained below.

    Customizing the SAC environment. When **sac** is invoked, it first looks for the per-system configuration script /etc/saf/_sysconfig. **sac** interprets _sysconfig to customize its own environment. The modifications made to the SAC environment by _sysconfig are inherited by all the children of the SAC. This inherited environment may be modified by the children.

    Starting port monitors. After it has interpreted the _sysconfig file, the **sac** reads its administrative file /etc/saf/_sactab. _sactab specifies which port monitors are to be started. For each port monitor to be started, **sac** forks a child [fork(2)] and creates a utmp entry with the *type* field set to LOGIN_PROCESS. Each child then interprets its per-port monitor configuration script /etc/saf/*pmtag*/_config, if the file exists. These modifications to the environment affect the port monitor and will be inherited by all its children. Finally, the child process **execs** the port monitor, using the command found in the _sactab entry. (See sacadm; this is the command given with the –c option when the port monitor is added to the system.)

    Polling port monitors to detect failure. The –t option sets the frequency with which **sac** polls the port monitors on the system. This time may also be thought of as half of the maximum latency required to detect that a port monitor has failed and that recovery action is necessary.

    Administrative functions. The Service Access Controller represents the administrative point of control for port monitors. Its administrative tasks are explained below.

    When queried (sacadm with either –l or –L), the Service Access Controller returns the status of the port monitors specified, which sacadm prints on the standard output. A port monitor may be in one of six states:

    ENABLED   The port monitor is currently running and is accepting connections. See sacadm(1M) with the –e option.

    DISABLED   The port monitor is currently running and is not accepting connections. See sacadm with the –d option, and see NOTRUNNING, below.

    STARTING   The port monitor is in the process of starting up. STARTING is an intermediate state on the way to ENABLED or DISABLED.

    FAILED   The port monitor was unable to start and remain running.

STOPPING   The port monitor has been manually terminated but has not
                  completed its shutdown procedure. STOPPING is an intermedi-
                  ate state on the way to NOTRUNNING.

NOTRUNNING   The port monitor is not currently running. (See sacadm with
                  −k.) This is the normal "not running" state. When a port mon-
                  itor is killed, all ports it was monitoring are inaccessible. It is
                  not possible for an external user to tell whether a port is not
                  being monitored or the system is down. If the port monitor is
                  not killed but is in the DISABLED state, it may be possible
                  (depending on the port monitor being used) to write a message
                  on the inaccessible port telling the user who is trying to access
                  the port that it is disabled. This is the advantage of having a
                  DISABLED state as well as the NOTRUNNING state.

When a port monitor terminates, the SAC removes the utmp entry for that port
monitor.

The SAC receives all requests to enable, disable, start, or stop port monitors and
takes the appropriate action.

The SAC is responsible for restarting port monitors that terminate. Whether or
not the SAC will restart a given port monitor depends on two things:

- the restart count specified for the port monitor when the port monitor
  was added by sacadm; this information is included in
  /etc/saf/pmtag/_sactab
- the number of times the port monitor has already been restarted

SEE ALSO

sacadm(1M), pmadm(1M).

FILES

/etc/saf/_sactab
/etc/saf/_sysconfig
/var/adm/utmp
/var/saf/_log

NAME

sacadm − service access controller administration

SYNOPSIS

sacadm −a −p *pmtag* −t *type* −c *cmd* −v *ver* [−f dx] [−n *count*] \
    [−y *comment*] [−z script]

sacadm −r −p *pmtag*

sacadm −s −p *pmtag*

sacadm −k −p *pmtag*

sacadm −e −p *pmtag*

sacadm −d −p *pmtag*

sacadm −l [−p *pmtag* | −t *type*]

sacadm −L [−p *pmtag* | −t *type*]

sacadm −g −p *pmtag* [−z *script*]

sacadm −G [−z script]

sacadm −x [−p *pmtag*]

DESCRIPTION

sacadm is the administrative command for the upper level of the Service Access Facility hierarchy, that is, for port monitor administration. sacadm performs the following functions:

- − adds or removes a port monitor
- − starts or stops a port monitor
- − enables or disables a port monitor
- − installs or replaces a per-system configuration script
- − installs or replaces a per-port monitor configuration script
- − prints requested port monitor information

Requests about the status of port monitors (−l and −L) and requests to print per-port monitor and per-system configuration scripts (−g and −G without the −z option) may be executed by any user on the system. Other sacadm commands may be executed only by a privileged user.

The options have the following meanings:

−a   Add a port monitor. When adding a port monitor, sacadm creates the supporting directory structure in /etc/saf and /var/saf and adds an entry for the new port monitor to /etc/saf/_sactab. The file _sactab already exists on the delivered system. Initially, it is empty except for a single line, which contains the version number of the Service Access Controller.

        Unless the command line that adds the new port monitor includes a −f option with the argument x, the new port monitor will be started. Because of the complexity of the options and arguments that follow the −a option, it may be convenient to use a command script or the menu system to add port monitors. If you use the menu system, enter sysadm ports and then choose the port_monitors option.

−c *cmd* Execute the command string *cmd* to start a port monitor. The −c option may be used only with a −a. A −a option requires a −c.

−d   Disable the port monitor *pmtag*.

−e   Enable the port monitor *pmtag*.

−f dx The −f option specifies one or both of the following two flags which are then included in the flags field of the _sactab entry for the new port monitor. If the −f option is not included on the command line, no flags are set and the default conditions prevail. By default, a port monitor is started. A −f option with no following argument is illegal.

          d   Do not enable the new port monitor.

          x   Do not start the new port monitor.

−g   The −g option is used to request output or to install or replace the per-port monitor configuration script /etc/saf/*pmtag*/_config. −g requires a −p option. The −g option with only a −p option prints the per-port monitor configuration script for port monitor *pmtag*. The −g option with a −p option and a −z option installs the file script as the per-port monitor configuration script for port monitor *pmtag*. Other combinations of options with −g are invalid.

−G   The −G option is used to request output or to install or replace the per-system configuration script /etc/saf/_sysconfig. The −G option by itself prints the per-system configuration script. The −G option in combination with a −z option installs the file script as the per-system configuration script. Other combinations of options with a −G option are invalid.

−k   Stop port monitor *pmtag*.

−l   The −l option is used to request port monitor information. The −l by itself lists all port monitors on the system. The −l option in combination with the −p option lists only the port monitor specified by *pmtag*. A −l in combination with the −t option lists all port monitors of type *type*. Any other combination of options with the −l option is invalid.

−L   The −L option is identical to the −l option except that the output appears in a condensed format.

−n *count*

      Set the restart count to *count*. If a restart count is not specified, count is set to 0. A count of 0 indicates that the port monitor is not to be restarted if it fails.

−p *pmtag*

      Specifies the tag associated with a port monitor.

-r   Remove port monitor *pmtag*. sacadm removes the port monitor entry from /etc/saf/_sactab. If the removed port monitor is not running, then no further action is taken. If the removed port monitor is running, the Service Access Controller (SAC) sends it SIGTERM to indicate that it should shut down. Note that the port monitor's directory structure remains intact.

-s   Start a port monitor. The SAC starts the port monitor *pmtag*.

-t *type* Specifies the port monitor type.

-v *ver* Specifies the version number of the port monitor. This version number may be given as

$$-v \text{ `pmspec } -V`$$

where *pmspec* is the special administrative command for port monitor *pmtag*. This special command is ttyadm for ttymon and nlsadmin for listen. The version stamp of the port monitor is known by the command and is returned when *pmspec* is invoked with a -V option.

-x   The -x option by itself tells the SAC to read its database file (_sactab). The -x option with the -p option tells port monitor *pmtag* to read its administrative file.

-y *comment*
      Include *comment* in the _sactab entry for port monitor *pmtag*.

-z *script*
      Used with the -g and -G options to specify the name of a file that contains a configuration script. With the -g option, script is a per-port monitor configuration script; with -G it is a per-system configuration script. Modifying a configuration script is a three-step procedure. First a copy of the existing script is made (-g or -G). Then the copy is edited. Finally, the copy is put in place over the existing script (-g or -G with -z).

OUTPUT

If successful, sacadm will exit with a status of 0. If sacadm fails for any reason, it will exit with a nonzero status. Options that request information will write the information on the standard output. In the condensed format (-L), port monitor information is printed as a sequence of colon-separated fields; empty fields are indicated by two successive colons. The standard format (-l) prints a header identifying the columns, and port monitor information is aligned under the appropriate headings. In this format, an empty field is indicated by a hyphen. The comment character is #.

EXAMPLES

The following command line adds a port monitor. The port monitor tag is npack; its type is listen; if necessary, it will restart three times before failing; its administrative command is nlsadmin; and the configuration script to be read is in the file script:

```
sacadm -a -p npack -t listen -c /usr/lib/saf/listen npack \
    -v `nlsadmin -V` -n 3 -z script
```

Remove a port monitor whose tag is pmtag:

    sacadm -r -p pmtag

Start the port monitor whose tag is pmtag:

    sacadm -s -p pmtag

Stop the port monitor whose tag is pmtag:

    sacadm -k -p pmtag

Enable the port monitor whose tag is pmtag:

    sacadm -e -p pmtag

Disable the port monitor whose tag is pmtag:

    sacadm -d -p pmtag

List status information for all port monitors:

    sacadm -l

List status information for the port monitor whose tag is pmtag:

    sacadm -l -p pmtag

List the same information in condensed format:

    sacadm -L -p pmtag

List status information for all port monitors whose type is listen:

    sacadm -l -t listen

Replace the per-port monitor configuration script associated with the port monitor whose tag is pmtag with the contents of the file file.config:

    sacadm -g -p pmtag -z file.config

SEE ALSO

doconfig(3N), pmadm(1M), sac(1M).

FILES

    /etc/saf/_sactab
    /etc/saf/_sysconfig
    /etc/saf/pmtag/_config

NAME

    sadp – disk access profiler

SYNOPSIS

    sadp [–th] [–d device[– drive]] s [n]

DESCRIPTION

    sadp reports disk access location and seek distance, in tabular or histogram form. It samples disk activity once every second during an interval of s seconds. This is done n times if n is specified. Cylinder usage and disk distance are recorded in units of 8 cylinders.

    Valid values of device are hdsk for integral disk, sdsk for the Small Computer Systems Interface (SCSI) disk, and fdsk for integral floppy. Neither XDC disks nor SCSI Release 1.0 disks can be profiled using sadp. sadp can profile only one device type per invocation. The –d option may be omitted if the system has only one device type.

    Drive specifies the disk drives and it may be:

            a drive number in the range supported by device,
            two numbers separated by a minus (indicating an inclusive range),

    or

            a list of drive numbers separated by commas.

    Up to 8 disk drives may be reported for device type hdsk or fdsk, and up to 56 for sdsk. If drive is not specified, sadp profiles all the disk drives specified by device, up to the maximum of 8 for hdsk and fdsk, or 56 for sdsk.

    The –t flag causes the data to be reported in tabular form. The –h flag produces a histogram of the data. The default is –t.

EXAMPLE

    The command:

        sadp –d hdsk– 0 900 4

    will generate four tabular reports, each describing cylinder usage and seek distance of hdsk disk drive 0 during a 15-minute interval.

FILES

    /dev/kmem

SEE ALSO

    mem(7).

NAME

sar: sa1, sa2, sadc – system activity report package

SYNOPSIS

/usr/lib/sa/sadc [t n] [ofile]

/usr/lib/sa/sa1 [t n]

/usr/lib/sa/sa2 [-ubdycwaqvmpgrkxDSAC] [-s time] [-e time] [-i sec]

DESCRIPTION

System activity data can be accessed at the special request of a user (see sar(1))
and automatically, on a routine basis, as described here. The operating system
contains several counters that are incremented as various system actions occur.
These include counters for CPU utilization, buffer usage, disk and tape I/O
activity, TTY device activity, switching and system-call activity, file-access, queue
activity, inter-process communications, paging, and Remote File Sharing.

sadc and two shell procedures, sa1 and sa2, are used to sample, save, and process this data.

sadc, the data collector, samples system data n times, with an interval of t
seconds between samples, and writes in binary format to *ofile* or to standard output. The sampling interval t should be greater than 5 seconds; otherwise, the
activity of sadc itself may affect the sample. If t and n are omitted, a special
record is written. This facility is used at system boot time, when booting to a
multiuser state, to mark the time at which the counters restart from zero. For
example, the /etc/init.d/perf file writes the restart mark to the daily data by
the command entry:

    su sys -c "/usr/lib/sa/sadc /var/adm/sa/sa`date +%d`"

The shell script sa1, a variant of sadc, is used to collect and store data in the
binary file /var/adm/sa/sa*dd*, where *dd* is the current day. The arguments t and
n cause records to be written n times at an interval of t seconds, or once if omitted. The following entries in /var/spool/cron/crontabs/sys will produce
records every 20 minutes during working hours and hourly otherwise:

    0 * * * 0-6 /usr/lib/sa/sa1
    20,40 8-17 * * 1-5 /usr/lib/sa/sa1

See crontab(1) for details.

The shell script sa2, a variant of sar, writes a daily report in the file
/var/adm/sa/sar*dd*. The options are explained in sar(1). The following entry
in /var/spool/cron/crontabs/sys will report important activities hourly during the working day:

    5 18 * * 1-5 /usr/lib/sa/sa2 -s 8:00 -e 18:01 -i 1200 -A

The structure of the binary daily data file is:

```
struct sa {
    struct sysinfo si;          /* see /usr/include/sys/sysinfo.h */
    struct minfo mi;            /* defined in sys/sysinfo.h */
    struct vminfo vmi;          /* defined in /usr/include/sys/sysinfo.h */
    rf_srv_info_t rf_srv;       /* defined in /usr/include/sys/fs/rf_acct.h */
    fsinfo_t rfs_in;
    fsinfo_t rfs_out;           /* defined in /usr/include/sys/sysinfo.h */
    rfc_info_t rfc;             /* defined in /usr/include/sys/fs/rf_acct.h */
    struct kmeminfo km;         /* defined in /usr/include/sys/sysinfo.h */
    struct bpbinfo bi[4];       /* Co-processor info defined in sys/sysinfo.h */
    int  bpb_utilize            /* Co-processor utilize flag */
    int  minserve, maxserve;    /* RFS server low and high water marks */
    int  szinode;               /* current size of inode table */
    int  szfile;                /* current size of file table */
    int  szproc;                /* current size of proc table */
    int  szlckf;                /* current size of file record header table */
    int  szlckr;                /* current size of file record lock table */
    int  mszinode;              /* size of inode table */
    int  mszfile;               /* size of file table */
    int  mszproc;               /* size of proc table */
    int  mszlckf;               /* maximum size of file record header table */
    int  mszlckr;               /* maximum size of file record lock table */
    long inodeovf;              /* cumulative overflows of inode table */
    long fileovf;               /* cumulative overflows of file table */
    long procovf;               /* cumulative overflows of proc table */
    time_t ts;                  /* time stamp, seconds */
    int apstate;                /* Co-processor flag */
    long devio[NDEVS][5];       /* device unit information */
#define IO_OPS      0           /* cumulative I/o requests */
#define IO_BCNT     1           /* cumulative blocks transferred */
#define IO_ACT      2           /* cumulative drive busy time in ticks */
#define IO_RESP     3           /* cumulative I/o resp time in ticks */
#define IO_ID       4
};
```

FILES

    /var/adm/sa/sadd   daily data file
    /var/adm/sa/sardd   daily report file
    /tmp/sa.adrfl   address file

SEE ALSO

    crontab(1), sag(1G), sar(1), timex(1).

NAME
    setclk – set system time from hardware clock

SYNOPSIS
    /sbin/setclk

DESCRIPTION
    setclk is used to set the internal system time from the hardware time-of-day
    clock. The command can be used only by the super-user. It is normally executed
    by an entry in the /sbin/inittab file when the system is initialized at boot time.
    Note that setclk checks the Nonvolatile Random Access Memory (NVRAM) only
    for the date. If the date is set, setclk runs silently. If the date is not set, setclk
    prompts the user to use sysadm datetime [see sysadm(1)] for the proper setting
    of the hardware clock.

SEE ALSO
    sysadm(1) in the *User's Reference Manual*.

NAME
     setmnt – establish mount table

SYNOPSIS
     /sbin/setmnt

DESCRIPTION
     setmnt creates the /etc/mnttab table which is needed for both the mount and
     umount commands. setmnt reads standard input and creates a mnttab entry for
     each line. Input lines have the format:

          filesys node

     where *filesys* is the name of the file system's "special file" (such as
     /dev/dsk/c?d?s?) and *node* is the root name of that file system. Thus *filesys*
     and *node* become the first two strings in the mount table entry.

FILES
     /etc/mnttab

SEE ALSO
     mount(1M).

BUGS
     Problems may occur if *filesys* or *node* are longer than 32 characters.
     setmnt silently enforces an upper limit on the maximum number of mnttab
     entries.

NAME

setuname – changes machine information

SYNOPSIS

setuname [–s *name*] [–n *node*] [–t]

DESCRIPTION

setuname changes the parameter value for the system name and node name. Each parameter can be changed using setuname and the appropriate option.

The options and arguments for this command are:

–s   Changes the system name. *name* specifies new system name and can consist of alphanumeric characters and the special characters dash, underbar, and dollar sign.

–n   Changes the node name. *node* specifies the new network node name and can consist of alphanumeric characters and the special characters dash, underbar, and dollar sign.

–t   Temporary change. No attempt will be made to create a permanent change.

Either or both the –s and –n options must be given when invoking setuname.

The system architecture may place requirements on the size of the system and network node name. The command will issue a fatal warning message and an error message if the name entered is incompatible with the system requirements.

NOTES

setuname attempts to change the parameter values in two places: the running kernel and, as necessary per implementation, to cross system reboots. A temporary change changes only the running kernel.

NAME
        setup – initialize system for first user
SYNOPSIS
        setup
DESCRIPTION
        The setup command, which is also accessible as a login by the same name,
        allows the first user to be established as the "owner" of the machine.

        The user can then set the date, time and time zone of the machine.

        The user can then set the node name of the machine.

        The user can then protect the system from unauthorized modification of the
        machine configuration and software by giving passwords to the administrative
        and maintenance functions. Normally, the first user of the machine enters this
        command through the setup login, which initially has no password, and then
        gives passwords to the various functions in the system. Any that the user leaves
        without password protection can be exercised by anyone.

        The user can then give passwords to system logins such as "root", "bin", etc. (*pro-*
        vided they do not already have passwords). Once given a password, each login can
        only be changed by that login or "root".

        Finally, the user is permitted to add the first logins to the system, usually starting
        with his or her own.

SEE ALSO
        passwd(1).
DIAGNOSTICS
        The passwd(1) command complains if the password provided does not meet its
        standards.
NOTES
        If the setup login is not under password control, anyone can put passwords on
        the other functions.

NAME
>   share – make local resource available for mounting by remote systems

SYNOPSIS
>   **share** [–F *fstype*] [–o *specific_options*] [–d *description*] [*pathname* [*resourcename*]]

DESCRIPTION
>   The **share** command makes a resource available for mounting through a remote
>   file system of type *fstype*. If the option –F *fstype* is omitted, the first file system
>   type listed in file **/etc/dfs/fstypes** will be used as the default. *Specific_options*
>   as well as the semantics of *resourcename* are specific to particular distributed file
>   systems. When invoked with only a file system type, **share** displays all resources
>   shared by the given file system to the local system. When invoked with no argu-
>   ments, **share** displays all resources shared by the local system.
>
>   The *access_spec* is used to control access of the shared resource. It may be one of
>   the following:
>
> | | |
> |---|---|
> | **rw** | *pathname* is shared read/write to all clients. This is also the default behavior. |
> | **rw**=*client*[:*client*]... | |
> | | *pathname* is shared read/write only to the listed clients. No other systems can access *resourcename*. |
> | **ro** | *pathname* is shared read-only to all clients. |
> | **ro**=*client*[:*client*]... | |
> | | *pathname* is shared read-only only to the listed clients. No other systems can access *pathname*. |
>
>   The –d flag may be used to provide a description of the resource being shared.

FILES
>   /etc/dfs/dfstab
>   /etc/dfs/sharetab
>   /etc/dfs/fstypes

SEE ALSO
>   unshare(1M)

NAME

share − make local NFS resource available for mounting by remote systems

SYNOPSIS

share [−F nfs] [−o *specific_options*] [−d *description*] *pathname*

DESCRIPTION

The **share** command makes local resources available for mounting by remote systems.

If no argument is specified, then **share** displays all resources currently shared, including NFS resources and resources shared through other distributed file system packages.

The following options are recognized:

−o *specific_options*

Specify options in a comma-separated list of keywords and attribute-value-assertions for interpretation by the file-system-type-specific command.

specific_options can be any combination of the following:

rw   Sharing will be read-write to all clients.

rw=*client*[: *client*]...

Sharing will be read-write to the listed clients; overrides the ro suboption for the clients specified.

ro   Sharing will be read-only to all clients.

ro=*client*[: *client*]...

Sharing will be read-only to the listed clients; overrides the rw suboption for the clients specified.

anon=*uid*

Set *uid* to be the effective user ID of unathenticated users if AUTH_DES authentication is used, or to be root if AUTH_UNIX authentication is used. By default, unknown users are given the effective user ID UID_NOBODY. If *uid* is set to −1, access is denied.

root=*host*[: *host*]...

Only root users from the specified hosts will have root access. By default, no host has root access.

secure

Clients must use the AUTH_DES authentication of RPC. AUTH_UNIX authentication is the default.

If *specific_options* is not specified, then by default sharing will be read-write to all clients.

−d *description*

Provide a comment that describes the resource to be shared.

pathname   Specify the pathname of the resource to be shared.

FILES

    /etc/dfs/fstypes
    /etc/dfs/sharetab

SEE ALSO

    unshare(1M)

NOTES

    The command will fail if both ro and rw are specified. If the same client name exists in both the ro= and rw= lists, the rw will override the ro, giving read/write access to the client specified.

    ro=, rw=, and root= are guaranteed to work over UDP but may not work over other transport providers.

    If a resource is shared with a ro= list and a root= list, any host that is on the root= list will be given only read-only access, regardless of whether that host is specified in the ro= list, unless rw is declared as the default, or the host is mentioned in a rw= list. The same is true if the resource is shared with ro as the default. For example, the following **share** commands will give read-only permissions to hostb:

        `share -F nfs -oro=hosta,root=hostb /var`

        `share -F nfs -oro,root=hostb /var`

    While the following will give read/write permissions to hostb:

        `share -F nfs -oro=hosta,rw=hostb,root=hostb /var`

        `share -F nfs -oroot=hostb /var`

NAME
share – make local RFS resource available for mounting by remote systems

SYNOPSIS
share [–F rfs] [–o *access_spec*] [–d *description*] [*pathname resourcename*]

DESCRIPTION
The **share** command makes a resource available for mounting through Remote
File Sharing. The –F flag may be omitted if rfs is the first file system type listed
in the file /etc/dfs/fstypes. When invoked with only a file system type (or no
arguments), **share** displays all local resources shared through Remote File Sharing.

The *access_spec* is used to control client access of the shared resource. Clients may
be specified in any of the following forms:

> *domain.*
> *domain.system*
> *system*

The *access_spec* can be one of the following:

rw   *resourcename* is shared read/write to all clients. This is also
                          the default behavior.

rw=*client*[:*client*]...
                          resourcename is shared read/write only to the listed clients.
                          No other systems can access *resourcename*.

ro   *resourcename* is shared read-only to all clients.

ro=*client*[:*client*]...
                          resourcename is shared read-only only to the listed clients.
                          No other systems can access *resourcename*.

The –d flag may be used to provide a description of the resource being shared.

ERRORS
If the network is not up and running or *pathname* is not a full path, an error message will be sent to standard error. If *pathname* isn't on a file system mounted
locally or the *client* is specified but syntactically incorrect, an error message will
be sent to standard error. If the same *resource* name in the network over the same
transport provider is to be shared more than once, an error message will be sent
to standard error.

FILES
/etc/dfs/dfstab
/etc/dfs/sharetab
/etc/dfs/fstypes

SEE ALSO
unshare(1M)

NAME
    shareall, unshareall – share, unshare multiple resources

SYNOPSIS
    shareall [–F fstype[,fstype...]] [– | file]
    unshareall [–F fstype[,fstype...]]

DESCRIPTION
    When used with no arguments, shareall shares all resources from *file*, which
    contains a list of share command lines. If the operand is a hyphen (–), then the
    share command lines are obtained from the standard input. Otherwise, if nei-
    ther a *file* nor a hyphen is specified, then the file /etc/dfs/dfstab is used as the
    default.

    Resources may be shared to specific file systems by specifying the file systems in
    a comma-separated list as an argument to –F.

    unshareall unshares all currently shared resources. Without a –F flag, it
    unshares resources for all distributed file system types.

FILES
    /etc/dfs/dfstab

SEE ALSO
    share(1M), unshare(1M).

NAME

shutdown – shut down system, change system state

SYNOPSIS

/usr/sbin/shutdown [-y] [-ggrace_period [-iinit_state]

DESCRIPTION

This command is executed by the super-user to change the state of the machine. In most cases, it is used to change from the multi-user state (state 2) to another state (see below).

By default, it brings the system to a state where only the console has access to the UNIX system. This state is called single-user (see below).

The command sends a warning message and a final message before it starts actual shutdown activities. By default, the command asks for confirmation before it starts shutting down daemons and killing processes. The options are used as follows:

-y   pre-answers the confirmation question so the command can be run without user intervention. A default of 60 seconds is allowed between the warning message and the final message. Another 60 seconds is allowed between the final message and the confirmation.

-ggrace_period
          allows the super-user to change the number of seconds from the 60-second default.

-iinit_state
          specifies the state that init is to be put in following the warnings, if any. By default, system state "s" is used.

Other recommended system state definitions are:

state 0   Shut the machine down so it is safe to remove the power. Have the machine remove power if it can. The rc0 procedure is called to do this work.

state 1   State 1 is referred to as the administrative state. In state 1 filesystems required for multi-user operations are mounted, and logins requiring access to multi-user filesystems can be used. When the system comes up from firmware mode into state 1, only the console is active and other multi-user (state 2) services are unavailable. Note that not all user processes are stopped when transitioning from multi-user state to state 1.

state s, S
          State s (or S) is referred to as the single-user state. All user processes are stopped on transitions to this state. In the single-user state, filesystems required for multi-user logins are unmounted and the system can only be accessed through the console. Logins requiring access to multi-user file systems cannot be used.

state 5   Stop the UNIX system and go to firmware mode.

state 6   Stop the UNIX system and reboot to the state defined by the `initde-`
`fault` entry in `/sbin/inittab`; configure a new bootable operating system, if necessary, before the reboot. The `rc6` procedure is called to do
this work.

SEE ALSO

init(1M), rc0(1M), rc2(1M), rc6(1M), inittab(4).

NAME

    `slink` – streams linker

SYNOPSIS

    `slink` [–v] [–p] [–u] [–f] [–c *file*] [func [*arg1 arg2 ...*]]

DESCRIPTION

    `slink` is a STREAMS configuration utility which is used to link together the various STREAMS modules and drivers required for STREAMS TCP/IP. Input to `slink` is in the form of a script specifying the STREAMS operations to be performed. Input is normally taken from the file `/etc/strcf`.

    The following options may be specified on the `slink` command line:

    –c *file*   Use *file* instead of `/etc/strcf`.

    –v   Verbose mode (each operation is logged to `stderr`).

    –p   Don't use persistent links (i.e., slink will remain in the background).

    –f   Don't use persistent links and don't fork (i.e., slink will remain in foreground).

    –u   Unlink persistent links (i.e., shut down network).

    The configuration file contains a list of *functions*, each of which is composed of a list of *commands*. Each command is a call to one of the functions defined in the configuration file or to one of a set of built-in functions. Among the built-in functions are the basic STREAMS operations `open`, `link`, and `push`, along with several TCP/IP-specific functions.

    `slink` processing consists of parsing the input file, then calling the user-defined function **boot**, which is normally used to set up the standard configuration at boot time. If a function is specified on the `slink` command line, that function will be called instead of **boot**.

    By default, `slink` establishes streams with persistent links (`I_PLINK`) and exits following the execution of the specified function. If the –p flag is specified, `slink` establishes streams with regular links (`I_LINK`) and remains idle in the background, holding open whatever file descriptors have been opened by the configuration commands. If the –f flag is specified, `slink` establishes streams with regular links (`I_LINK`) and remains in the foreground, holding open whatever file descriptors have been opened by the configuration commands.

    A function definition has the following form:

            `function-name {`
                `command1`
                `command2`
                `...`
        `}`

    The syntax for commands is:

        function arg1 arg2 arg3 ...

    or

        `var` = *function arg1 arg2 arg3 ...*

The placement of newlines is important: a newline must follow the left and right braces and every command. Extra newlines are allowed, i.e. where one newline is required, more than one may be used. A backslash (\) followed immediately by a newline is considered equivalent to a space, i.e. may be used to continue a command on a new line. The use of other white space characters (spaces and tabs) is at the discretion of the user, except that there must be white space separating the function name and the arguments of a command.

Comments are delimited by # and newline, and are considered equivalent to a newline.

Function and variable names may be any string of characters taken from A-Z, a-z, 0-9, and _, except that the first character cannot be a digit. Function names and variable names occupy separate name spaces. All functions are global and may be forward referenced. All variables are local to the functions in which they occur.

Variables are defined when they appear to the left of an equals (=) on a command line; for example,

        tcp = open /dev/tcp

The variable acquires the value returned by the command. In the above example, the value of the variable tcp will be the file descriptor returned by the open call.

Arguments to a command may be either variables, parameters, or strings.

A variable that appears as an argument must have been assigned a value on a previous command line in that function.

Parameters take the form of a dollar sign ($) followed by one or two decimal digits, and are replaced with the corresponding argument from the function call. If a given parameter was not specified in the function call, an error results (e.g. if a command references $3 and only two arguments were passed to the function, an execution error will occur).

Strings are sequences of characters optionally enclosed in double quotes ("). Quotes may be used to prevent a string from being interpreted as a variable name or a parameter, and to allow the inclusion of spaces, tabs, and the special characters {, }, =, and #. The backslash (\) may also be used to quote the characters {, }, =, #, ", and \ individually.

The following built-in functions are provided by slink:

open *path*	Open the device specified by pathname *path*. Returns a file descriptor referencing the open stream.
link *fd1 fd2*	Link the stream referenced by *fd2* beneath the stream referenced by *fd1*. Returns the link identifier associated with the link. Unless the −f or −p flag is specified on the command line, the streams will be linked with persistent links. Note: *fd2* cannot be used after this operation.
push *fd module*	Push the module *module* onto the stream referenced by *fd*.

sifname *fd link name*	Send a SIOCSIFNAME (set interface name) ioctl down the stream referenced by *fd* for the link associated with link identifier *link* specifying the name *name*.
unitsel *fd unit*	Send a IF_UNITSEL (unit select) ioctl down the stream referenced by *fd* specifying unit *unit*.
dlattach *fd unit*	Send a DL_ATTACH_REQ message down the stream referenced by *fd* specifying unit *unit*.
initqp *path qname lowat hiwat* ...	Send an INITQPARMS (initialize queue parameters) ioctl to the driver corresponding to pathname *path*. *qname* specifies the queue for which the low and high water marks will be set, and must be one of:

hd	stream head
rq	read queue
wq	write queue
muxrq	multiplexor read queue
muxwq	multiplexor write queue

lowat and *hiwat* specify the new low and high water marks for the queue. Both *lowat* and *hiwat* must be present. To change only one of these parameters, the other may be replaced with a dash (−). Up to five *qname lowat hiwat* triplets may be present.

strcat *str1 str2*	Concatenate strings *str1* and *str2* and return the resulting string.
return *val*	Set the return value for the current function to *val*. Note: executing a return command does not terminate execution of the current function.

FILES
/etc/strcf

SEE ALSO
strcf(4)

NAME

smtp – send SMTP mail to a remote host using Simple Mail Transfer Protocol

SYNOPSIS

smtp [–D] [–d *domain*] [–H *helohost*] *sender host recip* ...

DESCRIPTION

smtp sends a message to a remote host *host* using the Simple Mail Transfer Protocol (SMTP). The message is read from standard input. *sender* is used to identify the sender of the message and the *recip*s are used as the recipients.

When establishing a connection, smtp will use the first transport for which netdir_getbyname(3) returns an address, based on hostname, transport [returned from getnetpath(3)], and service smtp. Normally, this will be the "tcp" transport.

The options to smtp and their meanings are as follows:

–D   This option turns on debugging. Debugging information is printed on standard error.

–H *helohost*   This option can be used to set the hostname used in SMTP HELO message (this defaults to the system's name).

–d *domain*   This option can be used to set the domain name to be used for this host.

smtp is normally run by the smtpsched process to deliver mail queued in /var/spool/smtpq.

FILES

/var/spool/smtpq   where messages are queued

SEE ALSO

smtpsched(1M)
RFC821 – Simple Mail Transfer Protocol

NAME

smtpd – receive incoming SMTP messages

SYNOPSIS

smtpd [–n] [–H *helohost*] [–h *thishost*] [–L *loadlim*] [–l *maxprocs*]

DESCRIPTION

smtpd is a daemon that normally runs while in multi-user mode, waiting for requests from remote hosts to send mail. smtpd listens for these requests on any TLI-based network for which the SMTP service is defined (to netdir_getbyname(3)). Normally, this will only be the "tcp" network. As requests are received, smtpd will fork off child smtpd processes to handle each individual SMTP transaction.

The options to smtpd and their meanings are as follows:

–n   Do not create smtpsched processes to process the incoming mail. Rely on the hourly cron(1) invocation of smtpsched instead.

–H *helohost*   This option can be used to specify the name to be used for the host in the initial SMTP HELO message. If it is not specified, the name used in the HELO message defaults to the system node name.

–h *thishost*   Specify the network name to be prepended onto the sender path in the From line of the message. This option is passed through to the fromsmtp program.

–L *loadlim*   Specify the maximum load at which smtpd will create children. If this option is not specified, there is no limit to the load at which children may run. The load is determined by reading the kernel variable avenrun.

–l *maxprocs* This option is used to specify the maximum number of children of smtpd that can be running at once. Each child handles one SMTP conversation. If this option is not specified, there is no limit to the number of children that may run.

Mail that is successfully received is piped to the fromsmtp command, which in turn delivers the mail by piping it to rmail. A log of all smtpd's activities is kept in the file /var/spool/smtpq/LOG.

FILES

/dev/kmem	To get the current machine load (avenrun)
/etc/services	List of TCP/UDP services (SMTP should be 25/tcp)
/etc/net/*/services	List of other TLI networks' services
/usr/lib/mail/surrcmd/fromsmtp	
	Where incoming mail is piped to
/var/spool/smtpq/LOG	Log of smtpd transactions

SEE ALSO

cron(1M), fromsmtp(1M), smtp(1M)

NAME

smtpqer – queue mail for delivery by SMTP

SYNOPSIS

smtpqer [–nu] [–a *toaddr*] [–d *domain*] [–H *helohost*] *sender host recip ...*

DESCRIPTION

smtpqer queues the mail message it reads from standard input for eventual delivery by smtp. The message is queued for delivery to the host specified in the *to* address.

smtpqer should normally be invoked by the mail command by placing the following line in /etc/mail/mailsurr:

´.+´ ´([^!@]+)!(.+)´ ´< /usr/lib/mail/surrcmd/smtpqer %R \\1 \\2´

smtpqer will check the host name in the *to* address. If it is one that can be reached (i.e., if netdir_getbyname(3) can find it on at least one TLI network), the message will be queued, and smtpqer will exit with a return code of 0 (which means the mail was successfully queued). Otherwise, it will return with an exit code of 1, and the message will not be queued.

Messages that are queued are stored in a file under the SMTP queue directory (/var/spool/smtpq). If the –u option is not used, they are first converted to RFC822 format, by filtering them through the program tosmtp. Finally, smtpqer invokes the smtpsched program to deliver the mail.

The –H option is used to specify the host name that should be used in the SMTP HELO message. This option is passed to both the tosmtp and smtp programs.

The –d option is used to specify the domain name that should be used for your host. This option is passed to the tosmtp program. If this option is not used, and a domain has been specified in the mail configuration file *mailcnfg*, that domain will be used instead.

The –a option is used to specify the "to address" that is passed to the smtp program. Finally, the –n option is used to prevent smtpqer from starting an smtpsched process to deliver the mail.

FILES

/usr/bin/rmail	where mail originates from
/etc/hosts	database of remote hosts (for TCP/IP)
/etc/mail/mailcnfg	mail configuration file
/etc/net/*/hosts	database of remote hosts (for other TLI networks)
/etc/mail/mailsurr	control file containing rule to invoke smtpqer
/usr/lib/mail/surrcmd/smtpsched	
	program to process message queues
/usr/lib/mail/surrcmd/smtp	
	program that passes message to remote host

/usr/lib/mail/surrcmd/tosmtp
                          filter to convert to RFC822 format

/var/spool/smtpq   where messages are queued

SEE ALSO
rmail(1M), smtpsched(1M), smtp(1M), tosmtp(1M)
getdomainname(3) in the *Programmer's Reference Manual.*
RFC822 – Standard for the Format of ARPA Internet Text Messages

NAME
smtpsched – process messages queued in the SMTP mail queue

SYNOPSIS
smtpsched [–c] [–v] [–t] [–s *scheds*] [–r *days*] [–w *days*] [*qnames*]

DESCRIPTION
smtpsched is used to process the messages queued up in the SMTP mail queue
/var/spool/smtpq. It is invoked automatically by the SMTP mail surrogate
smtpqer, whenever mail is queued for SMTP delivery to a remote host, and by
smtpd whenever incoming mail arrives. It should also be run once per hour
(from cron) to attempt delivery of any mail that cannot be delivered immediately.

smtpsched will normally attempt to send all messages queued under all subdirectories of /var/spool/smtpq. However, if *qnames* are specified, only those listed
subdirectories of /var/spool/smtpq will be searched for messages to deliver.
The subdirectories each refer to a different remote host.

The options to smtpsched are as follows:

–c   Causes empty queue directories to be removed.

–v   Causes verbose logging to occur.

–t   Test mode. The actions smtpsched would take are logged but not
performed.

–s *scheds*   Specifies the maximum number of concurrent smtpscheds that may
be running at once. If more than this number is running,
smtpsched will exit.

–r *days*   Causes mail older than *days* days to be returned.

–w *days*   Any mail older than *days* days will trigger a warning message,
which is sent to the originator.

FILES

/usr/lib/mail/surrcmd/smtp	delivers the mail
/usr/lib/mail/surrcmd/smtpqer	queues the mail
/var/spool/smtpq	queued mail messages
/var/spool/smtpq/LOG*	log files
/var/spool/smtpq/*host*	mail messages queued for *host*

SEE ALSO
cron(1M), smtp(1M), smtpqer(1M)

NAME

strace – print STREAMS trace messages

SYNOPSIS

strace [*mid sid level*] ...

DESCRIPTION

strace without arguments writes all STREAMS event trace messages from all drivers and modules to its standard output. These messages are obtained from the STREAMS log driver [log(7)]. If arguments are provided they must be in triplets of the form *mid, sid, level*, where *mid* is a STREAMS module ID number, *sid* is a sub-ID number, and *level* is a tracing priority level. Each triplet indicates that tracing messages are to be received from the given module/driver, sub-ID (usually indicating minor device), and priority level equal to or less than the given level. The token all may be used for any member to indicate no restriction for that attribute.

The format of each trace message output is:

<seq> <time> <ticks> <level> <flags> <mid> <sid> <text>

<seq>	trace sequence number
<time>	time of message in *hh:mm:ss*
<ticks>	time of message in machine ticks since boot
<level>	tracing priority level
<flags>	E : message is also in the error log F : indicates a fatal error N : mail was sent to the system administrator
<mid>	module ID number of source
<sid>	sub-ID number of source
<text>	formatted text of the trace message

Once initiated, strace will continue to execute until terminated by the user.

EXAMPLES

Output all trace messages from the module or driver whose module ID is 41:

        strace 41 all all

Output those trace messages from driver/module ID 41 with sub-IDs 0, 1, or 2:

        strace 41 0 1 41 1 1 41 2 0

Messages from sub-IDs 0 and 1 must have a tracing level less than or equal to 1. Those from sub-ID 2 must have a tracing level of 0.

SEE ALSO

log(7)
Programmer's Guide: STREAMS

NOTES

Due to performance considerations, only one strace process is permitted to open the STREAMS log driver at a time. The log driver has a list of the triplets specified in the command invocation, and compares each potential trace message against this list to decide if it should be formatted and sent up to the **strace** process. Hence, long lists of triplets will have a greater impact on overall STREAMS performance. Running **strace** will have the most impact on the timing of the modules and drivers generating the trace messages that are sent to the **strace** process. If trace messages are generated faster than the **strace** process can handle them, then some of the messages will be lost. This last case can be determined by examining the sequence numbers on the trace messages output.

NAME
strclean – STREAMS error logger cleanup program

SYNOPSIS
strclean [–d *logdir*] [–a *age*]

DESCRIPTION
strclean is used to clean up the STREAMS error logger directory on a regular basis (for example, by using cron. By default, all files with names matching error.* in /var/adm/streams that have not been modified in the last three days are removed. A directory other than /var/adm/streams can be specified using the –d option. The maximum age in days for a log file can be changed using the –a option.

EXAMPLE
strclean –d /var/adm/streams –a 3

has the same result as running strclean with no arguments.

FILES
/var/adm/streams/error.*

SEE ALSO
cron(1M), strerr(1M)
Programmer's Guide: STREAMS

NOTES
strclean is typically run from cron on a daily or weekly basis.

NAME
strerr – STREAMS error logger daemon

SYNOPSIS
strerr

DESCRIPTION
strerr receives error log messages from the STREAMS log driver [log(7)] and appends them to a log file. The error log files produced reside in the directory /var/adm/streams, and are named error.*mm–dd*, where *mm* is the month and *dd* is the day of the messages contained in each log file.

The format of an error log message is:

<seq> <time> <ticks> <flags> <mid> <sid> <text>

<seq>	error sequence number
<time>	time of message in hh:mm:ss
<ticks>	time of message in machine ticks since boot priority level
<flags>	T : the message was also sent to a tracing process F : indicates a fatal error N : send mail to the system administrator
<mid>	module ID number of source
<sid>	sub-ID number of source
<text>	formatted text of the error message

Messages that appear in the error log are intended to report exceptional conditions that require the attention of the system administrator. Those messages which indicate the total failure of a STREAMS driver or module should have the F flag set. Those messages requiring the immediate attention of the administrator will have the N flag set, which causes the error logger to send the message to the system administrator via mail. The priority level usually has no meaning in the error log but will have meaning if the message is also sent to a tracer process.

Once initiated, strerr continues to execute until terminated by the user. It is commonly executed asynchronously.

FILES
/var/adm/streams/error.*mm–dd*

SEE ALSO
log(7)
Programmer's Guide: STREAMS

NOTES
Only one strerr process at a time is permitted to open the STREAMS log driver.

If a module or driver is generating a large number of error messages, running the error logger will cause a degradation in STREAMS performance. If a large burst of messages are generated in a short time, the log driver may not be able to deliver some of the messages. This situation is indicated by gaps in the sequence numbering of the messages in the log files.

NAME

    sttydefs – maintain line settings and hunt sequences for TTY ports

SYNOPSIS

    /usr/sbin/sttydefs –a *ttylabel* [–b] [–n *nextlabel*] [–i *initial-flags*] [–f *final-flags*]

    /usr/sbin/sttydefs –l [*ttylabel*]

    /usr/sbin/sttydefs –r *ttylabel*

DESCRIPTION

    sttydefs is an administrative command that maintains the line settings and hunt sequences for the system's TTY ports by making entries in and deleting entries from the /etc/ttydefs file.

    sttydefs with a –a or –r option may be invoked only by a privileged user. sttydefs with –l may be invoked by any user on the system.

    The options have the following meanings:

–l   If a *ttylabel* is specified, sttydefs will display the record from /etc/ttydefs whose TTY label matches the specified *ttylabel*. If no *ttylabel* is specified, sttydefs will display the entire contents of /etc/ttydefs. sttydefs will verify that each entry it displays is correct and that the entry's *nextlabel* field references an existing *ttylabel*.

–a *ttylabel*   Adds a record to the ttydefs file, using *ttylabel* as its label. The following describes the effect of the –b, –n, –i, or –f options when used in conjunction with the –a option:

–b   Specifies that autobaud should be enabled. Autobaud allows the system to set the line speed of a given TTY port to the line speed of the device connected to the port without the user's intervention.

–n *nextlabel*   Specifies the value to be used in the *nextlabel* field in /etc/ttydefs. If this option is not specified, sttydefs will set *nextlabel* equal to *ttylabel*.

–i *initial-flags* Specifies the value to be used in the *initial-flags* field in /etc/ttydefs. *initial-flags* must be in a format recognized by the stty command. These flags are used by ttymon when searching for the correct baud rate. They are set prior to writing the prompt.

                 If this option is not specified, sttydefs will set *initial-flags* equal to the termio(7) flag 9600.

–f *final-flags*   Specifies the value to be used in the *final-flags* field in /etc/ttydefs. *final-flags* must be in a format recognized by the stty command. *final-flags* are the termio(7) settings used by ttymon after receiving a successful connection request and immediately before invoking the service on the port. If this option is not specified, sttydefs will set *final-flags* equal to the termio(7) flags 9600 and sane.

−r *ttylabel*   Removes any record in the `ttydefs` file that has *ttylabel* as its
                 label.

OUTPUT

If successful, `sttydefs` will exit with a status of 0. `sttydefs −l` will generate
the requested information and send it to the standard output.

EXAMPLES

The following command will list all the entries in the `ttydefs` file and print an
error message for each invalid entry that is detected.

```
sttydefs −l
```

The following shows a command that requests information for a single label and
its output:

```
# sttydefs −l 9600

-----------------------------------------------------------------------
9600:9600 hupcl erase ^h:9600 sane ixany tab3 hupcl erase ^h::4800
-----------------------------------------------------------------------

ttylabel:        9600
initial flags:   9600 hupcl erase ^h
final flags:     9600 sane ixany tab3 hupcl erase ^h
autobaud:        no
nextlabel:       4800
```

The following sequence of commands will add the labels 1200, 2400, 4800, and
9600 and put them in a circular list:

```
sttydefs −a 1200 −n 2400 −i 1200 −f "1200 sane"
sttydefs −a 2400 −n 4800 −i 2400 −f "2400 sane"
sttydefs −a 4800 −n 9600 −i 4800 −f "4800 sane"
sttydefs −a 9600 −n 1200 −i 9600 −f "9600 sane"
```

FILES

/etc/ttydefs

SEE ALSO

System Administrator's Guide, "Terminal Line Settings."

NAME

su – become super-user or another user

SYNOPSIS

su [–] [*name* [*arg* ...]]

DESCRIPTION

su allows one to become another user without logging off. The default user *name* is root (that is, super-user).

To use **su**, the appropriate password must be supplied (unless one is already root). If the password is correct, **su** will execute a new shell with the real and effective user and group IDs and supplementary group list set to that of the specified user. The new shell will be the optional program named in the shell field of the specified user's password file entry [see passwd(4)] or /usr/bin/sh if none is specified [see sh(1)]. To restore normal user ID privileges, type an EOF character (CTRL–d) to the new shell.

Any additional arguments given on the command line are passed to the program invoked as the shell. When using programs such as sh, an *arg* of the form –c *string* executes *string* via the shell and an arg of –r gives the user a restricted shell.

The following statements are true only if the optional program named in the shell field of the specified user's password file entry is like sh. If the first argument to su is a –, the environment will be changed to what would be expected if the user actually logged in as the specified user. This is done by invoking the program used as the shell with an *arg0* value whose first character is –, thus causing first the system's profile (/etc/profile) and then the specified user's profile (.profile in the new HOME directory) to be executed. Otherwise, the environment is passed along with the possible exception of $PATH, which is set to /sbin:/usr/sbin:/usr/bin:/etc for root. Note that if the optional program used as the shell is /usr/bin/sh, the user's .profile can check *arg0* for –sh or –su to determine if it was invoked by login or su, respectively. If the user's program is other than /usr/bin/sh, then .profile is invoked with an *arg0* of –*program* by both login and su.

All attempts to become another user using su are logged in the log file /var/adm/sulog.

EXAMPLES

To become user bin while retaining your previously exported environment, execute:

    su bin

To become user bin but change the environment to what would be expected if bin had originally logged in, execute:

    su – bin

To execute *command* with the temporary environment and permissions of user bin, type:

    su – bin –c *"command args"*

FILES

/etc/passwd	system's password file
/etc/profile	system's profile
$HOME/.profile	user's profile
/var/adm/sulog	log file
/etc/default/su	the default parameters that live here are:

      SULOG: If defined, all attempts to su to
                another user are logged in the indicated file.

      CONSOLE: If defined, all attempts to suroot
                are logged on the console.

      PATH: Default path.

      SUPATH: Default path for a user invoking suroot.

SEE ALSO

env(1), login(1), sh(1) in the *User's Reference Manual.*
passwd(4), profile(4), environ(5) in the *Programmer's Reference Manual.*

NAME

    sulogin – access single-user mode

SYNOPSIS

    sulogin

DESCRIPTION

    sulogin is automatically invoked by init when the system is first started. It prompts the user to type the root password to enter system maintenance mode (single-user mode) or to type EOF (typically CTRL-d) for normal startup (multi-user mode). sulogin should never be directly invoked by the user.

FILES

    /etc/sulogin

SEE ALSO

    init(1M) in the *System Administrator's Reference Manual.*

NAME
    swap – swap administrative interface

SYNOPSIS
    /usr/sbin/swap −a *swapname swaplow swaplen*
    /usr/sbin/swap −d *swapname swaplow*
    /usr/sbin/swap −l [−s]
    /usr/sbin/swap −s

DESCRIPTION
    swap provides a method of adding, deleting, and monitoring the system swap
    areas used by the memory manager. The following options are recognized:

    −a   Add the specified swap area. *swapname* is the name of the block special par-
         tition, e.g., /dev/dsk/c1d0s1 or a regular file. *swaplow* is the offset in 512-
         byte blocks into the partition where the swap area should begin. *swaplen* is
         the length of the swap area in 512-byte blocks. This option can only be
         used by the super-user. If additional swap areas are added, it is normally
         done during the system start up routine /etc/rc when going into multi-
         user mode.

    −d   Delete the specified swap area. *swapname* is the name of block special parti-
         tion, e.g., /dev/dsk/c1d0s1 or a regular file. *swaplow* is the offset in 512-
         byte blocks into the the swap area to be deleted. Using this option marks
         the swap area as "INDEL" (in the process of being deleted). The system will
         not allocate any new blocks from the area, and will try to free swap blocks
         from it. The area will remain in use until all blocks from it are freed. This
         option can be used only by the super-user.

    −l   List the status of all the swap areas. The output has five columns:

         path   The path name for the swap area.

         dev   The major/minor device number in decimal if it is a block special
                 device; zeros otherwise.

         swaplo The *swaplow* value for the area in 512-byte blocks.

         blocks The *swaplen* value for the area in 512-byte blocks.

         free   The number of free 512-byte blocks in the area. If the swap area is
                 being deleted, the word INDEL will be printed to the right of this
                 number.

    −s   Print the following information about total swap space usage:

         allocated The amount of swap space (in 512-byte blocks) allocated to
                    private pages.

         reserved   The number of swap space (in 512-bytes blocks) not currently
                    allocated, but claimed by memory mappings that have not yet
                    created private pages.

         used   The total amount of swap space, in 512-byte blocks, that is
                    either allocated or reserved.

available   The total swap space, in 512-byte blocks, that is currently avail-
             able for future reservation and allocation.

WARNINGS

No check is done to see if a swap area being added overlaps with an existing file
system.

NAME

sync – update the super block

SYNOPSIS

sync

DESCRIPTION

sync executes the sync system primitive. If the system is to be stopped, sync must be called to insure file system integrity. It will flush all previously unwritten system buffers out to disk, thus assuring that all file modifications up to that point will be saved. See sync(2) for details.

NOTE

If you have done a write to a file on a remote machine in a Remote File Sharing environment, you cannot use sync to force buffers to be written out to disk on the remote machine. sync will only write local buffers to local disks.

SEE ALSO

sync(2) in the *Programmer's Reference Manual*.

NAME

sysadm – visual interface to perform system administration

SYNOPSIS

sysadm [*menu name* | *task name*]

DESCRIPTION

This command, when invoked without an argument, presents a set of menus that help you do administrative work. If you specify a menu or task on the command line, one of two things happens: if the requested menu or task is unique, it is immediately displayed; if the menu or task is not unique, a menu of choices is displayed.

The sysadm command may be given a password. To assign a password, use the password task under the system_setup menu. To change a password after it is assigned, use the password command.

The following twelve menus, which appear on the main sysadm menu, are available on a computer running UNIX System V Release 4:

        Backup Scheduling, Setup and Control

        Diagnosing System Errors

        File System Creation, Checking and Mounting

        Machine Configuration, Display and Powerdown

        Network Services Administration

        Port Access Services and Monitors

        Printer Configuration and Services

        Restore From Backup Data

        Software Installation and Removal

        Storage Device Operations and Definitions

        System Name, Date/Time and Initial Password Setup

        User Login and Group Administration

If you add software packages other than those delivered with UNIX System V Release 4 to your system, you will also see a menu entry called Administration for Available Applications on which those packages are listed.

Also, software packages that have not been updated to reflect UNIX System V Release 4 may require functionality provided with the pre-Release 4 sysadm menus that is not available with the Release 4 menus. To make this functionality available, the pre-Release 4 versions of the sysadm menus are installed along with any software packages that require their use. If you have such packages installed, the entry Pre-SVR4.0 System Administration will appear on your main menu.

The rest of this section describes each menu listed on the main menu.

- Backup Service Management

  This menu lists seven areas of administrative support for the backup services.

- • backup (Start Backup Jobs)

  This task starts the backup scheduled for the current day based on the default backup control table or the specified backup control table.

- • history (Backup History Management)

  This task lets you display reports of backup operations that have completed successfully.

- • reminder (Schedule Backup Reminder)

  This menu lets you schedule messages that will be sent to you to remind you to perform backups.

- • respond (Respond to Backup Job Prompts)

  This task lets you reply to operator prompts from backup jobs.

- • schedule (Schedule Automatic Backups)

  This menu lets you schedule backups so that they will run automatically. Because the backups are scheduled to run automatically and are not associated with a terminal, you must choose to run them in either automatic or background mode.

- • setup (Backup Control Table Management)

  This menu lets you modify or display backup registers.

- • status (Backup Status Management)

  This menu lets you manage backup requests that are in progress.

- Diagnosing System Errors

  This menu provides two tasks, diskreport and diskrepair, which allow you to look for and sometimes repair problems in the system.

- • diskrepair (Advises on Disk Error Repairs)

  This task advises you on how to repair errors that occur on a hard disk.

  WARNING: Because this is a repair function, it should be performed only by qualified service personnel.

  NOTE: Disk errors often cause files to be lost and/or data to be damaged. Be sure to restore a repaired disk from backup copies.

- • diskreport (Reports Disk Errors)

  This task shows you if the system has collected any information indicating that there have been errors while reading the hard disk. You can request either summary or full reports. A summary report provides sufficient information about disk errors to determine if a repair should be attempted. If the message no errors logged is part of the report, then

there is probably no damage. If a number of errors are reported, there is
damage and you should call for service. The full report gives additional
details for qualified service personnel who are trouble shooting complicated problems.

- Manage File Systems

  This menu provides eleven tasks that are part of file system management.
  These tasks include checking for and repairing errors on a specific file system, monitoring disk usage for all file systems, tracking files based on age
  or size, listing all file systems currently mounted on your system, creating
  a new file system, and mounting and unmounting file systems.

- • check (Check a File System)

  This task lets you check a file system for errors and fix them, either
  interactively or automatically.

- • defaults (Manage Defaults)

  This task identifies the percentage of hard disks currently occupied by
  files.

- • diskuse (Display Disk Usage)

  This task identifies the percentage of hard disks currently occupied by
  files. The information is presented as a list, organized by file system
  name.

- • display (Display Installed Types)

  This task displays a list of the file system types installed on your system.

- • fileage (List Files by Age)

  This task lets you print the names of old files in the directory you specify.
  If you do not specify an age, files older than 90 days are listed.

- • filesize (List Files by Size)

  This task lets you print the names of the largest files in a specific directory. If you do not request a particular number of files, the ten largest
  files are listed.

- • identify (Identify File System Type)

  This task tries to determine the type of any unmounted file system
  without damaging the data or the medium of the file system.

- • list (List Mounted File Systems)

  This task lets you list all file systems mounted on your computer.

- • make (Create a File System)

  This task lets you create a new file system on a removable medium which
  can then store data you do not want to keep on hard disk. When
  mounted, the file system has all the properties of a file kept on hard disk.

• • mount (Mount a File System)

This task lets you mount a file system located on a removable medium and make it available to users on your system. The file system may be unmounted using the unmount task.

WARNING: The medium must not be removed while the file system is still mounted.

• • unmount (Unmount a File System)

This task lets you unmount a file system and thus lets you remove the medium on which it resides. Both / and /usr are excluded because unmounting these file systems would cause a system crash. Once a file system has been unmounted, you may remove the medium on which it resided.

• Machine Configuration Display and Powerdown

This menu provides seven tasks for functions such as turning off the computer, rebooting it, and changing to firmware mode.

• • boot defaults (Assigns Boot Device Program)

This task lets you specify the default manual program to boot from firmware and/or the device to be used when automatically rebooting.

• • configuration (System Configuration Display)

This task allows you to check the current configuration of the system.

• • firmware (Stop All Running Programs and Enter Firmware Mode)

This task lets you stop all running programs, close any open files, write out information to the disk (such as directory information), and then cause the machine to enter the firmware mode. (Machine diagnostics and other special functions that are not available on the UNIX system are available in firmware mode.)

• • floppy key (Creates a Floppy Key Removable Diskette)

This task lets you create a software "key" to your system on floppy diskette. This key enables you to obtain access to the system even if you have forgotten the firmware password, by allowing you to enter firmware mode. Thus the "floppy key" is just that: a key to your system. Be sure to protect it as such.

• • powerdown (Stops All Running Programs and Turns Off Machine)

This task lets you stop all running programs, close any open files, write out information (such as directory information) to disk, and then turn off the power in the machine.

• • reboot (Stops All Running Programs and Reboots Machine)

This task lets you reboot the computer after all running programs have been stopped, any open files have been closed, and any necessary information (such as directory information) has been written out to disk, This procedure can be used to resolve some types of system trouble, such as a process that cannot be killed.

•• whos on (Displays List of Users Logged onto Machine)

This task prints the login ID, terminal device number, and sign-on time of all users who are currently using the computer.

• Network Services Management

This menu provides four functions for managing networks.

•• basic_networking (Basic Networking Utilities Management)

This menu allows you to set up administrative files for UUCP utilities.

•• remote_files (Distributed File System Management)

This menu allows you to set up administrative files for the Remote File Sharing (RFS) Utilities or the Network File Sharing (NFS) Utilities.

•• selection (Network Selection Management)

This menu allows you to set up administrative files for Network Selection; that is, for dynamically selecting a transport protocol.

•• name_to_address (Machine and Service Address Management)

This menu allows you to define machine addresses and service port information for the protocols that exist on the machine.

• Service Access Management

This menu provides functions for managing service access to the system.

•• port_monitors (Port Monitor Management)

This menu provides functions for managing port monitors under the Service Access Facility. Specifically, it allows you to add, disable, enable, list, modify, remove, start, and stop port monitors.

•• port_services (Port Service Management)

This menu provides functions for managing port services provides by port monitors. Specifically, it allows you to add, disable, enable, list, modify, and remove port services.

•• tty_settings (Terminal Line Setting Management)

This menu provides functions for managing tty line settings. Specifically, it allows you to create new tty settings and hunt sequences, and to display (on your screen) and remove those settings. To modify an existing tty line setting, remove the entry for it and then recreate it, including the modifications.

• Line Printer Services Configuration and Operation

This menu provides functions for managing the printers and print services you can make available to your users through the LP print service. Specifically, this menu can help you do the following: set up and control the LP print service; start and stop the print service, check the status of the print service and, if necessary, stop and start it; add new printers to your system, and change the configuration of existing printers; add, change, and mount forms, add, change, and change filters, and monitor users' print requests.

•• classes (Manage Classes of Related Printers)

This menu allows you to add new classes and to display a list of the current classes.

•• filters (Manage Filters for Special Processing)

This menu allows you to manage filters for special processing.

•• forms (Manage Pre-Printed Forms)

This menu allows you to manage pre-printed forms.

•• operations (Perform Daily Printer Service Operations)

This menu allows you to perform daily printer operations such as enabling printers, starting the print service, and mounting forms.

•• printers (Configure Printers for the Printer Service)

This menu allows you to configure printers for the LP print service.

•• priorities (Assign Print Queue Priorities to Users)

This menu allows you to assign priority in the queue for print requests.

•• requests (Manage Active Print Requests)

This menu allows you to hold and release pending print requests, to move print requests to new destinations, and to cancel print requests.

•• status (Display Status of Printer Service)

This menu allows you to display the current status of the LP print service.

•• systems (Configure Connections to Remote Systems)

This menu allows you to configure the connections between your LP print service system and any other LP print service.

• Restore Service Management

This menu provides tasks for restoring directories, files, file systems, and data partitions from archive volumes.

•• operator (Set/Display the Restore Operator)

This task lets you set up and display the restore operator.

•• respond (Respond to Restore Job Prompts)

> This task lets you respond to restore job prompts.

•• restore (Restore from Backup Archives)

> This task lets you request the restoration of files, directories, file systems, and data partitions from an archived version.

•• status (Modify/Report Pending Restore Request Status)

> This menu lets you display and change the status of pending restore requests.

• Software Installation and Information Management

> The tasks in this menu provide functions for software package installation, removal, and management of information pertaining to software packages. They include the ability to install and remove packages, and to check the accuracy of package installation. In addition, they include the ability to set installation defaults, store interactions with a particular package, store a package without actually installing it, and to list all installed packages.

•• check (Checks Accuracy of Installation)

> This task lets you check installed software packages for consistency, correct for inconsistencies, check for hidden files, and check the contents of files which are likely to have changed.

•• defaults (Sets Installation Defaults)

> This task allows you to decide, ahead of time, the way that the system should respond to an installation problem.

•• install (Installs Software Packages)

> This task lets you install software packages onto a spool, a hard disk, or a floppy diskette, and select the method that the system will use to respond to installation problems.

•• interact (Stores Interactions with Package)

> This task allows you to interact with the software installation process.

•• list (Displays Information about Packages)

> This task shows you the software packages that are installed on your system and tells you the name, location, and category of each.

•• read_in (Stores Packages Without Installing)

> This task lets you read in software packages without installing them.

•• remove (Removes Packages)

> This task lets you remove installed software packages.

* Storage Device Operations and Definitions

  This menu contains tasks for getting descriptions of device aliases and attributes and for assigning device groups.

** descriptions (Device Alias and Attribute Management)

  This menu contains tasks for listing, adding, removing, and modifying device descriptions and attributes. This menu also provides access to device reservation services.

** groups (Device Group Management)

  This menu provides access to tasks that let you list and administer device groups and their membership lists.

* System Name, Date Time and Initial Password Setup

  This menu lets you set up your machine. The tasks in this menu include setting the system date and time, setting the node name of your system, doing initial system setup, and assigning passwords to administrative logins on the system.

** datetime (System Date and Time Information)

  This task lets you tell the computer the date, time, time zone, and whether you observe Daylight Savings Time (DST). It is normally run once when the machine is first set up. If you observe DST, the computer automatically starts to observe it in the spring and returns to standard time in the fall. The machine must be turned off and turned back on again to guarantee that ALL times are reported correctly. Most times are correct the next time a user logs in.

** nodename (System Name and Network Node Name of the Machine)

  This task lets you change the node name and system name of this machine. These names are used by various communications networks to identify this machine.

** password (Assigns Administrative Login Passwords)

  This task lets you assign passwords to administrative logins.

** setup (Sets up System Information for First Time)

  This task lets you define the first login, set the initial passwords on administration logins, and set the time zone for your location.

* User Login and Group Administration

  This menu lets you manage the user IDs and groups on your machine. Tasks include the ability to add, modify, and delete users or groups defined on your machine. You can place users in groups so that they can share access to files belonging to members of the group but protect these files from access by members of other groups. In addition, you can set defaults that are used for subsequent user definitions on your machine, and you can define or redefine user password information.

•• add (Adds Users or Groups)

This task lets you define either a new user or a new group on your system.

•• defaults (Defines Defaults for Adding Users)

This task lets you change some of the default values used when the add user task creates a new login. Changing the default values does not affect any existing logins; it affects only those added subsequently.

•• list (Lists Users or Groups)

This task lets you examine the attributes of the users and groups on your system.

•• modify (Modifies Attributes of Users or Groups)

This task lets you modify either a user definition or a group definition on your system.

•• password ((Re-)defines User Password Information)

This task lets you define or change a user's password.

•• remove (Removes Users or Groups)

This task lets you remove a user from your system.

DIAGNOSTICS

The sysadm command exits with one of the following values:

0   Normal exit.
2   Invalid command syntax. Usage message of the sysadm command is displayed.
4   The menu or task name given as an argument does not exist.
5   The menu name given as an argument is an empty placeholder menu, and therefore not available for use.
7   The sysadm command is not available because it cannot invoke fmli. (The FMLI package may be corrupt or it may not have been installed.)

EXAMPLES

sysadm nodename

NOTES

Add-on system packages that have not been updated to System V Release 4 may still need functionality that existed with the pre-System V Release 4 sysadm but is not available with System V Release 4 sysadm. If so, when the package is added, those old sysadm tasks are added under a menu titled old_sysadm. The old_sysadm menu appears on the main menu.

SEE ALSO

backup(1M), bkexcept(1M), bkhistory(1M), bkoper(1M), bkreg(1M), bkstatus(1M), checkfsys(1M), delsysadm(1M), edsysadm(1M), groupadd(1M), groupdel(1M), groupmod(1M), makefsys(1M), mountfsys(1M), password(1M), powerdown(1M), restore(1M), rsnotify(1M), rsoper(1M), rsstatus(1M), setup(1M), urestore(1M), ursstatus(1M), useradd(1M), userdel(1M), usermod(1M).

NAME

sysdef − output system definition

SYNOPSIS

/usr/sbin/sysdef [-n *namelist* [-m *master*]]
/usr/sbin/sysdef -i

DESCRIPTION

sysdef outputs the current system definition in tabular form. It lists all hardware devices, their local bus addresses, and unit count, as well as pseudo devices, system devices, loadable modules, and the values of selected kernel tunable parameters.

It generates the output by analyzing the named bootable operating system file (*namelist*) and extracting the configuration information from it and files in the master directory. This directory contains the system configuration files used to build *namelist*.

The default system *namelist* is /stand/unix; the default *master* directory is /etc/master.d.

Valid options and parameters are:

-n *namelist*
> Specifies a *namelist* other than the default (/stand/unix). The *namelist* specified must be a valid bootable operating system [see cunix(1M)].

-m *master*
> Specifies a *master* directory other than the default (/etc/master.d). Can only be used with the −n option.

-i   Allows you read the configuration information from the kernel that is currently in memory (i.e., from /dev/kmem) rather than from a file.

DIAGNOSTICS

internal name list overflow
> If the master table contains more than an internally specified number of entries for use by nlist(3C).

FILES

/stand/unix   default operating system file (file that contains the system namelist)

/etc/master.d/*   default directory containing master files

SEE ALSO

cunix(1M), master(4).
nlist(3C) in the *Programmer's Reference Manual*.

NAME
        talkd, in.talkd – server for talk program

SYNOPSIS
        in.talkd

DESCRIPTION
        talkd is a server used by the talk(1) program. It listens at the UDP port indi-
        cated in the "talk" service description; see services(4). The actual conversation
        takes place on a TCP connection that is established by negotiation between the
        two machines involved.

SEE ALSO
        talk(1), inetd(1M), services(4).

NOTES
        The protocol is architecture dependent.

NAME

telnetd – DARPA TELNET protocol server

SYNOPSIS

in.telnetd

DESCRIPTION

telnetd is a server which supports the DARPA standard TELNET virtual terminal protocol. telnetd is invoked by the internet server [see inetd(1M)], normally for requests to connect to the TELNET port as indicated by the /etc/services file [see services(4)].

telnetd operates by allocating a pseudo-terminal device for a client, then creating a login process which has the slave side of the pseudo-terminal as its standard input, output, and error. telnetd manipulates the master side of the pseudo-terminal, implementing the TELNET protocol and passing characters between the remote client and the login process.

When a TELNET session is started up, telnetd sends TELNET options to the client side indicating a willingness to do *remote echo* of characters, to *suppress go ahead*, and to receive *terminal type information* from the remote client. If the remote client is willing, the remote terminal type is propagated in the environment of the created login process. The pseudo-terminal allocated to the client is configured to operate in cooked mode, and with XTABS, ICRNL, and ONLCR enabled [see termio(4)].

telnetd is willing to do: *echo, binary, suppress go ahead*, and *timing mark*. telnetd is willing to have the remote client do: *binary, terminal type*, and *suppress go ahead*.

SEE ALSO

telnet(1)

Postel, Jon, and Joyce Reynolds, "Telnet Protocol Specification," RFC 854, Network Information Center, SRI International, Menlo Park, Calif., May 1983.

NOTES

Some TELNET commands are only partially implemented.

The TELNET protocol allows for the exchange of the number of lines and columns on the user's terminal, but telnetd doesn't make use of them.

Binary mode has no common interpretation except between similar operating systems

The terminal type name received from the remote client is converted to lower case.

The *packet* interface to the pseudo-terminal should be used for more intelligent flushing of input and output queues.

telnetd never sends TELNET *go ahead* commands.

telnetd can only support 64 pseudo-terminals.

NAME

tftpd – DARPA Trivial File Transfer Protocol server

SYNOPSIS

in.tftpd [-s] [*homedir*]

DESCRIPTION

tftpd is a server that supports the DARPA Trivial File Transfer Protocol (TFTP). This server is normally started by inetd(1M) and operates at the port indicated in the tftp Internet service description in the /etc/inetd.conf file. By default, the entry for tftpd in etc/inetd.conf is commented out. To make tftpd operational, the comment character(s) must be deleted from the file. See inetd.conf(4) for details.

Before responding to a request, the server attempts to change its current directory to *homedir*; the default value is /tftpboot.

OPTIONS

-s   Secure. When specified, the directory change must succeed; and the daemon also changes its root directory to *homedir*.

The use of *tftp* does not require an account or password on the remote system. Due to the lack of authentication information, *tftpd* will allow only publicly readable files to be accessed. Files may be written only if they already exist and are publicly writable. Note that this extends the concept of public to include all users on all hosts that can be reached through the network; this may not be appropriate on all systems, and its implications should be considered before enabling this service.

tftpd runs with the user ID and group ID set to [GU]ID_NOBODY. -2, under the assumption that no files exist with that owner or group. However, nothing checks this assumption or enforces this restriction.

SEE ALSO

tftp(1), inetd(1M), ipallocd(1M), netconfig(4).

Sollins, K.R., *The TFTP Protocol (Revision 2)*, RFC 783, Network Information Center, SRI International, Menlo Park, Calif., June 1981.

NAME
tic – *terminfo* compiler

SYNOPSIS
tic [–v[*n*]] [–c] *file*

DESCRIPTION
The command tic translates a terminfo file from the source format into the compiled format. The results are placed in the directory /usr/share/lib/terminfo. The compiled format is necessary for use with the library routines in curses(3X).

–*vn*   specifies that (verbose) output be written to standard error trace information showing tic's progress. The optional integer *n* is a number from 1 to 10, inclusive, indicating the desired level of detail of information. If *n* is omitted, the default level is 1. If *n* is specified and greater than 1, the level of detail is increased.

–c   specifies to check only *file* for errors. Errors in use= links are not detected.

file   contains one or more terminfo terminal descriptions in source format [see terminfo(4)]. Each description in the file describes the capabilities of a particular terminal. When a use=*entry-name* field is discovered in a terminal entry currently being compiled, tic reads in the binary from /usr/share/lib/terminfo to complete the entry. (Entries created from *file* will be used first. If the environment variable TERMINFO is set, that directory is searched instead of /usr/share/lib/terminfo.) tic duplicates the capabilities in *entry-name* for the current entry, with the exception of those capabilities that explicitly are defined in the current entry.

If the environment variable TERMINFO is set, the compiled results are placed there instead of /usr/share/lib/terminfo.

Total compiled entries cannot exceed 4096 bytes. The name field cannot exceed 128 bytes. Terminal names exceeding 14 characters will be truncated to 14 characters and a warning message will be printed.

FILES
/usr/share/lib/terminfo/?/*   Compiled terminal description database.

NOTES
When an entry, e.g., entry_name_1, contains a use=*entry_name_2* field, any canceled capabilities in *entry_name_2* must also appear in entry_name_1 before use= for these capabilities to be canceled in entry_name_1.

SEE ALSO
curses(3X), captoinfo(1M), infocmp(1M), terminfo(4).

NAME

tnamed, in.tnamed – DARPA trivial name server

SYNOPSIS

in.tnamed [–v]

DESCRIPTION

tnamed is a server that supports the DARPA Name Server Protocol. The name server operates at the port indicated in the name service description [see services(4)], and is invoked by inetd(1M) when a request is made to the name server.

OPTIONS

–v   Invoke the daemon in verbose mode.

SEE ALSO

uucp(1C), inetd(1M), services(4).

Postel, Jon, *Internet Name Server*, IEN 116, SRI International, Menlo Park, California, August 1979.

NOTES

The protocol implemented by this program is obsolete. Its use should be phased out in favor of the Internet Domain Name Service (DNS) protocol. See named(1M).

NAME
     tosmtp – send mail to SMTP

SYNOPSIS
     tosmtp [–f] [–n] [–u] [–d *domain*] [–H *helohost*] *sender host recip ...*

DESCRIPTION
     tosmtp translates a UNIX System mail message (read from standard input), into
     an RFC822 mail message, which can then be delivered with SMTP. tosmtp is nor-
     mally invoked by smtpqer as part of the process of queueing mail for delivery.

     The options to tosmtp and their meanings are as follows:

     –d *domain*   Pass the specified *domain* directly to the smtp program.

     –f   Act as a filter. The RFC822 message is sent to the standard output.

     –H *helohost* This option can be used to specify the name to be used for the host
                    in the initial SMTP HELO message. This option is also passed to the
                    smtp program.

     –n   Do not place a To: line in the resulting RFC822 header.

     –u   Do no conversion. The standard input is sent directly to the stan-
                    dard output.

FILES
     /usr/lib/mail/surrcmd/smtp   Where the message is piped to

SEE ALSO
     smtp(1M), smtpqer(1M)
     RFC822 – Standard for the Format of ARPA Internet Text Messages

NAME
trpt – transliterate protocol trace

SYNOPSIS
trpt [-afjst] [-p *hex-address*] [*system* [*core*]]

DESCRIPTION
trpt interrogates the buffer of TCP trace records created when a socket is marked for debugging [see getsockopt(3N)], and prints a readable description of these records. When no options are supplied, trpt prints all the trace records found in the system grouped according to TCP connection protocol control block (PCB). The following options may be used to alter this behavior.

OPTIONS
-a   In addition to the normal output, print the values of the source and desti-nation addresses for each packet recorded.

-f   Follow the trace as it occurs, waiting a short time for additional records each time the end of the log is reached.

-j   Just give a list of the protocol control block addresses for which there are trace records.

-s   In addition to the normal output, print a detailed description of the packet sequencing information.

-t   In addition to the normal output, print the values for all timers at each point in the trace.

-p *hex-address*
Show only trace records associated with the protocol control block, the address of which follows.

The recommended use of trpt is as follows. Isolate the problem and enable debugging on the socket(s) involved in the connection. Find the address of the protocol control blocks associated with the sockets using the -A option to netstat(1M). Then run trpt with the -p option, supplying the associated proto-col control block addresses. The -f option can be used to follow the trace log once the trace is located. If there are many sockets using the debugging option, the -j option may be useful in checking to see if any trace records are present for the socket in question.

If debugging is being performed on a system or core file other than the default, the last two arguments may be used to supplant the defaults.

FILES
/stand/unix
/dev/kmem

SEE ALSO
netstat(1M), getsockopt(3N).

DIAGNOSTICS
no namelist
When the system image does not contain the proper symbols to find the trace buffer; others which should be self explanatory.

NOTES

Should also print the data for each input or output, but this is not saved in the trace record.

The output format is inscrutable and should be described here.

NAME

ttyadm – format and output port monitor-specific information

SYNOPSIS

/usr/sbin/ttyadm [–b] [–c] [–r count] [–h] [–i msg] [–m modules]
            –p prompt] [–t timeout] –d device –l ttylabel –s service

/usr/sbin/ttyadm –V

DESCRIPTION

The ttyadm command is an administrative command that formats ttymon-specific information and writes it to the standard output. The Service Access Facility (SAF) requires each port monitor to provide such a command. Note that the port monitor administrative file is updated by the Service Access Controller's administrative commands, sacadm and pmadm. ttyadm provides a means of presenting formatted port monitor-specific (i.e., ttymon-specific) data to these commands.

–b   Sets the "bidirectional port" flag. When this flag is set, the line can be used in both directions. ttymon will allow users to connect to the service associated with the port, but if the port is free, uucico, cu, or ct can use it for dialing out.

–c   Sets the connect-on-carrier flag for the port. If the –c flag is set, ttymon will invoke the port's associated service immediately when a connect indication is received (i.e., no prompt is printed and no baud-rate searching is done).

–d device   device is the full pathname of the device file for the TTY port.

–h   Sets the hangup flag for the port. If the –h flag is not set, ttymon will force a hangup on the line by setting the speed to zero before setting the speed to the default or specified value.

–i message Specifies the inactive (disabled) response message. This message will be sent to the TTY port if the port is disabled or the ttymon monitoring the port is disabled.

–l ttylabel Specifies which ttylabel in the /etc/ttydefs file to use as the starting point when searching for the proper baud rate.

–m modules Specifies a list of pushable STREAMS modules. The modules will be pushed, in the order in which they are specified, before the service is invoked. modules must be a comma-separated list of modules, with no white space included. Any modules currently on the stream will be popped before these modules are pushed.

–r count   When the –r option is invoked, ttymon will wait until it receives data from the port before it displays a prompt. If count is equal to zero, ttymon will wait until it receives any character. If count is greater than zero, ttymon will wait until count newlines have been received.

–p prompt   Specifies the prompt message, e.g., "login:."

−s *service*	*service* is the full pathname of the service to be invoked when a connection request is received. If arguments are required, the command and its arguments must be enclosed in double quotes.
−t *timeout*	Specifies that ttymon should close a port if the open on the port succeeds and no input data is received in *timeout* seconds.
−v	Displays the version number of the current /usr/lib/saf/ttymon command.

OUTPUT

If successful, ttyadm will generate the requested information, write it on the standard output, and exit with a status of 0. If ttyadm is invoked with an invalid number of arguments or invalid arguments, or if an incomplete option is specified, an error message will be written to the standard error and ttymon will exit with a non-zero status.

FILES

/etc/ttydefs

SEE ALSO

pmadm(1M), sacadm(1M), ttymon(1M).
System Administrator's Guide, "The Port Monitor ttymon."

NAME

    ttymon − port monitor for terminal ports

SYNOPSIS

    /usr/lib/saf/ttymon

    /usr/lib/saf/ttymon −g [−d *device*] [−h] [−t *timeout*] [−l *ttylabel*] \
      [−p *prompt*] [−m *modules*]

DESCRIPTION

    ttymon is a STREAMS-based TTY port monitor. Its function is to monitor ports, to set terminal modes, baud rates, and line disciplines for the ports, and to connect users or applications to services associated with the ports. Normally, ttymon is configured to run under the Service Access Controller, sac, as part of the Service Access Facility (SAF). It is configured using the sacadm command. Each instance of ttymon can monitor multiple ports. The ports monitored by an instance of ttymon are specified in the port monitor's administrative file. The administrative file is configured using the pmadm and ttyadm commands. When an instance of ttymon is invoked by the sac command, it starts to monitor its ports. For each port, ttymon first initializes the line disciplines, if they are specified, and the speed and terminal settings. The values used for initialization are taken from the appropriate entry in the TTY settings file. This file is maintained by the sttydefs command. Default line disciplines on ports are usually set up by the autopush command of the Autopush Facility.

    ttymon then writes the prompt and waits for user input. If the user indicates that the speed is inappropriate by pressing the BREAK key, ttymon tries the next speed and writes the prompt again. When valid input is received, ttymon interprets the per-service configuration file for the port, if one exists, creates a utmp entry if required, establishes the service environment, and then invokes the service associated with the port. Valid input consists of a string of at least one non-newline character, terminated by a carriage return. After the service terminates, ttymon cleans up the utmp entry, if one exists, and returns the port to its initial state.

    If *autobaud* is enabled for a port, ttymon will try to determine the baud rate on the port automatically. Users must enter a carriage return before ttymon can recognize the baud rate and print the prompt. Currently, the baud rates that can be determined by *autobaud* are 110, 1200, 2400, 4800, and 9600.

    If a port is configured as a bidirectional port, ttymon will allow users to connect to a service, and, if the port is free, will allow uucico, cu or ct to use it for dialing out. If a port is bidirectional, ttymon will wait to read a character before it prints a prompt.

    If the *connect-on-carrier* flag is set for a port, ttymon will immediately invoke the port's associated service when a connection request is received. The prompt message will not be sent.

    If a port is disabled, ttymon will not start any service on that port. If a disabled message is specified, ttymon will send out the disabled message when a connection request is received. If ttymon is disabled, all ports under that instance of ttymon will also be disabled.

SERVICE INVOCATION

The service ttymon invokes for a port is specified in the ttymon administrative file. ttymon will scan the character string giving the service to be invoked for this port, looking for a %d or a %% two-character sequence. If %d is found, ttymon will modify the service command to be executed by replacing those two characters by the full path name of this port (the device name). If %% is found, they will be replaced by a single %.

When the service is invoked, file descriptor 0, 1, and 2 are opened to the port device for reading and writing. The service is invoked with the user ID, group ID and current home directory set to that of the user name under which the service was registered with ttymon. Two environment variables, HOME and TTYPROMPT, are added to the service's environment by ttymon. HOME is set to the HOME directory of the user name under which the service is invoked. TTYPROMPT is set to the prompt string configured for the service on the port. This is provided so that a service invoked by ttymon has a means of determining if a prompt was actually issued by ttymon and, if so, what that prompt actually was.

See ttyadm(1M) for options that can be set for ports monitored by ttymon under the Service Access Controller.

INVOKING A STAND-ALONE ttymon PROCESS

A special invocation of ttymon is provided with the −g option. This form of the command should only be called by applications that need to set the correct baud rate and terminal settings on a port and then connect to login service, but that cannot be pre-configured under the SAC. The following combinations of options can be used with −g:

−d *device*   *device* is the full path name of the port to which ttymon is to attach. If this option is not specified, file descriptor 0 must be set up by the invoking process to a TTY port.

−h   If the -h flag is not set, ttymon will force a hangup on the line by setting the speed to zero before setting the speed to the default or specified speed.

−t *timeout*   Specifies that ttymon should exit if no one types anything in *timeout* seconds after the prompt is sent.

−l *ttylabel* *ttylabel* is a link to a speed and TTY definition in the ttydefs file. This definition tells ttymon at what speed to run initially, what the initial TTY settings are, and what speed to try next if the user indicates that the speed is inappropriate by pressing the BREAK key. The default speed is 9600 baud.

−p *prompt*   Allows the user to specify a prompt string. The default prompt is "Login: ".

−m *modules*   When initializing the port, ttymon will pop all modules on the port, and then push *modules* in the order specified. *modules* is a comma-separated list of pushable modules. Default modules on the ports are usually set up by the Autopush Facility.

SEE ALSO

pmadm(1M), sac(1M), sacadm(1M), ttyadm(1M).
System Administrator's Guide, "The Port Monitor ttymon."

NOTES

If a port is monitored by more than one ttymon, it is possible for the ttymons to send out prompt messages in such a way that they compete for input.

NAME
tunefs – tune up an existing file system

SYNOPSIS
tunefs [–a *maxcontig*] [–d *rotdelay*] [–e *maxbpg*] [–m *minfree*] [–o [s | t]] *special* | *filesystem*

DESCRIPTION
tunefs is designed to change the dynamic parameters of a file system which affect the layout policies. The file system must be unmounted before using tunefs. The parameters which are to be changed are indicated by the options given below:

The options are:

–a *maxcontig*   Specify the maximum number of contiguous blocks that will be laid out before forcing a rotational delay (see –d below). The default value is one, since most device drivers require an interrupt per disk transfer. Device drivers that can chain several buffers together in a single transfer should set this to the maximum chain length.

–d *rotdelay*   Specify the expected time (in milliseconds) to service a transfer completion interrupt and initiate a new transfer on the same disk. It is used to decide how much rotational spacing to place between successive blocks in a file.

–e *maxbpg*   Indicate the maximum number of blocks any single file can allocate out of a cylinder group before it is forced to begin allocating blocks from another cylinder group. Typically this value is set to approximately one quarter of the total blocks in a cylinder group. The intent is to prevent any single file from using up all the blocks in a single cylinder group, thus degrading access times for all files subsequently allocated in that cylinder group. The effect of this limit is to cause big files to do long seeks more frequently than if they were allowed to allocate all the blocks in a cylinder group before seeking elsewhere. For file systems with exclusively large files, this parameter should be set higher.

–m *minfree*   Specify the percentage of space held back from normal users; the minimum free space threshold. The default value used is 10%. This value can be set to zero, however up to a factor of three in throughput will be lost over the performance obtained at a 10% threshold. Note: if the value is raised above the current usage level, users will be unable to allocate files until enough files have been deleted to get under the higher threshold.

–o [s | t]   Change optimization strategy for the file system.

s - space (conserve space)
t - time (attempt to organize file layout to minimize access time.

Generally one should optimize for time unless the file system is over 90% full.

SEE ALSO

mkfs(1M), ufs(4). fork(2), terminfo(4) in the *Programmer's Reference Manual.*

NAME

uadmin – administrative control

SYNOPSIS

/sbin/uadmin *cmd fcn*

DESCRIPTION

The uadmin command provides control for basic administrative functions. This command is tightly coupled to the System Administration procedures and is not intended for general use. It may be invoked only by the super-user.

The arguments *cmd* (command) and *fcn* (function) are converted to integers and passed to the uadmin system call.

SEE ALSO

uadmin(2) in the *Programmer's Reference Manual.*

NAME

   ufsdump – incremental file system dump

SYNOPSIS

   ufsdump [*options*] *filesystem*

DESCRIPTION

   ufsdump backs up all files in *filesystem*, or files changed after a certain date, to
   magnetic tape; *options* is a string that specifies ufsdump options, as shown below.

   If no *options* are given, the default is 9u.

   The options are:

   0–9   The dump level. All files in the *filesystem* that have been modified since
         the last ufsdump at a lower dump level are copied to the volume. For
         instance, if you did a level 2 dump on Monday, followed by a level 4
         dump on Tuesday, a subsequent level 3 dump on Wednesday would con-
         tain all files modified or added since the level 2 (Monday) backup. A
         level 0 dump copies the entire filesystem to the dump volume.

   −b *factor*
         Blocking factor. Specify the blocking factor for tape writes. The default is
         20 blocks per write. Note: the blocking factor is specified in terms of 512
         bytes blocks, for compatibility with tar. The default blocking factor for
         tapes of density 6250BPI and greater is 64. The default blocking factor for
         cartridge tapes (−c option specified) is 126. The highest blocking factor
         available with most tape drives is 126.

   c   Cartridge. Use a cartridge instead of the standard half-inch reel. This sets
         the density to 1000BPI and the blocking factor to 126. The length is set to
         425 feet. This option is incompatible with the −d option, unless you
         specify a density of 1000BPI with that option.

   −d *bpi*   Tape density. The density of the tape, expressed in BPI, is taken from *bpi*.
         This is used to keep a running tab on the amount of tape used per reel.
         The default density is 1600 except for cartridge tape. Unless a higher den-
         sity is specified explicitly, ufsdump uses its default density — even if the
         tape drive is capable of higher-density operation (for instance, 6250BPI).
         Note: the density specified should correspond to the density of the tape
         device being used, or ufsdump will not be able to handle end-of-tape
         properly.

   −f *dump-file*
         Dump file. Use *dump-file* as the file to dump to, instead of /dev/rmt8 . If
         dump-file is specified as −, dump to the standard output.

   −n   Notify all operators in the operator group that ufsdump requires attention
         by sending messages to their terminals, in a manner similar to that used
         by the wall command.

-s *size*

Specify the *size* of the volume being dumped to. When the specified size is reached, ufsdump waits for you to change the volume. ufsdump interprets the specified size as the length in feet for tapes and cartridges, and as the number of 1024-byte blocks for diskettes. The following are defaults:

tape	2300 feet
cartridge	425 feet
diskette	1422 blocks (Corresponds to a 1.44 Mb diskette, with one cylinder reserved for bad block information.)

-t *tracks*

Specify the number of tracks for a cartridge tape. The default is 9 tracks. The -t option is not compatible with the -D option.

-u   Update the dump record. Add an entry to the file /etc/dumpdates, for each filesystem successfully dumped that includes the filesystem name, date, and dump level. This file can be edited by the super-user.

-w   List the file systems that need backing up. This information is gleaned from the files /etc/dumpdates and /etc/vfstab. When the -w option is used, all other options are ignored. After reporting, ufsdump exits immediately.

W   Similar to the -w option, except that the -W option includes all file systems that appear in /etc/dumpdates, along with information about their most recent dump dates and levels. Filesystems that need backing up are highlighted.

NOTES

Fewer than 32 read errors on the filesystem are ignored.

Each reel requires a new process, so parent processes for reels already written just hang around until the entire tape is written.

It is recommended that incremental dumps also be performed with the system running in single-user mode.

FILES

/dev/rmt8	default unit to dump to
/etc/dumpdates	dump date record
/etc/group	to find group operator
/etc/hosts	

SEE ALSO

tar(1), wall(1), shutdown(1M), ufsrestore(1M).

NAME
     ufsrestore – incremental file system restore

SYNOPSIS
     ufsrestore *options* [*filename...*]

DESCRIPTION
     ufsrestore restores files from backup tapes created with the ufsdump. com-
     mand. *options* is a string of at least one of the options listed below, along with
     any modifiers and arguments you supply. Remaining arguments to ufsrestore
     are the names of files (or directories whose files) are to be restored to disk.
     Unless the h modifier is in effect, a directory name refers to the files it contains,
     and (recursively) its subdirectories and the files they contain.

     The options are:

     -i   Interactive. After reading in the directory information from the tape,
           ufsrestore invokes an interactive interface that allows you to browse
           through the dump tape's directory hierarchy and select individual files to be
           extracted. See Interactive Commands, below, for a description of avail-
           able commands.

     -r   Restore the entire tape. Load the tape's full contents into the current direc-
           tory. This option should be used only to restore a complete dump tape onto
           a clear filesystem, or to restore an incremental dump tape after a full level 0
           restore.

     -R   Resume restoring. ufsrestore requests a particular tape of a multivolume
           set from which to resume a full restore (see the –r option above). This
           allows ufsrestore to start from a checkpoint when it is interrupted in the
           middle of a full restore.

     -t   Table of contents. List each *filename* that appears on the tape. If no *filename*
           argument is given, the root directory is listed. This results in a list of all
           files on the tape, unless the –h modifier is in effect.

     -x   Extract the named files from the tape. If a named file matches a directory
           whose contents were written onto the tape, and the –h modifier is not in
           effect, the directory is recursively extracted. The owner, modification time,
           and mode are restored (if possible). If no *filename* argument is given, the
           root directory is extracted. This results in the entire tape being extracted
           unless the –h modifier is in effect.

     -c   Convert the contents of the dump tape to the new filesystem format.

     -d   Debug. Turn on debugging output.

     h   Extract the actual directory, rather than the files that it references. This
           prevents hierarchical restoration of complete subtrees from the tape.

     m   Extract by inode numbers rather than by filename to avoid regenerating
           complete pathnames. This is useful if only a few files are being extracted.

     v   Verbose. ufsrestore displays the name of each file it restores, preceded by
           its file type.

y   Do not ask whether to abort the restore in the event of tape errors. ufsre-
        store tries to skip over the bad tape block(s) and continue as best it can.

b *factor*
        Blocking factor. Specify the blocking factor for tape reads. By default,
        ufsrestore will attempt to figure out the block size of the tape. Note: a
        tape block is 512 bytes.

f *dump-file*
        Use *dump-file* instead of /dev/rmt? as the file to restore from. If *dump-file*
        is specified as '−', ufsrestore reads from the standard input. This allows,
        ufsdump(1M) and ufsrestore to be used in a pipeline to dump and restore
        a file system:

        example# ufsdump 0f − /dev/rxy0g | (cd /mnt; ufsre-
        store xf −)

        If the name of the file is of the form *machine:device* the restore is done from
        the specified machine over the network using rmt(1M). Since ufsrestore
        is normally run by root, the name of the local machine must appear in the
        .rhosts file of the remote machine. If the file is specified as
        user!machine:device, ufsrestore will attempt to execute as the specified
        user on the remote machine. The specified user must have a .rhosts file
        on the remote machine that allows root from the local machine. If ufsre-
        store is called as ufsrrestore, the tape defaults to dumphost:/dev/rmt8.
        To direct the input from a desired remote machine, set up an alias for dum-
        phost in the file /etc/hosts.

s *n*   Skip to the *n*'th file when there are multiple dump files on the same tape.
        For example, the command:

        example# ufsrestore xfs /dev/nrar0 5

        would position you at the fifth file on the tape.

ufsrestore enters interactive mode when invoked with the i option. Interactive
commands are reminiscent of the shell. For those commands that accept an argument, the default is the current directory.

ls[*directory*]
        List files in directory or the current directory, represented by a '.'
        (period). Directories are appended with a '/' (backslash). Entries
        marked for extraction are prefixed with a '*' (asterisk). If the verbose
        option is in effect, inode numbers are also listed.

cd *directory*
        Change to directory directory (within the dump-tape).

pwd   Print the full pathname of the current working directory.

add[*filename*]
        Add the current directory, or the named file or directory directory to
        the list of files to extract. If a directory is specified, add that directory
        and its files (recursively) to the extraction list (unless the h modifier is
        in effect).

delete[*filename*]
> Delete the current directory, or the named file or directory from the list of files to extract. If a directory is specified, delete that directory and all its descendents from the extraction list (unless the h modifier is in effect). The most expedient way to extract a majority of files from a directory is to add that directory to the extraction list, and then delete specific files to omit.

extract
> Extract all files on the extraction list from the dump tape. ufsrestore asks which volume the user wishes to mount. The fastest way to extract a small number of files is to start with the last tape volume and work toward the first.

verbose
> Toggle the status of the v modifier. While v is in effect, the ls command lists the inode numbers of all entries, and ufsrestore displays information about each file as it is extracted.

help
> Display a summary of the available commands.

quit
> ufsrestore exits immediately, even if the extraction list is not empty.

NOTES

ufsrestore can get confused when doing incremental restores from dump tapes that were made on active file systems.

A level 0 dump must be done after a full restore. Because ufsrestore runs in user mode, it has no control over inode allocation; this means that ufsrestore repositions the files, although it does not change their contents. Thus, a full dump must be done to get a new set of directories reflecting the new file positions, so that later incremental dumps will be correct.

DIAGNOSTICS

ufsrestore complains about bad option characters.

Read errors result in complaints. If y has been specified, or the user responds y, ufsrestore will attempt to continue.

If the dump extends over more than one tape, ufsrestore asks the user to change tapes. If the x or i option has been specified, ufsrestore also asks which volume the user wishes to mount.

There are numerous consistency checks that can be listed by ufsrestore. Most checks are self-explanatory or can never happen. Common errors are given below.

Converting to new file system format.
> A dump tape created from the old file system has been loaded. It is automatically converted to the new file system format.

filename: not found on tape
> The specified file name was listed in the tape directory, but was not found on the tape. This is caused by tape read errors while looking for the file, and from using a dump tape created on an active file system.

expected next file *inumber*, got *inumber*
> A file that was not listed in the directory showed up. This can occur when using a dump tape created on an active file system.

Incremental tape too low
> When doing an incremental restore, a tape that was written before the previous incremental tape, or that has too low an incremental level has been loaded.

Incremental tape too high
> When doing incremental restore, a tape that does not begin its coverage where the previous incremental tape left off, or one that has too high an incremental level has been loaded.

Tape read error while restoring *filename*
Tape read error while skipping over inode *inumber*
Tape read error while trying to resynchronize
A tape read error has occurred.
> If a file name is specified, then its contents are probably partially wrong. If an inode is being skipped or the tape is trying to resynchronize, then no extracted files have been corrupted, though files may not be found on the tape.

resync ufsrestore, skipped *num*
> After a tape read error, ufsrestore may have to resynchronize itself. This message lists the number of blocks that were skipped over.

FILES

/dev/rmt8	the default tape drive
dumphost:/dev/rmt8	
	the default tape drive if called as ufsrrestore
/tmp/rstdir*	file containing directories on the tape
/tmp/rstmode*	owner, mode, and timestamps for directories
./restoresymtable	information passed between incremental restores

SEE ALSO
ufsdump(1M), mkfs(1M), mount(1M).

NAME

unshare – make local resource unavailable for mounting by remote systems

SYNOPSIS

unshare [–F *fstype*] [–o *specific_options*] [*pathname* | *resourcename*]

DESCRIPTION

The unshare command makes a shared local resource unavailable to file system type *fstype*. If the option –F *fstype* is omitted, then the first file system type listed in file /etc/dfs/fstypes will be used as the default. *Specific_options*, as well as the semantics of *resourcename*, are specific to particular distributed file systems.

FILES

/etc/dfs/fstypes
/etc/dfs/sharetab

SEE ALSO

share(1M), shareall(1M).

NOTES

If *pathname* or *resourcename* is not found in the shared information, an error message will be sent to standard error.

NAME

unshare – make local NFS resource unavailable for mounting by remote systems

SYNOPSIS

unshare [–F nfs] *pathname*

DESCRIPTION

The unshare command makes local resources unavailable for mounting by remote systems. The shared resource must correspond to a line with NFS as the *fstype* in the file /etc/dfs/sharetab. The –F option may be omitted if NFS is the first file system type listed in the files /etc/dfs/fstypes.

FILES

/etc/dfs/fstypes
/etc/dfs/sharetab

SEE ALSO

share(1M)

NAME

    unshare – make local RFS resource unavailable for mounting by remote systems

SYNOPSIS

    unshare [–F rfs] {*pathname* | *resourcename*}

DESCRIPTION

    The unshare command makes a shared resource unavailable through Remote File Sharing. The shared resource must correspond to a line with rfs as the *fstype* in the file /etc/dfs/sharetab. The –F flag may be omitted if RFS is the first file system type listed in the file /etc/dfs/fstypes.

FILES

    /etc/dfs/dfstab
    /etc/dfs/fstypes
    /etc/dfs/sharetab

SEE ALSO

    unshare(1M), share(1M)

NAME
   urestore – request restore of files and directories

SYNOPSIS
   urestore [–mn] [–s | v] [–o *target*] [–d *date*] –F *file* ...

   urestore [–mn] [–s | v] [–o *target*] [–d *date*] –D *dir* ...

   urestore –c *jobid*

DESCRIPTION
   urestore posts requests for files or directories to be restored from system-maintained archives. If the appropriate archive containing the requested files or directories is on-line, the files or directories are restored immediately. If not, a request to restore the specified files or directories is posted to a restore status table, /etc/bkup/rsstatus.tab. A restore request that has been posted must later be resolved by an operator (see rsoper(1M)). Each file or directory to be restored is assigned a restore job ID that can be used to monitor the progress of the restore (see ursstatus(1M)) or to cancel it.

   The user must have write permission for the current directory and any subdirectories to be traversed in storing the restored files or directories. Requests for restores may be made only by the user who owned the files or directories at the time the archive containing the files or directories was made, or by a user with superuser privileges.

Options
   –c *jobid*   Cancels a previously issued restore request.

   –d *date*   Restores the filesystem or directory as of *date*. (This may or may not be the latest archive.) See getdate(3C) for valid date formats.

   –m   If the restore cannot be carried out immediately, this option notifies the invoking user (via mail) when the request has been completed.

   –n   Displays a list of all archived versions of the filesystem or directory contained in the backup history log but does not attempt to restore the filesystem or directory.

   –o *target*   Instead of restoring directly to the specified file or directory, this option replaces the file or directory *target* with the archive of the specified file or directory.

   –s   While a restore operation is occurring, displays a "." for each 100 (512-byte) blocks transferred from the destination device.

   –v   Displays the name of each object as it is restored. Only those archiving methods that restore named directories and files (incfile, ffile) support this option.

   –D   Initiates a restore operation for directories.

   –F   Initiates a restore operation for files.

DIAGNOSTICS
   The exit codes for urestore are the following:

0 = the task completed successfully
1 = one or more parameters to urestore are invalid
2 = an error has occurred, causing urestore to fail to complete *all* portions of its task.

EXAMPLES

Example 1:

```
urestore -m -F bigfile
```

posts a request to restore the most current archived version of the file bigfile. If the restore operation cannot be carried out immediately, it notifies the invoking user when the request has been completed.

Example 2:

```
urestore -c rest-256a, rest-256b
```

cancels restore requests with job ID numbers rest-256a and rest-256b.

Example 3:

```
urestore -o /testfiles/myfile.b -F /testfiles/myfile.a
```

posts a request for the archived file /testfiles/myfile.a to be restored as /testfiles/myfile.b

Example 4:

```
urestore -d "december 1, 1987" -D /user1 -v
```

posts a request for the archived directory structure /user1, with all its files and subdirectories, to be restored as of December 1, 1987. If the restore is done immediately from an on-line archive, the name of each file will be displayed on standard output while the restore is underway.

Example 5:

```
urestore -n -D /pr3/reports
```

requests the system to display the backup dates and an ls -1 listing from the backup history log of all archived versions of the directory /pr3/reports. The directory is not restored.

FILES

/etc/bkup/bkhist.tab	–	contains the labels of all volumes that have been used for backup operations
/etc/bkup/rsstatus.tab	–	contains status information about all restore requests from users
/etc/bkup/rsnotify.tab	–	contains the electronic mail address of the operator to be notified whenever restore requests require operator intervention

SEE ALSO

restore(1M), ursstatus(1M).
mail(1) in the *User's Reference Manual*.
getdate(3C) in the *Programmer's Reference Manual*.

NAME
    ursstatus – report the status of posted user restore requests

SYNOPSIS
    ursstatus [–h] [–j *jobids*] [–f *field_separator*] [–d *ddev*] [–u *users*]

DESCRIPTION
    With no options, **ursstatus** reports the status of all pending user restore
    requests that are posted in the restore status table.

    This command can request a status report for only those restore requests that the
    user has initiated.

Options
    –h   Suppresses header for the report.

    –j *jobids* Restricts the report to the specified jobs. *jobids* is a list of restore job
                IDs (either comma-separated or blank-separated and surrounded by
                quotes). *jobids* must be valid for the user invoking the command.

    –f *field_separator*
                Suppresses field wrap and specifies an output field separator to be
                used. *field_separator* is the character that will appear as the field
                separator in the output displayed. A null *field_separator* will use a tab
                character as a separator.

    –d *ddev*   Restricts the report to pending restore jobs that could be satisfied by
                the specified device type or volumes. *ddev* describes the device or
                volumes used to select requests to be restored. *ddev* is of the form:

                    [*dtype*][: *dlabels*]

                dtype is a device type (such as diskette, cartridge tape, or 9-track tape).
                If specified, restrict the report to posted requests that could be
                satisfied by volumes of the type specified.

                dlabels is a list of volume names corresponding to the *volumename*
                displayed by the **labelit** command. *dlabels* may be either comma-
                separated or blank-separated and surrounded by quotes. If specified,
                restrict the report to posted requests that could be satisfied by an
                archive residing on the specified volumes.

    –u *users*   Restricts the report to requests submitted by the specified *users* (either
                comma-separated or blank-separated and surrounded by quotes).
                users must be listed in the **passwd** file.

DIAGNOSTICS
    The exit codes for **ursstatus** are the following:

    0 = successful completion of the task
    1 = one or more parameters to **ursstatus** are invalid.
    2 = an error has occurred which caused **ursstatus** to fail to
        complete *all* portions of its task.

EXAMPLE

        ursstatus -j rest-354a, rest-429b

reports the status of only the two posted restore requests with the specified job
IDs.

FILES

        /etc/bkup/rsstatus.tab   contains status report information for all restore
                                      requests from users

SEE ALSO

        restore(1M), rsstatus(1M), urestore(1M).

NAME

useradd – administer a new user login on the system

SYNOPSIS

useradd [–u *uid* [–o]] [–g *group*] [–G *group*[, *group*...] [–d *dir*] [–s *shell*]
    [–c *comment*] [–m [–k *skel_dir*]] [–f *inactive*] [–e *expire*] *login*

useradd –D [–g *group*] [–b *base_dir*] [–f *inactive*] [–e *expire*]

DESCRIPTION

Invoking **useradd** without the –D option adds a new user entry to the
/etc/passwd and /etc/shadow files. It also creates supplementary group
memberships for the user (–G option) and creates the home directory (–m option)
for the user if requested. The new login remains locked until the **passwd**(1M)
command is executed.

Invoking **useradd** –D with no additional options displays the default values for
group, base_dir, shel_dir, shell, inactive, and *expire.* The values for *group, base_dir,
inactive, expire,* and *shell* are used for invocations without the –D option.

Invoking **useradd** –D with –g, –b, –f, or –e (or any combination of these) sets
the default values for the respective fields. [As installed, the default group is
other (group ID of 1) and the default value of *base_dir* is /home]. Subsequent
invocations of **useradd** without the –D option use these arguments.

The system file entries created with this command have a limit of 512 characters
per line. Specifying long arguments to several options may exceed this limit.

The following options are available:

–u *uid*   The UID of the new user. This UID must be a non-negative decimal
integer below **MAXUID** as defined in <param.h>. The UID defaults to
the next available (unique) number above the highest number currently
assigned. For example, if UIDs 100, 105, and 200 are assigned, the next
default UID number will be 201. (UIDs from 0-99 are reserved.)

–o   This option allows a UID to be duplicated (non-unique).

–g *group*   An existing group's integer ID or character-string name. Without the
–D option, it defines the new user's primary group membership and
defaults to the default group. You can reset this default value by
invoking **useradd** –D –g *group*.

–G *group*   An existing group's integer ID or character-string name. It defines the
new user's supplementary group membership. Duplicates between
group with the –g and –G options are ignored. No more than
NGROUPS_MAX groups may be specified.

–d *dir*   The home directory of the new user. It defaults to *base_dir/login*, where
base_dir is the base directory for new login home directories and *login*
is the new login.

–s *shell*   Full pathname of the program used as the user's shell on login. It
defaults to an empty field causing the system to use /sbin/sh as the
default. The value of *shell* must be a valid executable file.

-c *comment*
> Any text string. It is generally a short description of the login, and is currently used as the field for the user's full name. This information is stored in the user's /etc/passwd entry.

-m
> Create the new user's home directory if it doesn't already exist. If the directory already exists, it must have read, write, and execute permissions by *group*, where *group* is the user's primary group.

-k *skel_dir*
> A directory that contains skeleton information (such as .profile) that can be copied into a new user's home directory. This directory must exist. The system provides a "skel" directory (/etc/skel) that can be used for this purpose.

-e *expire*
> The date on which a login can no longer be used; after this date, no user will be able to access this login. (This option is useful for creating temporary logins.) You may type the value of the argument *expire* (which is a date) in any format you like (except a Julian date). For example, you may enter 10/6/90 or October 6, 1990. A value of ''''' defeats the status of the expired date.

-f *inactive*
> The maximum number of days allowed between uses of a login ID before that login ID is declared valid. Normal values are positive integers. A value of -1 defeats the status.

login
> A string of printable characters that specifies the existing login name of the user. It must exist and may not contain a colon (:) or a newline (\n).

login
> A string of printable characters that specifies the new login name of the user. It may not contain a colon (:) or a newline (\n).

-b *base_dir*
> The default base directory for the system. If -d *dir* is not specified. *base_dir* is concatenated with the user's login to define the home directory. If the -m option is not used, base_dir must exist.

FILES
> /etc/passwd
> /etc/shadow
> /etc/group
> /etc/skel

SEE ALSO
> groupadd(1M),   groupdel(1M),   groupmod(1M),   logins(1M),   passwd(1), passwd(1M), userdel(1M), usermod(1M), users(1).

DIAGNOSTICS

The useradd command exits with one of the following values:

0   The command was executed successfully.

2   The command line syntax was invalid. A usage message for the useradd command is displayed.

3   An invalid argument was provided with an option.

4   The *uid* specified with the −u option is already in use.

6   The *group* specified with the −g option does not exist.

9   The specified *login* is not unique.

10   Cannot update /etc/group. The login was added to the /etc/passwd file but not to the /etc/group file.

12   Unable to create the home directory (with the −m option) or unable to complete the copy of *skel_dir* to the home directory.

NAME

userdel – delete a user's login from the system

SYNOPSIS

userdel [-r] *login*

DESCRIPTION

The userdel command deletes a user's login from the system and makes the appropriate login-related changes to the system file and file system.

The following options are available:

-r   Remove the user's home directory from the system. This directory must exist. The files and directories under the home directory will no longer be accessible following successful execution of the command.

login   A string of printable characters that specifies an existing login on the system. It may not contain a colon (:), or a newline (\n).

FILES

/etc/passwd
/etc/shadow
/etc/group
/etc/security/ia/index
/etc/security/ia/master
/etc/security/ia/uidage

SEE ALSO

groupadd(1M), groupdel(1M), groupmod(1M), logins(1M), passwd(1), passwd(1M), useradd(1M), usermod(1M), users(1).

DIAGNOSTICS

The userdel command exits with one of the following values:

0   Success.

2   Invalid command syntax. A usage message for the userdel command is displayed.

6   The login to be removed does not exist.

8   The login to be removed is in use.

10   Cannot update the /etc/group file but the login is removed from the /etc/passwd file.

12   Cannot remove or otherwise modify the home directory.

NAME
usermod – modify a user's login information on the system

SYNOPSIS
usermod [−u *uid* [−o]] [−g *group*] [−G *group*[, *group* . . .]   [−d *dir* [−m]] [−s *shell*]
[−c *comment*] [−l *new_logname*] [−f *inactive*] [−e *expire*] *login*

DESCRIPTION
The usermod command modifies a user's login definition on the system. It changes the definition of the specified login and makes the appropriate login-related system file and file system changes.

The system file entries created with this command have a limit of 512 characters per line. Specifying long arguments to several options may exceed this limit.

The following options are available:

−u *uid* New UID for the user. It must be a non-negative decimal integer below MAXUID as defined in <param.h>.

−o This option allows the specified UID to be duplicated (non-unique).

−g *group*
An existing group's integer ID or character-string name. It redefines the user's primary group membership.

−G *group*
An existing group's integer "ID" "," or character string name. It redefines the user's supplementary group membership. Duplicates between group with the −g and −G options are ignored. No more than NGROUPS_UMAX groups may be specified as defined in <param.h>.

−d *dir* The new home directory of the user. It defaults to *base_dir/login*, where *base_dir* is the base directory for new login home directories, and *login* is the new login.

−m Move the user's home directory to the new directory specified with the −d option. If the directory already exists, it must have permissions read/write/execute by *group*, where *group* is the user's primary group.

−s *shell*
Full pathname of the program that is used as the user's shell on login. The value of *shell* must be a valid executable file.

−c *comment*
Any text string. It is generally a short description of the login, and is currently used as the field for the user's full name. This information is stored in the user's /etc/passwd entry.

−l *new_logname*
A string of printable characters that specifies the new login name for the user. It may not contain a colon (:) or a newline (\n).

−e *expire*
The date on which a login can no longer be used; after this date, no user will be able to access this login. (This option is useful for creating temporary logins.) You may type the value of the argument *expire* (which is a date) in any format you like (except a Julian date). For example, you may

enter 10/6/90 or October 6, 1990. A value of `` '' defeats the status of the expired date.

-f *inactive*

The maximum number of days allowed between uses of a login ID before that login ID is declared valid. Normal values are positive integers. A value of −1 defeats the status.

login   A string of printable characters that specifies the existing login name of the user. It must exist and may not contain a colon (:), or a newline (\n).

FILES
/etc/passwd, /etc/shadow, /etc/group

SEE ALSO
groupadd(1M), groupdel(1M), groupmod(1M), logins(1M), passwd(1), passwd(1M), useradd(1M), userdel(1M), users(1).

DIAGNOSTICS
The usermod command exits with one of the following values:

0   The command was executed successfully.

2   The command syntax was invalid. A usage message for the usermod command is displayed.

3   An invalid argument was provided to an option.

4   The *uid* given with the −u option is already in use.

6   The login to be modified does not exist or *group* does not exist.

8   The login to be modified is in use.

9   The *new_logname* is already in use.

10   Cannot update the /etc/group file. Other update requests will be implemented.

11   Insufficient space to move the home directory (−m option). Other update requests will be implemented.

12   Unable to complete the move of the home directory to the new home directory.

NAME
     uucheck – check the uucp directories and permissions file

SYNOPSIS
     /usr/lib/uucp/uucheck [options]

DESCRIPTION
     uucheck checks for the presence of the uucp system required files and directories.
     uucheck   also   does   error   checking   of   the   *Permissions*   file
     (/etc/uucp/Permissions). uucheck has the following options:

     –v   Give a detailed (verbose) explanation of how the uucp programs will
                 interpret the *Permissions* file.

     –xdebug_level
                 debug_level is a number from 0 to 9. Higher numbers give more
                 detailed debugging information.

     uucheck is executed during package installation. Note that uucheck can only be
     used by the super-user or uucp.

FILES
     /etc/uucp/Systems
     /etc/uucp/Permissions
     /etc/uucp/Devices
     /etc/uucp/Limits
     /var/spool/uucp/*
     /var/spool/locks/*
     /var/spool/uucppublic/*

SEE ALSO
     uucico(1M), uusched(1M).
     uucp(1C), uustat(1C), uux(1C) in the *User's Reference Manual*.

BUGS
     The program does not check file/directory modes or some errors in the *Permis-
     sions* file such as duplicate login or machine name.

NAME

    uucico – file transport program for the uucp system

SYNOPSIS

    /usr/lib/uucp/uucico [options]

DESCRIPTION

    uucico is the file transport program for uucp work file transfers. The following options are available.

    –c*type*   The first field in the Devices file is the "Type" field. The –c option forces uucico to only use entries in the "Type" field that match the user specified *type*. The specified *type* is usually the name of a local area network.

    –d*spool_directory*

                This option specifies the directory *spool_directory* that contains the uucp work files to be transferred. The default spool directory is /var/spool/uucp.

    –f   This option is used to "force execution" of uucico by ignoring the limit on the maximum number of uucicos defined in the /etc/uucp/Limits file.

    –i*interface* This option defines the *interface* used with uucico. The interface only affects slave mode. Known interfaces are UNIX (default), TLI (basic Transport Layer Interface), and TLIS (Transport Layer Interface with Streams modules, read/write).

    –r*role_number*

                The *role_number* 1 is used for master mode. *role_number* 0 is used for slave mode (default). When uucico is started by a program or cron, *role_number* 1 should be used for master mode.

    –s*system_name*

                The –s option defines the remote system (*system_name*) that uucico will try to contact. It is required when the role is master; *system_name* must be defined in the Systems file.

    –x*debug_level*

                Both uux and uucp queue jobs that will be transferred by uucico. These jobs are normally started by the uusched scheduler, for debugging purposes, and can be started manually. For example, the shell Uutry starts uucico with debugging turned on. The *debug_level* is a number between 0 and 9. Higher numbers give more detailed debugging information.

FILES

    /etc/uucp/Systems
    /etc/uucp/Permissions
    /etc/uucp/Devices
    /etc/uucp/Devconfig
    /etc/uucp/Sysfiles
    /etc/uucp/Limits
    /var/spool/uucp/*

```
/var/spool/locks/*
/var/spool/uucppublic/*
```

SEE ALSO

cron(1M), uusched(1M), Uutry(1M).
uucp(1C), uustat(1C), uux(1C) in the *User's Reference Manual*.

NAME

uucleanup – uucp spool directory clean-up

SYNOPSIS

/usr/lib/uucp/uucleanup [options]

DESCRIPTION

uucleanup will scan the spool directories for old files and take appropriate action to remove them in a useful way:

Inform the requester of send/receive requests for systems that can not be reached.

Return undeliverable mail to the sender.

Deliver rnews files addressed to the local system.

Remove all other files.

In addition, there is a provision to warn users of requests that have been waiting for a given number of days (default 1). Note that uucleanup will process as if all option times were specified to the default values unless *time* is specifically set.

The following options are available.

−C*time*   Any C. files greater or equal to *time* days old will be removed with appropriate information to the requester. (default 7 days)

−D*time*   Any D. files greater or equal to *time* days old will be removed. An attempt will be made to deliver mail messages and execute rnews when appropriate. (default 7 days)

−W*time*   Any C. files equal to *time* days old will cause a mail message to be sent to the requester warning about the delay in contacting the remote. The message includes the *JOBID*, and in the case of mail, the mail message. The administrator may include a message line telling whom to call to check the problem (−m option). (default 1 day)

−X*time*   Any X. files greater or equal to *time* days old will be removed. The D. files are probably not present (if they were, the X. could get executed) But if there are D. files, they will be taken care of by D. processing. (default 2 days)

−m*string*   Include *string* in the warning message generated by the −W option.

−o*time*   Other files whose age is more than *time* days will be deleted. (default 2 days) The default line is "See your local administrator to locate the problem".

−s*system*   Execute for system spool directory only.

−x*debug_level*

The −x debug level is a single digit between 0 and 9; higher numbers give more detailed debugging information. (This option may not be available on all systems.)

This program is typically started by the shell *uudemon.cleanup*, which should be started by cron(1M).

FILES

/usr/lib/uucp   directory with commands used by uucleanup internally

/var/spool/uucp   spool directory

SEE ALSO

cron(1M).

uucp(1C), uux(1C) in the *User's Reference Manual*.

NAME
uusched – the scheduler for the uucp file transport program

SYNOPSIS
/usr/lib/uucp/uusched [options]

DESCRIPTION
uusched is the uucp(1C) file transport scheduler. It is usually started by the daemon *uudemon.hour* that is started by cron(1M) from an entry in
/var/spool/cron/crontab:

41,11 * * * * /usr/bin/su uucp -c "/usr/lib/uucp/uudemon.hour > /dev/null"

The options are for debugging purposes only. *debug_level* are numbers between 0
and 9. Higher numbers give more detailed debugging information:

−u*debug_level*   The −u *debug_level* option is passed to uucico(1M) as −x
                  debug_level.

−x*debug_level*   Outputs debugging messages from uusched(1M).

FILES
/etc/uucp/Systems
/etc/uucp/Permissions
/etc/uucp/Devices
/var/spool/uucp/*
/var/spool/locks/*
/var/spool/uucppublic/*

SEE ALSO
cron(1M), uucico(1M).
uucp(1C), uustat(1C), uux(1C) in the *User's Reference Manual.*

NAME

Uutry – try to contact remote system with debugging on

SYNOPSIS

/usr/lib/uucp/Uutry [options] system_name

DESCRIPTION

Uutry is a shell that is used to invoke uucico to call a remote site. Debugging is initially turned on and is set to the default value of 5. The debugging output is put in file /tmp/system_name. Here are the options:

-ctype   The first field in the Devices file is the "Type" field. The –c option forces uucico to only use entries in the "Type" field that match the user specified type. The specified type is usually the name of a local area network.

-r   This option overrides the retry time that is set in file /var/uucp/.status/system_name.

-xdebug_level

debug_level is a number from 0 to 9. Higher numbers give more detailed debugging information.

FILES

/etc/uucp/Systems
/etc/uucp/Permissions
/etc/uucp/Devices
/etc/uucp/Limits
/var/spool/uucp/*
/var/spool/locks/*
/var/spool/uucppublic/*
/tmp/system_name

SEE ALSO

uucico(1M).
uucp(1C), uux(1C) in the *User's Reference Manual*.

NAME
     uuxqt – execute remote command requests

SYNOPSIS
     /usr/lib/uucp/uuxqt [options]

DESCRIPTION
     uuxqt is the program that executes remote job requests from remote systems gen-
     erated by the use of the uux command. (*Mail* uses uux for remote mail requests).
     uuxqt searches the spool directories looking for execution requests. For each
     request, uuxqt checks to see if all the required data files are available, accessible,
     and the requested commands are permitted for the requesting system. The *Per-*
     missions file is used to validate file accessibility and command execution permis-
     sion.

     There are two environment variables that are set before the uuxqt command is
     executed:
     UU_MACHINE is the machine that sent the job (the previous one).
     UU_USER is the user that sent the job.
     These can be used in writing commands that remote systems can execute to pro-
     vide information, auditing, or restrictions. uuxqt has the following options:

     −s*system*   Specifies the remote system name.

     −x*debug_level*   *debug_level* is a number from 0 to 9. Higher numbers give more
                       detailed debugging information.

FILES
     /etc/uucp/Permissions
     /etc/uucp/Limits
     /var/spool/uucp/*
     /var/spool/locks/*

SEE ALSO
     uucico(1M).
     uucp(1C), uustat(1C), uux(1C), mail(1) in the *User's Reference Manual*.

NAME

volcopy (generic) – make literal copy of file system

SYNOPSIS

volcopy [–F *FSType*] [–V] [*current_options*] [–o *specific_options*] *operands*

DESCRIPTION

volcopy makes a literal copy of the file system.

current_options are options supported by the s5-specific module of volcopy. Other FSTypes do not necessarily support these options. *specific_options* indicate suboptions specified in a comma-separated list of suboptions and/or keyword-attribute pairs for interpretation by the *FSType*-specific module of the command.

operands generally include the device and volume names and are file system specific. A detailed description of the *operands* can be found on the *FSType*-specific man pages of volcopy.

The options are:

–F   Specify the *FSType* on which to operate. The *FSType* should either be specified here or be determinable from /etc/vfstab by matching the *operands* with an entry in the table.

–V   Echo the complete command line, but do not execute the command. The command line is generated by using the options and arguments provided by the user and adding to them information derived from /etc/vfstab. This option should be used to verify and validate the command line.

–o   Specify *FSType*-specific options.

NOTE

This command may not be supported for all FSTypes.

FILES

/etc/vfstab   list of default parameters for each file system

SEE ALSO

vfstab(4).

Manual pages for the FSType-specific modules of volcopy.

NAME

volcopy (s5) – make a literal copy of an s5 file system

SYNOPSIS

volcopy [–F s5] [*generic_options*] [–a] *fsname srcdevice volname1 destdevice volname2*

DESCRIPTION

generic_options are options supported by the generic volcopy command.

volcopy makes a literal copy of the s5 file system using a blocksize matched to the device.

The options are:

–F s5   Specify the s5-FSType.

–a   Invoke a verification sequence requiring a positive operator response instead of the standard 10 second delay before the copy is made.

The *fsname* argument represents the mounted name (e.g.: root, u1, etc.) of the filsystem being copied.

The *srcdevice* or *destdevice* should be the disk partition or tape (e.g.: /dev/rdsk/c1d0s8, /dev/rdsk/c1d1s8, etc.).

The *volname* is the physical volume name. Such label names are limited to six or fewer characters. *Volname* may be – to use the existing volume name.

Srcdevice and *volname1* are the device and volume from which the copy of the file system is being extracted. *Destdevice* and *volname2* are the target device and volume.

Fsname and *volname* are recorded in the superblock (char fsname[6], volname[6];).

NOTE

volcopy does not support tape-to-tape copying. Use dd(1M) for tape-to-tape copying.

FILES

/var/adm/filesave.log   a record of file systems/volumes copied

SEE ALSO

dd(1M), labelit(1M), generic volcopy(1M), cpio(4), fs(4).
cpio(1), sh(1) in the *Users Reference Manual*.

NAME

volcopy (ufs) – make a literal copy of a **ufs** file system

SYNOPSIS

volcopy [-F ufs] [*generic_options*] [-a] *fsname srcdevice volname1 destdevice vol-name2*

DESCRIPTION

generic_options are options supported by the generic volcopy command.

volcopy makes a literal copy of the **ufs** file system using a blocksize matched to the device.

The *fsname* argument represents the mounted name (for example, root, u1, etc.) of the file system being copied.

The *srcdevice* or *destdevice* should be the physical disk section or tape (for example, /dev/rdsk/cld0s8, /dev/rdsk/cld1s8, etc.).

The *volname* is the physical volume name. Such label names are limited to six or fewer characters. *volname* may be '–' to use the existing volume name.

srcdevice and *volname1* are the device and volume from which the copy of the file system is being extracted. *destdevice* and *volname2* are the target device and volume.

fsname and *volname* are recorded in the superblock.

The options are:

-F ufs
　　Specifies the ufs-FSType.

-a　　Invoke a verification sequence requiring a positive operator response instead of the standard ten-second delay before the copy is made.

NOTE

volcopy does not support tape-to-tape copying. Use dd(1M) for tape-to-tape copying.

FILES

/var/adm/filesave.log　　　a record of file systems/volumes copied

SEE ALSO

dd(1M), labelit(1M), generic volcopy(1M).
cpio(1) in the *User's Reference Manual*.
cpio(4), ufs(4) in the *Programmer's Reference Manual*.

NAME
wall – write to all users

SYNOPSIS
/usr/sbin/wall

DESCRIPTION
wall reads its standard input until an end-of-file. It then sends this message to all currently logged-in users preceded by:

> Broadcast Message from . . .

It is used to warn all users, typically prior to shutting down the system.

The sender must be super-user to override any protections the users may have invoked [see mesg(1)].

wall runs setgid() [see setuid(2)] to the group ID tty, in order to have write permissions on other user's terminals.

wall will detect non-printable characters before sending them to the user's terminal. Control characters will appear as a '^' followed by the appropriate ASCII character; characters with the high-order bit set will appear in meta notation. For example, '\003' is displayed as '^C' and '\372' as 'M-z'.

FILES
/dev/tty*

SEE ALSO
mesg(1), write(1).

NOTES
"Cannot send to ..." when the open on a user's tty file fails.

NAME

whodo – who is doing what

SYNOPSIS

/usr/sbin/whodo [-h] [-l] [*user*]

DESCRIPTION

whodo produces formatted and dated output from information in the /var/adm/utmp, /etc/ps_data, and /proc/pid files.

The display is headed by the date, time, and machine name. For each user logged in, device name, user-ID and login time is shown, followed by a list of active processes associated with the user-ID. The list includes the device name, process-ID, CPU minutes and seconds used, and process name.

If *user* is specified, output is restricted to all sessions pertaining to that user.

The following options are available:

-h   Suppress the heading.

-l   Produce a long form of output. The fields displayed are: the user's login name, the name of the tty the user is on, the time of day the user logged in (in *hours*:*minutes*), the idle time — that is, the time since the user last typed anything (in *hours*:*minutes*), the CPU time used by all processes and their children on that terminal (in *minutes*:*seconds*), the CPU time used by the currently active processes (in *minutes*:*seconds*), and the name and arguments of the current process.

EXAMPLE

The command:

whodo

produces a display like this:

```
Tue Mar 12 15:48:03 1985
bailey

tty09     mcn         8:51
    tty09    28158     0:29 sh

tty52     bdr        15:23
    tty52    21688     0:05 sh
    tty52    22788     0:01 whodo
    tty52    22017     0:03 vi
    tty52    22549     0:01 sh

xt162     lee        10:20
    tty08     6748     0:01 layers
    xt162     6751     0:01 sh
    xt163     6761     0:05 sh
    tty08     6536     0:05 sh
```

FILES

    /etc/passwd
    /etc/ps_data
    /var/adm/utmp
    /proc/pid

DIAGNOSTICS

If the PROC driver is not installed or configured or if /proc is not mounted, a message to that effect is issued and whodo will fail.

The exit status is zero on success, non-zero on failure.

SEE ALSO

ps(1), who(1) in the *User's Reference Manual*.

NAME

wtinit – object downloader for the 5620 DMD terminal

SYNOPSIS

/usr/lib/layersys/wtinit [–d] [–p] *file*

DESCRIPTION

The wtinit utility downloads the named *file* for execution in the AT&T 5620 DMD terminal connected to its standard output. *file* must be a DMD object file. wtinit performs all necessary bootstrap and protocol procedures.

There are two options.

–d   Prints out the sizes of the text, data, and bss portions of the downloaded *file* on standard error.

–p   Prints the down-loading protocol statistics and a trace on standard error.

The environment variable JPATH is the analog of the shell's PATH variable to define a set of directories in which to search for *file*.

If the environment variable DMDLOAD has the value hex, wtinit will use a hexadecimal download protocol that uses only printable characters.

Terminal Feature Packages for specific versions of AT&T windowing terminals will include terminal-specific versions of wtinit under those installation sub-directories. /usr/lib/layersys/wtinit is used for layers(1) initialization only when no Terminal Feature Package is in use (i.e., the $DMD shell variable is not set).

DIAGNOSTICS

Returns 0 upon successful completion, 1 otherwise.

WARNING

Standard error should be redirected when using the –d or –p options.

SEE ALSO

layers(1) in the *User's Reference Manual.*

NAME

    xts – extract and print xt driver statistics

SYNOPSIS

    xts [−f]

DESCRIPTION

    The xts command is a debugging tool for the xt(7) driver. It performs an XTIOCSTATS ioctl(2) call on its standard input file to extract the accumulated statistics for the attached group of channels. This call will fail if the standard input is not attached to an active xt(7) channel. The statistics are printed one item per line on the standard output.

    −f   Causes a "formfeed" character to be put out at the end of the output, for the benefit of page-display programs.

DIAGNOSTICS

    Returns 0 upon successful completion, 1 otherwise.

SEE ALSO

    layers(1) in the *User's Reference Manual.*
    xtt(1M), ioctl(2), xtproto(5).
    xt(7) in the *Programmer's Guide: STREAMS.*

NAME

   xtt – extract and print xt driver packet traces

SYNOPSIS

   xtt [-f] [-o]

DESCRIPTION

   The xtt command is a debugging tool for the xt(7) driver. It performs an
   XTIOCTRACE ioctl(2) call on its standard input file to turn on tracing and extract
   the circular packet trace buffer for the attached group of channels. This call will
   fail if the standard input is not attached to an active xt(7) channel. The packets
   are printed on the standard output.

   The optional flags are:

   -f   Causes a "formfeed" character to be put out at the end of the output, for
          the benefit of page-display programs.

   -o   Turns off further driver tracing.

DIAGNOSTICS

   Returns 0 upon successful completion, 1 otherwise.

NOTE

   If driver tracing has not been turned on for the terminal session by invoking
   layers(1) with the -t option, xtt will not generate any output the first time it is
   executed.

SEE ALSO

   layers(1) in the *User's Reference Manual.*
   xts(1M), ioctl(2), xtproto(5).
   xt(7) in the *Programmer's Guide: STREAMS.*

NAME
     zdump – time zone dumper

SYNOPSIS
     zdump [–v] [–c *cutoffyear*] [*zonename* ...]

DESCRIPTION
     The zdump command prints the current time in each *zonename* named on the com-
     mand line.

     The following options are available:

     –v   For each *zonename* on the command line, print the current time, the time at
             the lowest possible time value, the time one day after the lowest possible
             time value, the times both one second before and exactly at each time at
             which the rules for computing local time change, the time at the highest
             possible time value, and the time at one day less than the highest possible
             time value. Each line ends with isdst=1 if the given time is Daylight
             Saving Time or isdst=0 otherwise.

     –c *cutoffyear*
             Cut off the verbose output near the start of the year *cutoffyear*.

FILES
     /usr/lib/locale/TZ   standard zone information directory

SEE ALSO
     zic(1M), ctime(3C).

NAME
zic – time zone compiler

SYNOPSIS
zic [−v] [−d directory] [−l localtime] [*filename* ...]

DESCRIPTION
zic reads text from the file(s) named on the command line and creates the time conversion information files specified in this input. If a *filename* is '−', the standard input is read.

Input lines are made up of fields. Fields are separated by any number of white space characters. Leading and trailing white space on input lines is ignored. A pound sign (#) in the input introduces a comment which extends to the end of the line the pound sign appears on. White space characters and pound signs may be enclosed in double quotes (") if they're to be used as part of a field. Any line that is blank (after comment stripping) is ignored. Non-blank lines are expected to be of one of three types: rule lines, zone lines, and link lines.

A rule line has the form

        Rule *NAME FROM TO TYPE IN   ON   AT SAVE LETTER/S*

For example:

        Rule USA   1969 1973   −   Apr lastSun 2:00 1:00   D

The fields that make up a rule line are:

NAME   Gives the (arbitrary) name of the set of rules this rule is part of.

FROM   Gives the first year in which the rule applies. The word minimum (or an abbreviation) means the minimum year with a representable time value. The word maximum (or an abbreviation) means the maximum year with a representable time value.

TO   Gives the final year in which the rule applies. In addition to minimum and maximum (as above), the word only (or an abbreviation) may be used to repeat the value of the FROM field.

TYPE   Gives the type of year in which the rule applies. If TYPE is '−' then the rule applies in all years between FROM and TO inclusive; if TYPE is uspres, the rule applies in U.S. Presidential election years; if TYPE is nonpres, the rule applies in years other than U.S. Presidential election years. If TYPE is something else, then zic executes the command

        yearistype *year type*

to check the type of a year: an exit status of zero is taken to mean that the year is of the given type; an exit status of one is taken to mean that the year is not of the given type.

IN   Names the month in which the rule takes effect. Month names may be abbreviated.

ON   Gives the day on which the rule takes effect. Recognized forms include:

5	the fifth of the month
lastSun	the last Sunday in the month
lastMon	the last Monday in the month
Sun>=8	first Sunday on or after the eighth
Sun<=25	last Sunday on or before the 25th

Names of days of the week may be abbreviated or spelled out in full. Note: there must be no spaces within the ON field.

AT   Gives the time of day at which the rule takes effect. Recognized forms include:

2	time in hours
2:00	time in hours and minutes
15:00	24-hour format time (for times after noon)
1:28:14	time in hours, minutes, and seconds

Any of these forms may be followed by the letter w if the given time is local "wall clock" time or s if the given time is local "standard" time; in the absence of w or s, wall clock time is assumed.

SAVE   Gives the amount of time to be added to local standard time when the rule is in effect. This field has the same format as the AT field (although, of course, the w and s suffixes are not used).

LETTER/S

Gives the "variable part" (for example, the "S" or "D" in "EST" or "EDT") of time zone abbreviations to be used when this rule is in effect. If this field is '-', the variable part is null.

A zone line has the form

     Zone   *NAME*   *GMTOFF   RULES/SAVE   FORMAT   [UNTIL]*

For example:

     Zone Australia/South-west GMTOFF   RULES/SAVE   FORMAT

The fields that make up a zone line are:

NAME   The name of the time zone. This is the name used in creating the time conversion information file for the zone.

GMTOFF The amount of time to add to GMT to get standard time in this zone. This field has the same format as the AT and SAVE fields of rule lines; begin the field with a minus sign if time must be subtracted from GMT.

RULES/SAVE
The name of the rule(s) that apply in the time zone or, alternately, an amount of time to add to local standard time. If this field is '–' then standard time always applies in the time zone.

FORMAT   The format for time zone abbreviations in this time zone. The pair of characters %s is used to show where the "variable part" of the time zone abbreviation goes. UNTIL The time at which the GMT offset or the rule(s) change for a location. It is specified as a year, a month, a day, and a time of day. If this is specified, the time zone information is generated from the given GMT offset and rule change until the time specified.

The next line must be a "continuation" line; this has the same form as a zone line except that the string "Zone" and the name are omitted, as the continuation line will place information starting at the time specified as the UNTIL field in the previous line in the file used by the previous line. Continuation lines may contain an UNTIL field, just as zone lines do, indicating that the next line is a further continuation.

A link line has the form

        Link   LINK-FROM   LINK-TO

For example:

        Link   US/Eastern   EST5EDT

The LINK–FROM field should appear as the NAME field in some zone line; the LINK–TO field is used as an alternate name for that zone.

Except for continuation lines, lines may appear in any order in the input.

OPTIONS
-v   Complain if a year that appears in a data file is outside the range of years representable by system time values (0:00:00 AM GMT, January 1, 1970, to 3:14:07 AM GMT, January 19, 2038).

-d directory
Create time conversion information files in the directory **directory** rather than in the standard directory /usr/share/lib/zoneinfo.

-l timezone
Use the time zone **timezone** as local time. zic will act as if the file contained a link line of the form

                Link   *timezone*   localtime

FILES
/usr/share/lib/zoneinfo   standard directory used for created files

SEE ALSO

time(1), ctime(3)

NOTE

For areas with more than two types of local time, you may need to use local standard time in the AT field of the earliest transition time's rule to ensure that the earliest transition time recorded in the compiled file is correct.

NAME

    intro – introduction to file formats

DESCRIPTION

This section outlines the formats of various files. The C structure declarations for the file formats are given where applicable. Usually, the header files containing these structure declarations can be found in the directories /usr/include or /usr/include/sys. For inclusion in C language programs, however, the syntax #include <*filename.h*> or #include <sys/*filename.h*> should be used.

Because the UNIX operating system now allows the existence of multiple file system types, there are several instances of multiple manual pages with the same name. These pages all display the name of the FSType to which they pertain centered and in parentheses at the top of the page.

NAME

    acct – per-process accounting file format

SYNOPSIS

    #include <sys/types.h>
    #include <sys/acct.h>

DESCRIPTION

Files produced as a result of calling acct(2) have records in the form defined by
<sys/acct.h>, whose contents are:

```
typedef  ushort comp_t;      /* "floating point" */
              /* 13-bit fraction, 3-bit exponent  */

struct   acct
{
         char    ac_flag;     /* Accounting flag */
         char    ac_stat;     /* Exit status */
         uid_t   ac_uid;      /* Accounting user ID */
         gid_t   ac_gid;      /* Accounting group ID */
         dev_t   ac_tty;      /* control typewriter */
         time_t ac_btime;     /* Beginning time */
         comp_t ac_utime;     /* acctng user time in clock ticks */
         comp_t ac_stime;     /* acctng system time in clock ticks */
         comp_t ac_etime;     /* acctng elapsed time in clock ticks */
         comp_t ac_mem;       /* memory usage in clicks */
         comp_t ac_io;        /* chars trnsfrd by read/write */
         comp_t ac_rw;        /* number of block reads/writes */
         char    ac_comm[8];  /* command name */
};

extern   struct acct          acctbuf;
extern   struct vnode         *acctp;   /* vnode of accounting file */

#define AFORK  01             /* has executed fork, but no exec */
#define ASU    02             /* used super-user privileges */
#define ACCTF  0300           /* record type: 00 = acct */
#define AEXPND 040            /*Expanded Record Type*/
```

In ac_flag, the AFORK flag is turned on by each fork and turned off by an exec.
The ac_comm field is inherited from the parent process and is reset by any exec.
Each time the system charges the process with a clock tick, it also adds to ac_mem
the current process size, computed as follows:

>   *(data size) + (text size) / (number of in-core processes using text)*

The value of ac_mem/ (ac_stime + ac_utime) can be viewed as an approxima-
tion to the mean process size, as modified by text sharing.

The structure tacct, which resides with the source files of the accounting commands, represents the total accounting format used by the various accounting commands:

```
/*
 *  total accounting (for acct period), also for day
 */
struct tacct {
        uid_t           ta_uid;       /* userid */
        char            ta_name[8];   /* login name */
        float           ta_cpu[2];    /* cum. cpu time, p/np (mins) */
        float           ta_kcore[2];  /* cum kcore-minutes, p/np */
        float           ta_con[2];    /* cum. connect time, p/np, mins */
        float           ta_du;        /* cum. disk usage */
        long            ta_pc;        /* count of processes */
        unsigned short  ta_sc;        /* count of login sessions */
        unsigned short  ta_dc;        /* count of disk samples */
        unsigned short  ta_fee;       /* fee for special services */
};
```

SEE ALSO
acct(2), exec(2), fork(2).

acct(1M) in the *System Administrator's Reference Manual*.

acctcom(1) in the *User's Reference Manual*.

NOTES
The ac_mem value for a short-lived command gives little information about the actual size of the command, because ac_mem may be incremented while a different command (e.g., the shell) is being executed by the process.

NAME

   admin – installation defaults file

DESCRIPTION

   admin is a generic name for an ASCII file that defines default installation actions by assigning values to installation parameters. For example, it allows administrators to define how to proceed when the package being installed already exits on the system.

   /var/sadm/install/admin/default is the default admin file delivered with System V Release 4.0. The default file is not writable, so to assign values different from this file, create a new admin file. There are no naming restrictions for admin files. Name the file when installing a package with the –a option of pkgadd. If the –a option is not used, the default admin file is used.

   Each entry in the admin file is a line that establishes the value of a parameter in the following form:

   param=value

   Eleven parameters can be defined in an admin file. A file is not required to assign values to all eleven parameters. If a value is not assigned, pkgadd asks the installer how to proceed.

   The eleven parameters and their possible values are shown below except as noted. They may be specified in any order. Any of these parameters can be assigned the value ask, which means that if the situation occurs the installer is notified and asked to supply instructions at that time.

   basedir   Indicates the base directory where relocatable packages are to be installed. The value may contain $PKGINST to indicate a base directory that is to be a function of the package instance.

   mail   Defines a list of users to whom mail should be sent following installation of a package. If the list is empty, no mail is sent. If the parameter is not present in the admin file, the default value of root is used. The ask value cannot be used with this parameter.

   runlevel   Indicates resolution if the run level is not correct for the installation or removal of a package. Options are:

                      nocheck   Do not check for run level.

                      quit   Abort installation if run level is not met.

   conflict   Specifies what to do if an installation expects to overwrite a previously installed file, thus creating a conflict between packages. Options are:

                      nocheck   Do not check for conflict; files in conflict will be overwritten.

                      quit   Abort installation if conflict is detected.

nochange   Override installation of conflicting files; they will not be installed.

setuid   Checks for executables which will have setuid or setgid bits enabled after installation. Options are:

nocheck   Do not check for setuid executables.

quit   Abort installation if setuid processes are detected.

nochange   Override installation of setuid processes; processes will be installed without setuid bits enabled.

action   Determines if action scripts provided by package developers contain possible security impact. Options are:

nocheck   Ignore security impact of action scripts.

quit   Abort installation if action scripts may have a negative security impact.

partial   Checks to see if a version of the package is already partially installed on the system. Options are:

nocheck   Do not check for a partially installed package.

quit   Abort installation if a partially installed package exists.

instance   Determines how to handle installation if a previous version of the package (including a partially installed instance) already exists. Options are:

quit   Exit without installing if an instance of the package already exists (does not overwrite existing packages).

overwrite   Overwrite an existing package if only one instance exists. If there is more than one instance, but only one has the same architecture, it overwrites that instance. Otherwise, the installer is prompted with existing instances and asked which to overwrite.

unique   Do not overwrite an existing instance of a package. Instead, a new instance of the package is created. The new instance will be assigned the next available instance identifier.

idepend   Controls resolution if other packages depend on the one to be installed. Options are:

nocheck   Do not check package dependencies.

	quit	Abort installation if package dependencies are not met.

rdepend   Controls resolution if other packages depend on the one to be removed. Options are:

	nocheck	Do not check package dependencies.
	quit	Abort removal if package dependencies are not met.

space   Controls resolution if disk space requirements for package are not met. Options are:

	nocheck	Do not check space requirements (installation fails if it runs out of space).
	quit	Abort installation if space requirements are not met.

NOTES

The value `ask` should not be defined in an `admin` file that will be used for non-interactive installation (since by definition, there is no installer interaction). Doing so causes installation to fail when input is needed.

EXAMPLE

```
basedir=default
runlevel=quit
conflict=quit
setuid=quit
action=quit
partial=quit
instance=unique
idepend=quit
rdepend=quit
space=quit
```

NAME

ar – archive file format

SYNOPSIS

#include <ar.h>

DESCRIPTION

The archive command `ar` is used to combine several files into one. Archives are used mainly as libraries to be searched by the link editor `ld`.

Each archive begins with the archive magic string.

```
#define  ARMAG   "!<arch>\n"   /* magic string */
#define  SARMAG  8              /* length of magic string */
```

Following the archive magic string are the archive file members. Each file member is preceded by a file member header which is of the following format:

```
#define  ARFMAG     "`\n"  /* header trailer string */

struct  ar_hdr              /* file member header */
{
     char    ar_name[16];  /* '/' terminated file member name */
     char    ar_date[12];  /* file member date */
     char    ar_uid[6];    /* file member user identification */
     char    ar_gid[6];    /* file member group identification */
     char    ar_mode[8];   /* file member mode (octal) */
     char    ar_size[10];  /* file member size */
     char    ar_fmag[2];   /* header trailer string */
};
```

All information in the file member headers is in printable ASCII. The numeric information contained in the headers is stored as decimal numbers (except for *ar_mode* which is in octal). Thus, if the archive contains printable files, the archive itself is printable.

If the file member name fits, the *ar_name* field contains the name directly, and is terminated by a slash (/) and padded with blanks on the right. If the member's name does not fit, *ar_name* contains a slash (/) followed by a decimal representation of the name's offset in the archive string table described below.

The *ar_date* field is the modification date of the file at the time of its insertion into the archive. Common format archives can be moved from system to system as long as the portable archive command `ar` is used.

Each archive file member begins on an even byte boundary; a newline is inserted between files if necessary. Nevertheless, the size given reflects the actual size of the file exclusive of padding.

Notice there is no provision for empty areas in an archive file.

Each archive that contains object files [see **a.out**(4)] includes an archive symbol table. This symbol table is used by the link editor **ld** to determine which archive members must be loaded during the link edit process. The archive symbol table (if it exists) is always the first file in the archive (but is never listed) and is automatically created and/or updated by **ar**.

The archive symbol table has a zero length name (i.e., **ar_name[0]** is '**/**'), **ar_name[1]**==' ', etc.). All "words" in this symbol table have four bytes, using the machine-independent encoding shown below. (All machines use the encoding described here for the symbol table, even if the machine's "natural" byte order is different.)

	0	1	2	3
0x01020304	01	02	03	04

The contents of this file are as follows:

1.   The number of symbols. Length: 4 bytes.

2.   The array of offsets into the archive file. Length: 4 bytes * "the number of symbols".

3.   The name string table. Length: *ar_size* − 4 bytes * ("the number of symbols" + 1).

As an example, the following symbol table defines 4 symbols. The archive member at file offset 114 defines **name** and **object**. The archive member at file offset 426 defines **function** and a second version of **name**.

Offset	+0	+1	+2	+3	
0	4				4 offset entries
4	114				name
8	114				object
12	426				function
16	426				name
20	n	a	m	e	
24	\0	o	b	j	
28	e	c	t	\0	
32	f	u	n	c	
36	t	i	o	n	
40	\0	n	a	m	
44	e	\0			

The number of symbols and the array of offsets are managed with **sgetl** and **sputl**. The string table contains exactly as many null terminated strings as there are elements in the offsets array. Each offset from the array is associated with the corresponding name from the string table (in order). The names in the string table are all the defined global symbols found in the common object files in the archive. Each offset is the location of the archive header for the associated symbol.

If some archive member's name is more than 15 bytes long, a special archive member contains a table of file names, each followed by a slash and a new-line. This string table member, if present, will precede all "normal" archive members. The special archive symbol table is not a "normal" member, and must be first if it exists. The *ar_name* entry of the string table's member header holds a zero length name ar_name[0]=='/', followed by one trailing slash (ar_name[1]=='/'), followed by blanks (ar_name[2]==' ', etc.). Offsets into the string table begin at zero. Example *ar_name* values for short and long file names appear below.

Offset	+0	+1	+2	+3	+4	+5	+6	+7	+8	+9
0	f	i	l	e	_	n	a	m	e	_
10	s	a	m	p	l	e	/	\n	l	o
20	n	g	e	r	f	i	l	e	n	a
30	m	e	x	a	m	p	l	e	/	\n

Member Name	*ar_name*	Note
short–name	short–name/	Not in string table
file_name_sample	/0	Offset 0 in string table
longerfilenamexample	/18	Offset 18 in string table

SEE ALSO

ar(1), ld(1), strip(1), sputl(3X), a.out(4).

NOTES

strip will remove all archive symbol entries from the header. The archive symbol entries must be restored via the −ts options of the ar command before the archive can be used with the link editor ld.

NAME

archives - device header file

DESCRIPTION

```
/* Magic numbers */

#define CMN_ASC    0x070701   /* Cpio Magic Number for -c header */
#define CMN_BIN    070707     /* Cpio Magic Number for Binary header */
#define CMN_BBS    0143561    /* Cpio Magic Number for Byte-Swap header */
#define CMN_CRC    0x070702   /* Cpio Magic Number for CRC header */
#define CMS_ASC    "070701"   /* Cpio Magic String for -c header */
#define CMS_CHR    "070707"   /* Cpio Magic String for odc header */
#define CMS_CRC    "070702"   /* Cpio Magic String for CRC header */
#define CMS_LEN    6          /* Cpio Magic String length */

/* Various header and field lengths */

#define CHRSZ      76         /* -H odc size minus filename field */
#define ASCSZ      110        /* -c and CRC hdr size minus filename field */
#define TARSZ      512        /* TAR hdr size */

#define HNAMLEN    256        /* maximum filename length for binary and odc headers */
#define EXPNLEN    1024       /* maximum filename length for -c and CRC headers */
#define HTIMLEN    2          /* length of modification time field */
#define HSIZLEN    2          /* length of file size field */

/* cpio binary header definition */

struct hdr_cpio {
    short   h_magic,                    /* magic number field */
            h_dev;                      /* file system of file */
    ushort  h_ino,                      /* inode of file */
            h_mode,                     /* modes of file */
            h_uid,                      /* uid of file */
            h_gid;                      /* gid of file */
    short   h_nlink,                    /* number of links to file */
            h_rdev,                     /* maj/min numbers for special files */
            h_mtime[HTIMLEN],           /* modification time of file */
            h_namesize,                 /* length of filename */
            h_filesize[HSIZLEN];        /* size of file */
    char    h_name[HNAMLEN];            /* filename */
} ;

/* cpio -H odc header format */

struct c_hdr {
    char    c_magic[CMS_LEN],
            c_dev[6],
            c_ino[6],
            c_mode[6],
            c_uid[6],
            c_gid[6],
            c_nlink[6],
            c_rdev[6],
            c_mtime[11],
            c_namesz[6],
            c_filesz[11],
            c_name[HNAMLEN];
} ;
```

```
/* -c and CRC header format */

struct Exp_cpio_hdr {
    char    E_magic[CMS_LEN],
            E_ino[8],
            E_mode[8],
            E_uid[8],
            E_gid[8],
            E_nlink[8],
            E_mtime[8],
            E_filesize[8],
            E_maj[8],
            E_min[8],
            E_rmaj[8],
            E_rmin[8],
            E_namesize[8],
            E_chksum[8],
            E_name[EXPNLEN];
} ;

/* Tar header structure and format */

#define TBLOCK      512 /* length of tar header and data blocks */
#define TNAMLEN     100 /* maximum length for tar file names */
#define TMODLEN     8   /* length of mode field */
#define TUIDLEN     8   /* length of uid field */
#define TGIDLEN     8   /* length of gid field */
#define TSIZLEN     12  /* length of size field */
#define TTIMLEN     12  /* length of modification time field */
#define TCRCLEN     8   /* length of header checksum field */

/* tar header definition */

union tblock {
    char dummy[TBLOCK];
    struct header {
        char t_name[TNAMLEN];           /* name of file */
        char t_mode[TMODLEN];           /* mode of file */
        char t_uid[TUIDLEN];            /* uid of file */
        char t_gid[TGIDLEN];            /* gid of file */
        char t_size[TSIZLEN];           /* size of file in bytes */
        char t_mtime[TTIMLEN];          /* modification time of file */
        char t_chksum[TCRCLEN];         /* checksum of header */
        char t_typeflag;                /* flag to indicate type of file */
        char t_linkname[TNAMLEN];       /* file this file is linked with */
        char t_magic[6];                /* magic string always "ustar" */
        char t_version[2];              /* version strings always "00" */
        char t_uname[32];               /* owner of file in ASCII */
        char t_gname[32];               /* group of file in ASCII */
        char t_devmajor[8];             /* major number for special files */
        char t_devminor[8];             /* minor number for special files */
        char t_prefix[155];             /* pathname prefix */
    } tbuf;
};
```

```
/* volcopy tape label format and structure */

#define VMAGLEN 8
#define VVOLLEN 6
#define VFILLEN 464

struct volcopy_label {
    char    v_magic[VMAGLEN],
            v_volume[VVOLLEN],
            v_reels,
            v_reel;
    long    v_time,
                v_length,
            v_dens,
            v_reelblks,             /* u370 added field */
            v_blksize,              /* u370 added field */
            v_nblocks;              /* u370 added field */
    char    v_fill[VFILLEN];
    long    v_offset;               /* used with -e and -reel options */
    int     v_type;                 /* does tape have nblocks field? */
} ;
```

NAME

binarsys – remote system information for the ckbinarsys command

DESCRIPTION

binarsys contains lines of the form:

remote_system_name : *val*

where *val* is either Y or N. This line indicates whether that particular remote system can properly deal with messages having binary content. The absence of an entry for a particular system or absence of the binarsys file altogether will imply No.

Blank lines or lines beginning with # are considered comments and ignored. Should a line of Default=y be encountered, the default condition for missing entries described in the previous paragraph is reversed to be Yes. Another line of Default=n will restore the default condition to No.

mail is distributed with the binarsys file containing only a Default=y line.

FILES

/etc/mail/binarsys

SEE ALSO

ckbinarsys(1M), mailsurr(4)
mail(1) in the *User's Reference Manual*.

NAME

core − core image file

DESCRIPTION

The UNIX system writes out a core image of a process when it is terminated due to the receipt of some signals. The core image is called core and is written in the process's working directory (provided it can be; normal access controls apply). A process with an effective user ID different from the real user ID will not produce a core image.

The core file contains all the process information pertinent to debugging: contents of hardware registers, process status and process data. The format of a core file is object file specific.

For ELF executable programs [see a.out(4)], the core file generated is also an ELF file, containing ELF program and file headers. The e_type field in the file header has type ET_CORE. The program header contains an entry for every loadable and writeable segment that was part of the process address space, including shared library segments. The contents of the segments themselves are also part of the core image.

The program header of an ELF core file also contains a NOTE segment. This segment may contain the following entries. Each has entry name "CORE" and presents the contents of a system structure:

prstatus_t

> The entry containing this structure has a NOTE type of 1. This structure contains things of interest to a debugger from the operating system's u-area, such as the general registers, signal dispositions, state, reason for stopping, process ID and so forth. The structure is defined in <sys/procfs.h>.

fpregset_t

> This entry is present only if the process used the floating-point hardware. It has a NOTE type of 2 and contains the floating-point registers. The fpregset_t structure is defined in <sys/regset.h>.

prpsinfo_t

> The entry containing this structure has a NOTE type of 3. It contains information of interest to the ps(1) command, such as process status, cpu usage, "nice" value, controlling terminal, user ID, process ID, the name of the executable and so forth. The structure is defined in <sys/procfs.h>.

COFF executable programs produce core files consisting of two parts: the first section is a copy of the system's per-user data for the process, including the general registers. The format of this section is defined in the header files <sys/user.h> and <sys/reg.h>. The remainder of a COFF core image represents the actual contents of the process data space.

The size of the core file created by a process may be controlled by the user [see getrlimit(2)].

SEE ALSO
>   sdb(1), getrlimit(2), setuid(2), elf(3E), a.out(4), signal(5).
>   crash(1M) in the *System Administrator's Reference Manual.*
>   The "Object Files" chapter in the *Programmer's Guide: ANSI C and Programming Support Tools.*

NAME

dfstab – file containing commands for sharing resources

DESCRIPTION

dfstab resides in directory /etc/dfs and contains commands for sharing resources across a network. dfstab gives a system administrator a uniform method of controlling the automatic sharing of local resources.

Each line of the dfstab file consists of a share(1M) command. The dfstab file can be read by the shell directly to share all resources, or system administrators can prepare their own shell scripts to execute particular lines from dfstab.

The contents of dfstab are executed automatically when the system enters run level 3.

SEE ALSO

share(1M), shareall(1M).

NAME

dir (s5) − format of s5 directories

SYNOPSIS

```
#include <sys/types.h>
#include <sys/fs/s5dir.h>
```

DESCRIPTION

A directory behaves exactly like an ordinary file, save that no user may write into a directory. The fact that a file is a directory is indicated by a bit in the mode word of its i-node entry [see the s5-specific inode(4)]. The structure of a directory entry as given in the include file is:

```
#ifndef  DIRSIZ
#define  DIRSIZ  14
#endif
struct direct
{
        o_ino_t     d_ino;        /* s5 inode type */
        char        d_name[DIRSIZ];
};
```

By convention, the first two entries in each directory are . for the entry itself and .. for the parent directory. The meaning of .. is modified for the root directory of the master file system; there is no parent, so .. has the same meaning as . has.

SEE ALSO

s5_specific inode(4)

NAME
dir (ufs) − format of ufs directories

SYNOPSIS
```
#include <sys/param.h>
#include <sys/types.h>
#include <sys/fs/ufs_fsdir.h>
```

DESCRIPTION
A directory consists of some number of blocks of DIRBLKSIZ bytes, where DIRBLKSIZ is chosen such that it can be transferred to disk in a single atomic operation (e.g. 512 bytes on most machines).

Each DIRBLKSIZ-byte block contains some number of directory entry structures, which are of variable length. Each directory entry has a **struct direct** at the front of it, containing its inode number, the length of the entry, and the length of the name contained in the entry. These are followed by the name padded to a 4 byte boundary with null bytes. All names are guaranteed null-terminated. The maximum length of a name in a directory is MAXNAMLEN.

```
#define DIRBLKSIZ    DEV_BSIZE
#define MAXNAMLEN    256
struct      direct {
    u_long    d_ino;                      /* inode number of entry */
    u_short   d_reclen;                   /* length of this record */
    u_short   d_namlen;                   /* length of string in d_name */
    char      d_name[MAXNAMLEN + 1];      /* name must be no longer than this */
};
```

SEE ALSO
ufs-specific **fs**(4)

NAME

.environ, .pref, .variables – user-preference variable files for AT&T FACE

DESCRIPTION

The .environ, .pref, and .variables files contain variables that indicate user preferences for a variety of operations. The .environ and .variables files are located under the user's $HOME/pref directory. The .pref files are found under $HOME/FILECABINET, $HOME/WASTEBASKET, and any directory where preferences were set via the organize command. Names and descriptions for each variable are presented below. Variables are listed one per line and are of the form *variable=value*.

Variables found in .environ include:

LOGINWIN[1–4]   Windows that are opened when FACE is initialized

SORTMODE   Sort mode for file folder listings. Values include the following hexadecimal digits:

1   sorted alphabetically by name

2   files most recently modified first

800   sorted alphabetically by object type

The values above may be listed in reverse order by "ORing" the following value:

1000   list objects in reverse order. For example, a value of 1002 will produce a folder listing with files LEAST recently modified displayed first. A value of 1001 would produce a "reverse" alphabetical by name listing of the folder

DISPLAYMODE   Display mode for file folders. Values include the following hexadecimal digits:

0   file names only

4   file names and brief description

8   file names, description, plus additional information

WASTEPROMPT   Prompt before emptying wastebasket (yes/no)?

WASTEDAYS   Number of days before emptying wastebasket

PRINCMD[1–3]   Print command defined to print files.

UMASK   Holds default permissions that files will be created with.

Variables found in .pref are the following:

SORTMODE   which has the same values as the SORTMODE variable described in .environ above.

DISPMODE   which has the same values as the DISPLAYMODE variable described in .environ above.

Variables found in `.variables` include:

EDITOR   Default editor

PS1   UNIX shell prompt

FILES

```
$HOME/pref/.environ
$HOME/pref/.variables
$HOME/FILECABINET/.pref
$HOME/WASTEBASKET/.pref
```

NAME

ethers – Ethernet address to hostname database or domain

DESCRIPTION

The ethers file contains information regarding the known (48 bit) Ethernet addresses of hosts on the Internet. For each host on an Ethernet, a single line should be present with the following information:

Ethernet-address   official-host-name

Items are separated by any number of SPACE and/or TAB characters. A '#' indicates the beginning of a comment extending to the end of line.

The standard form for Ethernet addresses is $x:x:x:x:x:x$ where x is a hexadecimal number between 0 and ff, representing one byte. The address bytes are always in network order. Host names may contain any printable character other than a SPACE, TAB, NEWLINE, or comment character. It is intended that host names in the ethers file correspond to the host names in the hosts(4) file.

The ether_line routine from the Ethernet address manipulation library, ethers(3N) may be used to scan lines of the ethers file.

FILES

/etc/ethers

SEE ALSO

ethers(3N), hosts(4).

NAME

/dev/fd – file descriptor files

DESCRIPTION

These files, conventionally called /dev/fd/0, /dev/fd/1, /dev/fd/2, and so on, refer to files accessible through file descriptors. If file descriptor n is open, these two system calls have the same effect:

```
fd = open ("/dev/fd/n", mode);
fd = dup (n);
```

On these files creat(2) is equivalent to open, and mode is ignored. As with dup, subsequent reads or writes on fd fail unless the original file descriptor allows the operations.

For convenience in referring to standard input, standard output, and standard error, an additional set of names is provided: /dev/fd/0 is a synonym for /dev/fd/0, /dev/fd/1 for /dev/fd/1, and /dev/fd/2 for /dev/fd/2.

SEE ALSO

open(2), dup(2)

DIAGNOSTICS

open(2) returns −1 and EBADF if the associated file descriptor is not open.

NAME

filehdr – file header for common object files

SYNOPSIS

#include <filehdr.h>

DESCRIPTION

Every common object file begins with a 20-byte header. The following C struct declaration is used:

```
struct  filehdr
{
    unsigned short  f_magic ;    /* magic number */
    unsigned short  f_nscns ;    /* number of sections */
    long            f_timdat ;   /* time & date stamp */
    long            f_symptr ;   /* file ptr to symtab */
    long            f_nsyms ;    /* number of symtab entries */
    unsigned short  f_opthdr ;   /* sizeof(opt and header) */
    unsigned short  f_flags ;    /* flags */
} ;
```

f_symptr is the byte offset into the file at which the symbol table can be found. Its value can be used as the offset in fseek(3S) to position an I/O stream to the symbol table. The UNIX system optional header is 28 bytes. The valid magic numbers are given below:

```
#define I386MAGIC   0514    /* i386 Computer */
#define WE32MAGIC   0560    /* 3B2, 3B5, and 3B15 computers */
#define N3BMAGIC    0550    /* 3B20 computer */
#define NTVMAGIC    0551    /* 3B20 computer */

#define VAXWRMAGIC 0570     /* VAX writable text segments */
#define VAXROMAGIC 0575     /* VAX read only sharable
                               text segments */
```

The value in **f_timdat** is obtained from the time(2) system call. Flag bits currently defined are:

```
#define F_RELFLG  0000001    /* relocation entries stripped */
#define F_EXEC    0000002    /* file is executable */
#define F_LNNO    0000004    /* line numbers stripped */
#define F_LSYMS   0000010    /* local symbols stripped */
#define F_AR16WR  0000200    /* 16-bit DEC host */
#define F_AR32WR  0000400    /* 32-bit DEC host */
#define F_AR32W   0001000    /* non-DEC host */
#define F_BM32ID  0160000    /* WE32000 family ID field */
#define F_BM32B   0020000    /* file contains WE 32100 code */
#define F_BM32MAU 0040000    /* file reqs MAU to execute */
#define F_BM32RST 0010000    /* this object file contains restore
                                work around [3B5/3B2 only] */
```

SEE ALSO

time(2), fseek(3S), pa.out(4)

The "Common Object File Format (COFF)" chapter in the *Programmer's Guide*

NAME

fs (bfs) − format of the bfs file system volume

SYNOPSIS

#include <sys/types.h>
#include <sys/fs/bfs.h>

DESCRIPTION

The bfs superblock is stored on sector 0. Its format is:

```
struct bdsuper
{
        long bdsup_bfsmagic;      /* Magic number */
        off_t bdsup_start;        /* Filesystem data start offset */
        off_t bdsup_end;          /* Filesystem data end offset */

        /*
         * Sanity words
         */
        daddr_t bdcp_fromblock;   /* "From" block of current transfer */
        daddr_t bdcp_toblock;     /* "To" block of current transfer */
        daddr_t bdcpb_fromblock;  /* Backup of "from" block */
        daddr_t bdcpb_toblock;    /* Backup of "to" block */
};

#define BFS_MAGIC   0xBADFACE  /* bfs magic number */
```

The sanity words are used to promote sanity during compaction. They are used by fsck(1M) to recover from a system crash at any point during compaction. See "Storage Blocks under bfs" in the "The bfs File System" section of chapter 5 in the *System Administratror's Guide* for a description of compaction.

SEE ALSO

bfs-specific inode(4)

NAME

fs (s5) – format of s5 file system volume

SYNOPSIS

```
#include <sys/types.h>
#include <sys/param.h>
#include <sys/fs/s5filsys.h>
```

DESCRIPTION

Every file system storage volume has a common format for certain vital information. Every such volume is divided into a certain number of 512-byte long sectors. Sector 0 is unused and is available to contain a bootstrap program or other information.

Sector 1 is the super-block. The format of a super-block is:

```
struct      filsys
{
  ushort    s_isize;            /* size in blocks of i-list */
  daddr_t   s_fsize;            /* size in blocks of entire volume */
  short     s_nfree;            /* number of addresses in s_free */
  daddr_t   s_free[NICFREE];    /* free block list */
  short     s_ninode;           /* number of i-nodes in s_inode */
  o_ino_t   s_inode[NICINOD];   /* free i-node list */
  char      s_flock;            /* lock during free list */
                                /* manipulation */
  char      s_ilock;            /* lock during i-list manipulation */
  char      s_fmod;             /* super block modified flag */
  char      s_ronly;            /* mounted read-only flag */
  time_t    s_time;             /* last super block update */
  short     s_dinfo[4];         /* device information */
  daddr_t   s_tfree;            /* total free blocks*/
  o_ino_t   s_tinode;           /* total free i-nodes */
  char      s_fname[6];         /* file system name */
  char      s_fpack[6];         /* file system pack name */
  long      s_fill[12];         /* ADJUST to make */
                                /* sizeof filsys be 512 */
  long      s_state;            /* file system state */
  long      s_magic;            /* magic number to denote new file */
                                /* system */
  long      s_type;             /* type of new file system */
};

#define  FsMAGIC    0xfd187e20  /* s_magic number */

#define  Fs1b       1           /* 512-byte block */
#define  Fs2b       2           /* 1024-byte block */
#define  Fs4b       3           /* 2048-byte block */

#define  FsOKAY     0x7c269d38  /* s_state: clean */
#define  FsACTIVE   0x5e72d81a  /* s_state: active */
```

```
#define  FsBAD       0xcb096f43  /* s_state: bad root */
#define  FsBADBLK    0xbadbc14b  /* s_state: bad block */
                                 /* corrupted it */
```

s_type indicates the file system type. Currently, three types of file systems are supported: the original 512-byte logical block, the 1024-byte logical block, and the 2048-byte logical block. s_magic is used to distinguish the s5 file system from other FSTypes. The s_type field is used to determine the blocksize of the file system; 512-bytes, 1K, or 2K. The operating system takes care of all conversions from logical block numbers to physical sector numbers.

s_state indicates the state of the file system. A cleanly unmounted, not damaged file system is indicated by the FsOKAY state. After a file system has been mounted for update, the state changes to FsACTIVE. A special case is used for the root file system. If the root file system appears damaged at boot time, it is mounted but marked FsBAD. Lastly, after a file system has been unmounted, the state reverts to FsOKAY.

s_isize is the address of the first data block after the i-list; the i-list starts just after the super-block, namely in block 2; thus the i-list is s_isize−2 blocks long. s_fsize is the first block not potentially available for allocation to a file. These numbers are used by the system to check for bad block numbers; if an "impossible" block number is allocated from the free list or is freed, a diagnostic is written on the on-line console. Moreover, the free array is cleared, so as to prevent further allocation from a presumably corrupted free list.

The free list for each volume is maintained as follows. The s_free array contains, in s_free[1], ..., s_free[s_nfree−1], up to 49 numbers of free blocks. s_free[0] is the block number of the head of a chain of blocks constituting the free list. The first long in each free-chain block is the number (up to 50) of free-block numbers listed in the next 50 longs of this chain member. The first of these 50 blocks is the link to the next member of the chain. To allocate a block: decrement s_nfree, and the new block is s_free[s_nfree]. If the new block number is 0, there are no blocks left, so give an error. If s_nfree became 0, read in the block named by the new block number, replace s_nfree by its first word, and copy the block numbers in the next 50 longs into the s_free array. To free a block, check if s_nfree is 50; if so, copy s_nfree and the s_free array into it, write it out, and set s_nfree to 0. In any event set s_free[s_nfree] to the freed block's number and increment s_nfree.

s_tfree is the total free blocks available in the file system.

s_ninode is the number of free i-numbers in the s_inode array. To allocate an i-node: if s_ninode is greater than 0, decrement it and return s_inode[s_ninode]. If it was 0, read the i-list and place the numbers of all free i-nodes (up to 100) into the s_inode array, then try again. To free an i-node, provided s_ninode is less than 100, place its number into s_inode[s_ninode] and increment s_ninode. If s_ninode is already 100, do not bother to enter the freed i-node into any table. This list of i-nodes is only to speed up the allocation process; the information as to whether the i-node is really free or not is maintained in the i-node itself.

s_tinode is the total free i-nodes available in the file system.

s_flock and s_ilock are flags maintained in the core copy of the file system while it is mounted and their values on disk are immaterial. The value of s_fmod on disk is likewise immaterial; it is used as a flag to indicate that the super-block has changed and should be copied to the disk during the next periodic update of file system information.

s_ronly is a read-only flag to indicate write-protection.

s_time is the last time the super-block of the file system was changed, and is the number of seconds that have elapsed since 00:00 Jan. 1, 1970 (UTC). During a reboot, the s_time of the super-block for the root file system is used to set the system's idea of the time.

s_fname is the name of the file system and s_fpack is the name of the pack.

I-numbers begin at 1, and the storage for i-nodes begins in block 2. Also, i-nodes are 64 bytes long. I-node 1 is reserved for future use. I-node 2 is reserved for the root directory of the file system, but no other i-number has a built-in meaning. Each i-node represents one file. For the format of an i-node and its flags, see inode(4).

SEE ALSO

mount(2).

fsck(1M), fsdb(1M), mkfs(1M), s5-specific inode(4)

NAME

fs (ufs) – format of ufs file system volume

SYNOPSIS

```
#include <sys/param.h>
#include <sys/types.h>
#include <sys/fs/ufs_fs.h>
```

DESCRIPTION

Each disk drive contains some number of file systems. A file system consists of a number of cylinder groups. Each cylinder group has inodes and data.

A file system is described by its super-block, and by the information in the cylinder group blocks. The super-block is critical data and is replicated before each cylinder group block to protect against catastrophic loss. This is done at mkfs time; the critical super-block data does not change, so the copies need not normally be referenced further.

```
/*
 * Super block for a file system.
 */
#define FS_MAGIC      0x011954
#define FSACTIVE      0x5e72d81a      /* fs_state: mounted */
#define FSOKAY        0x7c269d38      /* fs_state: clean */
#define FSBAD         0xcb096f43      /* fs_state: bad root */

struct  fs {
        struct  fs *fs_link;          /* linked list of file systems */
        struct  fs *fs_rlink;         /* used for incore super blocks */
        daddr_t fs_sblkno;            /* addr of super-block in filesys */
        daddr_t fs_cblkno;            /* offset of cyl-block in filesys */
        daddr_t fs_iblkno;            /* offset of inode-blocks in filesys */
        daddr_t fs_dblkno;            /* offset of first data after cg */
        long    fs_cgoffset;          /* cylinder group offset in cylinder */
        long    fs_cgmask;            /* used to calc mod fs_ntrak */
        time_t  fs_time;              /* last time written */
        long    fs_size;              /* number of blocks in fs */
        long    fs_dsize;             /* number of data blocks in fs */
        long    fs_ncg;               /* number of cylinder groups */
        long    fs_bsize;             /* size of basic blocks in fs */
        long    fs_fsize;             /* size of frag blocks in fs */
        long    fs_frag;              /* number of frags in a block in fs */
/* these are configuration parameters */
        long    fs_minfree;           /* minimum percentage of free blocks */
        long    fs_rotdelay;          /* num of ms for optimal next block */
        long    fs_rps;               /* disk revolutions per second */
/* these fields can be computed from the others */
        long    fs_bmask;             /* ``blkoff'' calc of blk offsets */
        long    fs_fmask;             /* ``fragoff'' calc of frag offsets */
        long    fs_bshift;            /* ``lblkno'' calc of logical blkno */
        long    fs_fshift;            /* ``numfrags'' calc number of frags */
/* these are configuration parameters */
        long    fs_maxcontig;         /* max number of contiguous blks */
        long    fs_maxbpg;            /* max number of blks per cyl group */
```

```
        /* these fields can be computed from the others */
        long    fs_fragshift;           /* block to frag shift */
        long    fs_fsbtodb;             /* fsbtodb and dbtofsb shift constant */
        long    fs_sbsize;              /* actual size of super block */
        long    fs_csmask;              /* csum block offset */
        long    fs_csshift;             /* csum block number */
        long    fs_nindir;              /* value of NINDIR */
        long    fs_inopb;               /* value of INOPB */
        long    fs_nspf;                /* value of NSPF */
        long    fs_optim;               /* optimization preference, see below */
        long    fs_state;               /* file system state */
        long    fs_sparecon[2];         /* reserved for future constants */
/* a unique id for this filesystem (currently unused and unmaintained) */
        long    fs_id[2];               /* file system id */
/* sizes determined by number of cylinder groups and their sizes */
        daddr_t fs_csaddr;              /* blk addr of cyl grp summary area */
        long    fs_cssize;              /* size of cyl grp summary area */
        long    fs_cgsize;              /* cylinder group size */
/* these fields should be derived from the hardware */
        long    fs_ntrak;               /* tracks per cylinder */
        long    fs_nsect;               /* sectors per track */
        long    fs_spc;                 /* sectors per cylinder */
/* this comes from the disk driver partitioning */
        long    fs_ncyl;                /* cylinders in file system */
/* these fields can be computed from the others */
        long    fs_cpg;                 /* cylinders per group */
        long    fs_ipg;                 /* inodes per group */
        long    fs_fpg;                 /* blocks per group * fs_frag */
/* this data must be re-computed after crashes */
        struct  csum fs_cstotal;        /* cylinder summary information */
/* these fields are cleared at mount time */
        char    fs_fmod;                /* super block modified flag */
        char    fs_clean;               /* file system is clean flag */
        char    fs_ronly;               /* mounted read-only flag */
        char    fs_flags;               /* currently unused flag */
        char    fs_fsmnt[MAXMNTLEN];    /* name mounted on */
/* these fields retain the current block allocation info */
        long    fs_cgrotor;             /* last cg searched */
        struct  csum *fs_csp[MAXCSBUFS];/* list of fs_cs info buffers */
        long    fs_cpc;                 /* cyl per cycle in postbl */
        short   fs_postbl[MAXCPG][NRPOS];/* head of blocks for each rotation */
        long    fs_magic;               /* magic number */
        u_char  fs_rotbl[1];            /* list of blocks for each rotation */
};
/*
 * Cylinder group block for a file system.
 */

#define CG_MAGIC        0x090255
struct  cg {
        struct  cg *cg_link;            /* linked list of cyl groups */
        struct  cg *cg_rlink;           /* used for incore cyl groups */
        time_t  cg_time;                /* time last written */
        long    cg_cgx;                 /* we are the cgx'th cylinder group */
        short   cg_ncyl;                /* number of cyl's this cg */
```

```
        short    cg_niblk;              /* number of inode blocks this cg */
        long     cg_ndblk;              /* number of data blocks this cg */
        struct   csum cg_cs;            /* cylinder summary information */
        long     cg_rotor;             /* position of last used block */
        long     cg_frotor;            /* position of last used frag */
        long     cg_irotor;            /* position of last used inode */
        long     cg_frsum[MAXFRAG];     /* counts of available frags */
        long     cg_btot[MAXCPG];       /* block totals per cylinder */
        short    cg_b[MAXCPG][NRPOS];   /* positions of free blocks */
        char     cg_iused[MAXIPG/NBBY]; /* used inode map */
        long     cg_magic;             /* magic number */
        u_char   cg_free[1];           /* free block map */
    };
```

SEE ALSO

ufs-specific inode(4)

NAME

fspec – format specification in text files

DESCRIPTION

It is sometimes convenient to maintain text files on the UNIX system with non-standard tabs, (i.e., tabs that are not set at every eighth column). Such files must generally be converted to a standard format, frequently by replacing all tabs with the appropriate number of spaces, before they can be processed by UNIX system commands. A format specification occurring in the first line of a text file specifies how tabs are to be expanded in the remainder of the file.

A format specification consists of a sequence of parameters separated by blanks and surrounded by the brackets <: and :>. Each parameter consists of a keyletter, possibly followed immediately by a value. The following parameters are recognized:

ttabs The t parameter specifies the tab settings for the file. The value of **tabs** must be one of the following:

  1. a list of column numbers separated by commas, indicating tabs set at the specified columns

  2. a – followed immediately by an integer n, indicating tabs at intervals of n columns

  3. a – followed by the name of a "canned" tab specification

  Standard tabs are specified by t–8, or equivalently, t1, 9, 17, 25, etc. The canned tabs that are recognized are defined by the **tabs**(1) command.

ssize The s parameter specifies a maximum line size. The value of *size* must be an integer. Size checking is performed after tabs have been expanded, but before the margin is prepended.

mmargin The m parameter specifies a number of spaces to be prepended to each line. The value of *margin* must be an integer.

d The d parameter takes no value. Its presence indicates that the line containing the format specification is to be deleted from the converted file.

e The e parameter takes no value. Its presence indicates that the current format is to prevail only until another format specification is encountered in the file.

Default values, which are assumed for parameters not supplied, are t–8 and m0. If the s parameter is not specified, no size checking is performed. If the first line of a file does not contain a format specification, the above defaults are assumed for the entire file. The following is an example of a line containing a format specification:

    * <:t5, 10, 15 s72:> *

If a format specification can be disguised as a comment, it is not necessary to code the d parameter.

SEE ALSO
ed(1), newform(1), tabs(1) in the *User's Reference Manual*

NAME

fstypes – file that registers distributed file system packages

DESCRIPTION

fstypes resides in directory /etc/dfs and lists distributed file system utilities packages installed on the system. The file system indicated in the first line of the file is the default file system. When Distributed File System (DFS) Administration commands are entered without the option -F *fstypes*, the system takes the file system type from the first line of the fstypes file.

The default package can be changed by editing the fstypes file with any supported text editor.

SEE ALSO

dfmounts(1M), dfshares(1M), share(1M), shareall(1M), unshare(1M).

NAME

group – group file

DESCRIPTION

The file /etc/group contains for each group the following information:

```
group name
encrypted password
numerical group ID
comma-separated list of all users allowed in the group
```

group is an ASCII file. The fields are separated by colons; each group is separated from the next by a new-line.

Because of the encrypted passwords, the group file can and does have general read permission and can be used, for example, to map numerical group ID's to names.

During user identification and authentication, the supplementary group access list is initialized sequentially from information in this file. If a user is in more groups than the system is configured for, {NGROUPS_MAX}, a warning will be given and subsequent group specifications will be ignored.

SEE ALSO

groups(1), passwd(1) in the *User's Reference Manual*

newgrp(1M), setgroups(2), initgroups(3C), unistd(4)

NAME
> hosts – host name data base

SYNOPSIS
> /etc/hosts

DESCRIPTION
> The hosts file contains information regarding the known hosts on the DARPA Internet. For each host a single line should be present with the following information:
>
> > *Internet-address official-host-name aliases*
>
> Items are separated by any number of SPACE and/or TAB characters. A '#' indicates the beginning of a comment; characters up to the end of the line are not interpreted by routines which search the file. This file is normally created from the official host data base maintained at the Network Information Control Center (NIC), though local changes may be required to bring it up to date regarding unofficial aliases and/or unknown hosts.
>
> Network addresses are specified in the conventional '.' notation using the inet_addr routine from the Internet address manipulation library, inet(3N). Host names may contain any printable character other than a field delimiter, NEWLINE, or comment character.

EXAMPLE
> Here is a typical line from the /etc/hosts file:
>
> > 192.9.1.20   gaia   # John Smith

FILES
> /etc/hosts

SEE ALSO
> gethostent(3N), inet(3N).

NAME

hosts.equiv, .rhosts – trusted hosts by system and by user

DESCRIPTION

The /etc/hosts.equiv file contains a list of trusted hosts. When an rlogin(1) or rsh(1) request is received from a host listed in this file, and when the user making the request is listed in the /etc/passwd file, then the remote login is allowed with no further checking. The library routine ruserok (see rcmd(3N)) will make this verification. In this case, rlogin does not prompt for a password, and commands submitted through rsh are executed. Thus, a remote user with a local user ID is said to have equivalent access from a remote host named in this file.

The format of the hosts.equiv file consists of a one-line entry for each host, of the form:

   hostname [*username*]

The *hostname* field normally contains the name of a trusted host from which a remote login can be made. However, an entry consisting of a single '+' indicates that all known hosts are to be trusted. A hostname must be the official name as listed in the hosts(4) database. This is the first name given in the hosts database entry; hostname aliases are not recognized.

The User .rhosts File

Whenever a remote login is attempted, the remote login daemon checks for a .rhosts file in the home directory of the user attempting to log in. A user's .rhosts file has the same format as the hosts.equiv file, and is used to give or deny access only for the *specific user* attempting to log in from a given host. While an entry in the hosts.equiv file allows remote login access to *any* user from the indicated host, an entry in a user's .rhosts file only allows access from a named host to the user in whose home directory the .rhosts file appears. When this file is used, permissions in the user's home directory should allow read and search access by anyone, so it may be located and read. When a user attempts a remote login, his .rhosts file is, in effect, prepended to the hosts.equiv file for permission checking. Thus, if a host is specified in the user's .rhosts file, login access is allowed.

FILES

/etc/hosts.equiv
/etc/passwd
~/.rhosts
/etc

SEE ALSO

rlogin(1), rsh(1), rcmd(3N), hosts(4), passwd(4).

NAME

inetd.conf – Internet servers database

DESCRIPTION

The inetd.conf file contains the list of servers that inetd(1M) invokes when it receives an Internet request over a socket. Each server entry is composed of a single line of the form:

service-name socket-type protocol wait-status uid server-program server-arguments

Fields can be separated by either SPACE or TAB characters. A '#' (pound-sign) indicates the beginning of a comment; characters up to the end of the line are not interpreted by routines that search this file.

service-name   The name of a valid service listed in the file /etc/services. For RPC services, the value of the *service-name* field consists of the RPC service name, followed by a slash and either a version number or a range of version numbers (for example, mountd/1).

socket-type   Can be one of:

stream   for a stream socket,
dgram   for a datagram socket,
raw   for a raw socket,
seqpacket   for a sequenced packet socket

protocol   Must be a recognized protocol listed in the file /etc/protocols. For RPC services, the field consists of the string rpc followed by a slash and the name of the protocol (for example, rpc/udp for an RPC service using the UDP protocol as a transport mechanism).

wait-status   nowait for all but single-threaded datagram servers — servers which do not release the socket until a timeout occurs (such as comsat(1M) and talkd(1M)). These must have the status wait. Although tftpd(1M) establishes separate pseudo-connections, its forking behavior can lead to a race condition unless it is also given the status wait.

uid   The user ID under which the server should run. This allows servers to run with access privileges other than those for root.

server-program   Either the pathname of a server program to be invoked by inetd to perform the requested service, or the value internal if inetd itself provides the service.

server-arguments   If a server must be invoked with command-line arguments, the entire command line (including argument 0) must appear in this field (which consists of all remaining words in the entry). If the server expects inetd to pass it the address of its peer (for compatibility with 4.2BSD executable daemons), then the first argument to the command should be specified as '%A'.

FILES
        /etc/inetd.conf
        /etc/services
        /etc/protocols

SEE ALSO
        rlogin(1), rsh(1), comsat(1M), inetd(1M), talkd(1M), tftpd(1M), services(4).

NAME

    inittab – script for init

DESCRIPTION

The file /sbin/inittab controls process dispatching by init. The processes most typically dispatched by init are daemons.

The inittab file is composed of entries that are position dependent and have the following format:

    id : rstate : action : process

Each entry is delimited by a newline, however, a backslash (\) preceding a new-line indicates a continuation of the entry. Up to 512 characters per entry are per-mitted. Comments may be inserted in the *process* field using the convention for comments described in sh(1). There are no limits (other than maximum entry size) imposed on the number of entries in the inittab file. The entry fields are:

id   This is one or two characters used to uniquely identify an entry.

rstate   This defines the run level in which this entry is to be processed. Run-levels effectively correspond to a configuration of processes in the sys-tem. That is, each process spawned by init is assigned a run level or run levels in which it is allowed to exist. The run levels are represented by a number ranging from 0 through 6. As an example, if the system is in run level 1, only those entries having a 1 in the *rstate* field are pro-cessed. When init is requested to change run levels, all processes that do not have an entry in the *rstate* field for the target run level are sent the warning signal SIGTERM and allowed a 5-second grace period before being forcibly terminated by the kill signal SIGKILL. The *rstate* field can define multiple run levels for a process by selecting more than one run level in any combination from 0 through 6. If no run level is specified, then the process is assumed to be valid at all run levels 0 through 6. There are three other values, a, b and c, which can appear in the *rstate* field, even though they are not true run levels. Entries which have these characters in the *rstate* field are processed only when an init or telinit process requests them to be run (regardless of the current run level of the system). See init(1M). They differ from run levels in that init can never enter run level a, b or c. Also, a request for the execu-tion of any of these processes does not change the current run level. Furthermore, a process started by an a, b or c command is not killed when init changes levels. They are killed only if their line in inittab is marked off in the *action* field, their line is deleted entirely from init-tab, or init goes into single-user state.

action   Key words in this field tell init how to treat the process specified in the *process* field. The actions recognized by init are as follows:

          respawn   If the process does not exist, then start the process; do not wait for its termination (continue scanning the init-tab file), and when the process dies, restart the process. If the process currently exists, do nothing and continue scanning the inittab file.

wait	When init enters the run level that matches the entry's *rstate*, start the process and wait for its termination. All subsequent reads of the inittab file while init is in the same run level cause init to ignore this entry.
once	When init enters a run level that matches the entry's *rstate*, start the process, do not wait for its termination. When it dies, do not restart the process. If init enters a new run level and the process is still running from a previous run level change, the program is not restarted.
boot	The entry is to be processed only at init's boot-time read of the inittab file. init is to start the process, not wait for its termination; and when it dies, not restart the process. In order for this instruction to be meaningful, the *rstate* should be the default or it must match init's run level at boot time. This action is useful for an initialization function following a hardware reboot of the system.
bootwait	The entry is to be processed the first time init goes from single-user to multi-user state after the system is booted. (If initdefault is set to 2, the process runs right after the boot.) init starts the process, waits for its termination and, when it dies, does not restart the process.
powerfail	Execute the process associated with this entry only when init receives a power fail signal, SIGPWR [see signal(2)].
powerwait	Execute the process associated with this entry only when init receives a power fail signal, SIGPWR, and wait until it terminates before continuing any processing of inittab.
off	If the process associated with this entry is currently running, send the warning signal SIGTERM and wait 5 seconds before forcibly terminating the process with the kill signal SIGKILL. If the process is nonexistent, ignore the entry.
ondemand	This instruction is really a synonym for the respawn action. It is functionally identical to respawn but is given a different keyword in order to divorce its association with run levels. This instruction is used only with the a, b or c values described in the *rstate* field.
initdefault	An entry with this action is scanned only when init is initially invoked. init uses this entry, if it exists, to determine which run level to enter initially. It does this by taking the highest run level specified in the *rstate* field and using that as its initial state. If the *rstate* field is empty, this is interpreted as 0123456 and init therefore

enters run level 6. This will cause the system to loop, that is, it will go to firmware and reboot continuously. Additionally, if init does not find an initdefault entry in inittab, it requests an initial run level from the user at reboot time.

sysinit   Entries of this type are executed before init tries to access the console (i.e., before the Console Login: prompt). It is expected that this entry will be only used to initialize devices on which init might try to ask the run level question. These entries are executed and waited for before continuing.

process   This is a command to be executed. The entire process field is prefixed with exec and passed to a forked sh as sh −c 'exec *command*'. For this reason, any legal sh syntax can appear in the *process* field.

SEE ALSO

init(1M), ttymon(1M), exec(2), open(2), signal(2)

sh(1), who(1) in the *User's Reference Manual*

NAME

inode (bfs) – format of a bfs i-node

SYNOPSIS

```
#include <sys/types.h>
#include <sys/fs/bfs.h>
```

DESCRIPTION

```
struct bfs_dirent
{
        ushort  d_ino;                   /* inode number */
        daddr_t d_sblock;                /* Start block */
        daddr_t d_eblock;                /* End block */
        daddr_t d_eoffset;               /* EOF disk offset (absolute) */
        struct  bfsvattr d_fattr;        /* File attributes */
};
```

For the meaning of the defined type daddr_t see types(5). The bfsvattr structure appears in the header file <sys/fs/bfs.h>.

SEE ALSO

bfs-specific fs(4), types(5).

NAME

inode (s5) – format of an s5 i-node

SYNOPSIS

```
#include <sys/types.h>
#include <sys/fs/s5ino.h>
```

DESCRIPTION

An i-node for a plain file or directory in an s4 file system has the following structure defined by <sys/fs/s5ino.h>.

```
/* Inode structure as it appears on a disk block. */

struct dinode
{
        o_mode_t       di_mode;      /* mode and type of file */
        o_nlink_t      di_nlink;     /* number of links to file */
        o_uid_t        di_uid;       /* owner's user id */
        o_gid_t        di_gid;       /* owner's group id */
        off_t          di_size;      /* number of bytes in file */
        char           di_addr[39];  /* disk block addresses */
        unsigned char  di_gen;       /* file generation number */
        time_t         di_atime;     /* time last accessed */
        time_t         di_mtime;     /* time last modified */
        time_t         di_ctime;     /* time status last changed */
};

/*
 * Of the 40 address bytes:
 *     39 are used as disk addresses
 *     13 addresses of 3 bytes each
 *     and the 40th is used as a
 *     file generation number
 */
```

For the meaning of the defined types off_t and time_t see types(5).

SEE ALSO

stat(2), l3tot(3C), s5-specific fs(4), types(5)

NAME
    inode (ufs) − format of a ufs inode

SYNOPSIS
    #include <sys/param.h>
    #include <sys/types.h>
    #include <sys/vnode.h>
    #include <sys/fs/ufs_inode.h>

DESCRIPTION
    The I node is the focus of all local file activity in UNIX. There is a unique inode
    allocated for each active file, each current directory, each mounted-on file, each
    mapping, and the root. An inode is 'named' by its dev/inumber pair. Data in
    icommon is read in from permanent inode on the actual volume.

```
#define EFT_MAGIC 0x90909090    /* magic cookie for EFT */
#define NDADDR    12            /* direct addresses in inode */
#define NIADDR     3            /* indirect addresses in inode */

struct inode {
    struct    inode *i_chain[2];/* must be first */
    struct    vnode i_vnode;    /* vnode associated with this inode */
    struct    vnode *i_devvp;   /* vnode for block I/O */
    u_short   i_flag;
    dev_t     i_dev;            /* device where inode resides */
    ino_t     i_number;         /* i number, 1-to-1 with device address */
    off_t     i_diroff;         /* offset in dir, where we found last entry */
    struct    fs *i_fs;         /* file sys associated with this inode */
    struct    dquot *i_dquot;   /* quota structure controlling this file */
    short     i_owner;          /* proc index of process locking inode */
    short     i_count;          /* number of inode locks for i_owner */
    short     i_rwowner;        /* proc index of process holding rwlock */
    daddr_t   i_nextr;          /* next byte read offset (read-ahead) */
    struct inode  *i_freef;     /* free list forward */
    struct inode **i_freeb;     /* free list back */
    ulong     i_vcode;          /* version code attribute */
    ulong     i_mapcnt;         /* mappings to file pages */
    int       *i_map;           /* block list for the corresponding file */
    struct    icommon {
        o_mode_t ic_smode;      /* 0: mode and type of file */
        short    ic_nlink;      /* 2: number of links to file */
        o_uid_t  ic_suid;       /* 4: owner's user id */
        o_gid_t  ic_sgid;       /* 6: owner's group id */
        quad     ic_size;       /* 8: number of bytes in file */
#ifdef _KERNEL
        struct timeval ic_atime;/* 16: time last accessed */
        struct timeval ic_mtime;/* 24: time last modified */
        struct timeval ic_ctime;/* 32: last time inode changed */
#else
        time_t   ic_atime;      /* 16: time last accessed */
        long     ic_atspare;
        time_t   ic_mtime;      /* 24: time last modified */
        long     ic_mtspare;
        time_t   ic_ctime;      /* 32: last time inode changed */
        long     ic_ctspare;
```

```
        #endif
                daddr_t ic_db[NDADDR];  /* 40: disk block addresses */
                daddr_t ic_ib[NIADDR];  /* 88: indirect blocks */
                long    ic_flags;       /* 100: status, currently unused */
                long    ic_blocks;      /* 104: blocks actually held */
                long    ic_gen;         /* 108: generation number */
                mode_t  ic_mode;        /* 112: EFT version of mode*/
                uid_t   ic_uid;         /* 116: EFT version of uid */
                gid_t   ic_gid;         /* 120: EFT version of gid */
                ulong   ic_eftflag;     /* 124: indicate EFT version*/

        } i_ic;
    };

    struct dinode {
        union {
            struct  icommon di_icom;
            char    di_size[128];
        } di_un;
    };
```

SEE ALSO

ufs-specific fs(4)

NAME

   issue – issue identification file

DESCRIPTION

   The file /etc/issue contains the issue or project identification to be printed as a
   login prompt. issue is an ASCII file that is read by program getty and then
   written to any terminal spawned or respawned from the *lines* file.

FILES

   /etc/issue

SEE ALSO

   login(1) in the *User's Reference Manual.*

NAME

limits – header file for implementation-specific constants

SYNOPSIS

`#include <limits.h>`

DESCRIPTION

The header file limits.h is a list of minimal magnitude limitations imposed by a specific implementation of the operating system.

ARG_MAX	5120	/* max length of arguments to exec */
CHAR_BIT	8	/* max # of bits in a "char" */
CHAR_MAX	255	/* max value of a "char" */
CHAR_MIN	0	/* min value of a "char" */
CHILD_MAX	25	/* max # of processes per user id */
CLK_TCK	_sysconf(3)	/* clock ticks per second */
DBL_DIG	15	/* digits of precision of a "double" */
DBL_MAX	1.7976931348623157E+308	/* max decimal value of a "double"*/
DBL_MIN	2.2250738585072014E-308	/* min decimal value of a "double"*/
FCHR_MAX	1048576	/* max size of a file in bytes */
FLT_DIG	6	/* digits of precision of a "float" */
FLT_MAX	3.40282347e+38F	/* max decimal value of a "float" */
FLT_MIN	1.17549435E-38F	/* min decimal value of a "float" */
INT_MAX	2147483647	/* max value of an "int" */
INT_MIN	(-2147483647-1)	/* min value of an "int" */
LINK_MAX	1000	/* max # of links to a single file */
LOGNAME_MAX	8	/* max # of characters in a login name */
LONG_BIT	32	/* # of bits in a "long" */
LONG_MAX	2147483647	/* max value of a "long int" */
LONG_MIN	(-2147483647-1)	/* min value of a "long int" */
MAX_CANON	256	/* max bytes in a line for canonical processing */
MAX_INPUT	512	/* max size of a char input buffer */
MB_LEN_MAX	5	/* max # of bytes in a multibyte character */
NAME_MAX	14	/* max # of characters in a file name */
NGROUPS_MAX	16	/* max # of groups for a user */
NL_ARGMAX	9	/* max value of "digit" in calls to the NLS printf() and scanf() */
NL_LANGMAX	14	/* max # of bytes in a LANG name */
NL_MSGMAX	32767	/* max message number */
NL_NMAX	1	/* max # of bytes in N-to-1 mapping characters */
NL_SETMAX	255	/* max set number */
NL_TEXTMAX	255	/* max # of bytes in a message string */
NZERO	20	/* default process priority */
OPEN_MAX	20	/* max # of files a process can have open */
PASS_MAX	8	/* max # of characters in a password */

```
      PATH_MAX       1024           /* max # of characters in a path name */
      PID_MAX        30000          /* max value for a process ID */
      PIPE_BUF       5120           /* max # bytes atomic in write to a pipe */
      PIPE_MAX       5120           /* max # bytes written to a pipe
                                    in a write */
      SCHAR_MAX      127            /* max value of a "signed char" */
      SCHAR_MIN      (-128)         /* min value of a "signed char" */
      SHRT_MAX       32767          /* max value of a "short int" */
      SHRT_MIN       (-32768)       /* min value of a "short int" */
      STD_BLK        1024           /* # bytes in a physical I/O block */
      SYS_NMLN       257            /* 4.0 size of utsname elements */
                                    /* also defined in sys/utsname.h */
      SYSPID_MAX     1              /* max pid of system processes */
      TMP_MAX        17576          /* max # of unique names generated
                                    by tmpnam */
      UCHAR_MAX      255            /* max value of an "unsigned char" */
      UID_MAX        60000          /* max value for a user or group ID */
      UINT_MAX       4294967295     /* max value of an "unsigned int" */
      ULONG_MAX      4294967295     /* max value of an "unsigned long int" */
      USHRT_MAX      65535          /* max value of an "unsigned short int" */
      USI_MAX        4294967295     /* max decimal value of an "unsigned" */
      WORD_BIT       32             /* # of bits in a "word" or "int" */
```

The following POSIX definitions are the most restrictive values to be used by a POSIX conformant application. Conforming implementations shall provide values at least this large.

```
      _POSIX_ARG_MAX        4096   /* max length of arguments to exec */
      _POSIX_CHILD_MAX      6      /* max # of processes per user ID */
      _POSIX_LINK_MAX       8      /* max # of links to a single file */
      _POSIX_MAX_CANON      255    /* max # of bytes in a line of input */
      _POSIX_MAX_INPUT      255    /* max # of bytes in terminal
                                   input queue */
      _POSIX_NAME_MAX       14     /* # of bytes in a filename */
      _POSIX_NGROUPS_MAX    0      /* max # of groups in a process */
      _POSIX_OPEN_MAX       16     /* max # of files a process can have open */
      _POSIX_PATH_MAX       255    /* max # of characters in a pathname */
      _POSIX_PIPE_BUF       512    /* max # of bytes atomic in write
                                   to a pipe */
```

NAME

loginlog – log of failed login attempts

DESCRIPTION

After five unsuccessful login attempts, all the attempts are logged in the file /var/adm/loginlog. This file contains one record for each failed attempt. Each record contains the login name, tty specification, and time.

This is an ASCII file. Each field within each entry is separated from the next by a colon. Each entry is separated from the next by a new-line.

By default, loginlog does not exist, so no logging is done. To enable logging, the log file must be created with read and write permission for owner only. Owner must be **root** and group must be **sys**.

FILES

/var/adm/loginlog

SEE ALSO

login(1), passwd(1) in the *User's Reference Manual*

NAME
     mailcnfg – initialization information for mail and rmail

DESCRIPTION
     The /etc/mail/mailcnfg file contains initialization information for the mail and
     rmail commands. Each entry in mailcnfg consists of a line of the form

                              Keyword = *Value*

     Leading whitespace, whitespace surrounding the equal sign, and trailing whitespace is ignored. *Keyword* may not contain embedded whitespace, but whitespace may appear within *Value*. Undefined keywords or badly formed entries are silently ignored.

Keyword Definitions

     DEBUG   Takes the same values as the –x invocation option of mail.
                       This provides a way of setting a system-wide
                       debug/tracing level. Typically DEBUG is set to a value of 2,
                       which provides minimal diagnostics useful for debugging
                       mail and rmail failures. The value of the –x mail invoca-
                       tion option will override any specification of DEBUG in
                       mailcnfg.

     CLUSTER   To identify a closely coupled set of systems by one name to
                       all other systems, set *Value* to the cluster name. This string
                       is used to supply the ...remote from... information on
                       the From header line rather than the system nodename
                       returned by uname(2).

     FAILSAFE   In the event that the /var/mail directory is accessed via
                       RFS or NFS within a cluster (see CLUSTER above), provi-
                       sions must be made to allow for the directory not being
                       available when local mail is to be delivered (remote system
                       crash, RFS or NFS problems, etc.). *Value* is a string that
                       indicates where to forward the current message for
                       delivery. Typically this is the remote system that actually
                       owns /var/mail. In this way, the message is queued for
                       delivery to that system when it becomes available. For
                       example, assume a cluster of systems (sysa, sysb, sysc)
                       where /var/mail is physically mounted on sysc and made
                       available to the other machines via RFS or NFS. If sysc
                       were to crash, the RFS/NFS-accessible /var/mail would
                       become unavailable and local deliveries of mail would go
                       to /var/mail on the local system. When /var/mail is re-
                       mounted via RFS/NFS, all messages deposited in the local
                       directory would be hidden and essentially lost. To prevent
                       this, if FAILSAFE is defined in mailcnfg, mail and rmail
                       check for the existence of /var/mail/:saved, a required
                       subdirectory. If this subdirectory does not exist, mail
                       assumes that the RFS/NFS-accessible /var/mail is not
                       available and invokes the failsafe mechanism of automati-
                       cally forwarding the message to *Value*. In this example
                       Value would be sysc!%n. The %*n* keyword is expanded to

be the recipient name [see mail(1) for details] and thus the message would be forwarded to *sysc!recipient_name*. Because **sysc** is not available, the message remains on the local system until **sysc** is available, and then sent there for delivery.

DEL_EMPTY_MFILE   If not specified, the default action of mail and rmail is to delete empty mailfiles if the permissions are 0660 and to retain empty mailfiles if the permissions are anything else. If *Value* is **yes**, empty mailfiles are always deleted, regardless of file permissions. If *Value* is **no**, empty mailfiles are never deleted.

DOMAIN   This string is used to supply the system domain name in place of the domain name returned by getdomainname(3).

SMARTERHOST   This string may be set to a smarter host which may be referenced within the mail surrogate file via **%X**.

%*mailsurr_keyword*   As described in mailsurr(4), certain pre-defined single letter keywords are textually substituted in surrogate command fields before they are executed. While none of the predefined keywords may be changed in meaning, new ones may be defined to provide a shorthand notation for long strings (such as /usr/lib/mail/surrcmd) which may appear repeatedly within the mailsurr file. Upper case letters are reserved for future use and will be ignored if encountered here.

FILES

/etc/mail/mailcnfg
/etc/mail/mailsurr
/var/mail/:saved
/usr/lib/mail/surrcmd

SEE ALSO

mailsurr(4)
mail(1) in the *User's Reference Manual*
uname(2), getdomainname(3) in the *Programmer's Reference Manual*

NOTES

If /var/mail is accessed via RFS or NFS and the subdirectory /var/mail/:saved is not removed from the local system, the FAILSAFE mechanism will be subverted.

NAME

mailsurr – surrogate commands for routing and transport of mail

DESCRIPTION

The mailsurr file contains routing and transport surrogate commands used by the mail command. Each entry in mailsurr has three whitespace-separated, single quote delimited fields:

'sender'   'recipient'   'command'

or a line that begins

Defaults:

Entries and fields may span multiple lines, but leading whitespace on field continuation lines is ignored. Fields must be less than 1024 characters long after expansion (see below).

The sender and recipient fields are regular expressions. If the sender and recipient fields match those of the message currently being processed, the associated command is invoked.

The *command* field may have one of the following five forms:

A[ccept]
D[eny]
T[ranslate] R=[|]*string*
< S=...;C=...;F=...; *command*
> *command*

Regular Expressions

The sender and recipient fields are composed of regular expressions (REs) which are digested by the regexp(5) compile and advance procedures in the C library. The regular expressions matched are those from ed(1), with simple parentheses () playing the role of \(\) and the addition of the + and ? operators from egrep(1). Any single quotes embedded within the REs *must* be escaped by prepending them with a backslash or the RE is not interpreted properly.

The mail command prepends a circumflex (^) to the start and appends a dollar sign ($) to the end of each RE so that it matches the entire string. Therefore it would be an error to use ^RE$ in the sender and recipient fields. To provide case insensitivity, all REs are converted to lower case before compilation, and all sender and recipient information is converted to lower case before comparison. This conversion is done only for the purposes of RE pattern matching; the information contained within the message's header is *not* modified.

The sub-expression pattern matching capabilities of regexp may be used in the command field, that is, (...), where $1 \le n \le 9$. Any occurrences of \\n in the replacement string are themselves replaced by the corresponding (...) substring in the matched pattern. The sub-expression fields from both the sender and recipient fields are accessible, with the fields numbered 1 to 9 from left to right.

Accept and Deny Commands

Accept instructs rmail to continue its processing with the mailsurr file, but to ignore any subsequent matching Deny. That is, unconditionally accept this message for delivery processing. Deny instructs rmail to stop processing the mailsurr file and to send a negative delivery notification to the originator of the message. Whichever is encountered first takes precedence.

Translate Command

Translate allows optional on-the-fly translation of recipient address information. The *recipient* replacement string is specified as R=*string*.

For example, given a command line of the form

    '.+' '([^!]+)@(.+)\.EUO\.ATT\.com' 'Translate R=attmail!\\2!\\1'

and a recipient address of rob@sysa.EUO.ATT.COM the resulting recipient address would be attmail!sysa!rob.

Should the first character after the equal sign be a '|', the remainder of the string is taken as a command line to be directly executed by rmail. If any sh(1) syntax is required (metacharacters, redirection, etc.), then the surrogate command must be of the form:

    sh -c "*shell command line...*"

Special care must be taken to escape properly any embedded back-slashes and single or double quotes, since rmail uses double quoting to group whitespace delimited fields that are meant to be considered as a single argument to execl(2). It is assumed that the executed command will write one or more replacement strings on stdout, one per line. If more than one line is returned, each is assumed to be a different recipient for the message. This mechanism is useful for mailing list expansions. As stated above, any occurrences of *n* are replaced by the appropriate substring *before* the command is executed. If the invoked command does not return at least one replacement string (no output or just a newline), the original string is *not* modified. For example, the command line

    '.+' '(.+)' 'Translate R=|/usr/bin/findpath \\1'

allows local routing decisions to be made.

If the recipient address string is modified, mailsurr is rescanned from the beginning with the new address(es), and any prior determination of Accept (see above) is discarded.

< command

The intent of a < command is that it is invoked as part of the transport and delivery mechanism, with the ready-for-delivery message available to the command at its standard input. As such, there are three conditions possible when the command exits:

Success   The command successfully delivered the message. What actually constitutes successful delivery may be different within the context of different surrogates. The rmail process assumes that no more processing is required for the message for the current recipient.

Continue The command performed some function (logging remote message traffic, for example) but did not do what would be considered message delivery. The rmail process continues to scan the mailsurr file looking for some other delivery mechanism.

Failure   The command encountered some catastrophic failure. The
          rmail process stops processing the message and sends to the
          originator of the message a non-delivery notification that
          includes any stdout and stderr output generated by the com-
          mand.

The semantics of the < command field in the mailsurr file allow the specification
of exit codes that constitute success, continue, and failure for each surrogate command individually. The syntax of the exit state specification is:

> < WS [exit_state_id=ec[,ec[,...]];][exit_state_id=ec[,ec[,...]];
>   [...]]] WS surrogate_cmd_line

WS is whitespace. exit_state_id can have the value S, C, or F. exit_state_ids can be
specified in any order. ec can be:

any integer $0 \leq n \leq 255$ [Negative exit values are not possible. See exit(2)
and wait(2).]

a range of integers of the form lower_limit−upper_limit where the limits are
≥ 0 and ≤ 255, and

*, which implies anything

For example, a command field of the form:

> '< S=1-5,99;C=0,12;F=*;   command %R'

indicates that exit values of 1 through 5, and 99, are to be considered success,
values of 0 (zero) and 12 indicate continue, and that anything else implies failure.
If not explicitly supplied, default settings are S=0;C=*;.

It may be possible for ambiguous entries to exist if two exit states have the same
value, for example, S=12,23;C=*;F=23,52; or S=*;C=9;F=*;. To account for
this, rmail looks for explicit exit values (that is, not "*") in order of success, continue, failure. Not finding an explicit match, rmail then scans for "*" in the
same order.

It is possible to eliminate an exit state completely by setting that state's value to
an impossible number. Since exit values must be between 0 and 255 (inclusive), a
value of 256 is a good one to use. For example, if you had a surrogate command
that was to log all message traffic, a mailsurr entry of

> '(.+)' '(.+)' '<S=256;C=*; /usr/lib/mail/surrcmd/logger \\1 \\2'

would always indicate continue.

Surrogate commands are executed by rmail directly. If any shell syntax is
required (metacharacters, redirection, etc.), then the surrogate command must be
of the form:

> sh −c "shell command line..."

Special care must be taken to properly escape any embedded back-slashes and
other characters special to the shell as stated in the "Translate" section above.

If there are no matching < commands, or all matching < commands exit with a
continue indication, rmail attempts to deliver the message itself by assuming that
the recipient is local and delivering the message to /var/mail/*recipient*.

> command

The intent of a > command is that it is invoked *after* a successful delivery to do
any post-delivery processing that may be required. Matching > commands are
executed only if some < command indicates a successful delivery (see the previous section) or local delivery processing is successful. The mailsurr file is rescanned and all matching > commands, not just those following the successful <
command, are executed in order. The exit status of an > command is ignored.

Defaults: Line

The default settings may be redefined by creating a separate line in the mailsurr
file of the form

        Defaults: [S=...;][C=...;][F=...;]

Defaults: lines are honored and the indicated default values redefined when the
line is encountered during the normal processing of the mailsurr file. Therefore,
to redefine the defaults globally, the Defaults: line should be the first line in the
file. It is possible to have multiple Defaults: lines in the mailsurr file, where
each subsequent line overrides the previous one.

Surrogate Command Keyword Replacement.

Certain special sequences are textually-substituted in surrogate commands before
they are invoked:

%n	the recipient's full name.
%R	the full return path to the originator (useful for sending replies, delivery failure notifications, etc.)
%c	value of the Content-Type: header line if present.
%C	"text" or "binary", depending on an actual scan of the content. This is independent of the value of any Content-Type header line encountered (useful when calling ckbinarsys.)
%S	the value of the Subject: header line, if present.
%l	value of the Content-Length: header line.
%L	the local system name. This will be either CLUSTER from mailcnfg or the value returned by uname.
%U	the local system name, as returned by uname.
%X	the value of SMARTERHOST in mailcnfg.
%D	the local domain name. This will be either DOMAIN from mailcnfg, or the value returned by getdomainname.
n	as described above, the corresponding (...) substring in the matched patterns. This implies that the regexp limitation of 9 substrings is applied to the sender and recipient REs collectively.
%*keywords*	Other keywords as specified in /etc/mail/mailcnfg. See mailcnfg(4).

The sequences %L, %U, %D, and %*keywords* are permitted within the sender and recipient fields as well as in the command fields.

An example of the `mailsurr` entry that replaces the uux ''built-in'' of previous versions of `rmail` is:

```
'.+'  '([^@!]+)!(.+)'  '< /usr/bin/uux - \\1!rmail (\\2)'
```

Mail Surrogate Examples

Some examples of mail surrogates include the distribution of message-waiting notifications to LAN-based recipients and lighting Message-Waiting Lamps, the ability to mail output to printers, and the logging of all `rmail` requests between remote systems (messages passing through the local system). The following is a sample `mailsurr` file:

```
#
# Some common remote mail surrogates follow. To activate any
# or all of them, remove the '#' (comment indicators) from
# the beginning of the appropriate lines. Remember that they
# will be tried in the order they are encountered in the file,
# so put preferred surrogates first.

#       Prevent all shell meta-characters
'.+'  '.*[`;&|^<>()].*'        'Deny'

#       Map all names of the form local-machine!user -> user
'.+'  '%L!(.+)'               'Translate R=\1'

#       Map all names of the form uname!user -> user
#       Must be turned on when using mail in a cluster environment.
#'.+'  '%U!(.+)'               'Translate R=\1'

#       Map all names of the form user@host -> host!user
'.+'  '([^!@]+)@(.+)'          'Translate R=\2!\1'

#       Map all names of the form host.uucp!user -> host!user
'.+'  '([^!@]+)\.uucp!(.+)'  'Translate R=\1!\2'

#       Map all names of the form host.local-domain!user -> host!user
#       DOMAIN= within /etc/mail/mailcnfg will override getdomainame(3).
'.+'  '([^!@]+)%D!(.+)'        'Translate R=\1!\2'

#       Allow access to 'attmail' from remote system 'sysa'
'sysa!.*'  'attmail!.+'     'Accept'

#       Deny access to 'attmail' from all other remotes
'.+!.+'       'attmail!.+'     'Deny'

#       Send mail for 'laser' to attached laser printer
#       Make certain that failures are reported via return mail.
'.+'  'laser'      '< S=0;F=*; lp -dlaser'

#       Run all local names through the mail alias processor
#
```

```
     '.+'   '[^!@]+'              'Translate R=|/usr/bin/mailalias %n'

#       For remote mail via nusend
#'.+'  '([^!]+)!(.+)'    '< /usr/bin/nusend -d \\1 -s -e -!"rmail \\2" -'

#       For remote mail via usend
'.+'   '([^!]+)!(.+)'
                        '< /usr/bin/usend -s -d\\1 -uNoLogin -!"rmail \\2" - '

#       For remote mail via uucp
'.+'   '([^!@]+)!.+'    '<S=256;C=0;
              /usr/lib/mail/surrcmd/ckbinarsys -t %C -s \\1'
'.+'   '([^!@]+)!(.+)'    '< /usr/bin/uux - \\1!rmail (\\2)'

#       For remote mail via smtp
#'.+'  '([^!@]+)!(.+)'             '< /usr/lib/mail/surrcmd/smtpqer %R %n'

#       If none of the above work, then let a router change the address.
#'.+'  '.*[!@].*'       'Translate R=| /usr/lib/mail/surrcmd/smail -A %n'

#       If none of the above work, then ship remote mail off to a smarter host.
#       Make certain that SMARTERHOST= is defined within /etc/mail/mailcnfg.
#'.+'  '.*[!@].*'                  'Translate R=%X!%n'

#       Log successful message deliveries
'(.+)'  '(.+)'  '>/usr/lib/mail/surrcmd/logger \1 \2'
```

Note that invoking mail to read mail does not involve the mailsurr file or any surrogate processing.

Security

Surrogate commands execute with the permissions of rmail (user ID of the invoker, group ID of mail). This allows surrogate commands to validate themselves, checking that their effective group ID was mail at invocation time. This requires that all additions to mailsurr be scrutinized before insertion to prevent any unauthorized access to users' mail files. All surrogate commands are executed with the path /usr/lib/mail/surrcmd:/usr/bin.

Debugging New mailsurr Entries

To debug mailsurr files, use the −T option of the mail command. The −T option requires an argument that is taken as the pathname of a test mailsurr file. If null (as in −T ""), the system mailsurr file is used. Enter

      mail −T *test_file recipient*

and some trivial message (like "testing"), followed by a line with either just a dot (".") or a cntl-D. The result of using the −T option is displayed on standard output and shows the inputs and resulting transformations as mailsurr is processed by the mail command for the indicated *recipient*.

Mail messages will never be sent or delivered when using the −T option.

FILES

/etc/mail/mailsurr
/usr/lib/mail/surrcmd/*   surrogate commands
/etc/mail/mailcnfg   initialization information for mail

SEE ALSO

ckbinarsys(1M), mailcnfg(4)
mail(1), sh(1), uux(1), ed(1), egrep(1), in the *User's Reference Manual*
exec(2), exit(2), wait(2), popen(3), regexp(5), getdomainname(3) in the
Programmer's Reference Manual

NOTES

It would be unwise to install new entries into the system mailsurr file without
verifying at least their syntactical correctness via 'mail −T ...' as described above.

NAME

master – master configuration database

DESCRIPTION

The master configuration database is a collection of files. Each file contains configuration information for a device or module that may be included in the system. A file is named with the module name to which it applies. This collection of files is maintained in a directory called /etc/master.d. Each file has an identical format. For convenience, this collection of files will be referred to as the master file, as though it were a single file. Treating the master file as a single file allows a reference to the master file to be understood to mean the individual file in the master.d directory that corresponds to the name of a device or module. The file is used by the mkboot(1M) program to obtain device information to generate the device driver and configurable module files. It is also used by the sysdef(1M) program to obtain the names of supported devices. master consists of two parts; they are separated by a line with a dollar sign ($) in column 1. Part 1 contains device information for both hardware and software devices, and loadable modules. Part 2 contains parameter declarations used in Part 1. Any line with an asterisk (*) in column 1 is treated as a comment.

Part 1. Description

Hardware devices, software drivers and loadable modules are defined with a line containing the following information. Field 1 must begin in the left-most position on the line. Fields are separated by white space (tab or blank).

Field 1: element characteristics:

o	specify only once
r	required device
b	block device
c	character device
a	generate segment descriptor array
t	initialize cdevsw[].d_ttys
s	software driver
f	STREAMS driver
m	STREAMS module
x	not a driver; a loadable module
number	first interrupt vector for an integral device
none	no flags for this driver or module

Field 2: number of interrupt vectors required by a hardware device: "–" if none.

Field 3: handler prefix (4 characters maximum)

Field 4: software driver external major number; "–" if not a software driver, or to be assigned during execution of drvinstall(1M)

Field 5: number of sub-devices per device; "–" if none

Field 6: interrupt priority level of the device; "–" if none

Field 7: dependency list (optional); this is a comma-separated list of other drivers or modules that must be present in the configuration if this module is to be included

For each module, two classes of information are required by mkboot: external routine references and variable definitions. Routine and variable definition lines begin with white space and immediately follow the initial module specification line. These lines are free form, thus they may be continued arbitrarily between non-blank tokens as long as the first character of a line is white space.

Part 1. Routine Reference Lines

If the UNIX system kernel or other dependent module contains external references to a module, but the module is not configured, then these external references would be undefined. Therefore, the routine reference lines are used to provide the information necessary to generate appropriate dummy functions at boot time when the driver is not loaded. The format of a routine reference is as follows:

> *routine_name* () *action*

The valid actions and their meanings are:

{ }	*routine_name* () { }
{nosys}	{return nosys();
{nodev}	{return nodev();}
{false}	{return 0;}
{true}	{return 1;}
{nopkg}	{return nopkg();}
{noreach}	panic the system

Part 1. Variable Definition Lines

Variable definition lines are used to generate all variables required by the module. The variable generated may be of arbitrary size, be initialized or not, or be arrays containing an arbitrary number of elements. Variable references are defined as follows:

Field 1:	*variable_name*
Field 2:	[*expr*] − optional field used to indicate array size
Field 3:	(*length*) − required field indicating the size of the variable
Field 4:	={ *expr*, . . . } − optional field used to initialize individual elements of a variable

The *length* field is mandatory. It is an arbitrary sequence of length specifiers, each of which may be one of the following:

%i	an integer
%l	a long integer
%s	a short integer
%c	a single character
%*number*	a field which is *number* bytes long
%*number* c	a character string which is *number* bytes long

For example, the length field

> (%8c %l %0x58 %l %c %c)

could be used to identify a variable consisting of a character string 8-bytes long, a long integer, a 0x58 byte structure of any type, another long integer, and two characters. Appropriate alignment of each % specification is performed (%*number* is word-aligned) and the variable length is rounded up to the next word boundary during processing.

The expressions for the optional array size and initialization are infixed expressions consisting of the usual operators for addition, subtraction, multiplication, and division: +, −, *, and /. Multiplication and division have the higher precedence, but parentheses may be used to override the default order. The builtin functions min and max accept a pair of expressions, and return the appropriate value. The operands of the expression may be any mixture of the following:

  &name address of *name*, where *name* is any symbol defined by the kernel, any module loaded, or any variable definition line of any module loaded

  #*name* sizeof *name* where *name* is any variable name defined by a variable definition for any module loaded; the size is that of the individual variable—not the size of an entire array

  #C number of controllers present; this number is determined by the EDT for hardware devices, or by the number provided in the system file for non-hardware drivers or modules

  #C (*name*) number of controllers present for the module *name*; this number is determined by the EDT for hardware devices, or by the number provided in the system file for non-hardware drivers or modules

  #D number of devices per controller taken directly from the current master file entry

  #D (*name*) number of devices per controller taken directly from the master file entry for the module *name*

  #M the internal major number assigned to the current module if it is a device driver; zero of this module is not a device driver

  #M (*name*) the internal major number assigned to the module *name* if it is a device driver: zero if that module is not a device driver

  name value of a parameter as defined in the second part of master

  number arbitrary number (octal, decimal, or hex allowed)

  string a character string enclosed within double quotes (all of the character string conventions supported by the C language are allowed); this operand has a value which is the address of a character array containing the specified string

When initializing a variable, one initialization expression should be provided for each %i, %l, %s, or %c of the length field. The only initializers allowed for a %*number* c are either a character string (the string may not be longer than *number*), or an explicit zero. Initialization expressions must be separated by commas, and variable initialization proceeds element by element. Note that %*number* specification cannot be initialized—they are set to zero. Only the first element of an array can be initialized; the other elements are set to zero. If there are more initializers than size specifications, it is an error and execution of the mkboot program is aborted. If there are fewer initializations than size specifications, zeros will be used to pad the variable. For example:

```
={ "V2.L1", #C*#D, max(10,#D), #C(OTHER), #M(OTHER) }
```

would be a possible initialization of the variable whose length field was given in the preceding example.

Part 2. Description

Parameter declarations may be used to define a value symbolically. Values can be associated with identifiers and these identifiers may be used in the *variable definition* lines. Parameters are defined as follows:

> *identifier* = *value*

The *identifier* may have a maximum of 8 characters. The *value* may be a number (decimal, octal, or hex) or a string.

EXAMPLE

A sample master file for a tty device driver would be named atty if the device appeared in the EDT as ATTY. The driver is a character device, the driver prefix is at, two interrupt vectors are used, and the interrupt priority is 6. In addition, another driver named ATLOG is necessary for the correct operation of the software associated with this device.

```
*FLAG #VEC PREFIX SOFT #DEV IPL DEPENDENCIES/VARIABLES
 tca    2    at    -    2   6  ATLOG
                                atpoint(){false}
                                at_tty[#C*#D] (%0x58)
                                at_cnt(%i) ={ #C*#D }
                                at_logmaj(%i) ={ #M(ATLOG) }
                                at_id(%8c) ={ ATID }
                                at_table(%i%l%31%s)
                                    ={ max(#C,ATMAX),
                                       &at_tty,
                                       #C }

 $
 ATID = "fred"
 ATMAX = 6
```

This master file causes a routine named atpoint to be generated by the boot program if the ATTY driver is not loaded, and there is a reference to this routine from any other module loaded. When the driver is loaded, the variables at_tty, at_cnt, at_logmaj, at_id, and at_table are allocated and initialized as specified. Because of the t flag, the d_ttys field in the character device switch table is initialized to point to at_tty (the first variable definition line contains the variable whose address will be stored in d_ttys). The ATTY driver would reference these variables by coding:

```
extern struct tty at_tty[];
extern int at_cnt;
extern int at_logmaj;
extern char at_id[8];
extern struct {
        int member1;
        struct tty *member2;
        char junk[31];
        short member3;
        } at_table;
```

FILES
        /etc/master.d/*
SEE ALSO
        drvinstall(1M), mkboot(1M), sysdef(1M), system(4)

NAME

mnttab – mounted file system table

SYNOPSIS

#include <sys/mnttab.h>

DESCRIPTION

The file /etc/mnttab contains information about devices that have been mounted by the mount command. The information is in the following structure, defined in <sys/mnttab.h>:

```
struct  mnttab {
        char    *mnt_special;
        char    *mnt_mountp;
        char    *mnt_fstype;
        char    *mnt_mntopts;
        char    *mnt_time;
};
```

The fields in the mount table are space-separated and show the block special device, the mount point, the file system type of the mounted file system, the mount options, and the time at which the file system was mounted.

SEE ALSO

mount(1M), getmntent(1M), setmnt(1M)
Chapter 5 of the *System Administrator's Guide*

NAME
    netconfig – network configuration database

SYNOPSIS
    #include <netconfig.h>

DESCRIPTION

The network configuration database, /etc/netconfig, is a system file used to store information about networks connected to the system and available for use. The netconfig database and the routines that access it [see getnetconfig(3N)] are part of the UNIX System V Network Selection component. The Network Selection component also includes the environment variable NETPATH and a group of routines that access the netconfig database using NETPATH components as links to the netconfig entries. NETPATH is described in sh(1); the NETPATH access routines are discussed in getnetpath(3N).

netconfig contains an entry for each network available on the system. Entries are separated by newlines. Fields are separated by whitespace and occur in the order in which they are described below. Whitespace can be embedded as "*blank*" or "*tab*". Backslashes may be embedded as "\\". Each field corresponds to an element in the struct netconfig structure. struct netconfig and the identifiers described on this manual page are defined in /usr/include/netconfig.h.

network ID

    A string used to uniquely identify a network. *network ID* consists of non-null characters, and has a length of at least 1. No maximum length is specified. This namespace is locally significant and the local system administrator is the naming authority. All *network ID*s on a system must be unique.

semantics

    The *semantics* field is a string identifing the "semantics" of the network, i.e., the set of services it supports, by identifying the service interface it provides. The *semantics* field is mandatory. The following semantics are recognized.

        tpi_clts   Transport Provider Interface, connectionless

        tpi_cots   Transport Provider Interface, connection oriented

        tpi_cots_ord
                Transport Provider Interface, connection oriented, supports orderly release.

flag   The *flag* field records certain two-valued ("true" and "false") attributes of networks. *flag* is a string composed of a combination of characters, each of which indicates the value of the corresponding attribute. If the character is present, the attribute is "true." If the character is absent, the attribute is "false." "–" indicates that none of the attributes is present. Only one character is currently recognized:

v   Visible ("default") network. Used when the environment
                           variable NETPATH is unset.

protocol family
    The *protocol family* and *protocol name* fields are provided for protocol-specific applications.

    The *protocol family* field contains a string that identifies a protocol family. The *protocol family* identifier follows the same rules as those for *network IDs*, that is, the string consists of non-null characters; it has a length of at least 1; and there is no maximum length specified. A "–" in the *protocol family* field indicates that no protocol family identifier applies, that is, the network is experimental. The following are examples:

loopback	Loopback (local to host).
inet	Internetwork: UDP, TCP, etc.
implink	ARPANET imp addresses
pup	PUP protocols: e.g. BSP
chaos	MIT CHAOS protocols
ns	XEROX NS protocols
nbs	NBS protocols
ecma	European Computer Manufacturers Association
datakit	DATAKIT protocols
ccitt	CCITT protocols, X.25, etc.
sna	IBM SNA
decnet	DECNET
dli	Direct data link interface
lat	LAT
hylink	NSC Hyperchannel
appletalk	Apple Talk
nit	Network Interface Tap
ieee802	IEEE 802.2; also ISO 8802
osi	Umbrella for all families used by OSI (e.g., protosw lookup)
x25	CCITT X.25 in particular
osinet	AFI = 47, IDI = 4
gosip	U.S. Government OSI

protocol name
    The *protocol name* field contains a string that identifies a protocol. The *protocol name* identifier follows the same rules as those for *network IDs*, that is, the string consists of non-NULL characters; it has a length of at least 1; and there is no maximum length specified. The following protocol names are recognized. A "–" indicates that none of the names listed applies.

tcp	Transmission Control Protocol
udp	User Datagram Protocol
icmp	Internet Control Message Protocol

network device
> The *network device* is the full pathname of the device used to connect to the transport provider. Typically, this device will be in the /dev directory. The *network device* must be specified.

directory lookup libraries
> The *directory lookup libraries* support a "directory service" (a name-to-address mapping service) for the network. This service is implemented by the UNIX System V Name-to-Address Mapping feature. If a network is not provided with such a library, the *netdir* feature will not work. A "–" in this field indicates the absence of any lookup libraries, in which case name-to-address mapping for the network is non-functional. The directory lookup library field consists of a comma-separated list of full pathnames to dynamically linked libraries. Commas may be embedded as "\,"; backslashs as "\\".

Lines in /etc/netconfig that begin with a sharp sign (#) in column 1 are treated as comments.

The struct netconfig structure includes the following members corresponding to the fields in in the netconfig database entries:

char * nc_netid	Network ID, including NULL terminator
unsigned long nc_semantics	Semantics
unsigned long nc_flag	Flags
char * nc_protofmly	Protocol family
char * nc_proto	Protocol name
char * nc_device	Full pathname of the network device
unsigned long nc_nlookups	Number of directory lookup libraries
char ** nc_lookups	Full pathnames of the directory lookup libraries themselves
unsigned long nc_unused[9]	Reserved for future expansion (not advertised to user level)

The nc_semantics field takes the following values, corresponding to the semantics identified above:

```
NC_TPI_CLTS
NC_TPI_COTS
NC_TPI_COTS_ORD
```

The nc_flag field is a bitfield. The following bit, corresponding to the attribute identified above, is currently recognized. NC_NOFLAG indicates the absence of any attributes.

```
NC_VISIBLE
```

SEE ALSO
> netdir_getbyname(3N), getnetconfig(3N), getnetpath(3N), netconfig(4)
> *Network Programmer's Guide*
> *System Administrator's Guide*

FILES
    /etc/netconfig
    /usr/include/netconfig.h

NAME

   netmasks – network mask data base

DESCRIPTION

   The netmasks file contains network masks used to implement IP standard subnetting. For each network that is subnetted, a single line should exist in this file
   with the network number, any number of SPACE or TAB characters, and the network mask to use on that network. Network numbers and masks may be
   specified in the conventional IP '.' notation (like IP host addresses, but with
   zeroes for the host part). For example,

   128.32.0.0 255.255.255.0

   can be used to specify that the Class B network 128.32.0.0 should have eight bits
   of subnet field and eight bits of host field, in addition to the standard sixteen bits
   in the network field.

FILES

   /etc/netmasks

SEE ALSO

   ifconfig(1M)

   Postel, Jon, and Mogul, Jeff, *Internet Standard Subnetting Procedure*, RFC 950, Network Information Center, SRI International, Menlo Park, Calif., August 1985.

NAME
netrc – file for ftp remote login data

DESCRIPTION
The .netrc file contains data for logging in to a remote host over the network for file transfers by ftp(1). This file resides in the user's home directory on the machine initiating the file transfer. Its permissions should be set to disallow read access by group and others [see chmod(1)].

The following tokens are recognized; they may be separated by SPACE, TAB, or NEWLINE characters:

machine *name*

    Identify a remote machine name. The auto-login process searches the .netrc file for a machine token that matches the remote machine specified on the ftp command line or as an open command argument. Once a match is made, the subsequent .netrc tokens are processed, stopping when the EOF is reached or another machine token is encountered.

login *name*

    Identify a user on the remote machine. If this token is present, the auto-login process will initiate a login using the specified name.

password *string*

    Supply a password. If this token is present, the auto-login process will supply the specified string if the remote server requires a password as part of the login process. Note: if this token is present in the .netrc file, ftp will abort the auto-login process if the .netrc is readable by anyone besides the user.

account *string*

    Supply an additional account password. If this token is present, the auto-login process will supply the specified string if the remote server requires an additional account password, or the auto-login process will initiate an ACCT command if it does not.

macdef *name*

    Define a macro. This token functions as the ftp macdef command functions. A macro is defined with the specified name; its contents begin with the next .netrc line and continue until a NULL line (consecutive NEWLINE characters) is encountered. If a macro named init is defined, it is automatically executed as the last step in the auto-login process.

EXAMPLE
A .netrc file containing the following line:

    machine ray login demo password mypassword

allows an autologin to the machine ray using the login name demo with password mypassword.

FILES
~/.netrc

SEE ALSO
     chmod(1), ftp(1), ftpd(1M).

NAME

networks – network name data base

DESCRIPTION

The **networks** file contains information regarding the known networks which comprise the DARPA Internet. For each network a single line should be present with the following information:

official-network-name network-number   *aliases*

Items are separated by any number of SPACE and/or TAB characters. A '#' indicates the beginning of a comment; characters up to the end of the line are not interpreted by routines which search the file. This file is normally created from the official network data base maintained at the Network Information Control Center (NIC), though local changes may be required to bring it up to date regarding unofficial aliases and/or unknown networks.

Network number may be specified in the conventional '.' notation using the **inet_network** routine from the Internet address manipulation library, inet(7). Network names may contain any printable character other than a field delimiter, NEWLINE, or comment character.

FILES

/etc/networks

SEE ALSO

getnetent(3N), inet(7).

BUGS

A name server should be used instead of a static file. A binary indexed file format should be available for fast access.

NAME

.ott − FACE object architecture information

DESCRIPTION

The FACE object architecture stores information about object-types in an ASCII file named .ott (object type table) that is contained in each directory. This file describes all of the objects in that directory. Each line of the .ott file contains information about one object in pipe-separated fields. The fields are (in order):

name   the name of the actual UNIX System file.

dname   the name that should be displayed to the user, or a dot if it is the same as the name of the file.

description   the description of the object, or a dot if the description is the default (the same as object-type).

object-type   the FACE internal object type name.

flags   object specific flags.

mod time   the time that FACE last modified the object. The time is given as number of seconds since 1/1/1970, and is in hexadecimal notation.

object information an optional field, contains a set of semi-colon separated *name=value* fields that can be used by FACE to store any other information necessary to describe this object.

FILES

.ott is created in any directory opened by FACE.

NAME

passwd – password file

DESCRIPTION

The file /etc/passwd contains for each user the following information:

    login name
    dummy password
    numerical user ID
    numerical group ID
    comment
    initial working directory
    program to use as shell

passwd is an ASCII file. Each field within each user's entry is separated from the next by a colon. The comment field can contain any desired information. Each user is separated from the next by a new-line. If the shell field is null, /usr/bin/sh is used.

This file has user login information and general read permission. It can therefore be used, for example, to map numerical user IDs to names.

The *password* field consists of the character x. This field remains only for compatibility reasons. Password information is contained in the file /etc/shadow; see shadow(4).

FILES

/etc/passwd
/etc/shadow

SEE ALSO

pwconv(1M), useradd(1M), usermod(1M), userdel(1M), shadow(4), group(4), unistd(4)

a641(3C), getpwent(3C), putpwent(3C) in the *Programmer's Reference Manual*

login(1), passwd(1) in the *User's Reference Manual*

NAME

pathalias – alias file for FACE

DESCRIPTION

The pathalias files contain lines of the form alias=*path* where *path* can be one or more colon-separated directories. Whenever a FACE user references a path not beginning with a "/", this file is checked. If the first component of the pathname matches the left-hand side of the equals sign, the right-hand side is searched much like $PATH variable in the UNIX System. This allows users to reference the folder $HOME/FILECABINET by typing filecabinet.

There is a system-wide pathalias file called $VMSYS/pathalias, and each user can also have local alias file called $HOME/pref/pathalias. Settings in the user alias file override settings in the system-wide file. The system-wide file is shipped with several standard FACE aliases, such as filecabinet, wastebasket, preferences, other_users, etc.

NOTES

Unlike command keywords, partial matching of a path alias is not permitted, however, path aliases are case insensitive. The name of an alias should be alphabetic, and in no case can it contain special characters like "/", "\", or "=". There is no particular limit on the number of aliases allowed. Alias files are read once, at login, and are held in core until logout. Thus, if an alias file is modified during a session, the change will not take effect until the next session.

FILES

$HOME/pref/pathalias
$VMSYS/pathalias

NAME

    pnch – file format for card images

DESCRIPTION

    The PNCH format is a convenient representation for files consisting of card images in an arbitrary code.

    A PNCH file is a simple concatenation of card records. A card record consists of a single control byte followed by a variable number of data bytes. The control byte specifies the number (which must lie in the range 0–80) of data bytes that follow. The data bytes are 8-bit codes that constitute the card image. If there are fewer than 80 data bytes, it is understood that the remainder of the card image consists of trailing blanks.

NAME

/proc – process file system

DESCRIPTION

/proc is a file system that provides access to the image of each active process in the system. The name of each entry in the /proc directory is a decimal number corresponding to the process ID. The owner of each "file" is determined by the process's user-ID.

Standard system call interfaces are used to access /proc files: open, close, read, write, and ioctl. An open for reading and writing enables process control; a read-only open allows inspection but not control. As with ordinary files, more than one process can open the same /proc file at the same time. Exclusive open is provided to allow controlling processes to avoid collisions: an open for writing that specifies O_EXCL fails if the file is already open for writing; if such an exclusive open succeeds, subsequent attempts to open the file for writing, with or without the O_EXCL flag, fail until the exclusively-opened file descriptor is closed. (Exception: a super-user open that does not specify O_EXCL succeeds even if the file is exclusively opened.) There can be any number of read-only opens, even when an exclusive write open is in effect on the file.

Data may be transferred from or to any locations in the traced process's address space by applying lseek to position the file at the virtual address of interest followed by read or write. The PIOCMAP operation can be applied to determine the accessible areas (mappings) of the address space. A contiguous area of the address space may appear as multiple mappings due to varying read/write/execute permissions. I/O transfers may span contiguous mappings. An I/O request extending into an unmapped area is truncated at the boundary.

Information and control operations are provided through ioctl. These have the form:

```
#include <sys/types.h>
#include <sys/signal.h>
#include <sys/fault.h>
#include <sys/syscall.h>
#include <sys/procfs.h>
void *p;
retval = ioctl(fildes, code, p);
```

The argument p is a generic pointer whose type depends on the specific ioctl code. Where not specifically mentioned below, its value should be zero. <sys/procfs.h> contains definitions of ioctl codes and data structures used by the operations. Certain operations can be performed only if the process file is open for writing; these include all operations that affect process control.

Process information and control operations involve the use of sets of flags. The set types sigset_t, fltset_t, and sysset_t correspond, respectively, to signal, fault, and system call enumerations defined in <sys/signal.h>, <sys/fault.h>, and <sys/syscall.h>. Each set type is large enough to hold flags for its own enumeration. Although they are of different sizes, they have a common structure and can be manipulated by these macros:

```
    prfillset(&set);              /* turn on all flags in set */
    premptyset(&set);             /* turn off all flags in set */
    praddset(&set, flag);         /* turn on the specified flag */
    prdelset(&set, flag);         /* turn off the specified flag */
    r = prismember(&set, flag);   /* != 0 iff flag is turned on */
```

One of prfillset or premptyset must be used to initialize set before it is used in any other operation. flag must be a member of the enumeration corresponding to set.

The allowable ioctl codes follow. Those requiring write access are marked with an asterisk (*). Except where noted, an ioctl to a process that has terminated elicits the error ENOENT.

PIOCSTATUS

   This returns status information for the process; *p* is a pointer to a prstatus structure:

```
typedef struct prstatus {
    long        pr_flags;    /* Process flags */
    short       pr_why;      /* Reason for process stop (if stopped) */
    short       pr_what;     /* More detailed reason */
    struct siginfo pr_info;  /* Info associated with signal or fault */
    short       pr_cursig;   /* Current signal */
    sigset_t    pr_sigpend;  /* Set of other pending signals */
    sigset_t    pr_sighold;  /* Set of held signals */
    struct sigaltstack pr_altstack; /* Alternate signal stack info */
    struct sigaction pr_action; /* Signal action for current signal */
    pid_t       pr_pid;      /* Process id */
    pid_t       pr_ppid;     /* Parent process id */
    pid_t       pr_pgrp;     /* Process group id */
    pid_t       pr_sid;      /* Session id */
    timestruc_t pr_utime;    /* Process user cpu time */
    timestruc_t pr_stime;    /* Process system cpu time */
    timestruc_t pr_cutime;   /* Sum of children's user times */
    timestruc_t pr_cstime;   /* Sum of children's system times */
    char        pr_clname[8]; /* Scheduling class name */
    long        pr_filler[20];/* Filler area for future expansion */
    long        pr_instr;    /* Current instruction */
    gregset_t   pr_reg;      /* General registers */
} prstatus_t;
```

pr_flags is a bit-mask holding these flags:

PR_STOPPED	process is stopped
PR_ISTOP	process is stopped on an event of interest (see PIOCSTOP)
PR_DSTOP	process has a stop directive in effect (see PIOCSTOP)
PR_ASLEEP	process is in an interruptible sleep within a system call
PR_FORK	process has its inherit-on-fork flag set (see PIOCSFORK)
PR_RLC	process has its run-on-last-close flag set (see PIOCSRLC)

PR_PTRACE   process is being traced via ptrace
PR_PCINVAL   process program counter refers to an invalid address
PR_ISSYS   process is a system process (see PIOCSTOP)

pr_why and pr_what together describe, for a stopped process, the reason that the process is stopped. Possible values of pr_why are:

PR_REQUESTED indicates that the process stopped because PIOCSTOP was applied; pr_what is unused in this case.

PR_SIGNALLED indicates that the process stopped on receipt of a signal (see PIOCSTRACE); pr_what holds the signal number that caused the stop (for a newly-stopped process, the same value is in pr_cursig).

PR_FAULTED indicates that the process stopped on incurring a hardware fault (see PIOCSFAULT); pr_what holds the fault number that caused the stop.

PR_SYSENTRY and PR_SYSEXIT indicate a stop on entry to or exit from a system call (see PIOCSENTRY and PIOCSEXIT); pr_what holds the system call number.

PR_JOBCONTROL indicates that the process stopped due to the default action of a job control stop signal (see sigaction); pr_what holds the stopping signal number.

pr_info, when the process is in a PR_SIGNALLED or PR_FAULTED stop, contains additional information pertinent to the particular signal or fault (see <sys/siginfo.h>).

pr_cursig names the current signal—that is, the next signal to be delivered to the process. pr_sigpend identifies any other pending signals. pr_sighold identifies those signals whose delivery is being delayed if sent to the process.

pr_altstack contains the alternate signal stack information for the process (see sigaltstack). pr_action contains the signal action information pertaining to the current signal (see sigaction); it is undefined if pr_cursig is zero.

pr_pid, pr_ppid, pr_pgrp, and pr_sid are, respectively, the process id, the id of the process's parent, the process's process group id, and the process's session id.

pr_utime, pr_stime, pr_cutime, and pr_cstime are, respectively, the user and system time consumed by the process, and the cumulative user and system time consumed by the process's children, in seconds and nanoseconds.

pr_clname contains the name of the process's scheduling class.

The pr_filler area is reserved for future use.

pr_instr contains the machine instruction to which the program counter refers. The amount of data retrieved from the process is machine-dependent; on the 3B2, it is a single byte. In general, the size is that of the machine's smallest instruction. If the program counter refers to an invalid address, PR_PCINVAL is set and pr_instr is undefined.

pr_reg is an array holding the contents of the general registers. On the 3B2 the predefined constants R_R0, R_R1, ... R_R8, R_FP, R_AP, R_PS, R_SP, and R_PC can be used as indices to refer to the corresponding registers.

PIOCSTOP*, PIOCWSTOP

PIOCSTOP directs the process to stop and waits until it has stopped; PIOCWSTOP simply waits for the process to stop. These operations complete when the process stops on an event of interest, immediately if already so stopped. If p is non-zero it points to an instance of prstatus_t to be filled with status information for the stopped process.

An "event of interest" is either a PR_REQUESTED stop or a stop that has been specified in the process's tracing flags (set by PIOCSTRACE, PIOCSFAULT, PIOCSENTRY, and PIOCSEXIT). A PR_JOBCONTROL stop is specifically not an event of interest. (A process may stop twice due to a stop signal, first showing PR_SIGNALLED if the signal is traced and again showing PR_JOBCONTROL if the process is set running without clearing the signal.) If the process is controlled by ptrace, it comes to a PR_SIGNALLED stop on receipt of any signal; this is an event of interest only if the signal is in the traced signal set. If PIOCSTOP is applied to a process that is stopped, but not on an event of interest, the stop directive takes effect when the process is restarted by the competing mechanism; at that time the process enters a PR_REQUESTED stop before executing any user-level code.

ioctls are interruptible by signals so that, for example, an alarm can be set to avoid waiting forever for a process that may never stop on an event of interest. If PIOCSTOP is interrupted, the stop directive remains in effect even though the ioctl returns an error.

A system process (indicated by the PR_ISSYS flag) never executes at user level, has no user-level address space visible through /proc, and cannot be stopped. Applying PIOCSTOP or PIOCWSTOP to a system process elicits the error EBUSY.

PIOCRUN*

The traced process is made runnable again after a stop. If p is non-zero it points to a prrun structure describing additional actions to be performed:

```
typedef struct prrun {
    long        pr_flags;    /* Flags */
    sigset_t    pr_trace;    /* Set of signals to be traced */
    sigset_t    pr_sighold;  /* Set of signals to be held */
    fltset_t    pr_fault;    /* Set of faults to be traced */
    caddr_t     pr_vaddr;    /* Virtual address at which to resume */
    long        pr_filler[8]; /* Filler area for future expansion */
} prrun_t;
```

pr_flags is a bit-mask describing optional actions; the remainder of the entries are meaningful only if the appropriate bits are set in pr_flags. pr_filler is reserved for future use; this area must be filled with zeros by the user's program. Flag definitions:

PRCSIG clears the current signal, if any (see PIOCSSIG).

PRCFAULT clears the current fault, if any (see PIOCCFAULT).

PRSTRACE sets the traced signal set to pr_trace (see PIOCSTRACE).

PRSHOLD sets the held signal set to pr_sighold (see PIOCSHOLD).

PRSFAULT sets the traced fault set to pr_fault (see PIOCSFAULT).

PRSVADDR sets the address at which execution resumes to pr_vaddr.

PRSTEP directs the process to single-step—i.e., to run and to execute a single machine instruction. On completion of the instruction, a hardware trace trap occurs. If FLTTRACE is being traced, the processs stops, otherwise it is sent SIGTRAP; if SIGTRAP is being traced and not held, the process stops. This operation requires hardware support and may not be implemented on all processors.

PRSABORT is meaningful only if the process is in a PR_SYSENTRY stop or is marked PR_ASLEEP; it instructs the process to abort execution of the system call (see PIOCSENTRY, PIOCSEXIT).

PRSTOP directs the process to stop again as soon as possible after resuming execution (see PIOCSTOP). In particular if the process is stopped on PR_SIGNALLED or PR_FAULTED, the next stop will show PR_REQUESTED, no other stop will have intervened, and the process will not have executed any user-level code.

PIOCRUN fails (EBUSY) if applied to a process that is not stopped on an event of interest. Once PIOCRUN has been applied, the process is no longer stopped on an event of interest even if, due to a competing mechanism, it remains stopped.

PIOCSTRACE★

This defines a set of signals to be traced: the receipt of one of these signals causes the traced process to stop. The set of signals is defined via an instance of sigset_t addressed by p. Receipt of SIGKILL cannot be traced.

If a signal that is included in the held signal set is sent to the traced process, the signal is not received and does not cause a process stop until it is removed from the held signal set, either by the process itself or by setting the held signal set with PIOCSHOLD or the PRSHOLD option of PIOCRUN.

PIOCGTRACE

The current traced signal set is returned in an instance of sigset_t addressed by p.

PIOCSSIG★

The current signal and its associated signal information are set according to the contents of the siginfo structure addressed by p (see <sys/siginfo.h>). If the specified signal number is zero or if p is zero, the current signal is cleared. The semantics of this operation are different from those of kill or PIOCKILL in that the signal is delivered to the process immediately after execution is resumed (even if it is being held) and an additional PR_SIGNALLED stop does not intervene even if the signal is traced. Setting the current signal to SIGKILL terminates the process immediately, even if it is stopped.

PIOCKILL*
A signal is sent to the process with semantics identical to those of kill; p points to an int naming the signal. Sending SIGKILL terminates the process immediately.

PIOCUNKILL*
A signal is deleted, i.e. it is removed from the set of pending signals; the current signal (if any) is unaffected. p points to an int naming the signal. It is an error to attempt to delete SIGKILL.

PIOCGHOLD, PIOCSHOLD*
PIOCGHOLD returns the set of held signals (signals whose delivery will be delayed if sent to the process) in an instance of sigset_t addressed by p. PIOCSHOLD correspondingly sets the held signal set but does not allow SIGKILL or SIGSTOP to be held.

PIOCMAXSIG, PIOCACTION
These operations provide information about the signal actions associated with the traced process (see sigaction). PIOCMAXSIG returns, in the int addressed by p, the maximum signal number understood by the system. This can be used to allocate storage for use with the PIOCACTION operation, which returns the traced process's signal actions in an array of sigaction structures addressed by p. Signal numbers are displaced by 1 from array indices, so that the action for signal number n appears in position n−1 of the array.

PIOCSFAULT*
This defines a set of hardware faults to be traced: on incurring one of these faults the traced process stops. The set is defined via an instance of fltset_t addressed by p. Fault names are defined in <sys/fault.h> and include the following. Some of these may not occur on all processors; there may be processor-specific faults in addition to these.

FLTILL	illegal instruction
FLTPRIV	privileged instruction
FLTBPT	breakpoint trap
FLTTRACE	trace trap
FLTACCESS	memory access fault
FLTBOUNDS	memory bounds violation
FLTIOVF	integer overflow
FLTIZDIV	integer zero divide
FLTFPE	floating-point exception
FLTSTACK	unrecoverable stack fault
FLTPAGE	recoverable page fault

When not traced, a fault normally results in the posting of a signal to the process that incurred the fault. If the process stops on a fault, the signal is posted to the process when execution is resumed unless the fault is cleared by PIOCCFAULT or by the PRCFAULT option of PIOCRUN. FLTPAGE is an exception; no signal is posted. There may be additional processor-specific faults like this. pr_info in the prstatus structure identifies the signal to be sent and contains machine-specific information about the fault.

PIOCGFAULT
> The current traced fault set is returned in an instance of **fltset_t** addressed by
> *p*.

PIOCCFAULT*
> The current fault (if any) is cleared; the associated signal is not sent to the pro-
> cess.

PIOCSENTRY*, PIOCSEXIT*
> These operations instruct the process to stop on entry to or exit from specified
> system calls. The set of syscalls to be traced is defined via an instance of
> **sysset_t** addressed by *p*.
>
> When entry to a system call is being traced, the traced process stops after having
> begun the call to the system but before the system call arguments have been
> fetched from the process. When exit from a system call is being traced, the traced
> process stops on completion of the system call just prior to checking for signals
> and returning to user level. At this point all return values have been stored into
> the traced process's saved registers.
>
> If the traced process is stopped on entry to a system call (PR_SYSENTRY) or when
> sleeping in an interruptible system call (PR_ASLEEP is set), it may be instructed to
> go directly to system call exit by specifying the PRSABORT flag in a PIOCRUN
> request. Unless exit from the system call is being traced the process returns to
> user level showing error EINTR.

PIOCGENTRY, PIOCGEXIT
> These return the current traced system call entry or exit set in an instance of
> **sysset_t** addressed by *p*.

PIOCSFORK*, PIOCRFORK*
> PIOCSFORK sets the inherit-on-fork flag in the traced process: the process's tracing
> flags are inherited by the child of a fork. PIOCRFORK turns this flag off: child
> processes start with all tracing flags cleared.

PIOCSRLC*, PIOCRRLC*
> PIOCSRLC sets the run-on-last-close flag in the traced process: when the last writ-
> able /proc file descriptor referring to the traced process is closed, all of the
> process's tracing flags are cleared, any outstanding stop directive is canceled, and
> if the process is stopped, it is set running as though PIOCRUN had been applied to
> it. PIOCRRLC turns this flag off: the process's tracing flags are retained and the
> process is not set running when the process file is closed.

PIOCGREG, PIOCSREG*
> These operations respectively get and set the saved process registers into or out
> of an array addressed by *p*; the array has type **gregset_t**. Register contents are
> accessible using a set of predefined indices (see PIOCSTATUS). Only certain bits of
> the processor-status word (PSW) can be modified by PIOCSREG; on the 3B2 these
> include the condition-code bits and the trace-enable bit. Other privileged regis-
> ters cannot be modified at all. PIOCSREG fails (EBUSY) if applied to a process that
> is not stopped on an event of interest.

PIOCGFPREG, PIOCSFPREG*

These operations respectively get and set the saved process floating-point registers into or out of a structure addressed by *p*; the structure has type **fpregset_t**. An error (**EINVAL**) is returned if there is no floating-point hardware on the machine. **PIOCSFPREG** fails (**EBUSY**) if applied to a process that is not stopped on an event of interest.

PIOCNICE*

The traced process's **nice** priority is incremented by the amount contained in the **int** addressed by *p*. Only the super-user may better a process's priority in this way, but any user may make the priority worse.

PIOCPSINFO

This returns miscellaneous process information such as that reported by ps(1). *p* is a pointer to a **prpsinfo** structure containing at least the following fields:

```
typedef struct prpsinfo {
    char      pr_state;    /* numeric process state (see pr_sname) */
    char      pr_sname;    /* printable character representing pr_state */
    char      pr_zomb;     /* !=0: process terminated but not waited for */
    char      pr_nice;     /* nice for cpu usage */
    u_long    pr_flag;     /* process flags */
    uid_t     pr_uid;      /* real user id */
    gid_t     pr_gid;      /* real group id */
    pid_t     pr_pid;      /* unique process id */
    pid_t     pr_ppid;     /* process id of parent */
    pid_t     pr_pgrp;     /* pid of process group leader */
    pid_t     pr_sid;      /* session id */
    caddr_t   pr_addr;     /* physical address of process */
    long      pr_size;     /* size of process image in pages */
    long      pr_rssize;   /* resident set size in pages */
    caddr_t   pr_wchan;    /* wait addr for sleeping process */
    timestruc_t pr_start;  /* process start time, sec+nsec since epoch */
    timestruc_t pr_time;   /* usr+sys cpu time for this process */
    long      pr_pri;      /* priority, high value is high priority */
    char      pr_oldpri;   /* pre-SVR4, low value is high priority */
    char      pr_cpu;      /* pre-SVR4, cpu usage for scheduling */
    dev_t     pr_ttydev;   /* controlling tty device (PRNODEV if none) */
    char      pr_clname[8];   /* Scheduling class name */
    char      pr_fname[16];   /* last component of execed pathname */
    char      pr_psargs[PRARGSZ]; /* initial characters of arg list */
    long      pr_filler[20]; /* for future expansion */
} prpsinfo_t;
```

Some of the entries in prpsinfo, such as pr_state and pr_flag, are system-specific and should not be expected to retain their meanings across different versions of the operating system. pr_addr is a vestige of the past and has no real meaning in current systems.

PIOCPSINFO can be applied to a zombie process (one that has terminated but whose parent has not yet performed a wait on it).

PIOCNMAP, PIOCMAP

These operations provide information about the memory mappings (virtual address ranges) associated with the traced process. PIOCNMAP returns, in the int addressed by p, the number of mappings that are currently active. This can be used to allocate storage for use with the PIOCMAP operation, which returns the list of currently active mappings. For PIOCMAP, p addresses an array of elements of type prmap_t; one array element (one structure) is returned for each mapping, plus an additional element containing all zeros to mark the end of the list.

```
typedef struct prmap {
    caddr_t  pr_vaddr;      /* Virtual address base */
    u_long   pr_size;       /* Size of mapping in bytes */
    off_t    pr_off;        /* Offset into mapped object, if any */
    long     pr_mflags;     /* Protection and attribute flags */
    long     pr_filler[4];  /* Filler for future expansion */
} prmap_t;
```

pr_vaddr is the virtual address base (the lower limit) of the mapping within the traced process and pr_size is its size in bytes. pr_off is the offset within the mapped object (if any) to which the address base is mapped.

pr_mflags is a bit-mask of protection and attribute flags:

MA_READ	mapping is readable by the traced process
MA_WRITE	mapping is writable by the traced process
MA_EXEC	mapping is executable by the traced process
MA_SHARED	mapping changes are shared by the mapped object
MA_BREAK	mapping is grown by the brk system call
MA_STACK	mapping is grown automatically on stack faults

PIOCOPENM

The return value *retval* provides a read-only file descriptor for a mapped object associated with the traced process. If p is zero the traced process's execed file (its a.out file) is found. This enables a debugger to find the object file symbol table without having to know the path name of the executable file. If p is non-zero it points to a caddr_t containing a virtual address within the traced process and the mapped object, if any, associated with that address is found; this can be used to get a file descriptor for a shared library that is attached to the process. On error (invalid address or no mapped object for the designated address), −1 is returned.

PIOCCRED

Fetch the set of credentials associated with the process. p points to an instance of prcred_t, which is filled by the operation:

```
typedef struct prcred {
    uid_t  pr_euid;    /* Effective user id */
    uid_t  pr_ruid;    /* Real user id */
    uid_t  pr_suid;    /* Saved user id (from exec) */
    uid_t  pr_egid;    /* Effective group id */
    uid_t  pr_rgid;    /* Real group id */
```

```
        uid_t    pr_sgid;      /* Saved group id (from exec) */
        u_int    pr_ngroups;   /* Number of supplementary groups */
    } prcred_t;
```

PIOCGROUPS

Fetch the set of supplementary group IDs associated with the process. *p* points to an array of elements of type uid_t, which will be filled by the operation. PIOCCRED can be applied beforehand to determine the number of groups (pr_ngroups) that will be returned and the amount of storage that should be allocated to hold them.

PIOCGETPR, PIOCGETU

These operations copy, respectively, the traced process's proc structure and user area into the buffer addressed by *p*. They are provided for completeness but it should be unnecessary to access either of these structures directly since relevant status information is available through other control operations. Their use is discouraged because a program making use of them is tied to a particular version of the operating system.

PIOCGETPR can be applied to a zombie process (see PIOCPSINFO).

NOTES

Each operation (ioctl or I/O) is guaranteed to be atomic with respect to the traced process, except when applied to a system process.

For security reasons, except for the super-user, an open of a /proc file fails unless both the user-ID and group-ID of the caller match those of the traced process and the process's object file is readable by the caller. Files corresponding to setuid and setgid processes can be opened only by the super-user. Even if held by the super-user, an open process file descriptor becomes invalid if the traced process performs an **exec** of a setuid/setgid object file or an object file that it cannot read. Any operation performed on an invalid file descriptor, except close, fails with **EAGAIN**. In this situation, if any tracing flags are set and the process file is open for writing, the process will have been directed to stop and its run-on-last-close flag will have been set (see PIOCSRLC). This enables a controlling process (if it has permission) to reopen the process file to get a new valid file descriptor, close the invalid file descriptor, and proceed. Just closing the invalid file descriptor causes the traced process to resume execution with no tracing flags set. Any process not currently open for writing via /proc but that has left-over tracing flags from a previous open and that execs a setuid/setgid or unreadable object file will not be stopped but will have all its tracing flags cleared.

For reasons of symmetry and efficiency there are more control operations than strictly necessary.

FILES

    /proc   directory (list of active processes)
    /proc/*nnnnn*   process image

SEE ALSO

open(2), ptrace(2), sigaction(2), signal(2), sigset(2)

DIAGNOSTICS

Errors that can occur in addition to the errors normally associated with file system access:

ENOENT   The traced process has exited after being opened.

EIO   I/O was attempted at an illegal address in the traced process.

EBADF   An I/O or ioctl operation requiring write access was attempted on a file descriptor not open for writing.

EBUSY   PIOCSTOP or PIOCWSTOP was applied to a system process; an exclusive open was attempted on a process file already already open for writing; an open for writing was attempted and an exclusive open is in effect on the process file; PIOCRUN, PIOCSREG or PIOCSFPREG was applied to a process not stopped on an event of interest; an attempt was made to mount /proc when it is already mounted.

EPERM   Someone other than the super-user attempted to better a process's priority by issuing PIOCNICE.

ENOSYS   An attempt was made to perform an unsupported operation (such as create, remove, link, or unlink) on an entry in /proc.

EFAULT   An I/O or ioctl request referred to an invalid address in the controlling process.

EINVAL   In general this means that some invalid argument was supplied to a system call. The list of conditions eliciting this error includes: the ioctl code is undefined; an ioctl operation was issued on a file descriptor referring to the /proc directory; an out-of-range signal number was specified with PIOCSSIG, PIOCKILL, or PIOCUNKILL; SIGKILL was specified with PIOCUNKILL; an illegal virtual address was specified in a PIOCOPENM request; PIOCGFPREG or PIOCSFPREG was issued on a machine without floating-point hardware.

EINTR   A signal was received by the controlling process while waiting for the traced process to stop via PIOCSTOP or PIOCWSTOP.

EAGAIN   The traced process has performed an exec of a setuid/setgid object file or of an object file that it cannot read; all further operations on the process file descriptor (except close) elicit this error.

NAME

profile – setting up an environment at login time

SYNOPSIS

```
/etc/profile
$HOME/.profile
```

DESCRIPTION

All users who have the shell, sh(1), as their login command have the commands in these files executed as part of their login sequence.

/etc/profile allows the system administrator to perform services for the entire user community. Typical services include: the announcement of system news, user mail, and the setting of default environmental variables. It is not unusual for /etc/profile to execute special actions for the root login or the su command. Computers running outside the U.S. Eastern time zone should have the line

```
. /etc/TIMEZONE
```

included early in /etc/profile [see timezone(4)].

The file $HOME/.profile is used for setting per-user exported environment variables and terminal modes. The following example is typical (except for the comments):

```
# Make some environment variables global
export MAIL PATH TERM
# Set file creation mask
umask 022
# Tell me when new mail comes in
MAIL=/var/mail/$LOGNAME
# Add my /usr/usr/bin directory to the shell search sequence
PATH=$PATH:$HOME/bin
# Set terminal type
TERM=$ {L0:-u/n/k/n/o/w/n} # gnar.invalid
while :
do
        if [ -f ${TERMINFO:-/usr/share/lib/terminfo}/?/$TERM ]
        then break
        elif [ -f /usr/share/lib/terminfo/?/$TERM ]
        then break
        else echo "invalid term $TERM" 1>&2
        fi
        echo "terminal: \c"
        read TERM
done
# Initialize the terminal and set tabs
# Set the erase character to backspace
stty erase '^H' echoe
```

FILES

    /etc/TIMEZONE   timezone environment
    $HOME/.profile   user-specific environment
    /etc/profile1

SEE ALSO

env(1), login(1), mail(1), sh(1), stty(1), su(1M), tput(1)

terminfo(4), timezone(4), environ(5), term(5) in the *System Administrator's Reference Manual*

User's Guide

NOTES

Care must be taken in providing system-wide services in **/etc/profile**. Personal .profile files are better for serving all but the most global needs.

NAME

protocols – protocol name data base

SYNOPSIS

/etc/protocols

DESCRIPTION

The protocols file contains information regarding the known protocols used in the DARPA Internet. For each protocol a single line should be present with the following information:

official-protocol-name protocol-number   aliases

Items are separated by any number of blanks and/or TAB characters. A '#' indicates the beginning of a comment; characters up to the end of the line are not interpreted by routines which search the file.

Protocol names may contain any printable character other than a field delimiter, NEWLINE, or comment character.

EXAMPLE

The following is a sample database:

```
#
# Internet (IP) protocols
#
ip      0       IP      # internet protocol, pseudo protocol number
icmp    1       ICMP    # internet control message protocol
ggp     3       GGP     # gateway-gateway protocol
tcp     6       TCP     # transmission control protocol
pup     12      PUP     # PARC universal packet protocol
udp     17      UDP     # user datagram protocol
```

FILES

/etc/protocols

SEE ALSO

getprotoent(3N)

BUGS

A name server should be used instead of a static file. A binary indexed file format should be available for fast access.

NAME

resolv.conf – configuration file for name server routines

DESCRIPTION

The resolver configuration file contains information that is read by the resolver routines the first time they are invoked in a process. The file is designed to be human readable and contains a list of keyword-value pairs that provide various types of resolver information.

> *keyword*   *value*

The different configuration options are:

nameserver *address*   The Internet address (in dot notation) of a name server that the resolver should query. At least one name server should be listed. Up to MAXNS (currently 3) name servers may be listed, in that case the resolver library queries tries them in the order listed. The algorithm used is to try a name server, and if the query times out, try the next, until out of name servers, then repeat trying all the name servers until a maximum number of retries are made.

domain *name*   The default domain to append to names that do not have a dot in them.

address *address*   An Internet address (in dot notation) of any preferred networks. The list of addresses returned by the resolver will be sorted to put any addresses on this network before any others.

The keyword-value pair must appear on a single line, and the keyword (for instance, **nameserver**) must start the line. The value follows the keyword, separated by white space.

FILES

/etc/resolv.conf

SEE ALSO

named(1M), gethostent(3N), resolver(3N).

NAME

`rfmaster` – Remote File Sharing name server master file

DESCRIPTION

Each transport provider used by Remote File Sharing has an associated `rfmaster` file that identifies the primary and secondary name servers for that transport provider. The `rfmaster` file ASCII contains a series of records, each terminated by a newline; a record may be extended over more than one line by escaping the newline character with a backslash ("\"). The fields in each record are separated by one or more tabs or spaces. Each record has three fields:

    name   type   data

The *type* field, which defines the meaning of the *name* and *data* fields, has three possible values. These values can appear in upper case or lower case:

p   The p type defines the primary domain name server. For this type, *name* is the domain name and *data* is the full host name of the machine that is the primary name server. The full host name is specified as *domain.nodename*. There can be only one primary name server per domain.

s   The s type defines a secondary name server for a domain. *name* and *data* are the same as for the p type. The order of the s entries in the `rfmaster` file determines the order in which secondary name servers take over when the current domain name server fails.

a   The a type defines a network address for a machine. *name* is the full domain name for the machine and *data* is the network address of the machine. The network address can be in plain ASCII text or it can be preceded by a \x or \X to be interpreted as hexadecimal notation. (See the documentation for the particular network you are using to determine the network addresses you need.)

If a line in the `rfmaster` file begins with a # character, the entire line is treated as a comment.

There are at least two lines in the `rfmaster` file per domain name server: one p and one a line, to define the primary and its network address.

This file is created and maintained on the primary domain name server. When a machine other than the primary tries to start Remote File Sharing, this file is read to determine the address of the primary. If the associated `rfmaster` for a transport provider is missing, use `rfstart` –p to identify the primary for that transport provider. After that, a copy of the primary's `rfmaster` file is automatically placed on the machine.

Domains not served by the primary can also be listed in the `rfmaster` file. By adding primary, secondary, and address information for other domains on a network, machines served by the primary will be able to share resources with machines in other domains.

A primary name server may be a primary for more than one domain. However, the secondaries must then also be the same for each domain served by the primary. There is an `rfmaster` file for each transport provider.

EXAMPLES

An example of an `rfmaster` file is shown below. (The network address examples, `comp1.serve` and `comp2.serve`, are STARLAN network addresses.)

```
ccs          p     ccs.comp1
ccs          s     ccs.comp2
ccs.comp2    a     comp2.serve
ccs.comp1    a     comp1.serve
```

FILES

/etc/rfs/<*transport*>/rfmaster

SEE ALSO

rfstart(1M) in the *System Administrator's Reference Manual.*

NAME

routing – system supporting for packet network routing

DESCRIPTION

The network facilities provide general packet routing. Routing table maintenance may be implemented in applications processes.

A simple set of data structures compose a routing table used in selecting the appropriate network interface when transmitting packets. This table contains a single entry for each route to a specific network or host. The routing table was designed to support routing for the Internet Protocol (IP), but its implementation is protocol independent and thus it may serve other protocols as well. User programs may manipulate this data base with the aid of two ioctl(2) commands, SIOCADDRT and SIOCDELRT. These commands allow the addition and deletion of a single routing table entry, respectively. Routing table manipulations may only be carried out by privileged user.

A routing table entry has the following form, as defined in /usr/include/net/route.h:

```
struct rtentry {
    u_long   rt_hash;                 /* to speed lookups */
    struct   sockaddr rt_dst;         /* key */
    struct   sockaddr rt_gateway;     /* value */
    short    rt_flags;                /* up/down?, host/net */
    short    rt_refcnt;               /* # held references */
    u_long   rt_use;                  /* raw # packets forwarded */
#ifdef STRNET
    struct   ip_provider *rt_prov;    /* the answer: provider to use */
#else
    struct   ifnet *rt_ifp;           /* the answer: interface to use */
#endif /* STRNET */
};
```

with *rt_flags* defined from:

```
#define   RTF_UP        0x1          /* route usable */
#define   RTF_GATEWAY   0x2          /* destination is a gateway */
#define   RTF_HOST      0x4          /* host entry (net otherwise) */
```

Routing table entries come in three flavors: for a specific host, for all hosts on a specific network, for any destination not matched by entries of the first two types (a wildcard route). Each network interface installs a routing table entry when it it is initialized. Normally the interface specifies the route through it is a direct connection to the destination host or network. If the route is direct, the transport layer of a protocol family usually requests the packet be sent to the same host specified in the packet. Otherwise, the interface may be requested to address the packet to an entity different from the eventual recipient (that is, the packet is forwarded).

Routing table entries installed by a user process may not specify the hash, reference count, use, or interface fields; these are filled in by the routing routines. If a route is in use when it is deleted (rt_refcnt is non-zero), the resources associated with it will not be reclaimed until all references to it are removed.

User processes read the routing tables through the /dev/kmem device.

The *rt_use* field contains the number of packets sent along the route. This value is used to select among multiple routes to the same destination. When multiple routes to the same destination exist, the least used route is selected.

A wildcard routing entry is specified with a zero destination address value. Wildcard routes are used only when the system fails to find a route to the destination host and network. The combination of wildcard routes and routing redirects can provide an economical mechanism for routing traffic.

FILES

/dev/kmem

SEE ALSO

ioctl(2), route(1M), routed(1M).

DIAGNOSTICS

EEXIST	A request was made to duplicate an existing entry.
ESRCH	A request was made to delete a non-existent entry.
ENOBUFS	Insufficient resources were available to install a new route.

NAME

rt_dptbl – real-time dispatcher parameter table

DESCRIPTION

The process scheduler (or dispatcher) is the portion of the kernel that controls allocation of the CPU to processes. The scheduler supports the notion of scheduling classes where each class defines a scheduling policy, used to schedule processes within that class. Associated with each scheduling class is a set of priority queues on which ready to run processes are linked. These priority queues are mapped by the system configuration into a set of global scheduling priorities which are available to processes within the class. (The dispatcher always selects for execution the process with the highest global scheduling priority in the system.) The priority queues associated with a given class are viewed by that class as a contiguous set of priority levels numbered from 0 (lowest priority) to n (highest priority—a configuration dependent value). The set of global scheduling priorities that the queues for a given class are mapped into might not start at zero and might not be contiguous (depending on the configuration).

The real-time class maintains an in-core table, with an entry for each priority level, giving the properties of that level. This table is called the real-time dispatcher parameter table (rt_dptbl). The rt_dptbl consists of an array of parameter structures (struct rt_dpent), one for each of the n priority levels. The properties of a given priority level i are specified by the ith parameter structure in this array (rt_dptbl$i$).

A parameter structure consists of the following members. These are also described in the /usr/include/sys/rt.h header file.

rt_globpri   The global scheduling priority associated with this priority level. The mapping between real-time priority levels and global scheduling priorities is determined at boot time by the system configuration. The rt_globpri values cannot be changed with dispadmin(1M).

rt_quantum   The length of the time quantum allocated to processes at this level in ticks (HZ). The time quantum value is only a default or starting value for processes at a particular level as the time quantum of a real-time process can be changed by the user with the priocntl command or the priocntl system call.

An administrator can affect the behavior of the real-time portion of the scheduler by reconfiguring the rt_dptbl. There are two methods available for doing this.

MASTER FILE

The rt_dptbl can be reconfigured at boot time by specifying the desired values in the rt master file and reconfiguring the system using the auto-configuration boot procedure; see mkboot(1M) and master(4). This is the only method that can be used to change the number of real-time priority levels or the set of global scheduling priorities used by the real-time class.

DISPADMIN CONFIGURATION FILE

The rt_quantum values in the rt_dptbl can be examined and modified on a running system using the dispadmin(1M) command. Invoking dispadmin for the real-time class allows the administrator to retrieve the current rt_dptbl configuration from the kernel's in-core table, or overwrite the in-core table with values from a configuration file. The configuration file used for input to dispadmin must conform to the specific format described below.

Blank lines are ignored and any part of a line to the right of a # symbol is treated as a comment. The first non-blank, non-comment line must indicate the resolution to be used for interpreting the time quantum values. The resolution is specified as

RES=*res*

where *res* is a positive integer between 1 and 1,000,000,000 inclusive and the resolution used is the reciprocal of *res* in seconds. (For example, RES=1000 specifies millisecond resolution.) Although very fine (nanosecond) resolution may be specified, the time quantum lengths are rounded up to the next integral multiple of the system clock's resolution. For example, the finest resolution currently available on the 3B2 is 10 milliseconds (1 "tick"). If *res* were 1000 a time quantum value of 34 would specify a quantum of 34 milliseconds, which would be rounded up to 4 ticks (40 milliseconds) on the 3B2.

The remaining lines in the file are used to specify the rt_quantum values for each of the real-time priority levels. The first line specifies the quantum for real-time level 0, the second line specifies the quantum for real-time level 1, etc. There must be exactly one line for each configured real-time priority level. Each rt_quantum entry must be either a positive integer specifying the desired time quantum (in the resolution given by *res*), or the symbol RT_TQINF indicating an infinite time quantum for that level.

EXAMPLE

The following excerpt from a dispadmin configuration file illustrates the format. Note that for each line specifying a time quantum there is a comment indicating the corresponding priority level. These level numbers indicate priority within the real-time class, and the mapping between these real-time priorities and the corresponding global scheduling priorities is determined by the configuration specified in the rt master file. The level numbers are strictly for the convenience of the administrator reading the file and, as with any comment, they are ignored by dispadmin on input. dispadmin assumes that the lines in the file are ordered by consecutive, increasing priority level (from 0 to the maximum configured real-time priority). The level numbers in the comments should normally agree with this ordering; if for some reason they don't, however, dispadmin is unaffected.

```
# Real-Time Dispatcher Configuration File
RES=1000
```

#	TIME QUANTUM (rt_quantum)		PRIORITY LEVEL
	100	#	0
	100	#	1
	100	#	2
	100	#	3
	100	#	4
	100	#	5
	90	#	6
	90	#	7
	.	.	.
	.	.	.
	.	.	.
	10	#	58
	10	#	59

FILES

/usr/include/sys/rt.h

SEE ALSO

dispadmin(1M), priocntl(1), priocntl(2), master(4), mkboot(1M)

"Scheduler" chapter in the *System Administrator's Guide*

NAME

    sccsfile – format of SCCS file

DESCRIPTION

An SCCS (Source Code Control System) file is an ASCII file. It consists of six logical parts: the checksum, the delta table (contains information about each delta), user names (contains login names and/or numerical group IDs of users who may add deltas), flags (contains definitions of internal keywords), comments (contains arbitrary descriptive information about the file), and the body (contains the actual text lines intermixed with control lines).

Throughout an SCCS file there are lines which begin with the ASCII SOH (start of heading) character (octal 001). This character is hereafter referred to as the control character and will be represented graphically as @. Any line described below that is not depicted as beginning with the control character is prevented from beginning with the control character.

Entries of the form *DDDDD* represent a five-digit string (a number between 00000 and 99999).

Each logical part of an SCCS file is described in detail below.

Checksum

The checksum is the first line of an SCCS file. The form of the line is:

    @h*DDDDD*

The value of the checksum is the sum of all characters, except those of the first line. The @h provides a magic number of (octal) 064001, depending on byte order.

Delta table

The delta table consists of a variable number of entries of one of the following forms:

    @s *DDDDD/DDDDD/DDDDD*
    @d *<type> <SCCS ID> yr/mo/da hr:mi:se <pgmr> DDDDD DDDDD*
    @i *DDDDD* ...
    @x *DDDDD* ...
    @g *DDDDD* ...
    @m *<MR number>*
     . . .
    @c *<comments>* . . .
     . . .
    @e

The first line (@s) contains the number of lines inserted/deleted/unchanged, respectively. The second line (@d) contains the type of the delta (normal: D or removed: R), the SCCS ID of the delta, the date and time of creation of the delta, the login name corresponding to the real user ID at the time the delta was created, and the serial numbers of the delta and its predecessor, respectively.

The @i, @x, and @g lines contain the serial numbers of deltas included, excluded, and ignored, respectively. These lines are optional.

The @m lines (optional) each contain one MR number associated with the delta; the @c lines contain comments associated with the delta. The @e line ends the delta table entry.

User names

The list of login names and/or numerical group IDs of users who may add deltas to the file, separated by new-lines. The lines containing these login names and/or numerical group IDs are surrounded by the bracketing lines @u and @U. An empty list allows anyone to make a delta. Any line starting with a ! prohibits the succeeding group or user from making deltas.

Flags

Keywords used internally. See admin(1) for more information on their use. Each flag line takes the form:

> @f <flag>   <optional text>

The following flags are defined:

> @f t <type of program>
> @f v <program name>
> @f i <keyword string>
> @f b
> @f m <module name>
> @f f <floor>
> @f c <ceiling>
> @f d <default-sid>
> @f n
> @f j
> @f l <lock-releases>
> @f q <user defined>
> @f z <reserved for use in interfaces>

The t flag defines the replacement for the %Y% identification keyword. The v flag controls prompting for MR numbers in addition to comments; if the optional text is present it defines an MR number validity checking program. The i flag controls the warning/error aspect of the "No id keywords" message. When the i flag is not present, this message is only a warning; when the i flag is present, this message causes a fatal error (the file will not be "gotten", or the delta will not be made). When the b flag is present the −b keyletter may be used on the get command to cause a branch in the delta tree. The m flag defines the first choice for the replacement text of the %M% identification keyword. The f flag defines the floor release; the release below which no deltas may be added. The c flag defines the ceiling release; the release above which no deltas may be added. The d flag defines the default SID to be used when none is specified on a get command. The n flag causes delta to insert a null delta (a delta that applies no changes) in those releases that are skipped when a delta is made in a new release (e.g., when delta 5.1 is made after delta 2.7, releases 3 and 4 are skipped). The absence of the n flag causes skipped releases to be completely empty. The j flag causes get to allow concurrent edits of the same base SID. The l flag defines a *list* of releases that are locked against editing. The q flag defines the replacement for the %Q% identification keyword. The z flag is used in specialized interface programs.

Comments
Arbitrary text is surrounded by the bracketing lines @t and @T. The comments section typically will contain a description of the file's purpose.

Body
The body consists of text lines and control lines. Text lines do not begin with the control character, control lines do. There are three kinds of control lines: insert, delete, and end, represented by:

> @I *DDDDD*
> @D *DDDDD*
> @E *DDDDD*

respectively. The digit string is the serial number corresponding to the delta for the control line.

SEE ALSO
admin(1), delta(1), get(1), prs(1).

NAME

services – Internet services and aliases

DESCRIPTION

The **services** file contains an entry for each service available through the DARPA Internet. Each entry consists of a line of the form:

service-name   port / protocol   aliases

service-name   This is the official Internet service name.

port / protocol   This field is composed of the port number and protocol through which the service is provided (for instance, 512/tcp).

aliases   This is a list of alternate names by which the service might be requested.

Fields can be separated by any number of SPACE and/or TAB characters. A '#' (pound-sign) indicates the beginning of a comment; characters up to the end of the line are not interpreted by routines which search the file.

Service names may contain any printable character other than a field delimiter, NEWLINE, or comment character.

FILES

/etc/services

SEE ALSO

getservent(3N), inetd.conf(4).

BUGS

A name server should be used instead of a static file.

NAME

shadow – shadow password file

DESCRIPTION

/etc/shadow is an access-restricted ASCII system file. The fields for each user entry are separated by colons. Each user is separated from the next by a newline. Unlike the /etc/passwd file, /etc/shadow does not have general read permission.

Here are the fields in /etc/shadow:

username	The user's login name (ID).
password	A 13-character encrypted password for the user, a *lock* string to indicate that the login is not accessible, or no string to show that there is no password for the login.
lastchanged	The number of days between January 1, 1970, and the date that the password was last modified.
minimum	The minimum number of days required between password changes.
maximum	The maximum number of days the password is valid.
warn	The number of days before password expires that the user is warned.
inactive	The number of days of inactivity allowed for that user.
expire	An absolute date specifying when the login may no longer be used.
flag	Reserved for future use, set to zero. Currently not used.

The encrypted password consists of 13 characters chosen from a 64-character alphabet (., /, 0–9, A–Z, a–z).

To update this file, use the passwd, useradd, usermod, or userdel commands.

FILES

/etc/shadow

SEE ALSO

useradd(1M), usermod(1M), userdel(1M), passwd(4)
putspent(3X), getspent(3X) in the *Programmer's Reference Manual*
login(1), passwd(1) in the *User's Reference Manual*

NAME

 sharetab – shared file system table

DESCRIPTION

 sharetab resides in directory /etc/dfs and contains a table of local resources shared by the share command.

 Each line of the file consists of the following fields:

 pathname resource fstype specific_options description
 where

pathname	Indicates the pathname of the shared resource.
resource	Indicates the symbolic name by which remote systems can access the resource.
fstype	Indicates the file system type of the shared resource.
specific_options	Indicates file-system-type-specific options that were given to the share command when the resource was shared.
description	Is a description of the shared resource provided by the system administrator when the resource was shared.

SEE ALSO

 share(1M)

NAME

strcf – STREAMS Configuration File for STREAMS TCP/IP

DESCRIPTION

/etc/strcf contains the script that is executed by slink(1M) to perform the STREAMS configuration operations required for STREAMS TCP/IP.

The standard /etc/strcf file contains several functions that perform various configuration operations, along with a sample boot function. Normally, only the boot function must be modified to customize the configuration for a given installation. In some cases, however, it may be necessary to change existing functions or add new functions.

The following functions perform basic linking operations:

The tp function is used to set up the link between a transport provider, such as TCP, and IP.

```
#
# tp - configure transport provider (i.e. tcp, udp, icmp)
# usage: tp devname
#
tp {
      p = open $1
      ip = open /dev/ip
      link p ip
}
```

The linkint function links the specified streams and does a sifname operation with the given name.

```
#
# linkint - link interface to ip or arp
# usage: linkint top bottom ifname
#
linkint {
      x = link $1 $2
      sifname $1 x $3
}
```

The aplinkint function performs the same function as linkint for an interface that uses the app module.

```
#
# aplinkint - like linkint, but app is pushed on dev
# usage: aplinkint top bottom ifname
#
aplinkint {
      push $2 app
      linkint $1 $2 $3
}
```

The following functions are used to configure different types of Ethernet interfaces:

The uenet function is used to configure an Ethernet interface for a cloning device driver that uses the *unit select* ioctl to select the desired interface. The interface name is constructed by concatenating the supplied prefix and the unit number.

```
#
# uenet - configure ethernet-type interface for cloning driver using
#          unit select
# usage: uenet ip-fd devname ifprefix unit
#
uenet {
        ifname = strcat $3 $4
        dev = open $2
        unitsel dev $4
        aplinkint $1 dev ifname
        dev = open $2
        unitsel dev $4
        arp = open /dev/arp
        linkint arp dev ifname
}
```

The denet function performs the same function as uenet, except that DL_ATTACH is used instead of *unit select*.

```
#
# denet - configure ethernet-type interface for cloning driver using
#          DL_ATTACH
# usage: denet ip-fd devname ifprefix unit
#
denet {
        ifname = strcat $3 $4
        dev = open $2
        dlattach dev $4
        aplinkint $1 dev ifname
        dev = open $2
        dlattach dev $4
        arp = open /dev/arp
        linkint arp dev ifname
}
```

The cenet function is used to configure an Ethernet interface for a cloning device driver that uses a different major number for each interface. The device name is formed by concatenating the supplied device name prefix and the unit number. The interface name is formed in a similar manner using the interface name prefix.

```
#
# cenet - configure ethernet-type interface for cloning driver with
#          one major per interface
# usage: cenet ip-fd devprefix ifprefix unit
#
cenet {
```

```
            devname = strcat $2 $4
            ifname = strcat $3 $4
            dev = open devname
            aplinkint $1 dev ifname
            dev = open devname
            arp = open /dev/arp
            linkint arp dev ifname
      }
```

The senet function is used to configure an Ethernet interface for a non-cloning device driver. Two different device nodes must be specified for IP and ARP.

```
      #
      # senet - configure ethernet-type interface for non-cloning driver
      # usage: senet ip-fd ipdevname arpdevname ifname
      #
      senet {
            dev = open $2
            aplinkint $1 dev $4
            dev = open $3
            arp = open /dev/arp
            linkint arp dev $4
      }
```

The senetc function is like senet, except that it allows the specification of a convergence module to be used with the ethernet driver (such as, for the 3B2 emd driver).

```
      #
      # senetc - configure ethernet-type interface for non-cloning driver
      #          using convergence module
      # usage: senetc ip-fd convergence ipdevname arpdevname ifname
      #
      senetc {
            dev = open $3
            push dev $2
            aplinkint $1 dev $5
            dev = open $4
            push dev $2
            arp = open /dev/arp
            linkint arp dev $5
      }
```

The loopback function is used to configure the loopback interface.

```
      #
      # loopback - configure loopback device
      # usage: loopback ip-fd
      #
      loopback {
            dev = open /dev/loop
            linkint $1 dev lo0
      }
```

The `slip` function is used to configure a SLIP interface. This function is not normally executed at boot time. Rather, the `slattach`(1M) command runs `slink` specifying `slip` on the command line.

```
#
# slip - configure slip interface
# usage: slip unit
#
slip {
        ip = open /dev/ip
        s = open /dev/slip
        ifname = strcat sl $1
        unitsel s $1
        linkint ip s ifname
}
```

The `boot` function is called by default when `slink` is executed. Normally, only the *interfaces* section and possibly the *queue params* section will have to be customized for a given installation. Examples are provided for the various Ethernet driver types.

```
#
# boot - boot time configuration
#
boot {
        #
        # queue params
        #
        initqp /dev/udp rq 8192 40960
        initqp /dev/ip muxrq 8192 40960 rq 8192 40960
        #
        # transport
        #
        tp /dev/tcp
        tp /dev/udp
        tp /dev/icmp
        tp /dev/rawip
}
```

FILES

/etc/strcf

SEE ALSO

slattach(1M), slink(1M).

NAME
    strftime – language specific strings

DESCRIPTION
    There can exist one printable file per locale to specify its date and time formatting
    information. These files must be kept in the directory
    /usr/lib/locale/<*locale*>/LC_TIME. The contents of these files are:

    1. abbreviated month names (in order)

    2. month names (in order)

    3. abbreviated weekday names (in order)

    4. weekday names (in order)

    5. default strings that specify formats for locale time (%X) and
       locale date (%x).

    6. default format for cftime, if the argument for cftime is zero or null.

    7. AM (ante meridian) string

    8. PM (post meridian) string

    Each string is on a line by itself. All white space is significant. The order of the
    strings in the above list is the same order in which they must appear in the file.

EXAMPLE
    /usr/lib/locale/C/LC_TIME

    Jan
    Feb
     . . .
    January
    February
     . . .
    Sun
    Mon
     . . .
    Sunday
    Monday
     . . .
    %H:%M:%S
    %m/%d/%y
    %a %b %d %T %Z %Y
    AM
    PM

FILES
    /usr/lib/locale/<*locale*>/LC_TIME

SEE ALSO
    ctime(3C), setlocale(3C), strftime(3C).

NAME

   system – system configuration information file

DESCRIPTION

   The **system** file is used during the configuration of a new operating system to
   obtain configuration information that cannot be obtained from the Equipped Device Table (EDT). The system file is /stand/system.

   The **system** file generally contains a list of software drivers to include in the new
   bootable operating system, the assignment of system devices such as **swapdev**
   and **rootdev**, and instructions for excluding drivers from the configuration process.

   The parser for the **system** file is case-sensitive. All upper case strings in the syntax below should be upper case in the **system** file as well. Nonterminal symbols
   are enclosed in angle brackets <>, whereas optional arguments are enclosed in
   square brackets []. Ellipses (...) indicate optional repetition of the argument for
   that line.

   The symbols in the syntax description below are interpreted as follows:

<fname>	::=	pathname
<string>	::=	driver file name from /boot or EDT entry name
<device>	::=	special device name | DEV (*<major>*,*<minor>*)
<major>	::=	*<number>*
<minor>	::=	*<number>*
<number>	::=	decimal, octal or hex literal

   The lines listed below may appear in any order. Blank lines may be inserted at
   any point. Comment lines must begin with an asterisk. Entries for EXCLUDE and
   INCLUDE are cumulative. For all other entries, the last line to appear in the file is
   used—any earlier entries are ignored.

   BOOT: *<fname>*
   > Specifies the KERNEL object file to be used to build the bootable operating
   > system; if *<fname>* is the keyword DEFAULT, the configuration program
   > takes the KERNEL file from whatever boot directory it is using. For exam-
   > ple, if the user types cunix –b /my_boot_directory and the system file
   > contains the DEFAULT keyword for the BOOT directive, then the KERNEL file
   > used is /my_boot_directory/KERNEL. If no –b option is used then cunix
   > searches /boot by default; see cunix(1M).

   EXCLUDE: *<string>* ...
   > Specifies drivers to exclude from the configuration even if the device is
   > found in the EDT.

   INCLUDE: *<string>*[(*<number>*)] ...
   > Specifies software drivers or loadable modules to be included in the
   > configuration. The optional *<number>* (parentheses required) specifies the
   > number of devices to be controlled by the driver (defaults to 1). This
   > number corresponds to the builtin variable #C which may be referred to
   > by expressions in part one of the **master** file.

ROOTDEV: *<device>*
> Identifies the device containing the root file system.

SWAPDEV: *<device> <number> <number>*
> Identifies the device to be used as swap space. The *<device>* in this case may be a special device file name or a regular file. The *<number>*s correspond to the block number the swap space starts at and the number of swap blocks available.

FILES
> /stand/system

SEE ALSO
> crash(1M), cunix(1M), mkboot(1M), master(4).

NAME

> term – format of compiled term file

SYNOPSIS

> /usr/share/lib/terminfo/?/*

DESCRIPTION

> Compiled terminfo(4) descriptions are placed under the directory
> /usr/share/lib/terminfo. In order to avoid a linear search of a huge UNIX
> system directory, a two-level scheme is used: /usr/share/lib/terminfo/c/*name*
> where *name* is the name of the terminal, and *c* is the first character of *name*.
> Thus, att4425 can be found in the file /usr/share/lib/terminfo/a/att4425.
> Synonyms for the same terminal are implemented by multiple links to the same
> compiled file.

> The format has been chosen so that it is the same on all hardware. An 8-bit byte
> is assumed, but no assumptions about byte ordering or sign extension are made.
> Thus, these binary terminfo files can be transported to other hardware with 8-bit
> bytes.

> Short integers are stored in two 8-bit bytes. The first byte contains the least
> significant 8 bits of the value, and the second byte contains the most significant 8
> bits. (Thus, the value represented is 256*second+first*.) The value −1 is
> represented by 0377, 0377, and the value −2 is represented by 0376, 0377; other
> negative values are illegal. The −1 generally means that a capability is missing
> from this terminal. The −2 means that the capability has been cancelled in the
> terminfo source and also is to be considered missing.

> The compiled file is created from the source file descriptions of the terminals (see
> the −I option of infocmp) by using the terminfo compiler, tic, and read by the
> routine setupterm [see curses(3X).] The file is divided into six parts in the fol-
> lowing order: the header, terminal names, boolean flags, numbers, strings, and
> string table.

> The header section begins the file. This section contains six short integers in the
> format described below. These integers are (1) the magic number (octal 0432); (2)
> the size, in bytes, of the names section; (3) the number of bytes in the boolean
> section; (4) the number of short integers in the numbers section; (5) the number of
> offsets (short integers) in the strings section; (6) the size, in bytes, of the string
> table.

> The terminal names section comes next. It contains the first line of the terminfo
> description, listing the various names for the terminal, separated by the bar (|)
> character (see term(5)). The section is terminated with an ASCII NUL character.

> The boolean flags have one byte for each flag. This byte is either 0 or 1 as the
> flag is present or absent. The value of 2 means that the flag has been cancelled.
> The capabilities are in the same order as the file <term.h>.

> Between the boolean section and the number section, a null byte is inserted, if
> necessary, to ensure that the number section begins on an even byte offset. All
> short integers are aligned on a short word boundary.

The numbers section is similar to the boolean flags section. Each capability takes up two bytes, and is stored as a short integer. If the value represented is −1 or −2, the capability is taken to be missing.

The strings section is also similar. Each capability is stored as a short integer, in the format above. A value of −1 or −2 means the capability is missing. Otherwise, the value is taken as an offset from the beginning of the string table. Special characters in ^X or \c notation are stored in their interpreted form, not the printing representation. Padding information ($<nn>) and parameter information (%x) are stored intact in uninterpreted form.

The final section is the string table. It contains all the values of string capabilities referenced in the string section. Each string is null terminated.

Note that it is possible for **setupterm** to expect a different set of capabilities than are actually present in the file. Either the database may have been updated since **setupterm** has been recompiled (resulting in extra unrecognized entries in the file) or the program may have been recompiled more recently than the database was updated (resulting in missing entries). The routine **setupterm** must be prepared for both possibilities—this is why the numbers and sizes are included. Also, new capabilities must always be added at the end of the lists of boolean, number, and string capabilities.

As an example, here is terminal information on the AT&T Model 37 KSR terminal as output by the **infocmp −I tty37** command:

```
37|tty37|AT&T model 37 teletype,
    hc, os, xon,
    bel=^G, cr=\r, cub1=\b, cud1=\n, cuu1=\E7, hd=\E9,
    hu=\E8, ind=\n,
```

And here is an octal dump of the **term** file, produced by the **od −c /usr/share/lib/terminfo/t/tty37** command:

```
0000000 032 001      \0 032  \0 013  \0 021 001    3  \0    3    7    |    t
0000020   t    y   3   7    |   A    T    &    T        m    o    d    e    1
0000040   3    7        t    e    1    e    t    y    p    e   \0   \0   \0   \0   \0
0000060  \0   \0  \0 001  \0   \0   \0   \0   \0   \0   \0 001   \0   \0   \0   \0
0000100 001   \0  \0  \0   \0   \0 377 377 377 377 377 377 377 377 377 377
0000120 377 377 377 377 377 377 377 377 377 377 377 377 377 377    &   \0
0000140      \0 377 377 377 377 377 377 377 377 377 377 377 377 377 377
0000160 377 377    "   \0 377 377 377 377    (   \0 377 377 377 377 377 377
0000200 377 377    0   \0 377 377 377 377 377 377 377 377    −   \0 377 377
0000220 377 377 377 377 377 377 377 377 377 377 377 377 377 377 377 377
*
0000520 377 377 377 377 377 377 377 377 377 377 377 377 377 377    $   \0
0000540 377 377 377 377 377 377 377 377 377 377 377 377 377 377    *   \0
0000560 377 377 377 377 377 377 377 377 377 377 377 377 377 377 377 377
*
```

```
0001160 377 377 377 377 377 377 377 377 377 377 377 377 377 377   3   7
0001200   |   t   t   y   3   7   |   A   T   &   T       m   o   d   e
0001220   1       3   7       t   e   l   e   t   y   p   e  \0  \r  \0
0001240  \n  \0  \n  \0 007  \0  \b  \0 033   8  \0 033   9  \0 033   7
0001260  \0  \0
0001261
```

Some limitations: total compiled entries cannot exceed 4096 bytes; all entries in the name field cannot exceed 128 bytes.

FILES

/usr/share/lib/terminfo/?/*compiled terminal description database
/usr/include/term.h   terminfo header file

SEE ALSO

curses(3X).

infocmp(1M), terminfo(4), term(5)

NAME

terminfo – terminal capability data base

SYNOPSIS

/usr/share/lib/terminfo/?/*

DESCRIPTION

terminfo is a database produced by tic that describes the capabilities of devices such as terminals and printers. Devices are described in terminfo source files by specifying a set of capabilities, by quantifying certain aspects of the device, and by specifying character sequences that effect particular results. This database is often used by screen oriented applications such as vi and curses programs, as well as by some UNIX system commands such as ls and more. This usage allows them to work with a variety of devices without changes to the programs.

terminfo source files consist of one or more device descriptions. Each description consists of a header (beginning in column 1) and one or more lines that list the features for that particular device. Every line in a terminfo source file must end in a comma (,). Every line in a terminfo source file except the header must be indented with one or more white spaces (either spaces or tabs).

Entries in terminfo source files consist of a number of comma-separated fields. White space after each comma is ignored. Embedded commas must be escaped by using a backslash. The following example shows the format of a terminfo source file.

> $alias_1$ | $alias_2$ | ... | $alias_n$ | *longname,*
> *<white space>* am, lines #24,
> *<white space>* home=\Eeh,

The first line, commonly referred to as the header line, must begin in column one and must contain at least two aliases separated by vertical bars. The last field in the header line must be the long name of the device and it may contain any string. Alias names must be unique in the terminfo database and they must conform to UNIX system file naming conventions [see tic(1M)]; they cannot, for example, contain white space or slashes.

Every device must be assigned a name, such as "vt100". Device names (except the long name) should be chosen using the following conventions. The name should not contain hyphens because hyphens are reserved for use when adding suffixes that indicate special modes.

These special modes may be modes that the hardware can be in, or user preferences. To assign a special mode to a particular device, append a suffix consisting of a hyphen and an indicator of the mode to the device name. For example, the –w suffix means "wide mode"; when specified, it allows for a width of 132 columns instead of the standard 80 columns. Therefore, if you want to use a vt100 device set to wide mode, name the device "vt100-w." Use the following suffixes where possible.

Suffix	Meaning	Example
−w	Wide mode (more than 80 columns)	5410−w
−am	With auto. margins (usually default)	vt100−am
−nam	Without automatic margins	vt100−nam
−*n*	Number of lines on the screen	2300−40
−na	No arrow keys (leave them in local)	c100−na
−*n*p	Number of pages of memory	c100−4p
−rv	Reverse video	4415−rv

The terminfo reference manual page is organized in two sections: "DEVICE CAPABILITIES" and "PRINTER CAPABILITIES."

PART 1: DEVICE CAPABILITIES

Capabilities in terminfo are of three types: Boolean capabilities (which show that a device has or does not have a particular feature), numeric capabilities (which quantify particular features of a device), and string capabilities (which provide sequences that can be used to perform particular operations on devices).

In the following table, a **Variable** is the name by which a C programmer accesses a capability (at the terminfo level). A **Capname** is the short name for a capability specified in the terminfo source file. It is used by a person updating the source file and by the tput command. A **Termcap Code** is a two-letter sequence that corresponds to the termcap capability name. (Note that termcap is no longer supported.)

Capability names have no real length limit, but an informal limit of five characters has been adopted to keep them short. Whenever possible, capability names are chosen to be the same as or similar to those specified by the ANSI X3.64-1979 standard. Semantics are also intended to match those of the ANSI standard.

All string capabilities listed below may have padding specified, with the exception of those used for input. Input capabilities, listed under the **Strings** section in the following tables, have names beginning with **key_**. The #i symbol in the description field of the following tables refers to the *i*th parameter.

Booleans

Variable	Cap-name	Termcap Code	Description
auto_left_margin	bw	bw	cub1 wraps from column 0 to last column
auto_right_margin	am	am	Terminal has automatic margins
back_color_erase	bce	be	Screen erased with background color
can_change	ccc	cc	Terminal can re-define existing color
ceol_standout_glitch	xhp	xs	Standout not erased by overwriting (hp)
col_addr_glitch	xhpa	YA	Only positive motion for hpa/mhpa caps
cpi_changes_res	cpix	YF	Changing character pitch changes resolution
cr_cancels_micro_mode	crxm	YB	Using cr turns off micro mode

Variable	Cap-name	Termcap Code	Description
eat_newline_glitch	xenl	xn	Newline ignored after 80 columns (Concept)
erase_overstrike	eo	eo	Can erase overstrikes with a blank
generic_type	gn	gn	Generic line type (*e.g.*, dialup, switch)
hard_copy	hc	hc	Hardcopy terminal
hard_cursor	chts	HC	Cursor is hard to see
has_meta_key	km	km	Has a meta key (shift, sets parity bit)
has_print_wheel	daisy	YC	Printer needs operator to change character set
has_status_line	hs	hs	Has extra "status line"
hue_lightness_saturation	hls	hl	Terminal uses only HLS color notation (Tektronix)
insert_null_glitch	in	in	Insert mode distinguishes nulls
lpi_changes_res	lpix	YG	Changing line pitch changes resolution
memory_above	da	da	Display may be retained above the screen
memory_below	db	db	Display may be retained below the screen
move_insert_mode	mir	mi	Safe to move while in insert mode
move_standout_mode	msgr	ms	Safe to move in standout modes
needs_xon_xoff	nxon	nx	Padding won't work, xon/xoff required
no_esc_ctlc	xsb	xb	Beehive (f1=escape, f2=ctrl C)
non_rev_rmcup	nrrmc	NR	smcup does not reverse rmcup
no_pad_char	npc	NP	Pad character doesn't exist
over_strike	os	os	Terminal overstrikes on hard-copy terminal
prtr_silent	mc5i	5i	Printer won't echo on screen
row_addr_glitch	xvpa	YD	Only positive motion for vpa/mvpa caps
semi_auto_right_margin	sam	YE	Printing in last column causes cr
status_line_esc_ok	eslok	es	Escape can be used on the status line
dest_tabs_magic_smso	xt	xt	Destructive tabs, magic smso char (t1061)
tilde_glitch	hz	hz	Hazeltine; can't print tilde (˜)
transparent_underline	ul	ul	Underline character overstrikes
xon_xoff	xon	xo	Terminal uses xon/xoff handshaking

Numbers

Variable	Cap-name	Termcap Code	Description
buffer_capacity	bufsz	Ya	Number of bytes buffered before printing
columns	cols	co	Number of columns in a line
dot_vert_spacing	spinv	Yb	Spacing of pins vertically in pins per inch
dot_horz_spacing	spinh	Yc	Spacing of dots horizontally in dots per inch
init_tabs	it	it	Tabs initially every # spaces
label_height	lh	lh	Number of rows in each label
label_width	lw	lw	Number of columns in each label
lines	lines	li	Number of lines on a screen or a page

Variable	Cap-name	Termcap Code	Description
lines_of_memory	lm	lm	Lines of memory if > lines; 0 means varies
magic_cookie_glitch	xmc	sg	Number of blank characters left by smso or rmso
max_colors	colors	Co	Maximum number of colors on the screen
max_micro_address	maddr	Yd	Maximum value in micro_...._address
max_micro_jump	mjump	Ye	Maximum value in parm_...._micro
max_pairs	pairs	pa	Maximum number of color-pairs on the screen
micro_col_size	mcs	Yf	Character step size when in micro mode
micro_line_size	mls	Yg	Line step size when in micro mode
no_color_video	ncv	NC	Video attributes that can't be used with colors
number_of_pins	npins	Yh	Number of pins in print-head
num_labels	nlab	Nl	Number of labels on screen (start at 1)
output_res_char	orc	Yi	Horizontal resolution in units per character
output_res_line	orl	Yj	Vertical resolution in units per line
output_res_horz_inch	orhi	Yk	Horizontal resolution in units per inch
output_res_vert_inch	orvi	Yl	Vertical resolution in units per inch
padding_baud_rate	pb	pb	Lowest baud rate where padding needed
virtual_terminal	vt	vt	Virtual terminal number (UNIX system)
wide_char_size	widcs	Yn	Character step size when in double wide mode
width_status_line	wsl	ws	Number of columns in status line

Strings

Variable	Cap-name	Termcap Code	Description
acs_chars	acsc	ac	Graphic charset pairs aAbBcC
alt_scancode_esc	scesca	S8	Alternate escape for scancode emulation (default is for vt100)
back_tab	cbt	bt	Back tab
bell	bel	bl	Audible signal (bell)
bit_image_repeat	birep	Zy	Repeat bit-image cell #1 #2 times (use tparm)
bit_image_newline	binel	Zz	Move to next row of the bit image (use tparm)
bit_image_carriage_return	bicr	Yv	Move to beginning of same row (use tparm)
carriage_return	cr	cr	Carriage return
change_char_pitch	cpi	ZA	Change number of characters per inch
change_line_pitch	lpi	ZB	Change number of lines per inch
change_res_horz	chr	ZC	Change horizontal resolution
change_res_vert	cvr	ZD	Change vertical resolution
change_scroll_region	csr	cs	Change to lines #1 through #2 (vt100)
char_padding	rmp	rP	Like ip but when in replace mode
char_set_names	csnm	Zy	List of character set names
clear_all_tabs	tbc	ct	Clear all tab stops

Variable	Cap- name	Termcap Code	Description
clear_margins	mgc	MC	Clear all margins (top, bottom, and sides)
clear_screen	clear	cl	Clear screen and home cursor
clr_bol	el1	cb	Clear to beginning of line, inclusive
clr_eol	el	ce	Clear to end of line
clr_eos	ed	cd	Clear to end of display
code_set_init	csin	ci	Init sequence for multiple codesets
color_names	colornm	Yw	Give name for color #1
column_address	hpa	ch	Horizontal position absolute
command_character	cmdch	CC	Terminal settable cmd character in prototype
cursor_address	cup	cm	Move to row #1 col #2
cursor_down	cud1	do	Down one line
cursor_home	home	ho	Home cursor (if no cup)
cursor_invisible	civis	vi	Make cursor invisible
cursor_left	cub1	le	Move left one space.
cursor_mem_address	mrcup	CM	Memory relative cursor addressing
cursor_normal	cnorm	ve	Make cursor appear normal (undo vs/vi)
cursor_right	cuf1	nd	Non-destructive space (cursor or carriage right)
cursor_to_ll	ll	ll	Last line, first column (if no cup)
cursor_up	cuu1	up	Upline (cursor up)
cursor_visible	cvvis	vs	Make cursor very visible
define_bit_image_region	defbi	Yx	Define rectangular bit-image region (use tparm)
define_char	defc	ZE	Define a character in a character set †
delete_character	dch1	dc	Delete character
delete_line	dl1	dl	Delete line
device_type	devt	dv	Indicate language/codeset support
dis_status_line	dsl	ds	Disable status line
display_pc_char	dispc	S1	Display PC character
down_half_line	hd	hd	Half-line down (forward 1/2 linefeed)
ena_acs	enacs	eA	Enable alternate character set
end_bit_image_region	endbi	Yy	End a bit-image region (use tparm)
enter_alt_charset_mode	smacs	as	Start alternate character set
enter_am_mode	smam	SA	Turn on automatic margins
enter_blink_mode	blink	mb	Turn on blinking
enter_bold_mode	bold	md	Turn on bold (extra bright) mode
enter_ca_mode	smcup	ti	String to begin programs that use cup
enter_delete_mode	smdc	dm	Delete mode (enter)
enter_dim_mode	dim	mh	Turn on half-bright mode
enter_doublewide_mode	swidm	ZF	Enable double wide printing
enter_draft_quality	sdrfq	ZG	Set draft quality print
enter_insert_mode	smir	im	Insert mode (enter)

Variable	Cap-name	Termcap Code	Description
enter_italics_mode	sitm	ZH	Enable italics
enter_leftward_mode	slm	ZI	Enable leftward carriage motion
enter_micro_mode	smicm	ZJ	Enable micro motion capabilities
enter_near_letter_quality	snlq	ZK	Set near-letter quality print
enter_normal_quality	snrmq	ZL	Set normal quality print
enter_pc_charset_mode	smpch	S2	Enter PC character display mode
enter_protected_mode	prot	mp	Turn on protected mode
enter_reverse_mode	rev	mr	Turn on reverse video mode
enter_scancode_mode	smsc	S4	Enter PC scancode mode
enter_secure_mode	invis	mk	Turn on blank mode (characters invisible)
enter_shadow_mode	sshm	ZM	Enable shadow printing
enter_standout_mode	smso	so	Begin standout mode
enter_subscript_mode	ssubm	ZN	Enable subscript printing
enter_superscript_mode	ssupm	ZO	Enable superscript printing
enter_underline_mode	smul	us	Start underscore mode
enter_upward_mode	sum	ZP	Enable upward carriage motion
enter_xon_mode	smxon	SX	Turn on xon/xoff handshaking
erase_chars	ech	ec	Erase #1 characters
exit_alt_charset_mode	rmacs	ae	End alternate character set
exit_am_mode	rmam	RA	Turn off automatic margins
exit_attribute_mode	sgr0	me	Turn off all attributes
exit_ca_mode	rmcup	te	String to end programs that use cup
exit_delete_mode	rmdc	ed	End delete mode
exit_doublewide_mode	rwidm	ZQ	Disable double wide printing
exit_insert_mode	rmir	ei	End insert mode
exit_italics_mode	ritm	ZR	Disable italics
exit_leftward_mode	rlm	ZS	Enable rightward (normal) carriage motion
exit_micro_mode	rmicm	ZT	Disable micro motion capabilities
exit_pc_charset_mode	rmpch	S3	Disable PC character display mode
exit_scancode_mode	rmsc	S5	Disable PC scancode mode
exit_shadow_mode	rshm	ZU	Disable shadow printing
exit_standout_mode	rmso	se	End standout mode
exit_subscript_mode	rsubm	ZV	Disable subscript printing
exit_superscript_mode	rsupm	ZW	Disable superscript printing
exit_underline_mode	rmul	ue	End underscore mode
exit_upward_mode	rum	ZX	Enable downward (normal) carriage motion
exit_xon_mode	rmxon	RX	Turn off xon/xoff handshaking
flash_screen	flash	vb	Visible bell (may not move cursor)
form_feed	ff	ff	Hardcopy terminal page eject
from_status_line	fsl	fs	Return from status line
init_1string	is1	i1	Terminal or printer initialization string
init_2string	is2	is	Terminal or printer initialization string

Variable	Cap- name	Termcap Code	Description
init_3string	is3	i3	Terminal or printer initialization string
init_file	if	if	Name of initialization file
init_prog	iprog	iP	Path name of program for initialization
initialize_color	initc	Ic	Initialize the definition of color
initialize_pair	initp	Ip	Initialize color-pair
insert_character	ich1	ic	Insert character
insert_line	il1	al	Add new blank line
insert_padding	ip	ip	Insert pad after character inserted

The "key_" strings are sent by specific keys. The "key_" descriptions include the macro, defined in curses.h, for the code returned by the curses routine getch when the key is pressed [see curs_getch(3X)].

key_a1	ka1	K1	KEY_A1, upper left of keypad
key_a3	ka3	K3	KEY_A3, upper right of keypad
key_b2	kb2	K2	KEY_B2, center of keypad
key_backspace	kbs	kb	KEY_BACKSPACE, sent by backspace key
key_beg	kbeg	@1	KEY_BEG, sent by beg(inning) key
key_btab	kcbt	kB	KEY_BTAB, sent by back-tab key
key_c1	kc1	K4	KEY_C1, lower left of keypad
key_c3	kc3	K5	KEY_C3, lower right of keypad
key_cancel	kcan	@2	KEY_CANCEL, sent by cancel key
key_catab	ktbc	ka	KEY_CATAB, sent by clear-all-tabs key
key_clear	kclr	kC	KEY_CLEAR, sent by clear-screen or erase key
key_close	kclo	@3	KEY_CLOSE, sent by close key
key_command	kcmd	@4	KEY_COMMAND, sent by cmd (command) key
key_copy	kcpy	@5	KEY_COPY, sent by copy key
key_create	kcrt	@6	KEY_CREATE, sent by create key
key_ctab	kctab	kt	KEY_CTAB, sent by clear-tab key
key_dc	kdch1	kD	KEY_DC, sent by delete-character key
key_dl	kdl1	kL	KEY_DL, sent by delete-line key
key_down	kcud1	kd	KEY_DOWN, sent by terminal down-arrow key
key_eic	krmir	kM	KEY_EIC, sent by rmir or smir in insert mode
key_end	kend	@7	KEY_END, sent by end key
key_enter	kent	@8	KEY_ENTER, sent by enter/send key
key_eol	kel	kE	KEY_EOL, sent by clear-to-end-of-line key
key_eos	ked	kS	KEY_EOS, sent by clear-to-end-of-screen key
key_exit	kext	@9	KEY_EXIT, sent by exit key
key_f0	kf0	k0	KEY_F(0), sent by function key f0

Variable	Cap-name	Termcap Code	Description
key_f1	kf1	k1	KEY_F(1), sent by function key f1
key_f2	kf2	k2	KEY_F(2), sent by function key f2
key_f3	kf3	k3	KEY_F(3), sent by function key f3
key_f4	kf4	k4	KEY_F(4), sent by function key f4
key_f5	kf5	k5	KEY_F(5), sent by function key f5
key_f6	kf6	k6	KEY_F(6), sent by function key f6
key_f7	kf7	k7	KEY_F(7), sent by function key f7
key_f8	kf8	k8	KEY_F(8), sent by function key f8
key_f9	kf9	k9	KEY_F(9), sent by function key f9
key_f10	kf10	k;	KEY_F(10), sent by function key f10
key_f11	kf11	F1	KEY_F(11), sent by function key f11
key_f12	kf12	F2	KEY_F(12), sent by function key f12
key_f13	kf13	F3	KEY_F(13), sent by function key f13
key_f14	kf14	F4	KEY_F(14), sent by function key f14
key_f15	kf15	F5	KEY_F(15), sent by function key f15
key_f16	kf16	F6	KEY_F(16), sent by function key f16
key_f17	kf17	F7	KEY_F(17), sent by function key f17
key_f18	kf18	F8	KEY_F(18), sent by function key f18
key_f19	kf19	F9	KEY_F(19), sent by function key f19
key_f20	kf20	FA	KEY_F(20), sent by function key f20
key_f21	kf21	FB	KEY_F(21), sent by function key f21
key_f22	kf22	FC	KEY_F(22), sent by function key f22
key_f23	kf23	FD	KEY_F(23), sent by function key f23
key_f24	kf24	FE	KEY_F(24), sent by function key f24
key_f25	kf25	FF	KEY_F(25), sent by function key f25
key_f26	kf26	FG	KEY_F(26), sent by function key f26
key_f27	kf27	FH	KEY_F(27), sent by function key f27
key_f28	kf28	FI	KEY_F(28), sent by function key f28
key_f29	kf29	FJ	KEY_F(29), sent by function key f29
key_f30	kf30	FK	KEY_F(30), sent by function key f30
key_f31	kf31	FL	KEY_F(31), sent by function key f31
key_f32	kf32	FM	KEY_F(32), sent by function key f32
key_f33	kf33	FN	KEY_F(13), sent by function key f13
key_f34	kf34	FO	KEY_F(34), sent by function key f34
key_f35	kf35	FP	KEY_F(35), sent by function key f35
key_f36	kf36	FQ	KEY_F(36), sent by function key f36
key_f37	kf37	FR	KEY_F(37), sent by function key f37
key_f38	kf38	FS	KEY_F(38), sent by function key f38
key_f39	kf39	FT	KEY_F(39), sent by function key f39
key_f40	kf40	FU	KEY_F(40), sent by function key f40
key_f41	kf41	FV	KEY_F(41), sent by function key f41
key_f42	kf42	FW	KEY_F(42), sent by function key f42
key_f43	kf43	FX	KEY_F(43), sent by function key f43
key_f44	kf44	FY	KEY_F(44), sent by function key f44
key_f45	kf45	FZ	KEY_F(45), sent by function key f45

Variable	Cap- name	Termcap Code	Description
key_f46	kf46	Fa	KEY_F(46), sent by function key f46
key_f47	kf47	Fb	KEY_F(47), sent by function key f47
key_f48	kf48	Fc	KEY_F(48), sent by function key f48
key_f49	kf49	Fd	KEY_F(49), sent by function key f49
key_f50	kf50	Fe	KEY_F(50), sent by function key f50
key_f51	kf51	Ff	KEY_F(51), sent by function key f51
key_f52	kf52	Fg	KEY_F(52), sent by function key f52
key_f53	kf53	Fh	KEY_F(53), sent by function key f53
key_f54	kf54	Fi	KEY_F(54), sent by function key f54
key_f55	kf55	Fj	KEY_F(55), sent by function key f55
key_f56	kf56	Fk	KEY_F(56), sent by function key f56
key_f57	kf57	Fl	KEY_F(57), sent by function key f57
key_f58	kf58	Fm	KEY_F(58), sent by function key f58
key_f59	kf59	Fn	KEY_F(59), sent by function key f59
key_f60	kf60	Fo	KEY_F(60), sent by function key f60
key_f61	kf61	Fp	KEY_F(61), sent by function key f61
key_f62	kf62	Fq	KEY_F(62), sent by function key f62
key_f63	kf63	Fr	KEY_F(63), sent by function key f63
key_find	kfnd	@0	KEY_FIND, sent by find key
key_help	khlp	%1	KEY_HELP, sent by help key
key_home	khome	kh	KEY_HOME, sent by home key
key_ic	kich1	kI	KEY_IC, sent by ins-char/enter ins-mode key
key_il	kil1	kA	KEY_IL, sent by insert-line key
key_left	kcub1	kl	KEY_LEFT, sent by terminal left-arrow key
key_ll	kll	kH	KEY_LL, sent by home-down key
key_mark	kmrk	%2	KEY_MARK, sent by mark key
key_message	kmsg	%3	KEY_MESSAGE, sent by message key
key_move	kmov	%4	KEY_MOVE, sent by move key
key_next	knxt	%5	KEY_NEXT, sent by next-object key
key_npage	knp	kN	KEY_NPAGE, sent by next-page key
key_open	kopn	%6	KEY_OPEN, sent by open key
key_options	kopt	%7	KEY_OPTIONS, sent by options key
key_ppage	kpp	kP	KEY_PPAGE, sent by previous-page key
key_previous	kprv	%8	KEY_PREVIOUS, sent by previous-object key
key_print	kprt	%9	KEY_PRINT, sent by print or copy key
key_redo	krdo	%0	KEY_REDO, sent by redo key
key_reference	kref	&1	KEY_REFERENCE, sent by ref(erence) key
key_refresh	krfr	&2	KEY_REFRESH, sent by refresh key
key_replace	krpl	&3	KEY_REPLACE, sent by replace key
key_restart	krst	&4	KEY_RESTART, sent by restart key
key_resume	kres	&5	KEY_RESUME, sent by resume key

Variable	Cap-name	Termcap Code	Description
key_right	kcuf1	kr	KEY_RIGHT, sent by terminal right-arrow key
key_save	ksav	&6	KEY_SAVE, sent by save key
key_sbeg	kBEG	&9	KEY_SBEG, sent by shifted beginning key
key_scancel	kCAN	&0	KEY_SCANCEL, sent by shifted cancel key
key_scommand	kCMD	*1	KEY_SCOMMAND, sent by shifted command key
key_scopy	kCPY	*2	KEY_SCOPY, sent by shifted copy key
key_screate	kCRT	*3	KEY_SCREATE, sent by shifted create key
key_sdc	kDC	*4	KEY_SDC, sent by shifted delete-char key
key_sdl	kDL	*5	KEY_SDL, sent by shifted delete-line key
key_select	kslt	*6	KEY_SELECT, sent by select key
key_send	kEND	*7	KEY_SEND, sent by shifted end key
key_seol	kEOL	*8	KEY_SEOL, sent by shifted clear-line key
key_sexit	kEXT	*9	KEY_SEXIT, sent by shifted exit key
key_sf	kind	kF	KEY_SF, sent by scroll-forward/down key
key_sfind	kFND	*0	KEY_SFIND, sent by shifted find key
key_shelp	kHLP	#1	KEY_SHELP, sent by shifted help key
key_shome	kHOM	#2	KEY_SHOME, sent by shifted home key
key_sic	kIC	#3	KEY_SIC, sent by shifted input key
key_sleft	kLFT	#4	KEY_SLEFT, sent by shifted left-arrow key
key_smessage	kMSG	%a	KEY_SMESSAGE, sent by shifted message key
key_smove	kMOV	%b	KEY_SMOVE, sent by shifted move key
key_snext	kNXT	%c	KEY_SNEXT, sent by shifted next key
key_soptions	kOPT	%d	KEY_SOPTIONS, sent by shifted options key
key_sprevious	kPRV	%e	KEY_SPREVIOUS, sent by shifted prev key
key_sprint	kPRT	%f	KEY_SPRINT, sent by shifted print key
key_sr	kri	kR	KEY_SR, sent by scroll-backward/up key
key_sredo	kRDO	%g	KEY_SREDO, sent by shifted redo key
key_sreplace	kRPL	%h	KEY_SREPLACE, sent by shifted replace key
key_sright	kRIT	%i	KEY_SRIGHT, sent by shifted right-arrow key
key_srsume	kRES	%j	KEY_SRSUME, sent by shifted resume key
key_ssave	kSAV	!1	KEY_SSAVE, sent by shifted save key
key_ssuspend	kSPD	!2	KEY_SSUSPEND, sent by shifted suspend key
key_stab	khts	kT	KEY_STAB, sent by set-tab key

Variable	Cap- name	Termcap Code	Description
key_sundo	kUND	!3	KEY_SUNDO, sent by shifted undo key
key_suspend	kspd	&7	KEY_SUSPEND, sent by suspend key
key_undo	kund	&8	KEY_UNDO, sent by undo key
key_up	kcuu1	ku	KEY_UP, sent by terminal up-arrow key
keypad_local	rmkx	ke	Out of "keypad-transmit" mode
keypad_xmit	smkx	ks	Put terminal in "keypad-transmit" mode
lab_f0	lf0	l0	Labels on function key f0 if not f0
lab_f1	lf1	l1	Labels on function key f1 if not f1
lab_f2	lf2	l2	Labels on function key f2 if not f2
lab_f3	lf3	l3	Labels on function key f3 if not f3
lab_f4	lf4	l4	Labels on function key f4 if not f4
lab_f5	lf5	l5	Labels on function key f5 if not f5
lab_f6	lf6	l6	Labels on function key f6 if not f6
lab_f7	lf7	l7	Labels on function key f7 if not f7
lab_f8	lf8	l8	Labels on function key f8 if not f8
lab_f9	lf9	l9	Labels on function key f9 if not f9
lab_f10	lf10	la	Labels on function key f10 if not f10
label_off	rmln	LF	Turn off soft labels
label_on	smln	LO	Turn on soft labels
meta_off	rmm	mo	Turn off "meta mode"
meta_on	smm	mm	Turn on "meta mode" (8th bit)
micro_column_address	mhpa	ZY	Like column_address for micro adjustment
micro_down	mcud1	ZZ	Like cursor_down for micro adjustment
micro_left	mcub1	Za	Like cursor_left for micro adjustment
micro_right	mcuf1	Zb	Like cursor_right for micro adjustment
micro_row_address	mvpa	Zc	Like row_address for micro adjustment
micro_up	mcuu1	Zd	Like cursor_up for micro adjustment
newline	nel	nw	Newline (behaves like cr followed by lf)
order_of_pins	porder	Ze	Matches software bits to print-head pins
orig_colors	oc	oc	Set all color(-pair)s to the original ones
orig_pair	op	op	Set default color-pair to the original one
pad_char	pad	pc	Pad character (rather than null)
parm_dch	dch	DC	Delete #1 chars
parm_delete_line	dl	DL	Delete #1 lines
parm_down_cursor	cud	DO	Move down #1 lines.
parm_down_micro	mcud	Zf	Like parm_down_cursor for micro adjust.
parm_ich	ich	IC	Insert #1 blank chars
parm_index	indn	SF	Scroll forward #1 lines.
parm_insert_line	il	AL	Add #1 new blank lines
parm_left_cursor	cub	LE	Move cursor left #1 spaces

Variable	Cap-name	Termcap Code	Description
parm_left_micro	mcub	Zg	Like parm_left_cursor for micro adjust.
parm_right_cursor	cuf	RI	Move right #1 spaces.
parm_right_micro	mcuf	Zh	Like parm_right_cursor for micro adjust.
parm_rindex	rin	SR	Scroll backward #1 lines.
parm_up_cursor	cuu	UP	Move cursor up #1 lines.
parm_up_micro	mcuu	Zi	Like parm_up_cursor for micro adjust.
pc_term_options	pctrm	S6	PC terminal options
pkey_key	pfkey	pk	Prog funct key #1 to type string #2
pkey_local	pfloc	pl	Prog funct key #1 to execute string #2
pkey_plab	pfxl	xl	Prog key #1 to xmit string #2 and show string #3
pkey_xmit	pfx	px	Prog funct key #1 to xmit string #2
plab_norm	pln	pn	Prog label #1 to show string #2
print_screen	mc0	ps	Print contents of the screen
prtr_non	mc5p	pO	Turn on the printer for #1 bytes
prtr_off	mc4	pf	Turn off the printer
prtr_on	mc5	po	Turn on the printer
repeat_char	rep	rp	Repeat char #1 #2 times
req_for_input	rfi	RF	Send next input char (for ptys)
reset_1string	rs1	r1	Reset terminal completely to sane modes
reset_2string	rs2	r2	Reset terminal completely to sane modes
reset_3string	rs3	r3	Reset terminal completely to sane modes
reset_file	rf	rf	Name of file containing reset string
restore_cursor	rc	rc	Restore cursor to position of last sc
row_address	vpa	cv	Vertical position absolute
save_cursor	sc	sc	Save cursor position
scancode_escape	scesc	S7	Escape for scancode emulation
scroll_forward	ind	sf	Scroll text up
scroll_reverse	ri	sr	Scroll text down
select_char_set	scs	Zj	Select character set
set0_des_seq	s0ds	s0	Shift into codeset 0 (EUC set 0, ASCII)
set1_des_seq	s1ds	s1	Shift into codeset 1
set2_des_seq	s2ds	s2	Shift into codeset 2
set3_des_seq	s3ds	s3	Shift into codeset 3
set_a_background	setab	AB	Set background color using ANSI escape
set_a_foreground	setaf	AF	Set foreground color using ANSI escape
set_attributes	sgr	sa	Define the video attributes #1-#9
set_background	setb	Sb	Set current background color
set_bottom_margin	smgb	Zk	Set bottom margin at current line
set_bottom_margin_parm	smgbp	Zl	Set bottom margin at line #1 or #2 lines from bottom
set_color_band	setcolor	Yz	Change to ribbon color #1
set_color_pair	scp	sp	Set current color-pair
set_foreground	setf	Sf	Set current foreground color1

Variable	Cap-name	Termcap Code	Description
set_left_margin	smgl	ML	Set left margin at current line
set_left_margin_parm	smglp	Zm	Set left (right) margin at column #1 (#2)
set_lr_margin	smglr	ML	Sets both left and right margins
set_page_length	slines	YZ	Set page length to #1 lines (use tparm)
set_right_margin	smgr	MR	Set right margin at current column
set_right_margin_parm	smgrp	Zn	Set right margin at column #1
set_tab	hts	st	Set a tab in all rows, current column
set_tb_margin	smgtb	MT	Sets both top and bottom margins
set_top_margin	smgt	Zo	Set top margin at current line
set_top_margin_parm	smgtp	Zp	Set top (bottom) margin at line #1 (#2)
set_window	wind	wi	Current window is lines #1-#2 cols #3-#4
start_bit_image	sbim	Zq	Start printing bit image graphics
start_char_set_def	scsd	Zr	Start definition of a character set
stop_bit_image	rbim	Zs	End printing bit image graphics
stop_char_set_def	rcsd	Zt	End definition of a character set
subscript_characters	subcs	Zu	List of "subscript-able" characters
superscript_characters	supcs	Zv	List of "superscript-able" characters
tab	ht	ta	Tab to next 8-space hardware tab stop
these_cause_cr	docr	Zw	Printing any of these chars causes cr
to_status_line	tsl	ts	Go to status line, col #1
underline_char	uc	uc	Underscore one char and move past it
up_half_line	hu	hu	Half-line up (reverse 1/2 linefeed)
xoff_character	xoffc	XF	X-off character
xon_character	xonc	XN	X-on character
zero_motion	zerom	Zx	No motion for the subsequent character

Sample Entry

The following entry, which describes the AT&T 610 terminal, is among the more complex entries in the terminfo file as of this writing.

```
610 | 610bct | ATT610 | att610 | AT&T 610; 80 column; 98key keyboard
    am, eslok, hs, mir, msgr, xenl, xon,
    cols#80, it#8, lh#2, lines#24, lw#8, nlab#8, wsl#80,
    acsc=``aaffggjjkkllmmnnooppqqrrssttuuvvwwxxyyzz{{||}}~~,
    bel=^G, blink=\E[5m, bold=\E[1m, cbt=\E[Z,
    civis=\E[?251, clear=\E[H\E[J, cnorm=\E[?25h\E[?121,
    cr=\r, csr=\E[%i%p1%d;%p2%dr, cub=\E[%p1%dD, cub1=\b,
    cud=\E[%p1%dB, cud1=\E[B, cuf=\E[%p1%dC, cuf1=\E[C,
    cup=\E[%i%p1%d;%p2%dH, cuu=\E[%p1%dA, cuu1=\E[A,
    cvvis=\E[?12;25h, dch=\E[%p1%dP, dch1=\E[P, dim=\E[2m,
    dl=\E[%p1%dM, dl1=\E[M, ed=\E[J, el=\E[K, el1=\E[1K,
    flash=\E[?5h$<200>\E[?51, fsl=\E8, home=\E[H, ht=\t,
    ich=\E[%p1%d@, il=\E[%p1%dL, il1=\E[L, ind=\ED, .ind=\ED$<9>,
    invis=\E[8m,
    is1=\E[8;0 | \E[?3;4;5;13;151\E[13;201\E[?7h\E[12h\E(B\E)0,
    is2=\E[0m^O, is3=\E(B\E)0, kLFT=\E[\s@, kRIT=\E[\sA,
    kbs=^H, kcbt=\E[Z, kclr=\E[2J, kcub1=\E[D, kcud1=\E[B,
```

```
     kcuf1=\E[C, kcuu1=\E[A, kf1=\EOc, kf10=\ENp,
     kf11=\ENq, kf12=\ENr, kf13=\ENs, kf14=\ENt, kf2=\EOd,
     kf3=\EOe, kf4=\EOf, kf5=\EOg, kf6=\EOh, kf7=\EOi,
     kf8=\EOj, kf9=\ENo, khome=\E[H, kind=\E[S, kri=\E[T,
     ll=\E[24H, mc4=\E[?4i, mc5=\E[?5i, nel=\EE,
     pfxl=\E[%p1%d;%p2%l02dq%?%p1%{9}%<%t\s\s\sF%p1%1d\s\s\s\s\s
\s\s\s\s\s\s%;%p2%s,
     pln=\E[%p1%d;0;0;0q%p2%:-16.16s, rc=\E8, rev=\E[7m,
     ri=\EM, rmacs=^O, rmir=\E[41, rmln=\E[2p, rmso=\E[m,
     rmul=\E[m, rs2=\Ec\E[?31, sc=\E7,
     sgr=\E[0%?%p6%t;1%;%?%p5%t;2%;%?%p2%t;4%;%?%p4%t;5%;
%?%p3%p1% | %t;7%;%?%p7%t;8%;m%?%p9%t^N%e^O%;,
     sgr0=\E[m^O, smacs=^N, smir=\E[4h, smln=\E[p,
     smso=\E[7m, smul=\E[4m, tsl=\E7\E[25;%i%p1%dx,
```

Types of Capabilities in the Sample Entry

The sample entry shows the formats for the three types of terminfo capabilities listed: Boolean, numeric, and string. All capabilities specified in the terminfo source file must be followed by commas, including the last capability in the source file. In terminfo source files, capabilities are referenced by their capability names (as shown in the previous tables).

Boolean capabilities are specified simply by their comma separated cap names.

Numeric capabilities are followed by the character '#' and then a positive integer value. Thus, in the sample, cols (which shows the number of columns available on a device) is assigned the value 80 for the AT&T 610. (Values for numeric capabilities may be specified in decimal, octal, or hexadecimal, using normal C programming language conventions.)

Finally, string-valued capabilities such as el (clear to end of line sequence) are listed by a two- to five-character capname, an '=', and a string ended by the next occurrence of a comma. A delay in milliseconds may appear anywhere in such a capability, preceded by $ and enclosed in angle brackets, as in el=\EK$<3>. Padding characters are supplied by tput. The delay can be any of the following: a number, a number followed by an asterisk, such as 5*, a number followed by a slash, such as 5/, or a number followed by both, such as 5*/. A '*' shows that the padding required is proportional to the number of lines affected by the operation, and the amount given is the per-affected-unit padding required. (In the case of insert characters, the factor is still the number of lines affected. This is always 1 unless the device has in and the software uses it.) When a '*' is specified, it is sometimes useful to give a delay of the form 3.5 to specify a delay per unit to tenths of milliseconds. (Only one decimal place is allowed.)

A '/' indicates that the padding is mandatory. If a device has xon defined, the padding information is advisory and will only be used for cost estimates or when the device is in raw mode. Mandatory padding will be transmitted regardless of the setting of xon. If padding (whether advisory or mandatory) is specified for bel or flash, however, it will always be used, regardless of whether xon is specified.

terminfo offers notation for encoding special characters. Both \E and \e map to an ESCAPE character, ^x maps to a control x for any appropriate x, and the sequences \n, \l, \r, \t, \b, \f, and \s give a newline, linefeed, return, tab, backspace, formfeed, and space, respectively. Other escapes include: \^ for caret (^); \\ for backslash (\); \, for comma (,); \: for colon (:); and \0 for null. (\0 will actually produce \200, which does not terminate a string but behaves as a null character on most devices, providing CS7 is specified. [See stty(1).] Finally, characters may be given as three octal digits after a backslash (e.g., \123).

Sometimes individual capabilities must be commented out. To do this, put a period before the capability name. For example, see the second ind in the example above. Note that capabilities are defined in a left-to-right order and, therefore, a prior definition will override a later definition.

Preparing Descriptions

The most effective way to prepare a device description is by imitating the description of a similar device in terminfo and building up a description gradually, using partial descriptions with vi to check that they are correct. Be aware that a very unusual device may expose deficiencies in the ability of the terminfo file to describe it or the inability of vi to work with that device. To test a new device description, set the environment variable TERMINFO to the pathname of a directory containing the compiled description you are working on and programs will look there rather than in /usr/share/lib/terminfo. To get the padding for insert-line correct (if the device manufacturer did not document it) a severe test is to comment out xon, edit a large file at 9600 baud with vi, delete 16 or so lines from the middle of the screen, and then press the u key several times quickly. If the display is corrupted, more padding is usually needed. A similar test can be used for insert-character.

Section 1-1: Basic Capabilities

The number of columns on each line for the device is given by the cols numeric capability. If the device has a screen, then the number of lines on the screen is given by the lines capability. If the device wraps around to the beginning of the next line when it reaches the right margin, then it should have the am capability. If the terminal can clear its screen, leaving the cursor in the home position, then this is given by the clear string capability. If the terminal overstrikes (rather than clearing a position when a character is struck over) then it should have the os capability. If the device is a printing terminal, with no soft copy unit, specify both hc and os. If there is a way to move the cursor to the left edge of the current row, specify this as cr. (Normally this will be carriage return, control M.) If there is a way to produce an audible signal (such as a bell or a beep), specify it as bel. If, like most devices, the device uses the xon-xoff flow-control protocol, specify xon.

If there is a way to move the cursor one position to the left (such as backspace), that capability should be given as cub1. Similarly, sequences to move to the right, up, and down should be given as cuf1, cuu1, and cud1, respectively. These local cursor motions must not alter the text they pass over; for example, you would not normally use "cuf1=\s" because the space would erase the character moved over.

A very important point here is that the local cursor motions encoded in `terminfo` are undefined at the left and top edges of a screen terminal. Programs should never attempt to backspace around the left edge, unless `bw` is specified, and should never attempt to go up locally off the top. To scroll text up, a program goes to the bottom left corner of the screen and sends the `ind` (index) string.

To scroll text down, a program goes to the top left corner of the screen and sends the `ri` (reverse index) string. The strings `ind` and `ri` are undefined when not on their respective corners of the screen.

Parameterized versions of the scrolling sequences are `indn` and `rin`. These versions have the same semantics as `ind` and `ri`, except that they take one parameter and scroll the number of lines specified by that parameter. They are also undefined except at the appropriate edge of the screen.

The `am` capability tells whether the cursor sticks at the right edge of the screen when text is output, but this does not necessarily apply to a `cuf1` from the last column. Backward motion from the left edge of the screen is possible only when `bw` is specified. In this case, `cub1` will move to the right edge of the previous row. If `bw` is not given, the effect is undefined. This is useful for drawing a box around the edge of the screen, for example. If the device has switch selectable automatic margins, `am` should be specified in the `terminfo` source file. In this case, initialization strings should turn on this option, if possible. If the device has a command that moves to the first column of the next line, that command can be given as `nel` (newline). It does not matter if the command clears the remainder of the current line, so if the device has no `cr` and `lf` it may still be possible to craft a working `nel` out of one or both of them.

These capabilities suffice to describe hardcopy and screen terminals. Thus the AT&T 5320 hardcopy terminal is described as follows:

```
5320|att5320|AT&T 5320 hardcopy terminal,
    am, hc, os,
    cols#132,
    bel=^G, cr=\r, cub1=\b, cnd1=\n,
    dch1=\E[P, dl1=\E[M,
    ind=\n,
```

while the Lear Siegler ADM–3 is described as

```
adm3 | lsi adm3,
    am, bel=^G, clear=^Z, cols#80, cr=^M, cub1=^H,
    cud1=^J, ind=^J, lines#24,
```

Section 1-2: Parameterized Strings

Cursor addressing and other strings requiring parameters are described by a parameterized string capability, with `printf`-like escapes (%x) in it. For example, to address the cursor, the `cup` capability is given, using two parameters: the row and column to address to. (Rows and columns are numbered from zero and refer to the physical screen visible to the user, not to any unseen memory.) If the terminal has memory relative cursor addressing, that can be indicated by `mrcup`.

The parameter mechanism uses a stack and special % codes to manipulate the stack in the manner of Reverse Polish Notation (postfix). Typically a sequence will push one of the parameters onto the stack and then print it in some format. Often more complex operations are necessary. Operations are in postfix form with the operands in the usual order. That is, to subtract 5 from the first parameter, one would use %p1%{5}%-.

The % encodings have the following meanings:

%% outputs '%'

%[[:]*flags*][*width*[*.precision*]][doxXs]
 as in printf, flags are [-+#] and space

%c print pop gives %c

%p[1-9]
 push *i*th parm

%P[a-z]
 set dynamic variable [a-z] to pop

%g[a-z]
 get dynamic variable [a-z] and push it

%P[A-Z]
 set static variable [a-z] to pop

%g[A-Z]
 get static variable [a-z] and push it

%'*c*' push char constant *c*

%{*nn*} push decimal constant *nn*

%l push strlen(pop)

%+ %- %* %/ %m
 arithmetic (%m is mod): push(pop $integer_2$ op pop $integer_1$)

%& %| %^
 bit operations: push(pop $integer_2$ op pop $integer_1$)

%= %> %<
 logical operations: push(pop $integer_2$ op pop $integer_1$)

%A %O logical operations: and, or

%! %~ unary operations: push(op pop)

%i (for ANSI terminals) add 1 to first parm, if one parm present, or first two parms, if more than one parm present

%? *expr* %t *thenpart* %e *elsepart* %;
 if-then-else, %e *elsepart* is optional; else-if's are possible ala Algol 68: %? c_1 %t b_1 %e c_2 %t b_2 %e c_3 %t b_3 %e c_4 %t b_4 %e b_5%;
 c_i are conditions, b_i are bodies.

If the "−" flag is used with "%[doxXs]", then a colon (:) must be placed between the "%" and the "−" to differentiate the flag from the binary "%−" operator, *e.g.* ``%:-16.16s''.

Consider the Hewlett-Packard 2645, which, to get to row 3 and column 12, needs to be sent \E&a12c03Y padded for 6 milliseconds. Note that the order of the rows and columns is inverted here, and that the row and column are zero-padded as two digits. Thus its cup capability is:

cup=\E&a%p2%2.2dc%p1%2.2dY$<6>

The Micro-Term ACT-IV needs the current row and column sent preceded by a ^T, with the row and column simply encoded in binary, "cup=^T%p1%c%p2%c". Devices that use "%c" need to be able to backspace the cursor (cub1), and to move the cursor up one line on the screen (cuu1). This is necessary because it is not always safe to transmit \n, ^D, and \r, as the system may change or discard them. (The library routines dealing with terminfo set tty modes so that tabs are never expanded, so \t is safe to send. This turns out to be essential for the Ann Arbor 4080.)

A final example is the LSI ADM-3a, which uses row and column offset by a blank character, thus "cup=\E=%p1%'\s'%+%c%p2%'\s'%+%c". After sending "\E=", this pushes the first parameter, pushes the ASCII value for a space (32), adds them (pushing the sum on the stack in place of the two previous values), and outputs that value as a character. Then the same is done for the second parameter. More complex arithmetic is possible using the stack.

Section 1-3: Cursor Motions

If the terminal has a fast way to home the cursor (to very upper left corner of screen) then this can be given as home; similarly a fast way of getting to the lower left-hand corner can be given as ll; this may involve going up with cuu1 from the home position, but a program should never do this itself (unless ll does) because it can make no assumption about the effect of moving up from the home position. Note that the home position is the same as addressing to (0,0): to the top left corner of the screen, not of memory. (Thus, the \EH sequence on Hewlett-Packard terminals cannot be used for home without losing some of the other features on the terminal.)

If the device has row or column absolute-cursor addressing, these can be given as single parameter capabilities hpa (horizontal position absolute) and vpa (vertical position absolute). Sometimes these are shorter than the more general two-parameter sequence (as with the Hewlett-Packard 2645) and can be used in preference to cup. If there are parameterized local motions (*e.g.*, move *n* spaces to the right) these can be given as cud, cub, cuf, and cuu with a single parameter indicating how many spaces to move. These are primarily useful if the device does not have cup, such as the Tektronix 4025.

If the device needs to be in a special mode when running a program that uses these capabilities, the codes to enter and exit this mode can be given as smcup and rmcup. This arises, for example, from terminals, such as the Concept, with more than one page of memory. If the device has only memory relative cursor addressing and not screen relative cursor addressing, a one screen-sized window must be fixed into the device for cursor addressing to work properly. This is also used for the Tektronix 4025, where smcup sets the command character to be the one used by terminfo. If the smcup sequence will not restore the screen after an rmcup sequence is output (to the state prior to outputting rmcup), specify nrrmc.

Section 1-4: Area Clears

If the terminal can clear from the current position to the end of the line, leaving the cursor where it is, this should be given as el. If the terminal can clear from the beginning of the line to the current position inclusive, leaving the cursor where it is, this should be given as el1. If the terminal can clear from the current position to the end of the display, then this should be given as ed. ed is only defined from the first column of a line. (Thus, it can be simulated by a request to delete a large number of lines, if a true ed is not available.)

Section 1-5: Insert/Delete Line

If the terminal can open a new blank line before the line where the cursor is, this should be given as il1; this is done only from the first position of a line. The cursor must then appear on the newly blank line. If the terminal can delete the line which the cursor is on, then this should be given as dl1; this is done only from the first position on the line to be deleted. Versions of il1 and dl1 which take a single parameter and insert or delete that many lines can be given as il and dl.

If the terminal has a settable destructive scrolling region (like the VT100) the command to set this can be described with the csr capability, which takes two parameters: the top and bottom lines of the scrolling region. The cursor position is, alas, undefined after using this command. It is possible to get the effect of insert or delete line using this command — the sc and rc (save and restore cursor) commands are also useful. Inserting lines at the top or bottom of the screen can also be done using ri or ind on many terminals without a true insert/delete line, and is often faster even on terminals with those features.

To determine whether a terminal has destructive scrolling regions or non-destructive scrolling regions, create a scrolling region in the middle of the screen, place data on the bottom line of the scrolling region, move the cursor to the top line of the scrolling region, and do a reverse index (ri) followed by a delete line (dl1) or index (ind). If the data that was originally on the bottom line of the scrolling region was restored into the scrolling region by the dl1 or ind, then the terminal has non-destructive scrolling regions. Otherwise, it has destructive scrolling regions. Do not specify csr if the terminal has non-destructive scrolling regions, unless ind, ri, indn, rin, dl, and dl1 all simulate destructive scrolling.

If the terminal has the ability to define a window as part of memory, which all commands affect, it should be given as the parameterized string wind. The four parameters are the starting and ending lines in memory and the starting and ending columns in memory, in that order.

If the terminal can retain display memory above, then the da capability should be given; if display memory can be retained below, then db should be given. These indicate that deleting a line or scrolling a full screen may bring non-blank lines up from below or that scrolling back with ri may bring down non-blank lines.

Section 1-6: Insert/Delete Character

There are two basic kinds of intelligent terminals with respect to insert/delete character operations which can be described using terminfo. The most common insert/delete character operations affect only the characters on the current line and shift characters off the end of the line rigidly. Other terminals, such as the Concept 100 and the Perkin Elmer Owl, make a distinction between typed and untyped blanks on the screen, shifting upon an insert or delete only to an untyped blank on the screen which is either eliminated, or expanded to two untyped blanks. You can determine the kind of terminal you have by clearing the screen and then typing text separated by cursor motions. Type "abc   def" using local cursor motions (not spaces) between the abc and the def. Then position the cursor before the abc and put the terminal in insert mode. If typing characters causes the rest of the line to shift rigidly and characters to fall off the end, then your terminal does not distinguish between blanks and untyped positions. If the abc shifts over to the def which then move together around the end of the current line and onto the next as you insert, you have the second type of terminal, and should give the capability in, which stands for "insert null." While these are two logically separate attributes (one line versus multiline insert mode, and special treatment of untyped spaces) we have seen no terminals whose insert mode cannot be described with the single attribute.

terminfo can describe both terminals that have an insert mode and terminals which send a simple sequence to open a blank position on the current line. Give as smir the sequence to get into insert mode. Give as rmir the sequence to leave insert mode. Now give as ich1 any sequence needed to be sent just before sending the character to be inserted. Most terminals with a true insert mode will not give ich1; terminals that send a sequence to open a screen position should give it here. (If your terminal has both, insert mode is usually preferable to ich1. Do not give both unless the terminal actually requires both to be used in combination.) If post-insert padding is needed, give this as a number of milliseconds padding in ip (a string option). Any other sequence which may need to be sent after an insert of a single character may also be given in ip. If your terminal needs both to be placed into an 'insert mode' and a special code to precede each inserted character, then both smir/rmir and ich1 can be given, and both will be used. The ich capability, with one parameter, n, will insert n blanks.

If padding is necessary between characters typed while not in insert mode, give this as a number of milliseconds padding in rmp.

It is occasionally necessary to move around while in insert mode to delete characters on the same line (e.g., if there is a tab after the insertion position). If your terminal allows motion while in insert mode you can give the capability mir to speed up inserting in this case. Omitting mir will affect only speed. Some terminals (notably Datamedia's) must not have mir because of the way their insert mode works.

Finally, you can specify dch1 to delete a single character, dch with one parameter, n, to delete n characters, and delete mode by giving smdc and rmdc to enter and exit delete mode (any mode the terminal needs to be placed in for dch1 to work).

A command to erase *n* characters (equivalent to outputting *n* blanks without moving the cursor) can be given as ech with one parameter.

Section 1-7: Highlighting, Underlining, and Visible Bells

Your device may have one or more kinds of display attributes that allow you to highlight selected characters when they appear on the screen. The following display modes (shown with the names by which they are set) may be available: a blinking screen (blink), bold or extra-bright characters (bold), dim or half-bright characters (dim), blanking or invisible text (invis), protected text (prot), a reverse-video screen (rev), and an alternate character set (smacs to enter this mode and rmacs to exit it). (If a command is necessary before you can enter alternate character set mode, give the sequence in enacs or "enable alternate-character-set" mode.) Turning on any of these modes singly may or may not turn off other modes.

sgr0 should be used to turn off all video enhancement capabilities. It should always be specified because it represents the only way to turn off some capabilities, such as dim or blink.

You should choose one display method as *standout mode* [see curses(3X)] and use it to highlight error messages and other kinds of text to which you want to draw attention. Choose a form of display that provides strong contrast but that is easy on the eyes. (We recommend reverse-video plus half-bright or reverse-video alone.) The sequences to enter and exit standout mode are given as smso and rmso, respectively. If the code to change into or out of standout mode leaves one or even two blank spaces on the screen, as the TVI 912 and Teleray 1061 do, then xmc should be given to tell how many spaces are left.

Sequences to begin underlining and end underlining can be specified as smul and rmul , respectively. If the device has a sequence to underline the current character and to move the cursor one space to the right (such as the Micro-Term MIME), this sequence can be specified as uc.

Terminals with the "magic cookie" glitch (xmc) deposit special "cookies" when they receive mode-setting sequences, which affect the display algorithm rather than having extra bits for each character. Some terminals, such as the Hewlett-Packard 2621, automatically leave standout mode when they move to a new line or the cursor is addressed. Programs using standout mode should exit standout mode before moving the cursor or sending a newline, unless the msgr capability, asserting that it is safe to move in standout mode, is present.

If the terminal has a way of flashing the screen to indicate an error quietly (a bell replacement), then this can be given as flash; it must not move the cursor. A good flash can be done by changing the screen into reverse video, pad for 200 ms, then return the screen to normal video.

If the cursor needs to be made more visible than normal when it is not on the bottom line (to make, for example, a non-blinking underline into an easier to find block or blinking underline) give this sequence as cvvis. The boolean chts should also be given. If there is a way to make the cursor completely invisible, give that as civis. The capability cnorm should be given which undoes the effects of either of these modes.

If your terminal generates underlined characters by using the underline character (with no special sequences needed) even though it does not otherwise overstrike characters, then you should specify the capability ul. For devices on which a character overstriking another leaves both characters on the screen, specify the capability os. If overstrikes are erasable with a blank, then this should be indicated by specifying eo.

If there is a sequence to set arbitrary combinations of modes, this should be given as sgr (set attributes), taking nine parameters. Each parameter is either 0 or non-zero, as the corresponding attribute is on or off. The nine parameters are, in order: standout, underline, reverse, blink, dim, bold, blank, protect, alternate character set. Not all modes need to be supported by sgr; only those for which corresponding separate attribute commands exist should be supported. For example, let's assume that the terminal in question needs the following escape sequences to turn on various modes.

tparm parameter	attribute	escape sequence
	none	\E[0m
p1	standout	\E[0;4;7m
p2	underline	\E[0;3m
p3	reverse	\E[0;4m
p4	blink	\E[0;5m
p5	dim	\E[0;7m
p6	bold	\E[0;3;4m
p7	invis	\E[0;8m
p8	protect	not available
p9	altcharset	^O (off) ^N (on)

Note that each escape sequence requires a 0 to turn off other modes before turning on its own mode. Also note that, as suggested above, *standout* is set up to be the combination of *reverse* and *dim*. Also, because this terminal has no *bold* mode, *bold* is set up as the combination of *reverse* and *underline*. In addition, to allow combinations, such as *underline+blink*, the sequence to use would be \E[0;3;5m. The terminal doesn't have *protect* mode, either, but that cannot be simulated in any way, so p8 is ignored. The *altcharset* mode is different in that it is either ^O or ^N, depending on whether it is off or on. If all modes were to be turned on, the sequence would be \E[0;3;4;5;7;8m^N.

Now look at when different sequences are output. For example, ;3 is output when either p2 or p6 is true, that is, if either *underline* or *bold* modes are turned on. Writing out the above sequences, along with their dependencies, gives the following:

sequence	when to output	terminfo translation
\E[0	always	\E[0
;3	if p2 or p6	%?%p2%p6%|%t;3%;
;4	if p1 or p3 or p6	%?%p1%p3%|%p6%|%t;4%;
;5	if p4	%?%p4%t;5%;
;7	if p1 or p5	%?%p1%p5%|%t;7%;
;8	if p7	%?%p7%t;8%;
m	always	m
^N or ^O	if p9 ^N, else ^O	%?%p9%t^N%e^O%;

Putting this all together into the sgr sequence gives:

```
sgr=\E[0%?%p2%p6%|%t;3%;%?%p1%p3%|%p6%
    |%t;4%;%?%p5%t;5%;%?%p1%p5%
    |%t;7%;%?%p7%t;8%;m%?%p9%t^N%e^O%;,
```

Remember that sgr and sgr0 must always be specified.

Section 1-8: Keypad

If the device has a keypad that transmits sequences when the keys are pressed, this information can also be specified. Note that it is not possible to handle devices where the keypad only works in local (this applies, for example, to the unshifted Hewlett-Packard 2621 keys). If the keypad can be set to transmit or not transmit, specify these sequences as smkx and rmkx. Otherwise the keypad is assumed to always transmit.

The sequences sent by the left arrow, right arrow, up arrow, down arrow, and home keys can be given as kcub1, kcuf1, kcuu1, kcud1, and khome, respectively. If there are function keys such as f0, f1, ..., f63, the sequences they send can be specified as kf0, kf1, ..., kf63. If the first 11 keys have labels other than the default f0 through f10, the labels can be given as lf0, lf1, ..., lf10. The codes transmitted by certain other special keys can be given: kll (home down), kbs (backspace), ktbc (clear all tabs), kctab (clear the tab stop in this column), kclr (clear screen or erase key), kdch1 (delete character), kdl1 (delete line), krmir (exit insert mode), kel (clear to end of line), ked (clear to end of screen), kich1 (insert character or enter insert mode), kil1 (insert line), knp (next page), kpp (previous page), kind (scroll forward/down), kri (scroll backward/up), khts (set a tab stop in this column). In addition, if the keypad has a 3 by 3 array of keys including the four arrow keys, the other five keys can be given as ka1, ka3, kb2, kc1, and kc3. These keys are useful when the effects of a 3 by 3 directional pad are needed. Further keys are defined above in the capabilities list.

Strings to program function keys can be specified as pfkey, pfloc, and pfx. A string to program screen labels should be specified as pln. Each of these strings takes two parameters: a function key identifier and a string to program it with. pfkey causes pressing the given key to be the same as the user typing the given string; pfloc causes the string to be executed by the terminal in local mode; and pfx causes the string to be transmitted to the computer. The capabilities nlab, lw and lh define the number of programmable screen labels and their width and height. If there are commands to turn the labels on and off, give them in smln and rmln. smln is normally output after one or more pln sequences to make sure that the change becomes visible.

Section 1-9: Tabs and Initialization

If the device has hardware tabs, the command to advance to the next tab stop can be given as ht (usually control I). A "backtab" command that moves leftward to the next tab stop can be given as cbt. By convention, if tty modes show that tabs are being expanded by the computer rather than being sent to the device, programs should not use ht or cbt (even if they are present) because the user may not have the tab stops properly set. If the device has hardware tabs that are initially set every *n* spaces when the device is powered up, the numeric parameter it is given, showing the number of spaces the tabs are set to. This is normally used by tput init [see tput(1)] to determine whether to set the mode for hardware tab expansion and whether to set the tab stops. If the device has tab stops that can be saved in nonvolatile memory, the terminfo description can assume that they are properly set. If there are commands to set and clear tab stops, they can be given as tbc (clear all tab stops) and hts (set a tab stop in the current column of every row).

Other capabilities include: is1, is2, and is3, initialization strings for the device; iprog, the path name of a program to be run to initialize the device; and if, the name of a file containing long initialization strings. These strings are expected to set the device into modes consistent with the rest of the terminfo description. They must be sent to the device each time the user logs in and be output in the following order: run the program iprog; output is1; output is2; set the margins using mgc, smgl and smgr; set the tabs using tbc and hts; print the file if; and finally output is3. This is usually done using the init option of tput.

Most initialization is done with is2. Special device modes can be set up without duplicating strings by putting the common sequences in is2 and special cases in is1 and is3. Sequences that do a reset from a totally unknown state can be given as rs1, rs2, rf, and rs3, analogous to is1, is2, is3, and if. (The method using files, if and rf, is used for a few terminals, from /usr/share/lib/tabset/*; however, the recommended method is to use the initialization and reset strings.) These strings are output by tput reset, which is used when the terminal gets into a wedged state. Commands are normally placed in rs1, rs2, rs3, and rf only if they produce annoying effects on the screen and are not necessary when logging in. For example, the command to set a terminal into 80-column mode would normally be part of is2, but on some terminals it causes an annoying glitch on the screen and is not normally needed because the terminal is usually already in 80-column mode.

If a more complex sequence is needed to set the tabs than can be described by using tbc and hts, the sequence can be placed in is2 or if.

Any margin can be cleared with mgc. (For instructions on how to specify commands to set and clear margins, see "Margins" below under "PRINTER CAPABILITIES.")

Section 1-10: Delays

Certain capabilities control padding in the tty driver. These are primarily needed by hard-copy terminals, and are used by tput init to set tty modes appropriately. Delays embedded in the capabilities cr, ind, cub1, ff, and tab

can be used to set the appropriate delay bits to be set in the tty driver. If pb
(padding baud rate) is given, these values can be ignored at baud rates below the
value of pb.

Section 1-11: Status Lines

If the terminal has an extra "status line" that is not normally used by software,
this fact can be indicated. If the status line is viewed as an extra line below the
bottom line, into which one can cursor address normally (such as the Heathkit
h19's 25th line, or the 24th line of a VT100 which is set to a 23-line scrolling
region), the capability hs should be given. Special strings that go to a given
column of the status line and return from the status line can be given as tsl and
fsl. (fsl must leave the cursor position in the same place it was before tsl. If
necessary, the sc and rc strings can be included in tsl and fsl to get this
effect.) The capability tsl takes one parameter, which is the column number of
the status line the cursor is to be moved to.

If escape sequences and other special commands, such as tab, work while in the
status line, the flag eslok can be given. A string which turns off the status line
(or otherwise erases its contents) should be given as dsl. If the terminal has
commands to save and restore the position of the cursor, give them as sc and rc.
The status line is normally assumed to be the same width as the rest of the
screen, *e.g.*, cols. If the status line is a different width (possibly because the terminal does not allow an entire line to be loaded) the width, in columns, can be
indicated with the numeric parameter wsl.

Section 1-12: Line Graphics

If the device has a line drawing alternate character set, the mapping of glyph to
character would be given in acsc. The definition of this string is based on the
alternate character set used in the DEC VT100 terminal, extended slightly with
some characters from the AT&T 4410v1 terminal.

glyph name	vt100+ character
arrow pointing right	+
arrow pointing left	,
arrow pointing down	.
solid square block	0
lantern symbol	I
arrow pointing up	–
diamond	`
checker board (stipple)	a
degree symbol	f
plus/minus	g
board of squares	h
lower right corner	j
upper right corner	k
upper left corner	l
lower left corner	m
plus	n

scan line 1	o
horizontal line	q
scan line 9	s
left tee ($\vdash$)	t
right tee ($-\vert$)	u
bottom tee ($\perp$)	v
top tee ($\top$)	w
vertical line	x
bullet	~

The best way to describe a new device's line graphics set is to add a third column to the above table with the characters for the new device that produce the appropriate glyph when the device is in the alternate character set mode. For example,

glyph name	vt100+ char	new tty char
upper left corner	l	R
lower left corner	m	F
upper right corner	k	T
lower right corner	j	G
horizontal line	q	'
vertical line	x	.

Now write down the characters left to right, as in "acsc=lRmFkTjGq\,x.".

In addition, terminfo allows you to define multiple character sets. See Section 2-5 for details.

Section 1-13: Color Manipulation

Let us define two methods of color manipulation: the Tektronix method and the HP method. The Tektronix method uses a set of N predefined colors (usually 8) from which a user can select "current" foreground and background colors. Thus a terminal can support up to N colors mixed into N*N color-pairs to be displayed on the screen at the same time. When using an HP method the user cannot define the foreground independently of the background, or vice-versa. Instead, the user must define an entire color-pair at once. Up to M color-pairs, made from 2*M different colors, can be defined this way. Most existing color terminals belong to one of these two classes of terminals.

The numeric variables colors and pairs define the number of colors and color-pairs that can be displayed on the screen at the same time. If a terminal can change the definition of a color (for example, the Tektronix 4100 and 4200 series terminals), this should be specified with ccc (can change color). To change the definition of a color (Tektronix 4200 method), use initc (initialize color). It requires four arguments: color number (ranging from 0 to colors-1) and three RGB (red, green, and blue) values or three HLS colors (Hue, Lightness, Saturation). Ranges of RGB and HLS values are terminal dependent.

Tektronix 4100 series terminals only use HLS color notation. For such terminals (or dual-mode terminals to be operated in HLS mode) one must define a boolean variable hls; that would instruct the curses init_color routine to convert its RGB arguments to HLS before sending them to the terminal. The last three arguments to the initc string would then be HLS values.

If a terminal can change the definitions of colors, but uses a color notation different from RGB and HLS, a mapping to either RGB or HLS must be developed.

To set current foreground or background to a given color, use setaf (set ANSI foreground) and setab (set ANSI background). They require one parameter: the number of the color. To initialize a color-pair (HP method), use initp (initialize pair). It requires seven parameters: the number of a color-pair (range=0 to pairs-1), and six RGB values: three for the foreground followed by three for the background. (Each of these groups of three should be in the order RGB.) When initc or initp are used, RGB or HLS arguments should be in the order "red, green, blue" or "hue, lightness, saturation"), respectively. To make a color-pair current, use scp (set color-pair). It takes one parameter, the number of a color-pair.

Some terminals (for example, most color terminal emulators for PCs) erase areas of the screen with current background color. In such cases, bce (background color erase) should be defined. The variable op (original pair) contains a sequence for setting the foreground and the background colors to what they were at the terminal start-up time. Similarly, oc (original colors) contains a control sequence for setting all colors (for the Tektronix method) or color-pairs (for the HP method) to the values they had at the terminal start-up time.

Some color terminals substitute color for video attributes. Such video attributes should not be combined with colors. Information about these video attributes should be packed into the ncv (no color video) variable. There is a one-to-one correspondence between the nine least significant bits of that variable and the video attributes. The following table depicts this correspondence.

Attribute	Bit Position	Decimal Value
A_STANDOUT	0	1
A_UNDERLINE	1	2
A_REVERSE	2	4
A_BLINK	3	8
A_DIM	4	16
A_BOLD	5	32
A_INVIS	6	64
A_PROTECT	7	128
A_ALTCHARSET	8	256

When a particular video attribute should not be used with colors, the corresponding ncv bit should be set to 1; otherwise it should be set to zero. To determine the information to pack into the ncv variable, you must add together the decimal values corresponding to those attributes that cannot coexist with colors. For example, if the terminal uses colors to simulate reverse video (bit number 2 and decimal value 4) and bold (bit number 5 and decimal value 32), the resulting value for ncv will be 36 (4 + 32).

Section 1-14: Miscellaneous

If the terminal requires other than a null (zero) character as a pad, then this can be given as pad. Only the first character of the pad string is used. If the terminal does not have a pad character, specify npc.

If the terminal can move up or down half a line, this can be indicated with hu (half-line up) and hd (half-line down). This is primarily useful for superscripts and subscripts on hardcopy terminals. If a hardcopy terminal can eject to the next page (form feed), give this as ff (usually control L).

If there is a command to repeat a given character a given number of times (to save time transmitting a large number of identical characters) this can be indicated with the parameterized string rep. The first parameter is the character to be repeated and the second is the number of times to repeat it. Thus, tparm(repeat_char, 'x', 10) is the same as xxxxxxxxxx.

If the terminal has a settable command character, such as the Tektronix 4025, this can be indicated with cmdch. A prototype command character is chosen which is used in all capabilities. This character is given in the cmdch capability to identify it. The following convention is supported on some UNIX systems: If the environment variable CC exists, all occurrences of the prototype character are replaced with the character in CC.

Terminal descriptions that do not represent a specific kind of known terminal, such as *switch*, *dialup*, *patch*, and *network*, should include the gn (generic) capability so that programs can complain that they do not know how to talk to the terminal. (This capability does not apply to *virtual* terminal descriptions for which the escape sequences are known.) If the terminal is one of those supported by the UNIX system virtual terminal protocol, the terminal number can be given as vt. A line-turn-around sequence to be transmitted before doing reads should be specified in rfi.

If the device uses xon/xoff handshaking for flow control, give xon. Padding information should still be included so that routines can make better decisions about costs, but actual pad characters will not be transmitted. Sequences to turn on and off xon/xoff handshaking may be given in smxon and rmxon. If the characters used for handshaking are not ^S and ^Q, they may be specified with xonc and xoffc.

If the terminal has a "meta key" which acts as a shift key, setting the 8th bit of any character transmitted, this fact can be indicated with km. Otherwise, software will assume that the 8th bit is parity and it will usually be cleared. If strings exist to turn this "meta mode" on and off, they can be given as smm and rmm.

If the terminal has more lines of memory than will fit on the screen at once, the number of lines of memory can be indicated with lm. A value of lm#0 indicates that the number of lines is not fixed, but that there is still more memory than fits on the screen.

Media copy strings which control an auxiliary printer connected to the terminal can be given as mc0: print the contents of the screen, mc4: turn off the printer, and mc5: turn on the printer. When the printer is on, all text sent to the terminal will be sent to the printer. A variation, mc5p, takes one parameter, and leaves the printer on for as many characters as the value of the parameter, then turns the printer off. The parameter should not exceed 255. If the text is not displayed on the terminal screen when the printer is on, specify mc5i (silent printer). All text, including mc4, is transparently passed to the printer while an mc5p is in effect.

Section 1-15: Special Cases

The working model used by terminfo fits most terminals reasonably well. However, some terminals do not completely match that model, requiring special support by terminfo. These are not meant to be construed as deficiencies in the terminals; they are just differences between the working model and the actual hardware. They may be unusual devices or, for some reason, do not have all the features of the terminfo model implemented.

Terminals that cannot display tilde (˜) characters, such as certain Hazeltine terminals, should indicate hz.

Terminals that ignore a linefeed immediately after an am wrap, such as the Concept 100, should indicate xenl. Those terminals whose cursor remains on the right-most column until another character has been received, rather than wrapping immediately upon receiving the right-most character, such as the VT100, should also indicate xenl.

If el is required to get rid of standout (instead of writing normal text on top of it), xhp should be given.

Those Teleray terminals whose tabs turn all characters moved over to blanks, should indicate xt (destructive tabs). This capability is also taken to mean that it is not possible to position the cursor on top of a "magic cookie." Therefore, to erase standout mode, it is necessary, instead, to use delete and insert line.

Those Beehive Superbee terminals which do not transmit the escape or control–C characters, should specify xsb, indicating that the f1 key is to be used for escape and the f2 key for control C.

Section 1-16: Similar Terminals

If there are two very similar terminals, one can be defined as being just like the other with certain exceptions. The string capability use can be given with the name of the similar terminal. The capabilities given before use override those in the terminal type invoked by use. A capability can be canceled by placing xx@ to the left of the capability definition, where xx is the capability. For example, the entry

```
att4424-2|Teletype 4424 in display function group ii,
    rev@, sgr@, smul@, use=att4424,
```

defines an AT&T 4424 terminal that does not have the rev, sgr, and smul capabilities, and hence cannot do highlighting. This is useful for different modes for a terminal, or for different user preferences. More than one use capability may be given.

PART 2: PRINTER CAPABILITIES

The terminfo database allows you to define capabilities of printers as well as terminals. To find out what capabilities are available for printers as well as for terminals, see the two lists under "DEVICE CAPABILITIES" that list capabilities by variable and by capability name.

Section 2-1: Rounding Values

Because parameterized string capabilities work only with integer values, we recommend that terminfo designers create strings that expect numeric values that have been rounded. Application designers should note this and should always round values to the nearest integer before using them with a parameterized string capability.

Section 2-2: Printer Resolution

A printer's resolution is defined to be the smallest spacing of characters it can achieve. In general printers have independent resolution horizontally and vertically. Thus the vertical resolution of a printer can be determined by measuring the smallest achievable distance between consecutive printing baselines, while the horizontal resolution can be determined by measuring the smallest achievable distance between the left-most edges of consecutive printed, identical, characters.

All printers are assumed to be capable of printing with a uniform horizontal and vertical resolution. The view of printing that terminfo currently presents is one of printing inside a uniform matrix: All characters are printed at fixed positions relative to each "cell" in the matrix; furthermore, each cell has the same size given by the smallest horizontal and vertical step sizes dictated by the resolution. (The cell size can be changed as will be seen later.)

Many printers are capable of "proportional printing," where the horizontal spacing depends on the size of the character last printed. terminfo does not make use of this capability, although it does provide enough capability definitions to allow an application to simulate proportional printing.

A printer must not only be able to print characters as close together as the horizontal and vertical resolutions suggest, but also of "moving" to a position an integral multiple of the smallest distance away from a previous position. Thus printed characters can be spaced apart a distance that is an integral multiple of the smallest distance, up to the length or width of a single page.

Some printers can have different resolutions depending on different "modes." In "normal mode," the existing terminfo capabilities are assumed to work on columns and lines, just like a video terminal. Thus the old lines capability would give the length of a page in lines, and the cols capability would give the width of a page in columns. In "micro mode," many terminfo capabilities work on increments of lines and columns. With some printers the micro mode may be concomitant with normal mode, so that all the capabilities work at the same time.

Section 2-3: Specifying Printer Resolution

The printing resolution of a printer is given in several ways. Each specifies the resolution as the number of smallest steps per distance:

Specification of Printer Resolution

Characteristic	Number of Smallest Steps
orhi	Steps per inch horizontally
orvi	Steps per inch vertically
orc	Steps per column
orl	Steps per line

When printing in normal mode, each character printed causes movement to the next column, except in special cases described later; the distance moved is the same as the per-column resolution. Some printers cause an automatic movement to the next line when a character is printed in the rightmost position; the distance moved vertically is the same as the per-line resolution. When printing in micro mode, these distances can be different, and may be zero for some printers.

Specification of Printer Resolution
Automatic Motion after Printing

Normal Mode:	
orc	Steps moved horizontally
orl	Steps moved vertically

Micro Mode:	
mcs	Steps moved horizontally
mls	Steps moved vertically

Some printers are capable of printing wide characters. The distance moved when a wide character is printed in normal mode may be different from when a regular width character is printed. The distance moved when a wide character is printed in micro mode may also be different from when a regular character is printed in micro mode, but the differences are assumed to be related: If the distance moved for a regular character is the same whether in normal mode or micro mode (mcs=orc), then the distance moved for a wide character is also the same whether in normal mode or micro mode. This doesn't mean the normal character distance is necessarily the same as the wide character distance, just that the distances don't change with a change in normal to micro mode. However, if the distance moved for a regular character is different in micro mode from the distance moved in normal mode (mcs<orc), the micro mode distance is assumed to be the same for a wide character printed in micro mode, as the table below shows.

Specification of Printer Resolution
Automatic Motion after Printing Wide Character

Normal Mode or Micro Mode (mcs = orc):	
widcs	Steps moved horizontally

Micro Mode (mcs < orc):	
mcs	Steps moved horizontally

There may be control sequences to change the number of columns per inch (the character pitch) and to change the number of lines per inch (the line pitch). If these are used, the resolution of the printer changes, but the type of change depends on the printer:

Specification of Printer Resolution
Changing the Character/Line Pitches

cpi	Change character pitch
cpix	If set, cpi changes orhi, otherwise changes orc
lpi	Change line pitch
lpix	If set, lpi changes orvi, otherwise changes orl
chr	Change steps per column
cvr	Change steps per line

The cpi and lpi string capabilities are each used with a single argument, the pitch in columns (or characters) and lines per inch, respectively. The chr and cvr string capabilities are each used with a single argument, the number of steps per column and line, respectively.

Using any of the control sequences in these strings will imply a change in some of the values of orc, orhi, orl, and orvi. Also, the distance moved when a wide character is printed, widcs, changes in relation to orc. The distance moved when a character is printed in micro mode, mcs, changes similarly, with one exception: if the distance is 0 or 1, then no change is assumed (see items marked with † in the following table).

Programs that use cpi, lpi, chr, or cvr should recalculate the printer resolution (and should recalculate other values see "Effect of Changing Printing Resolution" under "Dot-Mapped Graphics").

Specification of Printer Resolution
Effects of Changing the Character/Line Pitches

Before	After
Using cpi with cpix clear:	
orhi′	orhi
orc′	$orc = \dfrac{orhi}{V_{cpi}}$
Using cpi with cpix set:	
orhi′	$orhi = orc \cdot V_{cpi}$
orc′	orc
Using lpi with lpix clear:	
orvi′	orvi
orl′	$orl = \dfrac{orvi}{V_{lpi}}$
Using lpi with lpix set:	
orvi′	$orvi = orl \cdot V_{lpi}$
orl′	orl
Using chr:	
orhi′	orhi

orc′	V_{chr}
Using cvr:	
orvi′	orvi
orl′	V_{cvr}
Using cpi or chr:	
widcs′	widcs=widcs′$\dfrac{\text{orc}}{\text{orc}′}$
mcs′	mcs=mcs′$\dfrac{\text{orc}}{\text{orc}′}$

V_{cpi}, V_{lpi}, V_{chr}, and V_{cvr} are the arguments used with cpi, lpi, chr, and cvr, respectively. The prime marks (′) indicate the old values.

Section 2-4: Capabilities that Cause Movement

In the following descriptions, "movement" refers to the motion of the "current position." With video terminals this would be the cursor; with some printers this is the carriage position. Other printers have different equivalents. In general, the current position is where a character would be displayed if printed.

terminfo has string capabilities for control sequences that cause movement a number of full columns or lines. It also has equivalent string capabilities for control sequences that cause movement a number of smallest steps.

String Capabilities for Motion

mcub1	Move 1 step left
mcuf1	Move 1 step right
mcuu1	Move 1 step up
mcud1	Move 1 step down
mcub	Move N steps left
mcuf	Move N steps right
mcuu	Move N steps up
mcud	Move N steps down
mhpa	Move N steps from the left
mvpa	Move N steps from the top

The latter six strings are each used with a single argument, N.

Sometimes the motion is limited to less than the width or length of a page. Also, some printers don't accept absolute motion to the left of the current position. terminfo has capabilities for specifying these limits.

Limits to Motion

mjump	Limit on use of mcub1, mcuf1, mcuu1, mcud1
maddr	Limit on use of mhpa, mvpa
xhpa	If set, hpa and mhpa can't move left
xvpa	If set, vpa and mvpa can't move up

If a printer needs to be in a "micro mode" for the motion capabilities described above to work, there are string capabilities defined to contain the control sequence to enter and exit this mode. A boolean is available for those printers where using a carriage return causes an automatic return to normal mode.

Entering/Exiting Micro Mode

smicm	Enter micro mode
rmicm	Exit micro mode
crxm	Using cr exits micro mode

The movement made when a character is printed in the rightmost position varies among printers. Some make no movement, some move to the beginning of the next line, others move to the beginning of the same line. terminfo has boolean capabilities for describing all three cases.

What Happens After Character Printed in Rightmost Position

sam	Automatic move to beginning of same line

Some printers can be put in a mode where the normal direction of motion is reversed. This mode can be especially useful when there are no capabilities for leftward or upward motion, because those capabilities can be built from the motion reversal capability and the rightward or downward motion capabilities. It is best to leave it up to an application to build the leftward or upward capabilities, though, and not enter them in the terminfo database. This allows several reverse motions to be strung together without intervening wasted steps that leave and reenter reverse mode.

Entering/Exiting Reverse Modes

slm	Reverse sense of horizontal motions
rlm	Restore sense of horizontal motions
sum	Reverse sense of vertical motions
rum	Restore sense of vertical motions

While sense of horizontal motions reversed:

mcub1	Move 1 step right
mcuf1	Move 1 step left
mcub	Move N steps right
mcuf	Move N steps left
cub1	Move 1 column right
cuf1	Move 1 column left
cub	Move N columns right
cuf	Move N columns left

While sense of vertical motions reversed:

mcuu1	Move 1 step down
mcud1	Move 1 step up
mcuu	Move N steps down
mcud	Move N steps up

cuu1	Move 1 line down
cud1	Move 1 line up
cuu	Move N lines down
cud	Move N lines up

The reverse motion modes should not affect the mvpa and mhpa absolute motion capabilities. The reverse vertical motion mode should, however, also reverse the action of the line "wrapping" that occurs when a character is printed in the right-most position. Thus printers that have the standard terminfo capability am defined should experience motion to the beginning of the previous line when a character is printed in the right-most position under reverse vertical motion mode.

The action when any other motion capabilities are used in reverse motion modes is not defined; thus, programs must exit reverse motion modes before using other motion capabilities.

Two miscellaneous capabilities complete the list of new motion capabilities. One of these is needed for printers that move the current position to the beginning of a line when certain control characters, such as "line-feed" or "form-feed," are used. The other is used for the capability of suspending the motion that normally occurs after printing a character.

Miscellaneous Motion Strings	
docr	List of control characters causing cr
zerom	Prevent auto motion after printing next single character

Margins

terminfo provides two strings for setting margins on terminals: one for the left and one for the right margin. Printers, however, have two additional margins, for the top and bottom margins of each page. Furthermore, some printers require not using motion strings to move the current position to a margin and then fixing the margin there, but require the specification of where a margin should be regardless of the current position. Therefore terminfo offers six additional strings for defining margins with printers.

Setting Margins	
smgl	Set left margin at current column
smgr	Set right margin at current column
smgb	Set bottom margin at current line
smgt	Set top margin at current line
smgbp	Set bottom margin at line N
smglp	Set left margin at column N
smgrp	Set right margin at column N
smgtp	Set top margin at line N

The last four strings are used with one or more arguments that give the position of the margin or margins to set. If both of smglp and smgrp are set, each is used with a single argument, N, that gives the column number of the left and right margin, respectively. If both of smgtp and smgbp are set, each is used to set the top and bottom margin, respectively: smgtp is used with a single argument, N, the line number of the top margin; however, smgbp is used with two arguments, N and M, that give the line number of the bottom margin, the first counting from the top of the page and the second counting from the bottom. This accommodates the two styles of specifying the bottom margin in different manufacturers' printers. When coding a terminfo entry for a printer that has a settable bottom margin, only the first or second parameter should be used, depending on the printer. When writing an application that uses smgbp to set the bottom margin, both arguments must be given.

If only one of smglp and smgrp is set, then it is used with two arguments, the column number of the left and right margins, in that order. Likewise, if only one of smgtp and smgbp is set, then it is used with two arguments that give the top and bottom margins, in that order, counting from the top of the page. Thus when coding a terminfo entry for a printer that requires setting both left and right or top and bottom margins simultaneously, only one of smglp and smgrp or smgtp and smgbp should be defined; the other should be left blank. When writing an application that uses these string capabilities, the pairs should be first checked to see if each in the pair is set or only one is set, and should then be used accordingly.

In counting lines or columns, line zero is the top line and column zero is the leftmost column. A zero value for the second argument with smgbp means the bottom line of the page.

All margins can be cleared with mgc.

Shadows, Italics, Wide Characters, Superscripts, Subscripts

Five new sets of strings are used to describe the capabilities printers have of enhancing printed text.

	Enhanced Printing
sshm	Enter shadow-printing mode
rshm	Exit shadow-printing mode
sitm	Enter italicizing mode
ritm	Exit italicizing mode
swidm	Enter wide character mode
rwidm	Exit wide character mode
ssupm	Enter superscript mode
rsupm	Exit superscript mode
supcs	List of characters available as superscripts
ssubm	Enter subscript mode
rsubm	Exit subscript mode
subcs	List of characters available as subscripts

If a printer requires the sshm control sequence before every character to be shadow-printed, the rshm string is left blank. Thus programs that find a control sequence in sshm but none in rshm should use the sshm control sequence before every character to be shadow-printed; otherwise, the sshm control sequence should be used once before the set of characters to be shadow-printed, followed by rshm. The same is also true of each of the sitm/ritm, swidm/rwidm, ssupm/rsupm, and ssubm/rsubm pairs.

Note that terminfo also has a capability for printing emboldened text (bold). While shadow printing and emboldened printing are similar in that they "darken" the text, many printers produce these two types of print in slightly different ways. Generally, emboldened printing is done by overstriking the same character one or more times. Shadow printing likewise usually involves overstriking, but with a slight movement up and/or to the side so that the character is "fatter."

It is assumed that enhanced printing modes are independent modes, so that it would be possible, for instance, to shadow print italicized subscripts.

As mentioned earlier, the amount of motion automatically made after printing a wide character should be given in widcs.

If only a subset of the printable ASCII characters can be printed as superscripts or subscripts, they should be listed in supcs or subcs strings, respectively. If the ssupm or ssubm strings contain control sequences, but the corresponding supcs or subcs strings are empty, it is assumed that all printable ASCII characters are available as superscripts or subscripts.

Automatic motion made after printing a superscript or subscript is assumed to be the same as for regular characters. Thus, for example, printing any of the following three examples will result in equivalent motion:

$$\text{Bi} \quad \text{B}_i \quad \text{B}^i$$

Note that the existing msgr boolean capability describes whether motion control sequences can be used while in "standout mode." This capability is extended to cover the enhanced printing modes added here. msgr should be set for those printers that accept any motion control sequences without affecting shadow, italicized, widened, superscript, or subscript printing. Conversely, if msgr is not set, a program should end these modes before attempting any motion.

Section 2-5: Alternate Character Sets

In addition to allowing you to define line graphics (described in Section 1-12), terminfo lets you define alternate character sets. The following capabilities cover printers and terminals with multiple selectable or definable character sets.

Alternate Character Sets	
scs	Select character set N
scsd	Start definition of character set N, M characters
defc	Define character A, B dots wide, descender D
rcsd	End definition of character set N
csnm	List of character set names
daisy	Printer has manually changed print-wheels

The scs, rcsd, and csnm strings are used with a single argument, N, a number from 0 to 63 that identifies the character set. The scsd string is also used with the argument N and another, M, that gives the number of characters in the set. The defc string is used with three arguments: A gives the ASCII code representation for the character, *B* gives the width of the character in dots, and *D* is zero or one depending on whether the character is a "descender" or not. The defc string is also followed by a string of "image-data" bytes that describe how the character looks (see below).

Character set 0 is the default character set present after the printer has been initialized. Not every printer has 64 character sets, of course; using scs with an argument that doesn't select an available character set should cause a null result from tparm.

If a character set has to be defined before it can be used, the scsd control sequence is to be used before defining the character set, and the rcsd is to be used after. They should also cause a null result from tparm when used with an argument *N* that doesn't apply. If a character set still has to be selected after being defined, the scs control sequence should follow the rcsd control sequence. By examining the results of using each of the scs, scsd, and rcsd strings with a character set number in a call to tparm, a program can determine which of the three are needed.

Between use of the scsd and rcsd strings, the defc string should be used to define each character. To print any character on printers covered by terminfo, the ASCII code is sent to the printer. This is true for characters in an alternate set as well as "normal" characters. Thus the definition of a character includes the ASCII code that represents it. In addition, the width of the character in dots is given, along with an indication of whether the character should descend below the print line (such as the lower case letter "g" in most character sets). The width of the character in dots also indicates the number of image-data bytes that will follow the defc string. These image-data bytes indicate where in a dot-matrix pattern ink should be applied to "draw" the character; the number of these bytes and their form are defined below under "Dot-Mapped Graphics."

It's easiest for the creator of terminfo entries to refer to each character set by number; however, these numbers will be meaningless to the application developer. The csnm string alleviates this problem by providing names for each number.

When used with a character set number in a call to tparm, the csnm string will produce the equivalent name. These names should be used as a reference only. No naming convention is implied, although anyone who creates a terminfo entry for a printer should use names consistent with the names found in user documents for the printer. Application developers should allow a user to specify a character set by number (leaving it up to the user to examine the csnm string to determine the correct number), or by name, where the application examines the csnm string to determine the corresponding character set number.

These capabilities are likely to be used only with dot-matrix printers. If they are not available, the strings should not be defined. For printers that have manually changed print-wheels or font cartridges, the boolean daisy is set.

Section 2-6: Dot-Matrix Graphics

Dot-matrix printers typically have the capability of reproducing "raster-graphics" images. Three new numeric capabilities and three new string capabilities can help a program draw raster-graphics images independent of the type of dot-matrix printer or the number of pins or dots the printer can handle at one time.

Dot-Matrix Graphics	
npins	Number of pins, N, in print-head
spinv	Spacing of pins vertically in pins per inch
spinh	Spacing of dots horizontally in dots per inch
porder	Matches software bits to print-head pins
sbim	Start printing bit image graphics, B bits wide
rbim	End printing bit image graphics

The sbim sring is used with a single argument, B, the width of the image in dots.

The model of dot-matrix or raster-graphics that terminfo presents is similar to the technique used for most dot-matrix printers: each pass of the printer's print-head is assumed to produce a dot-matrix that is N dots high and B dots wide. This is typically a wide, squat, rectangle of dots. The height of this rectangle in dots will vary from one printer to the next; this is given in the npins numeric capability. The size of the rectangle in fractions of an inch will also vary; it can be deduced from the spinv and spinh numeric capabilities. With these three values an application can divide a complete raster-graphics image into several horizontal strips, perhaps interpolating to account for different dot spacing vertically and horizontally.

The sbim and rbim strings are used to start and end a dot-matrix image, respectively. The sbim string is used with a single argument that gives the width of the dot-matrix in dots. A sequence of "image-data bytes" are sent to the printer after the sbim string and before the rbim string. The number of bytes is a integral multiple of the width of the dot-matrix; the multiple and the form of each byte is determined by the porder string as described below.

The porder string is a comma separated list of pin numbers optionally followed by an numerical offset. The offset, if given, is separated from the list with a semicolon. The position of each pin number in the list corresponds to a bit in an 8-bit data byte. The pins are numbered consecutively from 1 to npins, with 1 being the top pin. Note that the term "pin" is used loosely here; "ink-jet" dot-matrix printers don't have pins, but can be considered to have an equivalent method of applying a single dot of ink to paper. The bit positions in porder are in groups of 8, with the first position in each group the most significant bit and the last position the least significant bit. An application produces 8-bit bytes in the order of the groups in porder.

An application computes the "image-data bytes" from the internal image, mapping vertical dot positions in each print-head pass into 8-bit bytes, using a 1 bit where ink should be applied and 0 where no ink should be applied. This can be reversed (0 bit for ink, 1 bit for no ink) by giving a negative pin number. If a position is skipped in porder, a 0 bit is used. If a position has a lower case 'x' instead of a pin number, a 1 bit is used in the skipped position. For consistency, a lower case 'o' can be used to represent a 0 filled, skipped bit. There must be a multiple of 8 bit positions used or skipped in porder; if not, 0 bits are used to fill the last byte in the least significant bits. The offset, if given, is added to each data byte; the offset can be negative.

Some examples may help clarify the use of the porder string. The AT&T 470, AT&T 475 and C.Itoh 8510 printers provide eight pins for graphics. The pins are identified top to bottom by the 8 bits in a byte, from least significant to most. The porder strings for these printers would be 8, 7, 6, 5, 4, 3, 2, 1. The AT&T 478 and AT&T 479 printers also provide eight pins for graphics. However, the pins are identified in the reverse order. The porder strings for these printers would be 1, 2, 3, 4, 5, 6, 7, 8. The AT&T 5310, AT&T 5320, DEC LA100, and DEC LN03 printers provide six pins for graphics. The pins are identified top to bottom by the decimal values 1, 2, 4, 8, 16 and 32. These correspond to the low six bits in an 8-bit byte, although the decimal values are further offset by the value 63. The porder string for these printers would be , , 6, 5, 4, 3, 2, 1; 63, or alternately o, o, 6, 5, 4, 3, 2, 1; 63.

Section 2-7: Effect of Changing Printing Resolution

If the control sequences to change the character pitch or the line pitch are used, the pin or dot spacing may change:

Dot-Matrix Graphics
Changing the Character/Line Pitches

cpi	Change character pitch
cpix	If set, cpi changes spinh
lpi	Change line pitch
lpix	If set, lpi changes spinv

Programs that use cpi or lpi should recalculate the dot spacing:

Dot-Matrix Graphics
Effects of Changing the Character/Line Pitches

Before	After
Using cpi with cpix clear:	
spinh'	spinh
Using cpi with cpix set:	
spinh'	$spinh = spinh' \cdot \dfrac{orhi}{orhi'}$
Using lpi with lpix clear:	
spinv'	spinv
Using lpi with lpix set:	
spinv'	$spinv = spinv' \cdot \dfrac{orhi}{orhi'}$
Using chr:	
spinh'	spinh
Using cvr:	
spinv'	spinv

Dot-Matrix Graphics

Effects of Changing the Character/Line Pitches	
Before	*After*

orhi′ and **orhi** are the values of the horizontal resolution in steps per inch, before using cpi and after using cpi, respectively. Likewise, **orvi′** and **orvi** are the values of the vertical resolution in steps per inch, before using lpi and after using lpi, respectively. Thus, the changes in the dots per inch for dot-matrix graphics follow the changes in steps per inch for printer resolution.

Section 2-8: Print Quality

Many dot-matrix printers can alter the dot spacing of printed text to produce near "letter quality" printing or "draft quality" printing. Usually it is important to be able to choose one or the other because the rate of printing generally falls off as the quality improves. There are three new strings used to describe these capabilities.

Print Quality	
snlq	Set near-letter quality print
snrmq	Set normal quality print
sdrfq	Set draft quality print

The capabilities are listed in decreasing levels of quality. If a printer doesn't have all three levels, one or two of the strings should be left blank as appropriate.

Section 2-9: Printing Rate and Buffer Size

Because there is no standard protocol that can be used to keep a program synchronized with a printer, and because modern printers can buffer data before printing it, a program generally cannot determine at any time what has been printed. Two new numeric capabilities can help a program estimate what has been printed.

Print Rate/Buffer Size	
cps	Nominal print rate in characters per second
bufsz	Buffer capacity in characters

cps is the nominal or average rate at which the printer prints characters; if this value is not given, the rate should be estimated at one-tenth the prevailing baud rate. bufsz is the maximum number of subsequent characters buffered before the guaranteed printing of an earlier character, assuming proper flow control has been used. If this value is not given it is assumed that the printer does not buffer characters, but prints them as they are received.

As an example, if a printer has a 1000-character buffer, then sending the letter "a" followed by 1000 additional characters is guaranteed to cause the letter "a" to print. If the same printer prints at the rate of 100 characters per second, then it should take 10 seconds to print all the characters in the buffer, less if the buffer is not full. By keeping track of the characters sent to a printer, and knowing the print rate and buffer size, a program can synchronize itself with the printer.

Note that most printer manufacturers advertise the maximum print rate, not the nominal print rate. A good way to get a value to put in for cps is to generate a few pages of text, count the number of printable characters, and then see how long it takes to print the text.

Applications that use these values should recognize the variability in the print rate. Straight text, in short lines, with no embedded control sequences will probably print at close to the advertised print rate and probably faster than the rate in cps. Graphics data with a lot of control sequences, or very long lines of text, will print at well below the advertised rate and below the rate in cps. If the application is using cps to decide how long it should take a printer to print a block of text, the application should pad the estimate. If the application is using cps to decide how much text has already been printed, it should shrink the estimate. The application will thus err in favor of the user, who wants, above all, to see all the output in its correct place.

FILES

/usr/share/lib/terminfo/?/*	compiled terminal description database
/usr/share/lib/.COREterm/?/*	subset of compiled terminal description database
/usr/share/lib/tabset/*	tab settings for some terminals, in a format appropriate to be output to the terminal (escape sequences that set margins and tabs)

SEE ALSO

curses(3X), ls(1), pg(1), printf(3S), stty(1), tic(1M), tput(1), tty(1), vi(1).

NOTES

The most effective way to prepare a terminal description is by imitating the description of a similar terminal in terminfo and to build up a description gradually, using partial descriptions with a screen oriented editor, such as vi, to check that they are correct. To easily test a new terminal description the environment variable TERMINFO can be set to the pathname of a directory containing the compiled description, and programs will look there rather than in /usr/share/lib/terminfo.

NAME
       timezone – set default system time zone
SYNOPSIS
       /etc/TIMEZONE
DESCRIPTION
       This file sets and exports the time zone environmental variable TZ.

       This file is "dotted" into other files that must know the time zone.
EXAMPLES
       /etc/TIMEZONE for the east coast:

              #   Time Zone
              TZ=EST5EDT
              export TZ
SEE ALSO
       ctime(3C), environ(5).
       rc2(1M), profile(4) in the *System Administrator's Reference Manual.*

NAME

ts_dptbl – time-sharing dispatcher parameter table

DESCRIPTION

The process scheduler (or dispatcher) is the portion of the kernel that controls allocation of the CPU to processes. The scheduler supports the notion of scheduling classes where each class defines a scheduling policy, used to schedule processes within that class. Associated with each scheduling class is a set of priority queues on which ready to run processes are linked. These priority queues are mapped by the system configuration into a set of global scheduling priorities which are available to processes within the class. (The dispatcher always selects for execution the process with the highest global scheduling priority in the system.) The priority queues associated with a given class are viewed by that class as a contiguous set of priority levels numbered from 0 (lowest priority) to n (highest priority—a configuration-dependent value). The set of global scheduling priorities that the queues for a given class are mapped into might not start at zero and might not be contiguous (depending on the configuration).

Processes in the time-sharing class which are running in user mode (or in kernel mode before going to sleep) are scheduled according to the parameters in a time-sharing dispatcher parameter table (ts_dptbl). (Time-sharing processes running in kernel mode after sleeping are run within a special range of priorities reserved for such processes and are not affected by the parameters in the ts_dptbl until they return to user mode.) The ts_dptbl consists of an array of parameter structures (struct ts_dpent), one for each of the n priority levels used by time-sharing processes in user mode. The properties of a given priority level i are specified by the ith parameter structure in this array (ts_dptbl$i$).

A parameter structure consists of the following members. These are also described in the /usr/include/sys/ts.h header file.

ts_globpri   The global scheduling priority associated with this priority level. The mapping between time-sharing priority levels and global scheduling priorities is determined at boot time by the system configuration. ts_globpri is the only member of the ts_dptbl which cannot be changed with dispadmin(1M).

ts_quantum   The length of the time quantum allocated to processes at this level in ticks (HZ).

ts_tqexp   Priority level of the new queue on which to place a process running at the current level if it exceeds its time quantum. Normally this field links to a lower priority time-sharing level that has a larger quantum.

ts_slpret   Priority level of the new queue on which to place a process, that was previously in user mode at this level, when it returns to user mode after sleeping. Normally this field links to a higher priority level that has a smaller quantum.

ts_maxwait   A per process counter, ts_dispwait is initialized to zero each time a time-sharing process is placed back on the dispatcher queue after its time quantum has expired or when it is awakened (ts_dispwait is not reset to zero when a process is preempted by a higher priority process). This counter is incremented once per second for each process on the dispatcher queue. If a process's ts_dispwait value exceeds the ts_maxwait value for its level, the process's priority is changed to that indicated by ts_lwait. The purpose of this field is to prevent starvation.

ts_lwait   Move a process to this new priority level if ts_dispwait is greater than ts_maxwait.

An administrator can affect the behavior of the time-sharing portion of the scheduler by reconfiguring the ts_dptbl. There are two methods available for doing this.

MASTER FILE

The ts_dptbl can be reconfigured at boot time by specifying the desired values in the ts master file and reconfiguring the system using the auto-configuration boot procedure; see mkboot(1M) and master(4). This is the only method that can be used to change the number of time-sharing priority levels or the set of global scheduling priorities used by the time-sharing class.

DISPADMIN CONFIGURATION FILE

With the exception of ts_globpri all of the members of the ts_dptbl can be examined and modified on a running system using the dispadmin(1M) command. Invoking dispadmin for the time-sharing class allows the administrator to retrieve the current ts_dptbl configuration from the kernel's in-core table, or overwrite the in-core table with values from a configuration file. The configuration file used for input to dispadmin must conform to the specific format described below.

Blank lines are ignored and any part of a line to the right of a # symbol is treated as a comment. The first non-blank, non-comment line must indicate the resolution to be used for interpreting the ts_quantum time quantum values. The resolution is specified as

    RES=*res*

where *res* is a positive integer between 1 and 1,000,000,000 inclusive and the resolution used is the reciprocal of *res* in seconds (for example, RES=1000 specifies millisecond resolution). Although very fine (nanosecond) resolution may be specified, the time quantum lengths are rounded up to the next integral multiple of the system clock's resolution. For example, the finest resolution currently available on the 3B2 is 10 milliseconds (1 "tick"). If *res* were 1000 a time quantum value of 34 would specify a quantum of 34 milliseconds, which would be rounded up to 4 ticks (40 milliseconds) on the 3B2.

The remaining lines in the file are used to specify the parameter values for each of the time-sharing priority levels. The first line specifies the parameters for time-sharing level 0, the second line specifies the parameters for time-sharing level 1, etc. There must be exactly one line for each configured time-sharing priority level.

EXAMPLE

The following excerpt from a dispadmin configuration file illustrates the format. Note that for each line specifying a set of parameters there is a comment indicating the corresponding priority level. These level numbers indicate priority within the time-sharing class, and the mapping between these time-sharing priorities and the corresponding global scheduling priorities is determined by the configuration specified in the ts master file. The level numbers are strictly for the convenience of the administrator reading the file and, as with any comment, they are ignored by dispadmin. dispadmin assumes that the lines in the file are ordered by consecutive, increasing priority level (from 0 to the maximum configured time-sharing priority). The level numbers in the comments should normally agree with this ordering; if for some reason they don't, however, dispadmin is unaffected.

```
# Time-Sharing Dispatcher Configuration File
RES=1000
```

# ts_quantum	ts_tqexp	ts_slpret	ts_maxwait	ts_lwait	PRIORITY LEVEL
500	0	10	5	10	# 0
500	0	11	5	11	# 1
500	1	12	5	12	# 2
500	1	13	5	13	# 3
500	2	14	5	14	# 4
500	2	15	5	15	# 5
450	3	16	5	16	# 6
450	3	17	5	17	# 7
.	.	.	.	.	. .
.	.	.	.	.	. .
.	.	.	.	.	. .
50	48	59	5	59	# 58
50	49	59	5	59	# 59

FILES

/usr/include/sys/ts.h

SEE ALSO

dispadmin(1M), priocntl(1), priocntl(2), master(4), mkboot(1M)

"Scheduler" chapter in the *System Administrator's Guide*

NOTES

dispadmin does some limited sanity checking on the values supplied in the configuration file. The sanity checking is intended to ensure that the new ts_dptbl values do not cause the system to panic. The sanity checking does not attempt to analyze the effect that the new values will have on the performance of the system. Unusual ts_dptbl configurations may have a dramatic negative impact on the performance of the system.

No sanity checking is done on the ts_dptbl values specified in the ts master file. Specifying an inconsistent or nonsensical ts_dptbl configuration through the ts master file could cause serious performance problems and/or cause the system to panic.

NAME
    ttysrch — directory search list for ttyname

DESCRIPTION
    ttysrch is an optional file that is used by the ttyname library routine. This file
    contains the names of directories in /dev that contain terminal and terminal-
    related device files. The purpose of this file is to improve the performance of
    ttyname by indicating which subdirectories in /dev contain terminal-related dev-
    ice files and should be searched first. These subdirectory names must appear on
    separate lines and must begin with /dev. Those path names that do not begin
    with /dev will be ignored and a warning will be sent to the console. Blank lines
    (lines containing only white space) and lines beginning with the comment charac-
    ter "#" will be ignored. For each file listed (except for the special entry /dev),
    ttyname will recursively search through subdirectories looking for a match. If
    /dev appears in the ttysrch file, the /dev directory itself will be searched but
    there will not be a recursive search through its subdirectories.

    When ttyname searches through the device files, it tries to find a file whose
    major/minor device number, file system identifier, and inode number match that
    of the file descriptor it was given as an argument. If a match is not found, it will
    settle for a match of just major/minor device and file system identifier, if one can
    be found. However, if the file descriptor is associated with a cloned device (see
    clone(7)), this algorithm does not work efficiently because the inode number of
    the device file associated with a clonable device will never match the inode
    number of the file descriptor that was returned by the open of that clonable dev-
    ice. To help with these situations, entries can be put into the /etc/ttysrch file
    to improve performance when cloned devices are used as terminals on a system
    (e.g. for remote login). However, this is only useful if the minor devices related
    to a cloned device are put into a subdirectory. (It is important to note that device
    files need not exist for cloned devices and if that is the case, ttyname will eventu-
    ally fail.) For example if /dev/starlan is a cloned device, there could be a sub-
    directory /dev/slan that contains files 0, 1, 2, etc. that correspond to the minor
    devices of the starlan driver. An optional second field is used in the
    /etc/ttysrch file to indicate the matching criteria. This field is separated by
    white space (any combination of blanks or tabs). The letter M means major/minor
    device number, F means file system identifier, and I means inode number. If this
    field is not specified for an entry, the default is MFI which means try to match on
    all three. For cloned devices the field should be MF, which indicates that it is not
    necessary to match on the inode number.

    Without the /etc/ttysrch file, ttyname will search the /dev directory by first
    looking in the directories /dev/term, /dev/pts, and /dev/xt. If a system has
    terminal devices installed in directories other than these, it may help performance
    if the ttysrch file is created and contains that list of directories.

EXAMPLE
    A sample /etc/ttysrch file follows:

```
/dev/term  MFI
/dev/pts         MFI
/dev/xt          MFI
/dev/slan  MF
```

This file tells **ttyname** that it should first search through those directories listed and that when searching through the **/dev/slan** directory, if a file is encountered whose major/minor devices and file system identifier match that of the file descriptor argument to **ttyname**, this device name should be considered a match.

FILES

/etc/ttysrch

SEE ALSO

ttyname(3C), clone(7)

NAME

  unistd – header file for symbolic constants

SYNOPSIS

  `#include <unistd.h>`

DESCRIPTION

  The `<unistd.h>` header file defines the symbolic constants and structures which are not already defined or declared in some other header. The contents of this header are shown below.

  The following symbolic constants are defined for the **access** function [see access(2)]:

R_OK	Test for read permission
W_OK	Test for write permission
X_OK	Test for execute (search) permission
F_OK	Test for existence of file

  The constants F_OK, R_OK, W_OK and X_OK and the expressions R_OK | W_OK, R_OK | X_OK and R_OK | W_OK | X_OK all have distinct values.

  Declares the constant

  NULL   null pointer

  The following symbolic constants are defined for the **lockf** function [see lockf(3C)]:

F_ULOCK	Unlock a previously locked region
F_LOCK	Lock a region for exclusive use
F_TLOCK	Test and lock a region for exclusive use
F_TEST	Test a region for other processes locks

  The following symbolic constants are defined for the **lseek** [see lseek(2)] and **fcntl** [see fcntl(2)] functions (they have distinct values):

SEEK_SET	Set file offset to *offset*
SEEK_CUR	Set file offset to current plus *offset*
SEEK_END	Set file offset to EOF plus *offset*

  The following symbolic constants are defined (with fixed values):

_POSIX_VERSION	Integer value indicating version of the POSIX standard
_XOPEN_VERSION	integer value indicating version of the XPG to which system is compliant

The following symbolic constants are defined to indicate that the option is present:

_POSIX_JOB_CONTROL	implementation supports job control
_POSIX_SAVED_IDS	the exec functions [see exec(2)] save the effective user and group
_POSIX_VDISABLE	terminal special characters defined in <termios.h> [see termio(7)] can be disabled using this character

The following symbolic constants are defined for **sysconf** [see **sysconf**(3C)]:

```
_SC_ARG_MAX
_SC_CHILD_MAX
_SC_CLK_TCK
_SC_JOB_CONTROL
_SC_NGROUPS_MAX
_SC_OPEN_MAX
_SC_PAGESIZE
_SC_PASS_MAX
_SC_SAVED_IDS
_SC_VERSION
_SC_XOPEN_VERSION
```

The following symbolic constants are defined for **pathconf** [see fpathconf(3C)]:

```
_PC_CHOWN_RESTRICTED
_PC_LINK_MAX
_PC_MAX_CANON
_PC_MAX_INPUT
_PC_NAME_MAX
_PC_NO_TRUNC
_PC_PATH_MAX
_PC_PIPE_BUF
_PC_VDISABLE
```

The following symbolic constants are defined for file streams:

STDIN_FILENO	File number of stdin. It is 0.
STDOUT_FILENO	File number of stout. It is 1.
STDERR_FILENO	File number of stderr. It is 2.

The following pathnames are defined:

GF_PATH	Pathname of the group file.
PF_PATH	Pathname of the passwd file.

NOTES

The following values for constants are defined for this release of System V:

_POSIX_VERSION	198808L
_XOPEN_VERSION	3

SEE ALSO

access(2), exec(2), fcntl(2), lseek(2), termios(2), fpathconf(3C), sysconf(3C), group(4), passwd(4), termio(7).

NAME
utmp, wtmp – utmp and wtmp entry formats

SYNOPSIS
#include <utmp.h>

DESCRIPTION
These files, which hold user and accounting information for such commands as
who, write, and login, have the following structure, defined in <utmp.h>:

```
#define    UTMP_FILE     "/var/adm/utmp"
#define    WTMP_FILE     "/var/adm/wtmp"
#define    ut_name       ut_user

struct     utmp {
    char   ut_user[8];        /* user login name */
    char   ut_id[4];          /* /sbin/inittab id (created by */
                              /* process that puts entry in utmp) */
    char   ut_line[12];       /* device name (console, lnxx) */
    short  ut_pid;            /* process id */
    short  ut_type;           /* type of entry */
    struct exit_status {
       short  e_termination;  /* process termination status */
       short  e_exit;         /* process exit status */
    } ut_exit;                /* exit status of a process
                               * marked as DEAD_PROCESS */
    time_t ut_time;           /* time entry was made */
};

/*  Definitions for ut_type  */

#define EMPTY          0
#define RUN_LVL        1
#define BOOT_TIME      2
#define OLD_TIME       3
#define NEW_TIME       4
#define INIT_PROCESS   5    /* process spawned by "init" */
#define LOGIN_PROCESS  6    /* a "getty" process waiting for login */
#define USER_PROCESS   7    /* a user process */
#define DEAD_PROCESS   8
#define ACCOUNTING     9
#define UTMAXTYPE      ACCOUNTING /* max legal value of ut_type */

/*  Below are special strings or formats used in the "ut_line" */
/*  field when  accounting for something other than a process. */
/*  No string for the ut_line field can be more than 11 chars + */
/*  a null character in length. */
```

```
        #define RUNLVL_MSG    "run-level %c"
        #define BOOT_MSG      "system boot"
        #define OTIME_MSG     "old time"
        #define NTIME_MSG     "new time"
```

FILES

    /var/adm/utmp
    /var/adm/wtmp

SEE ALSO

    getut(3C).
    login(1), who(1), write(1) in the *User's Reference Manual*.

NAME

    utmpx, wtmpx – utmpx and wtmpx entry formats

SYNOPSIS

    #include <utmpx.h>

DESCRIPTION

    utmpx(4) is an extended version of utmp(4).

    These files, which hold user and accounting information for such commands as who, write, and login, have the following structure as defined by <utmpx.h>:

```
#define    UTMPX_FILE    "/var/adm/utmpx"
#define    WTMPX_FILE    "/var/adm/wtmpx"
#define    ut_name      ut_user
#define    ut_xtime     ut_tv.tv_sec

struct utmpx   {
   char   ut_user[32];          /* user login name */
   char   ut_id[4];             /* inittab id */
   char   ut_line[32];          /* device name (console, lnxx) */
   pid_t  ut_pid;               /* process id */
   short  ut_type;              /* type of entry */
   struct exit_status ut_exit;  /* process termination/exit status */
   struct timeval ut_tv;        /* time entry was made */
   long   ut_session;           /* session ID, used for windowing */
   long   pad[5];               /* reserved for future use */
   short  ut_syslen;            /* significant length of ut_host */
                                /* including terminating null */
   char   ut_host[257];         /* remote host name */
 } ;

/* Definitions for ut_type */

#define    EMPTY         0
#define    RUN_LVL       1
#define    BOOT_TIME     2
#define    OLD_TIME      3
#define    NEW_TIME      4
#define    INIT_PROCESS  5  /* Process spawned by "init" */
#define    LOGIN_PROCESS 6  /* A "getty" process waiting for login */
#define    USER_PROCESS  7  /* A user process */
#define    DEAD_PROCESS  8
#define    ACCOUNTING    9

#define    UTMAXTYPE ACCOUNTING  /* Largest legal value of ut_type */

/* Below are special strings or formats used in the "ut_line" */
/* field when accounting for something other than a process. */
/* No string for the ut_line field can be more than 11 chars + */
/* a null character in length. */

#define    RUNLVL_MSG    "run-level %c"
#define    BOOT_MSG      "system boot"
#define    OTIME_MSG     "old time"
#define    NTIME_MSG     "new time"
#define    MOD_WIN       10
```

FILES

    /var/adm/utmpx
    /var/adm/wtmpx

SEE ALSO

    getutx(3C).
    login(1), who(1), write(1) in the *User's Reference Manual.*

NAME
        vfstab – table of file system defaults

SYNOPSIS
        #include <sys/fstyp.h>
        #include <sys/param.h>
        #include <sys/vfstab.h>

DESCRIPTION
        The file etc/vfstab describes defaults for each file system. The information is in
        the following structure, defined in <sys/vfstab.h>:

```
struct vfstab {
        char    *vfs_special;
        char    *vfs_fsckdev;
        char    *vfs_mountp;
        char    *vfs_fstype;
        char    *vfs_fsckpass;
        char    *vfs_automnt;
        char    *vfs_mntopts;
};
```

The fields in the table are space-separated and show the block special or resource
name, the raw device to fsck, the default mount directory, the name of the file
system type, the number used by fsck to decide whether to check the file system
automatically, whether the file system should be mounted automatically by mountall, and the mount options. A '-' is used to indicate no entry in a field.

The getvfsent(3C) family of routines are used to read and write to
/etc/vfstab.

SEE ALSO
        fsck(1M), mount(1M), setmnt(1M)
        getvfsent(3C) in the *Programmer's Reference Manual*
        Chapter 5 in the *System Administrator's Guide*

NAME
    `intro` – introduction to miscellany

DESCRIPTION
    This section describes miscellaneous facilities such as macro packages, character
    set tables, etc.

NAME

>   ascii − map of ASCII character set

DESCRIPTION

>   ascii is a map of the ASCII character set, giving both octal and hexadecimal equivalents of each character, to be printed as needed. It contains:

```
|000 nul |001 soh |002 stx |003 etx |004 eot |005 enq |006 ack |007 bel |
|010 bs  |011 ht  |012 nl  |013 vt  |014 np  |015 cr  |016 so  |017 si  |
|020 dle |021 dc1 |022 dc2 |023 dc3 |024 dc4 |025 nak |026 syn |027 etb |
|030 can |031 em  |032 sub |033 esc |034 fs  |035 gs  |036 rs  |037 us  |
|040 sp  |041 !   |042 "   |043 #   |044 $   |045 %   |046 &   |047 ´   |
|050 (   |051 )   |052 *   |053 +   |054 ,   |055 −   |056 .   |057 /   |
|060 0   |061 1   |062 2   |063 3   |064 4   |065 5   |066 6   |067 7   |
|070 8   |071 9   |072 :   |073 ;   |074 <   |075 =   |076 >   |077 ?   |
|100 @   |101 A   |102 B   |103 C   |104 D   |105 E   |106 F   |107 G   |
|110 H   |111 I   |112 J   |113 K   |114 L   |115 M   |116 N   |117 O   |
|120 P   |121 Q   |122 R   |123 S   |124 T   |125 U   |126 V   |127 W   |
|130 X   |131 Y   |132 Z   |133 [   |134 \   |135 ]   |136 ^   |137 _   |
|140 `   |141 a   |142 b   |143 c   |144 d   |145 e   |146 f   |147 g   |
|150 h   |151 i   |152 j   |153 k   |154 l   |155 m   |156 n   |157 o   |
|160 p   |161 q   |162 r   |163 s   |164 t   |165 u   |166 v   |167 w   |
|170 x   |171 y   |172 z   |173 {   |174 |   |175 }   |176 ~   |177 del |


| 00 nul | 01 soh | 02 stx | 03 etx | 04 eot | 05 enq | 06 ack | 07 bel |
| 08 bs  | 09 ht  | 0a nl  | 0b vt  | 0c np  | 0d cr  | 0e so  | 0f si  |
| 10 dle | 11 dc1 | 12 dc2 | 13 dc3 | 14 dc4 | 15 nak | 16 syn | 17 etb |
| 18 can | 19 em  | 1a sub | 1b esc | 1c fs  | 1d gs  | 1e rs  | 1f us  |
| 20 sp  | 21 !   | 22 "   | 23 #   | 24 $   | 25 %   | 26 &   | 27 ´   |
| 28 (   | 29 )   | 2a *   | 2b +   | 2c ,   | 2d −   | 2e .   | 2f /   |
| 30 0   | 31 1   | 32 2   | 33 3   | 34 4   | 35 5   | 36 6   | 37 7   |
| 38 8   | 39 9   | 3a :   | 3b ;   | 3c <   | 3d =   | 3e >   | 3f ?   |
| 40 @   | 41 A   | 42 B   | 43 C   | 44 D   | 45 E   | 46 F   | 47 G   |
| 48 H   | 49 I   | 4a J   | 4b K   | 4c L   | 4d M   | 4e N   | 4f O   |
| 50 P   | 51 Q   | 52 R   | 53 S   | 54 T   | 55 U   | 56 V   | 57 W   |
| 58 X   | 59 Y   | 5a Z   | 5b [   | 5c \   | 5d ]   | 5e ^   | 5f _   |
| 60 `   | 61 a   | 62 b   | 63 c   | 64 d   | 65 e   | 66 f   | 67 g   |
| 68 h   | 69 i   | 6a j   | 6b k   | 6c l   | 6d m   | 6e n   | 6f o   |
| 70 p   | 71 q   | 72 r   | 73 s   | 74 t   | 75 u   | 76 v   | 77 w   |
| 78 x   | 79 y   | 7a z   | 7b {   | 7c |   | 7d }   | 7e ~   | 7f del |
```

FILES

>   /usr/pub/ascii

NAME

environ – user environment

DESCRIPTION

When a process begins execution, exec routines make available an array of strings called the environment [see exec(2)]. By convention, these strings have the form *variable=value*, for example, PATH=/sbin:/usr/sbin. These environmental variables provide a way to make information about a program's environment available to programs. The following environmental variables can be used by applications and are expected to be set in the target run-time environment.

HOME   The name of the user's login directory, set by login(1) from the password file (see passwd(4)).

LANG   The string used to specify localization information that allows users to work with different national conventions. The setlocale(3C) function looks for the LANG environment variable when it is called with "" as the *locale* argument. LANG is used as the default locale if the corresponding environment variable for a particular category is unset.

For example, when setlocale() is invoked as

            setlocale(LC_CTYPE, ""),

setlocale() will query the LC_CTYPE environment variable first to see if it is set and non-null. If LC_CTYPE is not set or null, then set-locale() will check the LANG environment variable to see if it is set and non-null. If both LANG and LC_CTYPE are unset or null, the default C locale will be used to set the LC_CTYPE category.

Most commands will invoke

            setlocale(LC_ALL, "")

prior to any other processing. This allows the command to be used with different national conventions by setting the appropriate environment variables.

The following environment variables are supported to correspond with each category of setlocale(3C):

LC_COLLATE   This category specifies the collation sequence being used. The information corresponding to this category is stored in a database created by the colltbl(1M) command. This environment variable affects strcoll(3C) and strxfrm(3C).

LC_CTYPE   This category specifies character classification, character conversion, and widths of multibyte characters. The information corresponding to this category is stored in a database created by the chrtbl(1M) command. The default C locale corresponds to the 7-bit ASCII character set. This environment variable is used by ctype(3C), mbchar(3C), and many commands; for example: cat(1), ed(1), ls(1), and vi(1).

LC_MESSAGES   This category specifies the language of the message database being used. For example, an application may have one message database with French messages, and another database with German messages. Message databases are created by the mkmsgs(1M) command. This environment variable is used by exstr(1), gettxt(1), gettxt(3C), and srchtxt(1).

LC_MONETARY   This category specifies the monetary symbols and delimiters used for a particular locale. The information corresponding to this category is stored in a database created by the montbl(1M) command. This environment variable is used by localeconv(3C).

LC_NUMERIC   This category specifies the decimal and thousands delimiters. The information corresponding to this category is stored in a database created by the chrtbl(1M) command. The default C locale corresponds to "." as the decimal delimiter and no thousands delimiter. This environment variable is used by localeconv(3C), printf(3C), and strtod(3C).

LC_TIME   This category specifies date and time formats. The information corresponding to this category is stored in a database specified in strftime(4). The default C locale corresponds to U.S. date and time formats. This environment variable is used by many commands and functions; for example: at(1), calendar(1), date(1), strftime(3C), and getdate(3C).

MSGVERB   Controls which standard format message components fmtmsg selects when messages are displayed to stderr [see fmtmsg(1) and fmtmsg(3C)].

SEV_LEVEL   Define severity levels and associate and print strings with them in standard format error messages [see addseverity(3C), fmtmsg(1), and fmtmsg(3C)].

NETPATH   A colon-separated list of network identifiers. A network identifier is a character string used by the Network Selection component of the system to provide application-specific default network search paths. A network identifier must consist of non-NULL characters and must have a length of at least 1. No maximum length is specified. Network identifiers are normally chosen by the system administrator. A network identifier is also the first field in any /etc/netconfig file entry. NETPATH thus provides a link into the /etc/netconfig file and the information about a network contained in that network's entry. /etc/netconfig is maintained by the system administrator. The library routines described in getnetpath(3N) access the NETPATH environment variable.

NLSPATH   Contains a sequence of templates which catopen(3C) uses when attempting to locate message catalogs. Each template consists of an optional prefix, one or more substitution fields, a filename and an optional suffix.

For example:

        NLSPATH="/system/nlslib/%N.cat"

defines that catopen() should look for all message catalogs in the directory /system/nlslib, where the catalog name should be constructed from the *name* parameter passed to catopen(), %N, with the suffix .cat.

Substitution fields consist of a % symbol, followed by a single-letter keyword. The following keywords are currently defined:

%N	The value of the *name* parameter passed to catopen().
%L	The value of LANG.
%l	The language element from LANG.
%t	The territory element from LANG.
%c	The codeset element from LANG.
%%	A single % character.

An empty string is substituted if the specified value is not currently defined. The separators "_" and "." are not included in %t and %c substitutions.

Templates defined in NLSPATH are separated by colons (:). A leading colon or two adjacent colons (::) is equivalent to specifying %N.

For example:

        NLSPATH=":%N.cat:/nlslib/%L/%N.cat"

indicates to catopen() that it should look for the requested message catalog in *name*, *name*.cat and /nlslib/$LANG/*name*.cat.

PATH   The sequence of directory prefixes that sh(1), time(1), nice(1), nohup(1), etc., apply in searching for a file known by an incomplete path name. The prefixes are separated by colons (:). login(1) sets PATH=/usr/bin. (For more detail, see sh(1).)

TERM   The kind of terminal for which output is to be prepared. This information is used by commands, such as mm(1) or vi(1), which may exploit special capabilities of that terminal.

TZ   Time zone information. The contents of the environment variable named TZ are used by the functions ctime(3C), localtime() (see ctime(3C)), strftime(3C) and mktime(3C) to override the default timezone. If the first character of TZ is a colon (:), the behavior is implementation defined, otherwise TZ has the form:

std offset [*dst* [*offset*] , [*start* [*/time*] , *end* [*/time*]]]

std and *dst*
> Three or more bytes that are the designation for the standard (*std*) and daylight savings time (*dst*) timezones. Only *std* is required, if *dst* is missing, then daylight savings time does not apply in this locale. Upper- and lower-case letters are allowed. Any characters except a leading colon (:), digits, a comma (,), a minus (−) or a plus (+) are allowed.

offset
> Indicates the value one must add to the local time to arrive at Coordinated Universal Time. The offset has the form:
>
> *hh* [: *mm* [: *ss*]]
>
> The minutes (*mm*) and seconds (*ss*) are optional. The hour (*hh*) is required and may be a single digit. The *offset* following *std* is required. If no *offset* follows *dst* , daylight savings time is assumed to be one hour ahead of standard time. One or more digits may be used; the value is always interpreted as a decimal number. The hour must be between 0 and 24, and the minutes (and seconds) if present between 0 and 59. Out of range values may cause unpredictable behavior. If preceded by a "−", the timezone is east of the Prime Meridian; otherwise it is west (which may be indicated by an optional preceding "+" sign).

start/*time*, *end*/*time*
> Indicates when to change to and back from daylight savings time, where *start*/*time* describes when the change from standard time to daylight savings time occurs, and *end*/*time* describes when the change back happens. Each *time* field describes when, in current local time, the change is made.

The formats of *start* and *end* are one of the following:

> J*n*   The Julian day *n* ($1 \le n \le 365$). Leap days are not counted. That is, in all years, February 28 is day 59 and March 1 is day 60. It is impossible to refer to the occasional February 29.

> *n*   The zero-based Julian day ($0 \le n \le 365$). Leap days are counted, and it is possible to refer to February 29.

> M*m.n.d*
> > The dth day, ($0 \le d \le 6$) of week *n* of month *m* of the year ($1 \le n \le 5$, $1 \le m \le 12$), where week 5 means "the last *d*-day in month *m*" which may occur in either the fourth or the fifth week). Week 1 is the first week in which the dth day occurs. Day zero is Sunday.

File access modes used for open and fcntl:
    O_RDONLY   Open for reading only
    O_RDWR   Open for reading and writing
    O_WRONLY   Open for writing only

The structure flock describes a file lock. It includes the following members:

```
short    l_type;       /* Type of lock */
short    l_whence;     /* Flag for starting offset */
off_t    l_start;      /* Relative offset in bytes */
off_t    l_len;        /* Size; if 0 then until EOF */
long     l_sysid;      /* Returned with F_GETLK */
pid_t    l_pid;        /* Returned with F_GETLK */
```

SEE ALSO

creat(2), exec(2), fcntl(2), open(2).

NAME

   iconv – code set conversion tables

DESCRIPTION

   The following code set conversions are supported:

Code Set Conversions Supported				
Code	Symbol	Target Code	Symbol	comment
ISO 646	646	ISO 8859-1	8859	US Ascii
ISO 646de	646de	ISO 8859-1	8859	German
ISO 646da	646da	ISO 8859-1	8859	Danish
ISO 646en	646en	ISO 8859-1	8859	English Ascii
ISO 646es	646es	ISO 8859-1	8859	Spanish
ISO 646fr	646fr	ISO 8859-1	8859	French
ISO 646it	646it	ISO 8859-1	8859	Italian
ISO 646sv	646sv	ISO 8859-1	8859	Swedish
ISO 8859-1	8859	ISO 646	646	7 bit Ascii
ISO 8859-1	8859	ISO 646de	646de	German
ISO 8859-1	8859	ISO 646da	646da	Danish
ISO 8859-1	8859	ISO 646en	646en	English Ascii
ISO 8859-1	8859	ISO 646es	646es	Spanish
ISO 8859-1	8859	ISO 646fr	646fr	French
ISO 8859-1	8859	ISO 646it	646it	Italian
ISO 8859-1	8859	ISO 646sv	646sv	Swedish

   The conversions are performed according to the tables following. All values in the tables are given in octal.

ISO 646 (US ASCII) to ISO 8859-1

   For the conversion of ISO 646 to ISO 8859-1 all characters in ISO 646 can be mapped unchanged to ISO 8859-1

ISO 646de (GERMAN) to ISO 8859-1

   For the conversion of ISO 646de to ISO 8859-1 all characters not in the following table are mapped unchanged.

Conversions Performed	
ISO 646de	ISO 8859-1
100	247
133	304
134	326
135	334
173	344
174	366
175	374
176	337

ISO 646da (DANISH) to ISO 8859-1

For the conversion of ISO 646da to ISO 8859-1 all characters not in the following table are mapped unchanged.

Conversions Peformed	
ISO 646da	ISO 8859-1
133	306
134	330
135	305
173	346
174	370
175	345

ISO 646en (ENGLISH ASCII) to ISO 8859-1

For the conversion of ISO 646en to ISO 8859-1 all characters not in the following table are mapped unchanged.

Conversions Peformed	
ISO 646en	ISO 8859-1
043	243

ISO 646fr (FRENCH) to ISO 8859-1

For the conversion of ISO 646fr to ISO 8859-1 all characters not in the following table are mapped unchanged.

Conversions Peformed	
ISO 646fr	ISO 8859-1
043	243
100	340
133	260
134	347
135	247
173	351
174	371
175	350
176	250

ISO 646it (ITALIAN) to ISO 8859-1

For the conversion of ISO 646it to ISO 8859-1 all characters not in the following table are mapped unchanged.

Conversions Peformed	
ISO 646it	ISO 8859-1
043	243
100	247
133	260
134	347
135	351
140	371
173	340
174	362
175	350
176	354

ISO 646es (SPANISH) to ISO 8859-1

For the conversion of ISO 646es to ISO 8859-1 all characters not in the following table are mapped unchanged.

Conversions Peformed	
ISO 646es	ISO 8859-1
100	247
133	241
134	321
135	277
173	260
174	361
175	347

A_CURRENT	followed by a two-byte channel number.
A_DELETE	followed by a two-byte channel number.
A_TOP	followed by a two-byte channel number.
A_BOTTOM	followed by a two-byte channel number.
A_MOVE	followed by a two-byte channel number and a point to move to (two two-byte coordinates).
A_RESHAPE	followed by a two-byte channel number and the new rectangle (four two-byte coordinates).
A_NEW	followed by a two-byte channel number and a rectangle structure (four two-byte coordinates).
A_EXIT	no parameters needed.
A_ROMVERSION	no parameters needed. The response packet contains the size byte, two-byte return code, two unused bytes, and the parameter part of the terminal ID string (e.g., 8;7;3).

JXTPROTO Set xt protocol type [see xtproto(5)]. The data consist of one byte specifying maximum size for the data part of regular xt packets sent from the host to the terminal. This number may be lower than the number returned by A_XTPROTO at lower baud rates or if the −m option was specified upon invocation of layers(1). A size of 1 specifies network xt protocol.

Packets from the windowing terminal to the UNIX System all take the following form:

   command, data ...

The single-byte commands are as follows:

C_SENDCHAR	Send the next byte to the UNIX System process.
C_NEW	Create a new UNIX System process group for this layer. Remember the window size parameters for this layer. The data for this command is in the form described by the jwinsize structure. The size of the window is specified by two 2-byte integers, sent low byte first.
C_UNBLK	Unblock transmission to this layer. There are no data for this command.
C_DELETE	Delete the UNIX System process group attached to this layer. There are no data for this command.
C_EXIT	Exit. Kill all UNIX System process groups associated with this terminal and terminate the session. There are no data for this command.
C_DEFUNCT	Layer program has died, send a terminate signal to the UNIX System process groups associated with this terminal. There are no data for this command.

C_SENDNCHARS	The rest of the data are characters to be passed to the UNIX System process.
C_RESHAPE	The layer has been reshaped. Change the window size parameters for this layer. The data take the same form as for the C_NEW command. A SIGWINCH signal is also sent to the process in the window, so that the process knows that the window has been reshaped and it can get the new window parameters.
C_NOFLOW	Disable network xt flow control [see xtproto(5)].
C_YESFLOW	Enable network xt flow control [see xtproto(5)].

FILES

/usr/include/windows.h
/usr/include/sys/jioctl.h

SEE ALSO

layers(1), libwindows(3X), jagent(5), xtproto(5).
xt(7) in the *Programmer's Guide: STREAMS*.

NAME
  nl_types – native language data types
SYNOPSIS
  #include <nl_types.h>
DESCRIPTION
  This header file contains the following definitions:

  nl_catd   used by the message catalog functions catopen, catgets and catclose to identify a catalogue

  nl_item   used by nl_langinfo to identify items of langinfo data. Values for objects of type nl_item are defined in langinfo.h.

  NL_SETD   used by gencat when no $set directive is specified in a message text source file. This constant can be used in subsequent calls to catgets as the value of the set identifier parameter.

  NL_MGSMAX   maximum number of messages per set

  NL_SETMAX   maximum number of sets per catalogue.

  NL_TEXTMAX maximum size of a message.

  DEF_NLSPATH the default search path for locating catalogues.
SEE ALSO
  catgets(3C), catopen(3C), nl_langinfo(3C), langinfo(5).
  gencat(1M) in the *System Administrator's Reference Manual*.

NAME

regexp: compile, step, advance – regular expression compile and match routines

SYNOPSIS

```
#define INIT declarations
#define GETC(void) getc code
#define PEEKC(void) peekc code
#define UNGETC(void) ungetc code
#define RETURN(ptr) return code
#define ERROR(val) error code

#include <regexp.h>

char *compile(char *instring, char *expbuf, char *endbuf, int eof);

int step(char *string, char *expbuf);

int advance(char *string, char *expbuf);

extern char *loc1, *loc2, *locs;
```

DESCRIPTION

These functions are general purpose regular expression matching routines to be used in programs that perform regular expression matching. These functions are defined by the <regexp.h> header file.

The functions step and advance do pattern matching given a character string and a compiled regular expression as input.

The function compile takes as input a regular expression as defined below and produces a compiled expression that can be used with step or advance.

A regular expression specifies a set of character strings. A member of this set of strings is said to be matched by the regular expression. Some characters have special meaning when used in a regular expression; other characters stand for themselves.

The regular expressions available for use with the regexp functions are constructed as follows:

Expression	Meaning
c	the character c where c is not a special character.
\\c	the character c where c is any character, except a digit in the range 1–9.
^	the beginning of the line being compared.
$	the end of the line being compared.
.	any character in the input.
[s]	any character in the set s, where s is a sequence of characters and/or a range of characters, *e.g.*, [c–c].

[^*s*]   any character not in the set *s*, where *s* is defined as above.

*r**   zero or more successive occurrences of the regular expression *r*. The longest leftmost match is chosen.

rx   the occurrence of regular expression *r* followed by the occurrence of regular expression *x*. (Concatenation)

r\\{*m*,*n*\\}   any number of *m* through *n* successive occurrences of the regular expression *r*. The regular expression *r*\\{*m*\\} matches exactly *m* occurrences; *r*\\{*m*,\\} matches at least *m* occurrences.

\\(*r*\\)   the regular expression *r*. When *n* (where *n* is a number greater than zero) appears in a constructed regular expression, it stands for the regular expression *x* where *x* is the *n*th regular expression enclosed in \\(and \\) that appeared earlier in the constructed regular expression. For example, \\(*r*\\)*x*\\(*y*\\)*z*\\2 is the concatenation of regular expressions *rxyzy*.

Characters that have special meaning except when they appear within square brackets ([ ]) or are preceded by \ are: ., *, [, \. Other special characters, such as $ have special meaning in more restricted contexts.

The character ^ at the beginning of an expression permits a successful match only immediately after a newline, and the character $ at the end of an expression requires a trailing newline.

Two characters have special meaning only when used within square brackets. The character – denotes a range, [*c*–*c*], unless it is just after the open bracket or before the closing bracket, [–*c*] or [*c*–] in which case it has no special meaning. When used within brackets, the character ^ has the meaning *complement of* if it immediately follows the open bracket (example: [^*c*]); elsewhere between brackets (example: [*c*^]) it stands for the ordinary character ^.

The special meaning of the \ operator can be escaped only by preceding it with another \, *e.g.* \\.

Programs must have the following five macros declared before the #include <regexp.h> statement. These macros are used by the compile routine. The macros GETC, PEEKC, and UNGETC operate on the regular expression given as input to compile.

GETC   This macro returns the value of the next character (byte) in the regular expression pattern. Successive calls to GETC should return successive characters of the regular expression.

PEEKC   This macro returns the next character (byte) in the regular expression. Immediately successive calls to PEEKC should return the same character, which should also be the next character returned by GETC.

UNGETC   This macro causes the argument c to be returned by the next call to GETC and PEEKC. No more than one character of pushback is ever needed and this character is guaranteed to be the last character read by GETC. The return value of the macro UNGETC(c) is always ignored.

RETURN *(ptr)*   This macro is used on normal exit of the compile routine. The value of the argument *ptr* is a pointer to the character after the last character of the compiled regular expression. This is useful to programs which have memory allocation to manage.

ERROR *(val)*   This macro is the abnormal return from the compile routine. The argument *val* is an error number [see ERRORS below for meanings]. This call should never return.

The syntax of the compile routine is as follows:

    compile (*instring, expbuf, endbuf, eof*)

The first parameter, *instring,* is never used explicitly by the compile routine but is useful for programs that pass down different pointers to input characters. It is sometimes used in the INIT declaration (see below). Programs which call functions to input characters or have characters in an external array can pass down a value of (char *)0 for this parameter.

The next parameter, *expbuf,* is a character pointer. It points to the place where the compiled regular expression will be placed.

The parameter *endbuf* is one more than the highest address where the compiled regular expression may be placed. If the compiled expression cannot fit in (endbuf−expbuf) bytes, a call to ERROR(50) is made.

The parameter *eof* is the character which marks the end of the regular expression. This character is usually a /.

Each program that includes the <regexp.h> header file must have a #define statement for INIT. It is used for dependent declarations and initializations. Most often it is used to set a register variable to point to the beginning of the regular expression so that this register variable can be used in the declarations for GETC, PEEKC, and UNGETC. Otherwise it can be used to declare external variables that might be used by GETC, PEEKC and UNGETC. [See EXAMPLE below.]

The first parameter to the step and advance functions is a pointer to a string of characters to be checked for a match. This string should be null terminated.

The second parameter, *expbuf,* is the compiled regular expression which was obtained by a call to the function compile.

The function step returns non-zero if some substring of *string* matches the regular expression in *expbuf* and zero if there is no match. If there is a match, two external character pointers are set as a side effect to the call to step. The variable loc1 points to the first character that matched the regular expression; the variable loc2 points to the character after the last character that matches the regular expression. Thus if the regular expression matches the entire input string, loc1 will point to the first character of *string* and loc2 will point to the null at the end of *string*.

The function advance returns non-zero if the initial substring of *string* matches the regular expression in *expbuf*. If there is a match, an external character pointer, loc2, is set as a side effect. The variable loc2 points to the next character in *string* after the last character that matched.

When **advance** encounters a * or \{ \} sequence in the regular expression, it will advance its pointer to the string to be matched as far as possible and will recursively call itself trying to match the rest of the string to the rest of the regular expression. As long as there is no match, advance will back up along the string until it finds a match or reaches the point in the string that initially matched the * or \{ \}. It is sometimes desirable to stop this backing up before the initial point in the string is reached. If the external character pointer **locs** is equal to the point in the string at sometime during the backing up process, **advance** will break out of the loop that backs up and will return zero.

The external variables **circf, sed,** and **nbra** are reserved.

DIAGNOSTICS

The function **compile** uses the macro RETURN on success and the macro ERROR on failure (see above). The functions **step** and **advance** return non-zero on a successful match and zero if there is no match. Errors are:

11   range endpoint too large.

16   bad number.

25   \ *digit* out of range.

36   illegal or missing delimiter.

41   no remembered search string.

42   \ (\) imbalance.

43   too many \ (.

44   more than 2 numbers given in \{ \}.

45   } expected after \.

46   first number exceeds second in \{ \}.

49   [ ] imbalance.

50   regular expression overflow.

EXAMPLE

The following is an example of how the regular expression macros and calls might be defined by an application program:

```
#define INIT          register char *sp = instring;
#define GETC          (*sp++)
#define PEEKC         (*sp)
#define UNGETC(c)     (--sp)
#define RETURN(*c)     return;
#define ERROR(c)      regerr

#include <regexp.h>

. . .
      (void) compile(*argv, expbuf, &expbuf[ESIZE],'\0');
. . .
      if (step(linebuf, expbuf))
                        succeed;
```

NAME
siginfo – signal generation information

SYNOPSIS
`#include <siginfo.h>`

DESCRIPTION
If a process is catching a signal, it may request information that tells why the system generated that signal [see `sigaction(2)`]. If a process is monitoring its children, it may receive information that tells why a child changed state [see `waitid(2)`]. In either case, the system returns the information in a structure of type `siginfo_t`, which includes the following information:

```
int si_signo    /* signal number */
int si_errno    /* error number */
int si_code     /* signal code */
```

`si_signo` contains the system-generated signal number. (For the `waitid(2)` function, `si_signo` is always `SIGCHLD`.)

If `si_errno` is non-zero, it contains an error number associated with this signal, as defined in `errno.h`.

`si_code` contains a code identifying the cause of the signal. If the value of `si_code` is less than or equal to 0, then the signal was generated by a user process [see `kill(2)` and `sigsend(2)`] and the `siginfo` structure contains the following additional information:

```
pid_t si_pid    /* sending process ID */
uid_t si_uid    /* sending user ID */
```

Otherwise, `si_code` contains a signal-specific reason why the signal was generated, as follows:

Signal	Code	Reason
SIGILL	ILL_ILLOPC	illegal opcode
	ILL_ILLOPN	illegal operand
	ILL_ILLADR	illegal addressing mode
	ILL_ILLTRP	illegal trap
	ILL_PRVOPC	privileged opcode
	ILL_PRVREG	privileged register
	ILL_COPROC	coprocessor error
	ILL_BADSTK	internal stack error
SIGFPE	FPE_INTDIV	integer divide by zero
	FPE_INTOVF	integer overflow
	FPE_FLTDIV	floating point divide by zero
	FPE_FLTOVF	floating point overflow
	FPE_FLTUND	floating point underflow
	FPE_FLTRES	floating point inexact result
	FPE_FLTINV	invalid floating point operation
	FPE_FLTSUB	subscript out of range

Signal	Code	Reason
SIGSEGV	SEGV_MAPERR	address not mapped to object
	SEGV_ACCERR	invalid permissions for mapped object
SIGBUS	BUS_ADRALN	invalid address alignment
	BUS_ADRERR	non-existent physical address
	BUS_OBJERR	object specific hardware error
SIGTRAP	TRAP_BRKPT	process breakpoint
	TRAP_TRACE	process trace trap
SIGCHLD	CLD_EXITED	child has exited
	CLD_KILLED	child was killed
	CLD_DUMPED	child terminated abnormally
	CLD_TRAPPED	traced child has trapped
	CLD_STOPPED	child has stopped
	CLD_CONTINUED	stopped child had continued
SIGPOLL	POLL_IN	data input available
	POLL_OUT	output buffers available
	POLL_MSG	input message available
	POLL_ERR	I/O error
	POLL_PRI	high priority input available
	POLL_HUP	device disconnected

In addition, the following signal-dependent information is available for kernel-generated signals:

Signal	Field	Value
SIGILL SIGFPE	caddr_t si_addr	address of faulting instruction
SIGSEGV SIGBUS	caddr_t si_addr	address of faulting memory reference
SIGCHLD	pid_t si_pid int si_status	child process ID exit value or signal
SIGPOLL	long si_band	band event for POLL_IN, POLL_OUT, or POLL_MSG

SEE ALSO

sigaction(2), waitid(2), signal(5).

NOTES

For SIGCHLD signals, if si_code is equal to CLD_EXITED, then si_status is equal to the exit value of the process; otherwise, it is equal to the signal that caused the process to change state. For some implementations, the exact value of si_addr may not be available; in that case, si_addr is guaranteed to be on the same page as the faulting instruction or memory reference.

NAME
     signal – base signals

SYNOPSIS
     #include <signal.h>

DESCRIPTION
     A signal is an asynchronous notification of an event. A signal is said to be gen-
     erated for (or sent to) a process when the event associated with that signal first
     occurs. Examples of such events include hardware faults, timer expiration and
     terminal activity, as well as the invocation of the kill or sigsend system calls.
     In some circumstances, the same event generates signals for multiple processes.
     A process may request a detailed notification of the source of the signal and the
     reason why it was generated [see siginfo(5)].

     Each process may specify a system action to be taken in response to each signal
     sent to it, called the signal's disposition. The set of system signal actions for a
     process is initialized from that of its parent. Once an action is installed for a
     specific signal, it usually remains installed until another disposition is explicitly
     requested by a call to either sigaction, signal or sigset, or until the process
     execs [see sigaction(2) and signal(2)]. When a process execs, all signals whose
     disposition has been set to catch the signal will be set to SIG_DFL. Alternatively,
     a process may request that the system automatically reset the disposition of a sig-
     nal to SIG_DFL after it has been caught [see sigaction(2) and signal(2)].

     A signal is said to be delivered to a process when the appropriate action for the
     process and signal is taken. During the time between the generation of a signal
     and its delivery, the signal is said to be pending [see sigpending(2)]. Ordinarily,
     this interval cannot be detected by an application. However, a signal can be
     blocked from delivery to a process [see signal(2) and sigprocmask(2)]. If the
     action associated with a blocked signal is anything other than to ignore the signal,
     and if that signal is generated for the process, the signal remains pending until
     either it is unblocked or the signal's disposition requests that the signal be
     ignored. If the signal disposition of a blocked signal requests that the signal be
     ignored, and if that signal is generated for the process, the signal is discarded
     immediately upon generation.

     Each process has a signal mask that defines the set of signals currently blocked
     from delivery to it [see sigprocmask(2)]. The signal mask for a process is initial-
     ized from that of its parent.

     The determination of which action is taken in response to a signal is made at the
     time the signal is delivered, allowing for any changes since the time of genera-
     tion. This determination is independent of the means by which the signal was ori-
     ginally generated.

     The signals currently defined in <signal.h> are as follows:

Name	Value	Default	Event
SIGHUP	1	Exit	Hangup [see termio(7)]
SIGINT	2	Exit	Interrupt [see termio(7)]
SIGQUIT	3	Core	Quit [see termio(7)]
SIGILL	4	Core	Illegal Instruction
SIGTRAP	5	Core	Trace/Breakpoint Trap
SIGABRT	6	Core	Abort
SIGEMT	7	Core	Emulation Trap
SIGFPE	8	Core	Arithmetic Exception
SIGKILL	9	Exit	Killed
SIGBUS	10	Core	Bus Error
SIGSEGV	11	Core	Segmentation Fault
SIGSYS	12	Core	Bad System Call
SIGPIPE	13	Exit	Broken Pipe
SIGALRM	14	Exit	Alarm Clock
SIGTERM	15	Exit	Terminated
SIGUSR1	16	Exit	User Signal 1
SIGUSR2	17	Exit	User Signal 2
SIGCHLD	18	Ignore	Child Status Changed
SIGPWR	19	Ignore	Power Fail/Restart
SIGWINCH	20	Ignore	Window Size Change
SIGURG	21	Ignore	Urgent Socket Condition
SIGPOLL	22	Exit	Pollable Event [see streamio(7)]
SIGSTOP	23	Stop	Stopped (signal)
SIGTSTP	24	Stop	Stopped (user) [see termio(7)]
SIGCONT	25	Ignore	Continued
SIGTTIN	26	Stop	Stopped (tty input) [see termio(7)]
SIGTTOU	27	Stop	Stopped (tty output) [see termio(7)]
SIGVTALRM	28	Exit	Virtual Timer Expired
SIGPROF	29	Exit	Profiling Timer Expired
SIGXCPU	30	Core	CPU time limit exceeded [see getrlimit(2)]
SIGXFSZ	31	Core	File size limit exceeded [see getrlimit(2)]

Using the signal, sigset or sigaction system call, a process may specify one of three dispositions for a signal: take the default action for the signal, ignore the signal, or catch the signal.

Default Action: SIG_DFL

A disposition of SIG_DFL specifies the default action. The default action for each signal is listed in the table above and is selected from the following:

Exit   When it gets the signal, the receiving process is to be terminated with all the consequences outlined in exit(2).

Core   When it gets the signal, the receiving process is to be terminated with all the consequences outlined in exit(2). In addition, a "core image" of the process is constructed in the current working directory.

Stop   When it gets the signal, the receiving process is to stop.

Ignore   When it gets the signal, the receiving process is to ignore it. This is identical to setting the disposition to `SIG_IGN`.

Ignore Signal: `SIG_IGN`

A disposition of `SIG_IGN` specifies that the signal is to be ignored.

Catch Signal: *function address*

A disposition that is a function address specifies that, when it gets the signal, the receiving process is to execute the signal handler at the specified address. Normally, the signal handler is passed the signal number as its only argument; if the disposition was set with the `sigaction` function however, additional arguments may be requested [see `sigaction(2)`]. When the signal handler returns, the receiving process resumes execution at the point it was interrupted, unless the signal handler makes other arrangements. If an invalid function address is specified, results are undefined.

If the disposition has been set with the `sigset` or `sigaction` function, the signal is automatically blocked by the system while the signal catcher is executing. If a `longjmp` [see `setjmp(3C)`] is used to leave the signal catcher, then the signal must be explicitly unblocked by the user [see `signal(2)` and `sigprocmask(2)`].

If execution of the signal handler interrupts a blocked system call, the handler is executed and the interrupted system call returns a −1 to the calling process with `errno` set to `EINTR`. However, if the `SA_RESTART` flag is set the system call will be transparently restarted.

NOTES

The dispositions of the `SIGKILL` and `SIGSTOP` signals cannot be altered from their default values. The system generates an error if this is attempted.

The `SIGKILL` and `SIGSTOP` signals cannot be blocked. The system silently enforces this restriction.

Whenever a process receives a `SIGSTOP`, `SIGTSTP`, `SIGTTIN`, or `SIGTTOU` signal, regardless of its disposition, any pending `SIGCONT` signal are discarded.

Whenever a process receives a `SIGCONT` signal, regardless of its disposition, any pending `SIGSTOP`, `SIGTSTP`, `SIGTTIN`, and `SIGTTOU` signals is discarded. In addition, if the process was stopped, it is continued.

`SIGPOLL` is issued when a file descriptor corresponding to a STREAMS [see `intro(2)`] file has a "selectable" event pending. A process must specifically request that this signal be sent using the `I_SETSIG` ioctl call. Otherwise, the process will never receive `SIGPOLL`.

If the disposition of the `SIGCHLD` signal has been set with `signal` or `sigset`, or with `sigaction` and the `SA_NOCLDSTOP` flag has been specified, it will only be sent to the calling process when its children exit; otherwise, it will also be sent when the calling process's children are stopped or continued due to job control.

The name `SIGCLD` is also defined in this header file and identifies the same signal as `SIGCHLD`. `SIGCLD` is provided for backward compatibility, new applications should use `SIGCHLD`.

The following macros are for POSIX conformance:

#define	S_ISBLK (mode)	block special file
#define	S_ISCHR (mode)	character special file
#define	S_ISDIR (mode)	directory file
#define	S_ISFIFO (mode)	pipe or fifo file
#define	S_ISREG (mode)	regular file

SEE ALSO

stat(2), types(5).

NAME

term – conventional names for terminals

DESCRIPTION

Terminal names are maintained as part of the shell environment in the environment variable TERM [see sh(1), profile(4), and environ(5)]. These names are used by certain commands [for example, tabs, tput, and vi] and certain functions [for example, see curses(3X)].

Files under /usr/share/lib/terminfo are used to name terminals and describe their capabilities. These files are in the format described in terminfo(4). Entries in terminfo source files consist of a number of comma-separated fields. To print a description of a terminal *term*, use the command infocmp -I *term* [see infocmp(1M)]. White space after each comma is ignored. The first line of each terminal description in the terminfo database gives the names by which terminfo knows the terminal, separated by bar (|) characters. The first name given is the most common abbreviation for the terminal [this is the one to use to set the environment variable TERMINFO in $HOME/.profile; see profile(4)], the last name given should be a long name fully identifying the terminal, and all others are understood as synonyms for the terminal name. All names but the last should contain no blanks and must be unique in the first 14 characters; the last name may contain blanks for readability.

Terminal names (except for the last, verbose entry) should be chosen using the following conventions. The particular piece of hardware making up the terminal should have a root name chosen, for example, for the AT&T 4425 terminal, att4425. This name should not contain hyphens, except that synonyms may be chosen that do not conflict with other names. Up to 8 characters, chosen from the set a through z and 0 through 9, make up a basic terminal name. Names should generally be based on original vendors rather than local distributors. A terminal acquired from one vendor should not have more than one distinct basic name. Terminal sub-models, operational modes that the hardware can be in, or user preferences should be indicated by appending a hyphen and an indicator of the mode. Thus, an AT&T 4425 terminal in 132 column mode is att4425-w. The following suffixes should be used where possible:

Suffix	Meaning	Example
-w	Wide mode (more than 80 columns)	att4425-w
-am	With auto. margins (usually default)	vt100-am
-nam	Without automatic margins	vt100-nam
-n	Number of lines on the screen	aaa-60
-na	No arrow keys (leave them in local)	c100-na
-np	Number of pages of memory	c100-4p
-rv	Reverse video	att4415-rv

To avoid conflicts with the naming conventions used in describing the different modes of a terminal (e.g., -w), it is recommended that a terminal's root name not contain hyphens. Further, it is good practice to make all terminal names used in the terminfo(4) database unique. Terminal entries that are present only for inclusion in other entries via the use= facilities should have a '+' in their name, as in 4415+nl.

Here are some of the known terminal names: (For a complete list, enter the command ls −C /usr/share/lib/terminfo/?.)

2621, hp2621	Hewlett-Packard 2621 series
2631	Hewlett-Packard 2631 line printer
2631−c	Hewlett-Packard 2631 line printer, compressed mode
2631−e	Hewlett-Packard 2631 line printer, expanded mode
2640, hp2640	Hewlett-Packard 2640 series
2645, hp2645	Hewlett-Packard 2645 series
3270	IBM Model 3270
33, tty33	AT&T Teletype Model 33 KSR
35, tty35	AT&T Teletype Model 35 KSR
37, tty37	AT&T Teletype Model 37 KSR
4000a	Trendata 4000a
4014, tek4014	TEKTRONIX 4014
40, tty40	AT&T Teletype Dataspeed 40/2
43, tty43	AT&T Teletype Model 43 KSR
4410, 5410	AT&T 4410/5410 in 80-column mode, version 2
4410−nfk, 5410−nfk	AT&T 4410/5410 without function keys, version 1
4410−nsl, 5410−nsl	AT&T 4410/5410 without pln defined
4410−w, 5410−w	AT&T 4410/5410 in 132-column mode
4410v1, 5410v1	AT&T 4410/5410 in 80-column mode, version 1
4410v1−w, 5410v1−w	AT&T 4410/5410 in 132-column mode, version 1
4415, 5420	AT&T 4415/5420 in 80-column mode
4415−nl, 5420−nl	AT&T 4415/5420 without changing labels
4415−rv, 5420−rv	AT&T 4415/5420 80 columns in reverse video
4415−rv−nl, 5420−rv−nl	AT&T 4415/5420 reverse video without changing labels
4415−w, 5420−w	AT&T 4415/5420 in 132-column mode
4415−w−nl, 5420−w−nl	AT&T 4415/5420 in 132-column mode without changing labels
4415−w−rv, 5420−w−rv	AT&T 4415/5420 132 columns in reverse video
4418, 5418	AT&T 5418 in 80-column mode
4418−w, 5418−w	AT&T 5418 in 132-column mode

4420	AT&T Teletype Model 4420
4424	AT&T Teletype Model 4424
4424-2	AT&T Teletype Model 4424 in display function group ii
4425,5425	AT&T 4425/5425
4425-fk, 5425-fk	AT&T 4425/5425 without function keys
4425-nl, 5425-nl	AT&T 4425/5425 without changing labels in 80-column mode
4425-w, 5425-w	AT&T 4425/5425 in 132-column mode
4425-w-fk, 5425-w-fk	AT&T 4425/5425 without function keys in 132-column mode
4425-nl-w, 5425-nl-w	AT&T 4425/5425 without changing labels in 132-column mode
4426	AT&T Teletype Model 4426S
450	DASI 450 (same as Diablo 1620)
450-12	DASI 450 in 12-pitch mode
500, att500	AT&T-IS 500 terminal
510, 510a	AT&T 510/510a in 80-column mode
513bct, att513	AT&T 513 bct terminal
5320	AT&T 5320 hardcopy terminal
5420_2	AT&T 5420 model 2 in 80-column mode
5420_2-w	AT&T 5420 model 2 in 132-column mode
5620, dmd	AT&T 5620 terminal 88 columns
5620-24, dmd-24	AT&T Teletype Model DMD 5620 in a 24x80 layer
5620-34, dmd-34	AT&T Teletype Model DMD 5620 in a 34x80 layer
610, 610bct	AT&T 610 bct terminal in 80-column mode
610-w, 610bct-w	AT&T 610 bct terminal in 132-column mode
630, 630MTG	AT&T 630 Multi-Tasking Graphics terminal
7300, pc7300, unix_pc	AT&T UNIX PC Model 7300
735, ti	Texas Instruments TI735 and TI725
745	Texas Instruments TI745
dumb	generic name for terminals that lack reverse line-feed and other special escape sequences
hp	Hewlett-Packard (same as 2645)
lp	generic name for a line printer
pt505	AT&T Personal Terminal 505 (22 lines)
pt505-24	AT&T Personal Terminal 505 (24-line mode)
sync	generic name for synchronous Teletype Model 4540-compatible terminals

Commands whose behavior depends on the type of terminal should accept arguments of the form −T*term* where *term* is one of the names given above; if no such argument is present, such commands should obtain the terminal type from the environment variable TERM, which, in turn, should contain *term*.

FILES

/usr/share/lib/terminfo/?/*   compiled terminal description database

SEE ALSO

infocmp(1M), profile(4), terminfo(4), environ(5) in the *System Administrator's Reference Manual*.

sh(1), stty(1), tabs(1), tput(1), vi(1) in the *User's Reference Manual* .

curses(3X).

NAME

xtproto – multiplexed channels protocol used by xt driver

DESCRIPTION

This xt protocol is used for communication between multiple UNIX System host processes and an AT&T windowing terminal operating under the layers command; see xt(7). It is a multiplexed protocol that directs traffic between host processes and terminal windows, thereby allowing multiple virtual terminal sessions over a single connection. The protocol is implemented by the xt host driver and corresponding firmware in a windowing terminal.

The xt driver implements two distinct low level protocols. Which protocol is used depends on the media used for communication with the terminal. The regular xt protocol is used when communicating over unreliable media such as RS-232. The regular xt protocol provides flow control and error correction, thereby guaranteeing error-free delivery of data. The network xt protocol is used when communicating over reliable media such as a local area network. In order to achieve maximum possible throughput, the network xt protocol relies on the underlying network to provide flow control and error correction.

The layers command queries the windowing terminal whether to use regular or network xt protocol through an A_XTPROTO JAGENT ioctl system call [see layers(5)]. The layers command then decides what protocol to use based on the return value of A_XTPROTO, baud rate, and the –m option of layers.

The regular xt protocol uses packets with a 2-byte header containing a 3-bit sequence number, 3-bit channel number, control flag, and one byte for data size. The data part of packets sent from the host to the terminal may not be larger than 252 bytes. The maximum data part size can be less than 252 at lower baud rates, or if the –m option of layers was specified. Also, when communicating with some earlier windowing terminals, maximum data part size is fixed at 32 bytes. The maximum data part size of packets sent from the terminal to the host is always fixed at 32 bytes. The trailer contains a CRC-16 code in 2 bytes. Each channel is double-buffered.

Correctly received regular xt packets in sequence are acknowledged with a control packet containing an ACK; however, out of sequence packets generate a control packet containing a NAK, which causes the retransmission in sequence of all unacknowledged packets.

Unacknowledged regular xt packets are retransmitted after a timeout interval that is dependent on baud rate. Another timeout parameter specifies the interval after which incomplete receive packets are discarded.

Network xt protocol uses a 3-byte header containing a 3-bit channel number, various control flags, and 2-bytes for data size. The data part of packets sent from the host to the terminal has no size limit. The data part of packets sent from the terminal to the host is restricted to 1025 bytes.

Since network xt protocol relies on the underlying media to guarantee error-free delivery of data, no CRC codes or timeouts are needed.

Network **xt** protocol provides a simple flow control mechanism to limit the amount of data sent to a window in the terminal before a NETWORK XT ACK acknowledgement is received by the host. The intent of this flow control is to limit the amount of data sent to a window in the terminal not reading its input because, for example, the user has pressed the scroll lock key. This is necessary to prevent data from backing up and blocking other data directed to other windows. To improve overall throughput, network **xt** flow control can be disabled by processes in the terminal that always read their input quickly.

FILES

/usr/include/sys/xtproto.h   channel multiplexing protocol definitions

SEE ALSO

jagent(5), layers(5).
layers(1) in the *User's Reference Manual.*
xt(7) in the *Programmer's Guide: STREAMS.*